Police Training Manual
Eighth Edition

Police Training Manual

Eighth Edition

Jack English

OBE, QPM, MA
*formerly Assistant Chief Constable, Northumbria Police
and Director of the Home Office Central Planning Unit*

Brian English

BSc
Northumbria Police

McGRAW-HILL BOOK COMPANY

London · New York · St Louis · San Francisco · Auckland
Bogotá · Caracas · Lisbon · Madrid · Mexico · Milan
Montreal · New Delhi · Panama · Paris · San Juan
São Paulo · Singapore · Sydney · Tokyo · Toronto

Published by
McGRAW-HILL Book Company Europe
Shoppenhangers Road, Maidenhead, Berkshire SL6 2QL, England
Telephone 01628 23432
Fax 01628 770224

British Library Cataloguing-in-Publication Data

English, Jack
    Police training manual. – 8Rev.ed
    I. Title II. English, Brian
    363.220941

    ISBN 0-07-709079-9

12345 CUP   9876

Typeset by BookEns Limited, Royston, Herts
and printed and bound in Great Britain at the University Press, Cambridge

Printed on permanent paper in compliance with ISO Standard 9706.

Contents

Module 4

Post-foundation training

Index

Note: As Module 3 comprises practical experience, Modules 1, 2, 4, and Post-foundation training only are covered in this book.

Preface

Following a review of police probationer training by a team from the University of East Anglia and selected police officers, a revised form of probationer training commenced in 1989.

The course is modular in structure, those subjects included in Module 1 being dealt with 'in-force' prior to the probationer constable's first visit to a Home Office Police Training Centre. Module 2 subjects are dealt with on the first occasion upon which a trainee attends the Training Centre, in the main by the medium of a core curriculum of case studies. Following Module 2, the trainee is to be given, within Module 3, opportunities to experience those situations which were discussed and examined within Modules 1 and 2, by being exposed to the real problems which arise in the course of a police officer's duties on the beat. Enriched by such experience, the trainee will return to a Training Centre where, within Module 4, there will be opportunities to consolidate the knowledge gained, by being involved in in-depth discussions with colleagues and experienced trainers. Some new subjects will be taught within Module 4 and these subjects are those which will be more readily understood after some experience of beat work.

The training programme is reinforced within a post-foundation training course which develops training experienced within the various modules and deals with further subjects which are more easily understood at a later stage in the training programme.

This book attempts, so far as is possible, to separate the subject matter related to law and police procedure which will be considered within Modules 1, 2 and 4 and within the post-foundation course. It will be appreciated, however, that it is not always possible to draw a distinct line between matters which will arise within one discussion, as opposed to another, or within one module as opposed to another. Each subject has, therefore, been dealt with completely on the first occasion upon which it is introduced into the training programme, but this is not universally true; subjects have been separated whenever it appeared to be realistic to do so.

There are exceptions to these general guidelines. Where post-foundation training represents a continuation of the consideration of subjects which have previously been encountered, for the sake of completeness, all of the material will appear in one place, usually at the point where the subject is first offered for consideration. Where the subject is met for the first time within post-foundation training, the material will appear under that heading.

As it is a practical module, Module 3 has not been included in the book.

This book seeks to provide police officers who are undergoing probationer training with details of the law and police procedures which are included within the probationary training programme. The 'law' content of the book has been considerably increased within this edition in the hope that it will be of value well beyond probationer training. It does not attempt to deal with the complex issues *which surround* policing; such social issues are best left to specialist trainers who combine knowledge of the subject with sound experience of policing at the front-line, and matters such as communications generally have been removed. The inclusion of such subjects would considerably increase the size of the book and its cost. The only exceptions to the rule that the book will confine itself to matters related to the law and approved procedures is where it is considered that 'background' material (unrelated to social issues) is not readily available elsewhere.

This book is written in recognition of the terms of s. 6 of the Interpretation Act 1978 which seeks to avoid the constant use of the terms 'he' and 'she'. This provides that, in all respects, words importing the feminine gender include the masculine and words importing the masculine gender include the feminine.

This edition assumes that the provisions of the Criminal Justice and Public Order Act 1994 will be in force on the date of publication. It also assumes that the amendments to the Police and Criminal Evidence Act 1984, which are concerned with the investigation of complaints (made by the Police and Magistrates' Courts Act 1994), are in force. It is possible that revised police discipline regulations will come into force shortly after publication.

Jack English
Brian English

Module 1

Police Regulations and conditions of service

Governing legislation

The Police Act 1964, s. 33, as amended by the Police and Magistrates' Courts Act 1994, s. 17, empowers the Home Secretary to make regulations in respect of police officers. The Police Regulations 1995 deal with the organisation of police forces, the appointment, promotion, retirement, personal records, duty, overtime, leave, allowances, housing, uniform and equipment, and pay of police officers. Discipline within the service is dealt with by the Police (Discipline) Regulations 1985, as amended. The main areas with which we are concerned are:

(a) conditions of service;
(b) promotion;
(c) discipline.

Disciplinary matters are dealt with in a later section of this book.

Conditions of service

We shall examine the following matters which are included in Police Regulations:

(1) *Restrictions on the private life of members*

It may, at first consideration, appear to be quite unfair that citizens who are appointed as constables and swear to uphold the peace should be subjected to additional restrictions upon their private lives. We tend to divorce our work from our home life and to think of them as separate matters. The labour organisations guarding the interests of workers in other fields would be unlikely to accept the idea of rules restricting, in any way, the private lives of their members, but it is important to recognise the unique position of a police constable.

The Police Regulations state that a constable shall at all times abstain from any activity which is likely to interfere with the impartial discharge of his duties, or which is likely to give rise to the impression among members of the public that it may so interfere. The importance of public confidence in the police is emphasised by the final words of this sentence within which it is made clear that nothing must be undertaken which suggests that a police officer may owe a certain allegiance to any section of society. If a constable was known to be working in the evenings as a steward in the local golf club, members of the public, knowing that in that capacity he or she was a servant of the members of the club, must doubt that constable's willingness to enforce the law in circumstances involving one of the members.

It is therefore not surprising to find that regulations also control a police officer's involvement in business, the term 'business interest' being so widely defined as to include any employment for hire or gain outside the police service which is not compatible with the office of constable, unless the previous consent of the appropriate chief officer of police has been gained. This regulation also applies to any shop or like business which is kept or carried on by a constable's spouse (not being separated from him) at any premises within the police area, or by any relative included in his family, at the premises where he resides, as any business interests in which they were involved which were not compatible with a police officer's duties, could be seen to have a similar effect upon the officer's willingness to discharge duties impartially. In particular, the regulation prohibits the member or his spouse (not being separated from him) or any relative in the family living with him, holding a liquor licence, licences and permits associated with betting and gaming or places of public entertainment, or holding a pecuniary interest in any such licence or permit. It is quite apparent, without the necessity for regulations to repeat it, that it is undesirable for police officers or their families to be responsible for the conduct of betting offices, public houses, night clubs and dance halls. These are some of the establishments in which breaches of the law are likely to take place from time to time, and it is inconceivable that a police officer should be directly connected with them. Although the regulation also includes a shop within the area of the police force in which the officer is serving, it is unlikely that a chief officer of police would refuse permission for an officer's husband or wife to open a shop which dealt with standard commodities, provided that the officer concerned did not intend to identify him or herself with it. It would be rather embarrassing to sell goods to a customer on one day and to report that person for an offence the following day. The purpose of such regulations is not to prevent police officers or their families from having other interests, but rather to ensure that their impartiality can never be questioned.

When a chief officer of police receives written notice of an intention to acquire a business interest, he must determine whether it is compatible with service as a constable and within 28 days, notify the constable of his decision. Within 10 days of that notification (or such longer period as the police authority may allow) the member may appeal to the police authority by written notice. On receipt of such notice the police authority must require the chief officer of police to provide it with a notice within 10 days setting out his reasons for refusal, together with any documents upon which he relied in support of his decision. The police authority must send copies of the notice and documents to the constable and afford him a reasonable time (not less than 14 days) to comment. Within 28 days of receipt of such comments, the police authority must determine the appeal. If it supports refusal a further appeal lies to the Secretary of State.

Active participation in politics is prohibited absolutely, although this does not preclude police officers from exercising their democratic right to vote at elections. Successive governments have always taken care to avoid legislation which suggested, even to the smallest degree, that police officers were subject to the dictates of central government or any political party temporarily in power. If police officers were to be seen adding vocal support at political meetings, the public could not be blamed for becoming alarmed at the significance. At times of industrial unrest, officers must be particularly careful to avoid identification with either side involved in the dispute, otherwise they will be accused of political bias.

Further restrictions with which we are concerned relate to a police officer's place of residence. The areas policed by most forces are quite considerable and it is the duty of a chief officer of police to ensure that all parts of his force area are efficiently policed. It is therefore essential that he has some control over the place at which a police officer shall live. In consequence, police officers have, for many years, been provided with free accommodation or a substantial allowance if they are owner-occupiers of residential property, or have rented property on their own behalf. It is therefore understandable that a police officer must obtain the approval of the chief officer of police as to his place of residence. In addition, an officer must not, without the previous consent of the chief officer of police, receive a lodger in a house or quarters with which he is provided by the police authority, nor must he sub-let any part of the premises. The situation is slightly different if the officer owns the house in which he receives a lodger, or sub-lets part of the property; in such a case he must give *written notice* to the chief officer before doing so. This allows the chief officer to make any adjustment to the allowance payable in respect of the property which recognises such arrangement.

The final requirement is that a police officer shall not wilfully refuse or neglect to discharge any lawful debt. This part of the regulations was not intended to discourage police officers from obtaining advances from building societies, or buying motor cars or house furnishings under hire purchase agreements. The intention is to prevent officers from incurring debts with local individuals who will then be in a position to exert some influence over them in the discharge of their duties, particularly if they are not in a position to clear the debt at the time.

(2) *Sick leave*

It is essential that force areas are efficiently policed for 24 hours each day. The right to strike has always been denied the police service as the public have a right to expect to be protected from the criminal section of society at all times. In the same way, steps have been taken to ensure that unnecessary absences from duty are prevented by requiring that all such absences are supported by a medical certificate.

All police authorities have taken advantage of the provisions of Police Regulations which permit them to consent to absence of not more than seven days on any one occasion without a medical certificate. The regulations make provision for a medical practitioner appointed or approved by the police authority to examine a police officer who is absent and in respect of whom a medical certificate is in force. If he considers the officer fit for duty, with the consent of the medical practitioner who issued the certificate, a third doctor may examine the officer within 28 days of the difference of opinion occurring. If the third medical practitioner considers the officer fit for duty, he must return to duty.

(3) *Personal records*

In any efficient organisation, it is essential that up-to-date records of employees are kept. Police Regulations require that such records be kept containing a constable's personal particulars together with details of his service. This will include his place and date of birth, and particulars of any marriage or children; military service or service in another force; passes or failures in qualifying examinations for promotion. When an officer, for example, is being considered for promotion to a higher rank details of previous promotions, the stations and departments in which he has served, his commendations by his chief officer or officers of courts of law, together with records of any punishments awarded under discipline regulations, must be readily available. A member of a police force is entitled, on request, to inspect his personal record. Punishments of a fine or reprimand shall be expunged after three years free of punishment other than a caution, or five years in other cases.

(4) *Probationary period and discharge of a probationer*

A police constable is on probation for the first two years of his service in his police force or for a longer period, not exceeding 12 months, where, in the opinion of the chief officer of police, the period of probation was seriously interrupted by a period of absence from duty by reason of injury or illness. Probation may also be extended by the chief officer of police for other reasons, but this must be with the consent of the Secretary of State. If an officer transfers from one force to another and has already successfully completed his probationary period in the first force, he may not be required to undergo probationary service once again. There are other exceptions to the rule which can be exercised at the discretion of a chief officer of police but the basic principle is that a constable in one way or another must undergo a full term of probationary service at the commencement of his police career.

This requirement is not surprising as it is quite impossible to determine, with certainty, that an applicant will be suited to a career in a police force on appointment to the office of constable. The police service is a disciplined service but peculiar in that the discipline required from individuals is mainly a self-discipline. The job is demanding. A constable patrols alone at all hours of the day and night; he is required to deal with distressing situations which can have some effect upon the individual, and he is required to enforce laws which are not always popular with members of the public. It is therefore necessary to have a period of time during which a fair assessment can be made of his suitability to hold the office of constable.

At any time during this probationary period a constable can be discharged if the chief officer considers that he is not fitted mentally or physically to perform the duties of his office, or is not likely to become an efficient or well conducted officer. By using the term 'mentally' it is not suggested that the officer is found to be of low IQ or unstable, but, as described above, the office of constable makes high demands upon men and women and all are not mentally equipped to hold such office. It can also be appreciated that the outdoor nature of police work demands some physical endurance, caused by changing tours of duty, peculiar hours of work, and the typically British winter season.

A constable whose services are dispensed with under these provisions may give notice to the police authority of his intention to retire. If he does so before the date upon which his services are to be dispensed with, he shall not be considered to have had his services dispensed with under these provisions.

A chief constable does not have an absolute discretion to dismiss a probationer constable at will. The action must be fair and in accordance with the rules of natural justice and must give the probationer constable an opportunity to offer any explanation or defence. In addition, it is only the chief constable, or an assistant commissioner in the case of the Metropolitan Police who can so dismiss, this function cannot be delegated to an assistant chief constable. The enquiry into the issue need not be conducted by the chief constable, who can delegate administrative matters, but the decision must be that of the chief constable alone.

Where a chief constable is considering dispensing with the services of a probationer constable under these regulations, the probationer constable must be shown any report containing judgments and opinions on the probationer. If the allegations against him amount to a disciplinary offence he must be charged and a disciplinary hearing held.

(5) *Qualification for promotion*

Matters concerning promotion are dealt with by the Police (Promotion) Regulations 1979. These regulations are quite brief and deal with qualification, selection, probationary service in the rank of sergeant, temporary promotion, and promotion of officers selected to attend the accelerated promotion course at the Police College.

The regulations require that a constable, to be qualified for promotion to the rank of sergeant, must have, before 1 December in any year, passed the constable's qualifying examination and practical tests, have completed two years' service and have completed his probationary service, and that sergeants, similarly, must have, before 1 December in any year, passed the sergeant's qualifying examination and practical tests and have completed two years' service in the rank of sergeant. Sergeants wishing to take the qualifying examination must hold the rank of sergeant (other than temporarily under Regulation 8) on 1 July in the year in which they wish to take it. Having been promoted to the rank of inspector there are no further qualifying examinations to be undertaken before being advanced to higher rank, nor are there minimum periods of service laid down to be completed within any rank. Further promotion is by selection of chief officers of police who are usually assisted in this difficult task by appraisal reports submitted by supervisory officers and the observations of members of interview boards set up by the chief officers for the purpose.

The Police (Promotion) Regulations prescribe two-part examinations: the first a written paper; the second a practical test. Passes in previous examinations remain valid. The content, form, the pass mark, and assessment criteria for each of the examinations is a matter for consideration by the Police Promotion Examinations Board. The Board is appointed by the Home Secretary and includes persons of suitable academic standing: a Home Office representative, representatives from police authorities, local government management board (which has undertaken the administrative arrangements in respect of the examinations), one of HM Inspectors of Constabulary, a representative from the Metropolitan Police, and representatives from the ranks of the chief officers, superintendents, and the federated ranks.

A member of a police force who is promoted to the rank of sergeant shall be on probation in that rank for a period of one year or for such longer period as the chief officer of police determines in the circumstances of a particular case. He may be reduced to the rank of constable at any time during his period of probation if the chief officer of police considers that he is not likely to perform satisfactorily the duties of a sergeant. This regulation merely provides an opportunity to examine an officer's potential to lead and direct people in an operational setting before confirming his rank. It is one thing to be an efficient police constable and as such to gain favourable mention by superior officers, but quite another to give effective leadership to a team of people.

Police Staff College – accelerated promotion course

(1) Objects

The courses are designed to give opportunities for accelerated promotion to officers who show potential to develop quickly and to reach high rank.

(2) Selection

Constables who are qualified for promotion to the rank of sergeant and existing sergeants who in either case are not more than 30 years of age and do not have more than 10 years' service, may make application to their chief officer to be considered for a place on the course. (The age limit may be extended to 35 years, at the discretion of the chief officer, in special circumstances.)

The second stage involves provincial and Metropolitan Police candidates being interviewed by a Central Selection Board which will recommend those officers considered to be suitable for interview by the Extended Interview Board which is the final stage of the process. The Extended Interview Board may recommend deferment for a period of one year, of the consideration of a particular candidate.

Those officers who have already been selected within the Graduate Entry Scheme are merely required to pass the qualifying examination for promotion to the rank of sergeant in order to receive a 'special interview' by the Extended Interview Board. However, such officers will be reported upon by their chief officers of police to ensure that they have equipped themselves in a way to justify selection and to merit attendance on the course. If such an entrant is not recommended, the report of the chief officer should be quite specific in relation to the reasons why that entrant is considered to be unsuitable.

(3) The nature of the course and promotion

An accelerated promotion course means a course for the time being recognised by the Secretary of State for the purposes of reg. 9 of the Police (Promotion) Regulations 1979, as amended, as the accelerated promotion course for sergeants APC(S), or the course recognised as the accelerated promotion course for inspectors APC(I). Such a course must entail periods of residence at the Police Staff College.

A constable who is qualified for promotion to the rank of sergeant and is selected to attend APC(S) shall be promoted to the rank of sergeant on the first day of his attendance. Such service is recognised as service in the rank of sergeant but the period of residence at the Police Staff College does not count as probationary service in that rank.

A sergeant so qualified and selected will similarly be promoted to the rank of inspector on the first day of his attendance but shall be on probation in that rank until he has completed one year's service in it.

Complaints against the police

Complaints

A 'complaint' for the purposes of the Police and Criminal Evidence Act 1984 is any complaint about the conduct of a police officer which is submitted by a member of the public, or on behalf of a member of the public and with his written consent. Complaints may be received directly from a member of the public or from some person or organisation which takes up his cause provided that such person gives his written consent.

Receipt and investigation of complaint

The chief officer of police is the disciplinary authority for his force and s. 84 of the Act of 1984 requires that where a complaint is submitted to a chief officer of police, it shall be his duty to take any steps that appear to him to be desirable for the purpose of obtaining or preserving evidence relating to the conduct complained of. He must determine whether he is the 'appropriate authority' in relation to the officer against whom the complaint is made. In relation to an officer in the Metropolitan Police, the 'authority' is the Commissioner, in the provinces it is the chief officer of police. If the conduct in respect of which the complaint has been made has already been the subject of criminal or disciplinary proceedings the complaint should not be recorded for investigation.

Otherwise, a chief officer must record the complaint and consider whether it is suitable for informal resolution. He can appoint an officer from his own force to assist with that decision. Complaints which are not suitable for informal resolution must be investigated and the chief officer must appoint an officer from his own or another force to carry out a formal investigation.

The investigating officer shall, as soon as possible (without prejudicing his or any other investigation in the matter), inform in writing the officer who is the subject of the complaint of the nature of that allegation or complaint. This may not be delayed until the conclusion of criminal proceedings against the complainant.

Informal resolution of complaints

Those complaints which appear to a chief officer to be capable of informal resolution may be so resolved and the chief officer may appoint an officer from his force to so resolve them. This can only be done with the consent of the complainant and the chief officer must be satisfied that even if proved, the conduct would not involve criminal or disciplinary proceedings against the officer concerned. If it appears that informal resolution will not be possible after attempts have been made, or that for any other reason the complaint is unsuitable for informal resolution, an investigating officer must be appointed. In these circumstances, the investigating officer must not be the officer who has been involved in attempts at informal resolution.

The investigating officer must submit his report to the chief officer of police, unless the complaint is one which is supervised by the 'Complaints Authority'. On occasions it is desirable to appoint an officer from another force to investigate a complaint and the chief officer of that other force is required by the Act to supply such an officer on request.

The officer appointed to resolve such a complaint informally is required by the Police (Complaints) (Informal Resolutions) Regulations 1985, as soon as practicable to seek the views of the complainant and the member concerned about the matter and take such other steps as appear to him appropriate. If it appears to the appointed officer that the complaint had in fact already been satisfactorily dealt with at the time it was brought to his notice he may, subject to any representation made by the complainant, treat it as having been informally resolved.

The appointed officer, taking into consideration the views of the complainant, shall take such steps as appear to him to be appropriate to resolve the complaint. He shall not, for the purpose of informally resolving a complaint, tender any apology to the complainant on behalf of the member concerned for his conduct unless he has admitted the conduct in question.

A complainant is entitled to a copy of the record of informal resolution within three months. No record shall be made in an officer's personal record.

Police Complaints Authority

Section 83 of the 1984 Act established a body to be known as the 'Police Complaints Authority' which consists of a chairman (which is a Crown appointment) and not less than eight other members who are appointed by the Home Secretary. Appointments are made for a period of three years at a time. Members may be removed from office by the Home Secretary for a number of reasons. The Authority is authorised to set up regional offices throughout England and Wales.

Under the Police (Dispensation from Requirement to Investigate Complaints) Regulations 1989 the Authority may dispense with complaints which are anonymous, repetitious, incapable of resolution, or which follow the informal resolution of a previous similar complaint; also where a complaint is vexatious or where there has been unreasonable delay (12 months without good reason for delay) in making a complaint.

References to the Authority

Complaints which allege that the conduct complained of resulted in the death or serious injury of some other person and other complaints which are to be specified in regulations, *must* be referred to the Complaints Authority. Other complaints may be referred to the Authority and the Authority *may require* the submission of any other complaint for its consideration.

The term 'serious injury' means any fracture, damage to an internal organ, impairment of bodily function, a deep cut or deep laceration. It will frequently be difficult for chief officers to decide upon those cuts which are deep as opposed to those which are not! The Act also permits the reference of matters to the Authority which appear to indicate that an officer may have committed a criminal offence or behaved in a manner which would justify disciplinary proceedings *which is not the subject of a complaint*, if it appears that it ought to be referred by reason of its gravity or exceptional circumstances. The words in italics were added by the Police and Magistrates' Courts Act 1994 and replaced the term 'offence against discipline' in preparation for the introduction of the new disciplinary procedures which allow minor matters to be dealt with outside formal disciplinary procedures.

The purpose is clear; there shall be an independent review of all complaints of a serious nature, those involving death or serious injury to a member of the public, of incidents in respect of which no complaint has been made but it appears that a serious criminal or disciplinary offence may have been committed and the circumstances are exceptional (e.g. comments by the media or statements made in either House of Parliament). In addition, the Authority always has the power to require the submission of the results of any investigation into a complaint.

By s. 87 of the Act of 1984 complaints alleging that the conduct complained of resulted in the death of or serious injury to some other person must be referred to the Complaints Authority. The section also requires reference of matters specified by regulations. The Police (Complaints) (Mandatory Referrals, etc.) Regulations 1985 require reference of complaints alleging conduct which, if shown to have occurred would constitute:

(a) assault occasioning actual bodily harm; or
(b) an offence under s. 1 of the Prevention of Corruption Act 1906; or
(c) a serious offence within the meaning of s. 116 of the Act of 1984.

The Authority is required to supervise the investigation of such complaints, or any in respect of which it is considered desirable to do so, in the public interest.

A member of the Complaints Authority is entitled to be present at the interviews of police officers subject to disciplinary proceedings following a complaint.

The Authority must either select or approve the appointment of the investigating officer in respect of all investigations which it supervises. The Authority is authorised to impose requirements upon the nature of the investigation and the investigating officer must submit his report to the Complaints Authority, sending a copy to the chief officer of police.

After consideration of such a report, the Authority must submit an 'appropriate statement' to the chief officer and if it is practicable to do so, it shall send a copy to the officer whose conduct has been investigated. If the investigation concerns a complaint and it is practicable to do so, a copy shall be sent to the person by, or on behalf of, whom the complaint was made. An 'appropriate statement' is one which:

(a) states whether the investigation was or was not conducted to the satisfaction of the Complaints Authority;

(b) specifies any respect in which it was not so conducted; and

(c) deals with any other matters specified by regulations.

Separate statements may be issued in respect of the 'criminal' or 'disciplinary' aspects of the investigation. Proceedings for either of these matters should not be commenced before the issue of the statement unless circumstances, in the view of the Director of Public Prosecutions, make it undesirable to wait.

Chief officer's duties after investigation

Section 90 of the 1984 Act as amended by the Police and Magistrates' Courts Act 1994 requires that, on receiving a report concerning the conduct of an officer (other than a senior officer) a chief officer must determine whether the report indicates that a criminal offence may have been committed. If he decides that it does, the report must be sent to the Director of Public Prosecutions. The Home Secretary is empowered by regulations to specify when a memorandum is to be sent to the Police Complaints Authority, after the Director has dealt with the issue of criminal proceedings, signed by the chief officer of police, stating whether he had brought (or proposes to bring) disciplinary proceedings in respect of the conduct which was the subject of the investigation and, if not, giving his reasons.

Where, in circumstances to be prescribed by regulations, a chief officer considers that the report does not indicate that a criminal offence may have been committed, he must send the Police Complaints Authority a memorandum to that effect, signed by him and stating whether he has brought (or proposes to bring) disciplinary proceedings in respect of the conduct which was the subject of the investigation and, if not, giving his reasons. Where the investigation related to conduct which was the subject of a complaint and it was not supervised by the Police Complaints Authority then, when the chief officer is required by regulations to send a memorandum to the Authority he must, at the same time, send a copy of the complaint, and a copy of the report of the investigation.

If the memorandum sent by the chief officer states that he proposes to bring disciplinary proceedings, it shall be his duty to bring and proceed with them and if such a memorandum states that he has brought such proceedings, it shall be his duty to proceed with them. If a memorandum states that a chief officer has not brought disciplinary proceedings or does not propose to do so, the Police Complaints Authority may recommend him to bring such proceedings. If, following such a recommendation and consultation with a chief officer of police, the chief officer is still unwilling to bring such disciplinary proceedings, the Authority may direct him to do so, providing a written statement of their reasons for doing so. Unless the Authority subsequently withdraws that direction, a chief officer must comply. The chief officer must advise the Authority of what action he has taken in respect to a recommendation or direction and furnish the Authority with such information as they may reasonably require for the purpose of discharging their functions under the section.

The duties of the chief officer described above, are usually discharged by an assistant chief constable when matters of discipline are involved. This must be so if the chief constable is to hear and determine those charges at a later stage. It is essential that assistant chief constables make decisions as to whether or not to prefer charges in the first instance and that they retain control over internal investigations. In this way the chief constable has no pre-knowledge of the facts of the case when he hears the charges.

Discipline hearing

At the time of writing, new discipline regulations are in the course of preparation and these will give effect to some of the changes for which the Police and Magistrates' Courts Act 1994 prepared the way. The following material may therefore be subject to change in the not too distant future. However, the content of such regulations, while the subject of much speculation as the 1994 Act passed through Parliament, was not available for scrutiny. Government Ministers revealed that they wished to find a way to accelerate the resolution of matters involving misconduct and poor performance. It was said that new methods would allow police managers to deal with failures of officers more flexibly, so as to encourage officers to improve their performance and behaviour. The system then being considered was one which would divide disciplinary matters into offences which would require proof beyond reasonable doubt and those which require a lesser standard of proof based upon probability. The first will be resolved by disciplinary procedures involving chief officers of police; the second are likely to be resolved at a lower level.

Disciplinary hearings at the time of writing may be held before the officer's chief officer of police; the chief officer of another force; an assistant chief constable of the officer's force (the rank of deputy chief having been abolished) in certain circumstances; or before a disciplinary tribunal.

The Police (Discipline) Regulations 1985 are made under s. 33 of the Police Act 1964. Regulations shall provide for the manner of the determination of whether offences against discipline have been committed and for the various punishments which may be awarded. The existing provisions of the Police and Criminal Evidence Act 1984, which permit the determination of questions of whether offences of discipline have been committed, by chief constables, assistant chief constables (appointed to act as deputies) and assistant chief constables, will be repealed by order when new discipline regulations are made under the amended Police Act 1964, s. 33(2)(e). These regulations will make particular arrangements for the hearing of charges by an officer's chief constable, a chief constable from another force, or by an assistant chief constable in prescribed circumstances in which punishment is limited. An officer found guilty and punished by an officer other than the chief constable will have a right of appeal to the chief constable.

Tribunals

Procedures existing at the time of writing allow the Authority to direct that the charges be heard by a tribunal. Such a tribunal shall consist of a chairman (a chief constable or Assistant Commissioner of the Metropolitan Police as prescribed by regulations) and two members of the Police Complaints Authority who have not been concerned with the case. The punishment to be awarded is a matter for the chairman after consultation with the other members of the tribunal. A decision as to guilt may be a majority decision. The Authority will always hold that majority. It is probable that new procedures will follow these lines.

Representation at disciplinary hearings

Section 102 of the Act of 1984 provides that on the hearing of a disciplinary offence, the punishments of dismissal, requirement to resign or reduction in rank shall not be awarded unless the officer has been given an opportunity to *elect* to be legally represented at the hearing. This representation may be by counsel or solicitor.

There is still, therefore, no general right to legal representation at a disciplinary hearing by counsel or solicitor, but in instances other than those which may merit such serious punishments, an officer may be represented by another member of a police force.

If an officer fails without reasonable cause to give notice that he wishes to be legally represented, or gives notice that he does not wish to be so represented, the punishments of dismissal, requirement to resign, or reduction in rank, may be awarded without the officer being legally represented. The Police Federation will offer advice in such cases and will no doubt arrange for legal representation in appropriate cases. Federation funds may be used to defray charges where officers have elected to be legally represented.

If an officer gives notice that he wishes to be legally represented in such a case, the case against him may be presented by counsel or a solicitor whether or not he is actually so represented.

Disciplinary appeals

The Police Act 1964, s. 37, provides that a member of a police force who is dismissed, required to resign or reduced in rank may appeal to a police appeals tribunal against the decision except where he has the right of appeal to some other person; and in that case he may appeal to a police appeals tribunal from the decision of that other person if it results in his dismissal, requirement to resign or reduction in rank. Where an appeals tribunal allows an appeal it may, if it considers it appropriate to do so, make an order dealing with the appellant in a way which is less severe and which is a way in which he could have been dealt with by the person making the decision.

Prior to the amendment made by the 1994 Act, police officers enjoyed a right of appeal to the Home Secretary against a conviction for any offence against discipline. The Home Secretary was empowered to refer the matter to a tribunal. Appeals will now be made directly to a tribunal, but are limited to those circumstances described above. Where other punishments are imposed, the only appeal which exists is to a chief officer, if the punishment was imposed by an officer other than the chief officer.

In determining appeals from officers other than senior officers (above the rank of superintendent) an appeals tribunal shall consist of four members. The chairman must be a person of seven years general qualification within the meaning of s. 71 of the Courts and Legal Services Act 1990 (a lawyer) who is nominated by the Lord Chancellor and the members shall be a member of the police authority, a member from a list of chief officers or past chief officers (within five years of their retirement) approved by the Home Secretary, and a retired police officer of appropriate rank. The chairman shall have a casting vote.

An appeals tribunal may determine a case without a hearing but shall not decide to do so unless both the appellant and respondent have been afforded an opportunity to make written or, if either so requests, oral representations and any such representations have been considered. At a hearing the appellant will have the right to appear by a serving member of a police force or by counsel or solicitor; and the respondent shall have the right to appear by officer of the police force or by the clerk or other officer of the police authority or by counsel or solicitor. Where an appeal is allowed the order which is made has the effect of substituting the tribunal's decision for the original decision. A reinstatement is effective from the date of the original disciplinary decision. Where there has been a suspension the order which is made must deal with that matter. An appellant shall pay his own costs (a reversal of the procedure which existed before the 1994 Act) unless the tribunal directs that the whole or any part of such costs is to be defrayed from police funds.

Double jeopardy

Prior to the Police and Magistrates' Courts Act 1994, s. 104 of the Police and Criminal Evidence Act 1984 provided that where a member of a police force has been convicted or acquitted of a criminal offence he shall not be liable to be charged with an offence against discipline which is in substance the same as the offence of which he had been convicted or acquitted. Section 37 of the 1994 Act repealed s. 104 of the 1984 Act.

There is now therefore no barrier to a police officer being charged with a disciplinary offence arising from circumstances which led to a criminal charge being preferred. The original proposal to bring about this change was defeated in the House of Lords but reinstated, in the face of considerable opposition, in the House of Commons. The Government argument, that a police disciplinary proceeding was not a court hearing, and therefore escaped the requirement that a man shall not be charged twice with the same offence, was strongly criticised and certainly appears to be contrived. Disciplinary offences are set out in a statutory instrument and are punishable by that instrument. Breaches of regulations set out in statutory instruments are, it is submitted, breaches of the law.

Police discipline code

Introduction

The following regulations are being reviewed at the time of writing. The need for formal discipline in the police service requires little explanation. The acceptance of the office of constable places considerable responsibility upon the individual and turns the public eye upon that person. The wearing of a uniform which symbolises the service which stands between the law-abiding majority and the reckless minority, demands a self-discipline unequalled in any other walk of life. Constables are subject to the laws of the land and, in addition, are subject to a discipline code which is set out in the Police (Discipline) Regulations 1985.

In justifying standards which do not apply elsewhere, one will often be told that the police service is a disciplined service, but it is important to dismiss from the mind any parity with the armed services in this respect. The nature of police training is such that men and women in the police force recognise a unique individual responsibility for their actions, and are trained to act alone, to make their own decisions and, to some degree, to set their own standards.

Police officers must obey the laws of the land in the same way as other citizens and they are answerable before the courts if they commit offences. The requirements of the police discipline code are additional requirements. The Police and Magistrates' Courts Act 1994 amended the Police Act 1964, s. 33. The amended section provides that one of the matters in respect of which regulations may be made will be related to the conduct, efficiency and effectiveness of members of police forces and the maintenance of discipline. It also requires that regulations shall establish, or make provision for the establishment of, procedures for cases in which a member of a police force may be dealt with by dismissal, requirement to resign, reduction in rank, reduction in rate of pay, fine, reprimand or caution.

The discipline code

If a constable is found guilty of an offence against the discipline code, he is liable to be punished. Punishments vary according to the gravity of the offence and, on occasions, according to the previous conduct of the individual concerned. These may be:

    (a) dismissal from the force;
    (b) requirement to resign as an alternative to dismissal;
    (c) reduction in rank;
    (d) fine;
    (e) reduction in rate of pay for up to one year;
    (f) reprimand;
    (g) caution.

The offences set out in the discipline code apply to all ranks except chief constables and assistant chief constables.

Offences against the discipline code

(1) Discreditable conduct

The offence lies in a member of a police force acting in a disorderly manner or a manner prejudicial to discipline or reasonably likely to bring discredit on the service. This offence is not confined to such acts committed while in uniform, or even while on duty, but applies to all occasions. It is intended to ensure that the police service retains the respect of the general public. Although a member of the public may be able to afford the luxury of becoming involved in a minor disturbance in a night club, it can be appreciated that a constable in a similar situation, when he is not enforcing the law but is an involved party, cannot be so easily forgiven.

(2) *Misconduct towards a member of a police force*

This offence is committed where a member of a police force engages in conduct towards another such member, which is oppressive or abusive, or a member of a police force assaults another such member.

(3) *Disobedience to orders*

This offence is committed where a member of a police force, without good and sufficient cause, disobeys or omits or neglects to carry out any lawful order, written or otherwise, or fails to comply with any requirement of a Code of Practice for the time being in force under s. 60 of the Act of 1984, or contravenes any provision of the Police Regulations containing restrictions on the private lives of members of police forces, or requiring him to notify the chief officer of police that he, or a relation included in the family, has a business interest, within the meaning of these regulations. Because of the inclusion of the words 'without good cause' a failure to carry out a task because of the pressure caused by other duties is not necessarily an offence. The offence embraces all forms of orders, spoken, written or provided by regulations. A chief constable's 'force orders', a formidable document, contains many hundreds of such orders.

(4) *Neglect of duty*

Where a member of a police force, without good cause omits or neglects or fails to work his beat in accordance with orders, or leaves his assigned place of duty (or fails to return promptly to it if left for an authorised purpose), is absent without leave from, or is late for any duty or fails to account properly for money or property received in the course of his duty. The words 'without good cause' automatically excluded occasions upon which the beat officer had been called to a serious incident such as a traffic accident. Many similar routine functions are to be carried out on most beats, for example, the checking of vulnerable property during tours of night duty.

(5) *Falsehood or prevarication*

Where a member of a police force 'knowingly or negligently' makes any false, misleading, or inaccurate oral or written statement, or entry in any official document or records. The offence is also committed when official documents or records are wilfully and without proper authority or through lack of care, destroyed, mutilated, or without good and sufficient cause altered, or erased, or added to, or when false, misleading or inaccurate statements have been knowingly or through neglect made in connection with his appointment to a police force.

The offences connected with false statements, oral or written, including entries in official records, merely emphasise the importance of police officers keeping fair and accurate records of matters with which they deal. For example, entries made in pocket notebooks may later become one of the most telling factors in determining the guilt or innocence of an accused person when he appears before a court. It is, therefore, important to ensure that all records kept by police officers are as accurate as possible. The important words in relation to such offences are 'knowingly or negligently', which tells us that such inaccuracies must have been deliberately or carelessly recorded before an offence is committed. The destruction or alteration of records must have been done wilfully and without proper authority, these words excluding occasions upon which records are destroyed because they no longer serve a useful purpose, as opposed to occasions when it may have been done to help a friend, by destroying records of his minor convictions. The term 'knowingly or through neglect', in connection with false statements made in connection with appointments, limits punishment to occasions when deliberate or reckless deception has been practised; for example, stating that one has not been convicted of any offence by a court, or that the candidate has a number of passes at GCSE, when such facts are untrue. Such a term would exclude instances in which an applicant merely made an honest mistake of fact, by alleging that he had perhaps six GCSEs when he in fact had only five. The test is: Did he deliberately attempt to deceive?

(6) *Improper disclosure of information*

Where a member of a police force, without proper authority, communicates to any person any information which he has in his possession as a member of a police force, he commits an offence. The offence also includes making anonymous communications to police authorities or any member of a police force or canvassing members of police authorities concerning force matters.

It can be appreciated that the office of constable is not one for gossips. The constable is in a privileged position and learns many things of a confidential nature not only concerning internal police matters, but affecting the lives and habits of citizens. This disciplinary offence merely ensures that the discretion which the public expect from their police officers is exercised. Anonymous communications to police authorities and other police officers are forbidden. If a member of a police force wishes to bring any matter to the attention of such persons, there are recognised procedures for doing so.

(7) *Corrupt or improper practice*

Where a member of a police force, in his capacity as such and without the consent of the chief officer of police or the police authority, directly or indirectly solicits or accepts any gratuity, present or subscription; or places himself under any pecuniary obligation to any person in such a manner as might affect his properly carrying out his duties; or improperly uses, or attempts so to use, his position as a member of the force for his private advantage; or in his capacity as a member of the force and without consent of the chief officer of police, writes, signs or gives a testimonial of character or other recommendation with the object of obtaining for any person or of supporting an application for the grant of a licence of any kind.

As long as there are laws to enforce, there will be people who are prepared to grant all kinds of privileges to constables in the hope that they will not be quite so vigorous in enforcing these laws. The simple test in relation to offers of favours, is one of determining whether or not such offers are being made to you in your capacity as John or Jane Citizen or in your capacity as a constable. All such approaches from other than your personal friends must be extremely suspect.

(8) *Abuse of authority*

This offence is committed where a member of a police force treats any person with whom he may be brought into contact in the execution of his duty in an oppressive manner and, without prejudice to the foregoing, in particular where he:

    (a) without good and sufficient cause conducts a search, or requires a person to submit to any test or procedure, or makes an arrest; or

    (b) uses any unnecessary violence towards any prisoner or any other person with whom he may be brought into contact in the execution of his duty, or improperly threatens any such person with violence; or

    (c) is abusive or uncivil to any member of the public.

The possibility of actions being considered as 'incivility' by members of the public should always be borne in mind as most complaints received from members of the public are rooted in the manner in which the officer dealt with a particular person. Always imagine that the person you are dealing with is a close relative and adopt the manner which you would adopt in those circumstances.

(9) *Racially discriminatory behaviour*

This offence is committed (without prejudice to the commission of any other offence) where a member of a police force:

    (a) while on duty, on the grounds of another person's colour, race, nationality or ethnic or national origins, acts towards that other person in a way involving abuse of authority (as defined above); or

    (b) in any other way, on any of these grounds, treats improperly a person with whom he may be brought into contact while on duty.

(10) *Improper dress or untidiness*

Where a member of a police force who is on duty is improperly dressed or untidy in appearance, without good and sufficient cause. The offence which can be committed while on duty is not restricted to the wearing of police uniform and equally applies to those in plain clothes. Additionally, the offence applies to the wearing of uniform, even when off duty, so covers the journey to and from a place of duty.

(11) *Neglect of health*

The instructions of any medical practitioner appointed by a police authority must be followed by all officers. Members of police forces who, without good and sufficient cause, neglect to do so, commit a disciplinary offence. However, an officer's duty to do all that he can to ensure an early return to duty from sick leave is not restricted to instructions from a doctor appointed by the police authority. If any act or any conduct likely to retard return to duty is carried out, the offence is committed.

19

(12) *Damage to police property*

There are two offences created by this regulation. The first is concerned with a member of a police force who wilfully, or through lack of care causes any waste, loss or damage to any police property. The second relates to failure to report as soon as reasonably practicable any such loss or damage to such property issued to, or used by him or entrusted to his care. Thus an officer who by negligence damages a police vehicle may be charged with this offence. If the incident occurs elsewhere than on a road, a charge under the Road Traffic Act would not apply. However, the degree of negligence should be sufficient to satisfy the requirements of criminal as opposed to civil proceedings. If such damage was 'wilful' it is likely that an offence contrary to the Criminal Damage Act 1971 would be preferred. Without regard to the issue of how the damage was occasioned, failure to report it is punishable under the second part of the regulation.

(13) *Drunkenness*

Where a member of a police force renders himself unfit through drink for duties which he is required to perform or may reasonably foresee having to perform. The offence can be committed when existing circumstances are such that a call out appears to be probable.

(14) *Drinking on duty or soliciting drink*

Where a member of a police force while on duty, without proper authority, drinks or receives from any other person intoxicating liquor or demands from any other person any intoxicating liquor he commits an offence.

Again the words 'without proper authority' appear as there are occasions upon which officers may be given authority by senior ranks to drink intoxicating liquor. On occasions, when duty is performed at some special outdoor function, the organisers may provide a bottle of beer with a lunch with the blessing of the officer in charge; this is permissible within the discipline regulations. However, the supervision of licensed premises and the dependence of licensees upon the assistance of constables from time to time, provide opportunities for police officers to drink while on duty and this must be discouraged.

(15) *Entering licensed premises*

Where a member of a police force while on duty, or while off duty but wearing a uniform, without good and sufficient cause, enters premises which are licensed in respect of intoxicating liquor, betting and gaming or the regulation of entertainment.

(16) *Criminal conduct*

Where a member of a police force has been found guilty by a court of law of a criminal offence. This disciplinary offence must be constantly in the minds of police officers. The term 'criminal offence' is not defined and is open to interpretation by chief officers of police. The widest interpretation could include all offences, including trivial breaches of regulations, even parking restrictions if those restrictions were imposed by regulations. At the extreme, this could lead to dismissal from the service. It is the author's view that this regulation was made to provide a means of getting rid of dishonest police officers and that the term 'criminal offence' should be restricted to those requiring some element of *mens rea*, that is a guilty or blameable condition of mind. However, the term is currently given wider interpretation by some chief officers.

(17) *Being an accessory to a discipline offence*

Where a member of a police force incites, connives at, or is knowingly an accessory to any offence against discipline.

Discipline and the Codes of Practice

The Police and Magistrates' Courts Act 1994 will repeal the Police and Criminal Evidence Act 1984, s. 67(8), which provided that a police officer would be liable to disciplinary proceedings for a failure to comply with any provisions of a Code of Practice. However, the repeal is proposed because of problems which have been caused in view of the many discretionary provisions of the codes. Similar disciplinary offences will be included in Police Regulations which follow the 1994 Act.

Police Federation and negotiating machinery

Terms of reference

The current legislation governing the Police Federation is s. 44 of the Police Act 1964, and under the authority of this section the Home Secretary may make regulations which prescribe the constitution and proceedings of the Police Federation. The Police Federation is the representative organisation of most members of police forces and stands in place of the usual trade union membership which is met in outside bodies. It is responsible for representing members of police forces in England and Wales in all matters affecting their welfare and efficiency other than questions of discipline and promotion affecting individuals. In a disciplined service, such as the police, it can be appreciated that matters of discipline and promotion affecting individuals must be excluded from the matters with which the Federation may make representation. The hearing of disciplinary proceedings, the decision to be made, and the selection of officers for promotion to a higher rank are matters solely for chief constables and tribunals. Members of a police force may be represented at the disciplinary hearing by another police officer, and appointed officers of the Police Federation may also accept this role but only in their capacity as members of a police force, not as officers of the Federation. Many chief constables allow Federation representatives to sit with the panel of senior officers charged with the task of interviewing candidates for promotion, on occasions to participate in the proceedings and at other times to act as observers.

Membership

The Home Secretary, in consultation with the Joint Central Committee of the Police Federation, makes provisions in regulations concerning membership. Currently, all members of police forces below the rank of superintendent and all police cadets are permitted to become members of the Federation. Superintendents have their own representative body, as do chief and assistant chief constables.

A branch of the Federation exists in every police force and in each are constituted three branch boards representing, separately, constables, sergeants, and inspectors. Female officers are represented by these three boards in the same way as their male colleagues. The Police Federation also protects the interests of police cadets. Meetings are held at force, divisional, or subdivisional level to establish the feelings of members upon matters then under consideration. Annual central conferences are also held, to which all forces send representatives at constable, sergeant, and inspector levels and such conferences provide an opportunity for discussion at national level on problems then existing for the federated ranks.

Having established a policy at national level, it next becomes necessary to present the view of the federated ranks to the Home Office. This is not done directly; it is necessary to form a smaller body of officers to discharge this duty. The Joint Central Committee has already been mentioned in the context of negotiation with the Home Secretary and is quite small in number. Its members are elected at the annual conference.

Although the procedure for ensuring that matters receive attention at national level has been outlined, it must be appreciated that local matters can be quite effectively dealt with at force level and local branch boards are usually afforded the opportunity to discuss problems with chief constables.

Desborough Committee

The Desborough Committee was set up in 1919 at a time when there was serious unrest in the police service. Prior to that date, police officers had no right to make any form of representation to their superiors, and between 1909 and 1919 the situation had deteriorated rapidly. In 1909 a promising young inspector in the Metropolitan Police became involved in a dispute with his superiors and accused them of oppressive conduct. His grievance received much attention from the national press and Inspector Syme, being an expressive individual, made public knowledge much material that was embarrassing to his superiors. Disciplinary charges were heard and he was dismissed from the force, but he continued to make allegations. He formed the National Union of Police and Prison Officers and, as a result of continued libellous statements aimed at the Commissioner, together with his attempts to cause disaffection among the police in wartime, found himself in and out of prison, being finally admitted to Broadmoor. In 1931 he received, from the Government, substantial compensation for his treatment.

To be a member of this Police Union was to risk dismissal, but conditions were rife for discontent, with police pay falling well below that of industrial workers, until it reached a stage at which the families of police officers could not be adequately clothed and fed. When a police officer was sacked for his Union activities in 1918, certain demands were made of the Home Secretary by the Union. The demands were not met and a strike was called. It was partly successful in that it resulted in a substantial pay rise for the Metropolitan Police; the constable who had been dismissed was reinstated, but the Prime Minister would not accept a police union. A form of representation for inspectors, sergeants, and constables was permitted but the scheme was not a success. The Union began to gain in strength and once again demanded recognition, which was refused. By this time the Desborough Committee had begun its work: an announcement had been made of a rise in the constable's starting pay from £1.10s. to £3.10s. per week and of the Government's intention to introduce an alternative form of representation, other than through a union. It was also made clear that police officers who went on strike would be dismissed, but the Union was determined to force its recognition and when the Police Bill was introduced into the House of Commons on 8 July 1919, providing for the establishment of a police federation and banning police officers from becoming members of a trade union, they called a second strike. It was doomed from the beginning. Many police officers felt that the service had achieved all it could hope for, a substantial pay increase and a representative body. The strike, by 2364 men from seven forces, soon collapsed. All strikers were dismissed from the service and none was ever reinstated.

It is probably fair to say that the sympathetic attitude of the members of the Desborough Committee avoided a period of major disruption in the police service. They accepted the description of a constable's duties as earlier reported by the Royal Commission of 1906–8:

'We are satisfied that a policeman has responsibilities and obligations which are peculiar to his calling and distinguish him from other public servants and municipal employees – the burden of individual discretion and responsibility placed upon a constable is much greater than that of any other public servant of subordinate rank,'

and as a result recommended (1) improvements in pay and conditions, (2) that these should be standardised, and, perhaps more important, (3) that they should be matters for the Home Secretary. For the first time pay and conditions of service were standardised and brought under central control. However, the large issue as to whether or not there should be a national police force resulted in a complete rejection of nationalisation on the grounds that such large organisations frequently get themselves into a groove.

At the same time the subsequent Police Act 1919 established the Police Council as a central advisory body to the Home Secretary and the Police Federation as the representative organisation of the police service. The structure of the Police Federation has already been considered.

The first meeting of the Police Council was a historic occasion. The Council was made up of representatives of the Home Office, local authorities, commissioners, and policemen of all ranks, and the Home Secretary himself took the chair. The Council proved to be the ideal medium for implementing the recommendations of the Desborough Committee and the advantages to be gained by assembling together representatives of all bodies affected by proposals ensured the efficient formation of the first Police Regulations. As was expected, local authorities were loath to surrender any measure of their control over police forces and the volume of their protests ensured that small borough forces survived until 1946, and watch committees – the public authorities for borough forces – retained control of appointment, promotion, and discipline until the passing of the Police Act 1964.

Oaksey Committee

Following the Desborough Committee and the 1919 Act, there was a long period of contentment in the police service, for although the service suffered two small reductions in pay as part of general government economic measures in 1922 and 1931, pay scales generally remained high in comparison with average incomes and the cost of living. The 1939–45 war and its aftermath benefited the industrial worker at the expense of those in public service, and the low pay of police officers severely affected recruiting. The position had become so grave that the Metropolitan force had fewer men than in 1901 and an immediate pay increase was granted by the Government in 1946 which placed the constable 17 per cent above the average earnings in industry. Part of the agreement was that a further increase would not be sought before 1950, but the effects of inflation were such that the value of this award was quickly eroded. The Police Federation pressed for an earlier review and initial government opposition was overcome by rising discontent within the service. In May 1948 a committee was set up under the chairmanship of Lord Oaksey to consider in the light of the need for the recruitment and retention of an adequate number of men and women for the police forces in England, Wales and Scotland, and to report on pay, emoluments, allowances, pensions, promotion, methods of representation and negotiation, and other conditions of service.

Two reports were presented by the Oaksey Committee: April and November 1949. The first dealt with pay, pensions, and conditions of service (and these findings proved to be disappointing, resulting in pay increases of about 15 per cent which had such little effect upon recruitment that a further increase of 20 per cent became necessary within two years); the second dealt with appointments, training, promotion, discipline, housing, amenities, and the establishment of negotiating machinery. The Committee recommended the setting up of a Police Council for Great Britain, which came into being in 1953. The Police Federation had for some time been dissatisfied with the Police Council, for although it had been successful in ensuring that representatives of all interested parties met regularly to discuss police affairs, it was considered that the Home Secretary could be over-sympathetic towards the views of police authorities in relation to pay, as both had an interest in keeping costs down. This new Council, which was not established on a statutory basis, consisted of three separate panels representing chief officers, superintendents, and federated ranks respectively. In turn each panel consisted of a staff side and an official side, but provision was made to allow the whole Council to sit together to consider general questions. Prior to the Police Council for Great Britain being set up, pay claims had not been permitted to be referred to arbitration, but provision was now made for a panel of three arbitrators to be appointed by the Prime Minister. An independent chairman was appointed and the official side was to include representatives of all police authorities and the Home Office. The Police Federation was also permitted at this time to collect voluntary subscriptions. It can be appreciated that previously, when all Federation activity was dependent upon official funds, the scope of such activities was limited. Subscriptions currently made by members to Federation funds are allocated proportionately to the national and local organisations.

Police Act 1964

By the time the Royal Commission reported in 1962 the scene had been set. The Federation had already made known its suspicion of the Police Council established by the Police Act 1919 and had indicated its support of the Police Council for Great Britain. The 1964 Act, therefore, gave statutory authority to the Police Council for Great Britain as the negotiating body and the old Police Council was replaced by the Police Advisory Board, which was set up to advise the Home Secretary on general questions affecting the service. The title was later changed to the Police Council for the United Kingdom.

Edmund Davies Committee

This Committee of Inquiry was appointed in 1977 to review the machinery for negotiating police pay following a period of discontent in which some members felt it was necessary to demand the right to strike in order to press claims which would otherwise be ignored. The inquiry led to a formula by which future pay settlements would be established and resulted in the eclipse of the old Police Council which was replaced by the Police Negotiating Board. The Board has an independent chairman and secretariat. The Police Federation ensures that the views of all federated ranks are made known to the Board, in all matters.

The Sheehy Inquiry

The Sheehy Inquiry into Police Responsibilities and Rewards, under the chairmanship of Sir Patrick Sheehy, produced a report which was presented to the Home Secretary in 1993. One of its recommendations was concerned with establishing a means by which police officers might be rewarded in accordance with their performance, skills and the job which they were asked to do. While the issue of performance-related pay was restricted in the Police and Magistrates' Courts Act 1994 to officers of the rank of superintendent and above (although the provisions in respect of superintendents were merely permissive), the report provided a means by which assessment of pay within the formula established by Lord Edmund Davies, was broken.

The efforts of the Police Federation, and those of the Association of Chief Police Officers and the Superintendents' Association were largely instrumental in ensuring that many of the proposals of this group were ignored by the Home Secretary. Perhaps the most significant of the proposals which were not taken up were those which would have led to fixed-term appointments for all police officers and a common retirement age of 60 years. While the Home Secretary included the proposals which would have led to the abolition of the ranks of both chief superintendent and chief inspector within the original Bill which led to the 1994 Act, strong opposition in both Houses of Parliament led to the retention of the rank of chief inspector.

Role of the Police Federation

The Police Federation has moved a long way since its formation following the demand for a police union during and after the First World War. It is quite clear that the Home Secretary and chief constables welcome the active participation of the Federation in matters affecting the welfare and efficiency of the service.

As had already been discussed, the Police Council for the United Kingdom was the usual medium through which the views of the Federation, the Association of Chief Police officers, and the Superintendents' Association were made known. It had five standing committees: (A) for matters affecting chief and assistant chief officers (ranks above chief superintendents); (B) for matters affecting chief superintendents and superintendents; (c) for matters affecting the federated ranks; (D) to consider problems peculiar to all ranks of the service; and finally (E) to consider police pensions. Before making regulations concerned with these matters, the Home Secretary had to take into account any recommendations made by the Council and had to provide the Council with a draft of such regulations.

The Police Advisory Board, which may consider any issues affecting the police service, is made up of the Home Secretary, who is its chairman, representatives of local authorities (police authorities), the Commissioner of the City of London Police, the receiver for the Metropolitan Police District, the Association of Chief Police Officers, the Superintendents' Association, the Police Federation, and the Home Office. The Police Federation is, therefore, able to have matters which it wishes to be discussed considered by the Police Advisory Board.

One might consider the Advisory Board as being a group of advisers immediately available to offer advice to the Home Secretary on general matters affecting the police, many of which would not need to be consolidated in Police Regulations. On the other hand, the Police Council for the United Kingdom was very much a debating chamber in which would be discussed all matters affecting, for example, pay, allowances, promotion, and discipline – all being matters dealt with by existing Police Regulations.

It is now standard practice for members of the Police Federation to be invited to join working parties and committees set up on behalf of the Advisory Board or the Home Office. In this way it is possible for such groups to be aware of the feelings of the members of the service on matters which are being considered.

The Police Council for the United Kingdom was abolished by the Police Negotiating Board Act 1980 which replaced the Council with the Police Negotiating Board for the United Kingdom. This Board is charged with the duty to consider the interests of police authorities, members of police forces and police cadets of the United Kingdom in questions related to hours of duty, leave, pay and allowances, pensions, or the issue, use and return of police clothing, personal equipment and accoutrements.

Each police force has a Joint Negotiating and Consultative Committee which was set up following recommendations of the Edmund Davies Committee. It consists of representatives of all ranks of the force and provides a medium by which local problems can be easily resolved.

Assistance given to individuals

The Police Federation Regulations 1969, as amended, permit Federation funds to be used, within Police Federation rules, for any purpose which the Federation considers to be necessary or expedient in the interests of the Federation or its members. The only ban upon the use of such funds is in the support of a political party or a person's candidature in an election, or the making of a contribution to the funds of such a party, or a trade union or an organisation unconnected with the police service, its welfare or a charity. Such funds are often used to provide legal assistance to members charged with traffic offences arising in the course of police duty while driving or in charge of a motor vehicle with proper authority. Quite often the police authority, having an interest in such matters, arranges for an accused officer's defence after consultation with the Police Federation.

Legal charges incurred by members in proceedings brought against them for causing death or injury to any person or for any assault are frequently met by the Police Federation. The Joint Central Committee may impose terms and conditions upon use in such circumstances.

The Police Federation is particularly helpful in proceedings concerning claims for damages, injuries, or in relation to National Insurance and pension matters. It can usefully be approached concerning any matter affecting welfare and deals sympathetically with appeals for assistance for officers who occasionally find themselves in financial difficulty. Although there is no suggestion that Federation funds can be used for such purposes, many branch boards manage schemes which allow loans to be made to members in particular circumstances. A personal liability group insurance scheme is maintained by the Police Federation on behalf of its members. A death benefit is payable to serving officers who contribute to the funds of the Police Federation. It also operates a return of premium group insurance scheme for those who wish to participate.

The Police Federation will also provide assistance and will guide an officer in the correct procedure to be followed in the completion of a claim of compensation from the state-financed Criminal Injuries Compensation Board, should an officer be injured in the course of his duties.

Police National Computer

Introduction

The Police National Computer became operational in 1974. It has become known as PNC2 and is now as essential a part of normal policing operations as the pocket notebook. Police officers on the beat can now talk to their computer which is filled with information about vehicles, drivers and wanted, suspected or missing persons, etc. The computer does not sleep and it is available throughout each working day. It provides a reliable source of information but it can be a mistake to rely upon it completely. Computers can only provide the information with which they have been programmed. The vehicle which is being checked may be stolen even though the computer holds no record of it. It may not have been reported as stolen at the time of the check.

Computer terminals are available in every police force in England, Scotland and Wales. Terminals are available at force control rooms and frequently at divisional or area stations. Information can only be obtained from the computer direct. Contact control by personal radio or from any telephone or other internal communication system and the PNC2 operator will make an instant check with the computer.

Confidentiality

The information stored on the Police National Computer is highly confidential and is for police use only. It must not be divulged to any unauthorised person or to another organisation. The disciplinary offences of improper disclosure of information may be committed by any police officer who provides information obtained from the computer to any external agency. In some cases, offences against the Data Protection Act 1984 may be committed.

Security

Most requests for information will come from a police officer on the beat who will use his personal radio. Although this system is not always secure, most operators at local controls are easily able to identify the voices of their fellow officers and security is easily maintained. However, requests received by Telecom lines should be carefully vetted. Once again, if the enquiry is local it is probable that the voice of the caller will be recognised but the PNC operator will require the name, rank and station of the caller so that, if necessary, his identity can be verified by means of a return call to a particular police station, before a reply is given. Force orders are always very specific in relation to the correct use of PNC2 and it is essential that these are studied carefully, as failure to follow the correct procedure will amount to a disciplinary offence.

Indexes

Information relating to different matters is stored in different indexes. In relation to vehicles, information is stored concerning owners, those vehicles listed as stolen or suspicious and chassis and engine numbers. Those concerned with persons include criminals, wanted and missing persons and drivers who are disqualified.

Owners' index

The details recorded on the vehicle owners' index are similar to those recorded by the Driver and Vehicle Licensing Agency, Swansea. The DVLA computer is of a different type to PNC2 and is basically designed to store information. The basis of these records is therefore stored in PNC2 in a different way to permit quick and easy access. Its aim is to give an immediate response to an enquiry, even in relation to special searches when only the description of the vehicle is available, or only part of its registration number. The index contains the names and addresses of the current keepers of all motor vehicles registered in England, Scotland and Wales together with their descriptions.

Although PNC2 does not store Northern Ireland registrations, vehicles imported from Northern Ireland may be permitted to retain their Northern Ireland registration numbers, so it is still advisable to check if immediate information is required.

Computer records are only as strong as the updating system. It must be remembered that not all changes of ownership are notified to DVLA. If they are not, then PNC2 records cannot be updated and the name and address of the previous owner may be given. Whenever a police officer making an enquiry finds that a change has not been notified, apart from any other action he might take, he should complete form V.79 which is concerned with incorrect information found on PNC2. Obviously, the computer does not contain details of foreign vehicles, military vehicles, trade plates or unregistered vehicles. Enquiries concerning the previous keepers of vehicles should be directed to DVLA on form VQ.1. DVLA will reply on form VQ.5.

Stolen and suspect vehicles' index

An index of vehicle registration marks (VRM) is maintained, listing those which are stolen, suspected or of interest to the police for any reason. This index has no relationship to the vehicle owners' index and any index mark may be included as the concern is with vehicles which are stolen or suspect. It therefore does not matter what type of plates they are carrying.

Property index

This contains details of parts of motor vehicles, their trailers, items of plant or equipment, boats and firearms , which have either been stolen or obtained by means of deception. Marine engines which have been reported stolen or found are also included in this index, which has become known as the property index because information is always recorded concerning identification marks.

Details from this index can be obtained by either giving the vehicle registration mark, the engine or chassis number or relevant serial number. On occasions, when checking a suspect vehicle an enquiring officer will want information from the vehicle owners' index and from the stolen vehicle index. Such a combined enquiry can be made and only the vehicle registration mark is required to allow both searches to be made.

With all enquiries the response may be that there is no trace of the vehicle on the records required to be searched, although this is highly unlikely in relation to searches of the vehicle owners' index. If the vehicle is recorded, then full information will be provided. Occasionally, the computer will not release information as the vehicle has been 'blocked' for particular reasons which means that information will not be given over the air or by telephone.

Names' index

This index contains the names and descriptive details of persons who have been convicted of crime or who are wanted or missing or are disqualified drivers. A name is required to initiate a search and identification is assisted if information is available concerning date of birth, sex, height, etc. The index contains the names of those persons with a Criminal Record Office (CRO) number in the United Kingdom. It also includes details of all aliases used by such persons. The updating of this index is carried out by means of updated information from Criminal Record Office. It is important to remember that the information given will draw attention to possible matches and can never be taken to be conclusive. It is the responsibility of the police officer making the enquiry to decide whether or not the person he is checking is the person recorded in the index.

This index includes the names of persons wanted by the police, suspected of being involved in particular offences or whose whereabouts are to be established for particular reasons, missing persons, found persons, absconders, absentees and deserters from the armed forces and life licensees. It is essential that all police officers are aware of the need to keep this index up to date. If wanted persons are found and dealt with, or missing persons are located and their relatives have been informed, the records must be amended. The enquirers must provide as much information as possible to assist identification.

Up-to-date records are maintained of all persons disqualified from driving by order of a court.

Warning signals

Additional information may be provided on occasions when an enquiry is made which may be of extreme importance. The person about whom the enquiry is made may prove to be wanted, but it may also be known that he is ill, perhaps suffering from heart disease. In such cases the officer will be informed so that the possibility of aggravation of his condition will be recognised. On other occasions, information may be given concerning weapons which are frequently carried, or a tendency to violence, or escape.

Methods of creating/updating or deleting records on PNC2

The records contained in the computer are the product of an awareness by police officers that certain information may be of use to their colleagues in the fight against crime. Whenever a situation is dealt with in which a person or vehicle is involved in the circumstances described, the officer should ensure that a record is made. On occasions, this will amount to creating a new record; the first time that a particular vehicle has been reported in suspicious circumstances or when a vehicle is reported to have been stolen. At other times additional information will come to hand, further descriptive particulars of a vehicle or person will become available or it will become necessary to delete records as vehicles are recovered or wanted persons are arrested. It is essential that this is done immediately by radio to control, or by telephone to the PNC operator, or by completion of the various forms provided for the purpose. The circumstances in each case will dictate the method to be used.

The completion of the various forms used for including information in the various indexes maintained is a matter which requires considerable care. We have all been critical of computers at times, usually when a bill is received which contains errors or a bill that has already been settled. Computers do not make mistakes, it is the people who use them who are the weak links.

Phoenix

At the time of writing, it is anticipated that the names' index will be enhanced and will become known as 'Phoenix'. This update will allow for the storage of up to 23 items of additional information such as descriptions, tattoos and addresses as well as details of arrests and summonses. This will assist when officers are dealing with criminals from other force areas who are not recorded within local intelligence records.

Constitutional position of the police

The origins of the police system

(1) *Collective responsibility*

The Danish and Anglo-Saxon invaders provided the foundation of the English police system. The nearest parallel to our modern police officer in those times was the Saxon 'tythingman' or 'headborough'. During the reign of King Alfred the system of collective responsibility was developed which has as its basis a form of mutual protection against serious crime. The 'tuns' or 'vills', which are roughly equivalent to modern parishes, were each required to assume responsibility for their own policing and groups of about ten families were formed and put in the charge of a tythingman. Every male of the age of 12 years or over was listed by the tythingman and was required to make himself available for police purposes. In this way, all adult male members of the community were made responsible for the good conduct of their fellows. If the group failed to produce a criminal for trial, it could be fined or forced to pay compensation. It is quite apparent that one of the weaknesses of the system was that minor crimes which did not appear to be easily solved might well be concealed.

The system was further developed by grouping the tything into 'hundreds' which were supervised by the hundred man, or royal reeve. At this stage a judicial function was introduced, as the hundred man exercised administrative and judicial powers through a hundred court and could, therefore, hear and determine offences. The hundred man was, in turn, under the control of a shire reeve, or sheriff, who was directly responsible to the King for the maintenance of the 'King's peace' within his shire. This system of policing was tribal in origin and could only be effectively carried out while there was little movement of population. In any particular area it was essential that each person was known to the remainder of the community. Strangers were looked upon with considerable suspicion; if they committed crime in the vill and moved on quickly to escape capture, the members of the particular community concerned were required to make good the loss. To give some protection against this type of situation, the shire reeve, in the King's name, was permitted to raise a *posse comitatus*, which consisted of every enrolled male in the shire. The system of hue and cry was developed which involved the posse setting off in pursuit of a felon and continuing such pursuit until the felon was apprehended or the chase was abandoned. With the necessity to pay compensation or a fine, the individuals of the community concerned were not likely to abandon pursuit prematurely.

(2) *The emergence of the office of constable*

The Norman invaders revised the Saxon system of collective responsibility by introducing the 'frankpledge'. As conquerors they were mainly concerned with the Saxon population, and the language difficulty did nothing to ease their task. The Normans required the sheriffs to ensure that all were pledged to enforce the peace, and the sheriffs held twice-yearly sessions of the hundred court to ascertain that all had enrolled and had given their pledge to keep the peace under fixed penalties. The Norman sheriffs were ruthless and savage men who imposed fines at the slightest excuse and, after showing little concern for available evidence, did not hesitate to hang those reported for petty theft.

The Assize of Clarendon in 1166 made matters much worse for the Saxon population as, in addition to surrendering thieves, they were required to report suspicions they might have concerning one another. Such suspicions were presented by the tythingman to a jury of 12 free men of the hundred, who, in turn, informed the sheriff of the more serious accusations.

In the course of time, resentment of the barbaric practices of the Normans, together with some intermarriage, caused much of the older system to return. The courts of the hundred were replaced by manorial courts, or 'courts leet' as they become known. The term 'constable', which had previously referred to officers of the court, keepers of castles, etc., now began to describe the constable of the vill, tything, or manor. However, the system of collective responsibility continued but the courts leet were given three distinct functions:

(a) they maintained the system of frankpledge;
(b) they awarded punishment either against an individual or a community;
(c) they appointed officers of the manor.

In exercising their functions, the courts leet relied upon the constables to present details of their suspicions in relation to offenders and crime generally within the area. Their status was considerably enhanced in 1252 by equating their authority to that of mayors and bailiffs, the office being recognised as a Crown appointment with responsibility for maintaining the peace. Such officers were appointed annually.

The Statute of Winchester in 1285 brought about the next significant development in our system of policing. It reinforced, but nevertheless confirmed, the best of previous systems and introduced 'watch and ward' in towns. The watch would consist of up to 16 men, stationed at the various gates to towns between sunset and sunrise, their duties being controlled by the constable. They had the power to arrest strangers at night and hand them over to the constable. All men of the town were required to perform these duties at the direction of the constable and were placed in the stocks if they refused. In addition to these measures, all male persons between the ages of 15 and 60 were to keep arms, according to their status, to enforce the 'peace'.

(3) *The breakdown of collective responsibility*

There was no significant change in the methods of law enforcement from this time until the nineteenth century which saw the introduction of modern police forces. The role of the justice of the peace emerged in 1195 when King Richard I commissioned knights to ensure that the peace was kept by all over 16 years of age. The knights, in time, became known as keepers of the peace and were given the authority to hear and give judgment for minor offences. The Justice of the Peace Act 1361 provided the new title of 'justices'. Justices were appointed by the Crown and their functions were partly judicial, partly administrative, and partly concerned with enforcement. In general practice the justice was often the lord of the manor who effectively controlled the court leet and, therefore, was responsible for the appointment of the constable. It is not surprising, therefore, that the constable was looked upon as almost a servant of the justice. The constable, being without uniform, was recognised by the staff or baton of his office.

From this time onwards the status of the office of constable began to decline, although it was still held in some esteem until the latter part of the sixteenth century. This erosion of dignity was caused by the reluctance of the better educated citizens to accept such an unpaid appointment for a period of one year. A stage was soon reached at which the office was recognised as being suitable for the old or infirm. If someone of higher status was appointed, he invariably paid a deputy to carry out his duties, which, by this time, involved a considerable amount of work. In 1827 a statute abolished the constable's duty to present matters connected with crime, vagabonds, etc., and the feudal system of policing was withdrawn without a substitute being offered.

It is interesting to note that the current Home Secretary (at the time of writing) has begun a process designed to reintroduce the 'parish constable' to provide a focal point for rural communities in the fight against crime. He is also experimenting with the introduction of 'neighbourhood patrols'; in effect, the eyes of volunteer members of the public assisting the police. Perhaps we are witnessing a return to collective responsibility. A high incidence of crime within the last century, created a situation in which collective responsibility of citizens was insufficient by itself and led to the appearance of the 'professional'. Perhaps we have now reached the stage at which only a sound professional service, fully supported by members of the public who accept the need for collective responsibility, will be sufficient to keep crime under control.

Formation of police forces

It might be imagined that in the years leading up to this situation there would have been an outcry for some effective form of policing, but the reverse was generally the case. Henry and John Fielding, as chief magistrates at Bow Street, made every effort to educate the public as to the dangers which faced society, but as late as 1820 many still believed that any organised form of policing would have a serious effect upon the liberty of the individual and that the state of considerable lawlessness which then existed was preferable.

(1) *The Metropolitan Police*

The Home Secretary, Robert Peel, introduced the Metropolitan Police Force Act 1829, having been given authority by Parliament to create an office of police under the control of the Home Secretary, who would be responsible for the policing of the metropolitan area, but not the City of London. Two justices were to take charge of the police office and were authorised to appoint sufficient men to police the district effectively. The justices later came to be known as commissioners, and a receiver was also appointed with a duty to provide the financial management of the force. The first commissioners were Lt Col. Charles Rowan, an army officer of distinction and a stern disciplinarian, and Richard Mayne, a young barrister with the legal knowledge necessary to administer such a new venture. The original force consisted of 3000 men organised into 17 divisions under the control of superintendents. Each superintendent was assisted by four inspectors and sixteen sergeants, each sergeant commanding nine constables. The origins of our present rank structure were established at that time. Realising that such an organisation was unlikely to be well received by a population which had previously been subject to little effective control, care was taken to select constables from all sections of the public, except the upper classes, and to introduce a uniform which, though distinctive, was not too military in appearance. This was a wise decision, but in spite of these efforts the first policeman to patrol the streets received a hostile reception.

(2) *Borough police*

The ultimate success of the Metropolitan Police Force ensured the general adoption of organised systems of policing. Criminals who found life difficult within the metropolitan area could not resist the temptation to operate within the comparatively unprotected boroughs, and this situation led to the passing of the Municipal Corporations Act 1835. This Act not only required boroughs to establish police forces but also reformed local government. Watch committees were appointed consisting of not more than one-third of the council members, and these committees were required to swear in a sufficient number of constables to preserve the peace in the borough. In England and Wales 178 boroughs which had charters of self-government were affected by this Act, and the significance of the establishment of police forces in this way is that local authorities were made responsible for the policing of their areas, thus preventing a national police force from being formed. The Home Secretary was given no authority to interfere with local arrangements and chief constables, when appointed, were therefore in no way responsible to central government. The situation is still in existence. Although having assumed an advisory role in the interests of standardisation and efficiency, the Home Secretary is still unable to dictate to chief constables or police authorities. However, as central government is responsible for the payment of the major part of local authorities' expenditure in respect of police forces, the Home Secretary reserves the right to suspend exchequer payments if HM Inspectors of Constabulary feel that a particular police force is inefficient.

The original arrangements made by watch committees for the policing of their boroughs were somewhat haphazard and this was almost inevitable as no direction was given concerning rate of pay or the types of men to be recruited. Many boroughs merely used their existing watchmen and gave little thought to their appointment of chief officers, while others looked to the existing Metropolitan Police for assistance.

(3) County police

One of the primary reasons for establishing police forces in counties was the sudden rise of Chartism. The Chartist Movement represented the discontent of the working classes, and when this discontent led to serious disorders it was at first necessary to use troops to suppress demonstrations. Even the Chelsea Pensioners were armed to act as a reserve unit. It was found then, and is still apparent today, that the armed services are well equipped to suppress disorder but are ill-equipped to carry out a true policing function as they are not trained in the processes of law.

The County Police Act 1839 empowered, but did not compel, county authorities to establish police forces. The magistrates in quarter sessions were given the authority to appoint constables for the whole, or a part, of their area. The number of constables appointed was not to exceed one for every 1000 of population. The cost of running police forces was to be met by local rates and the Home Secretary was given power to make rules concerning the pay of constables and the appointment of the chief constables. An element of central government control was thus established within this Act. Attempts at this stage to exercise more governmental control over police forces were bitterly resisted by the Tory Party which represented the view of the aristocracy, who were well represented in the ranks of the magistrates and preferred to retain local control.

(4) County and borough police

The County and Borough Police Act 1856 insisted upon the establishment of police forces in all areas. Approximately half of the counties had taken advantage of the permissive provisions of the 1839 Act and others had appointed constables only in some areas within their jurisdiction. Considerable lawlessness was becoming apparent in parts of England and Wales and the 1856 Act was passed by Parliament to ensure an efficient police force in all areas. Further control by central government was ensured by the appointment of three inspectors of constabulary who were to assess the efficiency of all forces. Those found to be efficient would be given an exchequer grant of one-quarter of the cost of pay and uniform, and encouragement was given to smaller boroughs to amalgamate by withholding financial assistance to forces serving populations of less than 5000.

The modern police service

(1) The constable

The modern police service has evolved since then, but although there have been many changes in the service itself, the office of constable has always retained the independence of a Crown appointment, which probably originated in 1662 when Charles II transferred to justices of the peace the power to appoint constables. The

35

justices required constables to take the oath to preserve the King's peace and thus established their individual responsibility for their actions. Being also 'members of police forces', they are made subject to control by chief officers of police.

Progress throughout the 100 years which followed saw the appointment of policewomen, the provision of rest days, an increase to 50 per cent of the cost of police forces being provided by central funds, and, following an unsuccessful strike by a number of police officers in support of a union, the formation of the Police Federation as a representative body. The process of the amalgamation of smaller forces was continued after the Second World War as a result of the Police Act 1946. Police training centres were also established, at first as a temporary measure, in order to train the large number of recruits available. In this way, responsibility for the initial training of recruits came for the first time within the scope of central government, as previously chief constables had been responsible for the training of their own constables on appointment.

(2) *County and borough police forces*

The Royal Commission which reported in 1962 was set up to examine a number of important factors, including the control of police forces, a fair rate of pay for police officers, the state of police/public relations, and the manner in which complaints were dealt with. The members of the Commission inevitably found themselves considering the desirability of local control of police forces as opposed to national control. The resulting Police Act 1964 abolished, or partly repealed, 61 Acts of Parliament, rejected the principle of national control (although they found many arguments in favour), and resolved that control should be exercised by a partnership involving the Home Secretary, police authorities and chief constables.

The Act gave the Home Secretary powers to promote efficiency in individual forces, to call for reports from chief constables, to approve the appointment of senior police officers, to compel the retirement of an inefficient chief constable, and to require the amalgamation of police areas. This final power has resulted in major reorganisations of police areas in the late 1960s and again in 1974.

The first series of amalgamations – made sometimes under voluntary and at other times under compulsory schemes – resulted in a number of combined police forces consisting of previous counties and county boroughs. In Nottinghamshire, for example, the new force thus created even took the title of Nottinghamshire Combined Constabulary. The second series of amalgamation schemes followed the Local Government Act 1972, as a result of which the county borough disappeared. Police areas were once again changed, but whereas in the first instance amalgamation schemes were prepared with a view to increasing the size of forces, the second schemes were necessary to allow police areas to remain compatible with those of the local authorities. The Police and Criminal Evidence Act 1984 made further provisions in relation to the powers and duties of the police.

(3) *Types of police forces*

(a) *Provincial police forces.* The existing provincial police forces have developed through a series of stages. In the beginning a large number of county borough and city police forces existed, each with its own chief constable. Many of these forces employed fewer police officers than are likely to be found in a modern police division. Within a series of amalgamation of police forces, the Home Office acted as midwife to the birth of the present police forces. This was done in the interests of efficiency. As the processes of law enforcement become more complex, it becomes increasingly necessary for forces to combine their resources in the interests of good service to the public. However, the policing provided tends to become less personal and the forces lose something by way of 'family' relationship.

Usually, the area covered by a police force roughly corresponds with a local authority boundary but this is not universally true. Experiments in the 1970s gave birth to some police forces which policed areas governed by new local authorities created to serve the 'metropolitan areas', or large city conurbations. Although these metropolitan authorities were later dismantled, the police forces created to police those areas have remained.

Section 1 of the Police Act 1964 was amended by the Police and Magistrates' Courts Act 1994 and now requires that England and Wales shall be divided into police areas. The 'police areas' will be those referred to in Schedule 1A. It also provides that the schedule may be amended by an order under the 1964 Act. Thus, the process of altering the boundaries of police forces is simplified for the future.

The police authorities for provincial police forces are composed of members of local councils, magistrates and independent members appointed by the Home Secretary.

(b) *The City of London Police.* The City of London Police are responsible for the policing of an area of approximately one square mile of the old City of London. It is commanded by a Commissioner and its police authority is the Common Council of that City.

(c) *The Metropolitan Police Force.* The Metropolitan Police Force operates within the Greater London area and its function are not controlled by the Police Act 1964. The force is commanded by a Commissioner and the Home Secretary is responsible for its efficiency, assuming the role fulfilled by police authorities in the provinces.

(d) *Private police forces.* Certain organisations have been allowed by statute to form police forces of their own. The British Transport Police, Ministry of Defence Police and the United Kingdom Atomic Energy Authority Constabulary are private forces which have been so created. The powers of officers appointed to those forces are generally limited to establishments in the occupation of those organisations, and a limited area which surrounds those establishments.

Organisation and administration of police forces

(1) *Central government*

The Secretary of State for the Home Department, generally known as the Home Secretary, is responsible for the internal security of the nation. Certain aspects are delegated to other departments but, in the main, internal security is a matter for the police. It is plain that the Home Secretary is finally responsible for ensuring that sufficient constables are appointed to ensure that law and order are maintained. To advise the Home Secretary upon this factor as well as the efficiency of police forces, Her Majesty's Inspectors of Constabulary and a Chief Inspector of Constabulary are appointed. The Chief Inspector of Constabulary is required to make an annual report to the Home Secretary, which is laid before Parliament and subsequently published.

The Home Secretary's control of police forces is exercised directly under powers provided by the Police Act 1964 as heavily amended by the Police and Magistrates' Courts Act 1994. He is responsible for the appointment of independent members of police authorities; for fixing the major objectives of policing in any year; for approving the appointment of chief officer; for allocating grants to police authorities towards the maintenance of their police forces; and for making regulations concerning the conditions of service, pay and discipline affecting members of police forces. While the Home Secretary no longer exercises direct control over the number of police officers employed by particular police authorities, he may find that a police force is not efficient or effective due to a deficiency of police officers. The number of officers in a police force is very much dependent upon the number of people within the police areas, the acreage to be policed, and local conditions including the incidence of crime and the presence of traffic. Chief officers of police, in turn, have administrative responsibilities of the highest order, as they must ensure that the members of their forces are deployed effectively throughout their police areas and that there is a satisfactory command structure.

Although chief officers of police and police authorities have retained control of their respective police forces, it is important to realise the significance of the powers of the Home Secretary. The Common Services Fund, to which forces contribute is managed by the Home Office and finances the police training centres, the Police College, research, wireless depots, central promotion examinations, the Police National Computer, the national coordination of regional crime squads, the Drugs and Illegal Immigration Intelligence Units, and many other bodies.

The 1994 Act amended the Police Act 1964 to permit the 'privatisation' of some specialist services. Where the Home Secretary feels that the best means of providing support to all forces is not the setting up of a service under his control, he may direct forces to use facilities provided by another agency. Forensic science services, one of the original common services provided by the Home Secretary, is well on the road to recovering its costs through direct charges to forces.

The Home Secretary frequently appoints working parties to examine in depth differing aspects of police work, and the advantages of planning on a national level – as opposed to within individual forces – are quite apparent.

(2) Police authorities

The 1964 Police Act was heavily amended by the Police and Magistrates' Courts Act 1994 in relation to police authorities. The Act now requires that a police authority shall be maintained for every police area. Police authorities shall consist of seventeen members: nine from relevant councils; five independent members appointed by the

Home Secretary; and three magistrates of the area. The Home Secretary is empowered to provide, by order, that the number of members shall be a specified number greater than seventeen. At the time of writing, the Home Secretary has made such orders in respect of Devon and Cornwall, Greater Manchester and Dyfed Powys.

It is the duty of a police authority to secure the maintenance of an efficient and effective police force for its area. In discharging its functions, a police authority must have regard to objectives determined by the Secretary of State; its own declared objectives; performance targets established by the authority; and a local policing plan issued by the authority. An authority must also have regard to any official 'Code of Practice'.

Local policing objectives must be determined for each year and these must be consistent with the objectives determined by the Secretary of State. Before setting the objectives, an authority must consult its chief constable and consider any views of the community on policing. The authority is also required to produce a 'local policing plan' which must include a statement of the authority's priorities for the year; the resources to be allocated; the objectives set both by the Secretary of State and the authority; and the performance targets set. The authority must consider a draft of a policing plan produced by the chief constable and before issuing a plan which differs from that draft, it must consult the chief constable. Policing plans must be published.

A police authority is required to publish an annual report which must include an assessment of the extent to which the local policing plan has been carried out. Since the revisions of 1994, police authorities are independent bodies.

The police authority appoints the chief constable and must determine the establishment of the force. It is also responsible for the maintenance of buildings, provisions, etc., of vehicles, apparatus, clothing and equipment and the selection of the deputy and assistant chief constables.

Police authorities form various liaison groups and committees to keep themselves informed of matters affecting the police force. Lord Scarman, in a report following inner city disturbances, placed considerable emphasis upon the need for police authorities to discharge their responsibilities firmly, ensuring that there is adequate liaison between police forces and the local communities. The Police and Criminal Evidence Act 1984 now requires police authorities to make arrangements for obtaining the views of the community.

(3) *The chief officer of a police force*

By s. 5 of the 1964 Act, as amended, a police force shall be under the direction and control of its chief constable. A chief constable is required to have regard to a police authority's policing plan. He is appointed by the police authority (subject to the Home Secretary's approval) and that authority may, with the approval of the Home Secretary, call upon him to retire in the interests of efficiency or effectiveness. The chief constable has complete control over the day-to day policing operations carried out in his area and operational priorities related to law enforcement. He also has complete control over civilian personnel.

The Police Act 1964 also defines the powers and duties of chief constables and places forces directly under their control by insisting that chief constables in all forces have the power to appoint, discipline, and promote subordinate ranks. The City of London Force is controlled by its commissioner and its police authority, the Court of Common Council; and the Metropolitan Force is controlled by its commissioner with the Home Secretary acting in the capacity of a police authority. The chief officer of police is in close liaison with his police authority throughout the year and attends meetings of that authority and reports upon policing within the area. An annual report is also prepared for members of the police authority.

(4) *The policeman*

The rank structure of the police service, being so associated with areas of responsibility, provides a chief constable with a command structure which, although allowing him to retain full control of his force, provides a medium for ensuring that his orders and policies are effectively implemented. At the same time, it is important to remember the unique nature of the office of constable demands that the holder of that office bears full personal responsibility for his actions. This is the major distinction which can be drawn between the police service, the armed services and other public bodies. A constable can never claim that he was merely acting upon orders if he performs acts which are legally or morally unacceptable.

(5) *General functions of a constable*

The primary function of a constable is the preservation of the Queen's peace. It is essential that all police officers remember their oath as set out in Schedule 2 of the Police Act 1964:

> 'I solemnly and sincerely declare and affirm that I will well and truly serve Our Sovereign Lady the Queen in the office of constable, without favour or affection, malice or ill-will, and I will to the best of my power cause the peace to be kept and preserved, and prevent all offences against all the persons and properties of Her Majesty's subjects, and that while I continue to hold the said office I will to the best of my skill and knowledge discharge all the duties thereof faithfully according to law.'

The appointment to the office of constable is a Crown appointment and the nature of that oath overcomes all other considerations. The officer is appointed to protect life and property, maintain order, prevent and detect crime and to bring about the prosecution of those who offend against the peace. When appointed to the office of constable, a police officer has the power and privileges of that office throughout England and Wales.

(6) *The role of constable*

The words of Sir Robert Peel, first commissioner, included in the first instructions to police officers, are always worth remembering:

'Therefore the constable will be civil and obliging to people of every rank and class. He must be particularly cautious not to interfere idly or unnecessarily in order to make a display of his authority; when required to act he will do so with decision and boldness. There is no qualification so indispensable to a police officer as perfect command of temper, never suffering himself to be moved in the slightest degree by any language or threat; if he does his duty in a quiet and determined manner, such conduct will probably excite the well disposed of the bystanders to assist him if he require them.'

These words still reflect the nature of the office of constable. He is a citizen, locally appointed, but having authority under the Crown to carry out his duties. He is essentially a member of the community which he serves and the nature of his oath to his Sovereign demands that he carries out his duties impartially and correctly. A rank structure exists in police forces to permit greater efficiency and a degree of organisation and control to the peace-keeping functions, but a constable remains responsible for his own actions as an independent officer of the Crown. The continuing support of members of the public is essential to the peace-keeping function. Criminals seldom commit offences within view of a constable but they are frequently seen by other members of the public. If the police service commands the respect and the trust of the society it serves, such members of the public will cooperate in bringing offenders to justice.

(7) Traffic wardens

To assist the police with the control of traffic and pedestrians in towns, the police authorities are permitted to appoint traffic wardens who are required to operate under the control of the Chief Officer of Police of that force. They are empowered to enforce certain aspects of road traffic law, but only while in uniform and on foot. They are only permitted to act in respect of a limited number of fixed penalty offences.

Pocket notebook rules

Introduction

The constable's pocket notebook is issued to enable written notes of an occurrence to be made either at the time or as soon after the occurrence as practicable. These notes will often form the basis of a written report or statement and it is, therefore, essential for a police officer to observe certain basic rules when making entries in his pocket notebook. They represent an officer's immediate recollection of an occurrence and although neatness is desirable it is secondary to the accuracy achieved by the immediate note made at the first opportunity. Accuracy is most important. All entries in a pocket notebook must be accurate whether they refer to times of duties performed or to facts connected with an offence or incident. Often a pocket notebook will be produced in court when a constable wishes to refresh his memory. In such a case the court is then entitled to examine the relevant entries, and if the notes are found to be inaccurate or untrustworthy this will considerably detract from the value of any evidence given by the constable.

41

In order to achieve accuracy all entries in a pocket notebook must be made at the time an incident occurs or as soon after it happened as practicable while the details of the event are still fresh in the officer's mind. All notes must be made in the pocket notebook; scraps of paper should only be used in exceptional circumstances and should be carefully preserved as the true record of an event. An example would be when a police officer in plain clothes is keeping observations inside premises and recording breaches of the law. Obviously, notes could not be made in a pocket notebook but could be made on the side of a newspaper, magazine, or even on a scrap of paper, later to be transferred and written out in full in the pocket notebook; the newspaper, magazine or scrap of paper being carefully preserved as the true record made at the time of observations.

Details required

At the start of a police officer's tour of duty he should commence his pocket book entries with the day and date in block capitals and this entry should be underlined. Whatever the entries which follow may illustrate, surnames should be written in capital letters so that they stand out when the entry is referred to. All matters of significance which occur during the tour of duty should be recorded and a note made of the time of occurrence or the time at which it was reported, or both. At the conclusion of the tour of duty, entries for the day should be finalised by the drawing of a continuous line across the page, immediately below the final entry.

It is essential to check force procedures in this respect as there are variations in requirements as to 'standard information' which should be recorded in pocket books.

Omissions and errors

The pages of a pocket notebook are numbered and a page should never be deliberately left blank. If a page is inadvertently left blank then a diagonal line should be drawn across the page from the top to the bottom and a note added indicating the reason why it was left blank, e.g. 'omitted in error'.

It would not be human to expect every entry to be free from mistakes, but no alterations or erasures should be made in a pocket notebook. If a mistake is made the offending word or words should be struck out neatly with a single line in such a way that the word or words can still be read and the deletion should be initialled. If the mistake is discovered before any further notes are made the correct words can then be substituted immediately after the entry, but where the mistake is followed by other notes, an asterisk should be made close to the struck-out words and repeated at the end of the entries, followed by the correction.

Collaboration by police officers in preparing notes

Where two or more police officers are present at the same interview, there is no objection to their consulting together when preparing their notes of the interview. However, as interviews which take place at police stations are now tape recorded, this is of less significance. Similarly, if two or more police officers have been keeping observations then collaboration may properly take place over the preparation of notes on the observations, but such notes must only reflect a genuine personal observation and recollection. In either case, where this is done the officers concerned should record in their pocket notebooks that such collaboration took place.

Off-duty note taking

It frequently occurs that a police officer is off duty when he sees something which is important, or when he is required to take action at the scene of some incident. He will not be in possession of his pocket notebook on many of these occasions and will be compelled to make notes upon pieces of paper in his possession or acquired at the scene. The important factor to remember is that it is the notes made upon the pieces of paper which represent the primary evidence for production in court. Any notes later made in a pocket notebook which are copied from, or are based upon these notes taken at the scene, are merely secondary evidence and are not admissible unless the court can be satisfied of good reason why the original notes cannot be produced. Original notes must be carefully preserved. It is good practice to pin such notes to the pages of the pocket notebook upon which copy entries have been made, unless otherwise instructed by a supervisory officer. Reports or statements should refer to the fact that such loose notes exist, and the manner of their preservation should be described. The originals must be taken to court in the event of a subsequent hearing. On occasions, orders require that the original notes be attached to the report.

Various forms of note taking

The form of note taking will vary with the nature of the incident but there are some general rules which assist.

(1) Non-offence occurrence

The police are called upon to deal with such a variety of incidents that it would be impossible to compile a comprehensive list of notes which should be made covering every eventuality; however, there are certain basic details which must always be recorded. Where the incident is not connected with any offence but will later be the subject of a report, e.g. a man collapsing in the street because of a serious illness, notes on the following matters will provide the basic information for a subsequent report.

(a) Time, day, and date.
(b) The exact place where the occurrence took place, giving the name of the street or road and the township or area, e.g. outside 21, High Street, Blacktown.
(c) Details of the particular occurrence in narrative form.
(d) Identity of the person concerned, that is name, age (date of birth), occupation, address, and telephone number where possible.
(e) Identity of any witness or informant including all of the particulars set out above. Details of witnesses should be obtained as soon as possible after an occurrence (otherwise a valuable witness may leave the scene before his

43

identity can be established). Arrangements should be made for the taking of a statement if it cannot be taken then.

(f) Action taken by police officer. A brief but accurate account should be included of all actions taken both at the scene and subsequently.

(g) Any other factors which need to be brought to the attention of supervisory officers.

(2) *Offence occurrence*

Where an incident involves the commission of an offence or suspected offence, extra details will be needed covering the various points which it is necessary to prove for that offence. While the following list is not designed to cover every type of offence, if these details are recorded correctly, together with the points to prove for the offence, they will provide the necessary data for any subsequent report.

(a) Time, day, and date.

(b) The exact place where the offence took place, giving the name of the street or road or township or area.

(c) Abbreviated reference to the offence, that is a description of the offence.

(d) The exact reply made by the offender, in direct speech, after the caution has been given in accordance with the Code of Practice. This should be recorded in capital letters for ease of reference at a later stage.

(e) Name, age (date of birth), occupation, address of the offender. If the offender is a child or young person the name of the school which he attends or last attended, should also be obtained together with the full name of his parent, usually the father, or his guardian where appropriate. If the offender is a commercial company obtain the full name of the company and the address of that company together with the name of the company secretary.

(f) Details of any article connected with the offence, e.g. the make, model, and registered number of any motor vehicle involved.

(g) Documents produced which relate to an offence disclosed or if they are required for any other purpose, for example, driving licence, excise licence, certificate of insurance or test certificate.

(h) Note, using block capitals, any reply made by the offender when told that he will be reported for the offence. This should be noted in direct speech. The Code of Practice states that it is not necessary to give or repeat a caution when informing a person who is not under arrest that he may be prosecuted for an offence. If already cautioned when the offence was pointed out, do not repeat the caution.

(i) Name and full particulars of any witness or the complainant in appropriate circumstances. This is extremely important in offence-based incidents as the evidence of such witnesses is likely to be essential to proving aspects of the offence. If the offence is of a sexual nature it is important to note the condition, appearance, and general demeanour of the complainant.

(j) A final entry in narrative form describing what the officer saw, heard or did, including all of the relevant facts which will be required in evidence.

(3) *Arrest occurrence*

The record made of an arrest is very similar in character to that made in relation to an offence and this is not surprising since most arrests will be in respect of offences. However, there are certain additional factors to be taken into account. The reason for the arrest must be explained to the offender and he must be cautioned in accordance with the Code of Practice if the arrest is to be lawful. This process should be carefully recorded, for example, 'I said to him, "I AM ARRESTING YOU FOR STEALING MONEY FROM A GAS METER AT A HOUSE AT 10, HIGH STREET", I cautioned him and he replied; "NOT ME".'

It is recognised that entries will not be made at the time of effecting an arrest as it will neither be practical nor sensible to try to do so. The entries should be made as soon as practicable. When prisoners have been taken to a police station following an arrest, the time of arrival at the police station should be recorded.

Module 2

1 Evidence and procedure

Functions of, and evidence accepted by, courts

Introduction

It is the responsibility of the police to enforce the law whether it is statute law laid down by Parliament in Acts and Regulations or the common law which recognises certain conduct as being criminal. It is not part of that responsibility to decide the guilt or the innocence of a person accused of a breach of the law; this is for the court of justice to determine. Police officers are required to bring offenders before the court and, depending on the nature of the proceedings, committal, trial or appeal, a number of courts may be involved but, except in certain rare cases, all criminal proceedings commence in the magistrates' court. There are certain instances in which discretion is allowed in relation to reporting offenders for offences, and guidance is usually given in force orders. Proceedings are instituted on behalf of the police by the Crown Prosecution Service. The head of that service is the Director of Public Prosecutions. The evidence gathered by police officers is used as a basis for a decision by Crown Prosecutors in respect of criminal proceedings against persons or bodies.

It is presumed in law that a person is innocent of any offence until proved guilty. It is the function of the courts to establish guilt or innocence and persons alleged to have committed offences will appear before courts by way of answering a summons, or having being arrested on the authority of a warrant, or having been arrested where authorised by law, without a warrant. The nature of these courts and their functions are described in some detail to assist understanding of the legal processes.

Magistrates' court

This is a court, composed of between two and seven justices of the peace, which sits in a court-house known as a petty sessional court-house. The county is divided into petty sessional areas, each having its own magistrates' court and although these courts deal mainly with matters arising in their own petty sessional areas, in certain circumstances they have the power to deal with criminal offences committed outside those areas. Where it appears to justices to be necessary or expedient, with a view to the better administration of justice, that a person charged with an offence should be tried jointly with, or in the same place as, some other person who is charged with an offence in that area, and who is in custody or is being proceeded against within their area, they have jurisdiction to try an offence committed outside their area. This could occur where a person is charged with driving a goods vehicle and failing to keep records of work and the operators of the vehicle are charged with associated offences connected with records kept at their premises.

Justices of the peace are generally not legally qualified and are members of the community appointed to the unpaid office of magistrate. The appointment is for life although most retire at the age of 70. A stipendiary magistrate may be appointed to some courts. This is a paid office granted to barristers or solicitors of not less than seven years' standing. A stipendiary magistrate sitting alone has all of the power of a bench of lay magistrates. Lay magistrates receive advice from a legally qualified clerk who advises upon points of law, procedure, and sentencing.

In criminal matters a magistrates' court has jurisdiction in relation to the following:

(a) *Offences triable only summarily*. A magistrates' court hears and determines information alleging any of the numerous statutory offences referred to as summary offences. These include all minor traffic offences such as exceeding the speed limit and contravention of the Road Vehicle (Construction and Use) Regulations. These summary offences form the bulk of all criminal offences. Although a single justice is empowered to deal with a few summary offences such as simple drunkenness, or idle and disorderly persons, as laid down by statute and with a limited power to impose punishment, the court usually consists of two or more justices but must not exceed seven in number.

(b) *Offences triable only on indictment*. In these cases the court proceeds with a view to transferring the proceedings for the offence to the Crown Court for trial. In such cases the prosecutor serves on the magistrates' court and on the accused a notice which specifies the charges, provides a set of documents and any other prescribed information. The accused may oppose such transfer by applying in writing for the charge, or any one of them, to be dismissed. The prosecutor may oppose such an application. These functions of a magistrates' court may be discharged by a single justice. Any magistrates' court is empowered to carry out this function. (See page 62 for further details of procedure which was altered by the Criminal Justice and Public Order Act 1994.)

(c) *Offences triable either way*. Certain offences listed in Schedule 1 of the Magistrates' Courts Act 1980 are triable either way, that is they may be tried either summarily or on indictment. Certain statutory offences are specified by the statute creating them as being triable either way. The accused must be present (the general exceptions being if he is too unruly to permit the proceedings to take place, or is absent for good reasons but legally represented), the charge must be read out, if not previously done, it must be written down and both the prosecutor and the accused must be given an opportunity to make representations concerning the mode of trial. Rules provide for the disclosure of advance information to an accused of the prosecutor's case in proceedings triable either way. The prosecutor must supply the accused with a written notice explaining this right. Where a request is made for advance information, the prosecutor must supply it unless it is likely to lead to interference with a witness or the course of justice. The court in reaching its decision must have regard to the nature of the case; whether the circumstances make it one of a serious character; whether the punishment a magistrates' court could inflict would be adequate and any other circumstances which appear to make one mode of trial more suitable than another. However, when the prosecution is being conducted by the Attorney General, Solicitor General or Director of Public Prosecutions, the court must proceed with a view to transfer. In addition when offences involving the use of firearms to resist arrest, or possessing firearms while committing certain offences are also involved, the magistrates must proceed as with a view to transfer.

If the magistrates decide that summary trial is the most suitable they must explain their decision to the accused in ordinary language, but inform him that the choice is finally his and he can still elect jury trial. They must also explain that if he is convicted summarily and the offence (or the offence and associated offences) turn out to be so serious, they may still commit him to a Crown Court for sentence if after hearing his character and antecedents they are of the opinion that a greater punishment is merited than can be inflicted by a magistrates' court.

The Criminal Justice Act 1988, s. 41, provides that a person transferred for trial in the Crown Court for an offence triable either way may also be committed for trial for a summary offence if such offence is punishable by imprisonment or involves obligatory or discretionary disqualification from driving and arises from the same or connected circumstances as the offence triable either way.

(d) *Binding over.* A magistrates' court may require a person to enter into a recognisance, that is an undertaking, with or without sureties, either to keep the peace or be of good behaviour. Justices have always had a power to bind over to keep the peace any person who it is feared will cause another or his family bodily harm if that other person declares on oath that he is in fear of such harm and has good cause for his fear. The power to bind over to be of good behaviour is more comprehensive than binding over to keep the peace. The Justice of the Peace Act 1361 gives justices the power to make an order binding over not only persons who have disturbed the peace but also those whose conduct is likely to cause a breach of the peace, even though no person is in fear of bodily harm. Protesters who put the Queen's peace at risk by their disorderly activities may be bound over where their conduct would have the natural consequence of provoking others to violence. It is not necessary to show that they put any person in bodily fear. Such orders are for a fixed period, usually 12 months, and if a person fails to comply with such an order the court may commit him to custody for a period not exceeding 6 months, or until he sooner complies with the order. Persons under 17 cannot be committed to custody and must be released if they refuse to be bound over.

Hearings in a magistrates' court, as a general rule, must be in open public court. The public may have access to the court-house to the extent to which the premises will contain them, but children under the age of 14 years must not enter the court unless they are babes in arms or are involved in the proceedings before the court. Examining justices enquiring into a case shall also sit in open court except where there is a statutory provision which permits the proceedings to be held in camera, and except where it appears to the court that the ends of justice would not be served by sitting in open court.

Youth court

A youth court is a court of summary jurisdiction. It is composed of justices chosen because of their special qualifications for dealing with juvenile cases. The court must sit in a different building or room from the usual magistrates' court if a sitting of that other court has been or will be held there within an hour of the sitting of the juvenile court. Not more than three justices may sit in a youth court and one of them must be a woman and one a man; however, in exceptional circumstances a court may sit without a woman or, as the case may be, without a man. There is no public right of access to a youth court.

A magistrates' court before which a person under 18 appears charged with an offence which, in the case of an adult, is triable only on indictment or triable either way must deal with it summarily unless:

(a) the charge is one of homicide; or
(b) he is a young person (i.e. aged 14–18) and the offence is so grave that under specific statutory powers he, if found guilty, may be sentenced to be detained for a long period; or
(c) he is jointly charged with an adult (i.e. a person who has attained the age of 18) and the court considers it necessary in the interests of justice to commit them both for trial.

(1) Jurisdiction

The general rule is that no charge against a child or young person may be heard by a magistrates' court other than a youth court. The exceptions to this general rule, which allow trial by a magistrates' court are:

(a) where the juvenile is charged jointly with an adult;
(b) where an adult is charged with aiding, abetting, counselling, procuring, allowing or permitting an offence with which a juvenile is charged;
(c) where the fact that the person is a juvenile is discovered in the course of proceedings in a magistrates' court, the court may hear and determine the proceedings;
(d) where a juvenile is charged with aiding, etc., an offence committed by an adult; and
(e) where the charge against a juvenile arises out of circumstances which are the same as, or connected with, those which give rise to an offence by an adult (e.g. theft by a juvenile and handling by an adult).

Any court by or before which a child or young person is found guilty of an offence other than homicide in any of the circumstances set out above, must send the case to a youth court to be dealt with as if he had been tried and found guilty by that court. In other words, they must send the case to a youth court for sentence.

The Act also gives an adult court discretion to remit a juvenile, who has been jointly charged with an adult, to a youth court for trial if the adult pleads guilty, is committed for trial or is discharged and the juvenile pleads not guilty.

When the offences charged are indictable, problems arise when these offences are committed by juveniles who have reached the age of 18 years when the offences come to trail. In such cases the appropriate date in relation to determining whether an accused has turned 18 for the purpose of proceedings is the date of his appearance before the court when it determines which mode of trial is to be adopted, which is not necessarily his first appearance.

The Crown Court

The Crown Court is part of the Supreme Court and may sit in any place in England and Wales. For administrative purposes the various locations of the Crown Court are grouped in six circuits, and within each circuit there are three tiers of the Crown Court. The first-tier centres deal with both civil and criminal cases and are served by High Court, circuit judges or recorders; second-tier centres deal with criminal cases only but are served by both High Court and circuit judges; while third-tier centres deal with criminal cases only and are served only by circuit judges. Offences are classified into one of four classes and, depending upon this classification, a magistrates' court when committing a person for trial shall specify the most convenient location of the Crown Court to deal with the offence.

The judge sits with a jury of 12 members of the public selected from the electoral register, advising the jury concerning legal matters and the extent of evidence required to prove offences. It is for the jury to decide guilt or innocence. The judge imposes the sentence upon those persons found guilty for a jury.

(1) *Jurisdiction*

In criminal matters the Crown Court has jurisdiction in relation to the following:

(a) *All proceedings on indictment.* These are either indictable offences or offences where an accused person has exercised a right to claim trial by jury, and a magistrates' court has committed the accused to the Crown Court for trial or for sentence.

(b) *Appeal against the decision of a magistrates' court.* A person convicted by a magistrates' court may appeal to the Crown Court against his sentence if he pleaded guilty, or against his conviction or sentence if he pleaded not guilty. The convicted person may also appeal against the making of certain 'orders'.

When the Crown Court sits in the City of London it is known as the Central Criminal Court.

Certain summary offences may be dealt with by a Crown Court where a person is committed for an offence which is triable either way; if such offences are punishable by imprisonment or involve obligatory or discretional disqualification from driving and arise from the same or connected circumstances.

Court of Appeal (Criminal Division)

This court consists of the Lord Chief Justice, Lords Justice of Appeal and judges of the Queen's Bench Division of the High Court. A circuit judge may take up one of these positions in certain specified circumstances. A person convicted of an offence on indictment may appeal to the Court of Appeal:

(a) without leave on any ground which involves a question of law alone;

(b) with the leave of the Court of Appeal or trial judge, on any ground which involves a question of fact alone, or a question of mixed fact or law; and

(c) with the leave of the Court of Appeal, on any ground which appears to the Court of Appeal to be sufficient ground for appeal.

The court can dismiss the appeal, quash the conviction, alter or vary the sentence, or substitute a conviction for another offence if it appears that the accused ought, on evidence, to have been convicted of that offence rather than the one of which he was actually convicted. The court may order a new trial where fresh evidence has come to light.

Queen's Bench Division

This court has an appellate and supervisory jurisdiction. The court hears appeals on points of law from magistrates' courts and from decisions of the Crown Court in relation to an appeal to the Crown Court from magistrates' courts. It also deals with the following orders and writs:

(a) *Mandamus*. This is an order of the court commanding a person, court, or other body to carry out its duty. An example would be where a magistrates' court disregards the law, considering it unjust, and refuses to exercise jurisdiction in a case. *Mandamus* would require the court to hear the case and come to a decision on the facts, disregarding personal views on whether the law was unjust.

(b) *Certiorari*. This order is used to quash a decision made by an inferior court. an example would be where it was alleged that the inferior court lacked jurisdiction because the justices had a pecuniary interest in the outcome of the proceedings or were biased.

(c) *Habeas corpus*. This is a writ for securing the release of a person who is unlawfully or unjustifiably detained, whether in private or in prison. It is available both in criminal and civil cases where an allegation is made that some person has been deprived of his liberty without lawful authority.

House of Lords

This is the highest court in the land and is composed of the Lord Chancellor, ex-Lord Chancellors, Lords of Appeal in Ordinary and any other peers holding or who have held high judicial office. The court hears appeals only from the Court of Appeal or the Queen's Bench Division on questions of law which are certified by the Court of Appeal or Queen's Bench Division to be questions of law involving general public importance, and the court is satisfied that the point of law is one which ought to be considered by the House, and leave to appeal has been given by the Court or the House itself.

The functions of a court

When dealing with courts of justice it was stated that a magistrates' court has jurisdiction in relation to summary offences. Persons accused of such offences appear before the court either by arrest with or without warrant, or by having received a summons to attend the court. There is a statutory provision enabling persons to plead guilty in certain cases without appearing before the court, but this procedure will be dealt with later.

When a person appears before the court the substance of the offence he is alleged to have committed will be read out to him and he will be asked by the court whether he pleads guilty or not guilty. It is for the court to decide whether an offence has been committed and if it was, whether or not it was committed by the defendant. The procedure which the court follows depends upon the plea.

Procedure on plea of guilty

The court must be satisfied that this is a clear unequivocal plea. If the accused pleads guilty and then says, for example, 'but I still don't think I was doing anything wrong', then clearly this is not a true plea of guilty and the court will, in practice, enter this plea as being 'not guilty'.

In a guilty plea the court may convict him without hearing any evidence although, in practice, the prosecution will usually give a brief outline of the facts in the case. If the accused wishes to dispute those facts, the court will normally require evidence on oath regarding the disputed facts. After the facts have been outlined or the evidence given, the accused will be asked if he wishes to say anything and this gives the accused an opportunity to put forward any mitigating facts which he wishes the court to consider when deciding his sentence. The court will hear any evidence of character and antecedents presented by the prosecution before reaching a decision as to the appropriate method of dealing with the accused, e.g. fine and/or imprisonment, probation, or discharge whether absolutely or conditionally and, where appropriate, endorsement of any driving licence or disqualification from driving.

Procedure on plea of not guilty

When an accused pleads not guilty to the offence with which he is charged, the court will hear the evidence before arriving at a decision and the presentation of evidence and speeches made to the court will follow a certain order.

Witnesses out of court

The court will, at the request of either party, make an order requiring the witnesses in the case to leave the court. This is done to ensure that each witness may be examined without having heard the evidence of previous witnesses, so that his testimony will not be influenced by what he has heard. In some courts it is an established practice for witnesses to leave the court during a hearing without the court making such an order, in others application is made to the court for an order. Should a witness remain after the making of an order to leave, the court must still hear his evidence but the value of his evidence may be diminished by his conduct in failing to leave the court.

Case for the prosecution

Prosecutions are now undertaken by the Crown Prosecution Service. This has relieved the police of any responsibility for acting in the capacity of 'prosecutor'. The prosecutor will be appointed by the Crown Prosecution Service.

The accused having made his plea of 'not guilty', the prosecutor may address the court when he will usually give a brief outline of the facts of the case. The witnesses for the prosecution will then be called one by one to give their evidence.

Examination-in-chief

A witness having taken the oath or affirmation will then give his evidence. As soon as the examination-in-chief reaches the facts in issue in the case, leading questions, that is, questions suggesting the answer which the prosecutor wishes or expects, may not be put to the accused. An example of such a leading question would be 'This occurred, did it not, at the junction of High Street with Maple Avenue?' Such leading questions can usually be answered by a 'yes' or 'no'. The question, to be properly asked, should have been, 'Where did this incident occur?'

Cross-examination

When a witness has finished giving his evidence the defence may then cross-examine him on the evidence he has given. At this stage the defence is permitted to ask leading questions, and the object of cross-examination is to test the accuracy, veracity, credibility, or to diminish the value of his evidence.

Re-examination

At the conclusion of the cross-examination the prosecutor has a right to re-examine the witness upon any new facts which have come to light or to clear up any ambiguity which has arisen during cross-examination. There is no right to ask leading questions or to introduce new evidence at this stage.

Written statements

In any proceeding a written statement by any person is admissible in evidence to the same extent as oral evidence if certain conditions and provisions are complied with. This means that instead of a witness attending court and giving oral evidence from the witness box, his written statement may be admitted without the need for him to attend court. By using this method, the evidence of witnesses which is not disputed by the defence or prosecution can be put before the court in the absence of the witnesses. The conditions which must be complied with before such a statement can be tendered in evidence are laid down in s. 9 of the Criminal Justice Act 1967, and are as follows:

(a) The statement purports to be signed by the person making it.
(b) The statement contains a declaration by that person to the effect that it is true to the best of his knowledge and belief and that he made the statement knowing that, if it were tendered in evidence, he would be liable to prosecution if he wilfully stated in it anything which he knew to be false or did not believe to be true.
(c) Before the hearing at which the statement is tendered in evidence, a copy of the statement is served by, or on behalf of, the party proposing to tender it (i.e. the prosecution or the defence) on each of the other parties to the proceedings.
(d) None of the other parties or their solicitors, within seven days from the service of the copy of the statement, serves a notice on the party so proposing objecting to the statement being tendered in evidence.

If the parties agree either before or during the hearing, the conditions at (c) and (d) above shall not apply. However, the following provisions also apply to such a statement:

(a) If it is made by a person under the age of 21, it shall give his age.
(b) It is made by a person who cannot read it, it shall be read to him before he signs it and shall be accompanied by a declaration by the person who so read the statement to the effect that it was read to the person making it.
(c) If it refers to any other document as an exhibit, the copy served on any other party to the proceedings shall be accompanied by a copy of that document or by such information as may be necessary in order to enable the other party to inspect or copy the document.

The court may, notwithstanding that a person's evidence is tendered by means of a written statement, require the witness to attend and give oral evidence.

At the conclusion of the case for the prosecution the accused or his legal representative may make a submission to the court that the prosecution has failed to establish a prima facie case; that is, sufficient evidence has not been produced to show that the accused may have committed the offence charged. If the court is satisfied that the prosecution has failed to make out a case to be answered, it may dismiss the information.

Case for the defence

It is important to consider the general position of the accused in relation to the issue of 'right to silence' before going on to consider the presentation of his case. It is possible that the prosecution will have already offered evidence of his failure or refusal to answer questions and may have invited the court to draw inferences from such failure.

(1) *Inferences from accused's silence*

When questioned or charged. Where, in any proceedings against a person for an offence evidence is given that the accused:

(a) at any time before he was charged with the offence, on being questioned under caution by a constable trying to discover whether or by whom the offence had been committed, failed to mention any fact relied on in his defence in those proceedings; or

(b) on being charged with the offence or officially informed that he might be prosecuted for it, failed to mention any such fact, being a fact, which in circumstances existing at the time, the accused could reasonably have been expected to mention when so questioned, charged or informed, as the case may be, a court may draw such inferences from the failure as appear proper.

However, these special provisions of the Criminal Justice and Public Order Act 1994, s. 34, do not affect the admissibility of evidence of silence or other reaction of an accused to things said in his presence relating to the conduct in respect of which he is charged, where such matters are admissible under other provisions. Nor do they preclude the drawing of any inference from any such silence or other reaction of the accused which could properly be drawn apart from the section. Thus, where an accused nods in response to a question, evidence of his seeming acceptance of the statement made to him, continues to be admissible as direct evidence.

Failure to account for objects, etc. Section 36 of the 1994 Act provides that where a person is arrested by a constable and there is:

(a) on his person; or
(b) in or on his clothing or footwear; or
(c) otherwise in his possession; or
(d) in any place in which he is at the time of his arrest,

any object, substance or mark, or there is any mark on any such object; and:

(a) the constable, or another investigating the case reasonably believes that the presence of the object, substance or mark may be attributable to the participation of the person arrested in the commission of an offence specified by the constable; and

(b) the constable informs the person arrested that he so believes, and requests him to account for the presence of the object substance or mark; and

(c) the person fails or refuses to do so,

the court may draw such inferences from the failure or refusal as appear proper.

Thus, an arrested person may be required to account for the presence of objects, substances or marks on his person, clothing, footwear or possessions. These provisions apply to the condition of clothing or footwear in addition to substances or marks thereon.

Such a person must be told in ordinary language of the consequences of his failure or refusal to comply with such a request. The section does not preclude the drawing of other inferences in these circumstances which could properly be drawn apart from the section.

Failure to account for presence in particular place. Section 37 of the 1994 Act makes similar provisions in respect of such a person failing or refusing to account for his presence at a particular place, where he was found at that place at or about the time the offence for which he is arrested is alleged to have been committed and the constable, or another investigating the offence reasonably believes that the presence of that person at that place and at that time may be attributable to his participation in the commission of the offence. Such a person must be informed of the belief and requested to account for his presence. The term 'place' includes any building or part of a building, any vehicle, vessel, aircraft or hovercraft and any other place whatsoever.

(2) *The position of the accused at trial*

At the trial of any person of 14 years or more for an offence, the court shall, at the conclusion of the evidence for the prosecution, satisfy itself (in the presence of the jury where appropriate) that the accused is aware that the stage has been reached at which evidence can be given for the defence and that he can, if he wishes, give evidence and that, if he chooses not to give evidence, or having been sworn, without good cause refuses to answer any question, it will be permissible for the court or jury to draw such inferences as appear proper from his failure to give evidence or his refusal, without good cause, to answer any question.

This does not apply where the accused's guilt is not in issue (so that where there is a guilty plea an accused cannot be required to give an account of his actions) or where the court considers that the accused's physical or mental condition is such that it is undesirable for him to give evidence nor where, at the conclusion of the evidence for the prosecution his legal representative informs the court that the accused will give evidence or, where he is unrepresented, the court ascertains from him that he will give evidence. In addition, the section makes it clear that an accused's right to silence remains, in that he is not compellable to give evidence and will not be in contempt by failure to do so. However, where a person has been sworn and then refuses to answer any question, he shall be considered to have done so without good cause unless he is entitled to do so on the grounds of privilege, or by some enactment, or the court in the exercise of its general discretion excuses him from answering it.

The accused or his representative may then address the court whether or not he calls evidence. If there are any witnesses for the defence they are called one by one to given evidence in exactly the same way as the witnesses for the prosecution: examination-in-chief, cross-examination, and re-examination. The accused person may also give evidence on his own behalf, but he cannot be compelled to give

59

evidence. He must give evidence first unless the court in its discretion allows otherwise.

An accused person who does give evidence may be asked questions in cross-examination about the offence with which he is charged, but he may not be questioned about any other offences he may have committed, or as to his character, unless:

(a) he has given evidence of his good character; or

(b) the defence has asked questions of the prosecution witnesses with a view to establishing the good character of the accused; or

(c) he has given evidence against another person charged in the same proceedings; or

(d) the fact that he has committed other offences is admissible in evidence against him.

Rebutting evidence

At the conclusion of the evidence for the defence the prosecution may, with leave of the court, call evidence to rebut new evidence introduced by the defence, but such rebutting evidence must be confined to a matter which has arisen unexpectedly in the course of the defence.

Unsworn statement by accused

When the accused does not give evidence on oath in his own defence he does not have the right to make an unsworn statement to the court. However, if unrepresented he may address the court or jury in any way which would have been allowed to his solicitor or barrister.

Final address

The accused or his representatives may address the court at the conclusion of the evidence for the defence, but only if he has not previously addressed the court, or where the court grants permission. Where the court grants leave to one party to address the court twice it shall not refuse leave to the other. Where both the prosecution and the defence have been granted leave to address the court twice the prosecution will address the court first, leaving the accused or his representative to have the last word.

Decision of the court

After hearing all the evidence the court will come to a decision and either convict the accused or dismiss the information. The court may adjourn before reaching a decision and may seek the advice of the magistrates' clerk; the clerk should not retire with the magistrate as a matter of course, but only where his advice is required, and even then he should leave the magistrates to arrive at a decision.

Where the court convicts the accused the court will ask if there is anything known about the accused, and the court may be given details of any previous convictions the accused may have and details of his character and antecedents.

The accused may ask the court to take into consideration other offences committed by him over which the court has jurisdiction. He may also call evidence of his character and put before the court any mitigating facts which he wishes the court to consider when determining his sentence.

The court may then proceed to sentence the accused, or the court may adjourn the case before sentencing for enquiries to be made as to the most suitable method of dealing with the accused. Such an adjournment must not be for more than four weeks, or three weeks if the accused is remanded in custody.

Plea of guilty by post in magistrates' court

A great many of the cases heard in a magistrates' court involve minor summary offences where a defendant pleads guilty to the charge made against him, and in order to allow a defendant to plead guilty by post, and for the case against him to be heard by the court in his absence, the Magistrates' Courts Act 1980 sets out a procedure which the prosecution can initiate. This permits such cases, where a defendant pleads guilty, to be heard without the need for the defendant to appear, or for any witnesses to be called.

The trial of such a case may take place in the absence of a defendant if:

(a) the case is one to be heard on summons (it does not apply to cases where a person has been arrested and bailed to appear before the court);

(b) the offence is not one for which the accused is likely to be sentenced to be imprisoned for a term exceeding three months, or an offence specified by the Secretary of State;

(c) the clerk of the court has been notified by the prosecutor that the accused, when served with the summons for the offence, was also served with a notice explaining the procedure under the Magistrates' Courts Act 1980, and a concise statement of the facts of the case which will be put before the court by or on behalf of the prosecutor if the accused pleads guilty without appearing before the court, and if any information relating to the accused will or may, in those circumstances, be placed before the court by the prosecutor, a notice containing or describing that information; and

(d) the accused or his solicitor has notified the magistrates' clerk that he wishes to plead guilty.

This procedure may be followed where a summons is issued in respect of a person who has attained the age of 16 years at the time when it is issued to appear before a youth court.

Where this procedure has been followed and the accused does not appear and it is proved to the satisfaction of the court, on oath or in such manner as may be prescribed, that the documents mentioned above have been served upon the accused with the summons, the court may proceed to hear and dispose of the case in the absence of the accused, whether or not the prosecutor is also absent, in like manner as if both parties had appeared and the accused had pleaded guilty. The court must cause the various documents referred to above together with any submission which the accused wishes to be brought to the attention of the court with a view to mitigation of the sentence, to be read out by the clerk of the court. No other information may be put before the court. Such an absent defendant cannot be sentenced to imprisonment or any disqualification in his absence.

If the defendant, after giving notice that he will have the case dealt with in his absence, appears before the court, the court may, with his consent, proceed as if he were absent and this also applies where no notification of an intention to plead guilty has been received and the defendant appears before the court. However, in such cases, before accepting the plea of guilty and convicting the accused under this procedure, the court must afford the defendant the opportunity to make an oral submission with a view to mitigation of sentence and where that is done any statement of mitigating circumstances submitted, becomes invalid.

In addition Home Office Circular 56/1981 recommends a further procedure to avoid unnecessary court attendances. If a defendant, on receipt of his summons and associated documents, notifies his intention to plead guilty, the case should continue without attendance of witnesses. If he intends to plead not guilty, the case should be adjourned to a later date for trial. If he does not notify his intentions, the case should be adjourned and he should be sent a notice of adjournment together with copies of statements of evidence under s. 9 of the Criminal Justice Act 1967. If no notice of objection to those statements is received, the court may deal with the case in the absence of the witnesses and defendant.

Offences triable on indictment

Where

(a) a person is charged before a magistrates' court with an offence which is triable only on indictment; or

(b) a person is charged before a magistrates' court with an offence triable either way and:
   (i) the court has decided that the offence is more suitable for triable on indictment, or
   (ii) the accused has not consented to be tried summarily,

the court and the prosecutor shall proceed with a view to transferring the proceedings for the offence to the Crown Court for trial.

In such cases the prosecutor serves notice of the charge(s), a set of documents containing relevant evidence and any other information prescribed. Such information must be sent to the accused. An accused may apply in writing to the magistrates' court for such charge/s to be dismissed and must send a copy of that application to the prosecutor who may oppose it in writing. An accused who has no legal representative may make oral representations to the court when his application is considered. There may be an oral hearing where an accused, who is represented, alleges that the complexity or difficulty of the case makes that course desirable. Whenever an accused is permitted to make oral representations, the court shall permit the prosecution to make similar representations. However, with the exception of such cases, the prosecutor and the accused shall not be entitled to be present when the court considers an application for dismissal. After considering written evidence and oral representations in the circumstances set out above, the court may dismiss a charge if it appears that there is not sufficient evidence against the accused to put him on trial before a jury.

Generally, where notice of the prosecution's case has been served on the magistrates' court and there is either no application for dismissal or such application has been rejected, the court shall transfer the proceedings to the Crown Court.

These are the provisions of the Criminal Justice and Public Order Act 1994, s. 44 and Schedule 4 which abolish the function of magistrates' courts to act as examining justices and substitute the transfer procedure.

In addition, under the provisions of the Criminal Justice Act 1991, s. 53 as amended by the 1994 Act, the following cases, where the Director of Public Prosecutions is of the opinion that there is sufficient evidence for the proceedings against the person charged to be transferred for trial and that a child who is alleged to be a person against whom the offence was committed, or is alleged to have witnessed the commission of the offence will be called as a witness at trial, and that for the purpose of avoiding any prejudice to the welfare of the child, the case should be taken over and proceeded with without delay by the Crown Court, the Director may serve a 'notice of transfer' on the magistrates' court in whose jurisdiction the offence has been charged:

(a) assault or injury;
(b) cruelty to a person under 16;
(c) matters of a sexual nature;
(d) indecent photographs.

Trial by jury

Before a criminal charge can be tried at the Crown Court a written accusation of the crime with which the accused is to be charged must be preferred before the Crown Court by delivering it to the appropriate officer of the court. This written accusation is called an indictment. An indictment may contain a number of charges, each of which is referred to as a count.

The accused is called to the bar of the court by name and the indictment is read over to him and explained if necessary. He is then asked whether he pleads guilty or not guilty to each count contained in the indictment. If the accused pleads not guilty to any charge a jury must be sworn to try the issue of whether or not he is guilty of the offence.

All trials on indictment take place before a jury consisting of 12 individuals chosen at random from a panel of jurors. Arrangements for these panels or list of persons liable for jury service are made by the Lord Chancellor, who is responsible for the summoning of jurors to attend for service at the Crown Court. An accused has certain rights to challenge the jury as a whole or individual persons summoned for jury service at his trial. If, during the course of the trial, a juror dies or has to be discharged through illness, but the number of jurors left does not fall below nine, the trial may still continue and a verdict may be reached. However, on a trial for murder or any offence punishable with death, this provision will not apply unless both the prosecution and defence agree in writing to continue to trial.

When an accused pleads not guilty, the witnesses give evidence for the prosecution and for the defence and the jury decides whether he is guilty or not. The jury in criminal proceedings need not be unanimous in reaching its verdict if:

(a) in a case where there are not less than 11 jurors, 10 of them agree on the verdict; and

(b) in a case where there are 10 jurors, 9 of them agree on the verdict;

and a verdict so reached is referred to as a majority verdict. Such a verdict shall not be accepted by the court unless the foreman of the jury states in open court the number of jurors who respectively agreed to and dissented from the verdict. Two hours must have elapsed between the time when the last member of the jury left the jury box to go to the jury room and the time when the jury returned to the jury box and is questioned concerning its verdict. The Crown Court may insist upon a longer period, bearing in mind the nature and complexity of the case.

If the accused is found guilty, the court will hear evidence of his character generally and of any previous convictions. The accused may ask the court to take into consideration other offences committed by him which are still untried, and the judge may properly take such offences into consideration when sentencing the accused.

Evidence

The basic functions of a court dealing with criminal matters are to determine:

(a) whether or not an offence has been committed, and if it is proved that an offence has been committed;

(b) whether or not the person accused before the court committed that offence, and finally, if this is proved;

(c) the most appropriate way of dealing with that person, i.e. by fine, by imprisonment, by conditional or absolute discharge, or by placing him on probation.

The proceedings before the court follow a process of enquiry: the prosecution attempting to prove certain facts and points to the court beyond reasonable doubt, and the defence attempting to disprove the same facts or points on the balance of probabilities. Like most other human activities the proceedings are governed by certain rules as to the manner in which any fact or point in issue or question may be proved or disproved, and these rules are known as the rules of evidence.

Any evidence brought before a court must relate to the 'facts in issue'; by this we mean the facts which the prosecution alleges constitute the offence charged, and which the defence disputes. If the police bring proceedings against a person for a minor summary offence – e.g. riding a pedal cycle on a road between sunset and sunrise without showing obligatory lights to the front and rear – the facts in issue in such a case would be:

(a) identity – that the person before the court was the person seen riding the pedal cycle;

(b) the place – that the offence took place on a road;

(c) the time – that the incident took place between sunset and sunrise; and

(d) the statutory provision breached – that the cycle was not showing the lights required by law.

An accused person may dispute all these facts in issue, in which case the prosecution must bring evidence to put all before the court and convince it beyond reasonable doubt that the facts alleged were true.

The accused may also bring evidence to put before the court to show that the facts in issue have not been proved against him. Because it is for the prosecution to prove to the court the facts it alleges, an accused only has to show to the court that on the balance of probabilities, the facts are not true; this is called 'the burden of proof', and the burden of proving an offence rests on the prosecution throughout the criminal proceedings.

Direct and circumstantial evidence

Direct evidence may be given of a particular fact which is in issue. If a person is found to be in possession of an explosive device, direct evidence will be given of this fact by the person who found him in possession of the device. The device will be produced to the court as direct evidence of its existence.

Circumstantial evidence is evidence of a fact, from which the existence of another fact can be inferred. Where a person is charged with murder, evidence from a witness who saw him shoot the victim, would be direct evidence. Evidence from a witness who did not see the actual shooting, but who saw the accused entering the victim's house carrying a gun shortly before the shot was fired, would be circumstantial evidence. It is evidence of a related fact from which the fact in issue (the accused's firing of the gun) may be inferred.

Presenting evidence

Evidence may be given to the court in the following manner.

(a) *Oral evidence*. This is a statement made by a witness before the court. In the example quoted, relating to the pedal cycle, it could be a police officer who, having been lawfully sworn, gives oral evidence that at a certain time, date and place, he saw the accused person riding the pedal cycle and at that time it was not displaying obligatory lights as required by law. Oral evidence is usually given by a witness concerning matters of which that person has knowledge; something they have seen, or heard, or felt, or smelt or touched.

(b) *Documentary evidence*. This is where the contents of a document are given to the court. Generally the document itself is also produced to the court, but in certain circumstances a verbal account of the contents may be given without the document itself being produced. An example of where the document is produced and the contents given is where an accused person has made a written statement under caution to a police officer and he produces the statement and reads it to the court.

(c) *Real evidence*. This is where an article connected with the circumstances of the case is produced to the court by a witness who usually gives a verbal

65

account of the article and its connection with the case. In an offence of theft it could be that a police officer produces to the court certain property which the accused is charged with stealing, and the officer states that he found the property in the possession of the accused, thus connecting the accused with the stolen property. Such articles are exhibits to be produced to the court and are the responsibility of the officer in charge of the case.

On occasions, difficulty is experienced in deciding whether certain types of documents are documentary or real evidence. This can be established by examining the reason why the evidence is produced. If, for example, a computer printout of telephone calls made at a hotel is produced merely to prove that certain calls were made, the printout would be real evidence; it would be documentary evidence if the printout was offered as evidence of the contents of the telephone calls. It can be seen that these three methods overlap each other; verbal or oral evidence is generally given in connection with documents and articles produced before a court.

Evidence by video live TV link

The Criminal Justice Act 1988 made provision for such evidence, with the leave of the court, to be given at a trial on indictment; in proceedings in a youth court or an appeal, through a live television link where the witness is outside the United Kingdom, or is under the age of 14 years, or is to be cross-examined following the admission of a video recording of his evidence, and the offence charged involves assault, threats of or injury; cruelty; sexual offences; offences of indecency with children, inciting incest with girls under 16, indecent photographs of a person under 16; and attempts, conspiracy, aiding and abetting such offences. This also applies where the witness is under 17 or is to be cross-examined following the admission of a video recording of his evidence, or the offence charged is one of the above sexual offences or an offence under the Protection of Children Act 1978.

(1) Evidence by video recording

In addition, the Criminal Justice Act 1988, s. 32A, makes provision for video recordings of testimony from child witnesses to be played in trials on indictment for such offences, or in proceedings in youth courts or in appeals. A video recording of an interview between an adult and a child who is not the accused or one of the accused and relates to any matter in issue in the proceedings may, with the leave of the court, be given in evidence. The court may exclude it, or parts of it. The child must still be called as a witness but will not be examined-in-chief on matters dealt with adequately in the recording. The court must estimate the weight to be attached to such evidence.

Subject to the court's power to exclude the whole or part of the video as being otherwise admissible in evidence, the court must give leave for the video recording to be given in evidence, unless:

(a) it appears that the child witness will not be available for cross-examination;
(b) rules concerning the disclosure of the circumstances in which the recording was made have not been complied with; or

(c) the court is of the opinion that, having regard to all the circumstances of the case, that in the interests of justice, the recording ought not to be admitted.

For the purposes of these provisions a 'child' is a person under 14 years of age, or if he was under that age when the video recording was made, is under 15 years of age, where the offence involves assault, injury or threat of injury to a person, or cruelty to a person under 16. It refers to a person under 17 years of age, or if he was under that age when the recording was made, is under 18 years of age, where the offence is one concerned with sexual matters, including indecency or incest, or the taking of indecent photographs.

A person charged with any of these offences shall not cross-examine in person a child or person who is to be cross-examined following the admission of video recorded testimony.

These provisions are 'special' to these particular circumstances but the section states that they do not prejudice the admissibility of other video recordings which would be admissible apart from the section. Such recordings would normally be supported by oral evidence from the person taking, or directing the taking of the recording.

Where proceedings are taking place in a youth court and suitable facilities for receiving such evidence are not available in any petty sessional court-house at which that court may sit, the court may sit for the purpose of the whole or any part of those proceedings at any place at which such facilities are available and has been appointed for that purpose. Such a place, if it is outside the petty sessional area concerned shall be deemed to be in that area for the purpose of the jurisdiction of the justices.

(2) Evidence by means of certificate

A further way in which evidence can be presented is by means of a statement or a certificate. Statements taken in accordance with s. 2 or s. 9 of the Criminal Justice Act 1967 can be put in evidence and be admissible to the same extent as oral evidence without the witness himself appearing before the court. This procedure is designed to avoid the necessity for a witness to appear at court when his evidence is not disputed. A police officer carrying out an enquiry for another force in connection with a criminal offence usually submits the result of his enquiries in the form of a statement under the Criminal Justice Act 1967, so that he does not have to attend any subsequent court proceedings if his statement is accepted in evidence by the court and the other party to the proceedings.

Certain certificates are accepted in evidence by a court; for example, a certificate, under s. 41(1) of the Criminal Justice Act 1948, certifying a drawing made to scale; a certificate, under s. 11 of the Road Traffic Offenders Act 1988, signed by a constable, certifying that a person made a statement to him regarding the driving, ownership, or the use of a motor vehicle on a particular occasion; and, of course, the analyst's certificate of his findings in relation to a laboratory specimen provided in a case of a person, who has more than the prescribed limit of alcohol in the blood, driving, attempting to drive, or being in charge of a motor vehicle.

Having outlined the ways in which evidence may be presented to the court, it is time to examine the extent to which evidence is acceptable by a court, i.e. its admissibility and the restrictions placed on the testimony of a witness.

Hearsay evidence

The general rule is that a witness may only testify to facts he perceived with his own senses, such facts being relevant to the proceedings before the court. This general rule excludes a witness giving in evidence a statement made by another person, not the accused. An example of this would be where a pedestrian, who has seen the driver of a motor vehicle commit an offence, writes down the registration number of the offending vehicle and later passes this information to a police officer. If proceedings are taken against the offending driver the police officer could not give in evidence the statement of the pedestrian, nor produce the paper on which the pedestrian took down the registered number, as this would be hearsay evidence. The only person who could give such evidence is the pedestrian, who could then be cross-examined by the defence. Thus, we might define hearsay evidence as being evidence of what someone else expressly or impliedly asserted orally, in writing or by conduct, when the object of that evidence is to establish the truth of what was said or written.

However, there is a difference between a person stating a fact and giving hearsay evidence. If a police officer says that a person complained to him of an indecent assault, this is a fact and the officer is entitled to say that the event took place. It would be different if he then attempted to give details of the allegation made, as those details are best given by the person assaulted. Where a police officer offered evidence, as a statement of fact, that a person whom he saw receiving a package was a heroin addict, the evidence was held to be hearsay unless the officer had first-hand knowledge of that fact based upon previous convictions; the observation of needle marks; or of that person's receipt of medical attention for drug addiction. That person's general reputation as an addict, without particular proof of addiction, was inadmissible hearsay.

Like many general rules in law there are a number of exceptions to the rule that hearsay evidence is not admissible, the more important of which are:

(a) *Dying declaration.* In cases of murder or manslaughter any statement made by the victim as to the fact and circumstances which caused his injuries is admissible in evidence. Such a declaration should give the actual words used and contain the fact that it is made in the hopeless expectation of imminent death. The person taking the declaration should date it, sign it, and get any other person present who had heard the declaration to sign to this effect. A judge will receive such a declaration in evidence if he is satisfied that
   (i) the declarant is dead and the manner of his death was the subject of the declaration;
   (ii) at the time it was made the declarant realised he was dying and had no hope of recovery.

(b) *Recent complaint in sexual offences.* In such cases the words of a complaint made by the victim of a sexual offence to some other person as soon as possible after the offence may be given by the person who received the complaint, not as proof of the act alleged or to corroborate other evidence but as evidence of the conduct of the victim and of the fact that the victim did not consent to the act. An example of this is where the victim of a rape runs to the nearest house, knocks on the door, and says to the householder: 'A man has just attacked and raped me.' The householder could give this statement in evidence.

(c) *Statements made by persons now deceased.* Such statements, to be admissible in evidence, must have been made contemporaneously in the regular course of duty or business. An example of such a written statement would be entries made in a police officer's notebook or an official police report.

(d) *Statements forming part of the* res gestae, i.e. things done or relevant to the matter before the court. Thus, if the victim in a poisoning case was heard by someone to say, 'I think the apple I just ate was poisoned', this could be put in evidence by the person who heard it. Police officers saw a man being jostled by two others. The assailant went into a shop doorway where the victim's wallet was found. The victim lunged at the men and said, 'They're the ones; these two mugged me of my wallet.' The victim did not give evidence. Could these statements (which were hearsay when repeated by the officers) be admitted as part of the *res gestae*? It was held that, looking at the incident as a whole, the statements were relevant and properly admitted.

(e) *First-hand hearsay and business or trade records.* Sections 23 and 24 of the Criminal Justice Act 1988 deal with these matters.

Section 23 permits a statement made in a document to be admissible as evidence of any fact stated therein of which direct oral evidence would be admissible if:

(1) any condition relating to the person who made the statement which is specified below is satisfied, that is
  (i) that the person who made the statement is dead or by reason of his bodily or mental condition, unfit to attend as a witness; or is outside the United Kingdom and it is not reasonably practicable to secure his attendance; or
  (ii) that all reasonable steps have been taken to find the person who made the statement but he cannot be found; or
(2) the statement was made to a police officer or some other person charged with the duty of investigating offences or charging offenders, and the person who made it does not give oral evidence through fear or because he is kept out of the way.

The words 'unfit to attend as a witness' apply not only to a person's physical inability to attend a court but also to his mental capacity. Where it is necessary to consider allowing a witness statement to be read on the grounds that it is not reasonably practicable to secure a witness's attendance, the judge must consider the matter as existing on the date of the application. It would be difficult to apply s. 23 with any certainty if the judge was required to consider future possibilities in relation to attendance.

The test of fear does not have to be based on reasonable grounds so long as the court is satisfied that the witness is in fear.

Section 24 is concerned with documents created or received by a person in the course of a business, profession or other occupation, or as the holder of a paid or unpaid office. If the information contained in such a document was supplied by a person who had, or may reasonably be supposed to have had, personal knowledge of the matter dealt with, a statement in the document is admissible in evidence in the same way as oral evidence would be admissible.

Particular rules are prescribed for written statements prepared in respect of pending or contemplated criminal proceedings or of a criminal investigation. Such statements are admissible if the requirements of s. 23(a) or (b) have been satisfied, or if the person who made the statement cannot reasonably be expected (having regard to the time that has elapsed and all the circumstances) to have any recollection of the matters dealt with in the statement.

Statements under s. 23 or 24 may be contested in the same way as oral testimony can be challenged. In estimating the weight to be attached to such a statement a court must consider all of the circumstances in assessing the accuracy or otherwise of the statement.

Statements which are prepared for the purpose of pending or contemplated criminal proceedings, etc., must not be admitted without the leave of the court which must not be given unless the court is of the opinion that the statement should be admitted in the interests of justice.

Evidence from *computer records* is admissible in accordance with s. 23 or 24 *and* the Police and Criminal Evidence Act 1994, s. 69. Section 69(1) states that, in any proceedings, a statement in a document produced by a computer shall not be admissible in evidence of *any fact stated therein* unless it is shown:

(1) that there are no reasonable grounds for believing that the statement is inaccurate because of improper use of the computer;
(2) that at all material times the computer was operating properly or, if not, that any respect in which it was not operating properly or was out of operation was not such as to affect the production of the document or the accuracy of its contents; and
(3) that any relevant conditions specified in rules made under the section are satisfied.

The High Court has indicated that it will be reluctant to accept that a document produced on a word processor, rather than in typescript or by pen, thereby becomes a document to which these provisions of the Police and Criminal Evidence Act 1984 apply. To accept such a proposition would be to accept that almost every business document produced today would be so admissible. That cannot have been the intention of Parliament.

Schedule 3 to the 1984 Act provides that where it is desired to give a statement in evidence in accordance with s. 69, a certificate

(1) identifying the printout containing the statement and describing the manner in which it was produced;
(2) giving such particulars of any device involved in the production of that printout as may be appropriate for the purpose of showing that the printout was produced by the computer;
(3) dealing with any matters mentioned in s. 69(1) above; and
(4) purporting to be signed by a person occupying a responsible position in relation to the operation of the computer,

is evidence of any matter stated therein. It is an offence to make such a statement which is false.

Such certificates will usually be offered in evidence where a computer operation is complex, involving for example, the storage of information in, and a printout from, a branch computer at a bank or building society. The computer procedure may in such circumstances involve a branch terminal and a mainframe computer operation to check personal identification numbers and account numbers. However, the Police and Criminal Evidence Act 1984, s. 69, does not render computer-generated evidence admissible in all circumstances if the conditions which it sets out are met. A document produced by a computer may be shown to be accurate and reliable, but still may be inadmissible, as hearsay evidence which does not satisfy the terms of the Criminal Justice Act 1988, ss. 23 and 24.

Although the provisions allow documentary 'first-hand' hearsay to be offered in such circumstances, this does not prevent oral evidence from being given concerning the workings of a computer and such evidence may be given by a person other than one who 'occupies a responsible position in relation to the operation of the computer'. Thus, a requirement in s. 69 of the 1984 Act, that the prosecution show that the computer had been operating satisfactorily, can be satisfied by the evidence of a person familiar with the operation of the computer who is not a computer expert. Here a store detective gave evidence that cash tills were operating satisfactorily, it was obvious to the court that she was familiar with computer-operated tills and the role of the central computer and knew that they were operating satisfactorily, even though she did not understand the technical operation of the computer. The House of Lords approved of such evidence being admitted.

(f) *Statements made by the accused.* Such statements are admissible as evidence when given by another person. For example, a police officer cautions a person and tells him he is being arrested on suspicion of theft. The prisoner's reply, 'Okay, I broke in and stole the gear', is hearsay evidence but may be given in evidence by the police officer.

(g) *Statement made in the presence and hearing of the accused.* Such statements are admissible but only to the extent to which the accused, by words or conduct, appeared to accept the statement as true. If he immediately denied the implication of the statement, the court would ignore the statement. For example, if a man is arrested at his home on suspicion of handling stolen property and his wife says, 'I told you not to bring that stuff here, you knew it was stolen' and the husband replies, 'I know, I am sorry', the evidence of the statement made by the wife and the reply of the accused could be given in evidence by the arresting officer.

(h) *Evidence by certificate* (see 'Presenting evidence', page 67).

(i) *Entries in certain public documents.* When a person has a public duty to keep records, such as the Registrar of Births and Deaths, etc., the records may be given in evidence as proof of the facts contained in the record which the person recording has a public duty to satisfy himself is correct.

(j) *Expert reports.* An expert report is admissible as evidence in criminal proceedings, whether or not the person making it attends to give oral evidence. However, if it is proposed that the maker of the report shall not give oral evidence, the report is only admissible with the leave of the court. Such a report must be written by a person dealing with matters on which he is (or would if living be) qualified to give expert evidence.

Evidence of opinion

The general rule is that the opinion of a witness is inadmissible unless he is an expert giving an opinion on matters which are outside the knowledge or experience of a court or jury, on points of science, art, or foreign law or is a witness who is familiar with the handwriting of a person and is giving evidence as to that handwriting, or the evidence relates to matters on which it is practically impossible for any witness to swear positively. For example, blame in relation to the driving of a motor car involved in an accident is a matter for the court or jury to decide. Thus, evidence of opinion to the effect that X was to blame for the accident is inadmissible because that is the matter to be determined by the court or jury. Evidence of opinion as to the speed at which the vehicle was travelling at the time of the accident may be admitted if given by an expert; being based upon scientific calculations, from evidence available at the scene of the accident or as a result of it. Examples of occasions when a police officer may give evidence of opinion are:

(a) the speed of a motor vehicle where it is alleged to have been exceeding the speed limit; and
(b) the condition of a person who is intoxicated.

Matters which need not be proved

A court, when hearing a case, will decide the matter on the facts put before it. Generally such facts must be proved by the side which places them before the court, but in relation to certain matters the court is obliged to take judicial notice of certain well-known facts such as the common law, statutes, the ordinary course of nature, and many other facts which it would be tedious to list, without the need to prove those facts. For example, it would not be necessary to prove that Christmas Day fell on 25 December each year.

Who may give evidence

So far we have covered the various types of evidence and the ways in which such evidence may be presented, and now we must examine the question of competency, i.e. who can be called to give evidence, and compellability, i.e. who can be ordered by the court to attend and give evidence

Competency and compellability

The general rule is that all persons are competent to give evidence (that is, their evidence will be accepted by the courts) and compellable (the court may insist that they do so). The general assumption may be set aside in relation to competency if the witness is obviously of such low intelligence that his evidence could have no relevance, or if he is so young that he could have no realisation of the matters in issue. In certain specific circumstances a witness may not be compelled to give evidence. Section 80 of the Police and Criminal Evidence Act 1984 deals with matters of competence and compellability.

A husband or wife of an accused person is usually competent to give evidence for the prosecution (unless he or she is jointly charged with his or her partner when he or she will only be competent if no longer liable to be convicted, either due to pleading guilty or for any other reason). He or she is always competent to give evidence on behalf of the accused or any person jointly charged with such person. Therefore the wife of a husband who is charged with burglary is competent to give evidence against her husband (provided that she is not jointly charged), if she wishes to do so.

The husband or wife of an accused shall only be compellable to give evidence for the prosecution or on behalf of any person jointly charged with the accused if:

(a) the offence charged involves an assault on, or injury or a threat of injury to, the wife or husband of the accused or a person who was at the material time under the age of 16; or

(b) the offence charged is a sexual offence alleged to have been committed in respect of a person who was at the material time under that age; or

(c) the offence charged consists of attempting or conspiring to commit, or of aiding, abetting, counselling or procuring or inciting the commissions of, the offences set out at (a) and (b) above.

For the purpose of (b) a sexual offence is an offence under the Sexual Offences Act of 1956 or 1967; the Indecency with Children Act of 1960; the Criminal Law Act of 1977, s. 5 (inciting girls under 16 to have an incestuous sexual relationship); and the Protection of Children Act of 1978.

A husband or wife is compellable to give evidence for the defence (unless jointly charged when he or she will only be compellable if no longer liable to be convicted, either due to pleading guilty or for any other reason). He or she is also compellable to give evidence in relation to the accused's co-defendant in the instances set out above.

These provisions apply to persons who are then married and do not apply to ex-spouses who are both competent and compellable to give evidence at all times. The failure of a husband or wife to give evidence shall not be commented upon by the prosecution.

Accomplices shall not be called by the prosecution unless they have pleaded guilty or no evidence has been offered against them.

The Children and Young Persons Act 1933, s. 33A provides that a child's evidence in criminal proceedings shall be given unsworn. It also provides that a deposition of a child's unsworn evidence may be taken for the purpose of criminal proceedings as if that evidence had been given on oath. For the purposes of this section a child is a person under 14 years of age. The power of a court in any criminal proceedings to determine that a particular person is not competent to give evidence shall apply to children of tender years as it applies to other persons.

Privilege

We have covered the ways of presenting evidence and the persons who are competent and compellable to give evidence before a court, but before leaving this subject we must examine the question of privilege, that is, the right of a person to refuse to give evidence on the grounds of privilege. Generally a person who refuses to give evidence can be treated as if he was in contempt of the court and would be liable to punishment, but in the following circumstances, where privilege is claimed, that person cannot be compelled to give evidence on the facts for which the privilege is claimed. It is interesting to note that the confession of a person to a priest is not privileged and, theoretically, a priest could be compelled to give in evidence the details of such a confession. Similarly communications between doctor and patient are not protected, but a court would have an overriding discretion to allow a doctor not to answer questions. The situations in which such privilege can be claimed are as follows:

(a) *Husband and wife.* There is no privilege in respect of communications between husband and wife. However, an answer to a question or the production of a document which would tend to expose the witness or his or her spouse to a criminal charge, is protected by privilege.

(b) *Self-incrimination.* A person cannot be compelled to answer any questions which might, in the opinion of the court, expose him to risk of punishment, penalty or forfeiture. This does not apply to an accused giving evidence on his own behalf.

(c) *Legal representative and client.* Communications between a client and his solicitor or counsel for the purpose of the proceedings before the court are confidential.

(d) *Public policy.* This is a matter for the court to decide, and a court will not compel a witness to give evidence of certain facts if it considers that to give such evidence would be contrary to the interest of the public, e.g. a police officer who does not wish to disclose an informant's identity should ask the court for a direction, and usually the court will rule that such information is privileged unless it is directly material to the case or necessary in the interests of the accused.

Corroboration

Corroboration is evidence from a source independent of the witness whose evidence is being corroborated which tends to confirm or support such evidence in a material particular. It is not generally required, but is always useful. However, the prosecution can discharge its burden of proof by the evidence of one witness whose evidence is not so supported.

Where corroboration is required by statute, a court cannot convict on the uncorroborated evidence of one witness. Such corroboration is required in the following cases:

(a) perjury (Perjury Act 1911); and
(b) speeding (Road Traffic Regulation Act 1984).

Character of the defendant

An accused may always give evidence of his own good character. When he does so the judge must direct the jury that evidence of good character is relevant in relation to their assessment of the credibility of the accused's evidence. It is also obligatory for the judge to direct that the previous good character of the accused may be regarded by them as a relevant factor when they are considering whether he is the kind of person who was likely to have behaved in the manner alleged.

The prosecution may generally not give evidence of the accused's bad character. However, such evidence may be admitted as evidence of similar facts (e.g. that the accused committed a previous offence which followed a particular and exclusive form which tends to identify him as the person responsible for the current offence), or where the accused seeks to establish his own good character during proceedings, either by giving direct evidence of that good character, or by cross-examination of a witness in order to establish it. In such circumstances the accused has raised the issue of good character and it is therefore permissible for the prosecution to offer evidence of his bad character.

In addition, there are certain statutes which permit evidence to be given of an accused's bad character, but these instances are rare.

Refreshing memory

A police officer will normally be called to give evidence about the facts of a case and he should ensure that he has refreshed his memory before attending court. There is nothing less professional than a police officer reading his evidence straight from his notebook as if he was reading a story for the first time, and while there is no objection to a police officer referring to his official notebook to refresh his memory on a specific point, this does not mean he can read all the evidence from his notebook.

A police constable, and any other witness, may refresh his memory while giving evidence by referring to a document or notebook provided that:

(a) the entry was made at the time of the event when the witness had a distinct recollection of the facts contained in the document or notebook; and

(b) the entry was made by the witness, or under his supervision if not made by him, and read over to him at a time when he had a distinct recollection of the facts contained in the document or notebook.

There is no objection to two witnesses who have acted together refreshing their memories from notes they collaborated in making; thus, two police officers engaged on observations together may later collaborate when making a record of their observations. If a witness refreshes his memory from a written statement before giving evidence, it is desirable, but not essential, that the defence is informed.

Exclusion of unfair evidence

The court has a right, provided by the Police and Criminal Evidence Act 1984, s. 78, to exclude any evidence (including confessions) if it appears to the court that, having regard to all the circumstances, including the circumstances in which the evidence was obtained, the admission of the evidence would have such an adverse effect upon the fairness of the proceedings that the court ought not to admit it. Where a man was convicted upon evidence obtained by way of a confession, after he had been falsely told by police that his fingerprints had been found at the scene of a crime, the confession was excluded because it posed a threat to the fairness of the proceedings. Similarly, breaches of the various Codes of Practice (see page 123) while collecting evidence, have led to its exclusion.

Where, following an incident of serious disorder on a bus, from which a man jumped and was killed, police arrested and properly recorded statements after caution which contained admissions from some of those involved in the disorder, the Court of Appeal accepted their claims that they had made the admissions because they thought that they were assisting police enquiries into the death and did not realise that they were in peril of prosecution and excluded those admissions. With respect to the court it is difficult to believe that a person arrested and told of the reason for that arrest, could be in any doubt that facts which he disclosed in a statement after caution, might be used within proceedings subsequent to that arrest.

How to give evidence

Introduction

A police officer giving evidence before a court is expected to be the perfect witness, and could be classed as a professional witness. It is part of his or her occupation to be a trained observer, to note facts, and be able to present those facts to a court correctly, impartially, and respectfully. The police officer's conduct while in the witness box must be of the highest order and be an example to others who may follow. To assist in attaining this ideal a police officer should constantly be aware of the importance of the following points.

Appearance

A police officer should ways look the part, particularly when giving evidence. The officer's bearing and appearance should always reflect favourably on him or her and the service to which he or she belongs. He or she should attend court in uniform unless employed on duties where he or she is allowed to wear civilian dress or unless directed by a senior officer to wear civilian clothes, e.g. when suffering from an injury.

Punctuality

A police officer should always be punctual, and when attending court to give evidence he or she should make sure he or she attends in good time to ensure that the witnesses for the prosecution are present and that details of any expenses they have incurred are known to the prosecutor so that, in the event of a conviction, he may inform the court so that it may consider awarding costs to the prosecution in suitable cases. A police officer should also be available before the court for consultation with the prosecutor, should this be required.

Witness – exhibits

It is the responsibility of the police officer in the case to ensure that all the witnesses are present. He must inform the senior officer in court, in the event of a witness not turning up as it may be necessary to apply to the court for an adjournment of the hearing. It is also the officer's responsibility to ensure that all of the exhibits, properly labelled, are present in court.

Place in court

Unless otherwise instructed, the police officer in charge of a case should be present in court before the hearing begins. In the event of a 'not guilty' plea witnesses will be asked to leave the courtroom and will be called to give their evidence separately.

Evidence

An officer's evidence is concerned with facts within his knowledge. He saw something, said something, heard something said by the defendant, or perhaps did something. These events should be described naturally and not recited in an artificial manner. The pocket notebook may be referred to with the permission of the court but should not be used as a basis for recitation.

Swearing witnesses

A witness giving evidence before a court takes the oath or makes an affirmation. As a general principle, the oath may be administered in such a form or made as accords with the religion of the witness. Christians are sworn on the New Testament, Jews on the Old Testament and with the head covered if the witness so wishes, Muhammedans on the Koran, and others according to the form prescribed by their particular religion. A Chinese witness has been sworn by kneeling down in the witness box, having a china saucer placed on his hand which he then struck against the rail in front of the witness box, breaking the saucer. The officer administering the oath then said: 'You shall tell the truth and the whole truth; the saucer is cracked, and if you do not tell the truth, your soul will be cracked like the saucer.'

When it is not reasonably practicable to administer an oath in the manner prescribed by the religion of a witness, he may be permitted to affirm. Similarly, where a person objects to being sworn and states, as the grounds of such objection, that he has no religious belief or that the taking of an oath is contrary to his religious belief, he shall be permitted to make an affirmation and this shall have the same effect as if he had taken an oath.

Form of oath

The form of oath taken in an adult court is as follows: 'I swear by Almighty God that the evidence I give shall be the truth, the whole truth, and nothing but the truth.'

In relation to juveniles, the beginning of the oath is changed slightly to read 'I promise before Almighty God ...'.

Giving evidence

A police officer called to give evidence should enter the witness box, raise the Testament in his right hand, and give the oath in a clear voice. He should then identify himself to court by giving his name, rank, number, force and the station at which he serves. He should then address the court and give his evidence in a clear voice which can be heard by the court. As far as possible he should give his evidence from memory, referring to his notebook only when necessary to refresh his memory.

When giving evidence a police officer should speak to the magistrates or, in the case of an indictable offence at the Crown Court, the judge and jury. Having completed his evidence he should remain in the witness box to answer any questions the prosecutor may wish to put to him and for the defence to cross-examine him on the evidence he has given to the court. When answering questions put to him in cross-examination, he should face the person asking the question; if he is in doubt about the question, he should ask for it to be repeated. Any answer given should be made to the magistrates or, in the case of the Crown Court, to the judge and jury. A police officer should beware of getting involved in an argument with the defence. Any question asked should be answered to the extent of a police officer's knowledge, and if the officer does not know the answer he should not be afraid to say so. Similarly, if the answer is favourable to the accused it must be given, as the police officer has a duty to serve the court. When answering a question, a police officer should not enlarge on his answer but should confine himself to the answer required.

When a police officer has completed his evidence and has been cross-examined by the defence and re-examined by the prosecution when necessary, he should leave the witness box but remain in the court unless, for some special reason, the court permits him to be released before the end of the hearing.

The officer in charge of a case is responsible for the civilian witnesses who have been called to give evidence. The result of a hearing frequently depends upon the evidence of an independent witness, and if such a witness is neglected and left to fend for himself at court he will not willingly attend court to give evidence on any further occasion and he will have formed a poor opinion of British justice, and the police service in particular. The success of our system of policing is entirely dependent upon the full cooperation of the public, and each police officer bears a heavy burden of responsibility in ensuring that the image of the service does not become tarnished. It is his duty, therefore, to establish good relationships with witnesses, through courtesy and helpfulness.

There are certain forms of address which a police officer giving evidence in court will be expected to use. Magistrates should be addressed as 'Your Worships', a recorder as 'Your Honour', a judge as 'Your Honour', and a High Court judge as 'My Lord'.

Common law and statute law

Law

The law of the land now falls into two categories – common law and statute law – and it is interesting to trace the process by which our laws have come into being. In modern times, when Parliament is so frequently in session, it is always possible to set down rules which members of the community must obey, and to include these rules in Acts of Parliament prescribing particular punishments which law breakers shall suffer. If we consider the position in the earliest times, when people began to live together in villages or communities, we realise that this was not possible. Citizens began to make their own rules to enforce a code of morality; as such, customs began to gain acceptance and the origins of an ordered society began to appear. In recognising these origins, it is not difficult to understand that the Sovereign, foreign Sovereigns, and their ambassadors were held to be above the law, for we are considering a time when Sovereigns and their official representatives were all-powerful.

Common law

The common customs of the people were recognised and developed by the judges of the Court of King's Bench between the twelfth and fourteenth centuries. While judges no longer claim the right to declare acts to be contrary to common law, this recognition, that the right no longer existed, is recent. Although many of the old common law offences have now been included in various Acts of Parliament, some offences still exist at common law only. No statutory definition of these offences can be found and the most notable of them is murder. Judges have so frequently defined the offence that no problems exist in relation to its recognition. The interesting factor is that the penalty for murder has so often become a matter for Parliamentary debate that the punishment has been set out in numerous Acts of Parliaments and is now governed by the Murder (Abolition of Death Penalty) Act 1965. Manslaughter similarly remains a common law offence, although the maximum penalty is set out in the Offences Against the Person Act 1861, and authority is given to the courts to pass such minimal sentences as that of a fine, conditional, or even absolute discharge, by the Powers of Criminal Courts Act 1973. The authority of the common law has, therefore, been firmly established. Although concerned on many occasions with the penalties for these common law offences, Parliament has acknowledged that their basis is firmly established in our common law and requires no further definition. Perhaps the most common example of the use of common law offences today is in respect of certain offences of conspiracy.

The common law has been built up on the doctrine of precedent. Decisions of the High Court are reported and officially set down, and subordinate courts are subsequently compelled to acknowledge the precedent which has been set. The majority of such rulings made by High Court judges involve a question of interpretation of the law. The power of High Court judges is considerable; Parliament may express its will by statute, but the meaning of all sections of any statute is a matter for interpretation by the High Court. Within the history of the common law, judges have frequently exercised a power to create new crimes, and having recognised that our common law consists of rules of conduct which have been acknowledged and approved by the courts, this is not surprising.

In the nineteenth century it had almost been recognised that judges would no longer exercise their power to declare new offences, in view of the relatively simple process of declaring acts to be contrary to statutes. In *R* v. *Price* (1884), Stephen, J. refused to declare it to be a criminal offence to cremate a dead body instead of burying it on the grounds that nothing should be punishable unless it is contrary to the law, and this seemed to be the end of judge-made law. However, in 1932 one Elizabeth Manley reported to the police that she had been robbed and provided them with a description of the man responsible. The police spent considerable time in enquiries which rendered innocent people liable to suspicion. Mrs Manley was charged with a common law offence of causing a public mischief by wasting the time of the police and placing innocent persons in peril of arrest. She was convicted on the grounds that all such acts or attempts as tend to the prejudice of the community are indictable, and once again judges of the High Court had exercised their right to declare such actions contrary to law. Many years later, the Criminal Law Act 1967 included the offence of causing the wasteful employment of the police, which can be punishable by six months' imprisonment.

In 1953, the Court of Criminal Appeal criticised the findings in *R* v. *Manley* and Lord Chief Justice Goddard gave the opinion that new crimes could only be created by statute. The position then seemed to be clear until *Shaw* v. *DPP* in 1962, when, in the House of Lords, Lord Simonds said:

'I entertain no doubt that there remains in the courts of law a residual power to enforce the supreme and fundamental purpose of the law, to conserve not only the safety and order but also the moral welfare of the state, and that it is their duty to guard it against attacks that may be the more insidious because they are novel and unprepared for.'

There is some merit in this point of view. It is no bad thing to have an independent chamber in which such matters can be considered impartially. It seems that our judges have reserved the right to consider acts which appear to be contrary to the common interest and, in circumstances of necessity, to declare such acts to be unlawful.

Statute law

The majority of crimes are set out in Acts of Parliament, approved by both Houses and given Royal assent. Most offences were first created in this manner, but many common law offences have been given statutory backing. It is quite common for statute law to change the definition of common law offences considerably.

As our society has become more complex, Parliament has found it increasingly necessary to regulate our way of life. Common law crimes can usually be described as acts which are in some way morally wrong, and for many years the freedom of the individual was so jealously guarded that matters outside this broad definition were not punishable. As our way of life, particularly in urban communities, became much more affected by the actions of others, the necessity to impose further controls became compelling. To prevent epidemics, legislation requiring the notification of certain diseases was passed, while, in the same way, the coming of the motor vehicle made further demands to impose restrictions upon the individual. The necessity to provide public services has led to an ever-increasing volume of social legislation, much of which restricts the freedom of members of the public to exercise an individual choice, in the interests of the majority. On occasions such individual choice has been eliminated by Parliament in circumstances in which the act required has no bearing upon the safety of the public at large, for example, the requirement for an adult to wear a seat belt. With the passing of each statute, the responsibility of the police service increases.

The process of passing an Act of Parliament through both the House of Commons and the House of Lords before seeking Royal assent is a much quicker process than having customs recognised by the courts as common law offences. There is, however, considerable pressure upon Parliamentary time and each Act requires three readings before the House and some debate in committee stage. For these reasons, Acts of Parliament may give power to some body such as the Queen in Council, a Minister of the Crown, or a local authority to make subordinate legislation and prescribe penalties for their breach.

All Acts of Parliament are divided into sections, each section dealing with specific offences, definitions of terms used within the Act and particular classes of persons may be exempted from provisions or particular circumstances in which a person may be exempt.

Subordinate legislation

The term 'subordinate' is almost self-explanatory and when applied to law it should be given this ordinary meaning. Because of the pressure of Parliamentary time, an Act of Parliament will frequently give a Minister authority to make regulations governing certain matters. The regulations may be called statutory instruments, by-laws, or some other form of regulations, but they all have in common a parent Act, in which authority has been given for their making. At first sight it may seem to be a procedure which allows a Minister of the Crown to assume the full powers of both Houses of Parliament, but a safeguard is provided in that such regulations in draft form must be made available for examination before they become law. We have already described how the Police Act 1964 and the Police and Criminal Evidence Act 1984 authorise the Home Secretary to make Police Regulations. Discipline regulations made in this way provide some punishments which are much more severe than those prescribed by Parliament for very serious offences. Dismissal, or a requirement to resign as an alternative to dismissal, is the heaviest of punishments and a reduction in pay over a period of one year can amount to a much more substantial fine than is usually imposed by magistrates' courts. Although classed as subordinate legislation, it is important to recognise that this form of legislation is just as necessary in our modern society as the common law and Acts of Parliament themselves. The frequency with which police officers enforce such regulations is ever-increasing.

A good example of the need for subordinate legislation is provided by the need to prescribe standards to which motor vehicles must be constructed. To debate before both Houses every detail of 'the safe motor vehicle' would be such a time-consuming process that the business of government would be seriously affected. Section 40 of the Road Traffic Act 1988 now provides authority for the Secretary of State to make regulations governing the use of motor vehicles and trailers on roads, their construction and equipment, and conditions under which they may be used. The Secretary of State for Transport has made, in consequence of the authority given to him, a statutory instrument (SI 1986 No.1078) which is given the title Road Vehicles (Construction and Use) Regulations 1986.

Subordinate legislation is, therefore, frequently referred to as delegated legislation and can be of two kinds. The more important, including Orders in Council (made in an emergency by the Queen in Privy Council) and such regulations as the Road Vehicles (Construction and Use) Regulations 1986, are known as statutory instruments and are made subject to Parliamentary control by the Statutory Instruments Act 1946 which deals with their publication, approval, and annulment. The less frequent and less important type of delegate legislation is the by-law. Particular statutes provide the power under which differing bodies may make by-laws. In certain instances Ministers are given power to make regulations by some means other than statutory instruments, but generally, if the problem is a national one, these forms of delegated legislation have little place.

Studying the law

The form of legal textbooks can be somewhat frightening to the student who is opening their pages for the first time, but there are some simple rules which can make their exploration much more easily achieved. Immediately following the title of the book and its preface, one usually finds a table of contents of the items as they occur, chapter by chapter. A general heading is normally given to the chapter, and if we consider the subject matter with which we have just dealt, we can imagine a general heading of 'English law' under which might be included the subheadings 'Common law', 'Statute law', 'Subordinate legislation', and 'Studying the law'. In this way, a table of contents gives a reader a quick reference to matters which are dealt with in each chapter.

Students of law will frequently know the particular Act of Parliament to which they must refer. A table of statutes is, therefore, usually found in one of two forms: either in chronological order according to the year, month, and date of the passing of the Act, or in alphabetical order. For example in the chronological table of statutes, older textbooks might begin with the Justices of the Peace Act 1361, which is closely followed by the Treason Act 1429. Knowing the date of the Act to which you wish to refer is therefore essential to its quick location in the book. In the case of alphabetical ordering, one would find, for example, under the heading 'Criminal Justice Act', references to all sections of the Acts of 1925, 1948, 1961, 1967, 1972, 1982, 1987, 1988, 1991 and 1993 listed in that order. With this type of table, the reader must be aware of the title of the Act and it is not so necessary to be certain of the date of its passing.

As the study of law intensifies, it becomes necessary to refer to particular cases, and the decisions of the High Court are identified by the title given at the time at which they were reported, for example, *Morton* v. *Chaney* [1960], a case which is

82

concerned with the meaning of 'sporting purposes' for the purposes of the exemption from the necessity to possess a firearm certificate, appears in the table before *Morton v. Confer* [1963], which is concerned with the burden of proof placed upon a defendant.

An alphabetical index is included in all legal textbooks and usually appears at the end. To form such an index, the key words likely to spring to the mind of the student are taken as the identifying factor. For example, research may be intended upon the law relating to brakes on motor cars, and recognising that there are likely to be two approaches in the minds of readers, either through the term 'motor car' or the term 'brakes', one usually finds that reference is made to the matter under both headings. In one instance it will be traced under the main headings 'Motor car' and the subheading 'Brakes', and in the other, under the main heading of 'Brakes' and the subheading 'Motor car'. A good index to a law book will lead you to the information which you require whatever the approach adopted.

Report writing rules

Introduction

The end product of the majority of police enquiries is a written report. A report is an official and confidential document containing all the relevant facts in a logical sequence. The skill in compiling a good report will only come with practice but, whether skilful or not, a report must always be legible, accurate, unambiguous, and to the point. Many police forces have introduced special report forms for use in connection with particular incidents, for example, accident report books, process cards, minor incident reports, and crime reports. All such documents are designed to ensure that a police officer obtains the required information by working through the various headings so that no detail is overlooked. The purpose of any report is to pass to others, usually senior officers, first-hand knowledge of an incident so that decisions can be taken as to action which needs to be taken.

Occurrence and offence reports

(1) *Occurrence report*

An occurrence report should accurately describe the details of an incident which does not involve the commission of an offence. It could refer to any street incident of such a nature that the attention of some other person needs to be drawn to it. Someone may collapse in the street and this may result in action being taken by a police officer which leads to that person being detained in a particular hospital. Quite apart from other considerations, the incident took place in public and it is likely that some form of enquiry will be made at the police station, perhaps by representatives of the local press or by relatives of the person concerned. It is important that supervisors and station officers are aware of such incidents. On occasions it may be necessary to do no more than make an entry in a station record book or update the command and control system; on many other occasions, a full report setting out the circumstances and detailing the action which was taken will be required. A patrolling officer may notice damaged road signs or road markings which are becoming obliterated and these matters need to be reported so the highway authority can be informed. In such cases a record should be made or the command and control system should be updated.

These reports provide a permanent record in police stations of incidents which occur elsewhere. The matters so recorded are brought to the attention of any external agency involved or which may be interested. It must be remembered that even though an offence is not involved, proceedings may frequently take place in civil courts when damages are sought for injuries which result from such incidents. Frequently such proceedings occur long after the incident took place and it is, therefore, essential that an accurate record is made at the time.

(2) *Offence report*

The purpose of this report is to report details of an offence committed by some person identified in the report. It is submitted to allow senior officers to decide whether proceedings should be taken before a court in respect of that offence. This report, in effect, forms the basis of the information which is given to a magistrate or a clerk to the magistrates for a decision as to whether or not to issue a summons.

Two factors are very important in report writing:

(a) *Accuracy*. One of the purposes of a police officer's notebook is to allow essential information to be recorded accurately at the time of the incident. These entries will form the basis of any subsequent report. Offence reports form the basis of the prosecution's case in court and the report on the reverse of the offence report is in every respect an offence statement as the contents follow that form and recognise the rules of evidence by containing only those facts which can be given in evidence. The contents of that report, supported by the oral evidence given by the constable, will to some considerable extent determine the guilt or innocence of the defendant.

It has already been said that occurrence reports may be referred to many years after their completion if proceedings arise in a civil court. Police officers may attend family disputes as a result of which there are no criminal proceedings. In most instances this will be an isolated incident, but on other occasions disputes will continue until some serious incident occurs and it becomes necessary to piece together events which have occurred over a number of years. It is, therefore, essential that reports are fully descriptive and accurate; sufficiently so to refresh the memory after the passage of a considerable time.

(b) *Legibility and clarity*. Reports are meant to be read by persons who have no direct knowledge of the incident described. It is, therefore, essential that the record is a written one and is legible. Many reports, which are of a standard type, are produced in a particular form to allow direct completion at the scene of an incident, e.g. an accident report. These are not subsequently typed or copied in another form. The original remains the permanent record. The clarity of any report must be proportionate to the circumstances of its completion. The correct use of the English language and the order in which the facts are assembled are important to its readability. Senior officers judge the efficiency of their constables to a marked degree, by the quality of the written work which they submit.

Contents of occurrence and offence reports

Reports generally contain certain standard information, quite regardless of the nature of the incident which they describe. A police officer must ensure that certain factors are included in any report:

(a) Time, day, and date of incident or offence.

(b) The exact location of the incident, naming not only the street or road but the district or town. It is essential to be precise and it is usual to refer to a fixed spot which is identifiable, for example, at the junction of High Street with Elm Street.

(c) How the incident came to notice; was it seen or reported by some other person, etc.?

(d) Action taken by the police; including not only the action taken by the reporting officer but action taken by any other police officers concerned with the incident. Where a person has been injured or property damaged, details of the persons concerned or the owner of the property should also be included. Where a person has been taken to hospital or some other establishment, the name of the hospital or building should be referred to in the report.

(e) Identities of all persons concerned. Surnames should be shown in capitals. Care must be taken to include ages and occupations as well as names and addresses. In relation to the person who is subject of the report, the manner in which that person came to the notice of the officer should also be included. The exact age of juveniles, together with the parents' details and those of the school attended should be included when offences are alleged to have been committed by juveniles.

(f) A clear account of events as they occurred and in the order of their happening is required. This gives the same sequence and flow to the report as the occurrence of the events themselves and this provides a clear picture to the reader.

(g) Any explanations given by persons must be in direct speech in the case of an offence report. It is helpful if this can be done in an occurrence report as the actual words used will always convey a clearer picture than any abstraction. However, when a lengthy occurrence has taken place requiring extensive and immediate action, this will not be possible.

(h) The officer submitting the report should sign it and include his rank and number.

(i) The report should be dated to show when it was submitted. On some occasions the time of submission will be extremely important as a matter of record.

Additional details

(1) *Occurrence reports*

Occurrence reports are frequently addressed to particular persons, recognising the nature of the incident which is reported upon. They are submitted through the normal channels involving supervisory officers. Such reports should be given a clear general heading which indicates the nature of the incident being reported upon. If the officer completing the report wishes that any particular outside body or person be informed of any action or requirement, this should be indicated in the report. It may, for example, be necessary to inform a highway authority of the dangerous condition of a section of roadway. Administrative staff will prepare a letter for the authority based upon the substance of the report.

(2) *Offence reports*

These must contain details of the full identity of all persons alleged to be offenders. Similar details should be included of witnesses. There must be an exact description of the offence committed and this is normally recorded on the front of the form. There must be a reference to the Act and section contravened. An example would be, 'Did use a motor vehicle, namely Ford motor car Registered Number A123 ABC on a certain road called Front Street, Dinnington, there not being in force in relation to the use of that vehicle such a policy of insurance or security in respect of third party risks as complies with the requirements of Part VI of the Road Traffic Act 1988, contrary to Section 143 Road Traffic Act 1988.'

When a registered company is the offender, for example when such a company is the owner of a defective vehicle, the name of the company secretary and the registered address of the company should also be included.

The basis of all good reports is a police officer's notebook. The essential details should always be noted carefully and an officer should rely upon remembering facts. The officer's notebook is issued primarily for the purpose of recording facts which may later be the subject of a report.

Introduction to statement writing

Introduction

A statement is a document made by or taken from a person containing details of the knowledge that person has of an incident. It is, therefore, a document containing a story told by or written by some person with a knowledge of an incident. A police officer recognises that it is necessary to record, in some particular way, most incidents dealt with. An officer will certainly make a record in a pocket notebook. From that record the officer may make out a report. On many occasions the officer will make out a statement of evidence personally, telling his or her own story of what occurred and the action which he or she took. Frequently the officer will record a statement made by some other person. A statement provides a means of informing senior officers and prosecution departments of the evidence which will be given by persons who will later attend a court and it is, therefore, important that it contains sufficient detail to make the facts quite clear.

Types of statements

The training of police recruits is fashioned on a need to know basis. Each lesson is examined to ensure that all aspects of law and procedure essential to the efficient discharge of a police officer's duties on the beat are explained. The approach to statement taking should be similar and we will examine different types of statements and their different levels of complexity. One form of statement writing is concerned with the commission of simple offences. It is the officer's statement describing that offence as he or she saw it committed and detailing the action taken. It will follow the rules of evidence. An occurrence statement contains all of the information concerning an incident which the person concerned can give. Its purpose is to gather all of the relevant information and it does not necessarily recognise the rules of evidence; hearsay and opinion might be included. For ease of reference we will call each of these types of statements, offence statements and occurrence statements.

Offence statements

We will look at the description 'offence statements' in the broadest possible manner by considering every statement which is taken in relation to every type of offence, from the most serious offence to a minor one. However, in introducing the concept of this type of statement it is helpful to consider the basic level of statement at the outset.

An offence statement is a written record of a person's first-hand knowledge of an incident which as far as practicable contains:

(a) *Factual details*
   (i) That is the exact time, day, date and place of the alleged offence, e.g. 'At 10 a.m. on Monday 5 March 1984 I was on duty in High Street, Longtown when I saw, etc.'. The details given by the officer or witness will be concerned with things which have been perceived by the senses — seen, heard, smelt, felt, or tasted, and it contains
   (ii) The identification of the alleged offender(s). This identification is essential. We are not concerned with formal identification of offenders, we are concerned with what the officer or a witness saw. Someone was driving the car; identify him. 'At 10 a.m. on Monday 5 March 1984, I was on duty in High Street, Longtown when I saw John Smith enter the Broadway Garage.' The manner of this identification tends to vary. Some senior officers prefer in instances where the man was unknown to the officer when the officer first saw him, that the statement reads, 'saw a man enter the Broadway Garage, whom I now know to be John Smith'. The form of identification is not so important as the identification itself. The important fact is that it was John Smith who entered and there is merit in describing that event as directly as possible.
      Frequently a positive identification cannot be made and it is then

87

important to describe the person concerned as fully as possible to provide every opportunity for an identification to be made. 'The man who stole my handbag was quite tall, about six feet, had brown wavy hair which was greying at the temples and he was wearing a navy blue half-length coat and faded blue jeans.' It may be that such a witness later saw the man being taken into police custody and her statement would then include that fact. 'I later saw the man who stole my handbag with PC Brown.' Assaults are frequently carried out by persons well known to the witness and a direct identification can be recorded in the statement. 'It was James Brown who hit me. I have known him for seven years.'

(b) *The offence details.* Sufficient detail must be included in the statement to prove every aspect of the offence alleged, which is within the knowledge of the officer or the particular witness. Often a number of statements are taken from different persons, each of whom can prove some of the points to be proved if that offence is to be established. Police officers frequently witness offences themselves and in such cases the statement of that officer is sufficient to prove all elements of the offence. If the offence is one of failing to stop at a stop sign the officer will have to prove that a particular person was driving a certain vehicle, in a particular road when he failed to cause the vehicle to stop at a stop line at a junction with another specified road. The time, day, and date, etc., will introduce the statement. Evidence will also be required of the presence of a 'stop' sign on the approach to the junction, an estimate of the speed of the vehicle as it passed over the stop line, together with details of the officer's action and the explanation, if any, given by the offender.

Dealing with offences of this nature provides a good opportunity to look at the beginnings of a file of evidence which really exists whenever there is more than one statement of evidence in relation to an offence. It may be that an officer observes a certain motor car drive past a stop sign while not in a position to stop the vehicle. In such a case the officer will be able to supply all of the factual details, i.e. time, day, date, place, particulars of the vehicle but is unlikely to be able to provide any evidence of the identification of the driver, unless he was previously known to the officer. Having traced the driver, if the officer is able to interview him personally, an offence statement can then be completed in every respect. The officer may recognise the man as he who was driving or, more probably, that person will admit that he was the driver at the time. However, if the driver lives many miles away it is more likely that he will be seen by another police officer. That officer will have no first-hand knowledge of the offence not having seen it being committed. This statement will, therefore, be concerned with identifying the man whom the officer interviews, as the man who was driving the car when it passed over the stop line. Such an officer will still commence his statement with a time, day, date, and place but these will be related to the interview with the alleged driver. His statement will then continue to give details of that interview, for example, I said to John Brown, 'Were you the driver of a Ford Escort motor car registered number, A123 YTN in High Street, Longtown at 10 a.m. on Monday 5 March 1984?' He replied, 'Yes, I was driving the car at that time.' I cautioned him and said 'At that time the Ford Escort A123 YTN passed over a stop line situated on the junction of Lime Grove with High Street without stopping at that line.' Brown said, 'I don't remember failing to stop at that junction but I was certainly driving the car at that time.' The remainder of the second officer's statement would be concerned with the technicalities of informing Brown that he would be reported, etc. Thus we have two statements to prove the offence. If two police officers had been on duty together and had both observed the original offence, there would have been three statements.

Offence statements are read by senior officers and by prosecuting solicitors to establish whether or not there is sufficient evidence to justify the prosecution of the alleged offender. If there is and proceedings follow, the statements are used by the prosecutor as a guide to the evidence which each witness will give. When that witness subsequently gives evidence in court, the statement will be used as a guide to the questions which the prosecutor should put to the witness.

Method of approach

A police officer is a trained observer and, therefore, begins to view things and to plan a course of action in an ordered way. An officer witnesses an incident and queries its nature; what is this? What am I dealing with? Do the actions which I see amount to an offence, that is directing attention towards the necessary points to prove in particular offences? What is that offence? How do I prove it? This final question is tied up with the entire concept of an offence statement. Its purpose is to include all of the information essential to prove particular points.

The points to remember are, therefore, quite logical. Follow the mental processes which are essential to establish whether an offence is being committed and, if so, which courses of action are open; shall I arrest, report, caution, search or seize property?

(a) What is the incident?
(b) Is it an offence?
(c) Which offence is it?
(d) How do I prove that particular offence?

These same processes give a skeleton to the process of statement taking.

Occurrence statement

An occurrence statement is a written record of an incident which contains all the relevant knowledge of that incident, held by the person making it. Such a statement can include hearsay evidence and evidence of opinion and is not subject to the Codes of Practice. Its purpose is merely to collate all of the relevant knowledge of an occurrence held by the person making the statement, so that a reader is aware of the whole picture. Occurrence statements are uncommon as most statements taken by the police tend to refer to the investigation of offences. Nevertheless, it is frequently necessary for a police officer to record all of the facts of an occurrence from a witness to an incident for the information of his or her senior officers. It may be that the officer is recording a statement from a person who witnessed a sudden death. A man walking down the street suddenly suffers a heart attack and falls to the ground. There is no suggestion of an offence by anyone, but a general description of the incident will be helpful to the officer's supervisor and to HM coroner. Disputes frequently occur involving families and neighbours and complaints are made to the police. Frequently there is no offence involved in respect of which the police can take action but the only way in which this can be established is for the officer to record full statements of the particular occurrence from all parties involved, if the issue seems to be complex in any way.

Occurrence statements generally allow the person concerned to tell his story in his own way, the role of the police officer being confined to recording the events in an ordered way which gives some flow and sequence to the events described. The basic factors remain the same: times, days, dates, etc., must be recorded. The use of hearsay and the inclusion of opinions is immaterial at this stage as the purpose of the statement is merely to record all of the circumstances, including the feelings of the people who are making the statement, so that a reader will be aware of the whole issue as seen through the eyes of the person making the statement. The information so gathered is of interest to supervisors, coroners, perhaps civil courts at some later stage, or insurance companies assessing fire claims. If it was decided that the information contained in an occurrence statement, or statements, disclosed an offence, offence statements which recognise the rules of evidence would then be taken from the witness for use in court by the prosecutor.

Usually civilian witnesses have no previous experience of providing statements following any particular occurrence. They, therefore, tend to begin in the middle and to describe the occurrence itself rather than to include the events leading up to that occurrence. It is an advantage to allow a witness to describe the event in his or her own words in the beginning and to follow this introduction with a series of questions designed to clarify the picture in the mind of the police officer making the enquiries. It is almost invariably a mistake to begin writing before a clear picture has developed. The usual results are to obtain a statement which lacks the detail necessary to permit supervisory officers to make a decision as to whether or not proceedings should follow, or to obtain an inaccurate account of events which will differ considerably from the story subsequently related to a court.

Certain basic rules assist in ensuring that a statement is sufficient in detail to describe events accurately, and these include:

(a) the recording of the events in the order in which they occurred;
(b) that there is sufficient detail to make the account accurate and free from ambiguity;
(c) that the writing is at least legible;
(d) that the words used are clear in meaning and convey the same impression to both the witness and the police officer; and
(e) that only information relevant to the investigation is included.

It is perhaps an oversimplification to say that only words which are clear in meaning should be used, as it is often possible to use words which are correct, but which are so wide in meaning that the picture in the mind of the reader differs considerably from that in the mind of the writer. Such terms are usually referred to as 'abstract terms' and a simple rule to follow is to ask yourself whether the words used will conjure up a sufficiently clear picture in the mind of the reader. Words have meaning when they represent something that can be readily identified, and communication takes place when the picture represented by those words is shared by two people. There must be a common understanding. A refugee from a foreign country arrived late for work at a factory and was told by a colleague that if he did this again he would be 'shot' by the foreman. He has not been seen since. Although the use of the word 'shot' as a replacement for 'reprimanded' is in common usage in this country it will not always convey the meaning intended. It is also possible to use terms which, although correct in themselves, are capable of a different meaning and for this reason they should be avoided.

Certain words which may be used carry a personal flavour and have a specific identity. Others which are more abstract have a collective meaning which is not so positive. If our children have a pet dog known as Rex, they have a clear picture of a particular animal when the word Rex is used. When they see other dogs outside they tend to identify them all as Rex. This requires an explanation that not all such animals are named Rex, but they are all dogs. When the term 'dog' is subsequently used, the picture in their mind becomes less distinct. A mixture of dogs and cats must be identified as 'pets' and the process of abstraction continues, using terms which are more collective and therefore less specific. In the course of statement taking, the process tends to appear in reverse order and a witness may say, 'The car approached me from the right', which might be extended by the addition of 'at a speed', which can be further extended to include the adjective 'fast' which still leaves the enquiring officer with a statement which is not very descriptive. Further details are still required concerning the terms 'car' and 'fast' before a clear picture can emerge.

Statement conclusion

All witness statements should include a declaration made by the witness to the effect that it is true to the best of his knowledge or belief, and is made in the knowledge that he will be subject to prosecution if it is later given in evidence and it is shown that he has wilfully stated something known to be false, or not believed to be true. The form of this declaration is as follows:

> 'This statement consisting of ... pages, signed by me is true to the best of my knowledge and belief and I make it knowing that, if it is tendered in evidence, I shall be liable to prosecution if I have wilfully stated in it anything which I know to be false or do not believe to be true.'

The witness must be required to read this declaration and to sign it if he is satisfied with the accuracy of the information included. If he is unable to read it, then it must be read to him and endorsed accordingly by the police officer. Finally, the police officer must record, on the statement form, the time at which the taking of the statement began and ended, the day and date, the place at which it was taken, his or her signature, rank, and number.

Statement writing rules

There are a certain number of general rules to be followed when recording statements and these are as follows:

(a) All statements should be recorded in ink (this prevents unauthorised alterations).

(b) Place names and surnames should be in block capitals (stand out to reader).

(c) Avoid police jargon (the witness's own words should be used as far as is practicable with understanding as this helps the prosecutor to assess the type of witness to be dealt with but the officer may suggest alternatives to terms which are not generally understood and should marshal the story in logical fashion).

(d) So that the original can still be read, errors should be crossed out with a single line through the words to be removed and these should be initialled by the witness, there must be no erasures.

(e) Where relevant use direct speech (I said to him, etc.).

(f) The normal rules of English grammar should apply, that is spelling, punctuation, and paragraphing.

(g) Each page of the statement must be signed by the witness as each part which can be separated must be authenticated.

(h) If the person making the statement is unable to read, it must be read over to him and the fact that this has been done must be noted on the statement by the police officer recording it.

(i) Persons making statements must sign the declaration provided on the statement to the effect that it is true, etc. (see above).

(j) The officer taking a statement must sign it and give his or her name, rank, and number.

Classification of offences and powers to arrest without warrant

Classification of offences

An offence is a disobedience of the common law or statute law which is punishable by the courts. It could be described as an act or omission which is forbidden by law on pain of punishment. Offences are divided into classes which indicate their mode of trial and the Interpretation Act 1978 defines the various classes of offences as:

(a) 'indictable offence' means an offence which, if committed by an adult, is triable on indictment, whether such an offence is exclusively so triable, or triable either way;

(b) 'summary offence' means an offence which, if committed by an adult, is triable only summarily; and

(c) 'an offence triable either way' means an offence which, if committed by an adult, is triable either on indictment or summarily.

Section 22 of the Magistrates Courts Act of 1980 provides special circumstances in which certain offences set out in Schedule 2 to the Act, which are triable either way, must be dealt with summarily if the 'value' involved in the offence is small.

Unless it is particularly provided by the statute creating the offence, a magistrates' court shall not try any information or hear a complaint in relation to a summary offence unless the information was laid or the complaint made within six months from the date when the offence was committed, or the complaint arose. Quite a number of statutes do extend the period within which information may be laid. There is no time in relation to indictable offences unless such a time limit is directly imposed by the statute. There is, therefore, no time limit upon a magistrates' court hearing an 'indictable offence' unless the statute particularly creates that limitation. The same provisions are applied to offences 'triable either way'.

Powers of arrest without a warrant

An arrest is the taking or depriving of a person of his liberty in order that he will be available to answer an alleged or suspected crime or offence. Powers to arrest are provided by the common law, the provisions of the Police and Criminal Evidence Act of 1984 which relate to 'arrestable offences' and the general, conditional power of arrest which is provided by the Act. A few powers to arrest are still provided by particular statutes.

Common law – powers of arrest

There are powers to arrest at common law in certain circumstances and these are unaffected by the provisions of the Police and Criminal Evidence Act 1984. These powers are associated with a 'breach of the peace' which occurs when an act is done or threatened to be done which:

(a) harms a person, or in his presence harms his property; or
(b) is likely to cause such harm; or
(c) puts someone in fear of such harm being done through an assault or serious disturbance.

At common law any person may arrest without warrant where:

(a) a breach of the peace is committed by the person arrested in the presence of the person making the arrest; or
(b) a breach of the peace has been committed by the person arrested and the person making the arrest reasonably believes that a renewal of it is threatened; or
(c) where the person making the arrest reasonably believes that such a breach will be committed in the immediate future, by the person whom he has arrested, although no breach has occurred at that stage (the threat of a breach of the peace must be more than an idle one);

and

a constable may arrest without warrant any person who assaults, or resists, or wilfully obstructs him in the lawful execution of his duty in circumstances which are likely to cause a breach of the peace. This final common law power given to a constable is almost identical to that given at (c) above.

These common law powers of arrest in relation to breaches of the peace are most important to police officers. They are not limited by the nature of the place in which the 'breach' occurs and arrests may be effected in public or private places. Once a constable reasonably foresees a breach of the peace, he is entitled to remain on the premises in which, until that time, he has been a trespasser. If persons fight, then regardless of all other considerations, a breach of the peace has occurred and an arrest is justified if it is necessary in the particular circumstances which are prevailing. If the stage of fighting has not been reached, the situation may exist in which it is apparent that the only way in which a fight will be prevented is to arrest some person. In other circumstances the fight may be over when a police officer arrives on the scene but it may be quite apparent that it will resume in the near future. The reason for the arrest is always to ensure the preservation of the peace.

Arrestable offence

Section 24(1) of the Police and Criminal Evidence Act of 1984 defines the term 'arrestable offence' as one specified in the section in respect of which powers of summary arrest are conferred. They are:

(a) offences for which the sentence is fixed by law (essentially murder);
(b) offences for which a person of 21 years of age or over (not previously convicted) may be sentenced to imprisonment for a term of five years (or might be so sentenced but for the restriction imposed by s. 33 of the Magistrates' Courts Act 1980); and
(c) offences to which subs. (2) of s. 24 of the Police and Criminal Evidence Act applies (offences declared to be 'arrestable offences').

Generally then, we are concerned with offences which are punishable by five years' imprisonment or more and this embraces a large proportion of the 'serious offences'. The powers given by s. 24 apply equally to common law and statutory offences.

The offences to which subs. (2) refers are:

(a) offences for which a person may be arrested under the customs and excise Acts as defined in s. 1(1) of the Customs and Excise Management Act 1979;
(b) offences under the Official Secrets Act 1920 that are not arrestable offences by virtue of the term of imprisonment for which a person may be sentenced in respect of them;
(bb) offences under any provision of the Official Secrets Act 1989 except s. 8(1), (4) or (5);
(c) offences under s. 22 (causing prostitution of women), or s. 23 (procuration of girl under 21) of the Sexual Offences Act 1956;
(d) offences under s. 12(1) (taking motor vehicle or other conveyance without authority, etc.) or s. 25(1) (going equipped for stealing, etc.) of the Theft Act 1968;
(e) any offence under the Football (Offences) Act 1991;
(f) an offence under s. 2 of the Obscene Publications Act 1959 (publication of obscene matter); and
(g) an offence under s. 1 of the Protection of Children Act 1978 (indecent photographs and pseudo-photographs of children);

(h) an offence under s. 166 of the Criminal Justice and Public Order Act 1994 (sale of tickets by unauthorised persons);

(i) an offence under s. 19 of the Public Order Act 1986 (publishing, etc., material intended or likely to stir up racial hatred);

(j) an offence under s. 167 of the Criminal Justice and Public Order Act 1994 (touting for hire car services).

Therefore certain offences are arrestable, regardless of the term of imprisonment which applies, because subs. (2) declares them to be so. An example of (a) would be an offence which we might describe as 'customs evasion'.

Section 24(3) states that without prejudice to s. 2 of the Criminal Attempts Act of 1981 the powers of arrest conferred in respect of arrestable offences shall also apply to offences of:

(a) conspiracy to commit any arrestable offence;

(b) attempting to commit any such offence other than an offence contrary to s. 12(1) of the Theft Act 1968;

(c) inciting, aiding, abetting, counselling or procuring such offences.

Arrestable offences – powers of arrest

Section 24 of the Act of 1984 provides that any person may arrest without warrant:

(a) anyone who is in the act of committing an arrestable offence;

(b) anyone whom he has reasonable grounds for suspecting to be committing such an offence;

and

where an arrestable offence has been committed, any person may arrest without warrant:

(a) anyone who is guilty of the offence; or

(b) anyone whom he has reasonable grounds for suspecting to be guilty of it.

It is important to note that an arrest purportedly on the basis that an arrestable offence has been committed will not be covered by the latter provision and will therefore be unlawful, not only if it transpires that no 'act' of theft was committed but also if it transpires that, while there was such an act, the person carrying it out lacked the necessary guilty intent to commit that act. With respect to the court, this is a bad decision as it is not possible for an officer to appreciate what is going on in the mind of the person who carries out such an act.

The section provides further powers for a constable to arrest without warrant as follows:

(a) where a constable has reasonable grounds for suspecting that an arrestable offence has been committed, he may arrest without warrant anyone whom he has reasonable grounds for suspecting to be guilty of the offence;

(b) anyone who is about to commit an arrestable offence;

(c) anyone whom he has reasonable grounds for suspecting to be about to commit an arrestable offence.

95

Understanding of these powers is assisted if practical circumstances are examined. It is predictable that constables and other citizens will have the power to arrest persons found, or believed to be in the act of, committing arrestable offences. They obviously could not be expected to ignore such activities. Where a constable, or a member of the public, observes someone in the act of stealing articles, or inflicting grievous bodily harm on another person, both are empowered to arrest such a person. It may be that a thief cannot be seen to be *in the act* of stealing. He may be standing at an unattended counter on which jewellery is displayed and may be seen to be placing some articles, the nature of which cannot be identified in the circumstances, into an inside pocket. In such circumstances it would be reasonable to suspect that he was committing an arrestable offence. In both of these situations the common factor is that *he is in the act* of doing something. But what if, having completed these various actions, the perpetrator runs away? He is no longer *in the act* or *reasonably suspected of being in the act*. However, his pursuers know that an arrestable offence has been committed, or reasonably suspect that this is so. In the circumstances of the first example, they know that the person committed it and in the circumstances of the second, have reasonable grounds for suspecting that he has committed it. Both the constable and the member of the public are therefore empowered to arrest that person without warrant.

The powers of arrest without warrant, which may only be exercised by a constable, are those set out finally at (a), (b) and (c) above. These powers are restricted to constables because the acts described are such that generally there may only be a *suspicion* that an arrestable offence has been or is about to be committed. If a constable stops a motor car owned and driven by X and finds that the boot is full of the type of silverware which one expects to find in a stately home, and X alleges that someone sold the silverware to him for a sum of £5, the constable will have reasonable grounds for suspecting that the property is stolen or unlawfully obtained (thus suspecting that an arrestable offence has been committed). In the absence of a satisfactory explanation he will no doubt suspect that X has committed an offence of burglary, theft or handling (each of which is an arrestable offence). It will be appreciated that members of the public, who have no suitable training, would be unlikely to be able to carry out a meaningful interrogation of X in these circumstances. If the powers of arrest were extended to members of the public, it is possible that unlawful arrests would be made in circumstances where a member of the public was offered an opportunity to buy goods cheaply.

Constables may also arrest without warrant any person who is about to commit an arrestable offence. Once again there is a question of judgment. If, for example, a person is about to throw a brick through a jeweller's window (which would amount to an offence of criminal damage which is an arrestable offence) a constable is empowered to arrest as he would be expected to know this. A member of the public is unlikely to know those offences which are 'arrestable' as opposed to merely being offences. In the same way, acts which constitute attempts to commit arrestable offences, will only be identifiable as such by police officers who have been trained to recognise acts which are more than merely preparatory to the commission of an arrestable offence.

The term 'reasonable grounds' means an honest belief founded on reasonable suspicion leading an ordinary, cautious man to the conclusion that the person arrested is guilty.

There may be grounds for arresting a suspect on the sole basis of the word of an informer but police officers must treat such information with considerable reserve. Where a store detective informed police officers that a woman had stolen property in the store, the Court of Appeal ruled that the employers of the detective were not liable in damages for false imprisonment where the police officers, acting upon that information, arrested the woman. The officers, acting upon that information, had acted in their own discretion.

The purpose of an arrest is to make a person answerable to a charge. Where a person is arrested on reasonable suspicion that he has committed an arrestable offence and the person arrested is able to prove that the arresting officer knew, at the time of the arrest, that there was no possibility of a charge being made, then the arrest would be unlawful because the arresting officer had acted on some irrelevant consideration or for an improper purpose. There is no reason why an arrest should not be made for the purpose of interviewing a person suspected of committing an arrestable offence in the hope of obtaining a confession as, in such a case, the possibility of prosecution still exists. However, arrests should not be made to 'teach a person a lesson' where there is no possibility of prosecution.

General conditional power to arrest

The power to arrest for other than arrestable offences and those offences specially mentioned is now provided by s. 25 of the Act of 1984. The section states:

> 'Where a constable has reasonable grounds for suspecting that any offence which is not an arrestable offence has been committed or attempted, or is being committed or attempted, he may arrest the *relevant person* if it appears to him that service of a summons is impracticable or inappropriate because any of the general arrest conditions is satisfied.'

The Act, therefore, provides a conditional power of arrest which can be applied to all other offences, while at the same time repealing all but a few statutory powers which previously existed. The section refers to 'relevant persons' and to the general arrest conditions.

A 'relevant person' is any person whom the constable has reasonable grounds to suspect of having committed or having attempted to commit the offence, or who has been in the course of committing or attempting to commit it. Therefore, such a person, committing any offence, may be arrested if the service of a summons is impracticable or inappropriate because any of the general arrest conditions is satisfied.

The general arrest conditions are:

(a) that the name of the relevant person is unknown to, and cannot be ascertained by, the constable;
(b) that the constable has reasonable grounds for doubting whether the name furnished by the relevant person as his name is his real name;
(c) that:
    (i)   the relevant person has failed to furnish a satisfactory address for service;
       or

(ii) that the constable has reasonable grounds for doubting whether an address furnished by the relevant person is a satisfactory address for service;

(d) that the constable has reasonable grounds for believing that arrest is necessary to prevent the relevant person:
  (i) causing physical harm to himself or some other person;
  (ii) suffering physical injury;
  (iii) causing loss of or damage to property;
  (iv) committing an offence against public decency; or
  (v) causing an unlawful obstruction of the highway;

(e) that the constable has reasonable grounds for believing that arrest is necessary to protect a child or other vulnerable person from the relevant person.

An arrest may, therefore, be made if identity or address cannot be established satisfactorily or if it is necessary to prevent harm to anyone, damage to property, a continuing affront to public decency, an obstruction of the highway, or for the protection of a child or other vulnerable person. Such arrests are necessary, either to prevent an offender from escaping the consequences of his acts, or for the protection of persons or property.

This general arrest provision is extremely helpful to police officers as such a power did not exist previous to the Act of 1984. Difficulties were encountered when persons gave names and addresses which were suspected of being false in respect of offences for which no power of arrest existed. In cases of doubt 'control' will be able to give considerable assistance in checking names and addresses given by offenders. Persons reasonably suspected of such offences should be given every opportunity to provide evidence of identity and address and the consequences of continued refusal should be explained to them. However, an arrest will be valid if the questions 'What is your name?' and 'What is your address?' lead to a refusal to answer, provided that the offender is told that he is being arrested in relation to a particular offence and for refusing to provide his name and address.

It is important to remember that the section does not require an offender to provide his residential address, it requires him to provide a satisfactory address for service of a summons. The section provides that an address is satisfactory if it appears to the constable that the relevant person will be at it for a sufficiently long period of time for it to be possible to serve him with a summons, or that some other persons specified by the relevant person will accept service of the summons for the relevant person at that address. Thus, if a foreign goods vehicle driver who commits an offence can give a satisfactory address at which service of a summons will be accepted on his behalf, that is all that the section requires. Such a form of service is authorised by Regulation 99(8) of the Magistrates' Courts Rules 1981.

The section also limits arrest for an offence against public decency. Such an arrest must not be made unless members of the public going about their normal business cannot reasonably be expected to avoid the person to be arrested.

There are, therefore, in effect, three major factors to be considered before effecting an arrest in respect of offences for which the power of arrest is conditional:

(a) Has an offence been committed or attempted (other than an arrestable

offence or one for which a statutory power of arrest is provided in which case the 'conditional' provisions would not apply)?
(b) Are there reasonable grounds to suspect that person of being responsible?
(c) Is the service of a summons impracticable or inappropriate because any of the general arrest conditions applies?

However, these questions need not be asked if the arrest is carried out in consequence of any of the circumstances set out at d(i) to (v) above.

Where the constable has reasonable grounds for believing that an arrest is necessary in such circumstances, his decision to arrest is not dependent upon doubts in relation to identification, or the existence of a satisfactory address for the service of a summons. If, for example, a man who was found in possession of indecent photographs of children, threatened to kill himself rather than face the consequences of his act, and the constable reasonably believed that he was likely to do so, the constable is empowered by this section to arrest the man even though his name and address are known. The same would apply if his threat was to do some harm to the person who supplied him with the photographs.

Where a person is found drunk upon a highway, a constable may have reasonable grounds to believe that he may cause himself injury by falling down or by walking into the roadway, and in such circumstances may arrest that person. It may be that there is such loss of bodily control that he may cause damage to property if he is allowed to continue, by falling into flower beds, gardens or even through shop windows. Where a man insists on sunbathing in the nude on a crowded beach, in an area where this is not permitted, it is obvious that it will be necessary to arrest him as members of the public cannot reasonably be expected to avoid him. Perhaps most importantly, the commission of the offence of unlawful obstruction of the highway may merit arrest, where the person or persons causing the obstruction refuse to move. Thus, 'sit-down' protesters may be removed, and if they persist, arrested.

Finally, the arrest of a person, where a constable has reasonable grounds to believe that arrest is necessary to protect a child or vulnerable person from the person who has committed an offence which is only subject to a provisional power of arrest, is authorised.

On none of these occasions is the establishment of the identity of the accused a central issue in relation to the arrest.

Statute law – powers to arrest without warrant

Section 26 of the Police and Criminal Evidence Act 1984 repeals all previous statutory powers to arrest (including those provided by local Acts) with the exception of certain powers which are specifically retained. These are listed in Schedule 2 to the Act, and are concerned with:

(a) the arrest of absentees and deserters from HM Forces and visiting forces;
(b) the arrest of persons under emergency powers or terrorism legislation;
(c) the arrest of persons who are absent from places of detention or who have broken bail;
(d) the arrest of trespassers on some military lands;

99

    (e)   offences relating to remaining on property contrary to ss. 6 to 10 of the Criminal Law Act 1977;

    (f)   drinking and driving, and driving while disqualified;

    (g)   offences contrary to s. 1 of the Public Order Act 1936 (prohibited uniforms); and

    (h)   the power to arrest a person suspected of impersonation at the direction of a presiding officer at a polling station.

Further statutory powers to arrest persons reasonably suspected of committing one of a number of offences under the Public Order Act 1986 and the Prevention of Terrorism (Temporary Provisions) Act 1989 have since been provided by those Acts. The Trade Union and Labour Relations (Consolidation) Act 1992, s. 241 has since provided a power of arrest for acts of intimidation of workers and their families. Section 2(4) of the Football Spectators Act 1989 empowers a constable to arrest a person on reasonable suspicion of committing the offence of unauthorised entering, or remaining at, a designated football match.

In addition, it has been held by the Divisional Court that, because s. 26 conflicts with other provisions in the Police and Criminal Evidence Act 1984 in this respect, a constable's powers under s. 91(1) of the Criminal Justice Act 1967, to arrest a person for the offence of being drunk and disorderly in a public place, has not been repealed by s. 26.

Cross-border powers of arrest

Under the Criminal Justice and Public Order Act 1994, s. 137, where the suspected offence is an arrestable offence, or in the case of another offence, it appears to the constable that the service of a summons is impracticable or inappropriate (the general arrest conditions), a constable of a police force in England and Wales, Scotland or Northern Ireland who has reasonable cause for suspecting that an offence has been committed or attempted in their respective countries, may arrest that person in any of the other countries. Where such arrests are effected by officers from England and Wales, the person arrested must be taken either to the nearest convenient designated police station in a police area in England and Wales, or to such a designated station in a police area in which the offence is being investigated. This must be done as soon as reasonably practicable.

In addition, s. 140 provides that where a constable in England and Wales would have a power to arrest a person under the Police and Criminal Evidence Act 1984, s. 24(6) or (7) or s. 25 (arrestable offences and general arrest conditions), those powers are also given to constables of Scotland and Northern Ireland. The same applies to powers which would exist in Northern Ireland under parallel provisions and to powers to arrest given to a constable in Scotland.

Summonses and warrants

Introduction

The subject of 'summonses and warrants' is associated with the process of prosecution of those who offend against the law. They provide a means by which such persons may be brought before a court. However, the procedure does not begin there; the responsibility for the conduct of criminal proceedings lies with the Director of Public Prosecutions who is head of the Crown Prosecution Service. With the exception of various minor traffic offences, where the defendant wishes to plead guilty by post (see page 61), the Crown Prosecution Service will conduct criminal proceedings instituted by the police.

Summons

One of the ways in which a person can be brought before a court is by way of a summons. This is a written order issued by a magistrate or a magistrate's clerk on behalf of a magistrate, directing the person named in the order to appear at a given time and date before a specified court to answer the allegation contained in the order.

A summons is obtained by the prosecutor laying information before a justice of the peace or the clerk to the justices on behalf of the justice and this process is explained below under the heading 'Defendant summons'. Any information need not be in writing (although it always is in practice), nor on oath. However, it should also be noted that a summons may also be issued by way of a complaint. A complaint is a written or verbal allegation to the effect that a person has committed a breach of the law which is not a *criminal offence*. A common example is a complaint to the effect that some person has committed, or is threatening to commit, a breach of the peace. If the justices find that this is so, the person against whom the complaint has been made may be asked to find surety of the peace, but he will not be punished in the accepted sense that he will not be fined or imprisoned, etc.

Contents of a summons

All summonses contain the full name of the person to whom they are addressed. They also contain a directive for that person to appear at a named court on a specified date at a particular time. If the summons is directed to an offender it will contain details of the offence, sufficient to make it clear to the defendant that he is answering a particular allegation. In the case of a witness summons it will direct him to give evidence in relation to a particular offence and perhaps to produce exhibits.

Defendant summons

This is the most usual method of bringing a person before a court to answer an allegation that he has committed an offence or act for which he is liable to be punished. The first stage in the sequence of events leading to the issue of a summons is the alleged offence being committed. To take a simple example: a constable sees a motor car without lights being driven along a road between sunset and sunrise. The constable stops the vehicle and, after pointing out the offence to the driver, records in his pocket notebook or process book particulars of the driver and his vehicle and the necessary evidence relating to the offence. The constable then submits a report to the supervisory officer and, on the basis of this report, the Crown Prosecution Service will make a decision whether or not the driver should be prosecuted for the offence. If it is decided that there should be a prosecution, information is laid before a magistrate to the effect that the driver, now called the defendant, has committed the offence of driving a motor car on a road between sunset and sunrise without showing the necessary lights required by law, specifying the time, date, and place where the offence is alleged to have occurred. The magistrates, or the magistrates' clerk on behalf of the magistrates, may then issue a summons directing the defendant to appear at the time, date, and court named in the summons to answer the allegation that he has committed the offence specified. It is only the appointed clerk to the justices who can consider the information on behalf of a magistrate. The clerk must do this personally and cannot delegate the function.

Service of a summons

Once a summons has been issued it then has to be served on the person to whom it is addressed, and generally it is the responsibility of the police to perform this task.

Whenever a constable is given a summons to serve he should first check the contents for errors and particularly that there is an original and a copy and that the original summons, which is the one which is served on the person named, is signed by the issuing magistrate or the magistrates' clerk on his behalf. Details of the summons should then be entered in the constable's pocket notebook. If there is an error, it should be returned to a supervisory officer.

The summons, if a defendant summons, can then be served by:

(a) delivering it to the defendant; or
(b) leaving it with a responsible adult at the defendant's last known or usual address; or
(c) sending it by post in a letter addressed to him at his last known or usual place of abode.

Service of a summons on a corporation may be effected by delivering it at, or sending it by post to:

(a) the registered office of the corporation, if that office is in the United kingdom; or
(b) any place in the United Kingdom where the corporation trades or conducts its business, if there is no registered office in the United Kingdom.

The Magistrates' Courts Rules provide that, in any instance in which a summons may be sent by post to a person's last known or usual place of abode, the rules shall have effect as if they provided also for the summons to be sent in the manner specified to an address given by that person for that purpose. In the case of summary offences, postal service will be satisfactorily proved if the summons was sent by post.

When the original summons has been served, the constable should then complete the certificate of service on the back of the copy summons, showing the method of service, the date, and the signature of the person who effected the service, i.e. the constable. He should then make an entry in his pocket notebook of the service of the summons.

Postal service of a summons issued in England and Wales is permitted throughout the United Kingdom. The Scots use a 'citation' instead of a summons and this may be served by post in England and Wales. Northern Irish summonses cannot be served by post in England and Wales.

Witness summons

The object of this type of summons is again to bring a person before a court, not to answer an allegation that he has committed an offence, but in order that he may give or produce evidence as a witness in proceedings before a magistrates' court. Such a summons is issued by a justice if he is satisfied that the person to whom it is addressed is likely to give material evidence or produce anything as evidence, and that this person will not voluntarily attend the court and give or produce such evidence. Unlike other summonses, a witness summons may not be served by post.

Warrants

A warrant is a written authority, signed by a magistrate, directing the person or persons named in the warrant to carry out the purpose for which it was issued, the purpose being stated in the warrant. This may be to arrest a person and bring him before a court, to take a person to prison, or to search premises and seize evidence.

Warrants to search premises

There are many statutes which provide particular powers to enter and search premises under the authority of a warrant. The Police and Criminal Evidence Act 1984 does not affect these provisions but additionally provides justices with a general power to issue warrants to enter and search premises. 'Premises' includes any place, vessel, aircraft or hovercraft or any offshore installation and any tent or moveable structure. The Act of 1984 also standardises procedure in relation to the obtaining of such warrants and the procedures to be followed regardless of the authority for the warrant.

Section 8(1) of the Act provides that if, on application made by a constable, a justice is satisfied that there are reasonable grounds for believing:

(a) that a serious arrestable offence has been committed; and
(b) that there is material on premises specified in the application which is likely to be of substantial value (whether by itself or with other material) to the investigation of the offence; and
(c) that the material is likely to be relevant (i.e. admissible) evidence; and
(d) that it does not consist of or include items subject to legal privilege, excluded material or special procedure material; and
(e) that any of the conditions specified in subs. (3) applies (see below);

the justice may issue a warrant authorising a constable to enter and search the premises. Subsection (2) authorises a constable to seize and retain anything for which a search has been authorised. All warrants to search, regardless of the statute which authorises them, must now be obtained by this procedure.

The conditions set out in subs. (3) are:

(a) that it is not practicable to communicate with a person entitled to grant entry to the premises;

(b) that it is practicable to communicate with a person entitled to grant entry to the premises but it is not practicable to communicate with any person entitled to grant access to the evidence;

(c) that entry to the premises will not be granted unless a warrant is produced;

(d) that the purpose of the search may be frustrated or seriously prejudiced unless a constable arriving at the premises can secure immediate entry to them.

The term 'serious arrestable offence' is not concerned with the term 'arrestable offence'. Schedule 5 to the Act declares certain offences to be serious arrestable offences, these are treason, murder, manslaughter, rape, kidnapping, incest with a girl under 13, buggery with a person under 16, an indecent assault which constitutes an act of gross indecency, causing an explosion likely to endanger life or property, intercourse with a girl under 13, possession of firearms with intent to endanger life or use to resist arrest or carrying a firearm with criminal intent, hostage taking, hi-jacking aircraft, torture, causing death by dangerous driving, causing death by careless driving when under the influence of drink or drugs, hi-jacking ships, endangering safety at aerodromes, seizing or exercising control of fixed platforms, indecent photographs and pseudo-photographs of children and publication of obscene matter. In addition, s. 116 of the 1984 Act specifies certain drug trafficking offences.

Section 116 states that any other arrestable offence is serious only if its commission has led to the consequences set out below, or is intended or likely to have such consequences:

(a) serious harm to the security of the State or to public order;

(b) serious interference with the administration of justice or with the investigation of offences or of a particular offence;

(c) the death of any person;

(d) serious injury to any person;

(e) substantial financial gain to any person; and

(f) serious financial loss to any person.

A loss is 'serious' for the purposes of the section if, having regard to all the circumstances, it is serious for the person who suffers it. The term 'injury' includes any disease and any impairment of a person's physical or mental condition. The seriousness of a loss is dependent upon the financial or other circumstances of the individual against whom the crime is committed. A theft of a large sum of money may not amount to a serious loss in the case of a multi-millionaire, while the theft of the small life-savings of a pensioner could be extremely serious in some cases.

Items subject to legal privilege are communications between lawyer and client and items enclosed with or referred to in such communications. Excluded material includes personal records (medical, trade, business, etc.), human tissue or fluid taken for medical purposes, journalistic material, etc.

The information supplied by the constable in order to obtain a warrant shall identify, so far as practicable, the articles or persons to be sought. Where the description of the articles provided by the warrant differed from that included in the information, the description not being so precisely phrased, the warrant was declared invalid. It will be insufficient in most circumstances to specify 'all records of the financial dealings of [company]' unless all dealings are under investigation. This is most improbable. If it is only the company's dealings with a particular body which are being examined, the information and the warrant should specify those dealings.

The conditions under which searches may be conducted are covered on pages 103–104.

Commitment or distress warrant

Such a warrant is issued by a magistrates' court where a person has defaulted in the payment of a fine or order of a magistrates' court. A warrant of distress is for the purpose of levying the sum which is unpaid. Such a warrant is usually executed by bailiffs but it may be directed to constables. It requires that goods be seized by labelling. Once labels are attached the goods are in legal custody. Property owned by public utilities cannot be seized, nor can clothes, bedding or tools or implements of a person's trade. It is an offence to move goods once they have been labelled. A warrant of commitment orders the defaulter to be arrested and taken to HM prison unless he pays the amount specified in the warrant. When such an arrest has been effected the person arrested should be taken to a designated police station for detention until transportation to the place specified in the warrant can be arranged. A receipt will be issued for the prisoner when he is handed over to the prison authorities.

Commitment warrants are usually issued where it appears that, on the return of a warrant of distress, the defaulter's assets are insufficient to satisfy the sum adjudged to be paid.

Arrest warrant

This type of warrant authorises the arrest of the person named or described in the warrant for the reason stated. To obtain a warrant to arrest, a written sworn information is laid before a magistrate who may then issue the warrant. A warrant to arrest for an offence shall not be issued unless the offence to which it relates is an indictable offence, or punishable with imprisonment, or the address of the defendant is not sufficiently established for a summons to be served.

A warrant to arrest an adult for failing to appear at a magistrates' court after being summoned for an offence shall not be issued unless there is proof of the service of the summons and the offence is punishable with imprisonment, or the court having convicted the defendant proposes to impose a disqualification on him.

If a magistrate is satisfied by evidence on oath that any person should give or produce evidence as a witness in criminal proceedings before a magistrates' court, and either that person has been served with a witness summons, or the magistrate is satisfied at the outset that such a summons would not procure his attendance at court, he may issue a warrant to arrest that person and bring him before the magistrates' court at a time and place specified in the warrant.

A warrant may be issued by a magistrate when a person has failed to pay a fine

105

imposed after conviction. If this fine is paid in full, the person concerned should not be arrested.

Execution of warrants

(1) Arrest warrants

A warrant is executed by carrying out the instructions contained in the warrant. If the warrant is to arrest for an offence and bring before the court, it is executed when the person named in the warrant is arrested. A warrant to arrest may be executed at any time and remains in force until it is withdrawn, even if the magistrate who issued the warrant dies or ceases to be a magistrate. If the warrant is for the arrest of a person for an offence and in some other circumstances set out on page 146 it need not be in the possession of the police office making the arrest, provided that the warrant is shown to the person as soon as possible after his arrest; in any other case the warrant is shown to that person as soon as possible after his arrest. In all other cases the warrant must be in the possession of the police officer who executes it.

The most common form of warrant a constable has to deal with is a warrant to arrest either for an offence or for non-payment of money which a court has ordered a person to pay. As with a summons, a constable receiving a warrant for execution must ensure that the warrant is in order and is signed. One particular point to check is if the warrant specifies that the person arrested should be taken before a court at a specified time and date. On occasions, because of difficulty in execution, this date is passed and it becomes necessary to return the warrant unexecuted so that a new warrant may be issued specifying a new time and date. This difficulty is avoided in most cases by the warrant merely specifying that the arrested person is brought before the next court after his arrest. Having checked the warrant, the constable should enter brief details of the document in his pocket notebook. The procedure for actually executing the warrant is that the constable should tell the person to whom it refers that he has a warrant for his arrest and show it to that person. In no circumstances must the warrant be handed over to him. It must be kept in the constable's possession. If the warrant is to arrest for an offence, that person should then be told he is being arrested for the offence specified in the warrant, and cautioned in accordance with the relevant Code of Practice. If the warrant is to arrest in default, then the person should be asked if he can pay the amount specified. If he can pay, the amount should be recorded in the constable's pocket notebook and he should ask the person to sign it. An official receipt will be delivered to him later, unless the constable is at the police station at this time when a receipt will be made out and handed over to the person paying the money. Remember, the full amount must be paid to satisfy the demand made by the warrant; if a smaller amount is offered, this should be accepted, recorded, and a receipt given but the person must still be arrested, the part payment possibly having the effect of reducing the period of imprisonment decided upon by the magistrates.

When a person is arrested on warrant it will frequently be found that the warrant will contain specific directions on the reverse. These are frequently concerned with directions to release the person arrested on bail to appear at a specified court. These directions should be studied carefully as the Police and Criminal Evidence Act 1984 makes provisions for such persons to be released on bail without being brought to a police station. If such a direction is not included, the person must be taken to a police station at which the sergeant or officer in charge of the police station will arrange for the person to be released on bail.

(2) *Search warrants*

The Police and Criminal Evidence Act 1984, s. 16, permits a search warrant to be executed by any constable. Other persons may be authorised to accompany a constable. Entry and search must be within one month of the issue of the warrant and must be at a reasonable hour unless the purpose of the search may be frustrated by entry at such a time.

Where the occupier of the premises is present, the constable must, before the search begins:

(a) identify himself (by warrant number in the case of terrorism enquiries) and, if not in uniform, show his warrant card (but in so doing in the case of terrorism enquiries, he need not reveal his name);

(b) produce the warrant to him; and

(c) supply him with a copy of it.

In the absence of the owner, the same procedure will be followed in relation to a person in charge of the premises. (See pages 154–157 for further information concerning the procedure to be followed when executing search warrants.)

(3) *Action after execution of warrant and powers*

Having executed a warrant the constable must endorse on the back of the warrant the time, date, place, and manner of execution and sign the endorsement. He should then enter brief details of the arrest in his pocket notebook. If money is received as directed in a warrant, this must be handed over to the sergeant or officer in charge of the police station as soon as practicable on arrival at the station, together with the endorsed warrant.

The Police and Criminal Evidence Act 1984, s. 17, permits a constable to enter and search premises including any vehicle, vessel, aircraft or tent for the purpose of executing any warrant of arrest issued in connection with or arising out of criminal proceedings, or a warrant of commitment issued under the Magistrates' Courts Act 1980, s. 76. The power is only exercisable where the constable has reasonable grounds for believing that the person he is seeking is on the premises. Where the premises consist of two or more separate dwellings, the entry and search is restricted to any common part of the building and the dwelling in which the constable reasonably believes that person may be. (See page 157 for action to be taken after executing search warrant. See page 155 in relation to forcible entry to premises.)

Cross-border enforcement of warrants

The Criminal Justice and Public Order Act 1994, s. 136, provides that warrants issued in respect of offences in England and Wales, Scotland and Northern Ireland may be executed without endorsement throughout the United Kingdom by constables of the country of issue or the country of execution. The provisions also apply to warrants of commitment, warrants to arrest a witness, and warrants to imprison (or to apprehend and imprison) issued in Scotland.

Questioning and treatment of persons

Introduction

The questioning and treatment of persons by the police is now controlled by ss. 53 to 65 of the Police and Criminal Evidence Act 1984; the Code of Practice for the Detention, Treatment, and Questioning of Persons by Police Officers; and the Code of Practice on Tape Recording. References throughout this chapter to the Act of 1984 will be references to 'the Act' and the Code of Practice for the Detention, Treatment, and Questioning of Persons by Police Officers will be referred to as the Detention Code. The Code of Practice on Tape Recording will be referred to as the Tape Recording Code.

These provisions replace all former controls upon police practice. Although references in the Detention Code are to persons 'detained' in police stations, those who are voluntarily in attendance must be treated with at least equal consideration. The procedures described must be carefully followed. Evidence which is obtained in a manner which breaches any provisions of the Code of Practice may be excluded at the trial judge's discretion. The breach will also involve the commission of a disciplinary offence.

The purpose of the Detention Code is to ensure that all persons in custody are dealt with expeditiously and are released as soon as the need for detention has ceased to apply. This and other Codes must be readily available at all police stations for consultation by police officers, detained persons, and members of the public. The Codes issued under the authority of the Act contain within them advice which is headed 'Notes for Guidance'. These notes are not provisions of the Codes themselves and are only intended to assist application and interpretation. There are also a number of Annexes to the Codes and these *are* parts of the Codes themselves and compliance with these provisions is essential.

Whenever the Detention Code requires a person to be given certain information, he does not have to be given it if he is incapable at the time of understanding what is said to him or is violent or likely to become violent or is in urgent need of medical attention, but he must be given it as soon as practicable.

The Code *does not apply* to persons arrested by officers from Scottish forces exercising their 'cross-border' powers; persons arrested for fingerprinting under the Asylum and Immigration Appeals Act 1993; persons served with a detention notice under the Immigration Act 1971; or convicted or remanded prisoners held in police cells on behalf of the prison service, but the provisions prescribing conditions of detention and treatment of detained persons must be considered as the minimum standard for such detained persons.

The Code *does apply* to all other persons who are in custody in police stations in England and Wales whether or not they have been arrested for an offence, and to those who have been removed to a police station as a place of safety under ss. 135 and 136 of the Mental Health Act 1983. However, s. 15 of the Code (reviews of extensions of detention) apply solely to people in police detention, for example, those brought to a police station under arrest or arrested at a police station for an offence after attending there voluntarily.

Nothing in the Tape Recording Code shall be taken as detracting in any way from the requirements of the Detention Code.

Enquiries prior to arrest

The Detention Code makes it clear that it does not affect the general principle that all citizens have a duty to help the police prevent crime and discover offenders. It stresses that this is a civic, rather than a legal duty, but that when a police officer is trying to discover whether, or by whom, an offence has been committed he is entitled to question any person from whom he thinks useful information can be obtained, subject to the restrictions which the Code imposes. A person's declaration that he is unwilling to reply does not alter the entitlement.

Thus the citizens' duty to assist the police is declared; the constable's right to ask questions is stated; that right continues to exist even though the person to whom the questions are addressed refuses to answer; and it is made clear that although a duty to assist exists, there is no requirement on the citizen's behalf to answer any of the questions addressed to him. These provisions provide a starting point to the process of criminal investigation. Whenever a person not under arrest is initially cautioned before or during an interview he must at the same time be told that he is not under arrest and is not obliged to remain with the officer. A person who accompanies a police officer voluntarily, when taken to a police station, or who is at a police station voluntarily is not under arrest and is free to leave at any time. In addition, the Codes of Practice do not prevent a police officer from asking questions at the scene of a crime to elicit an explanation which could provide the arrested person the opportunity to show that he was innocent.

If in the process of this questioning a point is reached at which there are grounds to suspect a person of an offence, that person must be cautioned before any questions about it (or further questions if it is his answers to previous questions that provide grounds for suspicion) are put to him regarding his involvement or suspected involvement in that offence if his answers or his silence (i.e. failure to answer a question or failure to answer satisfactorily) may be given in evidence in a court in a prosecution. He, therefore, need not be cautioned if questions are put to him for other purposes, for example, solely to establish his identity, or the ownership of any vehicle, or to obtain information in accordance with any relevant statutory requirement (where his refusal to supply a name or address may render him liable to detention, or where refusal to provide a specimen for analysis under the Road Traffic Act 1988, s. 7, may amount to an offence or make him liable to arrest), or in furtherance of, or the proper and effective conduct of a search (provided that the questioning does not concern the person's possible involvement in a criminal offence) or to seek verification of a written record of any comments made, including unsolicited comments which are outside the context of an interview which might be significant.

109

For these purposes a 'significant' statement or silence means one which appears capable of being used in evidence against the suspect, in particular a direct admission of guilt, or failure or refusal to answer a question (or failure to answer it satisfactorily) which might give rise to an inference under Part III of the Criminal Justice and Public Order Act 1994.

The Detention Code, therefore, requires police officers to administer a caution if the answer to the question posed is likely to be offered in evidence from the moment at which it is recognised that a particular person is guilty of an offence. It will be appreciated that questions which are put to establish identity or the ownership of a vehicle are questions, the answers to which, would merely establish that that person was the person who had committed the offences. If a motor car is found illegally parked and a person approaches that vehicle, it is not known that he is the person who parked the vehicle until the answers to such preliminary questions are obtained. Once it is established that he is the person responsible he must be cautioned, or put another way, advised to be careful concerning any further statements which he makes. It should be noted that if a person is under arrest, he must be cautioned when told that he will be prosecuted for an offence.

The Code also provides that when a person who is not under arrest is initially cautioned or is reminded that he is under caution he must at the same time be told that he is not under arrest and is not obliged to remain with the officer. An 'interview' is the questioning of a person regarding his involvement or suspected involvement in a criminal offence or offences which the Code of Practice would require to be carried out under caution. Any person attending a police station voluntarily for the purpose of assisting with an investigation may leave at will unless placed under arrest. If it is decided that he should not be allowed to do so then he must be informed at once that he is under arrest and brought before the custody officer, who is responsible for ensuring that he is notified of his rights in the same way as other detained persons. If he is not placed under arrest but is cautioned, the officer who gives the caution must at the same time inform him that he is not under arrest, that he is not obliged to remain at the police station but that if he remains at the police station he may obtain free legal advice if he wishes. If he asks about his entitlement to legal advice, he should be given a copy of the notice explaining the arrangements for obtaining legal advice. These provisions are difficult to understand. The process of investigation will frequently be hampered by the necessity almost to invite a suspect to leave at the moment at which the truth of the matter is beginning to emerge. If the interviewing officer, as he must do, is absolutely fair to the person by cautioning him immediately a suspicion arises and at the same time advises him that he may leave, this may lead to difficulties. However, the provisions of the Code must be complied with.

Action upon arrest

A person must be cautioned on arrest for an offence unless:

(a) it is impracticable to do so by reason of his condition or behaviour at the time; or

(b) he has already been cautioned prior to arrest as described above.

Action following arrest

Following an arrest, a police officer must caution that person (or cause him to be cautioned, or remind him that he remains under caution):

(a) before putting to him any questions or further questions for the purpose of obtaining evidence which may be given to a court in a prosecution (unless the questioning immediately follows arrest);
(b) when arresting him for any further offence in accordance with s. 31 of the Act;
(c) when charging him with an offence (or informing him that he may be prosecuted for it);
(d) when bringing to his notice a written statement or questioning him as permitted by the Detention Code.

In considering whether or not to caution again after a break, the officer should bear in mind that he may have to satisfy a court that the person understood that he was still under caution when the interview is resumed. If there is any doubt the caution should be given again in full. It is essential that interviewing officers recognise the importance of this requirement as it is probable that defence counsel will pay much attention to the issue of a suspect's continued awareness that he is under caution. Although it was obviously the intention of the writers of the Code that the reference to 'breaks' was a reference to official breaks for meals, etc., where a police officer cautioned the driver of a car who admitted possessing cannabis and two minutes later questioned him about the presence of heroin in the car, it was claimed that he should have been cautioned once more, or reminded that he was under caution, before questions were put concerning the heroin. The Court of Appeal held that the caution administered during the first period of questioning was sufficient to cover the second series of questions. However, the case illustrates the need for the utmost care in ensuring that an accused remains aware that he is under caution.

The officer who administers a caution must ensure that the significance of the caution is understood by the suspect. The person should not, however, be left with a false impression that non-cooperation will have no immediate effect upon his treatment as this may not be so. For example, his refusal to establish his identity may prevent his release from police detention. However, if such a person asks the officer directly what action will be taken in the event of his answering questions, making a statement or refusing to do either, then the officer may inform the person what action the police propose to take in that event provided that the action is itself proper and warranted.

The caution shall be in the following terms:

'You do not have to say anything. But it may harm your defence if you do not mention when questioned something which you later rely on in court. Anything you do say may be given in evidence.'

However, the Code provides that minor verbal deviations do not constitute a breach of this requirement provided that the sense of the caution is preserved. This is important when one recognises that a breach of the Code's requirements amounts to a disciplinary offence. It has long been the practice of defending solicitors and

111

counsel, when all else appeared to be failing, to ask a police office to recite the words of a caution. If a person does not understand the meaning of the caution, a constable should explain it to him. (See under heading 'Tape recorded interviews' below concerning special cautions which apply to all interviews, not merely those which are tape recorded, although interviews are, almost invariably, tape recorded.)

A person detained or cautioned during an interview must be told he is entitled to free independent legal advice and that he can speak to his solicitor on the telephone. If the suspect declines such advice, he should be invited to explain his reasons for doing so, which must be recorded. If such advice is requested, he may not be interviewed, or continue to be interviewed until he has received it.

The exercise of the right to legal advice may be delayed only in accordance with the provisions of the Code (Annex B). Whenever legal advice is requested (unless Annex B below applies) the custody officer must act without delay to secure the provision of such advice to the person concerned. If, on being informed or reminded of the right to legal advice, the person declines to speak to a solicitor in person, the officer shall point out that the right to legal advice includes the right to speak to a solicitor on the telephone and ask him if he wishes to do so. If the person continues to waive his right to legal advice the officer shall ask him the reasons for doing so, and any reasons shall be recorded on the custody record or the interview record as appropriate. Reminders as to the right to legal advice are required in many parts of the Code. Once it is clear that a person neither wants to speak to a solicitor in person nor by telephone he should cease to be asked his reasons. A person is not obliged to give such reasons and should not be pressed to do so.

Generally, the 'delay' provisions of Annex B permit an officer of the rank of superintendent or above to do so where he has reasonable grounds for believing that *either* the exercise of a right to have someone informed of arrest, *or* access to a legal adviser:

(a) will lead to interference with or harm to evidence connected with a serious arrestable offence or interference with or physical injury to other people; or

(b) will lead to the alerting of other people suspected of having committed such an offence but not yet arrested for it; or

(c) will hinder the recovery of property obtained as a result of such an offence.

Where a person asks for legal advice and the solicitor nominated by him or selected from a list, cannot be contacted; or has previously indicated that he does not wish to be contacted; or having been contacted has declined to attend; and the person concerned has been told of the duty solicitor scheme but has declined to ask for the duty solicitor, or the duty solicitor is unavailable, the interview must be started or continued without further delay provided that an officer of the rank of inspector or above has given agreement. However, where a solicitor chosen by a suspect is unavailable, the suspect may choose up to two alternatives. If these are unsuccessful, the custody officer may allow further attempts.

The same applies where a person who wanted legal advice changes his mind. Where this occurs, the inspector or above must enquire into the reasons for the change of mind before authorising the interview to proceed. All such details must be recorded on tape or in a written record.

For the purposes of the Code an 'interview' is the questioning of a person regarding his involvement or suspected involvement in a criminal offence or offences which, by virtue of the Code, is required to be carried out under caution. Procedures undertaken under s. 7 of the Road Traffic Act 1988 (provisions of specimens for analysis) do not constitute 'interviews' for the purposes of the Code.

A poster advertising the right to have legal advice must be prominently displayed in the charging area of every police station. See also 'Urgent interviews' on page 130.

An accurate record must be made of each interview with a person suspected of an offence, whether or not the interview takes place at a police station.

Tape recorded interviews

A special caution should be given at the beginning of the interview. When a suspect who is interviewed after arrest fails or refuses to answer certain questions, or to answer them satisfactorily, *after due warning*, a court or jury may draw such inferences as appear proper, under the Criminal Justice and Public Order Act 1994, ss. 36 and 37. This applies when:

(a) a suspect is arrested by a constable and there is found on his person or in or on his clothing or footwear, or otherwise in his possession or in the place where he was arrested, any objects, marks or substances, or marks on such objects, and the person fails or refuses to account for the objects, marks or substances found; or

(b) an arrested person was found by a constable at a place at or about the time the offence for which he was arrested, is alleged to have been committed, and the person fails or refuses to account for his presence at that place.

For an inference to be drawn from a suspect's failure or refusal to answer a question about one of these matters, or to answer it satisfactorily, the interviewing officer must first tell him in ordinary language:

(a) what offence he is investigating;

(b) what fact he is asking the suspect to account for;

(c) that he believes this fact may be due to the suspect's taking part in the commission of the offence in question;

(d) that the court may draw a proper inference from his silence if he fails or refuses to account for the fact about which he is being questioned; and

(e) that a record is being made of the interview and that it may be given in evidence if he is brought to trial.

The provisions of the latest Code, led to lawyer-driven media hype concerning the alleged intention of the Home Secretary to remove a suspect's 'right to silence'. These provisions do not remove that right. They merely provide that proper cognisance can be taken of the circumstances surrounding the exercise of that right, which is quite a different matter. If a police officer tells a suspect that he is investigating an offence of burglary and asks him to account for the fact that he was seen in the garden of the attacked dwelling-house at the approximate time at which the offence was committed and that he therefore believes that such presence in the garden may be due to his involvement in that offence, the magistrates or jury may draw a proper inference from his silence if he fails or refuses to account for his

113

presence. It will be important for police officers to ensure that the special caution as set out at (a) to (e) above is properly given and that a record is made of it. Procedural rules, and the extent to which they are followed, are becoming much more important than the question of guilt or innocence. It is certain that much time will be spent in the cross-examination of police officers concerning the nature of the warning given.

(1) *Nature of taped record*

Such a record, if it occurs at a police station, must be made in accordance with the Code of Practice on Tape Recording:

(a) with a person who has been cautioned in accordance with the Detention Code (grounds to suspect him of an offence) in respect of an indictable offence (including an offence triable either way);

(b) if it takes place as a result of a police officer exceptionally putting further questions to a suspect about such an offence at (a) after he has been charged with, or informed that he may be prosecuted for, that offence; or

(c) in which a police officer wishes to bring to the notice of a person, after he has been charged with, or informed that he may be prosecuted for, such an offence at (a), any written statement made by another person, or the content of an interview with another person. (This may be done by playing a tape recording.)

However, tape recordings at police stations may be made of interviews with persons cautioned for other offences, at police discretion, provided that the Code is complied with. This also applies to responses after charge in such situations.

The tape recording of an interview shall be carried out openly but unobtrusively and it must be made clear to the suspect that there is no opportunity to interfere with the tape recording or tapes. The 'master' tape will be sealed before it leaves the presence of the suspect. A 'master' tape may be either one of two tapes used in a twin-decked machine or the only tape used in a single-deck machine. A second tape will be used as a working copy and it may be either the other tape in the case of a twin-deck machine, or a copy of the master used in a single-deck machine. Such a copy must be made in the presence of the suspect and without the master tape having left his sight.

When a suspect is brought into the interview room the police officer will without delay, but in the sight of the suspect, load the tape recorder with previously unused tapes and set it to record. The tapes must be unwrapped or otherwise opened in the presence of the suspect. The police officer will then say:

(a) that the interview is being recorded;

(b) his name and rank and the name and rank of any other police officer present except in the case of enquiries linked to terrorism when the warrant or other identification number should be stated rather than names;

(c) the name of the suspect and any other party present (i.e. a solicitor);

(d) the date, time of commencement and place of the interview; and

(e) that the suspect will be given a notice about what will happen to the tapes.

The police must then caution the suspect in the usual way (see page 120 under heading (1) 'The interview itself', re legal advice and statements previously made) and he must be reminded of his right to free and independent legal advice and that he can speak to a solicitor on the telephone.

At the beginning of an interview carried out at a police station, the interviewing officer, after cautioning the suspect, shall put to him any significant statement or silence which occurred before his arrival at the police station, and shall ask him whether he confirms or denies that earlier statement or silence which occurred before his arrival at the police station, and shall ask him whether he confirms or denies that earlier statement or silence and whether he wishes to add anything.

A 'significant' statement or silence is one which appears capable of being used in evidence against the suspect, in particular a direct admission of guilt, or failure or refusal to answer a question or to answer it satisfactorily, which might give rise to an inference under Part III of the Criminal Justice and Public Order Act 1994.

If the suspect raises objections to such tape recording either at the outset, or during the interview, the officer shall explain the fact that the interview is being tape recorded and that the provisions of the Tape Recording Code require that the suspect's objections should be recorded on tape. When any objections have been recorded on tape or the suspect has refused to have his objections recorded, the police officer may turn off the recorder. In this eventuality, he must say that he is turning off the recorder and give his reasons for doing so and then turn it off. The police officer must then make a written record of the interview in accordance with the Detention Code (see below). If, however, the police officer reasonably considers that he may proceed to put questions to the suspect with the tape recorder still on, he may do so. He should bear in mind that a decision to continue recording against the wishes of the suspect may be subject to comment in court.

If a suspect indicates that he wishes to tell a police officer about matters not directly connected with the offence of which he is suspected and that he is unwilling for these matters to be recorded on tape, he must be given the opportunity to tell the police officer about these matters after the conclusion of the formal interview.

(2) Changing tapes and breaks

Where a tape is coming to an end, the police officer must inform the suspect and round off that part of the interview, remove the tapes and insert new tapes which will be unwrapped or otherwise opened in the suspect's presence. Tapes should be marked with an identification number immediately they are removed from the tape recorder. A suspect must not be left unattended in the interview room.

A break involving the suspect vacating the interview room must be recorded together with the reason for it and the time it was taken. The tape must then be removed from the machine and dealt with in the same manner as if the interview had been concluded (see below). A short break, in which both the suspect and the police officer remain in the room, must be recorded on the tape. The recorder may be switched off, but there is no need to remove the tapes. Recommencement should be recorded and the interviewing officer must ensure that the person being questioned is aware that he remains under caution. If there is a doubt, it must be renewed.

(3) *Equipment failure*

In the event of failure of equipment which can be rectified quickly, e.g. by inserting new tapes, this must be done following the procedures laid down in relation to the changing of tapes. The officer must record the reason and the time the interview recommences. Where the further use of the tape recorder is impossible and no alternative is readily available, the interview may continue without being tape recorded. The authority of the custody officer must be obtained.

(4) *Interview conclusion*

At the conclusion of an interview, including the taking and reading back of any written statement, the suspect must be offered the opportunity to clarify anything he has said and to add anything he wishes. The time must be recorded and the tape recorder switched off. The 'master tape' must then be sealed with a master tape label and treated as an exhibit. The police officer must sign the label and ask the suspect or any third party to sign it also. If either, or both, refuse to sign the label, an officer of at least the rank of inspector or, if one is not available, the custody officer, shall be called into the interview room and asked to sign it. In the case of enquiries linked to terrorism, an officer who signs the label shall use his warrant or other identification number. The suspect will be given a notice explaining the use which will be made of the tape recording and the arrangements for access to it.

(5) *Broken tape*

If one of the tapes breaks during an interview it should be sealed as a master tape in the presence of the suspect and the interview should be resumed where it left off. The unbroken tape should be copied and the original sealed in the usual way. If equipment for copying the unbroken tape is not readily available, both tapes must be sealed and the interview begun again. If a single-deck machine is being used and it is one on which a broken tape cannot be copied, the tape should be sealed in the usual way and the interview begun again.

(6) *Non-taped interviews*

Tape recording is not required in relation to interviews with persons arrested under the Prevention of Terrorism (Temporary Provisions) Act 1989, s. 14(1)(a), or Schedule 5, para. 6, or an interview with a person being questioned in respect of an offence where there are reasonable grounds for suspecting that it is connected with terrorism, or to interviews with persons reasonably suspected of an offence contrary to the Official Secrets Act 1911, s. 1.

In addition, the custody officer may authorise the interviewing officer not to tape record the interview:

(a) where it is not reasonably practicable to do so because of failure of the equipment or the non-availability of a suitable interview room or recorder and the custody officer considers on reasonable grounds that the interview should not be delayed until the failure has been rectified or a suitable room or recorder becomes available. Priority should be given to recording interviews with persons who are suspected of more serious offences.

(b) where it is clear from the outset that no prosecution will ensue, the custody officer may authorise the interviewing officer not to tape record the interview.

Written records following interviews

The police officer must make a note in his notebook of the fact that the interview has taken place and has been recorded on tape, its time, duration and date and the identification number of the master tape. Where no proceedings follow in respect of the person whose interview was recorded the tapes must nevertheless be kept securely in accordance with the Code. Where proceedings follow, the officer must prepare a written record of the interview and sign it. Any such written record of a tape recorded interview shall be made in accordance with national guidelines approved by the Secretary of State. The officer may refresh his memory by listening to the working copy of the tape to check its accuracy. The interview record shall be 'exhibited' to any written statement prepared by the officer. If the officer's evidence of the interview is accepted by the defence, the evidence shall refer to the fact that the evidence was tape recorded and may be presented to the court in the form of the interview record. However, acceptance of an agreed summary of a tape recorded interview does not exclude the later admission of the tapes before a jury. An issue may arise which can only be resolved by admitting the full tapes in evidence. Where such evidence is not so accepted, the officer must refer to and produce the master tape of the whole interview as an exhibit, informing the court of any transcription which has been made of which he is aware.

An interview record enables the prosecutor to make informed decisions; it is capable of use as an exhibit to an officer's witness statements and pursuant to the Criminal Justice Act 1967, s. 9, and the Magistrates Courts Act 1980; it enables the prosecutor to comply with the rules of advance disclosure; and where the record is accepted by the defence, facilitates the conduct of the case by the prosecution, the defence and the court. Such a record must, therefore, comprise a balanced account of the interview including points in mitigation, and/or defence, made by the suspect. Where an admission is made the question as well as the answer containing the admission shall be recorded verbatim in the record. Matters considered to be prejudicial or inadmissible should be brought to the attention of the prosecutor by means of a covering report.

It must be stressed that the general rules concerning the giving of a caution apply in the case of tape recorded interviews and the appropriate records of such cautions must be made.

Written records of interviews

Any written record (where such a procedure may be followed) must be made during the interview, unless in the investigating officer's view this would not be practicable or would interfere with the conduct of the interview. An accurate record must be made of each interview with a person suspected of an offence, whether or not the interview takes place at a police station. The record must state:

(a) the place of the interview;

(b) the time it begins and ends;

(c) the time the record is made (if different);

(d) details of breaks (including times); and

(e) the names of those present (subject to the provisions set out above in relation to terrorist offences);

(f) where legal advice is requested and interview proceeds without a solicitor, that fact, and

must constitute either a verbatim record or, failing this, an account of the interview which though not necessarily verbatim, adequately summarises it. Such a written record must be made on the appropriate forms or in the officer's pocket notebook or in accordance with the procedural guidance for the tape recording of police interviews. If the record is not made during the interview, it must be made as soon as practicable afterwards and the reason must be recorded in the police officer's notebook.

Unless it is impracticable the person interviewed must be given the opportunity to read the interview record and to sign it as correct or indicate the respects in which he considers it inaccurate. If the person concerned cannot read or refuses to read the record or sign it, the senior police officer present must read it over to him and ask him whether he would like to sign it as correct or to indicate the respects in which he considers it inaccurate. The police officer must then certify on the interview record itself what has occurred.

A written record should also be made of any comments made by a suspected person, including unsolicited comments which are outside the context of an interview but which might be relevant to the offence. Any such record must be timed and signed by the maker. Where practicable the person must be given the opportunity to read the record and to sign it as correct or to indicate the respects in which he considers it inaccurate. Any refusal to sign shall be recorded. Where an appropriate adult or the person's solicitor is present during an interview, he should also be given the opportunity to read and sign the interview record (or any statement written down by a police officer).

Where a suspect agrees to read records of interviews and of other comments and to sign them as correct, he should be asked to endorse the record with words such as 'I agree that this is a correct record of what was said' and add his signature. Where a suspect does not agree with the record, the officer should record the details of any disagreement and then ask the suspect to read these details and then sign them to the effect that they accurately reflect his disagreement. Any refusal to sign when asked to do so shall be recorded.

All entries in custody and written interview records (except those identifying the person to whom the record relates) must be timed and signed by the maker. Any refusal by a person to sign either a custody or interview record when asked to do so in accordance with the provisions of the Detention Code, must itself be recorded.

Decision to charge - procedure

The Detention Code also provides that as soon as a police officer who is making enquiries of any person about an offence believes that a prosecution should be brought against him and that there is sufficient evidence for it to succeed, he should ask the person if he has anything further to say. If the person indicates that he has nothing more to say the officer shall without delay cease to question him about that offence (with certain exceptions set out below) and bring him before a custody officer, who shall then be responsible for considering whether or not he should be charged. When a person is detained in respect of more than one offence it is permissible to delay bringing him before a custody officer until these conditions are satisfied in respect of all offences. A person in detention must be cautioned when charged or informed that he may be prosecuted for an offence. If charged, he must also be given at that time, a written notice showing particulars of the offence with which he is charged and including the name of the officer in the case (in terrorist cases, the officer's warrant or other identification number instead), his police station, and the station's reference number for the case. So far as possible the particulars of the charge shall be stated in simple terms, but they shall also show the precise offence in law with which he is charged. Thus, for practical purposes, although the nature of the offence may be simply stated, there should be a reference to the section and the Act offended against or a clear statement of the common law requirement which is breached. The notice which is given to a suspect shall begin with the following words:

'You are charged with the offence(s) shown below. You do not have to say anything. But it may harm your defence if you do not mention now something which you later rely on in court. Anything you do say may be given in evidence.'

Questions relating to an offence may not be put to a person after he has been charged with that offence, or informed that he may be prosecuted for it, unless they are necessary:

(a) to prevent or minimise harm or loss to some person or to the public; or
(b) to clear up ambiguity in a previous answer or statement; or
(c) where it is in the interests of justice that the person should have put to him and have an opportunity to comment upon any information concerning the offence which has come to light since he was charged or informed that he might be prosecuted.

However, before any such additional questions may be put, the person shall be warned that he does not have to say anything but that anything he does say may be given in evidence and reminded of his right to legal advice in accordance with the provisions of the Code.

Item (a) above is concerned with instances in which a person in detention may say prior to being charged, 'Yes, I broke into the High Street Electrical Stores and stole the property'. The prisoner has certainly caused the officer to decide that he is guilty of the offence and that he must be charged. However, there remains a duty to recover the stolen property to minimise the loss to the owner and the officer would, therefore, be entitled to ask, 'What did you do with the property?' In the case of (b) the prisoner may have referred to the name of a street without stating in which town, or a day of the week without clearly indicating which week of the year. This leads to ambiguity which can only be removed by further questioning. The purpose of (c) is to allow the prisoner an opportunity to comment upon further matters which had come to light since he was charged if it is in the interest of justice. Certain additional

119

evidence may come into the hands of the prosecution and it may well be that it is in the prisoner's interests to have the nature of that evidence brought to his notice and perhaps, additionally, that he should have the opportunity to comment upon it. It may be that a subsequent search of premises in the occupation of the prisoner, has revealed the presence of stolen property. It is possible that the prisoner will be able to give some account for its presence which relieves him of responsibility.

If any such questions are put after charge, the questions and answers given shall be contemporaneously recorded in full on the forms provided and the record shall be signed by that person. If he refuses, it shall be signed by the interviewing officer and any third parties present. In the case of tape recorded questions and answers, the procedural guide must be followed.

Interviews at police stations and procedural points

(1) *The interview itself*

An interview is the questioning of a person regarding his involvement or suspected involvement in a criminal offence or offences which by virtue of the Code is required to be carried out under caution. Procedures undertaken under s. 7 of the Road Traffic Act 1988 do not constitute interviews for the purpose of the Code.

At the beginning of an interview carried out in a police station, the interviewing officer, after cautioning the suspect, shall put to him any significant statement or silence which occurred before his arrival at the police station, and ask him whether he confirms or denies that earlier statement or silence and whether he wishes to add anything. Thus, at the beginning of an interview in a police station, there is an opportunity to 'tidy-up' any previous statements which may have been made before the formal interview takes place.

If a police officer wishes to interview, or conduct enquiries which require the presence of a detained person, the custody officer is responsible for deciding whether to deliver that detained person into the police officer's custody.

Following a decision to arrest a suspect he must not be interviewed about the relevant offence except at a police station (or other authorised place of detention) unless the consequent delay would be likely:

(a) to lead to interference or harm to evidence connected with an offence or interference or physical harm to other persons; or

(b) to lead to the altering of other persons suspected of having committed an offence but not yet arrested for it; or

(c) to hinder the recovery of property obtained in consequence of the commission of the offence.

Interviewing in any of these circumstances should cease once the relevant risk has been averted or the necessary questions have been put in order to avert that risk.

Immediately prior to the commencement or recommencement of any interview at a police station or other authorised place of detention, the interviewing officer should remind the suspect of his entitlement to free legal advice and that the interview can be delayed for him to obtain legal advice, unless the exceptions provided by the Code apply. It is the responsibility of the interviewing officer to ensure that all such reminders are noted in the interview record.

The Court of Appeal has recommended that if notes of an interview have, for any reason, not been shown to a suspect before the arrival of his solicitor, fairness both to the accused and to the police themselves requires that it be shown in the presence of his solicitor. If shown before the arrival of his solicitor, the solicitor should be informed of the facts when he arrives. If a court concludes that the police have acted less than fairly, the chances that the evidence of the conversation noted will be excluded will be increased considerably.

Where a solicitor is present at an interview he may seek to intervene in order to seek clarification or to challenge an improper question, or the manner in which it is put, or to advise his client not to reply to particular questions, or if he wishes to give his client further legal advice.

The solicitor may only be required to leave an interview if his conduct prevents or unreasonably obstructs proper questions being put to the suspect or his response being recorded. Examples of unacceptable conduct include answering questions on a suspect's behalf or providing written replies for him to quote.

No police officer may try to obtain answers to questions or to elicit a statement by the use of oppression or shall indicate, except in answer to a direct question, what action will be taken on the part of the police if the person being interviewed answers questions, makes a statement or refuses to do either. If the person asks the officer directly what action will be taken in the event of his answering questions, making a statement or refusing to do either, then the officer may inform the person what action the police propose to take in that event provided that the action is itself proper and warranted.

As soon as a police officer who is making enquiries of any person about an offence believes that a prosecution should be brought against him and that there is sufficient evidence for it to succeed, he should ask that person if he has anything further to say. If the person indicates that he has nothing more to say the officer must without delay cease to question him about that offence.

(2) *Conditions of detention*

The Code demands that in any period of 24 hours detained persons are allowed a continuous period of at least 8 hours for rest, free from questioning, travel or interruption by police officers in connection with the investigation concerned. Visits or rousing of detained persons made in accordance with the Code, or in accordance with medical advice, do not constitute an interruption to the rest period such that a fresh period must be allowed. (The Code requires hourly visits or half-hourly visits in the case of persons who are drunk.) Persons who are drunk must be aroused and spoken to on each visit. This period should normally be at night. It may not be interrupted except at the request of the person, his appropriate adult or his legal representative unless there are reasonable grounds for believing that this would:

(a) involve a risk of harm to persons or serious loss of, or damage to, property;
(b) delay unnecessarily the person's release from custody; or
(c) otherwise prejudice the outcome of the investigation.

These exceptions also apply in the case of necessity to delay breaks for rest or refreshment. Where a person is arrested at a police station after going there voluntarily, the period of 24 hours runs from the time of his arrest and not the time of his arrival at the police station.

As far as practicable, interviews shall take place in interview rooms which are adequately heated, lit and ventilated and persons being interviewed or making statements shall not be required to stand. Breaks shall be made at recognised meal times. Such breaks should normally be at least 45 minutes. Short breaks for refreshment shall also be provided at intervals of approximately two hours. These should last at least 15 minutes. If at any time during the course of an interview there is sufficient evidence to prosecute the person, the interviewing officer must immediately bring him before the custody officer.

A detained person may not be supplied with intoxicating liquor except on medical directions. No person who is unfit through drink or drugs to the extent that he is unable to appreciate the significance of questions put to him and his answers, may be questioned about an alleged offence, unless in accordance with the instructions of a police surgeon.

(3) *Complaints during interviews*

If, in the course of an interview, a complaint is made by the person being interviewed or on his behalf, concerning the provisions of the Detention Code or the Code on Tape Recording, then the interviewing officer shall record it in the interview record and inform the custody officer, who is then responsible for dealing with that complaint by a prescribed procedure. Where the interview is being tape recorded the tape recorder should be left running until the custody officer has entered the room and has spoken to the interviewee. Continuation or termination of the interview should be at the discretion of the interviewing officer pending action by an inspector under the Detention Code.

Where, during the course of an interview which is being tape recorded, a complaint is made about a matter not connected with the Detention Code or the Tape Recording Code the decision to continue the interview is at the discretion of the interviewing officer. If continued, the officer must inform the complainant that the complaint will be brought to the notice of the custody officer at the conclusion of the interview. This must be done as soon as practicable thereafter.

(4) *Nature of records and security of tapes*

An accurate record must be made of all interviews, whether or not they take place at a police station. If this record is for any reason not made during the course of an interview it must be made as soon as practicable after its completion and the reason for non-completion of the record during the interview must be recorded in the pocket notebook.

These records must state the place of the interview, the time it begins and ends, the time the record is made (if different), any breaks in the interview and the names of all those present (subject to the provisions set out above in relation to terrorist offences) and must be made on the forms provided for this purpose or in the officer's pocket notebook or in accordance with the Code of Practice on Tape Recording.

The security of master tapes is the responsibility of the officer in charge of each police station. Seals must not be broken on master tapes required for criminal proceedings, unless done in the presence of a representative of the Crown Prosecution Service. The defendant, or his legal adviser, shall be informed and shall be given a reasonable opportunity to be present. If either is present, he shall be invited to reseal and sign the master tape. If not present, or in the event of refusal, this will be done by the representative of the Crown Prosecution Service. If master tapes have been delivered to the Crown Court following committal, application must be made to the chief clerk of the Crown Court for the release of the tape for unsealing by the Crown Prosecutor.

Written interview records must be timed and signed by the maker. Any refusal by a person to sign an interview record when asked to do so in accordance with the provisions of the Code must itself be recorded.

(5) *Oppression and unreliability*

It is important to remember that a constable must not at any time try to obtain answers to questions or to elicit a statement from a person by oppression. Regardless of disciplinary issues, the Police and Criminal Evidence Act 1984, s. 76, states that statements obtained by oppression, or in consequence of anything said or done which was likely, in the circumstances existing at the time, to render unreliable any confession which might be made, shall be excluded by the court. If a prisoner is promised that if he is willing to give evidence against another he will not be prosecuted and is subsequently prosecuted, admissions made by him in consequence of that promise will not be admissible as they were gained by an inducement.

Where an accused was charged with theft in circumstances in which other offences may be discovered if other probable victims were interviewed, it was oppressive to threaten that such enquiries would be pursued in the absence of a confession, and any such confession must be excluded.

The inadmissibility of an original confession does not necessarily mean that any subsequent confession will be inadmissible. However, it is not sufficient that the second interview was conducted by a different police officer and that a caution was given. In such a case the suspect must have received appropriate legal advice between the first and second interviews. The Court of Appeal has directed that 'oppression' should be given its ordinary dictionary meaning. It denotes the exercise of power or authority in a burdensome, harsh or wrongful manner, or unjust or cruel treatment, or the imposition of unreasonable or unjust burdens, in circumstances which would almost always entail some impropriety on the part of the interrogator. Recent decisions of the High Court in relation to the meaning of 'oppression' indicate a strong need for care in this respect. Confessions have been excluded even where conducted under independent, expert supervision and where forceful, repetitious questioning has taken place.

Whether or not a drug addict is fit to be interviewed in the sense that his answers could be relied upon in the circumstances, is a matter for those present at the time. Where experienced police officers considered a person fit to be interviewed and a doctor who saw him after the interview was of the same opinion, there was no reason to believe that a confession was unreliable.

123

It is frequently claimed that a confession or admission is unreliable because the person concerned is of low IQ. Expert evidence may be admitted only where it is alleged that a defendant was suffering from a personality disorder so severe as to be categorised as mental disorder.

It may not be admitted to show that a defendant is of dull intelligence and very suggestible.

At the end of any interview with a detained person, the interviewing officer must inform the custody officer that the Code of Practice has been complied with.

Tape recordings in evidence

A tape recording of a police interview with a defendant is primary evidence which, when produced at a trial, becomes an exhibit. If the jury wish to hear it rather than rely upon a transcript, there is no reason why they should not be allowed to do so. It should be listened to in open court.

Written statements under caution

(1) *Written by person under caution*

A person shall always be given the opportunity to write down himself what he wants to say.

Where the person wishes to write it himself, he shall be asked to write out and sign before writing what he wants to say, the following:

> 'I make this statement of my own free will. I understand that I need not say anything but that it may harm my defence if I do not mention when questioned something which I later rely on in court. This statement may be given in evidence.'

Any person writing his own statement shall be allowed to do so without any prompting except that the police officer may indicate to him which matters are material or question any ambiguity in the statement.

(2) *Written by a police officer*

If a person says that he would like someone to write it for him, a police officer shall write the statement, but, before starting, he must ask him to sign or make his mark, to the following:

> 'I, . . ., wish to make a statement. I want someone to write down what I say. I understand that I need not say anything but that it may harm my defence if I do not mention when questioned something which I later rely on in court. This statement may be given in evidence.'

Where a police officer writes the statement, he must take down the exact words spoken by the person making it and he must not edit or paraphrase it. Any questions that are necessary (e.g. to make it more intelligible) and the answers given must be contemporaneously recorded on the statement form.

When the writing of a statement by a police officer is finished, the person making it shall be asked to read it and to make any corrections, alterations or additions he wishes. When he has finished reading it, he shall be asked to write and sign or make his mark on the following certificate at the end of the statement:

'I have read the above statement, and I have been able to correct, alter or add anything I wish. This statement is true. I have made it of my own free will.'

If the person making the statement cannot read, or refuses to read it, or to write the above-mentioned certificate at the end of it or to sign it, the senior police officer present shall read it over to him and ask him whether he would like to correct, alter or add anything and to put his signature or make his mark at the end. The police officer shall then certify on the statement itself what has occurred.

There is a difference between these two procedures. Annex D requires that where a person is to write a statement himself there is a requirement that he is asked *to write out and sign* the declaration. This is deliberately done to ensure that the person making the statement is fully aware of the implications of his actions. Where a statement is to be taken down by a police officer, the requirement is that the prisoner shall sign or make his mark to a declaration. It would therefore be quite proper to produce printed statement forms which carried that declaration and merely to require signature, etc.

The provisions concerning prompting merely follow the rules of common sense. Persons are not practised in the recording of statements of evidence and have no knowledge of the laws governing evidence. It is desirable that they be given general guidance in respect of those matters which are relevant and those which are not. It is similarly desirable that ambiguities, or conflicting statements which are included, are eliminated by some form of assistance by the officer.

General guidance – written statements made by alleged offenders

(a) All statements under caution should be written in ink on the statement form provided.
(b) An offender must be given the opportunity to write his own statement.
(c) If an offender dictates his statement, use only his words; do not edit or paraphrase.
(d) Do not leave spaces in the statement and avoid the use of paragraphs as this necessitates the leaving of spaces and admits the possibility of later allegations of words being inserted.
(e) Corrections should involve words being neatly crossed out, a single line being placed through the word, the correction being initialled by the person making the statement.
(f) The statement should be signed by the person making it at the bottom of each page.
(g) The purpose of an interview is to obtain from the person concerned his explanation of the facts, and not necessarily to obtain an admission.

Statements by co-accused

If at any time after a person has been charged with, or informed he may be prosecuted for an offence a police officer wishes to bring to the notice of that person any written statement made by another person or the content of an interview made by another person, he shall hand to that person a true copy of any such written statement or bring to his attention a copy of the interview record or play a relevant tape recording, but shall say or do nothing to invite any reply or comment save to warn him that he does not have to say anything but anything he does say may be given in evidence and to remind him of his right to legal advice.

If the person cannot read, the officer may read it to him. If he is a juvenile or mentally disordered or mentally handicapped the copy shall also be given, or the interview record shown, to the appropriate adult.

These provisions prevent verbal information being given to a person in detention concerning matters which are alleged to have been said by a co-accused who is also in detention. If such matters are to be brought to the attention of a prisoner, he must be shown and allowed to read the written record.

Persons at risk

A juvenile or someone who is mentally disordered or handicapped, whether suspected of crime or not, must not be interviewed in the absence of the 'appropriate adult' with the exception of the circumstances set out below, nor may he be asked to give or sign a written statement.

The 'appropriate adult' for the purpose of all Codes of Practice is:

(a) in the case of a juvenile, his parent or guardian (or if he is in care, the care authority or voluntary organisation. The term 'in care' is used in this Code to cover all cases in which a juvenile is 'looked after' by a local authority under the terms of the Children Act 1989) or a social worker, or failing either of these parties, another responsible adult, aged 18 or over, who is not a police officer or employed by the police.

A person, including a parent or guardian of a juvenile should not be the appropriate adult if he is suspected of involvement in the offence in question, is the victim, is a witness, is involved in the investigation or has received admissions prior to attending to act as the appropriate adult. If a parent or guardian of a juvenile is estranged from the juvenile he should not be asked to be the appropriate adult if the juvenile expressly and specifically objects to his presence.

If a juvenile admits an offence to or in the presence of a social worker other than during the time the social worker is acting as the appropriate adult for that juvenile, another social worker shall be the appropriate adult in the interests of fairness; and

(b) in the case of a person who is mentally disordered or mentally handicapped a relative, guardian or other person responsible for his care or custody; someone who is not a police officer or employed by the police who has experience of dealing with mentally disordered or mentally handicapped persons; or failing either of the above, some other responsible adult, aged 18 or over, who is not a police officer or employed by the police (such as an approved social worker as defined by the Mental Health Act 1983 or a specialist social worker).

It may, in some cases, be more satisfactory if the appropriate adult is someone who has experience or training in the case rather than a relative lacking those qualifications. However, if the person himself prefers a relative to a better qualified stranger, his wishes should, if practicable, be respected.

A solicitor who is present at the police station in a professional capacity may not act as the appropriate adult.

Where a suspect is mentally handicapped and is interviewed without such a person being present, the issue is not whether the confession obtained is true and can be relied upon; once it has been established that there has been a breach of the Code of Practice, the prosecution must prove beyond reasonable doubt that the confession was not obtained in breach of the Police and Criminal Evidence Act 1984, s. 76(2), and the 'circumstances existing at the time' are all important in relation to reliability. If the absence of an appropriate adult was likely to result in a confession being unreliable, the confession should be excluded.

The only exceptions to the general rule that interviews may not be conducted in the absence of the 'appropriate adult' are when the need to carry out the interview is urgent and such an interview is authorised by a superintendent. Such instances will be rare.

These provisions do not prevent a police officer from asking questions at the scene of a crime to elicit an explanation which could provide an arrested person an opportunity to show that he was innocent. If, in the course of such questions, the suspect, even if a juvenile, made a confession, it is prima facie admissible even though no adult was present provided that no advantage was taken of that fact. For example, if a juvenile was seen attempting to gain entry to a residence in suspicious circumstances, it would be quite proper for a police officer to ask why, and if he knew anyone who lived there. If he replies that he does not, it would be equally proper to offer a further chance to explain his actions by asking why he was attempting to gain entry. A reply of, 'Just to have a look around' leads naturally to a question such as, 'For what?' However, such questions must not go beyond that necessary to provide such a suspect with a reasonable opportunity to provide an *immediate* explanation at the scene.

Interviews – juveniles

Juveniles may only be interviewed at their place of education in exceptional circumstances and then only when the principal or his nominee agrees. Every effort must be made to contact both the parent(s) or other person responsible for the juvenile's welfare and the appropriate adult (if a different person) and a reasonable time should be allowed to enable the appropriate adult to attend. Where this would cause undue delay and unless the offence is against the educational establishment, the principal or his nominee can act as the appropriate adult for the purposes of the interview. It is preferable that a juvenile is not arrested at his place of education unless this is unavoidable. In that case, the principal or his nominee must be informed.

Detention of juveniles following charge

The Police and Criminal Evidence Act 1984, s. 38, requires that an arrested juvenile who is not released from custody after charge should be taken to local authority accommodation unless the custody officer certifies:

(a) that by reason of such circumstances as are specified in the certificate, it is impracticable to do so; or

(b) in the case of an arrested juvenile of at least 12 years of age, no secure accommodation is available and there is a risk to the public of serious harm from that juvenile.

At the time of writing, the age at (b) remains '15' but '12' will be substituted as the remaining sections of the Criminal Justice and Public Order Act 1994 are brought into force. Provision is made to reduce the age from 15 to 12 in stages, by statutory instrument. 'Secure accommodation' is that provided for the purpose of restricting liberty. In the case of arrested juveniles who are charged with a violent or sexual offence, references to protecting the public from serious harm shall be construed as references to protection from death or serious bodily injury, whether physical or psychological, occasioned by further such offences. The term 'sexual offence' in this context means an offence under the Sexual Offences Act 1956 (other than living on immoral earnings, woman exercising control over a prostitute or offences connected with brothels); an offence under the Mental Health Act 1959, s. 128 (sexual intercourse with patients); the Indecency with Children Act 1960; an offence under the Theft Act 1968, s. 9, of burglary with intent to rape; an offence under the Criminal Law Act 1977, s. 54 (inciting incest with girl under 16); the Protection of Children Act 1978; or a conspiracy or attempt to commit any of these offences or inciting such an offence. A 'violent offence' is an offence which leads, or is intended or likely to lead, to a person's death or to physical injury to a person, and includes an offence which is required to be charged as arson (whether or not it would otherwise fall within this definition).

However, except for these circumstances, neither a juvenile's behaviour nor the nature of the offence with which he is charged provides grounds for the custody officer to retain him in police custody rather than to seek to arrange for his transfer to the care of the local authority on the grounds of impracticability. Similarly, the lack of secure local authority accommodation shall not make it impracticable for the custody officer to transfer him. The availability of secure accommodation is only a factor in relation to a juvenile aged 12 or over for whom the local authority accommodation would not be adequate to protect the public from serious harm from the juvenile. The obligation to transfer a juvenile to local authority accommodation applies as much to a juvenile charged during the daytime as it does to a juvenile to be held overnight, subject to a requirement to bring the juvenile before a court under s. 46 of the Police and Criminal Evidence Act 1984.

Notes for guidance

All of these special groups may be particularly open to suggestion. Consequently special care should always be exercised in questioning such a person, and it is important to obtain corroboration of any facts admitted wherever possible.

Foreign languages, the deaf and the blind

The Detention Code provides:

(a) If a person has difficulty in understanding English, the interviewing officer cannot himself speak the person's own language or the person wishes an interpreter to be present, he must not be interviewed in the absence of an adult capable of acting as an interpreter, unless the urgent situation exists as described above.

(b) The interviewing officer must ensure that the interpreter makes a note of the interview at the time, in the language of the person being interviewed, for use in the event of his being called to give evidence and that he certifies its accuracy. However, in the case of a tape recorded interview there is no requirement on the interviewing officer to ensure that the interpreter makes a separate note of the interview, the interviewer must allow sufficient time for the interpreter to note each question and answer after it has been put or given and interpreted. The person being interviewed must be given an opportunity to read the record, sign it as correct, or indicate the respects in which he considers it to be inaccurate. If the interview is tape recorded the procedure set out in the Code or guide must be followed.

(c) In the case of a person making a statement in a language other than English:
  (i) the interpreter must take down the statement in the language in which it is made;
  (ii) the person making the statement must be invited to sign the statement; and
  (iii) an official English translation must be made in due course.

The provisions merely follow the rules of common sense. It would be unrealistic to record a statement in a language which the person who was making the statement could not read. The Community Relations Council can supply a list of interpreters for people being interviewed by the police and who do not understand English.

If a person is deaf or there is a doubt about his hearing ability he must not be interviewed in the absence of an interpreter unless he agrees in writing to be interviewed without one, or it is an 'urgent interview' as described above. An interpreter should also be called if a juvenile is interviewed and the parent or guardian present as the appropriate adult is deaf, unless he agrees in writing that the interview should proceed without one. The interviewing officer must ensure that the interpreter makes a note of the interview at the time for use in the event of his being called to give evidence, and that he certifies its accuracy. The person must be given an opportunity to read it and sign it as correct or indicate the respects in which he considers it inaccurate. Where an interview is being tape recorded and the suspect is deaf, or there is a doubt about his hearing ability, the police officer shall take a contemporaneous note of the interview as well as tape record it.

The Code directs that if a person appears to be blind or seriously visually handicapped, deaf, unable to read or communicate orally with the officer dealing with him at the time, he should be treated as such for the purpose of the Code in the absence of clear evidence to the contrary.

If a person is blind or seriously visually handicapped or is unable to read, the custody officer should ensure that his solicitor, relative, the appropriate adult or some other person likely to take an interest in him is available to help in any documentation. Where the Code requires consent or signification, then this person who is assisting may be asked to sign instead.

Where a person in detention cannot communicate with a solicitor, whether because of language or hearing difficulties, an interpreter must be called.

Interpreters should be provided at public expense and this must be made clear to the person concerned. The interpreter may not be a police officer when the interpretation is needed for the purpose of obtaining legal advice. In other cases a police officer may interpret if the detained person (or the appropriate adult) agrees in writing. The appropriate adult should not be the interpreter. If such an interview is tape recorded the appropriate rules must be followed.

Records are, once again, important. The action taken to call an interpreter must be recorded, together with any waiver of a right not to be interviewed in the absence of an interpreter. It must be remembered that as the interpreter will be required as a witness at the person's trial, a second interpreter will be needed to assist at the trial.

Urgent interviews

Annex C to the Detention Code is concerned with urgent interviews of particularly vulnerable people in exceptional circumstances. It overrides the usual bar upon interviews taking place in the absence of the 'appropriate adult'. If, and only if, an officer of the rank of superintendent (or above) considers that delay will involve an immediate risk of harm to persons or serious loss of or damage to property an arrested juvenile or person who is mentally disordered or mentally handicapped may be interviewed in the absence of the appropriate adult. This could occur where a woman who was mentally disordered, had stolen a child and was suspected of having abandoned that child in circumstances which involved risk to the life of the child. In such circumstances the primary aim of all concerned would be to find the child and a superintendent would, undoubtedly, authorise questioning to begin at once.

Questioning in these circumstances must not continue once sufficient evidence has been obtained to avert the immediate risk. In the example given above, this would occur when the location of the child had been discovered. At that point questioning would have to cease until the arrival of the 'appropriate adult'. A record must be made of the grounds for any decision to interview a person in the above circumstances.

In any circumstances in which such a 'person at risk' has been cautioned and interviewed prior to the attendance of the appropriate adult then the caution must be repeated in the adult's presence upon arrival (unless the interview has by then finished).

Annex C also permits such urgent interviews of persons heavily under the influence of drink or drugs, or persons who have difficulty in understanding English, or those with a hearing disability.

Access to solicitor

By s. 58 of the Police and Criminal Evidence Act 1984 a person arrested and held in police custody is entitled, if he so requests, to consult a solicitor privately at any time;

the consultation may be in person, in writing or by telephone. Where a suspect chooses to speak to a solicitor by telephone he should be allowed to do so in private unless this is impractical because of the design and layout of the custody area or the location of the telephones. If a person makes such a request he must be permitted to consult a solicitor as soon as practicable, and the custody officer must act without delay to secure the provision of such legal advice. 'Solicitor' means a solicitor who holds a current practising certificate, a trainee solicitor, a duty solicitor representative maintained by the Legal Aid Board. If a solicitor wishes to send a non-accredited or probationary representative to provide advice on his behalf, then that person shall be admitted to the police station for this purpose unless an officer of the rank of inspector or above considers that such a visit will hinder the investigation of crime and directs otherwise. Hindering the investigation of crime does not include giving proper legal advice to a detained person in accordance with the Code.

In exercising his discretion, the officer should take into account in particular whether the identity and the status of the non-accredited or probationary representative have been satisfactorily established; whether he is of suitable character to provide legal advice (a person with a criminal record is unlikely to be suitable unless the conviction was for a minor offence and is not of recent date) and any other matter in any written letter of authorisation provided by the solicitor concerned.

No police officer shall at any time do or say anything with the intention of dissuading a person in detention from obtaining legal advice. Whenever legal advice is requested (unless delay is authorised) a custody officer must, without delay, secure the provision of such advice. If, on being informed of this right, a person declines to speak to a solicitor in person, the officer shall point out that the right to legal advice includes the right to speak to a solicitor on the telephone and ask him if he wishes to do so. If the person continues to waive his right, the officer shall ask him his reasons for doing so, and any reasons shall be recorded on the custody record, or interview record. Once it is clear that a person neither wishes to speak to a solicitor in person, nor by telephone, he should cease to be asked his reasons. He is not obliged to give such reasons.

A person who asks for legal advice should be given an opportunity to consult a specific solicitor, or another solicitor from that firm, or the duty solicitor. If advice is not available by these means, or he does not wish to consult the duty solicitor, he should be allowed to choose from a list. If his choice is unavailable, he may choose up to two alternatives. The custody officer has discretion to allow two further attempts. A police officer must not advise the suspect about any particular firm of solicitors. Delay is permissible, but only if the person is in police detention for a serious arrestable offence and an officer of the *rank of superintendent or above authorises the delay*.

An arrested person must be informed of this right and must be given a notice to this effect. A record must be made of such matters in the custody records and the person should be asked to sign it. If video cameras are installed in the custody area notices which indicate that cameras are in use should be prominently displayed. Any request by any person to have such cameras switched off will be refused.

Where the right to legal advice has been exercised an interview may not be started or continued until such advice has been received unless special circumstances exist. A superintendent (or above) must decide whether such special circumstances exist.

However, where a person who wanted legal advice changes his mind, the interview may be started or continued without further delay providing that the person concerned has given his agreement in writing or on tape to being interviewed without receiving legal advice and an officer of the rank of inspector or above, having enquired into the suspect's reasons for his change of mind, has given approval for the interview to proceed. Confirmation of the person's agreement, his change of mind, his reasons where given and the name of the authorising officer shall be recorded in the taped or written interview record, at the beginning or recommencement of interview. The authorisation may be given over the telephone if the authorising officer satisfies himself as to the reason for the change of mind.

Inform someone of arrest

The Police and Criminal Evidence Act 1984, s. 56, provides that where a person has been arrested and is being held in custody at a police station or other premises, he shall be entitled, if he so requests, to have one friend or relative or other person who is known to him or is likely to take an interest in his welfare told, as soon as practicable, that he has been arrested and is being detained there. Where a person so chosen cannot be contacted the person being detained can make up to two alternative choices. In the event of it being impossible to contact either of them, the person in charge of his detention or of the investigation has discretion to allow further attempts until the information has been conveyed. Where delay is authorised, that delay may not be authorised beyond 36 hours after his arrest.

In addition, where an enquiry as to the whereabouts of the person is made by such persons this information shall be given if the person detained agrees and delay has not been authorised.

Delay is permitted where the person concerned is in police detention for a serious arrestable offence and an officer of at least the rank of superintendent authorises that delay. He may only do so where he has reasonable grounds for believing that the exercise of the right will lead to interference with or harm to evidence connected with a serious arrestable offence or interference with or physical injury to other persons; or will lead to the alerting of other persons suspected of having committed such an offence but not yet arrested for it; or will hinder the recovery of property obtained as a result of such an offence. The Code of Practice also extends the right of delay to drug trafficking offences (where proceeds of those crimes may be confiscated) and offences to which the Criminal Justice Act 1988, Part VI apply (confiscation orders) where disclosure may prevent the recovery of the proceeds of such crimes.

Generally, a person so detained shall be supplied with writing materials on request and allowed to speak on the telephone for a reasonable time to one person. However, where an officer of the rank of inspector or above considers that the sending of a letter or the making of a telephone call might result in the circumstances which are described in connection with the authorisation of a delay and the offence concerned is a serious arrestable offence, for which purpose any reference to a serious arrestable offence in Annex B (dealing with delay) includes an arrestable offence, or is one under the Prevention of Terrorism (Temporary Provisions) Act 1989 and may lead to similar consequences, the exercise of the privilege can be delayed or denied.

Before letters are sent, or telephone calls are made, the person detained must be told that what he says in the letter or call or message (other than in the case of a communication to a solicitor) may be read or listened to as appropriate and may be given in evidence. Such a telephone call may be terminated if it is being abused.

Records must be kept of such requests which are made and the action which is taken in consequence of them.

Stop and search

Introduction

There was no general power given to constables to stop and search persons before the Police and Criminal Evidence Act 1984. The Codes of Practice which accompany the Act lay down strict safeguards to ensure that these powers are not abused. The power to stop and search is in reality provided to give an officer an opportunity to establish whether or not certain types of offences have been committed without the necessity to arrest such a person on reasonable suspicion of his having committed an offence. A search, carried out in good faith, may render such an arrest unnecessary if no evidence of the suspected offence is found.

The Act provides special power for 'statutory undertakers', that is bodies authorised by enactments to carry out railway, road transport, water transport, canal, inland navigation, dock or harbour undertakings. Such constables may stop, detain and search any vehicle before it leaves a goods area wholly or mainly used for storage or handling of goods. In addition, existing powers to stop and search under s. 23 of the Misuse of Drugs Act 1971, s. 47 of the Firearms Act 1968 and s. 2 of the Poaching Prevention Act 1862 have been retained.

In addition, the Criminal Justice and Public Order Act 1994, s. 60, authorises a stop and search based on a reasonable belief that an incident involving serious violence may take place within a specific locality and a stop and search under s. 13A of the Prevention of Terrorism (Temporary Provisions) Act 1989 as amended by the 1994 Act. The provisions of the Search Code are applied to such stops and searches which may only be carried out by an officer in uniform. With these exceptions, a police officer's powers to stop and search are prescribed by the Act of 1984.

Powers to stop and search

(1) *Generally*

Section 1(2) of the Police and Criminal Evidence Act 1984 states that subject to sub s. (3) to (5) of the section a constable may search any person or vehicle (vehicle includes vessel, aircraft and hovercraft) *and* anything which is in or on a vehicle, for stolen or prohibited articles or articles to which s. 1(8A) applies and he may detain a person or vehicle for the purpose of such a search.

Subsection (3) requires that a constable must have reasonable grounds for suspecting that he will find stolen or prohibited articles or articles to which s. 1(8A) applies before carrying out such a search. Force may be used but every effort must be

133

made to persuade a person to cooperate. His willingness to cooperate must be established before a compulsory search is made.

It is important to understand what is meant by 'reasonable suspicion'. The Code of Practice sets out a number of considerations which must be applied.

Where a police officer has reasonable grounds to suspect that a person is in innocent possession of a stolen or prohibited article, the power to stop and search exists notwithstanding that there would be no power of arrest. However, every effort should be made to secure the voluntary production of the article before the power is resorted to.

Whether reasonable grounds for suspicion exist will depend on the circumstances in each case but there must be some objective basis for it. An officer will need to consider the nature of the article suspected of being carried in the context of other factors such as the time and the place, and the behaviour of the person concerned or those with him. Reasonable suspicion may exist, for example, where information has been received such as a description of an article being carried or of a suspected offender; a person is seen acting covertly or warily or attempting to hide something; or a person is carrying a certain type of article at an unusual time or in a place where a number of burglaries or thefts are known to have taken place recently. But the decision to stop and search must be based on all of the facts which bear on the likelihood that an article of a certain kind will be found.

Reasonable suspicion can never be supported on the basis of personal factors alone. A person's colour, age, hairstyle or manner of dress, or the fact that he is known to have a previous conviction for possession of an unlawful article, cannot be used alone or in combination with each other as the sole basis on which to search that person. Nor may it be founded on the basis of stereotyped images of certain persons or groups as more likely to be committing offences. Regardless of the power exercised all police officers should be careful to ensure that the selection and treatment of those questioned and searched is based upon objective factors and not upon personal prejudice.

(2) *Under the Criminal Justice and Public Order Act 1994, s. 60*

Where a police officer of or above the rank of superintendent reasonably believes that:

(a) incidents involving serious violence may take place in any locality in his area; and

(b) it is expedient to do so to prevent their occurrence,

he may give an authorisation that the powers to stop and search persons and vehicles conferred by this section shall be exercisable at any place within that locality for a period not exceeding 24 hours. Where such an authorisation has been given a constable in uniform has power:

(a) to stop any pedestrian and search him and anything carried by him for offensive weapons or dangerous instruments;

(b) to stop any vehicle and search the vehicle, its driver and any passenger for offensive weapons or dangerous instruments.

In these circumstances the constable may stop any person or any vehicle he thinks fit whether or not he has grounds for suspecting that the person or vehicle is carrying weapons or articles of that kind. He may seize dangerous instruments or articles which he has reasonable grounds for suspecting to be offensive. These powers apply to ships, aircraft and hovercraft (with the necessary modifications).

A person who fails to stop or (as the case may be) to stop the vehicle when required to do so commits an offence under the section which is punishable by one month's imprisonment, a level 3 fine, or both.

Such an authorisation must be in writing and must specify the locality and the validity of the authorisation. There is power, where the authorising officer feels that it is expedient to do so, having regard to offences which have, or are reasonably suspected to have been committed in connection with any incident falling within the authorisation, to extend it for a further six hours. The power to issue an authorisation is extended to a chief inspector or inspector where no superintendent is available.

Affected persons are entitled to the usual written statement of stop and search within 12 months.

The term 'dangerous instruments' means instruments which have a blade and are sharply pointed. The term 'vehicle' includes a caravan.

Similar powers are given under a new s. 13A of the Prevention of Terrorism (Temporary Provisions) Act 1989 to commanders and assistant chief constables where such powers are needed in relation to acts of terrorism, but such authorisations may extend to 28 days in the first instance and may subsequently be extended by similar periods. These provisions also include an offence of wilful obstruction of a constable in the exercise of such powers of search. Where a pedestrian is stopped under s. 13A a search may only be made of a bag, case or other thing carried by him. He may not be searched under this power.

It is important to ensure that powers to stop and search are used responsibly by those who exercise and those who authorise them. An officer should bear in mind that he may be required to justify the use of the powers to a senior officer and in court, and also that misuse of the powers is likely to be harmful to the police effort in the long term. This can lead to mistrust of the police by the community. It is also particularly important to ensure that any person searched is treated courteously and considerately.

The actions of police officers will be examined objectively in the light of the knowledge available to the officer at the time of his decision. The officer may have been given a *general description* of a person suspected of committing burglaries and, if he exercises a power to stop and search, the court will examine the issue objectively, by assuming that that person also had that general description. However, such a general description would be unlikely, in itself, to constitute sufficient grounds for search but observations of the actions of the suspect for a period of time may heighten the suspicion that he may be the person suspected of the offences of burglary.

It must be recognised that there is no power to stop and detain a person against his will in order to find grounds for a search.

The Stop and Search Code does not restrict an officer's right to speak to or question a person in the ordinary course of his duties (and in the absence of reasonable suspicion) without detaining him or exercising any element of compulsion, provided that the person concerned cooperates. It does not affect the principle that all citizens have a duty to help police officers prevent crime and discover offenders.

Where searches may be carried out

Section 1(1) of the Act of 1984 states that a constable may exercise these powers:

(a) in any place to which at the time when he proposes to exercise the power, the public or any section of the public has access, on payment or otherwise, as of a right or by virtue of express or implied permission; or

(b) in any other place to which people have ready access at the time when he proposes to exercise the power but which is not a dwelling.

The public have a general right of access to, and use of, a highway.

They certainly have express permission to enter places of entertainment as they are invited to pay a fee for entry to cinemas, sporting grounds, etc. A part of their express permission is conditioned on such persons remaining only for the duration of the particular entertainment; it is not a general permission to be there. By implication, people may enter supermarkets, stores, business premises, and public buildings. They also have 'implied' permission to enter the grounds of dwelling-houses to visit lawfully the householder or to call upon him. The term 'ready access' does not concern itself with lawful presence. It is concerned with whether or not ready access was in fact available to the building, premises, or land. The entry may well be a trespassory entry.

Section 1(4) of the Act of 1984 provides that persons in a garden or yard occupied with and used for the purpose of a dwelling, or on other land so occupied and used, may not be searched by a constable unless he has reasonable grounds for believing that such person does not reside in the dwelling and that he is not in the place in question with the express or implied permission of a person who resides in the dwelling. These provisions also apply to vehicles which are in such grounds unless they are not there with express or implied permission.

Stolen or prohibited articles

A 'prohibited article' is defined by the section as:

(a) an offensive weapon, which is any article made or adapted for use by causing injury, or intended by the person having it with him for such use by him or by some other person; or

(b) an article made or adapted for use in the course of or in connection with an offence of burglary, theft, taking a motor vehicle or other conveyance without authority and obtaining property by deception, or intended by the person having it with him for such use by him or by some other person.

(See 'Statutory preventive measures' on page 446 for explanation of these terms. The term 'stolen' is not defined and should be given its ordinary meaning.)

An 'article to which s. 1(8A) applies' is any article in relation to which a person has committed, or is committing or is going to commit an offence under s. 139 of the

Criminal Justice Act 1988. This section deals with possession in a public place of an article which has a blade or is sharply pointed, except a folding pocket knife. This section also applies to folding pocket knives if the cutting edge of its blade exceeds 3 inches. These provisions are discussed in greater depth under 'Offensive weapons' (see pages 449–450).

This is perhaps the moment at which to examine the current police practice of searching persons on football coaches for offensive weapons before allowing them into the ground. Firstly, the Act and Code require that the officer should, before carrying out the search of a particular person, ask himself if that person (not the persons on the coach as a whole), is reasonably suspected of possessing such a weapon. The Code does not allow a search if the suspicion is merely based upon the fact that he is a member of a group of disorderly soccer hooligans. There would have to be reason to suspect that person of possessing a weapon and little short of seeing him to be in such possession, is likely to satisfy these requirements. There is no doubt that the Code was not drafted with the intention of stopping this desirable practice in view of the attitude of Parliament to the problems caused by soccer hooligans, but nevertheless, this is the effect of the Code of Practice. In recognition of this, the Code contains the following note for guidance.

'Nothing in this Code affects the routine searching of persons entering sports grounds or other premises with their consent, or as a condition of entry.'

However, officers must bear in mind that notes for guidance are not provisions of the Code itself and that the Code insists that police officers must have reasonable suspicion related to an individual, that he is in possession of an offensive weapon in these circumstances. In addition, the note refers to 'entering sports grounds' which means that the searching of persons on football coaches as they approach a ground is not covered by the note for guidance. Such searches must be conducted under other powers in particular circumstances.

There can never be an objection to a search with true consent in these circumstances. However, the note is also concerned with the right of proprietors of sports grounds to make entry to the ground conditional upon those who seek entry permitting such a search, as a condition of entry. It is submitted that if this is done, the search should be conducted by persons other than police officers, whether or not the proprietors are paying for the police officer's services. It is no part of a police officer's duties to enforce a civil contract between the proprietors of the ground and those who seek entry to it. If it was otherwise, police officers could be employed as doormen by the owners of night clubs.

Information received from a third party may be taken into account when forming a reasonable suspicion, but the nature of the information and the credibility of the informant must be taken into account.

If such an article is found during a search an officer must satisfy himself that an offence has been committed; there is a reasonable suspicion that the person committed it and that a power to arrest exists in respect of that offence.

The Sporting Events (Control of Alcohol, etc.) Act 1985 gives a constable power to search a person at any time during the period of a designated sporting event when such a person is in the area of a designated sports ground from which the event may be directly viewed, or while entering or trying to enter at such times, if he has reasonable grounds to suspect that person of having intoxicating liquor, or a bottle, can or other portable container (even if crushed or broken) which is for holding drink, which is of a kind which, when empty, is normally discarded or returned, or left to be recovered by the supplier, or part of such an article.

The 1985 Act also empowers a constable to stop and search: (a) public service vehicles; and (b) vehicles adapted to carry more than eight passengers, which are being used for the principal purpose of carrying passengers for the whole or part of a journey to or from a designated sporting event (in case of (b) at least two persons must be carried), if he has reason to suspect that an offence is being committed in relation to the carriage of alcohol or an offence of drunkenness.

The Code's description of 'reasonable suspicion' must be applied to such searches.

The period of a designated sporting event is the period beginning two hours before the start of the event or (if earlier) two hours before the time at which it is advertised to start and ending one hour after the event. In the event of a postponement, the period is two hours before the advertised start to one hour after it.

Action to be taken on detaining a person for a search

In the first instance, an officer should remember that if a person is detained for the purpose of a search, that search need not be carried out if it subsequently appears to him that no search is required or that a search is impracticable. It is quite possible that, although a person was stopped and detained for the purpose of a search, such person easily satisfies the officer that there are no grounds for suspicion. In such a case it is unnecessary to search. The detention will not be unlawful merely because the search was not carried out.

Before a search of a detained person or attended vehicle takes place a police officer must:

(a) if he is not in uniform show his warrant card (if search is linked to terrorism he need not reveal his name);

(b) give his name and the name of the police station to which he is attached (except in the case of enquiries linked to the investigation of terrorism, in which case he shall give his warrant or other identification number);

(c) explain the object of the proposed search; and

(d) specify his grounds or authorisation for making that search;

(e) inform that person that he is entitled to a copy of the record of the search if he asks for it within one year. (On occasions this will not be possible in a particular sense as it will not be practicable to make such a record – perhaps following multiple searches.) If the person wishes to have a copy he should be advised to apply to the police officer's station.

Record of search

A constable who has carried out a search shall make a record of that search in writing, unless it is not practical to do so or where operational reasons, such as public disorder, dictate otherwise. A record is required for each person and each vehicle searched, except that, if a person is in a vehicle and both are searched for the same reason, only one record need be made. If it is not practical to do so then he must do so as soon as possible. The record should be made on the correct forms which are provided. The forms have been produced to comply with the requirements of s. 3(6) of the Act. The record includes:

(a) the name of the person searched, or (if he withholds it) a description of him (together in all cases with an indication of such descriptive features as may be required to be recorded in the national search record);

(b) a note of the person's ethnic origin;

(c) where a vehicle is searched, a description of it including its registration number;

(d) the object of the search;

(e) the grounds for making it;

(f) the date and time it was made;

(g) the place it was made;

(h) its results;

(i) a note of any injury or damage to property resulting from it;

(j) the identity of the officers making it except in the case of enquiries linked to an investigation into terrorism, when the warrant or other identification number and duty station of the officer(s) should be recorded.

The record of the grounds for making a search must, briefly but informatively, explain the reason for suspecting the person concerned, whether by his behaviour or other circumstances or, in the case of searches under the 1994 or 1989 Acts, by stating the authority provided to carry out such a search.

It is important to recognise that although record forms will include sections which require the name of the person, his address, and date of birth, there is no obligation upon such a person to provide that information and he may not be detained for the purpose of a check being made on his identity. If the record is made out on the spot in such a form that a copy is produced, it will be good practice to give the person searched a copy. He must be informed that he is entitled to such a copy at any time within 12 months from the date upon which the search was carried out, on request. If not given a copy at the time, he must be told at which police station the record will be available. The identity of all officers involved in a search must be recorded on the search record.

Searching unattended vehicles

If an unattended vehicle, or anything in or on such a vehicle is searched, the constable must leave a notice:

(a) stating that he searched it;

(b) giving the name of the police station to which he is attached;

(c) stating where a copy of the record of a search may be obtained at any time within 12 months;

(d) stating where any application for compensation should be directed.

A vehicle which has been searched must, if practicable, be left secure. The notice shall be left inside the vehicle if this can be done without damaging the vehicle.

A person may be detained for such time as is reasonably required to permit a search to be carried out either at the place where the person or vehicle was first detained, or nearby. The Code advises that the extent of the search will be related to the nature of the articles sought and the circumstances in which the search takes place. If a person is seen to place an article in a particular pocket, the search of that pocket should be sufficient. If the article sought is such that it may easily be concealed anywhere, the search may have to be more thorough.

The term 'nearby' is not defined. It should be interpreted narrowly. To move a vehicle off the main road to a side road would be reasonable. To move a person from the direct view of the general public, into a more private place would similarly be reasonable. This approach to the practicalities of such a search would appear to provide the reason for the word 'nearby'.

Removal of clothing

A constable may not require a person to remove any of his clothing in public other than an outer coat, jacket or gloves but he may search a person's mouth. This does not prevent the search of other garments provided they are not removed.

The Code of Practice restricts such searches to 'superficial examinations of outer clothing'. However, these restrictions upon search are applicable to those carried out in public. A more extensive search may only be carried out out of the view of the public. If such an extended search amounts to more than the removal of an outer coat, jacket, gloves, headgear or footwear, it may only be made by an officer of the same sex and may not be made in the presence of anyone of the opposite sex unless the person being searched specifically requests it.

All possible steps must be taken to avoid embarrassment. Paragraph 3A of the Search Code states:

'A search in a street itself should be regarded as being in public, even though the street is empty at the time the search begins. As a search of a person in public should be a superficial examination of outer clothing, such searches should be completed as soon as possible.'

Although there is no power to require a person to do so, there is nothing to prevent an officer from asking a person to voluntarily remove more than the outer coat, jacket or gloves in public.

An officer who is not in uniform may not stop a vehicle for the purpose of a search.

Seizure of articles

Articles which are suspected of being stolen or prohibited articles may be seized. The Code and the Act of 1984 require that the person who had the custody or control of the articles immediately before the search was carried out, or the person who occupied the vehicle is entitled, on request, to a record of the things seized and such a record must be supplied within a reasonable time. Persons from whom articles are seized are entitled to a photograph or copy of such articles.

Before 'stop and search' procedures are carried out an officer must have reasonable grounds to suspect that the person is in possession of stolen or prohibited articles. That suspicion must be a reasonable one which is based on a foundation of fact. Having stopped such a person who has directed such suspicion towards himself, it may be that an acceptable explanation may be given for that conduct which eliminates the need for a search. If that search must be carried out everything it is possible to do to remove likely causes of embarrassment should be done. Wherever possible, remove the person from the view of the general public before carrying out the search.

Most members of the public, although they are unlikely to be attracted to the idea of being searched, will accept the necessity for such a procedure if it is properly explained.

Nothing in the Code affects the ability of an officer to speak to or question a person in the course of his duties without detaining him or exercising any element of compulsion.

If a person to be searched, or in charge of a vehicle which is to be searched, does not understand what is being said or there is any doubt about his ability to understand English, the officer must take reasonable steps to bring the required information to his attention. If the person has someone with him, then the officer must establish whether that person can interpret or otherwise help him to give the required information.

Making an arrest and powers of entry without search warrant to arrest

Arrest – factors for consideration

Now that so general a power of arrest is available to police officers, the 'necessity' to arrest must be carefully considered. The members of the Royal Commission whose recommendations led to the passing of the Police and Criminal Evidence Act 1984 stressed the 'necessity principle'. It was not anticipated that every refusal to give a name and address would lead to an arrest on the occasion of the first refusal of an offender to provide these particulars. A refusal should lead to the officer explaining the consequences of continued refusal to provide a satisfactory name and address. Only in the event of continued refusal, should an arrest be effected.

In addition to these factors, officers should also consider their power to arrest in those particular circumstances as s. 25 of the Act 1984 demands that a constable has reasonable grounds for suspecting that an offence has been committed or attempted or is being committed or attempted. It is also essential that the gravity of the offence is taken into account before extreme measures are adopted. Most people who have committed a trivial offence will not continue to refuse to provide satisfactory evidence of identity if they are aware of the possibility of arrest in consequence of such failure. The intention of s. 25 is clearly to ensure that all offenders are given every opportunity to make themselves answerable for their offence by way of summons and arrest should be looked upon as an exceptional measure in most circumstances.

If an arrest is effected, s. 30 of the Act of 1984 demands that a person arrested by a constable at a place other than a police station, must be released if a constable is satisfied, before the person arrested reaches the police station, that there are no grounds for keeping him under arrest. If a person is arrested because of a failure to provide evidence of identity or a satisfactory address for the service of a summons and such information is subsequently provided or the person is identified in some other way, that person must be instantly released. A record of such a release must be made as soon as practicable after the release.

Object of arrest

An arrest consists of the seizing or touching of a person's body with a view to restraint. It amounts to the deprivation of a person's liberty to go where he pleases. It is possible to effect an arrest merely by words if they bring to a person's notice that he is under restraint and will be compelled to remain, and he submits to that compulsion. The purpose of such an arrest is to ensure that the person will answer an alleged offence.

Information to be given on arrest

Section 28 of the Act of 1984 provides that where a person is arrested, otherwise than by being informed that he is under arrest, the arrest is not lawful unless the person arrested is informed that he is under arrest as soon as practicable after his arrest. This is so whether or not the reason for his arrest is obvious.

In addition, the section requires that, if an arrest is to be lawful the person arrested must be informed of the grounds for his arrest at the time it takes place, or as soon as practicable thereafter and this is an absolute requirement in that it must be done regardless of the fact that the grounds must be obvious. There are two essential factors therefore: a person must be clearly told that he is under arrest; and he must also be told of the grounds for that arrest. In spite of television's assurances to the contrary, the words 'You are nicked' have no place in this procedure. These requirements will, on occasions, be easily satisfied. If a thief is seen leaving the premises of a jeweller carrying stolen property, it would be sufficient to say, 'I am arresting you for an offence of burglary which I have seen you commit'. If that person was seen leaving the grounds of a dwelling-house and found to be in possession of property which was not normally carried about the person, it would be sufficient to say, 'I am arresting you on reasonable suspicion of having committed an offence of burglary, having seen you leave the grounds of a dwelling-house which is not your own and having found you in possession of articles which I believe to have been taken from that dwelling-house'. Such persons are frequently stopped by an officer and found, on being searched, to be in possession of many household articles which are not normally carried in a street. The section requires that the officer makes it clear that such a person is being arrested, and why, and any explanation, which must be clear to the person arrested, will be satisfactory. 'I am arresting you on reasonable suspicion of an offence of burglary. I have found you to be in possession of household articles concerning which you are unable to provide a satisfactory explanation. I believe that these articles have been taken from the dwelling-house of some person, which you entered as a trespasser.'

The section provides an exception to these rules and this is limited to circumstances in which it was not reasonably practicable to do so by reason of the person's escape before the information could be given. Although this appears at first sight to be unimportant, the person who so escapes before being given this information is considered, for practical purposes, to have been arrested.

A constable who is in plain clothes at the time of an arrest must state that he is a police officer and show his warrant card.

Violence during arrest

If an arrest is effected outside, it is likely that some form of physical restraint will be applied as it is essential that a prisoner is not allowed to escape. However, when a quiet, elderly person is arrested it may be sufficient to effect that arrest merely by words which clearly indicate restraint as the issue of escape is unlikely and the possibility of successful escape remote.

It is important to remember that when unreasonable force is used in carrying out an arrest, the arrest is unlawful, whether or not the laid down procedures are followed. This is understandable. The person who is subjected to unnecessary and unreasonable force will not submit to such an arrest and to make such a person responsible for resisting a lawful arrest, would be unrealistic.

An officer must use no more than reasonable force; that is that which is necessary in the particular circumstances existing at the time. If violence is offered towards the constable he should request assistance so that the arrest may be made as effectively as possible. In any case 'control' should be made aware of all occasions in which a police officer expects to find himself in trouble. The use of handcuffs should be restricted to exceptional circumstances and handcuffs should never be used on women and children.

Use of the truncheon

A police truncheon is capable of causing considerable injury. Its use should, therefore, be restricted to situations of extreme emergency when the officer has no other means of defending himself against violent attack. The truncheon is issued for the officer's protection and not as a weapon of offence. Its use should be restricted to circumstances in which the officer is dealing with a violent person or persons; to prevent the escape of a violent prisoner *and* the officer is being overpowered.

When a truncheon is used it should be used with all of the care which the situation allows; if possible on the arms or legs of the assailant; particular care being taken to avoid a blow to the head. Many violent situations make the use of a truncheon, in any predetermined way, an impossibility but it is always possible to make every conscious effort to use it as a weapon of defence. The defensive use of a truncheon has been studied and perfected by the adviser to provincial police forces in methods of self-defence and is being introduced into police training programmes.

Following any occasion upon which a truncheon has been used, the police officer concerned must make a record of that use as soon as practicable and must inform the custody officer immediately upon his arrival at the police station. The use of the truncheon must be mentioned when evidence is given in relation to the arrest of the offender.

Plain clothes arrests

It is important that a person who is to be arrested is certain that the person who is carrying out the arrest is a police officer. If such a person assaults the officer, the issue of whether or not the person arrested knew that he was being arrested by a police officer is likely to be important.

It is essential, therefore, that an officer who is dressed in plain clothes at the time of the arrest clearly identifies himself as a police officer and produces his warrant card as proof of his identity.

Arrest – other than at a police station

Where a person is arrested by a constable for an offence, or is taken into custody by a constable having been arrested for an offence by some other person, at any place other than a police station, he shall be taken to a police station as soon as practicable. This is required by s. 30(1) of the Act of 1984.

The words 'as soon as practicable' allow for circumstances in which it would be unrealistic to take the person arrested immediately to a police station. Section 30(10) permits a delay in taking an arrested person to a police station if that person's presence elsewhere is necessary in order to carry out such investigations as it is reasonable to carry out immediately. This could occur where a person was seen to steal property from a motor car and on being arrested after a chase, was found to have disposed of the stolen property along the route of the chase. In such circumstances it would be both sensible and proper to take the prisoner back along that route for the purpose of recovering the property, provided that he was not resisting arrest and was securely held. It would be important to do this to recover valuable property which had been thrown away in a public place where it was likely to be quickly discovered by other persons. If the chase had been across private fields, the recovery of the property immediately would not be so important. If property is not in danger of being lost, the prisoner should be taken immediately to a police station.

If there is any delay in taking an arrested person to a police station, the reason for that delay must be recorded on first arrival there.

It must also be remembered that a person arrested elsewhere than at a police station, must be released if the constable is satisfied at any time before they reach the police station, that there are no grounds for keeping him in custody. If this occurs, the constable must make a record of that release as soon as practicable after it occurs.

Arrest – category of police station

Generally, a person arrested must be taken to a 'designated police station'. A 'designated police station' is one which the chief officer of police of the area has designated to be used for the purpose of detaining arrested persons. The chief officer of police has a duty to designate those stations which appear to him to have sufficient accommodation for that purpose. One or more custody officers must be appointed for each designated police station. A custody officer must be of at least the rank of sergeant. However, an officer of any rank may perform the functions of a custody officer at a designated police station if a custody officer is not readily available to perform them.

There are exceptional circumstances in which a person arrested may be taken to any police station. These are:

(a) where the constable is working in a locality covered by a police station which is not a designated police station; or

(b) where he is a constable belonging to a police force maintained by an authority other than a police authority (e.g. the British Transport Police).

The exception at (a) above recognises that many officers, in county forces in particular, may patrol a beat many miles from a designated police station. If the offence is such that the person arrested is likely to be released on bail more or less immediately, it would be unrealistic to require that he be transported many miles to a 'designated police station', only to be released on bail. There are limitations placed upon detention in non-designated police stations and a constable must not take a prisoner to such a station if it appears to him that it may be necessary to keep the arrested person in police detention for more than six hours.

Any constable may take an arrested person to any police station if:

(a) the constable has arrested him without the assistance of any other constable and no other constable is available to assist him; or

(b) the constable has taken him into custody from a person other than a constable without the assistance of any other constable and no other constable is available to assist him;

and (in either case) it appears to the constable that he will be unable to take the arrested person to a designated police station without the arrested person injuring himself, the constable or some other person.

There will be many occasions in which a police officer, acting upon his own, will encounter sufficient difficulty in attempting to take a resisting prisoner to the nearest police station. It would be unrealistic to require him to extend his journey in such circumstances.

When a person who is arrested is taken to a non-designated police station that police station will not have any appointed 'custody officer'. This means that another police officer must perform the duties of a custody officer while that prisoner remains in police detention.

Section 36(7) of the Act of 1984 allows that where an arrested person is taken to a police station which is not a designated police station, the functions of a custody officer shall be performed:

(a) by an officer who is not involved in the investigation of an offence for which he is in police detention, if such an officer is readily available; and

(b) if no such officer is readily available, by the officer who took him to the station, or any other officer.

Where the arresting officer is required to perform the duties of a custody officer at a police station to which he takes his prisoner, he shall inform an officer who is attached to a designated police station and is of at least the rank of inspector.

Arrest under the authority of a warrant

A warrant of arrest, or of commitment (or of distress, or a search warrant), may be executed anywhere in England and Wales by a constable acting in his police area. Special provisions are made by the Criminal Law Act 1977 to allow execution on each side of the Scottish border by officers of the forces surrounding those borders. Such warrants issued in the three parts of the United Kingdom (England and Wales, Scotland, or Northern Ireland) may be executed in one of the other parts by a constable in his own police area.

Certain warrants may be executed by a constable who does not have possession of the warrant at the time. These are:

(a) warrants to arrest a person in connection with an offence;

(b) warrants under the Army Act 1955, Air Force Act 1955, Naval Discipline Act 1957 or Reserve Forces Act 1980 (desertion, etc.);

(c) warrants for insufficiency of distress;

(d) warrants for the protection of a party to a marriage or of a child of the family (under s. 18 of the Domestic Proceedings and Magistrates' Courts Act 1978); and

(e) warrants relating to the non-appearance of a defendant, warrants of commitments and warrants to arrest a witness (under ss. 55, 76, 93 and 97 of the Magistrates' Courts Act 1980); but in such cases the warrants must, on demand of the person concerned, be shown to him as soon as practicable. The person arrested must be told of the existence of the warrant at the time of his arrest, as this is the reason for his arrest.

Where a warrant to arrest is in the possession of the officer at the time of the arrest, it must be shown to the person who is being arrested, but must not be given to him.

Searching of detained persons

The Police and Criminal Evidence Act 1984 removed all previous powers to search persons in custody. Section 54 of that Act charges a custody officer with a duty to ascertain the property which a person has with him when he is:

(a) brought to a police station after being arrested elsewhere or after being committed to custody by an order or a sentence of a court; or

(b) arrested at a police station or detained there following arrest for an offence or being detained thereafter answering police bail,

and to record particulars of that property in the person's custody record.

To discharge these responsibilities a person may be searched to the extent considered necessary by the custody officer, but an intimate search may not be carried out under this section and a strip search may only be carried out in specified circumstances. A strip search must be carried out by a constable who must be of the same sex as the person searched. Such searches may not, therefore, be carried out by a police matron unless she is also a special constable.

Articles other than those subject to legal privilege (e.g. letters from solicitors, etc.)

may be seized and retained but clothes and personal effects may only be seized if the custody officer believes that they may be used by that person:

(a) to cause physical injury to himself or another person;
(b) to damage property;
(c) to interfere with evidence;
(d) to assist him to escape; or
(e) if the custody officer has reasonable grounds for believing that they may be evidence of an offence.

A person in custody at a police station or elsewhere may be searched at any time by a constable in order to ascertain whether he is in possession of any such articles. A constable may seize and detain anything found in such a search, except that clothes and personal effects may only be seized in the circumstances outlined above.

Persons must be told the reason why articles are being seized unless they are violent, or likely to be violent, or are incapable of understanding. All such items at (a)–(d) must be returned to such a person when he is released from custody.

A detained person may retain clothing and 'personal effects' (which does not include cash) at his own risk subject to a custody officer's discretion to retain them if there is risk of harm to others or to property, or to interfere with evidence, or of their use in an escape. The level of responsibility placed on a custody officer is high. Is the mirror in a woman's make-up case dangerous? Obviously it is not when it remains in its original condition, but it is if it is subsequently broken. Is the woman likely to attempt to take her own life?

All such property must be recorded whether it is retained by the prisoner or retained by the custody officer. The detained person must be allowed to check the property record and to sign it. If articles are retained by the custody officer, the reason for doing so must be recorded.

Release of detained persons

The Police and Criminal Evidence Act 1984, s. 46, requires that where a person:

(a) is charged with an offence; and
(b) after being charged, is kept in police detention or (in the case of a juvenile) is detained by the local authority,

he must be brought before a magistrates' court as soon as practicable and in any event not later than the first sitting after he is charged (or, if he is brought before a magistrates' court in another area, not later than the first sitting of that court after his arrival in the area).

If there is no court due to sit, the custody officer must inform the clerk to the court and the clerk must arrange a sitting of the court not later than the day next following the day on which he is charged. Christmas Day, Good Friday and any Sunday do not count as 'days next following'. An exception to the rule is where a person is in hospital and is not well enough to appear.

(1) *Police bail of person charged – general*

Section 38 of the 1984 Act requires that where a person who is arrested otherwise than under a warrant authorised for bail is charged with an offence, the custody officer must (subject to the Criminal Justice and Public Order Act 1994, s. 25, which states that there must be no bail for defendants charged with homicide, rape or attempts to commit such offences, after a previous conviction for such an offence) order his release from police detention, either on bail or without bail, unless:

(a) his name and address cannot be ascertained or the custody officer has reasonable grounds for doubting the truth of a name and address provided by him;

(b) the custody officer has reasonable grounds for believing that the person arrested will fail to appear in court to answer bail;

(c) in the case of a person arrested for an imprisonable offence (one punishable with imprisonment), the custody officer has reasonable grounds for believing that the detention of the person arrested is necessary to prevent him from committing an offence;

(d) in the case of a person arrested for an offence which is not an imprisonable offence, the custody officer has reasonable grounds for believing that the detention of the person arrested is necessary to prevent him from causing physical injury to any other person or from causing loss of or damage to property;

(e) the custody officer has reasonable grounds for believing that the detention of the person arrested is necessary to prevent him from interfering with the administration of justice or the investigation of offences or of a particular offence; or

(f) the custody officer has reasonable grounds for believing that the detention of the person arrested is necessary for his own protection.

If the person charged is a juvenile it is also sufficient that the custody officer has reasonable grounds for believing that the juvenile should be detained in his own interests.

This section also requires that where a custody officer authorises an arrested juvenile to be kept in police detention, the custody officer shall secure that the arrested juvenile is taken to local authority accommodation unless the custody officer certifies:

(a) that by reason of such circumstances as are specified in the certificate, it is impracticable to do so; or

(b) in the case of a juvenile aged 12 that no secure accommodation is available and that keeping him in other local authority accommodation would not be adequate to protect the public from serious harm from him. However, there is likely to be a delay in bringing this into force because of the non-availability of suitable secure accommodation. (Interim provisions of the Criminal Justice and Public Order Act 1994 permit the existing age of 15 years to be reduced in stages by statutory instrument until the age of '12' is reached. No order has been made at the time of writing.)

In the case of juveniles charged with violent or sexual offences, references to protecting the public from serious harm refer to protection from death or serious personal injury, whether physical or psychological, occasioned by further offences. 'Sexual offence' means one under the Sexual Offences Act 1956 (other than man living on earnings of prostitution, woman exercising control over prostitute, keeping a brothel, landlord letting premises for use as a brothel, tenant permitting premises to be used as a brothel and tenant permitting premises to be used for prostitution); s. 128 of the Mental Health Act 1959 (sexual intercourse with patients); an offence under the Indecency with Children Act 1960; an offence under s. 9 of the Theft Act 1968 of burglary with intent to commit rape; an offence under s. 54 of the Criminal Law Act 1977 (inciting girl under 16 to incestuous sexual intercourse); an offence under the Protection of Children Act 1978; an offence under s. 1 of the Criminal Law Act 1977 of conspiracy to commit any of the above offences; an attempt to commit any of those offences; or inciting another to commit any of those offences. A 'violent offence' is one which leads, or is intended or likely to lead, to a person's death or physical injury, and includes an offence which is required to be charged as arson (whether or not it would otherwise fall within this definition).

By s. 47 of the 1984 Act a release on bail under the detention provisions of the Act shall be a release on bail granted in accordance with ss. 3, 3A, 5 and 5A of the Bail Act 1976 as they apply to bail granted by a constable. The normal powers to impose conditions of bail shall be available to him where a custody officer releases a person on bail under s. 38(1) (release after charge) *but not in any other case*. It may be subject to a duty to appear before a magistrates' court or to attend at a police station at a time and date appointed by the custody officer. A person so bailed promises to appear as prescribed. The Bail Act 1976 includes penalties for those who fail to appear in answer to bail. In serious cases an accused may be required to find one or more 'sureties', that is persons who undertake to secure his attendance. In such a case each surety enters into a recognisance to forfeit a specified sum to the Crown should the accused fail to appear. The parent or guardian of a juvenile may be required to act as a surety for a sum not exceeding £50 to secure a juvenile's compliance with a condition attached to bail, but he must consent to be so bound.

A record must be made of the decision to grant bail and the accused must be supplied with a copy of the record if he so requires. A magistrates' court may alter police bail to require attendance at a later time or to enlarge sureties.

Before a person is released on bail the court or the custody officer may require him to comply with specified conditions. A custody officer may impose requirements as appear to be necessary to secure that the person surrenders to custody; does not commit an offence while on bail; and does not interfere with witnesses or otherwise obstruct the course of justice whether in relation to himself or another person. However, he may not impose a requirement to live in a bail hostel. Where such conditions are imposed a record must be made of the reasons for doing so which will be available if requested by the person concerned. The same applies to variations which may be made to such conditions.

Before a custody officer decides to grant bail, he may wish to take into account the provisions of para. 2A to Schedule 1 of the Bail Act 1976 (added by the Criminal Justice and Public Order Act 1994) which state that a court need not grant bail if the offence being considered is an indictable one or is triable either way and it appears to the court that the person was on bail in criminal proceedings on the date of that offence. It would seem to be good practice in such cases to put that person before a court to allow such consideration to be given to the matter.

Where a custody officer has granted bail in criminal proceedings he or another custody officer serving at the same police station may, at the request of the person to whom it was granted, vary the conditions of bail, and in doing so he may impose conditions or more onerous conditions.

(2) *Delayed charges*

Where a custody officer decides, when an accused is brought before him, that there is insufficient evidence at that stage to charge the prisoner, but that there probably will be when further enquiries have been made, he may release a prisoner on bail, such bail being conditioned upon his appearance at a police station at a given time, as opposed to appearing at court. In such a way, an accused can be brought before a custody officer at a later stage, for the situation to be reassessed. This form of bail may be cancelled at any time by notice in writing from the custody officer. Where a person is detained, any previous time in custody must be included in any calculation of detention time. In practice, his old custody record will be continued. No conditions may be attached to such bail.

Police powers

A s. 46A was added to the 1984 Act by the Criminal Justice and Public Order Act 1994. It provides that a constable may arrest without warrant any person who, having been released on bail under these provisions subject to a duty to attend at a police station, fails to attend at that police station at the time appointed for him to do so.

A person who is arrested under this section shall be taken to a police station appointed as the place at which he is to surrender to custody as soon as practicable after his arrest.

Powers of entry without a search warrant to effect an arrest

The Act of 1984 abolishes all of the previous common law rules which gave a constable power to enter premises without a warrant for the purpose of effecting an arrest with the exception that the common law power still exists to enter premises to deal with a breach of the peace, or to prevent it. A constable may enter in such circumstances provided that he clearly states who he is and demands admission from the occupant. A power to enter in these circumstances merely recognises the urgency of certain situations. If urgent cries for help are heard coming from a dwelling, it would be unrealistic if a police officer was not entitled to enter. However, the power extends to 'preventing a breach of the peace'. This should be borne in mind when, having entered, the officer is required to leave by an occupant, other than the one in distress. The officer is entitled to remain to prevent a further breach of the peace.

Section 17 of the Police and Criminal Evidence Act 1984 provides that, without prejudice to any other enactment, a constable may enter and search any premises for the purpose:

(a) of executing a warrant of arrest issued in connection with or arising out of criminal proceedings, or a warrant of commitment issued under s. 76 of the Magistrates' Courts Act 1980;

(b) of arresting a person for an arrestable offence;

(c) of arresting a person for an offence under s. 1 of the Public Order Act 1936 (prohibited uniforms), or any enactment contained in ss. 6–8, or 10 of the Criminal Law Act 1977 (offences of entering or remaining on property) – in the latter case the arresting officer must be in uniform; s. 4 of Public Order Act 1986 (fear or provocation of violence) or s. 76 of the Criminal Justice and Public Order Act 1994 (failing to comply with interim possession order);

(d) failing to comply with interim possession order (squatters);

(e) of recapturing a person who is unlawfully at large and whom he is pursuing;

(f) of saving life or limb or preventing serious damage to property.

With the exception of the instances involving the saving of life or limb or preventing serious damage, powers of entry and search under s. 17 may only be exercised where the constable has reasonable grounds for believing that the person whom he is seeking is on the premises. A search under these provisions may only be to an extent that is reasonably required for the purpose.

In relation to premises consisting of two or more separate dwellings the power to search is limited to those parts used commonly by the residents and the particular dwelling in which the constable has reasonable grounds for believing that the person whom he is seeking may be.

Entry and search after arrest

There was no general right to enter a dwelling-house without a warrant to search for or to seize evidence after an arrest had been made, prior to the Police and Criminal Evidence Act 1984. If the occupier would not consent to such a search, in most circumstances a warrant was necessary. Section 18 of the Act of 1984 allows a constable to enter and search any premises occupied or controlled by a person who is under arrest for an arrestable offence, if there are reasonable grounds for suspecting that there is evidence on the premises which relates to that offence or to some other arrestable offence which is connected with, or is similar to, that offence. (The evidence must be such that it is not subject to legal privilege.) The section, therefore, authorises the search of the dwellings of those arrested for offences such as burglary, drug pushing, or thefts from motor vehicles, to recover evidence of the offence and further similar offences which might have been committed by the person arrested. A search of any person who has not been arrested, which is carried out during a search of premises, shall be carried out under the Stop and Search Code.

A constable is also authorised by the section to seize and retain articles found in consequence of such a search which relate to the offences for which a person has been arrested or to some other arrestable offence which is connected with or similar to that offence.

A search under the authority of s. 18 may only be made if it has been authorised in writing by an officer of the rank of inspector or above, unless it is carried out before a person is taken to a police station in circumstances where the presence of that person at the place in question is necessary for the effective investigation of the offence. Such an authorisation must be given on a document 'Notice of Powers and Rights' which should be given to or left for the occupier of the premises (see below). However, if a search is made in such circumstances without a written authority, the constable carrying out the search must inform an officer of the rank of inspector or above that the search has been made, as soon as practicable.

Thus, where a constable arrests a man who is a retailer of electrical goods in the living quarters above the shop, for thefts of electrical goods, the constable may search not only the living quarters, but also the shop premises as both are 'occupied and controlled' by the person arrested. If the shop premises are searched before the man is taken to the police station, the arresting officer must inform an officer of the rank of inspector or above that he has done so, as soon as practicable.

An officer who authorises a search or who is informed that a search has been made, must record in writing the grounds for the search and the nature of the evidence which was being sought. If the occupier of the premises is, at the time, in police custody, the record must be made in the custody record.

Use of force to enter and search

The Code of Practice for the Searching of Premises by Police Officers, etc., states that reasonable force may be used, if necessary, to enter premises if the officer in charge is satisfied that the premises are those specified in any warrant or other written authority. There are certain conditions which must be satisfied which are explained below. On any occasion upon which force is used, the use of such force must be justified. These provisions apply to all entries effected for the purpose of a search being made whether such entry is permitted by the Act of 1984 or any other statute.

The term 'premises' is defined by s. 23 of the Act of 1984 as including *any place* and, in particular, includes:

(a) any vehicle, vessel, aircraft or hovercraft;
(b) any offshore installation; and
(c) any tent or moveable structure.

The term 'offshore installation' has the meaning given to it by s. 1 of the Mineral Workings (Offshore Installations) Act 1971. It is, therefore, concerned with oil rigs, etc.

The local police/community consultative group or its equivalent should be informed as soon as practicable after a search where there is reason to believe that it might have an adverse effect on relations between the police and the community.

Searching premises with consent

If it is proposed to obtain consent to search premises, the officer in charge shall state the purpose of the proposed search to a person entitled to grant entry. He must also inform such person that he is not obliged to consent and that anything which is seized may be produced in evidence. In addition, if, at that time, such person is not suspected of an offence the officer shall tell him so when stating the purpose of the search. An officer cannot enter and search premises or continue to search premises if consent has been given under duress or is withdrawn before the search is completed. The consent of the person entitled to grant entry to the premises must, if practicable, be given in writing on the Notice of Powers and Rights before the search takes place. Such consent in writing is unnecessary where the consent is obtained although there is a warrant in force or if there is a power of entry and search without warrant.

It is unnecessary to seek consent, however, where in the circumstances, this would cause disproportionate inconvenience to the person concerned. This might occur where it is reasonable to assume that innocent occupiers would agree to, and expect that, police would take the proposed action. Examples are where a suspect has fled from the scene of a crime or to evade arrest and it is necessary quickly to check surrounding gardens and readily accessible places to see whether he is hiding; or where police have arrested someone in the night after a pursuit and it is necessary to make brief checks of gardens along the route of the pursuit to see whether stolen or incriminating articles have been discarded.

It is important that officers consult their supervisors before conducting such searches. It would be easy to forget that the searches of such gardens in other circumstances, in which the issue of inconvenience did not arise, should be consented to in writing. A garden is a 'place' which is included in the definition of the term 'premises'.

In the case of a lodging-house or similar accommodation, a search should not be made on the basis solely of the landlord's consent unless the tenant is unavailable and the matter is urgent.

Notice of powers and rights

An officer who conducts a search of premises under the above powers must, unless it is impractical to do so, provide the owner with a notice in standard format:

(a) specifying whether the search is made under warrant, or with consent, or in the exercise of statutory powers to search without warrant or consent;
(b) summarising the extent of the powers of search and seizure conferred in the Act;
(c) explaining the right of the occupier and the owner of property seized;
(d) explaining that compensation may be payable in appropriate cases for damage caused in entering and searching premises, and giving the address to which an application for compensation should be directed; and
(e) stating that a copy of the Search Code is available to be consulted at any police station.

If the occupier is present, copies of the notice, and of the warrant (if the search is made under warrant) should if practicable be given to the occupier before the search begins, unless the officer in charge of the search reasonably believes that to do so would frustrate the object of the search or endanger the officers concerned or other persons. If the occupier is not present, copies of the notice, and of the warrant where appropriate, should be left in a prominent place on the premises or appropriate part of the premises and endorsed with the name of the officer in charge of the search, the name of the police station to which he is attached and the date and time of the search. A warrant or other identification number will suffice where there is a terrorist connection. The warrant itself should be endorsed to show that this has been done.

Entry other than with consent

Searches made under the authority of a warrant must be made within one month from the date of issue of the warrant. They must be made at a reasonable hour unless this might frustrate the purpose of the search.

The officer in charge shall first attempt to communicate with the occupier or any other person entitled to grant access to the premises by explaining the authority under which he seeks to enter the premises, and ask the occupier to allow him to do so. Where the premises are occupied, the officer shall identify himself (by warrant or other identification number in the case of enquiries linked to terrorism) and if not in uniform produce his warrant card (but in so doing in the case of enquiries linked to the investigation of terrorism, the officer need not reveal his name) and state the purpose of the search and the grounds for undertaking it and shall produce the warrant and supply the occupier with a copy of it before a search begins, unless there are reasonable grounds to believe that to alert the occupier or any other person entitled to grant access would frustrate the search or endanger the officers concerned or other persons. Where warrants were issued which referred to schedules setting out the property to be seized, the search was held to be unlawful in consequence of the fact that the schedules had been removed before the copies were supplied to the occupier of the premises. The warrants were no longer 'complete'.

There are, therefore, technically two stages to the process: first attempt to communicate and explain authority to enter; then when entry has been gained, the officer should identify himself and state the purpose of the search and the grounds for making it. The logic of this is easy to establish, it would be unrealistic to demand that the constable shouted out the second stage information in the street, or through a letter box.

While there is no need for a constable to fulfil his obligations to identify himself, or to produce the various documents before entering if there are reasonable grounds to believe that this would frustrate the search or endanger the officer or others in such a case, he must do so at the earliest opportunity after entry and before starting to search (except that it is enough if he gives the copy of the warrant at the first reasonable opportunity thereafter).

The Code relating to Entry and Search states that it will not be necessary to carry out the above procedure if:

(a) the premises to be searched are known to be unoccupied;
(b) the occupier or any other person entitled to grant access is known to be absent;
(c) there are reasonable grounds to believe that to alert the occupier or any other persons entitled to grant access by attempting to communicate with him would frustrate the object of the search or endanger the officers concerned or other persons.

The circumstances embraced by (a) and (b) are self-explanatory. The provisions at (c) will cover a number of possibilities. The premises to be searched may be suspected to be housing a known, armed fugitive. To attempt to communicate with anyone inside the building would be likely to lead to the escape of such a fugitive, or to injury to the officers, or to the fugitive himself if the officers were armed. The provisions would also cover circumstances in which such warning of entry would provide the occupier with an opportunity to dispose of evidence, e.g. flushing drugs down a lavatory.

Reasonable force may be used if necessary to enter premises if the officer in charge is satisfied that the premises are those specified in any warrant or other written authority and where:

(a) the occupier or any other person entitled to grant access has refused a request to allow entry to his premises;

(b) it is impossible to communicate with the occupier or any other person entitled to grant access; or

(c) any of the conditions set out at (a) to (c) above apply.

Where premises have been entered by force the officer in charge shall, before leaving the premises, satisfy himself that they are secure either by arranging for the occupier or his agent to be present, or by any other appropriate means. This means that, in no circumstances, should premises which have been searched, be left insecure.

The local police/community consultative group or its equivalent should be informed as soon as practicable after a search where there is reason to believe that it might have an adverse effect on relations between the police and the community.

Searching of premises

All searches must be carried out at a reasonable hour, unless this would frustrate the purposes of the search. For example, if it was known that a criminal who was to be arrested was armed and dangerous, the purpose of the search would be to locate him and arrest him without injury being occasioned to any person. In such circumstances, a search during the daylight hours would be unlikely to be effective in this respect. One conducted at 3 a.m. would be much more likely to achieve that aim.

Premises may be searched only to the extent necessary to achieve the object of the search, having regard to the size and nature of whatever is being sought. If the search is for stolen television sets it would be unrealistic to search small drawers and bedside cabinets. A search under warrant may not continue under the authority of that warrant once all of the things specified in it have been found. If the warrant specifies three television sets of particular serial numbers, once these have been discovered and seized, the search must stop. On the other hand, once the officer in charge of the search is reasonably satisfied that the specified property or articles are not on the premises, the search must stop.

All searches must be conducted with due consideration for the property and the privacy of the occupier of the premises searched, with no more disturbance than necessary. If the search is for a stolen wallet or handbag, there is no necessity to remove personal articles of clothing from drawers. The presence or otherwise of the articles searched for can be established without the removal of such articles from the drawer. Reasonable force may be used only where this is necessary because the

155

cooperation of the occupier cannot be obtained or is insufficient for the purpose. It may be that the occupier, after admittance has been gained, obstructs the conduct of the search and some reasonable force may have to be used to effect a search within the terms of the authority. If the occupier of such premises wishes to ask a friend, neighbour or other person to witness the search, he must be allowed to do so, unless the officer has reasonable grounds to believe that this would seriously hinder the investigation or endanger the officers concerned or other people. A search need not be delayed for this purpose.

Seizure of property

The Police and Criminal Evidence Act 1984, s. 10, defines 'items subject to legal privilege' as:

(a) communications between a professional legal adviser and his client or any person representing his client made in connection with the giving of legal advice to the client;

(b) such communications made in connection with or in the contemplation of legal proceedings which are for the purpose of these proceedings; and

(c) items enclosed with, or referred to in such communications and in connection with the giving of legal advise or in contemplation of such legal proceedings.

An officer who is conducting such a search may seize anything covered by the warrant, other than an item which is subject to legal, professional privilege. However, he may also seize anything which he has reasonable grounds for believing is evidence of an offence, or has been obtained in consequence of the commission of an offence, where seizure is necessary to prevent its concealment, alteration, loss or destruction. It is apparent, therefore, that although warrants, etc., will specify material to be searched for, there is an authority to seize evidence of other offences if such evidence is discovered *in the course of searching for the specified articles*. This must be so, as the Code of Practice for the Searching of Premises, etc., allows a search only to the extent necessary to locate the specified articles. In the example previously quoted, of searching premises for stolen television sets, it could be accepted that the officers conducting the search would be likely to find stolen video recorders in the places which they would be likely to search for television sets. They would be searching cupboards, wardrobes, etc. In searching for such television sets, they could not realistically discover stolen postage stamps in a small drawer. In most circumstances, the seizure of property discovered will be necessary to prevent concealment, alteration, loss or destruction.

Should an officer decide that it is not appropriate to seize property because of an explanation given by the person holding it, but nevertheless has reasonable grounds for believing that it has been obtained in consequence of the commission of an offence by some person, he shall inform the holder of his suspicions and shall explain that, if he disposes of the property, he may be liable to civil or criminal proceedings. This would most probably occur where a person has innocently come into possession of property stolen by someone else.

A constable may photograph or copy, or have photographed or copied, any document or other article which he has power to seize. Where he considers that a computer may contain information that could be used in evidence, he may require the information to be produced in a form which can be taken away and in which it is visible and legible.

Such articles which have been seized can be retained as long as is necessary in the circumstances. They may be required for use as evidence; for forensic examination or for other investigation in connection with an offence or when stolen, etc., to establish their lawful owner. Property (other than that resulting from an offence) should not be retained if a photograph or copy would suffice (e.g. trading records).

Where seized property is retained the person who had custody or control of it immediately prior to its seizure must, on request, be provided with a list or description of the property within a reasonable time. He, or his representative, must be allowed supervised access to the property to examine it or have it photographed or copied, or must be provided with a photograph or copy, in either case within a reasonable time of any request and at his own expense unless the officer in charge of any investigation has reasonable grounds for believing that this would prejudice the investigation of the offence or any criminal proceedings. In such a case a record of the grounds must be made.

Action to be taken after searches

Where premises have been searched (other than when searched without consent because to seek it would cause disproportionate inconvenience, etc.) the officer in charge of the search shall, on arrival at a police station, make, or have made, a record of the search. The record shall include:

(a) the address of the premises searched;

(b) the date, time, and duration of the search;

(c) the authority under which the search was made. Where the search was made in exercise of a statutory power to search premises without a warrant the record shall include the power under which the search was made; and where the search was made under warrant or with written consent, a copy of the warrant or consent shall be appended to the record or kept in a place identified in the record;

(d) the names of the officers who conducted the search except in cases of enquiries linked to the investigation of terrorism, where the record must state the warrant or other identification number and the duty station of each officer;

(e) the names of any persons on the premises if they are known;

(f) either a list of any articles seized or a note of where such a list is kept and, if not covered by a warrant, the reason for their seizure;

(g) whether force was used and, if so, the reason why it was used;

(h) details of any damage caused during the search, and the circumstances in which it was caused.

A search register shall be maintained at each subdivisional police station. All records which are required to be made by the Code of Practice for the Searching of Premises, etc., shall be made, copied, or referred to in that register. If the wrong premises are searched by mistake, everything possible must be done at the earliest opportunity to allay any sense of grievance. In appropriate cases, assistance should be given to obtain compensation.

In instances in which premises have been searched under warrant, the warrant must be endorsed to show:

(a) whether any articles specified in the warrant were found;
(b) whether any other articles were seized;
(c) the date and time at which it was executed;
(d) the names of the officers who executed it (except in the case of enquiries linked to terrorism, in which case the warrant or other identification number and duty station of each officer shall be shown);
(e) whether a copy, together with the Notice of Powers and Rights, was handed to the occupier or whether it was enclosed with the date and time of the search and left on the premises and, if so, where on them.

It is essential to ensure that premises which have been entered by force are properly secured when the search has been completed. This will no doubt be done by the owner of the property or his agent if present, but if they are not it will be the responsibility of the officer in charge of the search to ensure that adequate steps are taken to safeguard the premises.

Any warrant which has not been executed within one month of its issue shall be returned to the clerk of the justices.

Safe custody of prisoners

Preliminary search after arrest

A constable has power to search a person at the time of his arrest for an offence. Section 32 of the Police and Criminal Evidence Act 1984 states:

'A constable may search an arrested person in any case where the person to be searched has been arrested at a place other than a police station, if the constable has reasonable grounds for believing that the arrested person may present a danger to himself or others.'

The inclusion of the words 'place other than a police station' recognises that any such search which was carried out in a police station would become the responsib.lity of the custody officer. The description of these powers extends to:

(a) the search of an arrested person for anything which he might use to assist him to escape from lawful custody; or which might be evidence relating to an offence; and
(b) entry and search of any premises in which he was when arrested or immediately before he was arrested for evidence relating to the offence for which he has been arrested.

These powers only extend to that which is reasonably required for the purpose of discovering any such thing or any such evidence and do not authorise the removal of clothing in a public place other than an outer coat, jacket or gloves. A constable must have reasonable grounds for believing, in the circumstances set out at (a), that the person may have concealed on him anything for which a search is permitted in those circumstances. The section is concerned with the search of an arrested person. The police acted beyond their powers under this section when they demanded the car keys of a person arrested for burglary. The keys did not relate to an offence of burglary. The same suspicion must exist in relation to the searching of premises as at (b). There must be reasonable grounds for believing that there is evidence to be found.

Thus a person may be searched 'on the spot' at the time of his arrest. Such a power is essential. The prisoner may be in possession of dangerous weapons or articles which may be used to injure the constable in order to effect an escape from custody. If a person who is arrested pulls out a knife and it is taken from him by a constable, the officer must have reason to believe that he may have some other concealed weapon and such a person must be searched. He has shown a will to escape and a willingness to use any article which might assist him. If that person has been arrested for a series of thefts it is probable that, on the way to the police station, he will attempt to dispose of any articles in his possession taken in the course of those thefts. If he is suspected of being in possession of such articles, he should be searched 'on the spot' to the extent necessary but not further, than allowed by s. 32, to take possession of such articles.

If an arrest is effected upon premises, similar considerations must apply. As a police officer approaches a building to arrest a person who is in it, it is certain that such person will quickly conceal any property associated with the commission of a crime. The position will not alter if the person to be arrested leaves the building immediately before the officer arrives at the door. He has been in that building and it is probable that the property or article will have been concealed within it. The section empowers a constable to enter and to search such premises to any reasonable extent necessary for the discovery of such articles. If a search is being conducted for stolen television sets, a search of desk drawers would be outside these powers. In the case of searches of premises the powers are limited to searches for evidence of the offence 'for which he has been arrested' under the terms of s. 32.

Some buildings will be found to be in 'communal occupation'. Bedsitters, hotels, etc., are such buildings. Where there are two or more separate dwellings the search must be limited to the premises in which the arrest took place or in which the arrested person was immediately before his arrest and any parts which are shared with the other occupants of the building. These would include common dining rooms, lounge, even shared kitchen facilities, but would not include the rooms of other occupants, unless the person arrested was known to have been in the room of one of the other occupiers immediately prior to his arrest. This could occur where a thief sees the approach of the officer and rushes into his neighbour's room and asks him to conceal property for him. If the officer knows this, he may search that other room also.

Constables exercising these powers may seize and retain anything which they find (other than an article subject to legal privilege), if they have reasonable grounds for believing:

(a) that it may be used to cause physical injury to the arrested person or to another; or

(b) that he might use it to assist him to escape from lawful custody; or

(c) that it is evidence of an offence or has been obtained in consequence of the commission of an offence.

The important factor in relation to the exercise of these powers is that the process should be reasonable. A man who is arrested for indecent assault who is known to be of a non-violent nature would not necessarily be searched 'on the spot'. There can be no evidence of the offence available and he is known to be non-violent.

Although a search may be carried out in the first instance to discover stolen property, the power set out at (c) above would allow the seizure of articles relating to other offences which were accidentally discovered during the course of that search. The extension of the power to things 'obtained in consequence of the commission of an offence' means that property obtained from the disposition of stolen goods, etc., may also be seized.

All searches must be carried out as soon as practicable and, so far as possible, out of the public view. The prime responsibilities of a constable when carrying out a preliminary search are to ensure that the prisoner does not escape during the process of that search; the preservation of evidence and his own protection, as well as the protection of any other persons who may be present.

Transport of a prisoner

All persons who are arrested should be taken to a police station as soon as possible. Section 30 of the Police and Criminal Evidence Act 1984 requires that the police station to which such a person is taken, shall be a designated police station. There are special circumstances in which a prisoner may be taken to a police station other than a designated police station.

Where it is necessary to use a motor vehicle to transport a prisoner to a police station the arresting officer should be accompanied by a driver. If escape is to be prevented and the possibility of harm eliminated, this is essential. However, it is recognised that certain non-violent criminals are 'picked up' by police officers on occasions when it is recognised that strict measures need not be taken. Where a prisoner is seated in a motor vehicle he should occupy a rear seat with the arresting officer alongside him. The prisoner should not be placed directly behind the driver. It is essential that a prisoner is carefully watched at all times while he is being transported to a police station. If given the opportunity he will dispose of all incriminating articles while on the journey. For these reasons, the vehicles must be thoroughly searched at the conclusion of the journey. Property is often concealed under the rear seat. It must be remembered that even though property may be discovered at this stage, the fact that the prisoner was allowed to dispose of it gives him the opportunity to allege that it was there as a result of another prisoner having been in the vehicle, or that it was planted by the police.

Arrival at the police station

The arresting officer, upon arrival at the police station, must report immediately with his prisoner to the custody officer. The custody officer will be at least of the rank of sergeant and he is responsible, in every respect, for the detention of persons in that police station. The arresting officer must satisfy the custody officer that there were grounds for making the arrest and that the arrest was correctly effected under existing powers. The custody officer should note on the detention record any comment made by the detained person in relation to the arresting officer's 'account' but should not invite comment. If the custody officer authorises his detention he must tell him why as soon as practicable and in any case before that person is questioned about any offence. The custody officer shall note any comment the person may make in respect of the decision to detain him but shall not invite comment. The custody officer must not put specific questions to the person regarding his involvement nor in respect of comments made in response to the arresting officer's account, or the decision to place him in detention. Such an exchange is likely to constitute an interview.

While a custody officer is required by the Code to deal with such a person as soon as it is practicable, the Code provides that a custody officer shall not be in breach in the event of delay provided that it is justifiable and all reasonable steps have been taken. This may occur where large numbers of suspects are brought to a police station simultaneously, or where all interview rooms are being used, or solicitors are awaited.

The custody officer must tell such a person (or a person attending a police station voluntarily) that he has:

(a) the right to have someone informed of his arrest;
(b) the right to consult privately with a solicitor and the fact that independent legal advice is available free of charge; and
(c) the right to consult the Codes of Practice.

He must also give such a person a written notice setting out such rights and his rights while in custody. Receipt, or refusal, must be noted on the custody record.

A custody officer is responsible for all persons in detention and for ensuring that they are properly treated in accordance with the Codes of Practice. He is also responsible for maintaining a chronological and contemporaneous record of every aspect of a person's treatment while in custody. There are occasions upon which officers other than specially appointed custody officers will have to assume the duties of such an officer, although this will always be for a short period of time and this means that most of the complexities of such an officer's duties do not need to be fully studied by all officers, but the general principles of 'correct detention' are essential to all. In these circumstances any officer at that police station may be called upon to carry out the duties of a custody officer during the brief detention of such a prisoner, or until he is transferred to the designated police station. Such an officer will be required to maintain the record of the prisoner's detention on the 'custody records' held in police stations. The officer who carries out these duties should not be involved in the investigation of the offence. In an emergency, where no other officer is available, the arresting officer is authorised to carry out these duties. In all circumstances in which an officer is required to perform the duties of a custody officer at a non-designated police station, such officer must inform an officer of at least the rank of inspector at a designated police station that he is doing so, as soon as it is practicable to do so. The officer will then act under the directions of such

161

senior officer. The provisions of the Detention Code, which apply to a custody officer, apply to an officer who is performing the function of a custody officer.

Detention in police cells

When persons are confined in police cells no additional restraints should be used within a locked cell unless absolutely necessary, and then only suitable handcuffs. In the case of a mentally handicapped or mentally disordered person, particular care must be taken when deciding whether to use handcuffs.

Further development of statement writing skills

Introduction

When statements were first considered we looked at offence statements and occurrence statements. A fairly clear separation was made. An offence statement is a written record of a person's first-hand knowledge of an incident which contains factual detail, that is the exact time, day, date and the place at which the offence occurred together with the identification of the offender, and sufficient evidence to prove the offence. Such a statement confined itself to those facts which were admissible in evidence. As it is required to include all detail, it is not bound by the rules of evidence and can virtually include any connected fact as its purpose is really to be fully descriptive of the incident.

On occasions it is desirable to combine some of the features of each, as the laws of evidence on occasions allow matters which would otherwise have been excluded, to be given in certain circumstances. This in effect means that when recording statements made by particular people, in particular circumstances, evidence of some other matters might be included.

Evidence of opinion

Generally the opinion of a witness is inadmissible and it is therefore not included in statements. There are occasions upon which evidence of opinion can be given:

(a) Statement of opinion can be given by recognised experts in science, art or trade, for example doctors, lawyers, forensic scientists and fingerprint experts who have knowledge of points outside the knowledge and experience of a jury. In such circumstances it is necessary to show that the witness has carried out some form of special study or has sufficient skill or experience to be accepted by a court as an expert witness. This must be borne in mind when a statement is being taken. If expert opinion is included, details of the qualifications and experience of the witness must also be shown so that the prosecutor is aware of the grounds upon which the court may consider whether or not to admit the evidence as expert evidence. This is a question which only the court can determine. A police officer with 15 years' experience as a traffic officer who had attended a course on accident investigation and had attended more than 400 fatal road accidents was accepted as an expert by the High Court.

(b) Opinion as to the identity, condition or age of a person or thing may be admitted. To some degree the identification of any person who was previously unknown to the witness must be a matter of opinion and so far as the recording of statements is concerned the police officer should attempt to gather as much information as he can as to identity. This may, on occasions, involve matters of opinion. Witnesses who cannot be sure that it was a particular person whom they saw committing a certain act, may be able to express the view that they are almost certain that it was a particular person. When this is done, support that statement with as much information as the witness can give as to why he formed this opinion. The same considerations would apply to property about which a conclusive identification may be possible. Opinions are sometimes expressed concerning the condition or age of persons or things. A witness may say that he formed the opinion that a person was under the influence of drugs. If he had previous experience of dealing with drug addicts the court may allow his evidence on the grounds that it was based upon matters within his knowledge. If he had little or no experience in this respect the court will allow him to give facts as to the way in which the person behaved and concerning his general appearance. The witness may be asked for his conclusions if his evidence of observation is sound. Such conclusions are best included in the statement and it is then a matter for the prosecutor to decide whether to ask him to express an opinion and, in the final analysis, for the court to decide whether he will be permitted to answer.

(c) Opinion as to appearance of illness or drunkenness may be permitted and should be included in a statement. Police officers frequently express the opinion that a man was drunk but courts accept that constables have considerable experience of dealing with such people and are prepared to accept such evidence, provided that it is supported by evidence of appearance and actions which is consistent with drunkenness.

(d) Opinion as to the speed of a vehicle may be accepted by a court. Although a person may not be convicted of an offence of speeding upon the evidence of witness as to his opinion of the speed at which a vehicle was travelling, this does not affect the general issue of giving evidence as to speed. It is important that drivers involved in motor accidents and witnesses to accidents are asked for their estimate as to the speed of vehicles. It is a matter, once again, for the court to attach weight to that evidence. A factual inclusion as to the length of time a driver has been driving and the extent of his experience can be extremely helpful to a prosecutor. Such an estimate from an experienced lorry driver will obviously be much more reliable than that of an old lady who has never driven. This does not mean that the old lady should not be asked if she could estimate the speed. She may be able to do so and may be a reliable witness, as she may have had many years of experience of travelling in other people's cars. Record that fact in the statement.

Negative statements

It is occasionally of advantage to record a statement from a person even though that statement amounts to no more than a denial of knowledge of a particular occurrence. Such a record can be helpful if subsequent enquiries reveal that some knowledge must have existed. Passengers in motor cars may allege that they have no knowledge of the circumstances leading up to an accident because they were either asleep or not paying attention. They may subsequently give evidence on behalf of the driver if he is charged with careless driving. It is useful to the prosecutor to be able to show that he previously denied knowledge of the events. The prosecutor does this by asking the witness if he made the negative statement, shows it to him and asks if it is his signature.

Attendance at court

The accuracy of statements is extremely important as there are times when a written statement may be offered in evidence without the necessity for the witness to attend court and give evidence on oath.

In criminal proceedings, a written statement by any person shall be admissible in evidence to the same extent as oral evidence if:

(a) the statement purports to be signed by the person who made it;

(b) the statement contains a declaration by that person to the effect that it is true to the best of his knowledge and belief and that he made the statement knowing that, if it were tendered in evidence, he would be liable to prosecution if he wilfully stated in it anything which he knew to be false or did not believe to be true;

(c) before the hearing at which the statement is tendered in evidence, a copy of the statement is served, by or on behalf of the party proposing to tender it, on each of the other parties to the proceedings; and

(d) none of the other parties or their solicitors, within seven days from the service of the copy of the statement, serves a notice on the party so proposing, objecting to the statement being tendered in evidence.

However, the conditions at (c) and (d) can be waived if the parties agree before or during the hearing to allow the statement to be tendered. If made by a person under 21, the age must be given and if read to a person who cannot read, a declaration must be included to that effect. If the statement refers to an exhibit, the defence must have the opportunity to inspect it.

In effect this means that if the contents of a statement are accepted by both sides as presenting a fair and accurate account, and they agree to its use, a witness need not be called. These provisions are used extensively when evidence is merely of a formal and non-contentious nature.

Linking exhibits with statements

Witnesses will frequently refer to articles when making a statement to a constable and it is essential that the article can be clearly identified so that it may be produced to the court at the appropriate time. To permit this to be done each exhibit is given a number and this number is shown in the statement at the point at which the witness refers to it. There is no standard way of doing this, sometimes the exhibit is given a number in a continuous way. The important thing is to do so in the manner followed in a particular police force or area and to ensure that each exhibit is individually identifiable. Labels are attached to exhibits at the time at which this identification is made. The labelling procedure does not apply to statements under caution, taken from defendants. If property was recovered from a thief by a police officer, the recovery of that property would be a part of the officer's evidence and he or she would produce the exhibits.

A police officer, Jane Smith, who arrested a thief who had stolen a ring from jeweller's shop, and subsequently found that ring in the thief's possession could include in her statement 'I searched the accused's jacket and in the breast pocket I found a diamond ring (J.S.1.)'. If later, the thief made a statement under caution, that statement would also become an exhibit to be produced by the officer who took the statement, and may become J.S.2 although it would not be labelled.

Hearsay

The admissibility of hearsay evidence was discussed when the functions of, and evidence accepted by courts were examined. In general terms it is not included in offence statements as it is inadmissible in evidence but there are exceptions to this rule and it must be remembered that oral statements made by an accused, and oral statements made in the presence and hearing of the accused may be included in statements as they may be given in evidence. This is also true of evidence of early complaint in sexual offences. However, the circumstances of the admissibility of such statements is worth recalling:

(a) *Oral statements made by the accused.* The general rule is that things said by another person may not be given in evidence if the purpose is to tender them as evidence of the truth of the matters asserted in them, unless they were made by a defendant and constitute admissions of facts relevant to these proceedings. The rule is founded in common sense. If Brown says to Green 'I saw Smith break a window in High Street', this is obviously not a matter for Green to give in evidence as it has no value. Green did not see the window broken and he is not permitted to give evidence of the fact. Brown saw Smith break the window and may give direct evidence of that fact and it should be included in Brown's statement. However, this does not apply to statements made by an accused person and this includes any incriminating statement, whether spoken or written, which is made by an accused person. If an accused says to a police officer, 'O.K. officer, I was in Woodbine Close that night and I did try to open the door of a blue car', the officer may include the words used by the accused in his statement of evidence and may repeat those words subsequently when giving evidence against the accused in court. The words amount to a verbal admission made to an officer which is relevant to the proceedings before the court.

(b) *Oral statements made in the presence and hearing of the accused.* This exception is better understood if it is considered in the context of facts which might be stated to an accused person in the course of an enquiry. Any such statement is only of value to the enquiry if it provokes some form of response

165

in the accused and it is only in such circumstances that it will be admitted. If a police officer says to an accused; 'Your sister told me that you brought a silver tea set home with you last Monday night', that statement would not normally be admissible as it is the sister who should give that evidence. If the accused then says 'Yes I did, I may as well admit that I stole the tea set', that statement would be admissible as a statement made by the accused, but it would be strange if the officer could not tell the court what he said to the accused to stimulate that response. Perhaps the accused may not reply at all, but merely shrug his shoulders and nod in the affirmative. In such circumstances the officer could describe what he said to the accused, because it is a statement made in the presence and hearing of the accused which did result in some form of acknowledgement of its truth.

(c) *Early complaint in sexual offences.* Generally complaints made to a police officer by a woman who had been the victim of a sexual offence would be inadmissible because those statements would be of matters best described to the court by the woman herself. However, the nature of such a complaint made by the victim of sexual offence should be included in a statement taken by a police officer in relation to an offence. Words may be admitted in evidence by the court, provided that they are not elicited by leading, inductive or intimidatory questions and the complaint was made as soon as possible after the act complained of, as was reasonable in the circumstances.

Such early complaints are admissible to prove the fact that a complaint was made, which fact is relevant to the question of consent. The words used by the complainant are also of value to the court as they will indicate the nature of the assault alleged and the complainant's reaction to that assault – these issues being, once again, relevant to the question of consent. The words used should be included in the statement made by the police officer receiving the complaint, or by any other witness who receives that complaint, together with details of the distress, etc., shown by the complainant. If a girl runs into her home and says to her mother, 'Mummy, a man put his hand up my skirt as I was walking home, I was frightened, I've run all the way home', the nature of that complaint and the fact that it was made straightaway is very important to the enquiry and full details must be recorded in the statement of the person who received the complaint.

In many police forces today, the procedure is to require investigating officers to include all information in a statement, whether or not the particular facts are admissible in evidence. It is then left to prosecution departments to decide what will be given in evidence.

Relevant facts in addition to points to prove

In general terms a court is concerned with evidence which directly points towards the particular points to prove in an offence but courts will admit relevant facts, that is additional matters which may assist the court, which are related to the offence being considered. The matters are:

(a) introductory and explanatory facts, being matters which prove identity; e.g., the witness himself, the objects, etc. referred to;

(b) facts showing opportunity; that a witness saw the accused in the area in which the crime was committed, if such an accused denies being there;

(c) motive such as expressions of ill-will towards a person or threats made against such person;

(d) preparation to commit the crime, evidence of the purchase of fire raising materials by an accused charged with arson;

(e) conduct of an accused after a crime is alleged to have been committed, for example the burning of clothing by a man charged with rape; or

(f) conduct of the victim of a crime after its commission, i.e. did he make a complaint (that is the fact that he made it, not the terms of the complaint itself).

In addition to these specific instances of related facts, a person recording such a statement from anyone should always ask himself the question, 'Is this information sufficiently connected with the offence to be of value to the court in establishing guilt or innocence?' If the answer to this question is 'yes' and the statement made is not specifically excluded by the laws of evidence, it will be a related fact. The general bearing, attitude or conduct of an accused before an offence is committed may be important as may the surrounding circumstances. If a man assaults a girl friend causing her bodily harm, the fact that he left a public house in any angry mood having said that he was going to look for her because he suspected that she was with another man, is a related fact and may be described by those witnesses who saw and heard these matters.

On many occasions related facts will explain why certain things occurred and provided that the explanation is relevant to a fact in issue, it may be given in evidence and should be included in a statement. The condition of a road, the condition of a vehicle, the nature of and make-up of the area in which a certain type of driving occurred are all issues related to charges of dangerous or careless driving.

Corroboration

A corroboration statement is a statement from another independent source which tends to support in a material particular the truthfulness or accuracy of a statement already obtained. It either confirms, supports or strengthens other evidence. In general circumstances the English common law merely requires the evidence of one competent witness. There are exceptions to this rule, perjury, and speeding, but they are quite limited in relation to the overall extent of our laws. The practice, however, is for police officers to gather as much corroborative evidence as possible in the circumstances of each case. A statement made by a traffic officer who pursued a motor vehicle which was being driven dangerously over a number of miles, can be corroborated by statements from witnesses who observed the manner of the driving at various points along the route. When taking corroborative statements it is helpful to remember certain desirable points of procedure which will add to the credibility of the evidence when presented to a court.

(a) Take the statements from each witness separately and, where possible, in the

167

absence of other witnesses from the immediate vicinity. Each account of happenings should be independently made without comment or prompting from other witnesses.

(b) The officer taking the statement should take care not to prompt the witness by using information which he has already gathered in the course of recording other statements. There is nothing wrong with questioning a witness at length, even before commencing to record a statement, provided that those questions are directed towards establishing with certainty the witness's own recollection of the incident.

(c) The corroborative evidence must be set out in detail, including all elements of information which support the truthfulness or accuracy of other statements. Do not set out merely to gain corroboration of one predetermined fact as the witness may have much more evidence to offer if his story is recorded in detail.

2 Traffic

Application of road traffic law

Classification of vehicles subject to legislation

The Road Traffic Acts and regulations deal with the use of all vehicles on roads. The term 'vehicle' includes any kind of carrier or conveyance, not necessarily a motor vehicle. In order to apply the law correctly it is important to distinguish between the various types of motor vehicles, particularly in relation to the Road Vehicle (Construction and Use) Regulations, and the type of licence required to drive certain classes of motor vehicle. The term 'motor vehicle' is defined in s. 185 of the Road Traffic Act 1988 as meaning: 'a mechanically propelled vehicle intended or adapted for use on roads'.

This definition applies for the purposes of the Road Traffic Act 1988 and regulations made thereunder, but it does not necessarily apply under the Vehicle Excise and Registration Act 1994; for the purposes of that Act, a mechanically propelled vehicle does not need to be intended or adapted for use on a road. 'Mechanically propelled' means constructed so that the vehicle can be propelled by mechanical means; thus, a motor assisted pedal cycle comes within the terms of the definition even while it is being propelled by the pedals. Similarly, a motor car with the engine removed is still classed as mechanically propelled if there is evidence that admits the possibility of the engine being restored. The term 'mechanically propelled' includes not only petrol and oil driven vehicles but also steam and electricity driven vehicles.

The test of whether a mechanically propelled vehicle is intended or adapted for use on roads is whether a reasonable person, looking at the vehicle, would say that its general use encompassed possible general use on a road. The particular use to which a particular person puts a vehicle is irrelevant. A vehicle which was originally manufactured for use on a road may cease to be a 'motor vehicle' for the purposes of s. 185 if it is subsequently altered, but only if such alterations are very substantial.

Classification of motor vehicles by unladen weight

Many motor vehicles are classified by means of their unladen weight; that is, the weight unladen of the vehicle inclusive of the body and all parts which are necessary to or ordinarily used with the vehicle when working on a road, but excluding the weight of water, fuel, batteries used for propulsion, and of loose tools and loose equipment. Loose equipment does not include loose boards fitted in slots at the side of a lorry to enable it to carry a heavier load but it would include moveable shelves fitted to slide on brackets in a baker's van. For our consideration vehicles can be divided into those which are solely used for the carriage of passengers; goods vehicles; those which carry permanent equipment (e.g. mobile cranes); and motor cycles. A description of all types of vehicles follows.

Types of motor vehicles

(1) *Invalid carriage*

The term 'invalid carriage' is defined by s. 185 of the Road Traffic Act 1988 as:

'a mechanically propelled vehicle, the weight of which unladen does not exceed 254 kilograms (5 cwt) and which is specially designed and constructed, and not merely adapted, for use of a person suffering from some physical defect or disability and is used solely by such person'.

When an invalid carriage exceeds 254 kg (5 cwt) in unladen weight it is classified as a motor car, or motor cycle, depending on its weight and number of wheels.

An invalid carriage must not only be specially designed and constructed for the sole use of a disabled person, but must only be used by such a person. When used by a person who is not disabled, the vehicle ceases to be an invalid carriage and any exemption granted by the Act or regulations to invalid carriages would cease to apply for the period when it was being used.

(2) *Motor cycle*

The term 'motor cycle' is defined in s. 185 of the Road Traffic Act 1988 as:

'a mechanically propelled vehicle, not being an invalid carriage, with less than four wheels and the weight of which unladen does not exceed 410 kilograms (8 cwt)'.

This general definition is sufficient for most purposes and covers all mechanically propelled vehicles with less than four wheels and not exceeding 410 kg. If you examine the various categories of motor vehicles for the purpose of driving licences, you will see that those vehicles which fit within this definition of a motor cycle are subdivided into classes:

(a) the standard motor bicycle having two wheels, whether fitted with a sidecar or not but which is not a pedestrian controlled vehicle, mowing machine or moped;

(b) mopeds first used before 1 August 1977, which have an engine with a cylinder capacity not exceeding 50 cc and are equipped with pedals by means of which the cycle is capable of being propelled;

(c) mopeds first used on or after 1 August 1977, which are motor cycles with a design speed not exceeding 30 mph, a kerbside weight not exceeding 250 kg and, if propelled by an internal combustion engine, and engine and a cylinder capacity not exceeding 50 cc. To enable police officers to easily identify 'mopeds' the Road Vehicles (Construction and Use) Regulations 1986, Regulation 69 and Schedule 9 require all motor cycles first used on or after 1 August 1977 (up to 150 cc if first used before 1 January 1982 and up to 125 cc if first used on or before that date) other than mowing machines or pedestrian controlled vehicles to be equipped with a plate, securely fixed and in a conspicuous and readily accessible position, which states whether the motor cycle is a 'standard motor cycle' or a 'moped' for driving licence purposes;

(d) the motor tricycle, having three wheels and with an unladen weight not exceeding 500 kg and with a maximum design speed exceeding 50 kph, but excluding mowing machines, pedestrian controlled vehicles, vehicles propelled by electrical power or mopeds.

An electrically assisted pedal cycle is not a motor cycle. It is not a motor vehicle of any description. In general terms an electrically assisted pedal cycle is one fitted with pedals and an electric motor which will not propel the vehicle in excess of 15 mph.

(3) *Motor car*

We are all familiar with this term, but again for the purposes of the Road Traffic Acts and Road Traffic Regulation Act and associated regulations the term is defined by s. 185 of the Road Traffic Act 1988 as being:

'A mechanically propelled vehicle, not being a motor cycle or an invalid carriage, which is constructed itself to carry a load or passengers and the weight of which unladen:

(a) if it is constructed solely for the carriage of passengers and their effects, is adapted to carry not more than seven passengers exclusive of the driver, and is fitted with tyres of such a type as may be specified in regulations made by the Secretary of State, does not exceed 3050 kg (3 tons);

(b) if it is constructed or adapted for use for the conveyance of goods or burden of any description, does not exceed 3050 kg (3 tons), or 3500 kg (3½ tons) if the vehicle carries a container or containers for holding for the purpose of propulsion of any fuel which is wholly gaseous at 17.5 °C under a pressure of 1.013 bar or plant and materials for producing such fuel;

(c) does not exceed 2540 kg (2½ tons) in a case falling within neither of the foregoing paragraphs.'

Let us examine these three categories. Sub-paragraph (a) refers to the type of vehicle which we know as the private motor car, the important point being that such vehicles are constructed solely for the carriage of passengers and their effects. Sub-paragraph (b) covers two types of motor cars, the first being a motor vehicle constructed or adapted for the carriage of goods or burden of any description which would include such things as a small van or light lorry, neither of which would exceed 3050 kg unladen weight, and the second type being a motor vehicle which uses gas as a fuel and carries the gas in containers fitted to the vehicle, or carries the plant and materials used for producing gas to power the engine. Gas fuelled motor vehicles not exceeding 3500 kg (3½ tons) and used for the carriage of goods are not common, although there have been press reports of people using methane gas as a substitute fuel for petrol at times when petrol was scarce. For the purpose of vehicle classification, articulated vehicles are declared to be goods vehicles, i.e. vehicles which are deemed to be constructed to carry a load. This applies to the towing unit when a trailer is not attached. In effect then at (b) we are talking about goods vehicles. Sub-paragraph (c) refers to vehicles which cannot be classified as (a) or (b), e.g. a minibus.

(4) *Heavy motor car*

This type of vehicle is often confused with a motor car; in fact, the most common examples you will find of a heavy motor car are either lorries constructed to carry goods or motor coaches constructed to carry passengers. Examine the definition as given by s. 195, and you will see that these two examples fit perfectly. The definition reads:

> 'a "heavy motor car" means a mechanically propelled vehicle, not being a motor car, which is constructed itself to carry a load or passengers and the weight of which unladen exceeds 2540 kg (2½ tons)'.

This definition covers a wide range of vehicles, from the small lorry or a coach to the juggernaut or the large double-decked public service vehicle. The important distinction to be made between this class of vehicle and the following three classes is that a heavy motor car is constructed to carry a load or passengers whereas the next three classes are not constructed to carry any load.

(5) *Motor tractor*

When one thinks of a motor tractor, immediately a picture of a tractor used on a farm springs to mind, but the term embraces a wider variety of vehicle than agricultural tractors. The important points to remember are that such a vehicle does not carry a load or passengers and has a maximum weight rather than a minimum weight as with heavy motor cars. If the vehicle exceeds this maximum weight then it falls into one of the next two classes of motor vehicle. The definition of a motor tractor is contained in s. 185, and reads:

> 'a "motor tractor" means a mechanically propelled vehicle which is not constructed itself to carry a load, other than the following articles, that is to say, water, fuel, accumulators and other equipment used for the purpose of propulsion, loose tools and loose equipment, and the weight of which unladen does not exceed 7370 kg (7¼ tons)'.

The type of motor tractor you will normally see used on roads is a large motor vehicle drawing a laden trailer. The drawing vehicle itself does not carry a load but provides the motive power to tow the trailer; a common example is the type used by travelling showmen to tow a trailer with fairground equipment, or the type used by Pickfords to draw a trailer carrying a large indivisible load.

(6) Light locomotive

The term 'locomotive' conjures up a picture of a railway engine, but the term also extends to wheeled vehicles used on roads and, like the motor tractor, this type of vehicle is not constructed to carry a load but issued to draw heavily laden trailers or for other purposes unconnected with the carriage of a load. The definition of a light locomotive is contained in s. 185, and reads:

> 'a "light locomotive" means a mechanically propelled vehicle which is not constructed itself to carry a load, other than articles used in connection with propulsion of the vehicle, loose tools and loose equipment, and the weight of which unladen does not exceed 11 690 kg (11½ tons) but does exceed 7370 kg (7¼ tons)'.

A light locomotive is thus distinguished from a motor tractor purely in terms of unladen weight.

(7) Heavy locomotive

This term also applies to wheeled vehicles used on roads and the points made above under light locomotive apply equally to this class of vehicles. The definition of this class of motor vehicle is contained in s. 185, which reads:

> 'a "heavy locomotive" means a mechanically propelled vehicle which is not constructed itself to carry a load other than any of the articles aforesaid (see under 'Motor tractor'), and the weight of which unladen exceeds 11 690 kg (11½ tons)'.

This is the largest type of motor vehicle which will be found in use on a road, other than a special type of vehicle the use of which has been specifically authorised by the Secretary of State.

Other types of vehicles

The next group of motor vehicles are distinguished by their construction and not by unladen weight, although they will also, by reason of their unladen weights, fall into one of the classes of motor vehicle dealt with above.

(1) Articulated vehicle

Generally, an articulated vehicle can be described as a vehicle so constructed that it can be divided into two parts both of which are vehicles and one of which is a motor vehicle. When we think of this in terms of goods vehicles we see a tractive unit with a trailer attached to it in such a way that a substantial part of the weight of the trailer is borne by the motor vehicle. The trailer is, therefore, resting on the back of the towing vehicle by superimposition, rather than being attached in the normal way, by a tow bar.

An 'articulated bus' is a passenger vehicle similarly constructed, but usually incapable of being divided other than in a workshop. Passengers must be able at all times, when the vehicle is coupled up, to move from one part to another.

(2) *Dual purpose vehicle*

As the title suggests, this is a motor vehicle which can be used either to carry passengers or goods, or both, if the vehicle is capable of transmitting the driving power of the engine to all the wheels of the vehicle or it is constructed in accordance with certain specifications and in either case the unladen weight of the vehicle does not exceed that specified. This definition of a dual purpose vehicle is contained in Regulation 3(2) Road Vehicles (Construction and Use) Regulations 1986 and reads:

'a "dual purpose vehicle" means a vehicle constructed or adapted for the carriage both of passengers and of goods or burden of any description, being a vehicle of which the unladen weight does not exceed 2040 kg which either:

(a) satisfies the conditions as to construction, or
(b) is so constructed or adapted that the driving power of the engine is, or by the appropriate use of controls of the vehicle can be, transmitted to all the wheels of the vehicle.'

The types of motor vehicles referred to at (b) above are Land Rovers, Jeeps and vehicles, not being track laying vehicles, which are designed to go over rough land as well as on roads.

The types of vehicles referred to at (a) are mainly shooting brakes, estate cars and utility brakes, which comply with certain conditions as to construction which are that:

(a) the vehicle must be fitted with a rigid roof, with or without a sliding panel;
(b) the area of the vehicle to the rear of the driver's seat must
   (i) be permanently fitted with at least one row of transverse seats (fixed or folding) for two or more passengers and those seats must be properly strung or cushioned and provided with upholstered backrests, attached either to the seats or to a side or the floor of the vehicle; and
   (ii) be lit on each side at the rear by a window or windows or other transparent material having an area or aggregate area of not less than 1850 square centimetres on each side and not less than 770 square centimetres at the rear;
(c) the distance between the rearmost part of the steering wheel and the backrests of the row of transverse seats (see above at (b) (i) or, if there is more than one such row of seats, the distance between the rearmost part of the steering wheel and the backrests of the rearmost such row) must, when the seats are ready for use, be not less than one-third of the distance between the rearmost part of the steering wheel and the rearmost part of the floor of the vehicle.

174   This all sounds rather technical, but if you examine any shooting brake or estate car you will find that all the above conditions are satisfied. The only difficulty that may be encountered is where a vehicle has been adapted by the owner to become a dual purpose vehicle, in which case you may find that the measurements specified in (b) and (c) above have not been complied with. The most important fact to remember is that a dual purpose vehicle must be for both passenger and goods. A Land Rover built purely for the carriage of passengers is not a dual purpose vehicle.

Classification of offenders

When we examine road traffic provisions we continually find that a person commits an offence if he 'uses, causes, or permits' some act or omission. These three terms are used disjunctively and have different meanings. For example, when we report offenders for breaches of the statutory provisions relating to the construction and use of motor vehicles, we have to state which of the three terms applies, whether the offender 'used' the vehicle, 'permitted' the use, or 'caused' the vehicle to be used. We must examine the ways in which the courts have interpreted these terms in order to understand fully their application.

Use

The term 'use' should be given its everyday, ordinary meaning. A person who drives a motor vehicle uses it and so does the person who owns it if it is used upon his business. The offence is one of strict liability, that is, awareness of the defective condition of a vehicle is irrelevant, as is the fact concerning whether or not a person should have known about it. To 'use' a vehicle there must be an element of controlling, operating or managing the vehicle as such.

If a person drives a motor lorry which proves to have a defective tyre, he 'uses' the vehicle; so does the owner of the vehicle if it is used upon his business. However, a person who lends his motor car to a friend without conditions, allowing the friend to use the vehicle in any way which he pleases, does not 'use' the motor car when it is being used solely for a purpose relevant to the friend. In such circumstances it is not being used for any purpose relevant to the owner.

Where the statutory provisions relate to 'using, causing, or permitting', the only persons who can be convicted of 'using' are the driver or the employer of the driver if the vehicle was being driven on the employer's business or the owner when he is being driven in his own vehicle for his purposes. However, offences under the Vehicle Excise and Registration Act can relate to the user of a vehicle or the keeper of the vehicle. When considering whether or not a vehicle is being used on a road without insurance, one should ask two questions. Is it a road in the ordinary sense, that is a definable way between two points over which vehicles can pass? Do the public, or a section of the public have access to that path which appears to be a definable way?

Cause or permit

The term 'cause' involves some degree of dominance or control, and it involves some express or positive command or direction to the other person. A general manager of five depots, each of which was independently supervised, was held not to have

175

'caused' a vehicle to be used on a road in a dangerous condition. If the general manager had ordered one of the vehicles to be used for a specific purpose, he could have been 'causing' the use in those circumstances.

The term 'permit' is somewhat looser than 'cause'. There is not the same express or positive mandate as in 'cause'. It includes those cases when permission may be inferred. For example, a person requests the loan of your vehicle and you tell him that he can use the vehicle any time he likes, and give him the keys. It cannot be said that you 'caused' him to use the vehicle, but you certainly 'permitted' him to use the vehicle.

'Causing' and 'permitting' always refer to another person. A person should not be reported for causing or permitting himself to commit an offence. It is often difficult to differentiate between the two terms and if in doubt choose 'permitting', which does not require the control or positive mandate required by the term 'causing'. The essential element of each, as opposed to 'using', is that *mens rea* is necessary for these two offences.

Aid, abet, counsel, or procure

If a person aids, abets, counsels, or procures another to commit an offence then he is liable to be tried and punished as if here were a principal, i.e. the offender himself. When the offence is summary, the relevant statutory provision is s. 44 of the Magistrates' Courts Act 1980, and where the offence is indictable it is s. 8 of the Accessories and Abettors Act 1861. Now, let us examine these terms to get their true meaning in relation to offences.

A person aids and abets an offence if, knowing all the circumstances which constitute the offence, he assists the principal in committing the offence. In such circumstances he may be said to be an aider and abettor. It is not necessary for the defendant to realise that the facts known to him amount to an offence. To use a simple example: the holder of a provisional licence is riding his solo motor cycle with a pillion passenger who knows that the driver has a provisional driving licence. The motor cycle is not displaying 'L' plates. The driver commits the offences of (a) carrying a passenger and (b) failing to display 'L' plates as required by his licence. He could not commit the first offence unless the passenger actively assisted by being on the vehicle; thus, the passenger commits the offence of aiding and abetting the offence at (a), but unless there was evidence that he actively assisted the driver to remove the 'L' plates, or to persuade him to drive without the plates, he does not aid and abet the offence at (b) merely because he was being carried on the vehicle.

If a person shuts his eyes to the obvious he may be guilty of aiding and abetting, although in most circumstances inactivity will be insufficient to constitute assistance. However, if a person deliberately refrains from making enquiries the results of which he may not wish to know and that nature of the offence is such that it is obvious, an aiding and abetting may occur.

In relation to the supervisor of a learner driver, the supervisor has a special relationship with the driver which places him under certain obligations. If the supervisor permitted the learner driver to drive without 'L' plates, he would be aiding and abetting the offence notwithstanding that he did not actively assist in the removal of the 'L' plates.

176

The words 'aid, abet, counsel, or procure' create only one offence and all the words can be used in a charge.

Motor vehicles – registration and licensing

Registration

The Secretary of State for Transport has a duty to register all mechanically propelled vehicles used or kept on public roads in Great Britain. All records related to mechanically propelled vehicles are held by the DVLA at Swansea and stored in a computer.

Registration is completed when the details of the vehicle – such as colour, body, chassis, and engine number – are recorded, together with the name and address of the person who is the owner or keeper of the vehicle. On registering a vehicle the Secretary of State will assign a registration mark and issue a registration document which contains the registered particulars of the vehicle. The provisions in respect of motor dealers allow the Secretary of State to issue 'blocks' of registration numbers to suitable motor dealers who are then in a position to allocate particular numbers to vehicles purchased by customers, supply the necessary registration plates and send details of each vehicle and its owner to the DVLA. This registration document is not to be treated as proof that the person shown as the owner or keeper of the vehicle referred to in the registration document is the owner of the vehicle.

(1) *Mechanically propelled*

The term 'mechanically propelled vehicle' is wider than the term 'motor vehicle' as defined in the Road Traffic Act 1988, which states that a motor vehicle is a mechanically propelled vehicle intended or adapted for use on a road. The Vehicle Excise and Registration Act 1994 and regulations made under that Act apply to all mechanically propelled vehicles used or kept on public roads, whether or not the vehicle was intended or adapted for such use. If, for example, a go-kart was seen being used on a public road, then, because such a vehicle has been held not to be a motor vehicle intended or adapted for use on a road, any breach of the provisions contained in the Road Traffic Act or regulations made under the Act would not be an offence, but, because the go-kart is a mechanically propelled vehicle, any use on a public road is a breach of the provisions contained in the Vehicle Excise and Registration Act 1994 or any regulations made under the Act.

(2) *Used or kept*

A person 'keeps' a mechanically propelled vehicle on a public road if he causes it to be on such a road for any period, however short, when it is not in use there. From this it appears that the mere sight of a vehicle stationary and unattended on a public road is sufficient evidence to show that the vehicle was kept there, and evidence of any 'use' is sufficient to show that the vehicle was being used on a public road. Where the driver is an employee of the owner or keeper of the vehicle and is using it on his master's business, but is not responsible for registering or licensing the vehicle, it was held that it would be oppressive to take action against the driver and proceedings should be limited to the owner or keeper who would also be deemed to be using the vehicle in such circumstances. (See 'Vehicle excise licence', page 181.)

(3) *Public road*

This means 'a road repairable at public expense', therefore it does not include privately maintained roads such as those that may be found in a dock area or enclosed factory complex. It should be noted that this definition is much narrower than the definition of road contained in the Road Traffic Act 1988. A situation may arise where a mechanically propelled vehicle is seen being used on a road in contravention of a provision contained in the Vehicle Excise and Registration Act 1994 or regulations made under the Act, but because the road is not repairable at public expense the statutory provisions would not apply; however, if it could be proved that there was public access to this road the provision of the Road Traffic Act 1988 would apply and a check may reveal offences under that Act or associated regulations.

Vehicle registration document

When a mechanically propelled vehicle is first licensed to be used or kept on a public road, the Secretary of State for Transport has a duty to register the vehicle, issue a registration document (unless a registration mark has already been assigned by a dealer who has been allocated a 'block' of registration numbers), and assign a registration mark to the vehicle. Where a mechanically propelled vehicle is exempt from the requirement to be licensed but is to be used or kept on a public road, it still requires to be registered and a registration document issued and registration mark allocated. The registration document contains the registered particulars of the vehicle together with the name and address of the person shown in the register as the owner or keeper of the vehicle. If a registration document is lost, stolen, destroyed, mutilated or accidentally defaced, or the figures and particulars contained therein have become illegible or the colour of the licence has become altered by fading or otherwise, the owner of the vehicle, on application to the Secretary of State, will be issued with a duplicate registration document.

The Secretary of State has the power to assign different registration numbers to a vehicle. This gives rise to the trade in personalised number plates.

(1) *Change of ownership*

When there is a change of ownership of a mechanically propelled vehicle the previous owner of the vehicle shall deliver the registration document (and may deliver any current licence) to the new owner and shall forthwith notify in writing the change of ownership to the Secretary of State, stating the registration mark of the new vehicle, its make and class, and the name and address of the new owner. The vehicle registration document carries a tear off slip upon which such a report can be made. It is entitled 'Notification of sale or transfer'.

The new owner of a vehicle shall:

(a) if he intends to use or keep the vehicle upon public roads, otherwise than under a trade licence (see 'Trade licences', page 184), forthwith enter his name and address in the space provided in the registration document, and deliver it to the Secretary of State;

(b) if he does not intend to use or keep the vehicle on public roads, forthwith notify the Secretary of State in writing that he is the owner of the vehicle, and state the registration mark, its make and class, the name and address of the previous owner, and the fact that he does not intend to use or keep the vehicle on public roads;

(c) if he intends to use the vehicle upon public roads solely under a trade licence (see 'Trade licences'), at the expiration of three months from the date when he became the owner of the vehicle, or if a further change of ownership occurs, on the date of that change, whichever is the sooner, notify the Secretary of State in writing of his name and address and those of the previous owner.

Provision (c) above relates to dealers in mechanically propelled vehicles who are able to buy second-hand vehicles and keep them for up to three months or until the vehicle is sold, whichever is the sooner, without any notification. This is why you rarely see the name and address of a garage or dealer in the registration document; the vehicle is usually sold within three months of being purchased.

(2) *Change of address*

When the person registered as the owner or keeper of a vehicle changes his address he shall enter his new address in the space provided in the registration document and send the document to the Secretary of State.

(3) *Change of registered particulars*

When any alteration is made to a mechanically propelled vehicle which affects the particulars contained in the registration document, the owner of the vehicle shall notify the Secretary of State in writing of the alteration and forward the registration document for amendment. An example of such an alteration would be where the vehicle is re-painted a different colour, or when a new engine is fitted; in each case the particulars contained in the registration document would be incorrect and require amendment.

(4) *Destruction or permanent export*

When any vehicle is broken up, destroyed , or sent permanently out of Great Britain, the owner must notify the Secretary of State of the fact and surrender the registration document to him.

Police powers

A police officer may require the owner of a mechanically propelled vehicle to produce the registration document for inspection at any reasonable time.

Failure to produce the registration document or to comply with any of the above requirements relating to changes in ownership, registered particulars, etc., is a summary offence. However, it should be noted that the offence by the previous owner is committed when the change is effected.

If there is ever any suspicion that a vehicle may be stolen or the documents forged, an examination of the registration document may provide evidence to confirm a suspicion. Thieves steal vehicles and either strip them of all parts and accessories or respray the body and pass it off as a newly built vehicle which had been previously written off. The engine number should tally with that given in the registration document and any evidence of filing or punching of the metal round an engine number should be viewed with suspicion.

Registration mark

The registration mark assigned to a vehicle is a combination of letters and figures which serve to identify the vehicle and is often referred to as the registered number of the vehicle. The size, shape, and character of any registration mark is governed by Schedule 2 of the Road Vehicles (Registration and Licensing) Regulations 1971 as amended.

There are two methods of exhibiting the registration mark: the first is where the letters and figures are white, silver, or light grey upon a black background; the second is where the letters and figures are exhibited on a plate of reflecting material, in which case the mark shown to the front consists of black letters and figures on a white background, and the mark shown to the rear consists of black letters and figures on a yellow background. Vehicles first used before 1 January 1973 may use the first method. A vehicle first registered on or after 1 January 1973 must use the second method of exhibiting the registration mark unless the vehicle is a goods vehicle of unladen weight exceeding 3 tons, fitted with an approved rear marking, a stage carriage, works truck, or agricultural machine. In relation to a bicycle, invalid carriage, or a pedestrian controlled vehicle registered on or after 1 January 1973, the mark exhibited to the front and rear shall be black letters and figures on a yellow background. Motor cycles are no longer required to carry a front registration mark.

It is a summary offence to use or keep, on a public road, a mechanically propelled vehicle not having the registration marks properly fixed to the front and rear of the vehicle, or with a registration mark which is obscured or not easily distinguishable. It is a defence to a charge of using, etc., a vehicle which does not have a plate so affixed where the accused proves that there has been no reasonable opportunity to register the vehicle and that the vehicle was being driven on a public road for the purpose of being registered. It is a defence to a charge in relation to an obscured plate, to prove that all reasonable steps were taken to prevent the driving of the like from taking place.

Where a plate is not easily distinguishable, etc., the person driving the vehicle, or if it is not being driven, the person keeping it, commits an offence. It is a summary offence contrary to the Road Vehicles Lighting Regulations 1989, to use or keep such a vehicle on a public road and fail to illuminate the registration mark fixed to the rear of the vehicle. In instances where motor vehicles may be lawfully parked without lights within the period between sunset and sunrise, there is no legal requirement to have the registration mark illuminated.

The name and address of the registered keeper of a motor vehicle can be obtained from the Secretary of State for Transport or, more easily, through the Police National Computer on most occasions.

Vehicle excise licence

With certain exceptions, every mechanically propelled vehicle used or kept on a public road must have in force in relation to that vehicle an excise licence issued by the Secretary of State. An application may be made for a licence up to 14 days before the licence is to have effect. The application form containing the prescribed particulars must be accompanied by a test certificate (if applicable), a certificate of insurance covering the use of that vehicle, the registration document relating to the vehicle, and the amount of duty payable on the licence. When checking whether or not a person has a current excise licence in force for a vehicle the owner or keeper will often state that his application is in the post. In such a case ask the person to produce his certificate of insurance and test certificate, if applicable. If these documents are produced, this usually shows that no application has been made as these documents would not have been available for production if an application had been made for a licence – they would be with his application form.

(1) *Vehicles exempt from licence duty*

Under the Vehicle Excise and Registration Act 1994, a number of mechanically propelled vehicles are exempt from the requirement to have an excise licence when used or kept on public roads. The main exceptions are:

(a) electrically propelled vehicles;
(b) fire engines and mine rescue vehicles;
(c) vehicles kept by a fire authority while being used or kept for the purposes of fire fighting;
(d) ambulances, including veterinary ambulances and vehicles being used as such by NHS approved bodies;
(e) road rollers;
(f) vehicles used on tram lines;
(g) vehicles used or kept on a road solely for haulage of lifeboats and their equipment;
(h) vehicles (including pedal cycles with an attachment for propelling them by mechanical power) which do not exceed 10 cwt (508 kg) and are adapted and used or left on a road, for invalids, or vehicles used or kept for use by or for the purposes of a disabled person who is in receipt of some form of mobility supplement;
(i) road construction vehicles;
(j) vehicles constructed, or adapted, and used solely for the conveyance of machinery for spreading materials on roads to deal with frost, ice or snow;
(k) local authority watering vehicles;
(l) tower wagons used solely in connection with installing or maintaining materials or apparatus for street lighting;

181

(m) vehicles being used or kept for snow clearance;

(n) vehicles purchased by overseas residents;

(o) vehicles travelling to or from a previously arranged test in connection with a test certificate, or to or from a place where work is to be or has to be done on it to remedy defects for which a test certificate has been refused; or when towed to be broken up;

(p) during a test by an authorised person;

(q) vehicles specially exempted which are intended to be used on public roads:

    (i) only in passing from land occupied by the owner of the vehicle to other land occupied by him and

    (ii) for distances not exceeding a total of six miles in any one week.

The Road Vehicles (Exemptions from Duty) Regulations 1986 exempt vehicles imported by members of visiting forces, members of a headquarters of organisation, or a dependant of such person. This exemption lasts for a period of 12 months only.

Recovery vehicles and works trucks attract lower rates of duty under the Act. Recovery vehicles are only entitled to operate under a reduced rate licence if they are used solely for that purpose. They must be constructed or permanently adapted primarily for the purpose of lifting, towing and transporting a disabled vehicle, or for any one or more of those purposes. They are recovery vehicles only if they are used for the recovery, repair or removal of disabled vehicles and the transport of the occupants of the disabled vehicle and its load to places of repair, or in the case of persons, to their destination. It is not a recovery vehicle if it is used to recover more than two vehicles at a time.

Works trucks are designed for use on private premises. Dumper trucks are such vehicles. They may only be used on a road while operating at a reduced rate of duty when going from one part of premises to another in the 'immediate vicinity'. To be so placed, premises must enjoy a very considerable degree of closeness.

(2) *Duration of licence*

Vehicle excise licences for most vehicles may be issued for periods of twelve or six months. Licences valid for six months are limited to vehicles for which the annual rate of duty exceeds £50. The Secretary of State may also issue temporary licences for 14 days, or such other period as may be prescribed. Applications for a licence may be made by any person who makes out a declaration and furnishes the prescribed particulars. The licence is issued to the vehicle, not to any person, and must either be transferred with the vehicle if it is sold, or returned to the DVLA for a rebate. It has become a practice to allow up to 14 days after a licence has expired as a period of grace in which road users may make application for the renewal of a licence, but such a licence will commence on the first day of the month following the expiry of the previous licence.

(3) *Exhibition of licence*

Every licence issued under the Act shall be fixed to the vehicle in a holder sufficient to protect the licence from the effects of the weather to which it would otherwise be exposed. This means that if the licence is exhibited outside the vehicle or in an exposed position, it must be in a waterproof holder. The licence shall be exhibited on the vehicle so that the particulars are clearly visible in daylight from the nearside of the road:

(a) in the case of an invalid carriage, tricycle, or bicycle, on the nearside in front of the driving seat;

(b) in the case of a bicycle drawing a sidecar, on the nearside of the handlebars or the nearside of the sidecar;

(c) in the case of a vehicle having a windscreen, on the nearside of the windscreen;

(d) on any other vehicle, on the nearside window of the driver's cab (if it has one) or on the nearside of the vehicle in front of the driver's seat, or towards the front of the vehicle in the case of a pedestrian-controlled vehicle.

(4) *Offences*

There are a number of offences which can be committed in connection with an excise licence, the most common of which can be summarised as follows:

(a) using or keeping a mechanically propelled vehicle on a public road without having in force an excise licence – s. 29;

(b) failing to display an excise licence – s. 33;

(c) to forge, fraudulently alter or use, or fraudulently lend or allow to be used by any other person, an excise licence – s. 44;

(d) to alter, deface, mutilate, or add anything to an excise licence, or to exhibit on any vehicle such a licence – Regulation 7(1), The Road Vehicles (Registration and Licensing) Regulations 1971 and s. 59;

(e) to exhibit anything which is intended to be or could be mistaken for a licence – Regulation 7(2) and s. 59;

(f) to make a false declaration in an application for the issue of a licence – s. 45.

Where an excise licence is alleged to be forged, the issue does not surround whether there was an intention to avoid payment of excise duty. It must be proved that there was an intention by deceit to cause a person exercising a public duty to act or refrain from acting, in a way which he would not otherwise have done. Thus, the alteration of an excise licence with the intention of avoiding the attention of police officers being drawn to the car while an application for a licence is pending, contravenes the section.

Police powers

Although there is no statutory power given to a police officer to seize any licence plate, or registration document which he suspects to be forged, altered, or otherwise fraudulently used, it is an accepted practice to seize such articles to ensure their availability as evidence of the offence in any subsequent court proceedings.

Where a police officer finds a mechanically propelled vehicle exhibiting an excise licence issued in respect of another vehicle, he should not only bear in mind offences under the Vehicles Excise and Registration Act 1994, but remember that there could be a theft or handling of stolen property involved. If there is any suspicion of either offence, then there would be a power of arrest without warrant, both offences being arrestable offences. A common explanation given when a vehicle is found displaying a licence issued to another vehicle is that the owner of the vehicle bought if from a stranger in a public house, which could be an offence of handling stolen property, or that he had found it lying in the road, which would be theft.

In relation to certain offences under the Act, the most important of which is the offence under s. 29 of the using or keeping a mechanically propelled vehicle on a public road without having an excise licence in force, s. 46 of the Act gives the police certain powers to require persons to give information. If it is alleged that a vehicle has been used or kept in breach of the provisions of s. 29, then:

(a) the person keeping the vehicle shall give such information as he may be required by or on behalf of a chief officer of police (or the Secretary of State) to give as to the identity of the persons who were driving or using or keeping the vehicle at the time of the alleged offence;

(b) any other person shall, if required as above, give such information as it is in his power to give as to the identity of any of the persons concerned – i.e. the driver, user, or keeper of the vehicle – at the time of the alleged offence;

(c) the person who is alleged to have used the vehicle at the time of the alleged offence shall, if required as above, give such information as it is in his power to give as to the identity of the person by whom the vehicle was kept at that time.

A failure to give this information when required to do so under the provisions of s. 46 is a summary offence, but a person coming within (a) above shall not be convicted if he shows to the satisfaction of the court that he did not know and could not, with reasonable diligence, have ascertained the identity of the person or persons concerned.

Evidence of driving

Where it is proved that such a requirement has been made of such a person, the Vehicle Excise and Registration Act 1994, s. 51, permits proof that a person was the driver, user or keeper of the vehicle on a particular occasion, by proof of service by post of a request under s. 46, together with the production of a signed statement from the accused to the effect that he was the driver, user or keeper on that occasion. This does not apply, of course, where the recipient of the form identifies some other person.

Trade licences

When dealing with the registration and licensing of mechanically propelled vehicles used or kept on public roads, it was stated that, with certain exceptions, all mechanically propelled vehicles must have a current excise licence in force in relation to that vehicle, one licence to each vehicle. Trade licences, however, can be used on vehicles and are a type of excise licence issued to a motor trader or vehicle tester by the Secretary of State for use in connection with his business as a motor trader or vehicle tester. The term 'motor trader' is defined in s. 62(1) of the Vehicle Excise and Registration Act 1994 as:

(a) a manufacturer or repairer of, or dealer in, vehicles, or (b) any other description of person who carries on a business of such description as may be prescribed by regulations made by the Secretary of State, and a person is treated as a dealer in vehicles if he carries on a business consisting wholly or mainly of collecting and delivering vehicles, and not including any other activities except activities as a manufacturer or repairer of, or dealer in, vehicles'.

In addition, a person whose business is that of modifying vehicles (by fitting accessories or otherwise), or of 'valeting' (i.e. thorough cleaning, including removing wax and grease) prior to first registration or in order to prepare it for sale is also a 'motor trader'. Thus, persons entitled to trade licences are clearly defined and private motorists and similar persons are clearly excluded.

The term 'vehicle tester' means a person, other than a motor trader, who regularly in the course of his business engages in the testing on roads of mechanically propelled vehicles to other persons.

Applications for a trade licence or for two or more trade licences must be made to the Secretary of State and, if the licence is granted, the holder of the licence will be issued with two plates, referred to as 'trade plates', showing the general registration mark assigned to the holder of the licence, and one of the plates shall contain means whereby the licence can be fixed to that plate.

Trade licences are granted for periods of 12 months or such shorter period as may be prescribed. The annual duty payable for a 12-month licence is currently that for a vehicle excise licence for motor cars or for motor cycles as the case may be.

Trade plates

The holder of a trade licence is issued with two plates in respect of each licence held by him, and provided he satisfies the Secretary of State that the vehicle which he will use include bicycles as well as other vehicles, he shall be entitled to be issued free of charge with an additional plate for use on such bicycles. The plates remain the property of the Secretary of State and shall be returned to him when the person to whom they were issued ceases to be the holder of a trade licence. The plates themselves contain the registration mark assigned to the licence, the letters and figures of which are red against a white background. These plates should be exhibited to the front and rear of the vehicle in the same manner as the ordinary registration mark is displayed. It is an offence to fail to do so.

Display of licence

The trade licence is put in a holder fixed to the trade plate which is exhibited at the front of the vehicle so as to be at all times clearly visible by daylight. In addition to the contents of an ordinary excise licence, the trade licence contains the name and address of the person who holds the licence. Motor cycles may display a rear plate only, and if this is so, the licence will be contained on that plate. It is an offence,

185

contrary to s. 59 of the Act and Regulation 33 of the Road Vehicles (Registration and Licensing) Regulations 1971 to fail to display a licence.

Use of a trade licence by its holder

The Vehicle Excise and Registration Act 1994, s. 12, places limitations upon the use of the licence by its holder. He is not entitled:

(a) to use more than one mechanically propelled vehicle at any one time; or
(b) to use any vehicle for any purpose other than a permitted one (see below); or
(c) to keep any vehicle on a road if it is not being used thereon, except in such circumstances as may be prescribed.

However, this refers to a particular licence and there is nothing to prevent a trader from holding more than one licence so that he may use plates on more than one vehicle at any one time. It is an offence to use more than the number of vehicles permitted by such licences.

It is made quite clear in (c) above that a trade licence cannot be used in respect of a vehicle which is being 'kept' rather than being 'used' on a road.

Restrictions on the use of trade licences

The Road Vehicles (Registration and Licensing) Regulations 1971, Regulation 34, prohibits the use of a vehicle under trade plates by a person who is not the holder of the licence but this does not prevent a person driving a vehicle on a road with the consent of the licence holder, if it is being used on the licence holder's business. An employee is therefore permitted to drive such a vehicle on his employer's business.

However, outside these generalised permitted purposes, the Road Vehicles (Registration and Licensing) Regulations 1971, Regulations 33–37, are concerned with more specific permitted purposes.

Permitted purposes

Regulation 35 limits use by the licence holder under the authority of the licence, to instances in which that use of a vehicle on a road is a use of a vehicle temporarily in his possession in the course of business. The regulation goes on to require that such vehicles will not be used in any case outside the terms of use which are declared to be *permitted purposes:*

(a) for the test or trial of the vehicle, or its equipment or accessories in the ordinary course of construction, modification or repair, or after completion in either case;
(b) for proceeding to or from a public weighbridge to ascertain its unladen weight, or to or from any place for its first registration or inspection by someone acting on behalf of the Secretary of State;
(c) for its test or trial for the benefit of a prospective purchaser, including going either to or from a place of such test or trial at the instance of the prospective purchaser;

(d) for its test or trial for the benefit of a person interested in promoting publicity in regard to the vehicle, including going either to or from a place of such test or trial at the instance of such person;

(e) for delivering it to a purchaser;

(f) for demonstrating the operation of the vehicle or its accessories or equipment when handed over to a purchaser;

(g) for delivering it between parts of the motor trader's own premises or to the premises of another manufacturer, dealer or repairer, or bringing it back therefrom directly to his own premises;

(h) for proceeding to or from a workshop where a body, or a special type of equipment or accessories, is to be or has been fitted to it or where it is to be or has been, painted, valeted or repaired;

(i) for proceeding from the premises of a manufacturer, repairer or dealer to a railway station, airfield or shipping dock for the purpose of transportation, or for proceeding to such premises from a railway station, etc., to which it has been transported;

(j) for proceeding to or from any garage, auction room or storage place where vehicles are usually stored or offered for sale and at which the vehicle is to be or has been stored or offered for sale as the case may be;

(k) for proceeding to or from a place of testing or to a place to be broken up or otherwise dismantled.

A 'business purpose' is a purpose connected with the motor trader's business as a manufacturer or repairer of, or dealer in, mechanically propelled vehicles, or a purpose connected with such a business in relation to trailers provided that that business is carried on in conjunction with his business as a motor trader, or a purpose connected with the business of modifying vehicles prior to their first registration with the Secretary of State, or of valeting vehicles.

The use of a vehicle with a trailer is authorised under a trade licence.

Manufacturers may use a trade licence for research and development purposes. Vehicle testers may use a trade licence for testing vehicles and trailers drawn by those vehicles, or any accessory or equipment on the vehicle or trailer.

The purposes set out above are the only purposes for which a trade licence may be used. A motor trader who returns to his home in the evening using a car which is being driven on a road under the authority of a trade licence, commits an offence. He would commit a further offence if he then used the vehicle to go to a restaurant. If an employee used trade plates to take his personal car to a car auction, he would commit an offence. The offence would be one of using a motor vehicle without a current excise licence.

Carriage of goods

The use of a motor vehicle under trade plates for the carriage of goods or burden of any description is prohibited by Regulation 38 with the exception of:

(a) a load which is carried by a vehicle being used for the purpose of demonstrating or testing the vehicle, or its accessories or equipment, within the terms of (a), (c), (d) or (f) above, and is carried solely for that purpose,

187

and which is returned to the place of loading without having been removed from the vehicle (except in the case of an accident or for demonstrating its operation to a purchaser when handed over to him, or when the load consists of water, fertiliser or refuse);

(aa) in the case of a vehicle which is being delivered or collected and is being used for a relevant purpose, a load consisting of another vehicle used or to be used for travel from or to the place of delivery or collection;

(b) any load built in as a permanent part of the vehicle or permanently attached to it;

(c) a load consisting of parts, accessories or equipment designed to be fitted to the vehicle and tools for so fitting them, when the vehicle is being moved between premises in the course of manufacture or transhipment; or

(d) a load consisting of a trailer, the vehicle carrying the trailer being used to deliver the trailer to a purchaser, or to move it between premises in the course of manufacture, or to take it to a place of transhipment.

Although there appears to be, at first sight, a lot of exceptions, their effect is narrow. It can be appreciated that the test and trial of a goods vehicle may often lead to the carriage of a load. However, there should be no reason for that load not being returned to the premises of the trader and this is demanded. Vehicles which have an in-built load such as engineering plant could not conveniently be stripped of that load for the purpose of a test and that purpose could well be affected by the removal of machinery which is an essential part of such a specialised vehicle. Similar restrictions apply to use by researchers and vehicle testers.

Carriage of passengers

Regulation 40 prohibits use under a trade licence for carrying any person in or on the vehicle, or on a trailer drawn by that vehicle, except a person carried in connection with the permitted purpose for which the vehicle is being used. While such a vehicle may carry prospective purchasers, it could not carry an employee of the trader who was merely taking a lift home.

Offences in relation to trade licences and plates

The use of a vehicle under a trade licence for an unauthorised purpose has the effect of making the use of that vehicle, an unlicensed use.

Regulation 32 of the 1971 Regulations creates offences of altering, defacing, mutilating, or adding to, trade plates, or the exhibition of plates which have been so treated.

The Vehicle Excise and Registration Act 1994, s. 44, applies the offences of forgery, fraudulent alteration or use, or fraudulent lending or allowing to be used by any other person, which are created by the Act in respect of excise licences and registration marks, to such acts if committed in respect of trade licences or trade plates.

Driving licences, insurance, and test certificates

The general rule is that before a person can drive a motor vehicle on a road he must be the holder of a current driving licence covering the category of vehicle he is driving, and there must be in force in relation to the use of the vehicle a valid policy of insurance or other approved form of insurance. The object behind the need to hold a driving licence is to ensure that all drivers possess the necessary basic skill to drive a motor vehicle on a road in a manner which is not likely to endanger other road users. To enable persons to practise driving in order to reach the standard required to pass a driving test, a person may be granted a provisional driving licence but, when driving, such persons must conform to certain conditions, the object of which is to indicate to other drivers that the driver is a 'learner' and, in the case of most motor vehicles, to ensure that such a 'learner' is under the supervision of a competent driver in or on the vehicle who is in such a position that he can supervise the actions of the learner driver. We will examine the various types of driving licence, the grant and issue of licences, the conditions that may be imposed, and the powers of the police as regards production and inspection. We will also examine the legal requirements relating to insurance and police powers relating to production, etc.

For the purposes of this legislation the term 'road' includes any highway and any other road to which the public has access and includes bridges over which a road passes. We are, therefore, considering roads used by the public, who have a right of access to them. However, some roads, although they may be considered to be 'private' by their owners, may be public roads, for the purpose of the Road Traffic Acts if there is an unrestricted access. A highway allows members of the public a right of way on foot, riding, accompanied by a beast of burden or with vehicles, or cattle. The term, therefore, embraces all forms of 'public passage'. Vehicles such as motor cycles which use public paths may be subject to the provisions of the Road Traffic Acts if public usage can be proved. If it is possible to show that the place is a 'road' (which includes a highway), and that members of the public generally use it, without trespass, then the provisions of the Road Traffic Acts apply. The common offences are driving otherwise than in accordance with a licence for a particular category of vehicle and for some other person to cause or permit another to drive a motor vehicle on a road otherwise than in accordance with such licence. The essence of driving is using the controls of the vehicle to control its movements. Persons 'free-wheeling' in a motor vehicle, or being towed (provided they have steerage) are driving. Someone who is pushing a vehicle is not driving it, even if his hand is placed through the window and on to the steering wheel.

Driving licences

A driving licence is an authority to drive a motor vehicle on a road, and the onus is upon a person to show that he has this authority if he is found driving a motor vehicle on a road. The offence of driving otherwise than in accordance with a driving licence is contained in s. 87 of the Road Traffic Act 1988. It is also an offence to cause or permit a person to drive on a road a motor vehicle of any class otherwise than in accordance with a licence authorising him to drive a motor vehicle of that class. It can be seen, therefore, that employers have a responsibility to ensure that

189

persons employed as drivers must be licensed. However, notwithstanding these provisions, a person may drive or cause or permit another person to drive a vehicle of any class if:

(a) the driver has held:
    (i) a licence under Part III of the Act (which deals with driving licences) to drive vehicles of that or a corresponding class; or
    (ii) a Northern Ireland licence to drive vehicles of that or a corresponding class; or
    (iii) a British External licence or British Forces licence to drive vehicles of that or a corresponding class; or
    (iv) an exchangeable licence (community licence or that of an associated country) to drive vehicles of that or a corresponding class; and

(b) either:
    (i) a qualifying application by the driver for the grant of a licence to drive vehicles of that class for a period which includes that time has been received by the Secretary of State; or
    (ii) a licence to drive vehicles of that class granted to him has been revoked or surrendered (for endorsement or alteration of details) otherwise than by reason of a current disqualification or of its being granted in error; and

(c) in relation to a provisional driving licence, the conditions relating to such a licence are being complied with. This exemption only applies to the renewal of a licence. A person applying for his first licence must not drive until the licence is issued.

However, the significance of these provisions was lessened by legislation extending the validity of driving licences until the age of 70. However, the Road Traffic (Driver Licensing and Information Systems) Act 1989 provides that licences which authorise the holder to drive large goods or large passenger-carrying vehicles shall be renewable on the holder's 45th birthday, or after five years, whichever is the *longer*, or where the licence is issued to a person between 45 and 65, for the period ending on his 66th birthday or after five years whichever is the shorter. After the age of 65, such a licence will remain in force for one year only.

Before the coming into force of provisions originating within the 1989 Act, drivers of heavy goods vehicles and public service vehicles were required to have two driving licences; a DVLA licence for the particular class of vehicle being driven and a separate licence issued by a traffic commissioner authorising the driving of the heavy goods vehicle or public service vehicle.

The categories of vehicles embraced by the DVLA licence have been extended to include all categories of large goods vehicles and large passenger-carrying vehicles. However, all existing separate licences issued by a traffic commissioner (and those which are still being issued during a transitory period) continue to be valid. While, with the coming into force of the 1989 Act, a driver who is found driving such a vehicle otherwise than in accordance with an appropriate DVLA licence, should be charged with an offence contrary to the Road Traffic Act 1988, s. 87 (driving otherwise than in accordance with an appropriate DVLA licence), para. 11 of Schedule 1 to the 1989 Act provides that a person who holds a valid licence issued by a traffic commissioner, may drive such vehicles notwithstanding that his DVLA licence does not cover the category of vehicle which he is driving. Many such licences issued by traffic commissioners will be valid for some years to come.

Minimum age for driving classes of motor vehicles

Section 101 of the Road Traffic Act 1988 and the Motor Vehicles (Driving Licences) Regulations 1987, Regulation 4, make it an offence for a person to drive a motor vehicle on a road if he is under the age specified as the minimum age to drive that class of vehicle. The classes of vehicles and minimum ages are as follows:

(a) *16 yrs. Invalid carriages* not exceeding 510 kg unladen weight.

Mopeds, if first used on or after 1 August 1977 of a maximum design speed of 30 mph, kerbside weight not exceeding 250 kg, and engine not exceeding 50 cc. If first used before 1 August 1977, engine not exceeding 50 cc and having pedals by which it may be propelled.

Mowing machines or pedestrian controlled vehicle, if classed as motor cycles, therefore having less than four wheels and an unladen weight not exceeding 410 kg.

Agricultural tractors, if wheeled vehicles not exceeding 2.45 metres in width and driven without a trailer, other than a two wheeled trailer (or close coupled four wheeled trailer not exceeding 2.45 metres in width). A 16-year-old who has not passed a test may not drive a tractor on a road unless while taking, proceeding to or returning from such a test.

Mobility allowance, a 16-year-old who is in receipt of a mobility allowance under the Social Security Contributions and Benefit Act 1992 may drive small passenger or small goods vehicles.

(b) *17 yrs. Motor cycles*

Road rollers if not capable of carrying or handling goods (if not it would be 21 years), or if propelled by steam and not exceeding 11 690 kg unladen weight and not constructed or adapted to carry a load other than tools and equipment and which is not fitted with a soft or elastic tyre.

Small passenger vehicles, constructed solely to carry passengers and their effects and not adapted to carry more than nine persons inclusive of the driver.

Small goods vehicles, constructed or adapted to carry or haul goods and not adapted to carry more than nine persons inclusive of the driver and of a permissible maximum weight which does not exceed 3.5 tonnes.

(c) *18 yrs. Medium sized goods vehicles*, constructed or adapted to carry or haul goods and not adapted to carry more than nine persons inclusive of the driver, with a permissible maximum weight exceeding 3.5 tonnes, but exceeding 7.5 tonnes.

(d) *21 yrs. Large passenger vehicles*, that is passenger vehicles with more than nine seats inclusive of the driver (18 yrs. for PSV driving licence holder under test, on some short routes not exceeding 50 kilometres and in some vehicles equipped to carry not more than 17 persons including the driver on a national transport operation).

191

Large goods vehicles, that is exceeding 7.5 tonnes.

All other vehicles, which embrace vehicles which do not normally carry passengers or carry or haul a load, e.g. plant.

Members of the armed services may drive medium and large goods vehicles owned and used by the armed services at 17 years of age. Other persons may drive large goods vehicles at 18 years of age if they and their employer are registered under the HGV training scheme, or such use is in connection with a HGV training establishment; similarly if the heavy goods vehicle is brought temporarily into Great Britain.

An 18-year-old person may also drive a large vehicle for the purposes of an ambulance service of a Health Authority or, in Scotland, the Common Services Agency.

Disqualification

Persons below the ages specified above in relation to particular classes of vehicle are disqualified by reason of their age from driving. However, while s. 103 of the Road Traffic Act 1988 creates offences of obtaining a driving licence while disqualified for holding or obtaining such a licence; and driving a motor vehicle on a road while so disqualified; these offences do not apply where the disqualification is by reason of age. Sections 34–36 of the Road Traffic Offenders Act 1988 deal with disqualification for certain offences; disqualification for repeated offences; and disqualification until a test is passed.

Where a person is convicted of an offence involving obligatory disqualification, the court must order him to be disqualified for such period, not less than 12 months, as the court thinks fit unless the court for special reasons thinks fit to order him to be disqualified for a shorter period or not to order him to be disqualified. The term 'special reasons' relates to circumstances peculiar to the offence, rather than to the offender. A lorry driver who stands to lose his livelihood cannot plead that these are special reasons for non-disqualification where that disqualification is in respect of a particular offence. The reasons are peculiar to the driver not the offence. However, a doctor called out to a serious accident, or a police officer ordered back to duty in an emergency where instant attendance was essential, could plead that these amounted to special reasons for driving while a little over the prescribed limit. It would be a matter for the court to decide whether or not their conduct was such that it might be 'special' to the case.

The offences that involve obligatory disqualification are:

(a) manslaughter;
(b) causing death by dangerous driving;
(c) dangerous driving;
(d) causing death by careless driving when under the influence of drink;
(e) driving or attempting to drive when unfit through drink or drugs;
(f) driving or attempting to drive with alcohol concentration above the prescribed limit;
(g) failing to provide a specimen for analysis in (e) and (f) above; and
(h) motor racing or taking part in special trials on highways, or aggravated vehicle-taking under the Theft Act 1968, s. 12A.

The offences of manslaughter (or in Scotland culpable homicide); causing death by dangerous driving and that of causing death by careless driving while under the influence of drink or drugs involve obligatory disqualification for a period of two years. This will also apply where a person has been disqualified within the three years immediately preceding the commission of the offence, for more than one fixed period of 56 days. If the conviction is for any of the offences which are connected with the drink/driving laws, that is an offence under s. 3A, 4(1), or 5(1)(a) of the 1988 Act, and there has been a previous conviction for such an offence within the preceding ten years, a court must order disqualification for a period of not less than three years unless there are special reasons for not doing so.

There are a number of other offences in respect of which a court may, at its discretion, order disqualification for such period as the court may think fit, but this must not be an indefinite period although it may be for life. Examples of these offences are careless and inconsiderate driving, the offences of being in charge of vehicles while unfit, etc., failing to stop after an accident and give particulars, driving otherwise than in accordance with a licence, driving with uncorrected eyesight and using an uninsured vehicle. Offences which carry discretional disqualification usually carry obligatory endorsement. However, The Road Traffic Act 1991 removed the requirement for obligatory endorsement for offences of stealing motor vehicles or taking them without consent.

Disqualification may also result from the accumulation of penalty points on conviction for certain offences. If, for any reason, persons who are convicted of offences for which there should be obligatory or discretional disqualification, are not disqualified, the particulars of the offence and the date upon which it was committed must be endorsed on the licence or counterpart together with the number of penalty points awarded by the court. Where a defendant is convicted of two or more offences committed on the same occasion, the number of penalty points to be awarded must be the number, or generally, the highest number which could be awarded for one of those offences. Where a person is convicted for aiding and abetting offences involving obligatory disqualification the number of penalty points to be attributed is ten.

On conviction for an offence, when the penalty points awarded bring the total to 12 or more in respect of offences within the preceding three years, the court must order disqualification for a minimum of six months unless the court is satisfied, having regard to all the circumstances, that there are grounds for mitigating the normal consequences of the conviction and thinks fit to order disqualification for a shorter period or not to order disqualification at all. In such cases the magistrates may consider *all of the circumstances*, but no account must be taken of any circumstances which are alleged to make the offence other than a serious one, nor of any hardship other than exceptional hardship. Once such a disqualification has been imposed the driving licence is in effect wiped clean. However, 'wiping clean' is restricted to such disqualification for repeated offences. Where a disqualification is imposed under the Road Traffic Offenders Act 1988, s. 34, for a specific offence, the penalty points previously accumulated are to remain effective at the end of the period of disqualification until the expiry of three years from the date of the offence for which they were imposed. The penalty points for particular offences are listed in Schedule 2 to Road Traffic Offenders Act 1988. Some examples are:

Dangerous driving 3–11
Careless driving 3–9
In charge of vehicle while unfit, etc., 10
Failing to comply with traffic directions 3
Failing to stop after accident 5–10
Driving otherwise than in accordance with a licence 3–6
Motor vehicle insurance offences 6–8
Contravention of pedestrian crossing regulations 3
Exceeding speed limit 3–6 (or 3 fixed penalty)
Construction and use offences in relation to tyres, brakes, or steering 3

A constable in uniform may arrest without warrant any person driving or attempting to drive a motor vehicle on a road whom he has reasonable cause to suspect of being disqualified. This power does not extend to circumstances in which the person is disqualified by reason of age.

Removal of disqualification

The Road Traffic Offenders Act 1988, s. 42, provides that a person who has been disqualified by a court may apply to have the disqualification removed as follows:

(a) if the disqualification is for less than four years, after two years;
(b) if it is for less than ten but more than four years, when half the disqualification has expired; or
(c) in any other case (life or ten or more years), when five years have passed.

Disqualification until test is passed

The Road Traffic Offenders Act 1988, s. 36, provides that where a person is disqualified under s. 34 (obligatory disqualification) on conviction for manslaughter by the driver of a motor vehicle, or an offence of causing death by dangerous driving, or is disqualified under s. 34 or 35 (repeated offences) in such circumstances or for such period as the Secretary of State may prescribe, or is convicted of an offence involving obligatory endorsement which may be prescribed by the Secretary of State, the court *must* order him to be disqualified until he has passed the appropriate driving test. The term 'appropriate driving test' means an extended driving test where a person is convicted of an offence involving obligatory disqualification or an offence prescribed by the Secretary of State, or is disqualified under s. 35, and the ordinary driving test in any other circumstances. At the time of writing, the Secretary of State has not prescribed any circumstances, period or offences for the purpose of these provisions.

In any case not covered by the above paragraph, where a person is convicted of an offence involving obligatory endorsement, the court *may* order him to be disqualified until he passes the ordinary driving test (whether or not he has previously passed such a test).

Types of driving licences

The purpose of holding a driving licence is to be able to offer instant proof to a police officer of a qualification to drive a particular class of motor vehicle on a road.

In order to become qualified it is necessary to become used to driving motor vehicles on roads and to allow persons to gain the necessary experience, provisional licences are issued. Once a satisfactory degree of proficiency has been achieved and the test successfully completed, a full licence can be issued in respect of the category of vehicle concerned and any other categories which the regulations allow. The categories are generally as follows:

A	Motor bicycles (with or without sidecar).
B	Motor vehicles 'not exceeding' (n.e.) 3.5 tonnes and not more than eight seats in addition to the driver's seat (including trailer n.e. 750 kg).
B1	Motor tricycle n.e. 500 kg and with maximum design speed exceeding 50 kph.
C1	Goods vehicles exceeding 3.5 tonnes but n.e. 7.5 tonnes (including trailer n.e. 750 kg).
D1	Passenger vehicles (not used for hire or reward) with more than 8 seats but not more than 16 seats, in addition to the driver's seat (including trailer n.e. 750 kg).
B plus E	Combination of a motor vehicle in B and trailer exceeding 750 kg.
C1 plus E	Combination of a motor vehicle in C1 and trailer exceeding 750 kg where the maximum authorised mass of the combination does not exceed 8.25 tonnes.
D1 plus E	Combination of a motor vehicle in D1 and a trailer exceeding 750 kg
F	Agricultural tractor.
G	Road roller.
H	Track-laying vehicle.
K	Mowing machine or pedestrian-controlled vehicle.
L	Electrically propelled vehicle.
N	Vehicle exempt from excise – limited use on road.
P	Moped.

This satisfactorily deals with the British national who produces either a full or provisional licence to a police officer. Not all drivers on our roads today are British nationals, therefore, many drivers will produce a foreign document. The term 'convention permit' refers to a driving licence issued under the authority of a country outside the United Kingdom within the terms of the Motor Vehicles (International Circulation) Order 1975 as amended and issued in accordance with various international conventions on road traffic. The document will be headed 'International Driving Permit'.

A 'Domestic Driving Permit' is a document issued under the law of a country outside the United Kingdom authorising the holder to drive vehicles of a specified class or classes. It refers to a driving licence of that country.

Persons holding either of these documents or a 'British Forces Germany' (BFG) document may drive vehicles of the classes authorised for a period of 12 months from the last date of entry into the United Kingdom. EC residents who have the domestic driving permit of their own country or an international driving permit may drive any large goods vehicle or any large passenger-carrying vehicle if authorised to drive those categories of vehicle by their permit.

Other holders of such permits may only drive such vehicles brought temporarily into Great Britain. EU holders of relevant BFGs may drive any large passenger-carrying vehicle; non-EU holders may only drive such vehicles brought temporarily into Great Britain. The need for this legislation is quite obvious. As trade has become international and tourism a part of everyone's life, it would be ridiculous to insist that drivers took tests in each country which they visited or passed through. Licences of member States of the EU can be exchanged for UK licences if the EU citizen becomes normally resident in the United Kingdom, without a test being taken. This must be done before such person has been resident for more than one year. The 'one year rule' applies to any other foreign driver who is resident. He must take a test.

Provisional driving licence

The object of a provisional driving licence is to enable a person to drive a motor vehicle on a road, subject to certain conditions, so that he can gain the necessary experience and be given the necessary tuition to prepare him for a test by a traffic examiner, the passing of which entitles such a person to be granted a full driving licence for certain classes of vehicles, specified in the licence, e.g. entitled to drive motor vehicles of certain categories.

A provisional licence is granted by the Secretary of State for Transport and lasts for such period as may be prescribed. An ordinary driving licence, authorising its holder to drive motor vehicles of certain classes, shall also authorise its holder to drive motor vehicles of all other categories subject to the same conditions which apply to the holder of a provisional licence. Thus, a person who has an ordinary licence authorising him to drive motor cars but not motor cycles could use his ordinary driving licence as a provisional licence in order to learn to drive a motor cycle, providing he complies with the conditions applicable to the holder of a provisional licence. However, a full licence may not be treated as a provisional licence where the person is below the age required to drive, or in the case of a motor cycle, if the machine to be used is not a 'learner motor cycle' (not exceeding 125 cc) as defined by s. 97 of the Road Traffic Act 1988, or if the licence is restricted to specially adapted vehicles for the disabled, or for pedestrian-controlled vehicles only. A provisional licence does not authorise a person before he has passed a test of competence to drive, to drive on a road a motor bicycle except where he has successfully completed an approved training course for motor cyclists or is undergoing training on such a course and is driving a motor cycle on a road as part of the training. Certificates will be issued to those who have successfully completed such courses.

A person who held a provisional licence immediately before 1 December 1990 and who exchanged that licence for a full licence to drive vehicles of category B (small passenger and goods vehicles) may use his category B licence as a provisional licence to ride motor bicycles and may do so without having successfully completed an approved training course for motor cyclists provided that he has not since been disqualified until he passes an appropriate test. Persons who have been disqualified until they pass an appropriate motor cycle test who have previously passed a test on a moped or motor bicycle may also ride motor cycles on a road without having successfully completed an approved course for motor cyclists.

The test for solo motor cyclists is divided into two parts, Part I seeking to establish basic mastery over the machine. A learner motor cyclist is not authorised, before passing a test of competence to drive, to drive a motor bicycle on a road unless he has successfully completed an approved training course, unless that driving on a road is a part of that training course, or the driving is permitted by regulations. Nor will he be able to take a test in Part II unless he furnishes the prescribed certificate of completion of an approved training course for motor cyclists, either with his application for a test, or to the person who is to conduct it.

Part II examines road craft. If a test for a category A motor cycle is not taken within two years as an 'L' driver, a further provisional licence may be refused. Provisional licences for motor cycles are limited to two years. Renewal shall be refused for one year, where renewal is sought for motor cycles of category A, that is those other than tricycles or mopeds.

Conditions applicable to a provisional licence holder

These conditions are set out in the Motor Vehicles (Driving Licences) Regulations 1987, and can be summarised as follows:

(a) He should not drive or ride a motor vehicle otherwise than under the supervision of a qualified driver who is present with him in or on the vehicle, except
   (i) when undergoing a test or a test of competence to drive; or
   (ii) when driving a vehicle (not being a motor car) not constructed or adapted to carry more than one person; or
   (iii) when driving an electrically propelled vehicle constructed or adapted to carry only one person, constructed or adapted for the carriage of goods or burden of any description, and not exceeding 815 kg unladen weight; or
   (iv) when driving a road roller the unladen weight of which does not exceed 3050 kg being a vehicle constructed or adapted for the carriage of goods or burden of any description; or
   (v) when riding a motor bicycle whether or not having attached thereto a sidecar.

(b) He should not drive or ride a motor vehicle unless there is displayed in a conspicuous manner on the front and the back 'L' plates of the prescribed form and colour.

(c) He should not drive or ride a motor vehicle while it is drawing a trailer, except
   (i) when driving an agricultural tractor; or
   (ii) when driving an articulated vehicle.

(d) In the case of a motor bicycle not having a sidecar attached, he should not ride the vehicle while carrying on it any other person, except when he has passed a test authorising him to hold a full licence. (This does not apply to a tandem pedal cycle with an auxiliary engine.)

(e) He should not ride a motor cycle having two wheels only, unless it is a learner

197

motor cycle. 'Learner motor cycle' means a motor cycle which does not exceed 125 cc. There are other additional provisions in respect of those first used on or after 1 January 1982, to include those propelled by electric power and those with certain power outputs measured in kilowatts, within those which may be ridden.

Any breach of the conditions constitutes an offence of driving a motor vehicle on a road otherwise than in accordance with the licence, contrary to the Road Traffic Act 1988, s. 87(1). This is an opportune time to mention a practical point. When a police officer discovers an offence of driving without a driving licence and no licence could have been granted to the offender or the only type of licence that could have been granted to him is a provisional licence, the police officer should include in his report whether or not at the time of the offence there was any breach of the conditions applicable to the holder of a provisional licence. The reason for this additional information is that if such a person is convicted of driving otherwise than in accordance with a driving licence, the magistrates' court has a discretion whether or not to order disqualification and is obliged to order endorsement of any licence or subsequent licence, if the conditions applicable to learner drivers were not being observed. A qualified driver for the purpose of these regulations is a person who holds a full licence to drive the motor vehicle being driven by the learner, and who, except in the case of a member of the armed forces of the Crown acting in the course of his duties, is at least 21 years of age and has held such a licence for at least three years.

Examination of driving licences

The following particulars should be noted: the type of licence (provisional or full), the serial number; the driver number which indicates date of birth and sex of holder; the name of the person to whom the licence was issued; date of issue; date of expiry; the categories of vehicles which may be driven and the signature of the holder. Licence holders must sign their licence in ink forthwith. They must also notify any change of address forthwith. Offences are committed if they do not.

Defective eyesight

If a person drives a motor vehicle on a road while his eyesight is such (whether through a defect which cannot be or is not for the time being sufficiently corrected) that he cannot comply with the eyesight requirements (read a number plate at a distance of 20.5 m), he commits an offence.

A police officer having reason to suspect that a person with defective eyesight is driving a motor vehicle may require the driver to submit to a test to ascertain whether, using no other means of correction than he used at the time of driving, he can comply with the requirements as to eyesight. Refusal to submit to a test is an offence against s. 96 of the Road Traffic Act 1988. It should be noted that the test must be carried out in good daylight, and it is usual to request the assistance of the traffic branch to arrange for such a test to be carried out.

Sections 173, 174 and 175 of the Road Traffic Act 1988 deal with the various offences of forgery and false statements in relation to certain documents, which include driving licences and certificates of insurance or documents purporting to be evidence of insurance, and we will deal with the various offences in order.

Section 173 states that a person shall be guilty of an offence, who, with intent to deceive:

(a) forges, or alters, or uses or lends to, or allows to be used by any other person, a document to which this section applies;

(b) makes or has in his possession any document or other thing so closely resembling a document or other thing to which this section applies as to be calculated to deceive.

The most common form of this offence is when a person produces a driving licence or certificate of insurance relating to another person, intending to pass it off as his own. It can be seen that in such circumstances there may be an offence of 'lending or allowing to be used with intent to deceive' as well as 'using with intent to deceive'.

Section 174 deals with false statements and withholding material information. The relevant provisions are set out below:

'(1) A person shall be guilty of an offence who knowingly makes a false statement for the purpose of:

(a) obtaining the grant of a licence under any part of this Act to himself or any other person (this includes a driving licence); or

(b) preventing the grant of any licence; or

(c) procuring the imposition of a condition or limitation in relation to such licence [s. 174(1)].

(2) A person shall be guilty of an offence who makes a false statement or withholds any material information for the purpose of obtaining the issue:

(a) of a certificate of insurance or certificate of security; or

(b) of any document issued under regulations made by the Secretary of State which may be produced in lieu of a certificate of insurance or a certificate of security' [s. 174(5)].'

The question whether there is any gain or advantage derived from the making of a false statement is immaterial. Where a person whose name is 'Jones' shows another name, e.g. 'Brown' on a proposal form for insurance purposes he is guilty of an offence under this section.

The final offence under this heading deals with the issue of false documents, and by virtue of s. 175 of the Act a person is guilty of an offence if he issues a certificate of insurance, certificate of security, or any other document which may be produced in lieu of such certificates as evidence of insurance, if the document or certificate so issued is, to his knowledge, false in a material particular. The accused must know that the document or certificate is false. The most common form of this offence is where a person issues a cover note for insurance and back dates the issue of the cover note, falsely showing that a vehicle was covered prior to the note being issued. The section also covers test certificates.

Police powers

If a constable has reasonable cause to believe that a document which is produced to him under the provisions of the Road Traffic Act 1988 is a document in relation to which an offence has been committed under s. 173, 174 or 175 of the Act, he may seize the document.

Section 164 of the Road Traffic Act 1988 authorises a constable to require a person to state his date of birth in circumstances which are now prescribed by the Motor Vehicles (Driving Licences) Regulations 1987:

(a) where that person fails to produce forthwith for examination his driving licence on being required to do so by a constable; or

(b) where, on being so required, that person produces a licence which the constable has reason to suspect:
  (i)   was not granted to that person, or
  (ii) was granted to him in error, or
  (iii) contains an alteration in its particulars made with intent to deceive; or

(c) where, on being required, that person produces a licence in which the driver number has been altered, erased or defaced;

(d) in the case of the supervisor of a learner driver; where the constable has reason to suspect that he is under 21 years of age.

It is an offence to fail to state a date of birth when so required.

Insurance

(1) *The requirement*

The purpose of requiring every user of a motor vehicle on a road or public place to be insured is to ensure that monetary compensation is available for any injury or damage resulting from the use of a motor vehicle on a road or other public place.

Section 143(1) of the Road Traffic Act 1988 reads:

'Subject to the provisions of this part of the Act –
  (a) a person must not use a motor vehicle on a road unless there is in force in relation to the use of the vehicle by that person such a policy of insurance or such a security in respect of third party risks as complies with the requirements of this part of this Act, and
  (b) a person must not cause or permit any other person to use a motor vehicle on a road unless there is in force in relation to the use of the vehicle by that other person such a policy of insurance or such a security in respect of a third party risks as complies with the requirements of this part of the Act.
A person who acts in contravention of these provisions is guilty of an offence.'

A policy must be issued by an authorised insurer and must provide the minimum third party cover for such person, persons or classes of persons as may be specified in it in respect of the death or bodily injury to any person (other than the driver) or damage to property up to a maximum value of £250 000, caused by, or arising out of the use of the vehicle, as well as provide for emergency treatment. It must also cover a policy holder against any liability which may be incurred in respect of the use

200

within the territory of any member of the EU of a vehicle normally based in Great Britain, according to the law on compulsory motor insurance against liability in that State or, if it would give higher cover, the law which would be applicable if the vehicle was used in Great Britain when the event occurred.

It is common to find that the use of a vehicle in particular circumstances, or by a particular person, is not covered by the certificate of insurance produced. If the certificate refers to social, domestic, and pleasure purposes only, then the policy-holder is not covered, if he uses the vehicle for his business. If it covers the policy-holder and his spouse, then this is precisely what it means and no one else may drive. It is the terms of the certificate which are important, as the test is whether or not the terms of the certificate cover the use, not whether the insurance company says it would have accepted the risk. Vehicles are frequently driven by persons not covered by the policy-holder's certificate, but they may be covered by their own certificate of insurance, which allows them to drive other vehicles which they do not own or hire.

The test to be applied is concerned with whether or not there is a binding contract of insurance in force and not with the opinion of insurers as to whether or not they are liable. When a man obtained a cover note without disclosing that he was disqualified from driving, it was held that this contract was not void from the outset, but merely voidable and that until the insurers took steps to void the contract, it remained in force.

'Use' in relation to insurance offences may be interpreted in its widest sense as previously discussed. It is not necessarily something done by a driver, or even an owner and a group of persons, if acting in concert in relation to their usage of a motor vehicle they may be using without insurance. There is a 'use' for the purposes of motor vehicle insurance, if there is any element of controlling, managing or operating the vehicle as a vehicle. However, there may also be a use where a vehicle is parked even if, because of some defect, the vehicle is incapable of moving, for example, where the brakes are seized.

It is worth noting that the Road Traffic Act 1988 requires, *inter alia*, that judgment in respect of third-party liabilities must be met by authorised insurers even where the vehicle has been illegally used. Where insurance is limited to use by specified persons, judgments in respect of use by other persons shall be met as if the policy related to 'all persons'. However, although insurers must meet such liabilities, the test in relation to offences of uninsured use is concerned with the risks which are covered by the terms of the policy of insurance.

A UK motor vehicle insurance covers the legal requirements in relation to use in any EU country or in countries with which we have an agreement. The use of vehicles from those countries in the UK is similarly covered, as is the use of Northern Ireland vehicles if they are properly insured in Northern Ireland. Other foreign visitors must have an international insurance card, known as the 'green card insurance'.

(2) *Permitting uninsured use*

Where a person borrows a motor vehicle subject to an implied limitation, of which he knows, and he uses the vehicle outside that limitation, the use is uninsured if the policy demands that the use was with the consent of the owner.

Where a person permits another to have the use of his vehicle subject to an express condition that sufficient insurance cover is obtained in relation to its use, he *may* or *may not* permit the use of the vehicle without insurance. The situation is that, if the condition is *directly* communicated to the person who uses the vehicle without insurance, the person imposing the condition does not permit uninsured use. This is quite clear; a person cannot be said to have permitted something which he has expressly forbidden. However, the Divisional Court has ruled that if such a condition as to use has not been *directly* communicated to the user but has been passed on by someone else (as would occur if the vehicle was borrowed by A, but subsequently driven by B who had not spoken to the owner), the owner will be guilty of permitting uninsured use by B. The rule appears to be that any condition which would rule out 'permitting' must be directly between the two parties concerned.

(3) *Particular use of vehicles and trailers*

A policy which covers social, domestic and pleasure purposes only does not cover business use. However, giving a lift to a friend who is 'on business' does not amount to a business use by the user of the vehicle. Most non-business policies will exclude use 'for hire or reward' and it may be that a vehicle used to assist a friend to move personal possessions is used for hire or reward if payment is made in respect of that use. While payments made to cover expenses may be considered to be outside the term 'hire or reward' the dividing line will often be a fine one.

Policies frequently permit a person to drive with the permission of the policy-holder if such driver 'holds or has held a licence to drive' and is not disqualified. If that person has at any time held a licence, whether full or provisional, it is sufficient in law to satisfy that requirement. It may be that on other occasions, a policy will refer to a person holding or having held a licence in respect of that category of vehicle, which is more restrictive.

In Great Britain, the use of trailers does not expressly need to be covered in respect of third-party risks. This cover is essential in other EU countries. In practice, in most cases in Great Britain, the use of trailers is covered and in any case, such 'use' would appear to be within the 'use' of the motor vehicle. Any relevant injury or damage caused by a trailer must be due to the use of the towing motor vehicle on a road.

When a person is apprehended for taking a motor vehicle without consent it is possible that his own motor vehicle insurance will cover him for use of the vehicle concerned. It is the terms of the policy which are important. If the policy covers the use by him of another vehicle not owned by him or hired to him under a hire purchase agreement, the policy will cover such use even though the vehicle has been illegally taken. It would be different if the use covered was similar but 'with the consent of the owner of that other vehicle'.

Proof of insurance

Depending on the type of insurance a person has, any of the following documents may be produced as evidence that the use of a vehicle was lawfully covered for the purpose of s. 143 of the Road Traffic Act 1988:

(a) A certificate of motor insurance signed by the insuring company and containing the date of commencement and expiry, the person or persons entitled to drive, the limitations as to use, and a reference to the vehicle covered by the certificate.

(b) A cover note issued by an insurance company, pending the issue of a certificate of insurance, is valid proof of insurance.

(c) An international motor insurance card.

(d) A Northern Ireland certificate of insurance.

(e) Any EU certificate of insurance is valid in the UK.

There are other, quite rare documents, which may be held by large undertakings.

(a) A certificate of security signed by an authorised person and containing the name of the holder, the date of commencement and expiry, and any conditions to which the certificate of security is subject.

(b) A certificate signed by the owner of the motor vehicle, or by a person authorised by him, that the owner has deposited the sum of £500 000 with the Attorney-General of the Supreme Court (referred to as a certificate of deposit).

(c) In relation to a vehicle owned by a specified body, a police authority, or the Receiver for the Metropolitan Police District, a certificate of ownership signed by an authorised person of that body, authority, or Receiver as the case may be.

Exemptions from insurance

The use, on a road or public place, of a motor vehicle which falls into one of the following classifications does not require to be covered by a policy of insurance. These vehicles are:

(a) a vehicle owned by a local authority at a time when it is being driven under the owner's control;

(b) a vehicle owned by a police authority, or the Receiver for the Metropolitan Police District, at a time when it is being driven under the owner's control;

(c) a vehicle when it is being driven for police purposes by or under the direction of a police constable or a person employed by a police authority or Receiver as the case may be;

(d) a vehicle being used for salvage purposes pursuant to Part IX of the Merchant Shipping Act 1984;

(e) a vehicle being used for the purpose of it being provided under a direction of the Army Act 1955 or the Air Force Act 1955;

(f) a vehicle which is owned by a Health Service body, an ambulance owned by a Health Service Trust or a vehicle made available by the Secretary of State to any person, body or local authority in pursuance of s. 23 or 26 of the National Health Service Act 1977 when used as authorised;

(g) a vehicle which is made available by the Secretary of State to any local authority, education authority or voluntary organisation in Scotland in pursuance of s. 15 or 16 of the National Health Service (Scotland) Act 1978 when used as authorised.

It should be noted, however, that although a vehicle being driven for a police purpose by or under the direction of a police constable (see (c) above) does not require to be covered by a policy of insurance, the driver will be liable for any injury or damage caused by the use of such a motor vehicle on a road. Most police forces carry motor vehicle insurance and have standing instructions concerning police officers authorised to drive various classes of vehicles. Caution should, therefore, be exercised when stolen or abandoned motor vehicles are driven by police officers who, if not specifically authorised to drive such vehicles, may find themselves personally liable for any injury or damage caused arising out of the use of the vehicle on a road under their direction.

Particulars to note

When a certificate of insurance is examined the following factors should be checked: the number of the certificate; date of issue; date of expiry; the name and address of the insurance company; the authorised uses of the vehicle as measured against the use to which it is being put; the vehicle which is insured and the persons entitled to drive the insured vehicle.

Defence

However, if a person is charged with using a motor vehicle without being covered by a policy of insurance he shall not be convicted if he proves that the vehicle does not belong to him and was not in his possession under a contract of hiring or of loan, that he was using the vehicle in the course of his employment, and that he neither knew nor had reason to believe that there was not in force in relation to the vehicle a valid policy of insurance or security. This provision is to safeguard a person who, if employed as a driver, should not be made responsible for the insurance in relation to his employer's vehicles.

Test certificate

The increased use of motorways places greater stress upon motor vehicles, and the consequences of mechanical defects occurring in vehicles using these roads can be so serious that legislation was introduced to ensure that older motor vehicles were examined from time to time and that no major defects existed which were likely to make their presence on a road a danger both to the driver and to others using the road.

Section 45 of the Road Traffic Act 1988 authorises the Secretary of State for Transport to make regulations setting out the requirements for such examinations. He is permitted to authorise particular persons to carry out these tests, and approved testing stations display a sign consisting of three white triangles on a blue background, carrying the words 'Vehicle Testing Station'.

A person offends against the Road Traffic Act 1988, s. 47(1), if he uses a motor vehicle, or causes or permits it to be used on a road, without an appropriate test certificate.

Examination of motor vehicles

The Motor Vehicles (Tests) Regulations 1981 require that with effect from 1 January 1993 specified parts of motor cars and heavy motor cars in Class IV, that is all vehicles except those falling within Classes I to III (motor cycles and light vehicles) or Classes V or VI (large passenger-carrying vehicles for more than 12 passengers, public service vehicles, etc.) or Class VII (goods vehicles of design gross weight exceeding 3000 kg but not exceeding 3500 kg) be tested. These include wheels and tyres, steering, audible warning instrument, front position lamps, rear retro reflectors, stop lamps, direction indicators, rear registration plate lamps, rear fog lamps, hazard warning signal devices, braking, glass and field of vision, mirrors, windscreen cleaning, fuel tanks and pipes, seat belts and anchorages, exhaust (general condition), exhaust (emissions), vehicle identification number, structure and suspension (body, chassis, subframe, mounting or suspension which prejudices steering, braking or seat belt mountings or may otherwise cause danger), seats, doors and other openings to the extent that their condition may cause danger, and registration marks.

The tests are even more extensive for vehicles which fall within Classes V and VI including speedometers, speed limiters and speed limiter plates, in addition to examination of many interior fittings. Class VII vehicles are inspected in a similar but extended fashion to those in Class IV, the test including such items are tyre loads and speed ratings.

When a test certificate is refused, the examiner must give a notice of refusal stating the reasons for failure. He must also provide in relation to all vehicles, other than motor cycles, an inspection check list on an approved form, giving details of the examination. Test certificates must be embossed by the stamp of the examiner or council on whose behalf it is issued. There is a right of appeal to the Secretary of State for Transport.

Motor vehicles requiring test certificates

Motor vehicles which are more than three years old, following the date of their original registration, must be examined annually and may only be used on a road if a test certificate is issued. On some occasions it is their date of manufacture which is taken into consideration if the vehicle has been used for some time before registration. This might occur when the vehicle has been used in the United Kingdom by one of Her Majesty's Services and is not registered until sold by auction to a private individual. For these purposes, date of manufacture is taken to be the last day of the year in which the vehicle was finally assembled or modified. The provisions apply to passenger vehicles with not more than eight seats, excluding the driver's seat; goods vehicles, the design gross weight of which does not exceed 3,500 kg; dual-purpose vehicles; motor cycles (including three-wheelers and mopeds); and motor caravans. Motor vehicles used for the carriage of passengers and with more than eight seats, excluding the driver's seat (mainly public service vehicles), taxis and ambulances should be tested when they are one year old and annually thereafter.

It is important, therefore, that when a person is reported for an offence of using a motor vehicle without there being a test certificate in force, the date of the vehicle's first registration is obtained. This will be recorded in the vehicle registration document and at DVLA, Swansea.

Exemptions

Certain vehicles are exempt from these provisions, and on a number of occasions they are exempt because they are subject to other testing requirements, or are owned by public services which have their own rules concerning inspection. Examples of such vehicles are goods vehicles (most of which are subject to ss. 49–53 of the 1988 Act and the Goods Vehicles (Plating and Testing) Regulations 1988) and taxis licensed to ply for hire, which are subject to local inspection.

Vehicles temporarily in Great Britain (but only for the first year of their stay) are also exempt from these requirements. Vehicles in respect of which a Northern Ireland Test Certificate has been issued are also exempt during its validity.

Special exemptions

In certain circumstances the use of vehicles which require a test certificate is permitted without such a certificate being in force, but such use is limited and is always associated with the test itself. It is quite possible that the owner of a motor vehicle will forget that an annual test is due and, if there were no exceptions to the rule concerning use, he could not drive the vehicle to a testing station on realising his omission. Use of vehicles without a test certificate is, therefore, permitted when going to, coming from, or during a pre-arranged test. The test must have been booked. On occasions a vehicle may fail the test and it may be necessary to remove it to some place for repair, and in these circumstances it may be driven directly to that place. If the owner decides to scrap the vehicle, it may be lawfully towed to a breaker's yard.

Police officers and customs officials must occasionally remove vehicles under statutory powers, for example, when abandoned on roads or when seized; and test certificates are unnecessary in such circumstances.

Contents of certificate

The form of test certificate is not set out within the regulations. It shall be in a form supplied by the Secretary of State. Each certificate will generally have a serial number and contain a statement to the effect that the vehicle complied with the statutory requirements on the date of the examination. The registration number, vehicle testing station number, date of issue, date of expiry, and the signature of the person issuing the certificate are currently shown. If the previous certificate was out of date at the time of examination, the number of that certificate may be included. The testing station name and address is embossed on the certificate.

It is an offence to use, cause, or permit to be used, a motor vehicle more than three years old (from the date of its first registration) on a road without a current test certificate.

Evidence of first registration

As the offences of using, causing, or permitting a motor vehicle to be used on a road without a current test certificate apply to motor vehicles of age decided upon by the Secretary of State for Transport (currently three years old), it is important in each case to prove the date of the original registration of the vehicle. This information can be obtained from the registration document, and the Motor Vehicles (Registration and Licensing) Regulations 1971 require the registered owner of a mechanically propelled vehicle, in respect of which a vehicle registration document has been issued, to produce it for inspection at any reasonable time if required to do so by a police officer or a local taxation officer. In the event of such a document having been lost, the owner must apply for a duplicate.

Police powers; production of driving licences and other documents

Sections 164 and 165 of the Road Traffic Act 1988 give a constable or vehicle examiner power to demand production of driving licences and their counterparts, insurance and test certificates, from any person:

(a) driving a motor vehicle on a road; or
(b) whom a constable or vehicle examiner has reasonable cause to believe to have been the driver of a motor vehicle at a time when an accident occurred owing to its presence on a road; or
(c) whom a constable or vehicle examiner has reasonable cause to believe to have committed an offence in relation to the use of a motor vehicle on a road.

In addition, a constable or vehicle examiner may require a person who supervises the holder of a provisional driving licence, in the circumstances described at (a) to (c), to produce his driving licence and its counterpart.

Where a constable is demanding production of a driving licence under these provisions the person concerned must, in prescribed circumstances, state his date of birth. The prescribed circumstances are those involving that person's failure to produce his driving licence forthwith or where the constable has reason to suspect that the licence was not granted to that person, or was granted to that person in error, or that it contains an alteration made with intent to deceive, or contains a driver number which has been altered, removed or defaced.

The purpose of the production of a driving licence is to enable the constable or vehicle examiner to ascertain the name and address of the holder of the licence, its date of issue and the authority by which it was issued. A person so required to produce his certificate of insurance or test certificate may also be required to give his name and address and the name and address of the owner of the vehicle.

The 'counterpart' to a driving licence means a document in such a form as the Secretary of State may determine, issued with the licence, containing such information as he determines and designed for the endorsement of particulars relating to the licence.

A person so required to produce such documents who fails to do so is guilty of an offence, but a person shall not be convicted of such an offence by reason only of failure to produce any such document if in proceedings against him for any such offence he shows that:

(a) within seven days after the production was required, that document (and in the case of a licence, its counterpart) was produced at such police station as may have been specified by him at the time when its production was required (in person in the case of a driving licence); or

(b) it was produced there as soon as reasonably practicable (in person in the case of a driving licence); or

(c) it was not reasonably practicable for it to be produced there before the day on which the proceedings were commenced.

The laying of the information shall, for the purposes of these requirements, be treated as the commencement of the proceedings.

The usual practice, where a person fails to produce his vehicle documents as required by these sections, on the demand of a constable, is to issue him with a form HO/RT 1, but this only represents police procedure and a failure to issue a person with a form HO/RT 1 does not affect the liability of the person concerned should he fail to produce in accordance with a police requirement. However, it is not an offence to fail to produce a driving licence if requested to do so by a constable for the purpose of issuing a fixed penalty notice.

These offences are committed *at the time of the demand* which is made in relation to production. In the event of a subsequent non-production, the driver should be charged with driving a motor vehicle on a road without having such a document in force *and* with the offence of non-production. It will then be for him to prove to the court that such a document, or documents, was in force at the time as these are matters particularly within his knowledge. If he produces the relevant document(s) to the court, he will still be convicted of an offence of non-production should the circumstances described above not apply in his case.

There is no power to require the driver of an invalid carriage to produce a certificate of insurance or a test certificate, as these provisions do not apply to such vehicles.

Section 164 of the Road Traffic Act 1988 allows the production of a receipt for a driving licence in place of a driving licence subject to the same conditions as to production which are applied to the licence itself, provided that if the person producing such a receipt is required to do so, he produces the licence and its counterpart in person, immediately on its return, at such police station as may have been specified. Receipts are issued under the authority of s. 56 of the Road Traffic Offenders Act 1988 where a licence is surrendered within the fixed penalty procedure.

Where a provisional licence has been produced to a constable by a person driving a motor bicycle and the constable has reasonable cause to believe that the holder was not driving that motor bicycle as part of the training being provided on a training course for motor cyclists, the constable may require him to produce the prescribed certificate of a training course for motor cyclists. The provisions at (a) to (c) as set out above apply to such production.

A traffic warden is empowered by s. 164 to require the production of a driving licence where the offence is one concerned with stopping on a pedestrian crossing or leaving a vehicle in a dangerous position and, where employed to perform functions in connection with the custody of vehicles removed because they were illegally, obstructively or dangerously parked, and he has reasonable cause to believe that the offence was committed by that person.

Road vehicles – construction and use

The first horseless carriages to be manufactured were not subject to any form of control during the production process. This is not difficult to imagine, as we have already traced the processes which bring about the need for new kinds of laws. The coming of the first motor cars made necessary legal controls to ensure the safety of their drivers and that of other road users. Speed limits were so low that it was a simple matter to require a man to walk ahead of the vehicle carrying a red flag, but such measures were likely to prevent the introduction of the motor vehicle as an efficient form of transport, rather than to control its use in such a way that it could be both properly developed and used. The Road Vehicles (Construction and Use) Regulations 1986 now regulate the use of motor vehicles and trailers on roads, their construction, equipment, and the conditions under which they may be used. Their purpose is to provide for the safety of drivers and other road users.

Many modern vehicles are exempt from various provisions of the 1986 Regulations because they comply with certain international requirements in relation to the construction and use of motor vehicles. The requirements are commonly referred to as 'Type Approval' requirements. When vehicles are so exempt, this is stated in the particular regulation which refers to the alternative standards which they must meet.

Construction and use offences: general

The Road Traffic Act 1988, ss. 40A, 41A, 41B provide various offences which may be committed in relation to the use of a vehicle in a dangerous condition and/or in contravention of the regulations.

Section 40A makes it an offence for a person to use, cause or permit another to use a motor vehicle or a trailer on a road when:

(a) the condition of the motor vehicle or trailer, or of its accessories or equipment, or
(b) the purpose for which it is used, or
(c) the number of passengers carried by it, or the manner in which they are carried, or
(d) the weight, position or distribution of its load, or the manner in which it is secured,

is such that the use of the motor vehicle or trailer involves danger of injury to any person.

Section 41A makes it an offence for a person to:

(a) contravene or fail to comply with a construction and use requirement as to brakes, steering gear or tyres; or
(b) use on a road a motor vehicle or trailer which does not comply with such a requirement, or cause or permit a motor vehicle or trailer to be so used.

Offences against ss. 40A and 41A carry discretional disqualification; the endorsement of three penalty points is obligatory.

Section 41B punishes offences in relation to weight. A person who:

(a) contravenes or fails to comply with a construction and use requirement as to any description of weight applicable to
  (i) a goods vehicle, or
  (ii) a motor vehicle or trailer adapted to carry more than eight passengers, or
(b) uses on a road a vehicle which does not comply with such a requirement, or causes or permits a vehicle to be so used, commits an offence against the section.

Section 41B(2) provides a defence where the alleged contravention relates to any description of weight applicable to a goods vehicle. It provides that in such a case it is a defence to prove either that the vehicle was going to or coming from a weighbridge or, where the relevant weight limit is not exceeded by more than 5 per cent, that the weight was not exceeded at the time of loading and that the load had not been added to.

Section 42 is concerned with the contravention of a construction and use requirement other than those relating to brakes, steering gear or tyres, or those relating to weight, which are dealt with by s. 41A or 41B. It provides that a person who:

(a) contravenes or fails to comply with such a requirement; or
(b) uses on a road a motor vehicle or trailer which does not comply with such a requirement, or causes or permits a motor vehicle or trailer to be so used, commits an offence.

Those who contravene s. 41B or 42 are not liable to disqualification or to obligatory endorsement under these sections.

An offence of using on a road a trailer which does not comply with regulations is an offence distinct from that of using a defective motor vehicle.

Since the relevant provisions are concerned with persons who *use, cause* or *permit* the use of motor vehicles or trailers in contravention of the regulations, it is important that police officers understand the meaning of these terms.

To use

The term 'use' should be given its ordinary meaning and indicates absolute liability by persons who are using the motor vehicle. It is quite obvious that the driver is using the vehicle, but if the journey is being made on an employer's business, the employer is also using it, although he may be many miles distant at the time. The term 'absolute liability' means that we must usually let the facts speak for themselves; if the vehicle is being driven and there is a defect existing in it, then persons using it are guilty of an offence and it is not necessary to prove that they were aware of the defect at the time. However, the High Court has advised that in circumstances in which a sudden defect occurs, such as a brake failure, the police should not prosecute. The rule appears to be that if the user is morally guiltless and has not been negligent, no charge should be preferred. An example of the strict liability of users is given by the following circumstance. A driver was convicted of using a motor vehicle with a load which had not been properly secured, although he took no part in the loading, which was carried out by loaders employed for the purpose. A vehicle is in 'use' when it is stationary on a road for loading or unloading. It has also been held that it is in use even when left with a defective engine and without a battery or petrol, on the grounds that it could still be moved by pushing or releasing the brake. It is, therefore, plain that the term 'use' does not imply that the vehicle must be in motion, or have previously been in motion within a short period of time.

An employee used a motor vehicle with defective brakes. Although the owner had told him to take it to a garage whenever it required maintenance, it was held that as the vehicle was being used on the owner's business, he was guilty of using it with defective brakes as the Construction and Use Regulations generally impose absolute liability upon those contravening them. This decision provides a good summary of instances in which persons may be alleged to be using a motor vehicle in contravention of the regulations.

Perhaps the clearest indication of the limitation of charges of 'using' was given when the owner of a stock car was convicted at a magistrates' court of seven offences contrary to the Road Vehicles (Construction and Use) Regulations. There was no evidence to show that the driver of the car was a servant of the owner and it was held that only the driver and his employer could be said to 'use' the vehicle. The Lord Chief Justice said that when an employer–servant relationship could not be proved, a charge of 'permitting' would be correct.

To cause

Judges of the High Court have suggested that the term 'causing' as well as the term 'permitting' deal with offences of being an accessory or aider and abettor, and in circumstances in which one is considering the position of the aider or abettor in respect of Construction and Use offences, one of these terms will fit the appropriate circumstances.

The term 'cause' suggests that the person 'causing' has some authority over the person connected. The person charged with such an offence must have had the necessary authority to cause the vehicle to be used, and must have directly or indirectly ordered or directed the use of the vehicle. If an employee uses a vehicle without authority, the employer has neither caused nor permitted its use as he has no guilty knowledge, which is now recognised to be essential in such cases. Such guilty knowledge may be proved by showing that he knew of the defect in the vehicle, or was wilfully blind towards his responsibilities. There must be some evidence linking the person charged, more or less directly, with the use of the vehicle on the particular occasion. Where a manager was responsible for five vehicle depots, at each of which there was a vehicle superintendent, he was found not guilty of causing it to be used in a defective condition, having no opportunity to exercise local control.

It is also possible for the driver of a vehicle to be charged with offences of 'causing' in certain circumstances, as some offences can only be committed by persons causing or permitting them. A bus driver who left his bus and reported off duty without handing over to his relief driver was convicted of causing it to stand so as to cause unnecessary obstruction. A driver who is towing another vehicle is causing it to be used.

To permit

The term 'permit' covers instances in which either a general or a particular permission has been given to use the vehicle. The owner, or any person who has control on the owner's behalf – for example, a company manager – can permit the use of a vehicle. It is necessary to prove that the use of the vehicle in its defective condition was permitted by a responsible officer of the company, and this can be done by allowing it to be used in a known defective condition, or by closing the eyes to the possibility of such use.

A vehicle belonging to a company left its premises in good condition and, while out of the control of the responsible officers of the company, the crew coupled up a trailer in such a manner that the brakes were defective. It was held that the company was not guilty of 'permitting' the use of the vehicle with defective brakes as there was no evidence of any kind of permission by a responsible officer of the company. The observation was made, however, that as the vehicle was on company business at the time, the company could be said to be 'using' it. Similarly, where a man was the owner of a lorry driven on a road by his employee while the brakes were defective , it was held that for a charge of permitting to succeed there must be proof of actual knowledge or recklessness on the part of the owner. It has been held that the essence of 'permitting' offences is knowledge, and when such knowledge cannot be proved directly, there must be sufficient proof that the person charged had ignored the obvious or there had been recklessness as to whether it was allowed to occur. In 1972 the High Court set aside a conviction, the circumstances of which were that a company had been found guilty of permitting a vehicle to be used with inefficient brakes, in that the managing director should have ensured that the vehicle was lubricated more frequently than at four-weekly intervals and that he should have ensured that it was done correctly. The company employed an experienced foreman fitter, and it was held that the manager had not been sufficiently reckless to justify a charge of permitting.

The position appears to be that if an employee can be shown to be negligent, it is not sufficient to assume that responsible officers of the company are aware of this and, therefore, guilty of permitting. In certain circumstances, if responsibility for maintenance is delegated to an unskilled employee, the officers of the company may be liable.

In relation to offences under the Road Vehicles (Construction and Use) Regulations 1986, charges of permitting should be restricted to instances in which it can be shown that responsible officers of the company were aware of the condition of the vehicle or had closed their eyes to the obvious. Employers are not necessarily guilty of permitting use in instances in which the defect is due to the negligence of a skilled mechanic. Charges of 'using' are better made when the vehicle is being used by a servant on his master's business.

Vehicle classification

The Road Vehicles (Construction and Use) Regulations make references to all forms of motor vehicles but make special references to dual purpose vehicles and motor cars. These terms have already been considered but it will assist understanding to remember that dual purpose vehicles can be either shooting brakes or four wheel drive vehicles and that the term 'motor car' embraces certain goods vehicles as well as passenger-carrying vehicles. In brief they are:

(a) *Dual purpose vehicle.* A vehicle constructed or adapted to carry both passengers and goods and of weight unladen not exceeding 2040 kg which is either:
   (i) constructed according to certain specifications with regard to roof, seats and windows; or
   (ii) is such that all wheels are capable of being driven (Land Rover type).

(b) *Motor car.* A mechanically propelled vehicle (not being a motor cycle) or invalid carriage which is constructed itself to carry a load or passengers and the weight of which unladen:
   (i) if it constructed solely for the carriage of passengers and their effects and is adapted to carry not more than seven passengers exclusive of the driver and does not exceed 3050 kg;
   (ii) a goods vehicle having an unladen weight not exceeding 3050 kg; or
   (iii) in any other case, has an unladen weight not exceeding 2540 kg (for example, if it did not have pneumatic tyres).

Construction and maintenance of vehicles

The Road Vehicles (Construction and Use) Regulations 1986 create offences in relation to the fitting and maintenance of parts and accessories of motor vehicles. We will examine the provisions of these regulations which create offences most commonly dealt with by police officers.

Audible warning instrument

The regulations deal with the requirements in relation to the fitting of a horn to motor vehicles and also place restrictions upon the use of such instruments in certain circumstances.

(1) *Fitting of horn and its use*

All motor vehicles, which have a maximum speed of more than 20 mph, or in the case of an agricultural vehicle, if it is being driven at more than 20 mph, require a horn. In recent years there has been a tendency to fit warning instruments which play the first notes of 'Colonel Bogey' or other ear-catching tunes, and although this will still be lawful in the case of older vehicles, vehicles first used on or after 1 August 1973 must have a horn which gives a continuous and uniform sound.

Motor vehicles used by emergency services, all of which are specified in the regulations and include police, fire brigade, ambulance, and the emergency vehicles

213

used by other services for fire fighting or rescue operations, may be fitted with gongs, bells, sirens or two-tone horns. Vehicles used for the sale of goods from the vehicle, e.g. ice cream vans, may be fitted with an instrument, other than a two-tone horn, to advertise their presence. They must, additionally, have a normal warning instrument fitted. Bells, gongs or sirens may be fitted to a vehicle if their purpose is to prevent theft or attempted theft of the vehicle or its contents. They may also be fitted to large passenger-carrying vehicles if the purpose is to summon help for the driver, conductor or an inspector. Such anti-theft alarms must be fitted with a device which switches the alarm off after a period of five minutes.

It is an offence for any person to sound or cause or permit the sounding of the warning instrument of a motor vehicle which is stationary on a road at any time other than when there is danger due to another moving vehicle on or near the road. Horns shall not be sounded between the hours of 23.30 and 0700 hours on a moving vehicle on a restricted road (roads to which a 30 mph speed limit applies). These generally occur in built-up areas and these provisions are to prevent unnecessary annoyance to residents.

(2) Reversing alarms

The regulations permit 'reversing alarms' to be fitted to certain vehicles in addition to horns. These are devices to warn persons that the vehicle is reversing or about to reverse. Such a device is exempted from the requirement that the sound of a warning instrument shall be continuous and uniform and from restrictions affecting restricted roads.

Such alarms may be fitted to goods vehicles with a maximum gross weight not less than 2000 kg, buses, refuse vehicles, engineering plant and works trucks. The sound emitted must be such that it is not likely to be confused with the sound emitted from a pedestrian crossing.

A reversing alarm may only be used on a stationary vehicle if the vehicle's engine is running and it is about to move backwards or the vehicle is in danger from another moving vehicle.

(3) Maintenance

Horns and other audible warning instruments must be maintained in good and efficient working order at all times.

Brakes

(1) Fitting of brakes

There are a number of regulations which provide for the provision of effective braking systems upon motor vehicles. The common factor is that no matter what system of braking the regulations require to be fitted to particular types of vehicles, every part of the system and its means of operation must be maintained in good and efficient working order and must be properly adjusted. Foot braking systems should be capable of stopping the vehicle within a reasonable distance, and tables of braking distances are set out in the Highway Code. For example, at a speed of 30 mph, the overall stopping distance is 75 feet.

Regulation 15 of the 1986 Regulations sets out the requirements in respect of braking systems fitted to wheeled vehicles first used on or after 1 April 1983 or which, in the case of a trailer, are manufactured on or after 1 October 1982. Such vehicles must comply with the requirements of Community Directive 79/489. This Directive covers most vehicles first used since that date. However, some vehicles first used on or after 1 April 1989 must comply with Community Directive 85/647 and others must comply if first used on or after 1 April 1990. Other motor vehicles (with certain exceptions) first used on or after 1 April 1992 and trailers manufactured on or after 1 October 1991 must comply with Community Directive 88/194. Other vehicles may comply with this Directive as an alternative to complying with other Community Directives or Regulation 16 or 17 of the 1986 Regulations. All such vehicles as specified above first used on or after 1 April 1995 and trailers manufactured on or after that date must comply with Community Directive 91/422.

Vehicles first used before 1 April 1983 and those not covered by the Community Directive are dealt with by Regulation 16, but such vehicles may, as an alternative, comply with the Community Directive.

Generally, heavy motor cars and motor cars first used on or after 1 January 1968 must be equipped with one efficient braking system having two means of operation, or an efficient split braking system with one means of operation, or two efficient systems with separate means of operation. Such systems must be so designed that in the event of failure (of other than a fixed member or a brake shoe anchor pin), there shall still be sufficient braking power to bring the vehicle to rest within a reasonable distance. Such brakes must be applied to at least one wheel of a three-wheeler, otherwise to at least half of the wheels of the vehicle. The parking brake must be independent and able to hold the vehicle stationary on a gradient of at least 16 per cent. The full braking system of such vehicles must apply to all the wheels.

The provisions set out above also apply, to a large degree, to heavy motor cars and motor cars first used before 1 January 1968. There are small variations, perhaps the most significant being that the parking brake must be such that it can be set so as to prevent the rotation of at least one wheel in the case of a three-wheeler, and at least two wheels in the case of a vehicle having more than three wheels and the requirement that the full braking system must apply to all wheels does not apply to such vehicles.

Two-wheeled motor cycles must have either an efficient braking system with two means of operation, or two efficient independent systems. Trailers, with limited exceptions, require brakes if they have a maximum gross weight exceeding 750 kg. However, where a trailer which does not exceed that maximum gross weight is fitted with a braking system, that system must be maintained in efficient working order, even though it is not *required* to have any brakes. The brakes will apply to all wheels, and in the event of failure, brakes must be left for one wheel in the case of a trailer with two wheels, and for at least two wheels if it has more than two wheels. Brakes may be of the 'overrun' type. They must have a parking brake which can be applied by a person on the ground, by a means of operation fitted to the trailer. There are minor differences if the trailer is pre-1 January 1968, particularly in relation to the

215

main system, in that the brakes need only apply to two wheels if there are no more than four wheels and to at least half of the wheels if there are more than four.

(2) *Efficiency and maintenance*

Regulation 18 deals with the efficiency of braking systems, requiring that they shall be maintained in good and efficient working order and be properly adjusted. Defects arising within ABS braking systems during the course of a journey, or use while the vehicle is being taken to a place of repair, are removed from the requirement that every part of a braking system shall be maintained in good and efficient working order. However, the affected braking system must still meet the braking efficiencies specified in Regulation 18(3).

Service and secondary systems are required to meet minimum percentage efficiencies as measured by a testing meter. Most vehicles are required to have a service braking system of 50 per cent efficiency and a secondary system of 25 per cent efficiency. These percentages are usually reduced if the vehicle is drawing a trailer. The regulation also deals with the efficiency of parking brakes, requiring that all vehicles shall have parking brakes so maintained that the brakes are capable, without the assistance of stored energy, of holding the vehicle stationary on a gradient of at least 16 per cent. If a trailer is attached to a vehicle which complies with Community Directive 79/489, this requirement is reduced to 12 per cent.

Mirrors

The requirements of the regulations in relation to mirrors are very much affected by the date of first use of a motor vehicle. The important date is 1 June 1978. As the more recent vehicles have the more extensive requirements, we will consider them first.

(1) *First used on or after 1 June 1978*

Every passenger vehicle, goods vehicle or dual purpose vehicle first used on or after 1 June 1978 must be equipped with an interior rear view mirror and at least one exterior rear view mirror fitted to the offside of the vehicle. If, for any reason, the interior rear view mirror does not provide an adequate view to the rear, the vehicle must also have an exterior rear view mirror fitted to the nearside of the vehicle. If we consider these requirements in relation to the family car, it *must* have an interior mirror and an exterior mirror on the offside, both giving an adequate rearwards view. If, on returning from holiday, the rear of the vehicle has been filled with luggage, etc., the interior mirror may not afford a rearwards view. However, the regulation provides that if the vehicle has an exterior mirror on the nearside, no offence will be committed. The relevant date of first use in the case of Ford Transit vehicles is 10 July 1978.

(2) *First used before 1 June 1978*

In the case of vehicles first used before 1 June 1978, passenger vehicles adapted to

216

carry more than eight passengers exclusive of the driver, goods vehicles and dual purpose vehicles (except locomotives and motor tractors), require two mirrors, one fitted externally on the offside of the vehicle and the second *either* internally or externally on the nearside of the vehicle. However, the remainder of vehicles, including the family car, merely require one mirror fitted either internally or externally in such a way that the driver can become aware of traffic to the rear of the vehicle.

Although this appears to permit the fitting of a mirror anywhere, it must be remembered that its purpose is to allow the driver to become aware of traffic to the rear. Most nearside mirrors would not satisfy this requirement as there would be no view to the offside rear of the vehicle.

(3) *Motor cycles and special vehicles*

There is no requirement for mirrors in relation to a two-wheeled motor cycle. However, if mirrors are fitted to motor cycles first used on or after 1 October 1978 they must be of a type which complies with the regulations. Other 'excepted vehicles' are motor vehicles drawing trailers upon which there is some person who can communicate to the driver the intentions of other vehicles to the rear, works trucks which afford a clear view to the rear, pedestrian controlled vehicles and a chassis being driven to a body plant. Motor tractors, agricultural and forestry tractors, locomotives, works trucks and some vehicles with limited design speed (16 mph), are only required to be fitted with one mirror, fitted on the offside of the vehicle.

(4) *Manner of fitting*

General provisions contained in the regulations include requirements that mirrors shall be fixed to a vehicle first used on or after 1 June 1978 in such a way that they remain steady under normal driving conditions; each exterior mirror shall be visible to the driver from his driving position, either through a side window or area of the windscreen swept by a wiper blade. Interior mirrors and those fitted to the offside shall be capable of adjustment by the driver from his driving position, except where the exterior mirror is a 'spring back' model. However, the offside mirror may be locked into position from the outside of the vehicle.

If the bottom edge of an exterior mirror is less than 2 metres from the road surface when the vehicle is laden, projection must not exceed 20 centimetres. If drawing a trailer which is wider than the towing vehicle, projection must not exceed the trailer width by more than 20 centimetres. This proviso permits the use of extended mirrors on motor cars towing caravans. All mirrors fitted after these dates must bear approval marks described in the Motor Vehicles (Designation of Approval Marks) Regulations.

Silencer and exhaust system

All vehicles propelled by an internal combustion engine must be fitted with an exhaust system including a silencer and the exhaust gases from the engine shall not escape into the atmosphere without first passing through the silencer. Most silencers

217

consist of a series of baffle plates which the gases strike, breaking their velocity and so reducing the noise. The removal of plates results in an increase of noise. This can be popular with young motor cyclists. It is an offence to alter any exhaust system in such a way as to increase the noise. Alterations or replacements to exhaust systems are not permitted if they have the effect of increasing the noise.

Seat belts

The regulations requiring the fitting of seat belts to some motor vehicles provide a good example of the increasing tendency of government to legislate for the public good. Although the lack of seat belts is likely to result in injury only to the driver or his passenger, research has shown that many unnecessary injuries result from front seat passengers being thrown forward when the vehicle is in collision.

Motor cars first used on or after 1 January 1965; every three-wheeled motor cycle the unladen weight of which exceeds 255 kg and which was first used on or after 1 September 1970; and every heavy motor car first used on or after 1 October 1988 must be fitted with anchorage points and seat belts as specified. These provisions do not apply to goods vehicles (other than dual purpose vehicles) which were first used:

(a) before 1 April 1967; or

(b) on or after 1 April 1980 and before 1 October 1988 which have a gross weight exceeding 3500 kg; or

(c) before 1 April 1980 or, if a model manufactured before 1 October 1979, was first used before 1 April 1982 and in either case, has an unladen weight exceeding 1525 kg.

Other exempted vehicles include buses (minibuses if first used before 1 October 1988 which are constructed or adapted to carry more than 12 passengers; if first used on or after 1 October 1988, which have a gross weight exceeding 3500 kg) and large buses other than coaches first used on or after 1 October 1988; agricultural vehicles; motor tractors; works trucks; pedestrian controlled vehicles; electrically propelled goods vehicles first used before 1 October 1988; used imported vehicles while travelling to be fitted, etc.; and vehicles having a maximum speed not exceeding 16 mph.

Vehicles first used before 1 April 1982 shall be equipped with anchorage points for seat belts in respect of the driver's seat and specified passenger's seat. A 'specified passenger seat' is a forward-facing front passenger seat. Where there is more than one forward-facing front passenger seat, the term is applied to the one furthest from the driver's seat. Passenger and dual purpose vehicles first used on or after that date must have anchorage points for every forward-facing seat constructed or adapted to accommodate one adult, with the exception that minibuses, motor ambulances and motor caravans first used before 1 October 1988 need only be provided with anchorage points for the driver's seat and specified passenger's seat. Such vehicles which are first used on or after 1 October 1988 must have anchorage points for the driver's seat and all forward-facing seats.

Vehicles first used before 1 April 1981 must have seat belts for the driver's seat and the specified passenger's seat. They must be of an approved type and in respect of these vehicles, they may be 'diagonal'. Those first used on or after 1 April 1981 must be provided with three-point seat belts for both the driver's seat and the specified passenger's seat.

Passenger and dual purpose vehicles and all other vehicles fitted with anchorage points as required by Regulation 46 (other than minibuses, motor ambulances and motor caravans), which are first used on or after 1 April 1987, must be fitted with three-point, lap or disabled person's belts for every forward-facing front seat which is not a specified passenger's seat. Thus, the 'Transit' type of vehicle will be required to have seat belts for *all* front seats. All passenger or dual purpose vehicles first used on or after this date must also be fitted with rear seat belts for passengers sitting in the rear of the vehicles who are using forward-facing seats. The regulation requires that belts be provided as follows:

(a) vehicles with not more than two forward-facing seats behind the driver's seat must have either an inertia reel belt for at least one of those seats, or a three-point, lap, disabled person's or child restraint belt for each of those seats;

(b) vehicles having more than two forward-facing seats behind the driver's seat, with either:

(i)   an inertia reel belt for one of those seats being an outboard seat, and a three-point, lap disabled person's or child restraint belt for at least one other of those seats;

(ii) a three-point belt for one of those seats and either a child restraint or disabled person's belt for at least one other of those seats; or

(iii) a three-point, lap, disabled person's or child restraint belt for each of those seats.

The rear seat belt provisions become a little easier to understand if one imagines that an inertia reel will count as two in the case of a vehicle with two rear seats, and that an inertia reel or a three-point belt will count as two in the case of a vehicle with more than two rear seats.

Minibuses, motor ambulances and motor caravans first used on or after 1 October 1988 must have three-point belts for the driver's and specified passenger's seat and a three-point or lap belt for any other forward-facing front seat.

It is an offence to fail to maintain seat belts and their anchorage points. Buckles must be maintained so that they can be readily fastened and unfastened, and they must be kept free of any obstruction which would prevent them from becoming readily accessible to a person using the seat. Each end of a seat belt must be securely fastened to its anchorage point and the webbing must be free of cuts and other visible faults likely to affect its performance under stress. Within 30 cm of a seat belt anchorage point, the load bearing members or panelling of the vehicle structure must be maintained in sound condition.

Wearing of seat belts

The circumstances in which seat belts must be worn by passengers in a motor vehicle are prescribed in the Motor Vehicles (Wearing of Seat Belts) Regulations 1993 and the Motor Vehicles (Wearing of Seat Belts by Children in Front Seats) Regulations 1993. The 1993 Regulations implement the requirements of Council Directive 91/671/EEC which only applies to vehicles of less than 3.5 tonnes which have four or

219

more wheels and a design speed of more than 25 kph. The Directive does not apply to passenger vehicles with more than eight passenger seats if they are designed to carry standing passengers. Vehicles within the scope of the Directive with not more than eight seats in addition to the driver's seat are referred to in the regulations as 'passenger cars'.

The offences committed by breaches of the regulations are punishable under the Road Traffic Act 1988, ss. 14 and 15 as amended by the Road Traffic Act 1988 (Amendment) Regulations 1992. The requirements created by the 1993 Regulations are not always confined to the description of vehicles set out in the Directive.

(1) *Front seat adult passengers*

Regulation 5 of the Motor Vehicles (Wearing of Seat Belts) Regulations 1993 requires that every person driving or riding in the front seat of a motor vehicle (other than a two-wheeled motor cycle with or without sidecar) must wear an adult seat belt. The regulation does not apply to a person under the age of 14 years. Nor does it apply if no seat belt is provided for a driver, or is available for a front seat passenger. Failure to comply with Regulation 5 is an offence under the Road Traffic Act 1988, s. 14(3).

Regulation 6 provides the following exemptions from the requirement to wear a seat belt made by Regulation 5:

(a) a person holding a medical certificate (including that of a member State);
(b) a person using a vehicle constructed or adapted for the delivery of goods or mail to consumers or addresses, while engaged in making local rounds of deliveries or collections;
(c) a person performing a manoeuvre which includes reversing;
(d) a qualified driver supervising a learner carrying out such a manoeuvre;
(e) a person undergoing a driving test where wearing a seat belt would endanger himself or another person;
(f) a person driving or riding in a vehicle being used for fire brigade or police purposes or for carrying a person in lawful custody (this includes the prisoner);
(g) the driver of a licensed taxi while being used to seek hire or answer a call, or when carrying a passenger for hire, or a private hire car while it is being used to carry a passenger for hire;
(h) a person in a vehicle being used under a trade licence for investigating or remedying a fault;
(j) a disabled person who is wearing a disabled person's belt; or
(k) a person riding in a vehicle while it is in a Crown procession.

In addition to (k), a person who is riding in a vehicle which is taking part in a procession which is being held to commemorate an event if either the procession is one commonly or customarily held in a police area or areas, or notice in respect of the procession has been given in accordance with the Public Order Act 1986, s. 11 (see page 475).

(2) *Rear seat adult passengers*

Regulation 5 also prohibits an adult person (i.e. someone aged 14 or over) from riding in the rear seat of a motor car, or of a passenger car which is not a motor car, if he is not wearing an adult seat belt provided in the vehicle. Persons who fail to comply offend against the Road Traffic Act 1988, s. 14(3).

(3) *Front seat child passengers*

It is an offence contrary to the Road Traffic Act 1988, s. 15(1) and (2) for a person, without reasonable excuse, to drive a motor vehicle on a road in which a child under the age of 14 is in the front of that vehicle unless the child is wearing a seat belt in conformity with the Motor Vehicles (Wearing of Seat Belts by Children in Front Seats) Regulations 1993. Generally, it is irrelevant that a seat belt is not provided for the seat. The regulations set out the rules with which a driver must conform. A 'front seat' is one which is wholly or partially in the front of the vehicle. The regulations do not apply to two-wheeled motor cycles, with or without sidecars.

The description of the seat belts which satisfy the requirements of the regulations is prescribed in Regulation 5:

(a) in the case of a 'small child' travelling in a passenger car, light goods vehicle (not exceeding 3.5 tonnes) or a small bus (more than eight passenger seats not exceeding 3.5 tonnes) the seat belt must be a child restraint with a marking required under the Road Vehicles (Construction and Use) Regulations 1986, Regulation 47(7) or a child restraint approved by another member State;

(b) in the case of a 'small child' in any other vehicle, the seat belt must be a child restraint approved under Regulation 47(7);

(c) in the case of a 'large child', the seat belt must be a child restraint approved under Regulation 47(7) or an adult belt.

A 'small child' is a child who is under 12 and under 150 centimetres in height and a 'large child is a child under 14 who is not a 'small child'.

Regulation 7 exempts from these provisions:

(a) a 'small child' aged three or more if a prescribed seat belt is not available for him *in the front or rear* of the vehicle and he is wearing an adult belt;

(b) a child for whom there is a medical certificate (including one issued in a member State);

(c) a child under the age of one in a carry cot provided that it is restrained by straps;

(d) a disabled child who is wearing a disabled person's belt; or

(e) a child riding in a motor car first used before 1 January 1965 if:
    (i) the vehicle has no rear seat; and
    (ii) apart from the driver's seat, no seat in the vehicle is provided with a seat belt which is appropriate for that child.

In addition, the prohibition created by s. 15 does not apply in relation to a child riding in a vehicle which is being used to provide a local service within the meaning of the Transport Act 1985 and is neither a motor car nor a passenger car. The prohibition does not apply in relation to a 'large child' if no appropriate seat belt is available for him in the front of the vehicle.

(4) *Rear seat child passengers*

The Road Traffic Act 1988, s. 15(3) and (3A) make it an offence for a person, without reasonable excuse, to drive a motor vehicle on a road if there is a child of under 14 in the rear of it who is not wearing a seat belt fitted there or, in the case of a 'small child', if there is no rear seat belt and there is an unoccupied seat in the front which is fitted with an appropriate seat belt. Exemption from these requirements is provided by the Motor Vehicles (Wearing of Seat Belts) Regulations 1993, Regulation 9. An offence is not committed where the vehicle is neither a motor car nor a passenger car or where the vehicle is a licensed taxi or licensed hire car in which (in each case) the rear seats are separated from the driver by a fixed partition. Further exemptions are provided by Regulation 10:

(a) where a seat belt of a description prescribed by Regulation 8 (i.e. an approved child restraint) is not available to a 'small child' aged three or more in the front or rear of the vehicle and he is wearing an adult seat belt;

(b) where the child holds an approved medical certificate (including that of a member State);

(c) where a child under the age of one is being carried in a carry cot provided that it is restrained by straps; and

(d) where a disabled child is wearing a disabled person's belt.

The prohibition against the carriage of a child in the rear of a vehicle who is not wearing a seat belt does not apply in relation to a 'small child' in a passenger car if no appropriate seat belt is available to him in the front or rear of the vehicle. Nor does it apply to such a child in the rear of a vehicle other than a passenger car in such circumstances. There is also an exemption in favour of a 'large child' where, in any vehicle, no appropriate seat belt is available to him.

An adult seat is now treated as being suitable for a child aged three or over where no booster cushion is used.

(5) *Availability of seat belts*

Schedule 2 of the 1993 Regulations describes the circumstances in which a seat belt will be regarded as not being available. They are where:

(a) another person is wearing the relevant belt;

(b) a child is occupying the relevant seat and wearing a child restraint which is an appropriate child restraint for that child and this renders use of the seat belt impracticable;

(c) a person holding a medical certificate is occupying the relevant seat;

(d) a disabled person (not being the person in question) is occupying the relevant seat and wearing a disabled person's belt and this renders use of the seat impracticable;

(e) by reason of his disability, it would not be practicable for the person in question to wear the relevant belt;

(f) the seat is occupied by a carry cot containing a child under one and that cot is secured by straps and it would not be practicable to carry the cot, suitably restrained, elsewhere;

(g) the person in question is prevented from occupying the relevant seat by the presence of a child restraint which could not readily be removed without the use of tools; or

(h) the relevant seat is so designed that it can be adjusted to increase the space available for goods and effects and when it is so adjusted the seat cannot be used.

Steering gear

All steering gear fitted to a motor vehicle shall, at all times when the vehicle is used on a road, be maintained in good and efficient working order and shall be properly adjusted. This regulation is general in nature and there are so many moving parts in a steering system that a defect may exist in many places. Defective steering systems are usually detected by over-stiffness in movement, which indicates lack of lubrication, or by excessive movement at the steering wheel without any movement being transmitted to the appropriate road wheels, which suggests lack of adjustment or excessive wear in joints.

Tyres

(1) *Tyre defects*

No person shall use, cause or permit to be used on a road, a motor vehicle or trailer of which a tyre:

(a) is unsuitable for the use to which the vehicle, etc., is being put;

(b) is wrongly inflated for that use;

(c) has a cut exceeding 25 mm or 10 per cent of the section width of the tyre, whichever is the greater, in any direction and reaching the ply or body cords;

(d) has a lump, bulge or tear caused by separation or partial failure of the structure;

(e) has a portion of the ply or cord structure exposed;

(f) possesses any groove which showed in the original tread pattern of the tyre and which is not clearly visible; or

(g) either, does not have a depth of 1 mm in the grooves of the tread pattern throughout a continuous band measuring at least three-quarters of the breadth of the tyre and round its entire circumference, or, if the grooves of the original tread pattern of the tyre did not extend beyond three-quarters of the breadth of the tread, any groove which showed in the original tread pattern does not have a depth of at least 1 mm (see below for requirement of 1.6 mm on some vehicles); or

(h) is not maintained in such condition as to be fit for the use to which the vehicle or trailer is being put or has a defect which may in any way cause damage to the surface of the road or damage to persons on or in the vehicle or to other persons using the road.

223

This regulation is extremely comprehensive. Any defect in a tyre which may cause danger is covered by these requirements. The contact area of a tyre must have visible tread which must be at least 1 mm deep for three-quarters of the contact area. The regulations make special provisions to allow the use of a tyre which will operate satisfactorily when deflated. It also prohibits the use of recut pneumatic tyres if the ply or cord has been exposed in the recutting process.

With effect from 1 January 1992:

(i)   passenger vehicles other than motor cycles constructed or adapted to carry no more than eight seated passengers in addition to the driver;

(ii) goods vehicles with a maximum gross weight which does not exceed 3500 kg; and

(iii) light trailers not falling within sub-paragraph (ii);

first used on or after 3 January 1933 are not subject to the provisions set out at (f) and (g) above. With regard to such vehicles, these provisions are replaced by a requirement that the grooves of the tread pattern shall be of a depth of at least *1.6 mm* throughout a continuous band comprising the central three-quarters of the breadth of tread and round the entire circumference of the tyre.

(2) *Mixture of tyres*

No person shall use or cause or permit to be used on a road a vehicle if pneumatic tyres of different types of structure are fitted to the same axle of the vehicle. The regulations mention three types of tyres:

(a)   diagonal-ply tyres which are commonly known as cross-ply tyres;

(b)   bias-belted tyres which are as above but have a reinforcing band around the outer circumference of the tyre, under the tread, but on top of the cords;

(c)   radial-ply tyres.

The regulation also provides that a motor vehicle, having only two axles, must not be fitted with the following combination of tyres; cross-ply or bias-belted tyres on the rear axle and radials on the front; and cross-ply on the rear axle and bias-belted on the front. These provisions are designed to prevent a 'gripping' tyre from being fitted to the steering wheels while a tyre which is not so stable, is fitted to the rear.

(3) *Tyre checks*

It can be seen, therefore, that there are many statutory requirements in relation to tyres, and vehicle checks must be thorough. A check might begin with an examination for a mixture of tyres on the same axle and if there are cross-plies on the rear axle a check that radials or bias-belted are not fitted to the front axle. Individual tyres should be examined for depth of tread (gauges are provided for this purpose), and defects such as bulges, cuts, incorrect tyre pressures, or exposed cord. The references to the base of any groove showing in the original tread not being visible refer to smooth patches where the tread has disappeared.

Windscreen wipers and washers

All vehicles which are fitted with windscreens must be fitted with at least one automatic efficient windscreen wiper which is capable of clearing the windscreen sufficiently to give an adequate view to the front of both sides of the vehicle and to the front of it. The only exceptions are in respect of vehicles which have a windscreen which opens (now quite rare) or which it is possible to see over. Windscreen wipers required by the regulation must be properly maintained at all times when the vehicle is used on a road. However, it must be remembered that only one wiper, that for the driver, is required by law and it is not necessarily an offence to fail to maintain a wiper fitted to the passenger side of a vehicle, unless two wipers are necessary to give the driver an adequate view to the front, of both sides of the vehicle and to the front of it. The provision of wipers would be of little effect if vehicles which are required to have wipers were not also required to have windscreen washers fitted. The washers must be capable of cleaning, with the assistance of the wiper, the area swept by the wiper blade. Washers must be fitted to all such vehicles, except vehicles incapable of exceeding 20 mph; agricultural motor vehicles; and vehicles being used to provide a local bus service.

Instruments for measuring and controlling speed

(1) *Speedometer*

The general rule is that all motor vehicles must be fitted with a speedometer. However, some vehicles are exempt; these are invalid carriages, motor cycles not exceeding 100 cc and works trucks (provided that in each case they were first used before 1 April 1984); agricultural vehicles which are not driven at more than 20 mph; vehicles which legally or physically cannot exceed 25 mph; and those which have an alternative type approved instrument. Vehicles first used before 1 October 1937 are also exempt.

Speedometers must be kept free of any obstruction which might prevent them from being easily read and must at all times be kept in good working order. It is a defence to prove that a defect arose in the course of the journey then being undertaken or that steps had already been taken to have repairs or replacements effected as soon as possible. These defences eliminate the possibility of charges in all but those cases in which there is an admission of a long standing defect by the driver or, where there is a defect, that the condition of the parts indicates that the instrument has not been working for some time.

(2) *Speed limiter*

Most buses and goods vehicles which exceed 7.5 tonnes maximum gross weight are required to be fitted with speed limiters. Where such requirements exist the vehicle will be fitted with a plate in a conspicuous position in the driving compartment of the vehicle. The plate will be clearly and indelibly marked with the speed at which the speed limiter has been set. Such buses will be limited to 70 or 65 mph and goods vehicles to 60 or 56 mph depending upon their maximum gross weight and date of first use.

All such speed limiters must be sealed against improper interference or adjustment and against interference with the power supply and must be maintained in good and efficient working order.

Defences exist where a defect has occurred in the course of a journey or where the vehicle is being taken to a place where a speed limiter is to be installed, calibrated, repaired or replaced. Vehicles used by some Crown and emergency services are specifically exempted.

Maintenance of glass

All glass or other transparent material fitted to a motor vehicle shall be maintained in such condition that it does not obscure the vision of the driver while the vehicle is being driven on a road. The provisions of this regulation are frequently ignored by early morning drivers following a severe frost. It is not enough to clear a small portion of glass through which a driver can see. *All* glass or transparent material must be maintained in a suitable condition.

Petrol tank

All fuel tanks must be constructed and maintained so that leakage of any liquid or vapour from the tank is adequately prevented. Where filler caps are lost, vapour will escape from the tank unless it is adequately plugged and this cannot be done with porous material. However, it must be remembered that a driver who loses his filler cap will reasonably expect that he will be allowed to proceed to a garage or accessory shop to replace it provided that he has made reasonable provisions to prevent leakage.

Wings

All invalid carriages, heavy motor cars and motor cycles, not being agricultural vehicles or pedestrian-controlled vehicles shall be fitted with wings or similar fittings to catch, as far as practicable, mud or water thrown up by the wheels, unless adequate protection is afforded by the body of the vehicle. There are certain exceptions, which include unfinished vehicles and articulated vehicles used only for the carriage of round timber.

The rear wheels of trailers must be fitted with wings, where the trailer has more than two wheels.

Duties of drivers and others

Some of the regulations contained in the Road Vehicles (Construction and Use) Regulations 1986 are concerned with prohibiting the driver of a vehicle from carrying out certain actions. We will examine some of these.

(1) Position of driver

A driver must always be in such a position that he has proper control of the vehicle and a full view of the road and traffic ahead. It is also an offence for any other

226

person to cause or permit a driver to be in such a position that he does not retain full control of the vehicle.

(2) *Danger*

Reference has already been made on page 209 to the offences under the Road Traffic Act 1988, s. 40A, of using, causing or permitting the use of a motor vehicle or trailer which is in a dangerous condition because of the condition of the vehicle's accessories or equipment, the purpose of its use, the number of passengers carried or the manner of their carriage and the weight, or distribution or security of the load, etc. It is submitted that most offences involving dangerous vehicles will now be charged under the Road Traffic Act 1988, s. 40A, and not under s. 42 (which covers most construction and use offences) since a conviction of an offence under s. 40A involves the risk of discretionary disqualification and requires the obligatory endorsement of three penalty points. Where there is a conviction under s. 42 for a breach of Regulation 100 there can be no disqualification or endorsement of the offender's driving licence. Regulation 100(1) requires that all motor vehicles and trailers and all parts and accessories must always be in such a condition that no danger is caused or is likely to be caused to persons being carried, or on a road. The regulation is concerned with the correct maintenance of all parts and accessories of vehicles which must always be in good working order. It was, therefore, held that when a ball and socket unit connecting a lorry to a trailer was in good repair, but incorrectly coupled, they were not in efficient working order. It is important to remember that, in any charge alleging failure to maintain a vehicle, the particular defects must be specified in the charge. Separate and distinct offences are involved in using a defective motor vehicle and a defective trailer on a road. This equally applies to articulated vehicles.

A breach of Regulation 100(1) is also committed if the number of passengers in a vehicle is excessive, or, because of the manner of their carriage, danger may be caused. When a small car designed to carry four passengers was driven with eight persons aboard, it was found that at any speed other than a low one, the steering of the vehicle was affected and that this constituted an offence of driving in an unsafe or unroadworthy condition.

One of the most common offences committed under Regulation 100(1) is that of faulty loading, or security of the load. Unfortunately, these offences often become apparent when the load, or part of it, has fallen from the vehicle. It must be stressed that Regulation 100(1) is concerned with badly loaded vehicles which cause danger by the manner in which the load is carried. Regulation 100(2) requires that loads, where necessary, must be secured by physical restraint other than their own weight and that loads must be so positioned that neither danger nor nuisance is likely to be caused to persons or property by reason of the load, or part of it, falling or being blown from the vehicle, or by reason of movement of the load or vehicle. Where two large vats were knocked from a vehicle when it was driven under a pedestrian bridge, the High Court ruled that something 'fell' from a vehicle whether it fell because it was not securely strapped to the vehicle or because it had been knocked off the vehicle. In deciding whether a load was so secured that neither danger nor nuisance was likely to be caused four things must be considered:

227

(a) the nature of the journey;
(b) the way in which the load was secured;
(c) the way in which the load was positioned; and
(d) the journey to be taken.

What might be secure for one journey in fine weather and on good roads might not be secure for another journey in poor weather and on less good roads.

It is an offence contrary to Regulation 100(3) to use a vehicle or trailer for a purpose for which it is unsuitable, so as to cause such danger, or nuisance to persons in or on that vehicle, or trailer or on a road.

However, where a vehicle or trailer is designed for the purpose of carrying goods and is capable of carrying those goods without danger if properly loaded, it is suitable for that purpose. Thus, if a trailer is loaded with a machine which would pass under a bridge with that load if properly loaded, an offence does not lie under Regulation 100(3) if the load strikes the bridge. A charge under Regulation 100(2) would have been appropriate.

The responsibility of the driver is absolute and it is no defence that the loading was carried out by some other persons, although such person may also be in breach of the regulation. It has been held that where crates fall from a lorry when taking a bend, the driver may be convicted though the crates were loaded by another person. Remember, however, that in all circumstances where danger can be proved the most appropriate charge will probably be one contrary to the Road Traffic Act 1988, s. 40A.

(3) *Noise*

Permitted noise levels of vehicles are prescribed by the Construction and Use Regulations and are measured at the time of manufacture by a device known as a sound level meter. Drivers are also required to prevent the use of vehicles on roads in a manner which causes excessive noise which could reasonably have been avoided. This last offence is committed by those drivers, particularly motor cyclists, who 'rev' up the engines of their vehicles while stationary.

(4) *Unnecessary obstruction*

A person in charge of a motor vehicle must not cause or permit that vehicle to stand on a road so as to cause unnecessary obstruction. It has been held that to leave a vehicle on a road for an 'unreasonable' time may constitute an unnecessary obstruction, but if the driver has only left his car for a 'reasonable' time, this does not amount to an unnecessary obstruction. The duration of an obstruction; the characteristics of the road at the particular place; the purpose for which the vehicle was parked; and the actual degree of obstruction caused are all matters which the court will consider in deciding whether or not an obstruction had been caused.

Exemptions provided by 'no-waiting' orders in favour of loading and unloading have led to many goods vehicle drivers double-parking, often completely blocking a road. This is an obstruction and it will be so where a road, which normally permits two-way traffic, is reduced to a one-way flow.

(5) *Doors*

No person shall open, or cause to permit to be opened, any door of a motor vehicle or trailer while it is on a road, so as to cause injury or danger to any person.

(6) *Quitting*

It is an offence for a person to leave or cause or permit a motor vehicle to be left on a road which is unattended by a person who is licensed to drive it unless the engine has been stopped and the brake set. Fire engines at work, or vehicles being used for police or ambulance purposes, are included in the exemptions. The peculiarity of this charge is that the word 'and' is used and it is, therefore, apparent that the driver is required to do two things: to stop the engine and set the handbrake. If he fails to do one or the other he is guilty of the offence.

(7) *Reversing*

The offence lies in causing or permitting a motor vehicle to travel backwards for a greater distance or time than may be required for the safety or reasonable convenience of the occupants of the vehicle, or other traffic on the road. This regulation is provided to reinforce the common-sense assumption that the safest way to propel a motor vehicle is in a forward direction, when the driver has a full view of traffic ahead and to both sides. Reversing is at times necessary, but can only safely be carried out for a limited time due to the necessity for the driver either to look over his shoulder or to rely upon driving mirrors. If it is unreasonable, and drivers have been known to reverse at fast speeds over considerable distances, then an offence has been committed. The presence of other traffic and pedestrians, combined with other factors such as the passing of possible turning points and the overall distance travelled, can combine to provide good evidence of such an offence. It is always a good guide to respond only to situations which make you fear for the safety of the public.

(8) *Tow ropes*

Where a motor vehicle is drawing a trailer by means of a rope or chain, the rope or chain shall be of such a length that the nearest points of both vehicles are no more than 4.5 metres (15 feet) apart. In assessing this distance, towing attachments shall be disregarded. If a tow rope or chain exceeds 1.5 metres (5 feet), it must be made clearly visible to all road users within a reasonable distance on each side.

Testing and inspection

(1) *On a road*

The powers of constables and examiners to inspect vehicles are contained in the Road Traffic Act 1988 and the Road Vehicles (Construction and Use) Regulations 1986.

The Road Traffic Act permits authorised examiners to test a motor vehicle on a road for the purpose of ascertaining whether the requirements relating to construction and use and the requirement that the condition of the vehicle is not such that its use on a road would involve danger of injury to any person, are being complied with.

For the purposes of testing a vehicle an examiner may require the driver to comply with his reasonable instructions and may drive the vehicle. The term 'authorised examiners' includes vehicle examiners appointed under s. 66A of the Road Traffic Act 1988 by the Secretary of State and constables authorised by their chief officer of police. Only a constable in uniform may stop vehicles for a test. In the case of normal checks, the driver may elect that the test be deferred. In certain circumstances – for example, following an accident on a road or where, in his opinion, the vehicle is apparently so defective that it should not be allowed to proceed without being tested – the constable may require the test to be carried out immediately. If the constable concerned is not himself authorised by his chief officer of police to carry out such tests, he may insist that the vehicle is not removed before testing.

However, this does not mean that the provisions of the Road Vehicles (Construction and Use) Regulations 1986 can only be enforced by authorised constables. Particular offences may and should be dealt with by any constable. If this is not done the right to defer examination will be exercised where a full vehicle examination is proposed and the defect will be remedied before that examination takes place. Where a constable who was not an authorised examiner tested the efficiency of a handbrake with the driver's consent, evidence of his findings was admitted. There is a difference between a formal examination of a vehicle and dealing with infringements of the regulations.

(2) Prohibition of unfit vehicles

The Road Traffic Act 1988, s. 69, empowers an authorised constable to issue an immediate prohibition notice, if on inspection under s. 41, 45, 49, 61, 67, 68 or 77 it appears to him that owing to any defects in the vehicle driving it (or driving it for any particular purpose or purposes or for any except one or more particular purposes) would involve a danger of injury to any person. The sections referred to deal with powers in relation to construction and use; test certificates generally; inspections related to plated weights of goods vehicles, public service vehicles and vehicles adapted to carry more than eight passengers which are not public service vehicles; and the testing of the condition of used vehicles at sale rooms, etc. A notice under s. 69 may prohibit use absolutely, or for one or more specified purposes, or except for one or more specified purposes.

Vehicle examiners appointed under s. 66A have a similar power.

The Road Vehicles (Prohibition) Regulations 1992 make provision for a vehicle which is subject to a prohibition issued by an authorised constable or vehicle examiner to be used on a road for the purpose of submitting it, by arrangement, for test with a view to the removal of that prohibition, within three miles from where it is being, or has been repaired, solely for the purpose of test or trial, and during any test for the purpose of the removal of the prohibition. Evidence that a vehicle is being driven in contravention of a prohibition order may be some evidence of its being used in contravention of the Road Traffic Act 1988, s. 2.

(3) *Off-road*

The Construction and Use Regulations are concerned with the testing of motor vehicles on premises. Constables in uniform and authorised examiners may carry out such tests with the permission of the owner of the premises. If the owner of the vehicle refuses permission, notice may be served upon him, not less than 48 hours before the time of the proposed test (or 72 hours before if by recorded delivery service), setting out the date and time of the proposed test. However, if the test and inspection are made within 48 hours of an accident which is required to be reported by law, such notice will not be necessary. The owner, for the purpose of this regulation, is the registered owner, or if used under a trade licence, the holder of the licence.

Public service vehicles

What are public service vehicles?

The most likely encounter, for a beat officer, with the legislation dealing with public service vehicles, will be one involving a breach of the Public Service Vehicles (Conduct of Drivers, Inspectors, Conductors and Passengers) Regulations 1990. As these offences are only committed in respect of public service vehicles, it is essential to recognise those vehicles to which the legislation applies.

For the purposes of these regulations a public service vehicle is defined by s. 1 of the Public Passenger Vehicles Act 1981 as:

(a) being a vehicle adapted to carry more than eight passengers is carrying passengers for hire or reward; or
(b) being a vehicle not so adapted is used for carrying passengers for hire or reward at separate fares, in the course of a business of carrying passengers.

It will be seen that the definition is wide enough to embrace many types of vehicle which may be operating as a public service vehicle. However, public service vehicles are easily identified by discs which are carried on the windscreen.

How may they be identified?

To operate a business involving the use of public service vehicles, the operator must have a licence. It may be a standard licence (which authorises the use of public service vehicles of any size) or a restricted licence (for the smaller, transit-type of vehicle). In either case there will be a disc displayed on the windscreen which gives details of the licence.

The Transport Act 1985 permits certain organisations to operate vehicles in circumstances in which they would be regarded as public service vehicles, but without it being necessary for those organisations to have operators' licences. The Road Traffic Act 1988, as amended by the Road Traffic (Driver Licensing and Information Systems) Act 1989, now requires that those who drive public service vehicles (now referred to as large passenger-carrying vehicles) are the holders of a DVLA licence covering the category of vehicle to which that large passenger-carrying vehicle belongs. However, those who hold a current public service vehicle driver's licence issued by a traffic commissioner (in addition to a DVLA licence for the old group of vehicles to which the appropriate public service vehicle belonged), commit no offence if their DVLA licence does not cover the new category of vehicle which they are driving, provided that the public service vehicle driver's licence does. As public service vehicle drivers' licences issued by traffic commissioners are valid for five years they will still be encountered. The 1989 Act introduced new categories of vehicles, together with the appropriate amendments to the Motor Vehicles (Driving Licences) Regulations 1987.

The vehicles which may be so operated are:

(a) *Minibuses* which will carry a disc bearing the words 'Transport Act 1985, section 19 permit vehicles'; or

(b) *Community buses* which will carry a disc bearing those words.

Conduct of drivers, conductors, and passengers

The Public Service Vehicles (Conduct of Drivers, Inspectors, Conductors and Passengers) Regulations 1990 regulate behaviour on public service vehicles. Contravention of any of the following regulations is an offence.

A driver shall not:

(a) while the vehicle is in motion, hold a microphone or any attachment thereto unless it is necessary for him, either in an emergency or on the grounds of safety, to speak into that microphone;

(b) speak to any person either directly or by means of a microphone, while the vehicle is in motion, except that he may do so in an emergency or on the grounds of safety, or when speaking to a relevant person in relation to the operation of the vehicle. The driver of a public service vehicle which is providing a service for the carriage of passengers for hire or reward at separate fares which is not an excursion or sightseeing tour may make short statements from time to time limited to indicating the location of the vehicle or operational matters provided that he can do so without distraction;

(c) fail to stop as close as is reasonably practicable to the left or nearside of the road when picking up or setting down passengers.

Drivers and conductors must:

(a) take all reasonable precautions to ensure the safety of passengers who are on, or who are entering or leaving a public service vehicle;

(b) if requested by a constable or other person having reasonable cause (this also applies to inspectors) give their name and that of any person by whom they are employed and a driver must give particulars of the licence by virtue of which he drives the vehicle;

(c) not smoke, except where the vehicle is not available for the carriage of passengers and it takes place in a 'smoking' area, or where the vehicle is hired as a whole and the person concerned has the permission of the operator and the hirer.

A conductor must not:

while the vehicle is in motion and without reasonable cause, distract the driver's attention and obstruct his vision.

Passengers must not:

(a) put at risk or unreasonably impede or cause discomfort to any person travelling on or entering or leaving the vehicle, or to the driver, inspector or conductor, or employee of the operator when doing his work on that vehicle;

(b) smoke or carry lighted tobacco or light a match or cigarette lighter in or on any part of the vehicle where passengers are by a notice informed that smoking is prohibited, unless the vehicle has been hired as a whole and both the operator and hirer have given their permission to the contrary;

(c) speak to the driver (other than for safety reasons or to request him to stop);

(d) without reasonable cause, distract the driver's attention or obstruct his vision or give a signal which might reasonably be interpreted by the driver as a signal to stop the vehicle in an emergency, or to stop the vehicle;

(e) remain on the vehicle when directed to leave by the driver, an inspector or conductor on the grounds that their remaining on the vehicle would result in the number of passengers exceeding the maximum seating capacity marked on the vehicle in accordance with the Public Service Vehicles (Carrying Capacity) Regulations 1984 or that they had been causing a nuisance, or their condition was such that they would be likely to cause offence to a reasonable passenger, or that the condition of their clothing was such that their remaining on the vehicle would be reasonably expected to soil the fittings of the vehicle or the clothing of other passengers;

(f) play or operate a musical instrument or sound reproducing equipment to the annoyance of any person on the vehicle or in a manner which is likely to cause such annoyance;

(g) fail to place an article, substance or animal where directed by the driver, conductor or inspector, or fail to remove same from the vehicle on such a direction being given (this refers to bulky or cumbersome articles and those likely to cause annoyance, risk of injury or damage; there are certain exceptions in favour of guide dogs).

Certain other offences may be committed by passengers on a vehicle being used for the carriage of passengers at separate fares:

(a) using a ticket which has been altered or defaced or which has been issued to another person and was not transferable;

(b) failing to declare the journey to be taken when requested to do so;

(c) failing to pay the driver or insert the fare in a machine on one-man buses;

(d) failing to pay the appropriate fare to the conductor immediately upon his request;

(e) failing to accept or retain a ticket for the remainder of the journey;

(f) failing to produce a ticket to a driver, inspector or conductor during the currency of a journey:

(g) failing to leave the vehicle or pay an excess fare at the end of the journey paid for; and

(h) being a person who was reasonably suspected by the driver, inspector or conductor of contravening these provisions, failing to give name and address to such person.

Some of the offences which existed within the replaced regulations have not been preserved. However, the conduct which would have given rise to such offences is punishable elsewhere. Staff or passengers who are rude or disorderly will probably be guilty of offences under the Public Order Act 1986. The responsibility for seeing that the details of the service are displayed have been transferred from the conductor to the operator of local services by the Public Service Vehicles (Registration of Local Services) Regulations 1986. Passengers who spit upon, soil or deface any part of a public service vehicle would probably commit an offence under the Criminal Damage Act 1971.

Powers

Certain powers are given to drivers, conductors and the police by the PSV (Conduct of Drivers, Conductors, Inspectors and Passengers) Regulations 1990.

Passengers contravening the Regulations may be removed from the vehicle by the driver or conductor. On the request of the driver or conductor, such persons may be removed by a police constable.

A passenger reasonably suspected of contravening the regulations must give his name and address to the driver, inspector or conductor on demand.

While offences related to taxis are primarily the concern of local authorities, it is helpful to know that the Criminal Justice and Public Order Act 1994, s. 167, created a nuisance offence related to 'taxi touts'. It is an offence for a person, in a public place, to solicit persons to hire vehicles to carry them as passengers. However, as this offence is aimed at unauthorised persons, it does not apply where the soliciting is permitted by a taxi-sharing scheme under the Transport Act 1985 in accordance with any taxi code. Where this is so, there will be an indication on the vehicle that it is an authorised vehicle. The offence is an arrestable offence.

Lights on vehicles

Introduction

The Act of Parliament which controls the lighting of vehicles used on roads during the hours of darkness is the Road Traffic Act 1988. It authorises the Secretary of State for Transport to make regulations. The Road Vehicles Lighting Regulations 1989 currently set out the details of road vehicle lighting requirements. There is a general requirement that all vehicles must display lights of various types while being driven or used on a road between sunset and sunrise or during the hours of darkness. There are additional requirements when visibility is seriously reduced during times other than 'hours of darkness'. It will be appreciated that certain lights must be used at all times whether it is light or dark. Direction indicators are used at all times and the purpose of stop lights is not to make the vehicle visible when it is dark, it is to warn following drivers that the brakes are being applied. The regulations therefore seek to ensure the provision of satisfactory lighting so that vehicles may be seen at night; so that drivers can see the road ahead at night; so that manoeuvres of vehicles can be anticipated and to ensure the safety of other road users generally.

Roads

The term 'road' is defined as meaning any length of highway or of any other road to which the public has access, and includes bridges over which a road passes. The Act and Regulations are concerned with vehicles which are 'on a road'. It has been established that a motor vehicle is on a road if it is partly on a road and partly on private land and that the forecourt of an hotel can be deemed to be part of a highway if there is no obstruction separating it from the road and it is frequently used by the public to pass from one street to another. However, other cases involving such private property have resulted in different rulings, but always on the grounds that where there was no separation from the highway, there was no evidence of public use. Normally, a highway is described as the area of right of way as defined by its fences. Grass verges may be a part of the highway, but this is dependent upon who erected the fences. If they were erected by the highway authority, it raises a presumption that the fences define the extent of the highway itself. Whether a road is public or private is dependent upon the evidence available of public use, rather than ownership. A private road leading to a farmhouse which was maintained by the farmer, but had no gate, was held to be a road to which the public had access, evidence being given that it was used by people who had no business at the farm.

Daytime hours

This means the time between half an hour before sunrise and half and hour after sunset.

Hours of darkness

This means the time between half an hour after sunset and half an hour before sunrise. The term 'sunset' means sunset according to local, not Greenwich time and as lighting up times vary from place to place within Great Britain, lighting up times are frequently published in force orders. All local newspapers publish local lighting up times.

Obligatory lights and reflectors

The term 'obligatory' is defined by the regulations. It means, in relation to a lamp, reflector, rear marking or device; a lamp, reflector, rear marking or device with which a vehicle, its load or equipment is required by the regulations to be fitted. The 1989 Regulations, and particularly the schedules to these regulations, specify quite precisely the lights, etc., the performance expected from those lights, etc., and the permitted uses of such lights, etc.

Optional lamps and reflectors

The regulations state that 'optional', in relation to a lamp, reflector, rear marking or device means a lamp, reflector, rear marking or device, with which a vehicle, its load or equipment is not required by the regulations to be fitted.

There are quite a number of lights which are permitted to be fitted by the regulations as 'optional extras' but if they are fitted, the nature of the lamps, etc., the positions in which they may be fitted, their performance and their use are nevertheless controlled by the regulations.

The situation generally is that certain lamps, etc., must be fitted to vehicles and certain additional lamps, etc., may be fitted. If additional optional lamps, etc., are fitted they must comply with the provisions of the 1989 Regulations. In this way, the law ensures that a multiplicity of lamps, reflectors, etc., are not fitted to vehicles in such a way that confusion and danger may be caused to other road users.

Types of lamps and reflectors which are obligatory on most motor vehicles

(1) Headlamps

The regulations define two types of headlamps, main beam and dipped headlamps. Although separately defined most vehicles carry headlamps. A 'main beam' means a beam of light emitted by a lamp which illuminates the road over a long distance ahead of the vehicle. A 'dipped beam' means a beam of light emitted by a lamp which illuminates the road ahead of the vehicle without causing undue dazzle or discomfort to oncoming drivers or other road users.

In most circumstances two dipped beam headlamps are required by motor vehicles with three or more wheels. The maximum permitted distance from the side of the vehicle is usually 400 mm (except vehicles first used before 1 January 1972, agricultural, engineering, and industrial tractors). There is no minimum distance by which the two lamps need to be separated. Solo motor bicycles or combinations and three wheelers first used before 1 January 1972, and certain others, require only one headlamp on the centre line of the motor vehicle itself. Buses first used before 1 October 1969 need only have one dipped beam headlamp.

Dipped beam headlamps should generally be not more than 1200 mm and not less than 500 mm from the ground. There are no minimum requirements for vehicles first used before 1 January 1956 and no maximum for vehicles first used before 1 January 1952 or regardless of date, for agricultural, emergency or home forces vehicles. They must be of the same colour and intensity and switch off and on together.

The light which must be emitted by a dipped beam headlamp must be either white or yellow. The lamp must be such that the direction of the beam of light can be adjusted while the vehicle is stationary. Where two dipped beam lamps are required to be fitted, they must form a matched pair and be capable of being switched on and off simultaneously and not otherwise.

The provisions concerning main beam headlamps are the same with the exception that buses first used before 1 October 1969 are required to have two main beam headlamps. They must have two headlamps but only one of them needs to be capable of dipping. Main beam headlamps must be such that they can be deflected at the will of the driver to become a dipped beam, or so that they can be extinguished by a device which at the same time switches on dipped beam, or causes another lamp to emit a dipped beam. 'Long range' driving lamps are invariably fitted by manufacturers so that they are extinguished by the dip switch operating the normal headlamps.

The 1989 Regulations require that vehicles first used on or after 1 April 1987 shall be fitted with 'dim-dip' lighting devices. The devices are capable of causing a dipped-beam headlamp to operate at reduced intensity. Alternatively, vehicles may be equipped with a 'running lamp' which is a lamp used to make the presence of a moving vehicle readily visible from the front. Vehicles having a maximum speed of 40 mph, home forces vehicles and those complying with Community Directives are exempt.

Headlamps may not be used so as to cause undue dazzle or discomfort to other persons using the road and shall not be lit when a vehicle is parked.

(2) *Front and rear position lamps*

These terms replace previous references to 'side lights'. A 'front position lamp' is one which is used to indicate the presence and width of a vehicle when viewed from the front. A 'rear position lamp' indicates its presence and width from the rear.

Vehicles with three or more wheels (other than invalid carriages and pedal tricycles) require two front and two rear position lamps. Front position lamps shall be white in colour, unless they are incorporated in a yellow headlamp, in which case they may be yellow. All rear position lamps must be red in colour.

Front position lamps on vehicles first used before 1 April 1986 must not be more than 510 mm from the side of the vehicle. Motor vehicles first used after that date must have front position lamps not more than 400 mm from the side. Pedal cycles, solo motor bicycles, and invalid carriages require only one front position lamp which must be fitted on the centre line or offside of the vehicle. Motor cycle combinations with a headlamp on the motor bicycle require a front position lamp on the centre line of the sidecar, or on the side of the sidecar furthest from the motor bicycle. Solo motor bicycles fitted with a headlamp need not be fitted with a front position lamp.

Certain vehicles do not require two rear position lamps. Those which require only one include buses first used before 1 April 1955, solo motor cycles, pedal cycles with less than four wheels, trailers drawn by pedal cycles, trailers (the overall width of which does not exceed 800 mm) drawn by solo or motor cycle combinations, invalid carriages having a maximum speed not exceeding 4 mph, and vehicles propelled by hand. (There is a general exemption for some hand propelled vehicles not exceeding 800 mm in width.) Rear position lamps, where two are required to be fitted on vehicles first used before 1 April 1986, shall not be more than 800 mm from the side of the vehicle. After that date the distance will be reduced to 400 mm. In cases in which only one rear position lamp is required it must be fitted on the centre line of the vehicle or on its offside. Because of the tendency of enthusiasts to fit extra rear position lamps, it is helpful to know that the maximum permitted height of such lights on motor vehicles first used before 1 April 1986 other than buses, or trailers manufactured before 1 October 1985 and other specialist exemptions is 2100 mm. Vehicles first used after 1 April 1986 will have a permitted maximum of 1500 mm unless the structure of the vehicle makes this impracticable, when the height of 2100 mm will apply.

The provisions concerning rear position lamps also apply to trailers.

(3) *Rear registration lamps*

Every motor vehicle which is required to be fitted with a rear registration plate must have lighting, which is capable of adequately illuminating the rear registration plate.

(4) *Stop lamps*

All motor vehicles having three or more wheels, and trailers drawn by motor vehicles must, unless otherwise stated in the regulations, be fitted with two stop lamps. Solo motor bicycles, combinations, invalid carriages and trailers drawn by motor cycles and motor vehicles or trailers first used before 1 January 1971 need only be fitted with one stop lamp. Motor cycles of less than 50 cc, if first used before 1 April 1986, are exempt.

If two are fitted they should be one each side of the longitudinal axis of the vehicle. If there is only one it should be on the centre line or offside of the vehicle. Stop lights must be separated by a distance of at least 400 mm and they should not be more than 1500 mm from the ground, or if the structure of the vehicle makes this impracticable 2100 mm. The minimum height is 350 mm. There are no maximum or minimum height specifications for vehicles first used before 1 January 1971. Those first used before 1 January 1936 do not require stop lamps, nor do vehicles with a maximum speed of 25 mph or less; or agricultural vehicles or works trucks first used before 1 April 1986.

Stop lamps must be operated by the application of a service braking system. If there are two, they must form a pair. It is common practice for enthusiasts to fit additional stop lamps and there is no restriction upon the number of such lights which may be fitted. If additional lights are fitted they must comply with all of the provisions of Schedule 12 to the regulations, except the requirements as to number, position, and angles of visibility. Motor vehicles, other than motor bicycles, first used on or after 1 April 1991 are subject to control in relation to the intensity of the light projected through rear windows.

(5) *Direction indicators*

Motor vehicles first used before 1 April 1936 and trailers manufactured before that date may have any arrangement of indicators which makes the intentions of the driver clear to other road users but they are not required to have any indicators at all. Motor vehicles first used on or after that date and before 1 April 1986 (or trailers manufactured between 1 January 1936 and 1 October 1985) must be provided with any arrangement of indicator so as to satisfy the requirements for angles of visibility. They may not have more than one front indicator on each side and two rear indicators on each side.

Motor vehicles first used on or after 1 April 1986 and trailers manufactured on or after 1 October 1985, if having more than three wheels, must have a front and rear indicator and a side repeater indicator on each side of the vehicle. They must also have at least one side repeater indicator on each side. Trailers may have one or two rear indicators on each side. Motor bicycles and combinations, first used on or after 1 April 1986, must have one single front and one single rear indicator on each side of the vehicle.

All indicators shall be operated by one switch. There must be a tell-tale to show that the indicators are in operation. Flashing indicators must flash at a constant rate of not less than 60 and not more than 120 times per minute.

(6) *Rear retro reflectors*

It is generally required that all vehicles and trailers will be equipped with two retro reflectors. Some vehicles only require one rear retro reflector; they are solo motor bicycles; pedal cycles with less than four wheels (with or without a sidecar); trailers drawn by pedal cycles generally; trailers not exceeding 800 mm drawn by solo motor cycles or combinations; invalid carriages having a maximum speed not exceeding 4 mph; and hand propelled vehicles. There are some vehicles which are restricted in respect of speed (maximum of 25 mph) which require four reflectors.

Reflectors must be fitted at or near the rear of the vehicle. Motor vehicles first used before 1 April 1986 and manufactured before 1 October 1985 must have their obligatory reflectors fitted no more than 610 mm from the side. After these dates the distance is reduced to 400 mm. Where only one reflector is fitted it must be on the centre line or offside of the vehicle. Before the 1 April 1986 deadline, the maximum permitted height of reflectors is 1525 mm for motor vehicles. After that date the height is reduced to 900 mm unless the structure of the vehicle makes it impracticable (when it may be 1200 mm). All rear reflectors must be red.

(7) *Rear fog lamps*

All motor vehicles having three or more wheels, and all trailers drawn by motor vehicles must (unless specifically dealt with in some other way) have at least one rear fog lamp fitted, at or near the rear, on the centre line or offside of the vehicle. If there are two lamps fitted there is no requirement concerning the distance at which the lamps are placed from the sides of the vehicle. The maximum height from the ground is 100 mm (except agricultural, engineering plant and motor tractors) and the minimum height is 250 mm. Rear fog lamps must be separated from the stop lamps of the vehicle by a minimum distance of 100 mm. No more than two lamps may be fitted.

Rear fog lamps must show a red light. They must not be fitted so that they are illuminated by the braking of the vehicle. There must be a tell-tale fitted to show that the light(s) are on. If two lamps are fitted to a motor vehicle first used on or after 1 April 1986, they must be a matched pair.

Vehicles first used before 1 April 1980 (or manufactured before 1 October 1979) are not required to have rear fog lamps. These are limited exceptions. If they do have them, there are no restrictions in respect of number, but they must be separated from stop lamps by a distance of at least 1000 mm and must not be capable of illumination by the braking system.

Motor vehicles either used or manufactured on or after these dates are not permitted to have more than two rear fog lamps and both must comply with all of the conditions set out above.

Rear fog lamps must not be used so as to cause undue dazzle or discomfort to other following drivers. They must not be used when a vehicle, other than an emergency vehicle, is parked. Their use generally is restricted to conditions of seriously reduced visibility.

Trailers, the overall width of which does not exceed 1300 mm, do not require rear fog lamps.

(8) *Hazard warning signals*

A hazard warning signal device is one which is capable of causing all the direction indicators with which a vehicle, or a combination of vehicles, is fitted to operate simultaneously.

The device must be operated by one switch which causes all of the direction indicators with which the vehicle (or combination of vehicles) is equipped to flash in phase. There must be a tell-tale in the vehicle and the device must be capable of operation without the ignition being switched on.

The fitting of hazard warning signal devices is obligatory on vehicles having three or more wheels and first used on or after 1 April 1986 with the exception of vehicles which are not required to be fitted with indicators.

Hazard warning signals may only be used on a motor vehicle while it is stationary to warn road users of a temporary obstruction or of the presence of a school bus which is loading or unloading or on a motorway or unrestricted dual carriageway, to warn of a temporary obstruction ahead, or in the case of a bus to summon assistance. A bus which is fitted with a sign of yellow reflective material (including black figures of school children) may use hazard warning lights when it is stationary and children are entering or leaving the vehicle, or are about to enter or leave, or have just left the vehicle.

Types of lamps which are commonly found as 'optional lamps' on motor vehicles

(1) *Reversing lamps*

A vehicle may not be fitted with more than two reversing lamps. They are fitted to vehicles to indicate when the vehicle is reversing and to illuminate the road to the rear. The light shown must be white.

The reversing lamps must be wired so that the only way in which the light can be switched on is by selecting reverse gear, or by using a switch which shows a tell-tale light when the lamps are in use. Such lamps may not be used for any purpose, other than reversing the vehicle.

(2) *Front fog lamps*

The term 'fog lamp' clearly indicates the intended use of these optional lamps. They are lamps used to improve the illumination of the road in front of a motor vehicle in conditions of seriously reduced visibility and are fitted in a low position to allow light to seek out the road in poor visibility conditions when a headlamp light tends to become scattered by fog or falling snow. They must be white or yellow lights. Where they are used in conditions of seriously reduced visibility in place of the obligatory headlamps they must not be more than 400 mm from the side of the vehicle. This is logical; they are being used as headlights and should give a clear indication of the approximate width of the vehicle. They may not be placed more than 1200 mm from the ground, there is no minimum height requirement. (The maximum height permits the usual exceptions – as with headlamps.)

If the front fog lamps are used in place of the obligatory headlamps they must be a matched pair. These lights may only be used, when the vehicle is on a road, in conditions of seriously reduced visibility. They must not be lit if this causes undue dazzle or discomfort to other road users and must not be lit when the vehicle is parked. Motor vehicles (other than motor bicycles) first used on or after 1 April 1991 may not have more than two front fog lamps.

(3) Warning beacons

Certain vehicles are permitted to show blue, amber, green (yellow on limited occasions) rotating lights to indicate to other road uses the presence of those vehicles on a road in special circumstances.

A blue and white chequered light is permitted from a domed lamp fitted to a police control vehicle and intended for use at the scene of an emergency; a blue lamp is permitted from a warning beacon, or rear special warning lamp on an emergency vehicle.

Amber lamps are authorised on road clearance, refuse, breakdown vehicles, vehicles when not exceeding 25 mph, those with an overall width exceeding 2.9 m, road service vehicles, special vehicles carrying abnormal loads (and escorts) and vehicles of HM Customs and Excise (fuel testing vehicles). Motor vehicles first used before 1 January 1947 with a maximum speed not exceeding 25 mph must show, or show on any trailer, at least one amber warning beacon when on an unrestricted dual carriageway road (other than a motorway). This does not apply to such vehicles merely crossing such a road.

Green lights are limited to registered medical practitioners, who may only use such lights in an emergency.

Yellow lights (as opposed to amber) are quite rare. They are used by airport vehicles.

All warning beacons must be mounted so that the centre of the lamp is not less than 1200 mm from the ground. They must flash between 60 and 240 times per minute at constant intervals.

Trailers – obligatory lights and reflectors

(1) General rule

The general rule is that trailers require the same obligatory lamps as the towing vehicle, with the obvious exception of headlamps. On occasions, trailers do not require front position lamps; if they do not exceed 1600 mm width; pre-October 1985 vehicles if their length, excluding draw bar, does not exceed 2300 mm, or boat trailers. Obviously, there are no exceptions in respect of rear position lamps.

Trailers which are not fitted with lights may lawfully be used on a road during daylight hours.

(2) Side marker lamps

Side marker lamps, that is lamps fitted to the side of a vehicle or its load and used to render the vehicle more visible to other road users, must be fitted to some trailers (and motor vehicles). Exemption exists in favour of trailers the overall length of which, excluding any drawbar and any fitting for its attachment, does not exceed 6 m or 9.15 m if manufactured before 1 October 1990. The obligatory requirements are to have two side marker lamps on each side and as many more as are sufficient to ensure that the maximum distance from the front of the vehicle (including any drawbar) to the first lamp is 4 m and the maximum distance from the rear in respect of the rearmost side marker lamp is 1 m. The maximum separation distance of adjacent obligatory side marker lamps on the same side of the vehicle is 3 m or, if this is not practicable, 4 m. (Motor vehicles first used before 1 April 1991 are exempt from these provisions.) Additional side marker lamps are required to be fitted to a vehicle, or a combination of vehicles the overall length of which (including any load) exceeds 18.3 m, one lamp being no more than 9.15 m from the foremost part of the vehicle or vehicles and one lamp no more than 3.05 m from the rear (including loads in both instances). Other lamps must be placed to ensure that no more than 3.05 m separates lamps. Where the length exceeds 12.2 m but not 18.3 m and the load is supported by any two vehicles, there shall be lamps placed behind the rearmost part of the drawing vehicle, but not more than 1530 mm to the rear of that point. If the supported load extends more than 9.15 m to the rear of the drawing vehicle, the lamp shall not be forward of, or more than 1530 mm to the rear of, the centre of the length of the load. These last provisions do not apply to articulated vehicles. Lamps must be no more than 2300 mm from the ground. There is no minimum height restriction.

(3) End-outline marker lamps

Trailers (and motor vehicles) with an overall width exceeding 2100 mm require end-outline marker lamps. These are lamps fitted near the outer edge of a vehicle in addition to the front and rear position lamps to indicate the presence of a wide vehicle. There must be two visible from the front and two visible from the rear. They must be no more than 400 mm from the side of the vehicle. These provisions apply to trailers manufactured on or after 1 October 1990 (and to motor vehicles first used on or after 1 April 1991). Any number *may* be fitted.

(4) Side retro reflectors

Side retro reflectors are obligatory on certain trailers (and motor vehicles). The provisions do not apply to passenger vehicles, nor to goods vehicles whose overall length does not exceed 6 m (if first used on or after 1 April 1986); or whose overall length does not exceed 8 m (if first used before that date). We are, therefore, considering long goods vehicles. In the case of such vehicles first used before 1 April 1986 and trailers manufactured before 1 October 1985, there must be two side retro reflectors on each side of the vehicle. In the case of those first used or manufactured on or after those dates, there must be two on each side of the vehicle and as many more as are required by para. 2(a) of Schedule 17 to the regulations. Side retro reflectors must be amber or, within 1 m of the rear of the vehicle, they may be red. They must not be triangular in shape.

(5) *Rear markings*

The provisions concerning *rear markings* are dealt with here as they are more commonly associated with articulated vehicles and are therefore primarily concerned with trailers. These are 'long vehicle' markings. Such long vehicles which are first used before 1 April 1996 which do not exceed 13 m in length need only carry marker boards with diagonal lines of fluorescent yellow and red. Those which exceed that length must have boards which also display the words 'long vehicle' in black on a yellow background surrounded by a red border, or as an alternative, boards of yellow retro reflective material surrounded by a red fluorescent border. Those used on or after 1 April 1996 which do not exceed 13 m must carry boards of red and yellow diagonal stripes and those which exceed 13 m, boards of yellow retro reflective material surrounded by a red fluorescent border. Trailers forming part of a combination of vehicles are similarly affected; if, in the case of a trailer manufactured before 1 October 1995, the overall length does not exceed 11 m the marking must be of the diagonal line variety; if between 11 m and 13 m the marking may be of any approved variety; and if it exceeds 13 m it must be of the 'long vehicle' type, or a board of yellow reflective material surrounded by a red fluorescent border. In the case of a trailer manufactured on or after 1 October 1995 which does not exceed 11 m, it must carry a board of red and yellow diagonal stripes; if it exceeds 11 m but not 13 m it may carry boards of such red and yellow stripes or of yellow surrounded by red; and if it exceeds 13 m, the boards must be of yellow surrounded by red.

(6) *General exceptions*

Within the requirements set out above there are a number of vehicles which are exempt, but those exemptions are predictable. They are, for example, works trailers, agricultural trailers, on occasions, boat trailers and incomplete trailers. Itemised provisions are set out in Schedule 1, Table VI, concerning exceptions to the general rules and the particular provisions relating to each type of lamp are set out in following schedules.

Overhanging and projecting loads

Regulation 21 prohibits any person from using, or causing or permitting to be used on a road:

(a) any trailer which projects laterally beyond the preceding vehicle in the combination; or

243

(b) any vehicle or combination of vehicles which carries a load or equipment which (in either case) does not comply with the specifications set out in the regulation.

The specifications with which we are concerned are:

(a) a trailer which (or whose load) projects laterally more than 400 mm from the outermost part of the obligatory front position lamp on that side of the vehicle in front of it, must have white lights to the front which are not more than 400 mm from the outermost projection of the trailer (or, as the case may be, of the load);

(b) a vehicle whose load projects laterally more than 400 mm must have lights at the front and rear not more than 400 mm from the outermost projection of the load;

(c) a vehicle whose load projects more than 1 m to the front or to the rear must have a front or rear lamp not more than 1 m from the foremost or rearmost projection of the load (except that that distance is 2 m in the case of an agricultural vehicle or vehicle carrying a fire escape); or

(d) a vehicle carrying a load which obscures any obligatory lamps, reflector or rear markings must show a lamp, etc., in the prescribed position.

These restrictions only apply while the vehicle is being used between sunset and sunrise or in conditions of reduced visibility, except that in relation to stop lights and direction indicators in the circumstances set out at (d) the requirement applies at any time.

Pedal cycles – lamps and reflectors

There is no daytime requirement in relation to pedal cycles. They need only be fitted with obligatory lamps and reflectors if used during the hours of darkness. They require one front position lamp which shows a white light, one rear position lamp which shows a red light and one rear, red reflex reflector.

Pedal cycles which are manufactured after September 1985 must be fitted with amber reflectors on the leading and trailing edge of each pedal.

Use of obligatory lamps during the hours of darkness

A person must not use, or cause or permit to be used, on a road, a vehicle which is fitted with obligatory dipped beam headlamps unless every such lamp is kept lit:

(a) during the hours of darkness, except on a road which is a restricted road by virtue of a system of street lighting with lamps not more than 200 yards apart which are lit; and

(b) in seriously reduced visibility (i.e. during daylight hours).

It must be remembered that in (b), front fog lamps, as previously discussed, may be used as an alternative to headlamps but only if they are fitted as described.

In addition, the regulations prohibit a person using, or causing or permitting to be used, a vehicle on a road between sunset and sunrise or (while the vehicle is in motion) during daytime hours in seriously reduced visibility unless every front position lamp, rear position lamp, rear registration plate lamp required by the regulations to be fitted is kept lit. The term 'seriously reduced visibility' is not defined by the regulations. Common sense requires that the various forms of lighting should be used when the daytime situation requires them in the interests of road safety.

The provisions do not apply to a solo motor cycle or pedal cycle which is being pushed along the left-hand edge of the carriageway; a pedal cycle waiting to proceed provided it is kept to the left-hand or nearside edge of a carriageway; or a vehicle which is parked in an area outlined by lamps or traffic signs so as to prevent the presence of the vehicle, its load or equipment being a danger to persons using the road.

The regulations also exempt vehicles of certain classes which are parked during the hours of darkness on roads which are subject to speed limits of 30 mph or less, from showing such lights. The vehicles which are exempt are goods vehicles not exceeding 1525 kg; passenger vehicles other than buses, invalid carriages, and motor cycles and pedal cycles (in either case with or without a sidecar). If a trailer is attached to such vehicles the exemption does not apply, nor does it apply if the vehicle is carrying a load which requires lamps. The regulations only apply to particular places:

(a) designated parking places on roads; or
(b) a lay-by which is clearly shown to be such; or
(c) elsewhere provided, if the vehicle is parked on a one-way road, it is facing in the correct direction on either side of the road as close as possible to the kerb or, if it is parked on an ordinary road, it is properly parked and facing the correct way, and in either case no part of the vehicle is less than 10 m from a junction with the road upon which it is parked, whether the junction is on the same side of the road or not. For the purposes of measuring the distance from a junction where a curving kerb exists, the junction is regarded as beginning where the kerb begins to curve.

Light goods vehicles, passenger vehicles, combinations, solo cycles and invalid carriageways may therefore park on restricted roads provided that they are in a designated parking place, a lay-by, or *elsewhere* on a one-way street or ordinary road provided that they are not within 10 m of a junction on either side of the road.

The person who parks without lights outside the permitted exceptions commits the offence of allowing the vehicle to remain at rest, or cause or permit to be allowed to remain at rest, on a road, between sunset and sunrise, without the front and rear position lamps, and/or rear registration plate lamp, being kept lit.

General control on parking at night

The Road Vehicles (Construction and Use) Regulations prohibit any person, without the permission of a police constable in uniform, causing or permitting any motor vehicle to stand on any road between sunset and sunrise otherwise than with the left or nearside of the vehicle as close as may be to the edge of the carriageway. The usual exemptions apply in respect of emergency and public utility vehicles and, of course, in one-way streets.

This offence is not concerned with the Road Vehicles Lighting Regulations of

1989, it is concerned with vehicles being parked facing the wrong way at night. If the vehicles are unlit, in circumstances in which they should be lit, then a second offence is committed.

Maintenance of lamps and reflectors

It is an offence for a person to use, or cause or permit to be used, on a road any vehicle unless every front position lamp, rear position lamp, headlamp, rear registration plate lamp, rear fog lamp, retro reflector with which it is required to be fitted, is in good working order and in the case of a lamp, clean.

The regulations require the correct maintenance of all lamps, reflectors and devices which the vehicle is required to have fitted. Additionally, they demand that every stop lamp and direction indicator, even if they are in excess of the number required to be fitted, be maintained at all times. The provisions concerning rear fog lamps do not apply to a vehicle which is drawing a trailer (as the rear fog lamp will not show in any case). There is also a proviso which excuses a defective lamp of any character if the defect arose in the course of a daytime journey (but this would not excuse use at night), or if arrangements have been made to have the defect remedied with all reasonable expedition. Thus, a vehicle with a defective wiring loom might be used during the daytime if it had been 'booked in' for repair. Similarly a vehicle may be driven to a garage to have a new bulb or fuse fitted.

Dipped beam headlamps, front fog lamps, rear fog lamps and reversing lamps must be so maintained so that their aim will not cause undue dazzle or discomfort to other persons using the road. These provisions apply to all lamps fitted, whether required by the regulations to be fitted or not. It is an offence to use, cause or permit to be used, on a road, a vehicle with such lamps not so maintained.

Fitting and use of lamps and reflectors

The 1989 Regulations require that obligatory lamps, reflectors, devices, etc., are fitted to vehicles and are performing satisfactorily at all times. These requirements, however, do not apply to incomplete vehicles which are proceeding to a works for completion, pedal cycles, pedestrian controlled vehicles, horse drawn vehicles, hand propelled vehicles and certain combat vehicles of HM Forces.

The exemption also applies to a vehicle which is not fitted with any front or rear position lamps. If an enthusiast is building a car from parts and has not yet installed a lighting system, he will not commit an offence by using the car during the daytime. (He would, of course, if he used it at night.) For the purposes of the regulations a lamp shall not be treated as a lamp if it is painted over or masked so that it is not capable of being immediately used or readily put to use, or if it is an electric lamp which is not provided with any system of wiring by means of which that lamp is (or can readily be) connected with a source of electricity. Headlamps, etc., which are masked over or are not wired up, could not be used in such a way that they would cause undue dazzle or inconvenience, so the exemption, during daylight hours is logical. The vehicle could not be used generally, upon the roads at night as it could not display headlights in the circumstances required. Equally it could not be used in conditions of seriously reduced visibility.

Offences by owners and drivers

Motor cycles and mopeds

For the definitions of the terms 'motor cycle' and 'moped', see page 170.

Passengers on motor cycles

The Road Traffic Act 1988, s. 23, provides that no more than one person, in addition to the driver, shall be carried on a two-wheeled motor cycle. Such a passenger must be carried sitting astride the cycle, on a proper seat securely fixed to the cycle behind the driver's seat. It is important to recognise that the duties are those of the driver, who commits the offence of carrying more than one passenger, or of carrying a passenger otherwise than astride the machine on a seat securely fixed behind the driver. The person carried may be proceeded against for aiding, abetting, counselling, or procuring the commission of the offence, if sufficient evidence of 'joint enterprise' is available.

Footrests for passengers

The Road Vehicles (Construction and Use) Regulations 1986, Regulation 102 provides that if any person, in addition to the driver, is carried astride any two-wheeled motor cycle (whether a sidecar is attached or not), suitable supports or rests for the feet shall be available on the cycle.

The offence is one of using, causing, or permitting a two-wheeled motor cycle to be used on a road, upon which a person in addition to the driver was carried astride, there not being available on the cycle for that person suitable supports or rests for the feet.

Protective headgear

Every person driving or riding a motor bicycle on a road (otherwise than in a sidecar) shall wear protective headgear of approved design. If he does not, he commits an offence under the Road Traffic Act 1988, s. 16(4). The regulations which are contravened are the Motor Cycles (Protective Helmets) Regulations 1980. Turban wearing followers of the Sikh religion are exempted. There is no requirement to wear a crash helmet when pushing a motor cycle. A driver is not liable in respect of a passenger who does not wear a crash helmet, unless that passenger is under 16 years.

Passengers on pedal cycles

By the Road Traffic Act 1988, s. 24, it is not lawful for more than one person to be carried on a road on a bicycle not propelled by mechanical power unless it is constructed or adapted for the carriage of more than one person. If a cycle is ridden in contravention of this section, each of the persons carried is guilty of an offence. A tandem machine provides a good example of a cycle which is constructed for the

247

carriage of more than one person. Cycles are frequently seen which have been adapted by the owner to allow a child to be carried by attaching a seat securely to the cross bar, with footrests provided below it. The test as to whether or not there has been an adaptation can be applied by asking the question. 'If the vehicle had been originally produced in this form, would it have been produced for the carriage of two persons?'

Riding on a footpath

The offence of wilfully riding a pedal cycle on a footpath by the side of a road and set apart for pedestrians is one contrary to s. 72 of the Highways Act 1835. There are, frequently, local by-laws controlling the use of pedal cycles in particular places.

Brakes on pedal cycles

The Pedal Cycles (Construction and Use) Regulations 1983 are not the most easily understood regulations to appear in legal textbooks. It is helpful to imagine in the first instance, the types of pedal cycles which are likely to be seen in use on a road and to consider in each case the braking systems which are required. We must think in terms of children's cycles, all forms of bicycles, passenger and goods tricycles and, since these regulations also deal with the new concept of electrically assisted pedal cycles, we must also consider the separate provisions made for such cycles. No person under 14 may ride an electrically assisted pedal cycle. Such a cycle is not a motor vehicle. In addition the 1983 Regulations make different provisions in respect of cycles manufactured before the 1 August 1984.

Let us first consider cycles manufactured before 1 August 1984. Generally in the case of two-wheeled machines with wheels exceeding 460 mm in outside diameter, including the fully inflated tyre, there are two types of pedal cycle to consider. The first has a fixed wheel (a wheel which cannot rotate independently of the pedals) and the other has two free wheels. The fixed wheel is really a braking system in itself and it is possible to bring the cycle to a halt by progressively slowing down the pedalling action. It is not surprising to find that such a cycle requires only one braking system operating on the front wheel. If such a bicycle is free wheel then it is obvious that it will require two independent systems operating on each wheel.

Cycles with a lesser wheel diameter than that prescribed require only one braking system, e.g. a child's cycle, although some children's cycles are exempt entirely from these provisions.

Tricycles with wheels exceeding 460 mm are more rare than bicycles and most that still exist are passenger (that is non-goods) tricycles. In such cases it is sufficient to have two independent braking systems operating on the single wheel of the machine. Although it is now unusual to see a goods tricycle, some still do exist which are used for the sale of 'hot dogs', etc. They are tricycles which are constructed or adapted for the carriage of goods and they require, if fixed wheel, a system of operating on all front wheels. (There may be one or two depending upon the construction of the tricycle.) If it is free wheel it must have braking systems operating on both the front and rear wheels and the front system must act on all of the wheels (there may be one or two), but that fitted to the rear need only act on one wheel (whether one or two are fitted).

Pedal cycles manufactured on or after the 1 August 1984 must be equipped with at least one braking system. If they have a saddle, the height of which is 635 mm (the part of the seat furthest from the ground) or more, or have four or more wheels they must in the case of fixed wheel cycles have a braking system operating on the front wheel(s) and in the case of a free wheel cycle, two independent systems: one operating on the front wheel(s) and the other on the rear wheel(s).

These provisions must apply to at least two wheels where there is more than one wheel, although perhaps this did not need to be said as the likelihood of finding a cycle with three wheels at either the front or the rear is at present remote. In general terms, as most cycles with which police officers deal are bicycles, those manufactured on or after 1 August 1984 are treated in the same way as those manufactured before that date, with the substitution of saddle height for wheel diameter as the criterion.

Offences are committed by those who ride, or cause or permit to be ridden on a road, a pedal cycle which does not comply with the regulations concerning the fitting of brakes on pedal cycles.

The regulations introduce legislation governing pedal cycles to which the Electrically Assisted Pedal Cycle Regulations 1983 apply. An electrically assisted pedal cycle is one which has pedals by which the cycle may be propelled and a kerbside weight not exceeding 40 kg and a continuously rated electrical output not exceeding 0.2 kilowatts. All of these cycles must be such that the electric motor will not operate when the cycle is travelling at more than 15 mph. Tandems and tricycles may weigh 60 kg and their rated output may be 0.25 kilowatts.

No person shall ride or cause or permit to be ridden on a road, a pedal cycle to which the Electrically Assisted Pedal Cycle Regulations 1983 apply unless it is fitted with braking systems which are so designed and constructed that, in the case of a bicycle, they comply with clause 6 of the British Standard and in the case of a tricycle they comply with standards no less than those set out for a bicycle in that standard. These provisions are also included in the Pedal Cycles (Construction and Use) Regulations 1983 and, therefore, follow the pattern of the Road Vehicle (Construction and Use) Regulations in being directed towards manufacturers in matters regarding safety. It can be safely assumed that the braking requirements for electrically assisted pedal cycles will have been met by the manufacturers. It is only in instances of 'amateur conversions' that police officers may have to refer to the British Standard. Copies (which will be required for production in court in any case) can be obtained from the British Standards Institution at 195 Pentonville Road, London N1 9ND.

The most likely offence is one of failure to maintain a braking system and this offence can be committed by a person who rides, causes or permits such an electrically assisted cycle to be ridden on a road when the braking systems are not in efficient working order.

These cycles are also required to carry a securely fixed plate showing the name of the manufacturer, the voltage of the battery and the rated output. The battery must not leak and there must be a device, biased to the off position, which allows power from the battery only when it is operated. An offence is committed by anyone who rides, causes or permits the riding on a road of such a cycle if the plate is not fixed, or if the battery leaks or if there is not such a device.

Maintenance of brakes

All braking systems required by the Pedal Cycle (Construction and Use) Regulations must be efficient and kept in proper working order, and it is an offence if they are not. Any system fitted to a cycle which operates directly on the tyre of any wheel is not permitted.

Exemptions

Persons who are resident outside Great Britain, who are staying temporarily, may use cycles which do not comply with these Regulations. However, certain safety standards are set down by the Geneva Convention on Road Traffic. There is also an exemption in respect of cycles which are so constructed that the pedals act directly upon any wheel or the axle of such wheel. Examples are the penny farthing bicycle and the small tricycles with solid wheels to which pedals are attached, used by small children.

Police powers

Any police officer in uniform may test and inspect the brakes of any cycle being used on a road at any time. Inspections may also be carried out on premises within 48 hours of an accident, provided that the owner of the premises consents.

Vehicles – dangerous position

A person in charge of a vehicle commits an offence if he causes or permits the vehicle or its trailer to remain at rest on a road in such a position, or in such a condition, or in such circumstances as to be likely to cause danger to other persons using the road. A person is in charge of a vehicle from the moment he takes it out on to the road until he puts it away again or hands it over to some person, thus surrendering his charge of it. This offence is committed in relation to vehicles (not necessarily motor vehicles). The common element is danger but the section describes three ways in which that danger might be caused. It may be the way it is parked; it may be its condition (although other offences contrary to the Road Vehicles (Construction and Use) Regulations might also be considered in such circumstances) or the total circumstances surrounding the presence of the vehicle and its condition may be taken cumulatively to cause that danger.

A traffic warden may require a person whom he has reasonable cause to believe to have committed such an offence, to produce his driving licence.

Causing danger to road users

By s. 22A of the 1988 Act, a person is guilty of an offence if he intentionally and without lawful authority or reasonable excuse:

(a) causes anything to be on or over a road; or

(b) interferes with a motor vehicle, trailer or cycle; or

(c) interferes (directly or indirectly) with traffic equipment in such circumstances that it would be obvious to a reasonable person that to do so would be dangerous. The term 'danger' for the purposes of this offence relates to danger either of injury to any person while on or near a road, or of serious damage to property on or near a road. In determining what would be obvious to a reasonable person in a particular case, regard shall be had not only to the circumstances of which he could be expected to be aware but also to circumstances shown to have been within the knowledge of the accused.

Where a person hangs out washing in a back street, that person certainly causes articles to be over a road. However, it could be argued that those actions were not 'dangerous' as opposed to being a nuisance. Washing can easily be seen and such danger is unlikely. He who deflates a tyre to a low pressure, or who interferes with the brakes or steering of a vehicle, clearly interferes with those parts for the purposes of (b) above in such circumstances that it would be obvious to a reasonable person that to do so would be dangerous.

'Traffic equipment' for the purposes of the section means anything placed on or near a road by a highway authority or some other person, or any fence, barrier or light so placed to protect street works or undertakings, or items placed by a constable or person acting on the instructions (whether general or specific) of a chief officer of police.

Things so placed shall be deemed to have been lawfully placed unless the contrary is proved. Thus, official road signs, those indicating temporary works or obstructions, road accidents or diversions are covered by the section. It must be remembered that the interference with traffic equipment must have created an obvious danger. A person may remove a light from road workings without causing such danger. If the lights were closely placed, it is unlikely that a court will find that the necessary element of danger was present. However, if a group of persons are together and each removes a light, their joint enterprise will be such that such danger could be caused. A person who removes a 'Stop' sign undoubtedly commits an offence against this section. He who removes a sign which merely indicates the direction of a town may have caused a nuisance, but he is unlikely to have caused obvious danger.

Removal of vehicles

A constable may require a vehicle to be removed by the owner, driver or other person in control or charge of any vehicle which has broken down, or has been permitted to remain at rest on a road in such a position, condition or circumstances as to cause obstruction or be likely to cause danger to other road users. He may also require its removal if the vehicle is parked in contravention of statutory restrictions, such as those imposed by no waiting signs, traffic regulation orders, motorway regulations, pedestrian crossing restrictions or local Acts controlling traffic. Part of the constable's requirement may be to remove the vehicle to some place which is not on a road.

It is an offence to fail to remove the vehicle as soon as practicable on being required to do so by a constable. Although the powers of removal are set out in the Removal and Disposal of Vehicles Regulations 1986, the offence is contrary to s. 91 of the Road Traffic Offenders Act 1988.

Vehicles which have been left on a road in any of these circumstances are either a danger to other road users or are likely to cause serious inconvenience, and the provisions allow a constable to ensure that vehicles are moved in addition to dealing with the driver for particular offences. A constable may remove or arrange for the removal of a vehicle which is on a road in the circumstances described above. He may also do so if the vehicle, having broken down on a road or on any land in the open air, appears to have been abandoned without lawful authority, or if the vehicle has been permitted to remain at rest on a road or on any land in the open air in such a position or circumstances as to appear to the constable to have been abandoned without lawful authority. The power to remove vehicles from land occupied by any person, is subject to giving notice as prescribed by s. 99 of the Road Traffic Regulation Act 1984 and Regulation 8 of the Removal and Disposal of Vehicles Regulations 1986.

Traffic wardens may remove a vehicle parked or broken down in a road in circumstances where it is causing an obstruction; it is likely to cause danger to road users; or an offence is being committed under certain enactments by or under which prohibitions or restrictions are imposed upon the waiting of vehicles on roads.

It is now quite common to see vehicles which have apparently been abandoned at the side of motorways, many of them having been stripped of all identifying marks. In these circumstances it is often impossible to trace the owner in order to require its removal and it was obviously not the intention of the legislators to have police officers acting as refuse collectors. Local authorities are, therefore, also empowered by these regulations to remove vehicles apparently abandoned on roads and on land in the open air, but in addition, the Refuse Disposal (Amenity) Act 1978 places upon them the duty to provide places where such vehicles may be deposited. This Act also gives local authorities the power to remove vehicles which appear to have been abandoned on open land or land which forms part of a highway, to dispose of them, and to recover the expenses involved in doing so.

Section 2 of the Refuse Disposal (Amenity) Act 1978 makes it an offence for any person, without lawful authority, to abandon a motor vehicle or part of a vehicle removed during the course of dismantling it in these places or to abandon anything other than a motor vehicle. If motor vehicles or other things are left in circumstances or for such a period of time that they reasonably appear to have been abandoned, the burden of proof is upon the defendant to prove that there was no abandonment.

The provisions of the Refuse Disposal (Amenity) Act 1978 allow local authorities to remove such waste material and additionally enable the prosecution of those responsible. Police officers may institute proceedings under this Act.

Heavy commercial vehicles – parking on footways, etc.

An offence is committed by a person who parks a heavy commercial vehicle wholly or partly on the verge of a road or any land situated between two carriageways which is not a footway, or on any footways. For the purposes of s. 19 of the Road Traffic Act 1988, which creates this offence, a heavy commercial vehicle is a goods vehicle with an operating weight exceeding 7.5 tonnes. The 'operating weight' is the maximum laden weight of the vehicle and all its trailers. Parking is banned on verges (grass strips), central reservations, and footpaths because of the damage which may be caused.

The exceptions to this rule are logical. A police officer may give permission for such parking to take place. He may wish, for example, to authorise such parking to remove an obstruction caused by a broken down or damaged vehicle. Such vehicles may also park in such places in order to save life or extinguish fire. This provision allows usage by emergency vehicles. Finally, these vehicles may park on a verge or a footway for the purpose of loading or unloading, if that loading or unloading could not have been performed if the vehicle had not been so parked, provided that the vehicle is not left unattended at any time while so parked. This final exemption is not intended to authorise such parking generally; the nature of the loading, etc., must be such that it could not be effectively carried out in any other way.

The Road Traffic Act 1991, ss. 76, 77 and Schedule 3 make provisions for 'special parking areas'. London and provincial authorities can apply to the Secretary of State for an order designating an area as a special parking area. Where such an order is in force it has the effect of making all parking offences within that area offences which lead to a parking penalty, recoverable by civil process. This offence becomes so punishable within a special parking area and the criminal offence ceases to apply. At the time of writing there are no special parking areas outside London.

Notice of intended prosecution

Section 1 of the Road Traffic Offenders Act 1988 requires that, for certain offences, the offender must have been warned at the time of the possibility of a prosecution, have been served with a summons within 14 days, or, alternatively, the prosecutor must have sent a notice of intended prosecution within 14 days of the offence to either the driver or registered keeper of the motor vehicle. If the offence is one involving the use of a pedal cycle (dangerous or careless cycling), notice must be sent to the rider of the cycle. The requirements of s. 1 are deemed to have been complied with unless and until the contrary is proved. The words 'at the time of the offence' mean at the time of the incident and not *the moment of the offence*.

The offences in respect of which such warning must be given are:

(a) Road Traffic Act 1988
  Section 2   Dangerous driving
  Section 3   Careless and inconsiderate driving
  Section 22   Leaving a vehicle in a dangerous position
  Section 28   Dangerous cycling
  Section 29   Careless and inconsiderate cycling
  Section 35   Failing to conform with the indication given by a constable engaged in the regulation of traffic
  Section 36   Failing to comply with the indication given by a traffic sign.
(b) Road Traffic Regulation Act 1984
  Section 16   Exceeding temporary speed restrictions imposed under s. 14
  Section 17(4)   Exceeding speed restriction on special road
  Section 88(7)   Exceeding temporary speed limit imposed by order
  Section 89(1)   Speeding offences generally.

A written notice of intended prosecution must specify the nature of the offence and the time and place where it is alleged to have been committed. It may be served by delivering it to the person; by addressing it to him and leaving it at his last known address; or by sending it by registered post, recorded delivery service or first class post addressed to such a person at his last known address. A notice so dispatched is deemed to be served where it was sent by registered post or recorded delivery service, notwithstanding that the notice was returned as undelivered or, for some other reason, it was not received by the person to whom it was addressed. It is assumed that the provisions of this section of the Act have been complied with unless the contrary is proved.

To prevent offenders escaping the consequences of their acts, if the name and address of the driver or registered keeper could not with reasonable diligence have been discovered in time for service, or if the accused by his own conduct contributed to the failure, failure to serve a notice or a summons shall not be a bar to conviction.

(1) *Points of procedure*

(a) A general warning at the time, which does not indicate the offence clearly, is insufficient. A constable must say: 'You will be reported for consideration of the question of prosecuting you for ...' followed by clear words describing the offence.

(b) A warning given 35 minutes after the offence was committed, but as soon as possible after the arrival of police officers on the scene, has been held to be sufficient. A warning given after a man had been in custody for three hours for driving while unfit through drink was also held to be satisfactory as there was an unbroken chain of circumstances taking place which was connected with the incident.

(c) Common sense should be used in determining whether or not there is sufficient information in the notice. The object is 'to take back the recollection of the motorist to the facts upon which reliance is to be placed'.

(d) A notice is deemed to have been served within 14 days if it is posted within that period.

(e) In considering the 14 days within which the notice must be served, the date of the commission of the offence is excluded.

(f) Some police forces send a written notice of intended prosecution in all cases although the driver may have been warned at the time. This provides an added safeguard against an allegation by a driver that he has not been warned.

(g) It is not necessary to comply with the provisions in relation to notices of intended prosecution if, at the time of the offence or immediately thereafter, an accident occurs owing to the presence on a road of the vehicle in respect of which the offence was committed. If any of the actions specified above results at the time, or immediately afterwards in an accident, there is no need to comply with the provisions of this section. However, before this can apply, the offender must have been aware that the accident had occurred. In addition, where a driver who is seriously injured in an accident has no recollection of the accident occurring, there is no bar to prosecution because no notice has been given. The Divisional Court has ruled that Parliament cannot have intended oral warnings to be given to unconscious survivors of serious road accidents nor the giving of written notices to survivors so badly injured as to be unable to read them or understand their effect.

(h) The provisions of this section need not be complied with in relation to an offence in respect of which a full or provisional fixed penalty notice has been given or fixed under the provisions of the Road Traffic Offenders Act 1988.

Accidents – law

Introduction

Police officers are called upon to deal with many types of accidents, but those involving motor vehicles warrant special attention and the Road Traffic Act 1988 contains provisions dealing with the obligations of drivers of mechanically propelled vehicles involved in accidents on roads. Not all road accidents are covered by those statutory provisions, and it is important to distinguish between those to which the Road Traffic Act 1988 applies, referred to as 'reportable accidents', and those outside the Act.

The statutory provisions are concerned with mechanically propelled vehicles. The words 'mechanically propelled' immediately exclude vehicles not propelled by mechanical means such as carts drawn by horses, cycles without motors attached, and any other type of vehicle which is not mechanically propelled.

A vehicle does not necessarily cease to be mechanically propelled merely because of a mechanical fault which can be rectified or because the mechanical means of propulsion was not being used at that time. Thus, a motor car with the engine removed remains a mechanically propelled vehicle if there is evidence of the possibility that the engine may shortly be replaced. Similarly, a motor-assisted pedal cycle remains a mechanically propelled vehicle while it is being propelled only by the pedals.

A 'road', for the purpose of the Act, means any length of highway or of any other road to which the public has access, and includes bridges over which a road passes. This definition will embrace the footpath as well as the carriageway, a cul-de-sac made up with houses on both sides, and a quayside over which the public walk and motor without a legal right. It is really a question of fact, each case being decided on its own merit. Places which have been held not to have been 'roads' within the terms of the above definition include a car park maintained by a local authority, an occupation road leading to a farm and caravan site where there was no evidence of general use by the public, and a yard, not being a thoroughfare, to which the public had access.

Having briefly examined the basic elements of what constitutes a mechanically propelled vehicle to which the Act applies and where reportable accidents can occur, it is now necessary to examine the statutory provisions relating to reportable accidents.

Road accidents

Section 170 of the Road Traffic Act 1988 applies in a case where, owing to the presence of a mechanically propelled vehicle on a road, an accident occurs by which personal injury is caused to a person other than the driver of that mechanically propelled vehicle or a trailer drawn by it or to an animal other than an animal in or on it or trailer drawn by that mechanically propelled vehicle or to any other property constructed on, fixed to, growing in or otherwise forming part of the land on which the road in question is situated, or land adjacent to such land, the driver of the mechanically propelled vehicle shall stop and, if required so to do by any person having reasonable grounds for so requiring, give his name and address, and also the name and address of the owner and the identification marks of the vehicle. If, for any reason, such a driver does not give his name and address to any such person as aforesaid, he shall report the accident at a police station or to a constable as soon as reasonably practicable, and in any case within 24 hours of the occurrence thereof.

Note that the mechanically propelled vehicle does not have to be in motion before these provisions apply, the mere presence of the vehicle on a road could be sufficient, for example, if a person parks his car on the road outside a shop while he goes for cigarettes and because his car is parked there an accident occurs, causing damage or injury to another vehicle or another person, this would be a reportable accident. The word 'driver' means the person who takes out the vehicle and he remains the driver until the journey is complete.

There must a direct causal connection between the presence of the mechanically propelled vehicle and the occurrence of the accident. Where a driver, who is approaching a pedestrian crossing at a fast speed, causes a pedestrian to turn quickly to regain the pavement and in doing so the pedestrian falls and injures himself, there has been an 'accident' as there is a direct causal link between the mechanically propelled vehicle and the accident. If a cyclist collides with a stationary car there is such a link; the accident could not have occurred without the presence of the motor vehicle. On the other hand, if a cyclist who merely moves to the nearside of the road to allow a car to pass, oversteers, and because of his own actions, falls from the cycle, the causal connection with the motor car would be too remote.

It has been held that an 'accident' has occurred where the situation is such that an ordinary person would say that an accident had occurred. Thus, where a driver deliberately drives into another vehicle or property, an 'accident' has occurred because that is how the ordinary man would describe it. It is not necessary that a mechanically propelled vehicle is involved in a collision. If the actions of the driver are such that he causes other vehicles to collide, he is involved in an accident and the obligations imposed by the section apply. There can be an accident where a part of the injury or damage was deliberate. If a person deliberately drives into a wall there has been an accident because that is how an ordinary member of the public would describe it.

(1) Personal injury

Where personal injury is involved as a result of the accident, this means personal injury to any person other than the driver of the mechanically propelled vehicle concerned. It includes any passengers in his mechanically propelled vehicle, the driver and passengers in any other vehicle , and pedestrians, etc. It would cover the situation where a public service vehicle loaded with passengers swerved violently, resulting in a number of the passengers being injured, or any circumstances in which there is any direct connection between the presence of the vehicle on a road and the injury. Sometimes it is difficult to decide whether there is an injury; quite often there is only shock, and a good guide as to whether to class shock as an injury is whether the shock is severe enough to require medical treatment. If this is the case, then shock is classed as personal injury (see also 'Additional information in personal injury accidents', page 259).

(2) *Damage to an animal*

Where an animal is injured in a road accident it must be an animal other than one carried in or on the mechanically propelled vehicle concerned or in or on a trailer drawn by such a motor vehicle. Thus, if the driver of a mechanically propelled vehicle pulling a trailer full of pigs had to brake sharply and, as a result, one of the pigs suffered a broken leg, this would not be a reportable accident. The term 'animal' is defined for the purpose of s. 170 as meaning any horse, cattle, ass, mule, sheep, pig, goat, or dog. The notable omission is a cat, so if the animal injured is a cat or some other animal not included in the definition then the accident does not come within the provisions of s. 170 of the Act.

(3) *Damage*

The statutory provisions concern the driver of a mechanically propelled vehicle involved in a reportable accident, but it should be noted that where, owing to the presence of a mechanically propelled vehicle on a road, damage is caused to another vehicle, not necessarily a mechanically propelled vehicle, this is a reportable accident. An example would be where the other vehicle involved was a pedal cycle or a horse and cart; if the cycle or car was damaged, this would be a reportable accident.

(4) *Property damage*

Damage to property, not being a vehicle, is covered by the Act. Where a mechanically propelled vehicle collides with a lamp standard, the Act places an obligation on the driver of the motor vehicle to report the accident. Similarly, damage to buildings, fences, hedgerows, traffic signs, etc., would be included within the provisions of the section.

(5) *Driver's obligations*

(a) *Stopping*. Where a mechanically propelled vehicle is involved in an accident to which s. 170 applies, the driver must stop. This appears simple enough but it has caused some difficulty, particularly on how long the driver should stop at the scene. It has been held that 'stop' means that the driver should stop and remain where he has stopped for such a period of time as in the prevailing circumstances, having regard in particular to the character of the road or place where the accident happened, will provide sufficient time to enable persons who have the right to do so, and reasonable ground for so doing, to require from the driver directly and personally the information the driver is required to supply under the Act. Thus, where a mechanically propelled vehicle collided with a parked motor vehicle causing damage to that other vehicle and the driver, having stopped, instructed an employee to wait by this vehicle to supply the necessary information and the driver left the scene, it was held that he had failed to stop after the accident, because having stopped he did not remain at the scene for such a period as would have enabled the owner of the other vehicle concerned to require him to supply the information he was obliged to give. If a driver who is supervising a learner driver, allows the learner to walk away from the scene of an accident without remaining there for the purpose of discharging his duties, he aids and abets the offence if he took no steps to ensure that the driver remained at the scene.

(b) *Supplying information.* Having stopped, the driver of a mechanically propelled vehicle involved in a reportable accident has an obligation to supply certain information at the scene, but only if he is required by some person having reasonable grounds for requiring such information. While that person will usually be the driver of the other vehicle or the owner of the property, a relative or friend, or person acting on his behalf, can be such a person. If the requirement is made by any person having such grounds, s. 170 obliges the driver to give:

(i)   his name and address;

(ii) the name and address of the owner of the vehicle; and

(iii) the identification mark of the vehicle.

Section 170(2), which requires a driver to stop and to give this information is concerned with one offence which can be committed in two ways; either by failing to stop, or if, having stopped; failing to provide the information which is required to be given.

If at the scene of an accident the driver is not required to supply the necessary information, then s. 170 places an obligation on the driver to report the accident at a police station or to a constable as soon as practicable, and in any case within 24 hours. Thus, if he supplies the necessary information at the scene of the accident, this relieves him of any obligation to report the matter to the police. However, this does not mean that if he refuses to supply the information at the scene when required by a person having reasonable grounds for so requiring, and later reports the accident to the police, that he has fulfilled his obligations under the Act; an offence is committed if he refuses such information at the scene, even if he later reports the accident to the police. Where a driver is already known by the person reasonably requiring his name and address, he must give the information required.

(c) *Reporting to the police.* If for any reason the driver of the mechanically propelled vehicle does not give his *name and address* to a person having reasonable grounds for so requiring he must report the accident at a police station or to a constable as soon as reasonably practicable, and in any case within 24 hours of the occurrence of the accident. The obligation to report arises whenever the driver has not given his name and address at the scene of the accident, whether or not he was required to do so. This does not give a driver leave to report the accident at any time within 24 hours; thus, where a driver involved in an accident is traced and interviewed by police who obtain his name and address, the name and address of the owner of the vehicle, and the identification marks of his vehicle, this does not amount to compliance with the provisions of s. 170 of the Act, and it may be, having regard to the time which has elapsed since the time of the accident and any opportunity that the driver had of reporting the accident to the police, that the driver has committed an offence of failing to report the accident, notwithstanding that he was interviewed before 24 hours had elapsed from the time of the accident. It should be noted that s. 170(3) requires a driver to report an accident, if for any reason he does not give his *name and address*. It does not specify the other particulars required by s. 170(2).

The duty to report is a personal one; the report must be made by the driver to a police constable or at a police station. A telephone call will not suffice, nor will informing a friend who happens to be a police officer. What is 'reasonably practicable' is a matter for the court.

(6) *Additional information in personal injury accidents*

Where a reportable accident involves personal injury to a person other than the driver of the mechanically propelled vehicle involved, then, in addition to his obligations under s. 170 of the Act, a driver has to produce evidence of insurance or security. If the driver of the mechanically propelled vehicle does not at the time of the accident produce a certificate of insurance or security to a constable or to some other person who, having reasonable grounds for so doing, has required its production, the driver shall as soon as possible, and in any case within 24 hours of the occurrence of the accident, report the accident at a police station or to a constable and produce a certificate of insurance or security. If he fails to do so he commits an offence.

However, it is important that we recognise that there are no circumstances therefore in which a driver must report an accident to the police if he provides all of the necessary information at the scene of the accident and, in addition, if personal injury to someone results, he produces a certificate of insurance to a person having reasonable grounds for requiring it. It would not, of course, be sufficient for a driver to wave a certificate of insurance before the eyes of such a person. It must be produced so that a person can take particulars if required and can satisfy himself that proper insurance is in force.

However, if at the time of reporting the accident he is unable to produce a certificate of insurance or security, he may produce it subject to the usual conditions set out in the Road Traffic Act 1988.

General

While the provisions examined above are concerned with legal requirements to report accidents, the high incidence of accident reports has led to force procedures being adapted to meet the situation. It may be that police officers are not required to record all of the details set out above on every occasion. This is equally true of the process of the police investigation of accidents as set out in the following section.

In many areas the CPS has given guidance as to the types of accidents which are likely to result in proceedings before a court and police action has been adapted to recognise such guidance.

Accidents – police action

Introduction

Prompt action by the first police officer at the scene of a road accident often prevents further accidents occurring, saves lives, and provides evidence of possible offences committed by the drivers of vehicles involved in the accident. No two accidents are exactly the same but certain basic rules will apply to the handling of all accidents, and by following these basic rules a police officer should be competent to deal with any road accident except where a specialist knowledge is required, e.g. accidents on motorways, where special procedures apply.

Receipt of information

When a police officer receives a report of an accident he should note the time he receives the report. If the report is received from a member of the public he should, in addition, record the name and address of the informant and as much information about the accident as possible, e.g. the time and place of the accident, the number of vehicles involved, and the presence of any injured. The informant should be asked if he witnessed the accident and, if so, arrangements can be made for him to be subsequently interviewed and a statement obtained, if necessary. Speed is essential, however, and these details should be obtained with a minimum of delay.

If the report of an accident is received from a non-police source, then a radio message should be sent to control; it may be that a police officer is nearer to the scene or even already at the scene, in which case the presence of another police officer may not be required.

Initial action and safety precautions

A police officer's duty is to preserve life and attend to any injured. Quickly ascertain if an ambulance has been called; if not, or if there is any doubt, summon an ambulance. Where there is danger of petrol being ignited, warn spectators not to smoke; ensure that the ignition of a motor vehicle is switched off or, where this is not possible, disconnect the battery. If people are trapped in a motor vehicle, summon assistance immediately; the fire service have cutting equipment and jacking equipment specially designed to cope with situations. Remember, it might also be necessary to have a doctor at the scene to give medical attention to a trapped and injured person, pending his release from the vehicle.

Where injured persons are removed from the scene by ambulance, obtain the name of the hospital to which they will be taken and, if possible, the names and addresses of the injured persons. This information can be passed by radio to control so that relatives can be informed. Where there are a large number of persons requiring medical attention, it may be necessary to warn the hospital as soon as possible so that the hospital staff are in a position to deal with the injured when they arrive.

On arriving at the scene of a road accident it is a police officer's duty to prevent any further accidents and to safeguard his own life. Where a police officer is in possession of a fluorescent jacket or white coat, this should be worn at all times to minimise the risk of being injured by other traffic. This applies particularly at night when a police uniform is hard to distinguish against a dark background. If particular vehicles are involved which present hazards because of the dangerous loads which they carry, check the markings on the vehicle and inform control giving the details of the hazard warning panel, including the telephone number to be contacted for advice. It is essential to obtain assistance from the fire service when there is a danger from hazardous substances.

Witnesses

Witnesses should be located as soon as possible after arrival at the scene. If any witness is unable to wait at the scene, his name and address should be obtained and arrangements can be made later for the witness to be interviewed and a statement obtained.

When statements are taken from witnesses either at the scene or at a police station, this should be done out of the presence and hearing of other witnesses. It is often a good idea to see if a witness can indicate on the rough sketch of the scene exactly where he or she was standing at the time of the accident.

It is often useful to ask a witness about his own driving experience and to endorse this on his written statement. If there is a subsequent prosecution, this information may guide the prosecuting officer, particularly where a witness has estimated the speed of a vehicle. Non-drivers may have very little idea of vehicle speeds; in one instance a speed described as very fast was later put at 45 mph when in fact other evidence indicated a speed of 80 mph.

Position of vehicles

The position of the vehicles involved in a road accident often produces valuable evidence as to the cause of an accident. It is important to ascertain if any of the vehicles have been moved from the positions they occupied immediately after the accident. If the vehicles have been moved, there is no evidential value in taking measurements fixing their positions. If the vehicles have not been moved after the accident they should not be moved until their relative positions have been fixed by means of measurements, unless it is essential to move the vehicles to save life or in some other emergency. Where it is necessary to move the vehicles, try to mark their positions; the yellow sticks of wax crayon used in the tyre industry are very good for marking the position of motor vehicles on a road. Unlike chalk marks which fade very quickly when traffic passes over the marks, yellow crayon marks last some hours and can also be used where the road surface is wet.

It is not only essential to fix the position of vehicles involved in an accident, a record should be made of any other marks or debris which may prove to have evidential value. The point of impact can usually be ascertained by debris on the road where dried mud, etc., has fallen from under the wheel arches at the moment of impact. Black tyre marks on the road should be measured; such skid marks may often be an indication of the speed of a motor vehicle immediately before the accident.

Any measurements taken and notes made should, if possible, be made in the presence of drivers concerned, who then have an opportunity of corroborating the accuracy of the measurements and may have some relevant comment to make about marks found on the road.

The accident report book provides space for a sketch of the scene of the accident which should, where possible, show the relative position of vehicles and the fixed objects from which measurements are taken. As the sketch will perhaps be later referred to by those concerned with conducting prosecutions which arise from such accidents, it should be as accurate as possible in the circumstances existing at the time. While it is usually referred to as a 'rough sketch', 'rough' distinguishes the sketch from a scale plan which may subsequently be prepared. Make sure that everything which is relevant is included in the sketch; the names of roads; the position of traffic signs; hedges, etc., which may affect the line of vision of a driver approaching a junction; the marked positions of vehicles involved in the accident; and additionally, the positions of any other vehicle or vehicles on the road or roads concerned, the presence of which may have some bearing on the cause of the accident.

The measurements which are taken should be taken from at least two fixed points such as lamp posts, the corners of walls or drain covers; anything which will always be there and thus merits the description 'fixed point'. In selecting your fixed points keep in mind that it is a good idea to select two which are some distance apart, so that the 'triangle' which you produce has a fairly wide base. The triangle will consist of, at its base, your two fixed points, and at its apex, the particular corner of the motor vehicle, or the position of the debris, which you are seeking to fix. The sketch will be easier to follow if you indicate these three points with chosen letters, for example FP 1 or FP 2 for the fixed points, together with letters of the alphabet to mark the apex of the triangle. If this is done, the measurements can then be listed at some place on the plan which is well separated from the actual scene of the impact. The measurements can be listed, for example as A to FP 1 = 3.6 m. Listing the actual distances in this way, as opposed to attempting to indicate the distance above the line which is drawn between the appropriate part of the vehicle, avoids 'cluttering up' the sketch in the area surrounding the vehicles.

Accident booklet

The accident report booklet is to be used for all original entries at the scene of an accident. The booklet, not the police officer's notebook, is the original record which must be examined when giving evidence in court. The entry made in the officer's notebook should merely itemise brief details of the occurrence and all original entries must be made in the accident report booklet.

If the accident is serious, and particularly if there is a likelihood that a person will die from injuries received, then this information should be passed by radio to control as soon as possible in order that a supervising officer may attend at the scene together with other officers, such as a photographer, to assist the reporting officer.

If there is any suspicion that a mechanical failure in any of the vehicles involved contributed to the accident, then arrangements should be made for the vehicle to be examined. A police officer has the power to detain any vehicle for the purpose of such an examination where such a vehicle has been involved in a road accident.

In case of hit and run accidents it is possible that you will be required to take and submit paint samples to the Forensic Laboratory for examination. Although the taking of such samples is sometimes considered to be a job for a specialist, it will not always be practicable to receive immediate assistance. It must be recognised that this procedure will be restricted to serious accidents which are likely to give rise to serious criminal charges. If it becomes necessary to take samples, there are a number of rules which should be observed.

(a) Take a control sample of paint from the vehicle which has been struck. A control sample is a sample of uncontaminated paint, taken from a point close to the damaged area, but away from an area on which there may be transferred material.

(b) Take a sample from the damaged area, to include some of the vehicle's own paint and some of the transferred material. Even if no transferred material can be seen, take the sample, as the microscope may well pick out transferred material.

(c) It may be possible to take a sample of debris at the scene which might include fittings, glass, paint or filler.

(d) Paint samples should be taken by scraping down to the bare metal to include all layers of paint. Avoid contamination which might occur by using the same scraper on two different spots. You should take enough paint to cover a circle of about 2.5 cm diameter.

(e) Place each paint sample on a separate sheet of plain paper and enclose the sample by wrapping in the manner of a Beecham's powder. Seal it with Sellotape and place the folded, sealed paper in an envelope or polythene bag, then seal and attach a label giving details of the sample.

(f) Do not put samples directly into envelopes which may leak at the corners. Do not use polybags or fixed penalty bags as the paint tends to stick to these bags. For the same reasons, Sellotape lifts should not be used, as the adhesive contaminates the sample.

(g) The following information must be given to the laboratory with the samples:
  (i) time, date, and place of occurrence;
  (ii) make, model, and registration mark of vehicle(s);
  (iii) the colours of vehicle(s), locations, and extent of damage;
  (iv) the name of any suspect or accused; and
  (v) the name, location and telephone number of the OIC case.

Similar samples must be taken from suspect vehicles when traced and submitted to the laboratory in the same way.

Property

Any property found at the scene of an accident should be taken into police custody if it cannot be immediately identified and returned to the owner. Where it is necessary to remove damaged vehicles from the scene, the driver should be asked if he wishes to have the vehicle removed by any particular garage. If the driver does not nominate a particular garage, or the driver is absent from the scene, control should be asked to arrange for a breakdown truck to remove the vehicle. The driver should be asked to remove any property from the vehicle or to secure any property by locking it in the boot of the car.

Interviewing drivers

There is certain essential information to be obtained when interviewing drivers who have been involved in accidents. Each driver must be identified with a particular vehicle and the direction of travel of the vehicle must be clearly established. It is helpful if a compass direction can be given, but this is not essential. The vehicle must have been travelling along a particular road, from one place to another. The driver's estimate of speed is helpful as it may later establish the reliability of his story as there are scientific ways of determining the speed of a vehicle when the circumstances of the accident justify a thorough investigation. The position which the vehicle occupied on the road is most important as are the manoeuvres of the vehicle immediately prior to the collision, including any avoiding action taken. Any information which helps to establish the point of impact must be recorded as should information which helps to establish where the vehicle came to rest.

When interviewing a driver of a motor vehicle involved in a road accident it is necessary to obtain certain details to complete the accident report. These reports usually take the form of a booklet and are self-explanatory. The police officer should go through the report carefully, filling in the necessary information.

General

A police officer must take charge at the scene of an accident as the public will look to him for leadership. The speed with which an accident is dealt with is related to the degree of calm, method, and logic which the officer brings to the incident.

It is frequently necessary to use the accident report book and the statements taken from the drivers and witnesses in order to prepare a file of evidence in respect of offences disclosed. This is more effectively done while all of the facts are still fresh in the mind of the reporting officer. The file should be completed without delay.

On some occasions it may be necessary to inform relatives or friends of those injured in road accidents as it will be unlikely that the injured will be in a position to do so themselves. However, hospitals usually make such contacts but it is advisable to check. There is nothing to be gained by informing such relatives or friends twice. The question of providing first aid at the scene should be answered in recognition of existing circumstances. Where injuries are of a minor nature and medical help is readily available, there may be more urgent matters to deal with as a first priority if a dangerous situation exists because of the presence of damaged vehicles or debris at the scene.

Many accidents occur in consequence of drivers failing to distinguish road markings which have become faded, or to recognise traffic signs which have been vandalised. Accidents can be avoided if such matters are reported to the highway authority.

Traffic signs and pedestrian crossings

Traffic signs

Traffic signs are used to control and guide traffic and to promote road safety. The term 'traffic sign' means any object or device (whether fixed or portable) for conveying to traffic on roads or any specified class of traffic, warnings, information, requirements, restrictions or prohibitions of any description which are specified by regulations. The bulk of legislation concerning the placing of traffic signs is to be found in the Road Traffic Regulation Act 1984 and the Traffic Signs Regulations and General Directions 1994.

Traffic signs may be placed on or near a road by the highway authority and in certain circumstances police officers may also place signs. There are many types of signs prescribed by statute and it would make the enforcement of the law unnecessarily tedious if, upon each occasion when proceedings were taken against an offender, it was essential to prove that the sign complied in form and content with the regulations. The Road Traffic Act 1988, therefore, states that a traffic sign placed on or near a road shall be deemed to be of the prescribed size, colour, and type authorised by the Minister unless the contrary is proved. The burden of proof, therefore, lies upon the defendant to prove that a sign is defective. However, if the issue is raised by the defence it will be for the prosecution to prove that the sign and road markings were in order. Account must therefore be taken of such matters. There is also a presumption that automatic traffic lights are in working order unless the contrary is proved.

In offences of non-compliance with the directions given by a traffic sign, it is no defence for a driver to allege that he did not see the sign, as guilty knowledge is not essential and the requirement to comply is absolute. It may be a defence that a sudden mechanical defect occurred in the vehicle which the driver could not have foreseen. Although various types of signs are described in the regulations, the offences are contrary to s. 36 of the Road Traffic Act 1988, which provides the penalty for non-compliance with the directions given by a traffic sign.

Traffic signs placed by the police

A constable, or other person directed to do so by a chief officer of police, may in certain circumstances place traffic signs upon a highway. There are particular instances in which this can be done, as authorised by certain Acts of Parliament, but the most used power is that given by the Road Traffic Regulation Act 1984 to place signs necessary to prevent or mitigate congestion or obstruction of traffic, or danger to or from traffic in extraordinary circumstances. These signs may only be maintained for a period of seven days. Frequent use of 'Police – No Waiting' signs is made under the authority of this Act; in particular, emergencies such as the holding of street markets, air displays, and other functions which cause the assembly of unusual numbers of motor vehicles. The 'time-clock' in relation to such a period of seven days starts when the signs are placed so that a sign placed at 9 a.m. on a particular day must be removed by 9 a.m. seven days after placement.

Failure to comply with such a sign constitutes an offence against the Road Traffic Act 1988, s. 36.

Failing to conform to traffic signs

Section 36 of the Road Traffic Act 1988 creates the offence of failing to comply with the indication given by a traffic sign. Section 35 deals with the offence of failing to comply with a signal given by a constable or traffic warden who is engaged in the regulation of traffic on a road. An offence is committed by a driver who neglects or refuses to stop the vehicle, or to make it proceed in, or keep to, a particular line of traffic when directed to do so by a constable or traffic warden in the execution of his duty. The section, therefore, gives statutory backing to the signals given by a constable on point duty.

In addition, s. 163 of the Road Traffic Act 1988 requires the drivers of motor vehicles and riders of pedal cycles to stop on being so required by a constable in uniform. It is an offence to fail to do so.

The police officer observes many failures to comply with traffic signs in the course of his duties and common offences include parking in contravention of emergency signs placed by the police; failing to stop at 'Stop' signs; or to give way at 'Give way' signs; failures to comply with stop/go signs at road works; light signals at junctions and at railway crossings; failing to keep left or right as required; failing to comply with double white lines in the middle of the road; ignoring 'No entry' signs or the signals of a police officer regulating traffic. All of these offences require notice of intended prosecution.

Meaning of certain traffic signs

(1) Traffic lights

The red signal given by a traffic light indicates that traffic shall not proceed beyond the stop line on the carriageway provided in conjunction with the signal. If that line has become obscured or there is no line, traffic must not pass the post or object in which the light signals are contained.

The only exception to the rule that all traffic must halt at a red light relates to vehicles being used for police, fire or ambulance purposes if observance would hinder the use to which the vehicle was then being put, but this exception is not absolute and those vehicles must not proceed beyond such signals in such a manner or at such time as is likely to cause danger to the driver of any other vehicle, on that or any other road controlled by those lights or so as to necessitate the other driver to change speed or course in order to avoid an accident. The exception is, therefore, limited to cautious progress across such a junction when no other traffic will be interfered with.

Amber with red denotes an impending change to green but does not alter the prohibition set out above. It is an offence to pass the red with amber light. Amber on its own conveys a prohibition and vehicles may not pass unless, when the signal first appears the vehicle is so close to the signal that it cannot safely be stopped before passing. This frequently occurs when a continuous stream of traffic is passing the traffic lights. When a sudden change to amber occurs when a moving vehicle is up to the light, the driver must consider the advisability of braking if following traffic is close behind him. Discretion must be used in such instances; there is a considerable difference between the driver who is close to the signal at the time of the change and chooses to proceed, and the driver who tries to beat the lights.

A green signal indicates that vehicular traffic may pass the signals and may proceed straight on or to the left or to the right. A green arrow indicates that traffic may proceed in the direction shown by the arrow, regardless of the signals shown by other lights.

(2) Stop signs

The modern stop sign is octagonal and coloured red with the word 'Stop' in white capitals on it. The sign is used in conjunction with two solid white transverse lines marking the point at which a vehicle must stop on the road. The word 'Stop' is also painted on the roadway. The sign requires that every vehicle shall, before entering the major road, stop at the transverse lines at the junction, or if these lines are not visible, at the junction with the major road.

No vehicle shall proceed past the transverse line or the junction as the case may be, so as to enter into the major road in such a manner or at such a time as is likely to cause danger to the driver of another vehicle on the major road, or to cause the driver to change speed or direction to avoid an accident. It will be seen that it is not sufficient to stop; the vehicle must not proceed at any time at which it is likely to interfere with traffic on the major road.

(3) Give way signs

A 'Give way' sign consists of a red inverted triangle with the words 'Give way' in black lettering on a white background. These signs are used in conjunction with two broken white lines at the junction of the road with the major road and an inverted white triangle on the road surface of the minor road at the approach to the junction.

Although there is no requirement to stop, a driver must give way to traffic on the major road and he must not enter the major road in such a manner as to be likely to cause danger or a collision with a vehicle on the major road or to cause that vehicle to change its speed or course. The offence is quite a common one and it is important for a constable to recognise that all that is needed to prove the offence is that the vehicle proceeded beyond the broken white lines or in to the major road and caused danger, etc. On many occasions when accidents occur at such junctions and a plea of not guilty is entered, the defendant experiences great difficulty in explaining how it is that he emerged from the junction safely, but nevertheless an accident occurred. The usual allegation is that he did not see the vehicle which he hit. If it was there and he did not see it, it is submitted that he is also guilty of careless driving.

'Stop' and 'Give way' signs must be illuminated during the hours of darkness if they are within 50 metres of an electric street lamp. Those signs not within 50 metres of an electric street lamp and which are not illuminated must be of reflective material. It will be appreciated that it would be quite impossible to illuminate such signs in the middle of the countryside.

Carriageway markings (double white lines)

The Road Traffic Regulation Act 1984 permits certain lines or marks on the road to be regarded as traffic signs in themselves without necessarily being supported by signs of any description. The single white lines marked on the road are not traffic signs in the sense that they are not connected with offences against s. 36 of the Road Traffic Act 1988. However, the presence of such lines on the road might be significant in a prosecution for careless driving.

Regulation 26 of the 1994 Traffic Signs, etc., Regulations authorises the placing of double white lines, which may consist of two continuous white lines or one continuous white line together with a broken white line. Any white unbroken line must be immediately preceded with a white warning arrow painted on the road, otherwise the line is not an authorised traffic sign. If there are two continuous white lines, vehicles travelling in both directions must at all times keep to the nearside of the nearest continuous line. If there is a continuous line with a broken line, the vehicles are required to keep to the nearside of the continuous line when it is the nearer of those two lines to that vehicle. Those drivers who find the broken line nearest to their vehicles, must not cross or straddle the line unless it is seen by the driver of the vehicle to be safe to do so.

However, these prohibitions upon crossing a continuous white line shall not apply to a vehicle which has to do so to obtain access to another road, land or premises, therefore, right turns made across the line into other roads, driveways or on to land are not prohibited. Drivers may also cross the line in order to pass stationary vehicles, to overtake a road maintenance vehicle, pedal cycle or horse moving at no more than 10 mph, or in circumstances outside the control of the driver or in order to avoid an accident, or for the purpose of complying with a direction given by a police constable in uniform or a traffic warden in uniform. These are merely common-sense exceptions to allow drivers to turn into their own access roads and to allow broken down or damaged vehicles to be overtaken with care, either by the driver himself or with the assistance of a constable or traffic warden who is controlling traffic.

No vehicle may stop on any length of road along which double white line markings have been placed. There are certain permitted stoppages and they are mainly predictable:

(a) to enable a person to board or alight from the vehicle;
(b) to enable goods to be loaded on to or unloaded from the vehicle;
(c) to enable essential road works;
(d) in connection with building operations or demolition;
(e) police, fire, and ambulance usage;
(f) pedal cycles with sidecars (including power assisted);
(g) in circumstances where the driver is required by law to stop, or to avoid an accident, or in circumstances beyond the driver's control;

(h)   when permission is given by a police constable in uniform or a traffic warden in uniform;

The various types of traffic signs

The understanding of the legislation concerning traffic signs is made easier if they are considered in relation to their purpose. Do they set out to inform, direct, warn, regulate or prohibit?

(1) *Informatory signs*

When undertaking long journeys it can be extremely helpful to have certain points of information available concerning facilities which are provided in particular places. Informatory signs have, therefore, been placed to assist motorists. Examples of such signs, which usually consist of white lettering on a blue background, are the letter 'P' indicating a parking place. 'Dual carriageway ahead', 'Unsuitable for motors', 'Single track road with passing places', 'H' for hospital, 'Road clear', and 'Forton Services ½ m'.

(2) *Directional signs*

The colouring and types of directional signs vary according to the types of roads upon which they are displayed. On primary roads other than motorways, directional signs will carry white letters and symbols on a green background, the classifications of the roads approached being shown in gold letters and figures. To give more local information, other signs will appear at the roadside indicating the direction and the distance of local towns and villages, and these will be black lettering on a white background. Signs show the relative importance of each road by differing widths of the route symbol. Motorway signs consist of white symbols, letters, and figures on a blue background. If travelling on a motorway *en route* for some town or village, the first sign to be met will indicate the turn off towards the nearest large town in the vicinity of our destination and will be of white symbols, letters, and figures on a blue background. The directional arrow pointing ahead may show 'The North, Sheffield, Leeds' while the turn off arrow indicates 'Nottingham A52'. On leaving the motorway and joining the A52, which is a primary road, it is probable that the next sign to be met will be white lettering on a green background, which will indicate the direction of Nottingham and other large towns in the area. Steering towards the nearest town to our destination we may then meet a local sign of black lettering on a white background showing the turn off towards the village which we are seeking. When travelling the journey in reverse, the signs are met in opposite order, but those indicating the approach to primary roads and motorways include this information on the sign. As the A52 is approached the local sign will show its direction and will carry a small green square with the letter and figures 'A52' in gold, below the directional arrow. The approach to a motorway is similarly shown by a blue square with letters and figures in white below the directional arrow.

Other types of directional signs are authorised, many of which provide local information. Examples of these signs are arrowheaded signs carrying such

269

information as 'Public Library', 'Council Offices', 'Free Car Park', 'Toilets'. Only traffic signs which are authorised by statute may be placed on or near a highway, and this control ensures that motorists experience little difficulty in recognising traffic signs as their colour, size, and type become familiar.

(3) *Warning signs*

The Romans probably eliminated the need for warning signs by making all of their roads straight, keeping junctions to a minimum, and thus avoiding many of the hazards which our modern roads provide. If we consider this situation and add to it our modern motor vehicles which are capable of travelling at great speed, a need for warning signs begins to appear. One of the penalties which results from making all roads straight is that they must be taken over ranges of hills rather than around them, and gradients begin to appear. Our first warning signs, therefore, become necessary to indicate steep hills. Warning signs consist of an upright red triangle surrounding black symbols on a white background, the symbols depicting the particular hazard to be met. On occasions letters or figures are also included in the sign to provide additional information. Our first sign, would, therefore, show a hill up or a hill down, supported by the figures 1 : 10 for example, to inform approaching drivers of the slope to be met.

As road development continues and tributary roads are constructed, the need to warn drivers of the presence of road junctions arises and warning signs appear showing the types of junctions which lie ahead, the presence of roundabouts, double bends, the fact that the road narrows, or that there is a hump backed bridge. In each case, a diagram in black sets out the particular hazard which is to be encountered.

(4) *Mandatory signs*

This title can be given to both regulatory and prohibitory signs. They must be obeyed and an offence is committed if the driver of a motor car fails either to do what he is told to do or does that which is prohibited.

(a) *Regulatory signs.* The types of action which these signs require motorists to perform are to 'Stop' or 'Give way' and this requirement may be conveyed by a sign or by a light signal. The recognition of a regulatory sign lies in its message, rather than its form, as drivers will also face white arrows on a blue circular background, indicating the direction in which they must proceed, or white arrows with a right angle bend, on the circular background, meaning turn left or right ahead, as the case may be. The common factor is that the driver's actions are regulated by requiring him to do something in order to comply with the sign.

(b) *Prohibitory signs.* 'No right turn', 'No left turn', 'No U turns', 'All motor vehicles prohibited', 'Lorries prohibited', 'No overtaking' are all examples of actions which a motorist can be prohibited from doing by traffic signs. These types of signs are often without written instructions of any kind, the symbol included in the sign being sufficient for identification. The advantage of such signs is that their message is quite clear to all drivers, whether they are capable of reading the English language or not. The sign itself often consists of a red circle with a symbol contained inside it in black, on a white background. Thus a sign prohibiting right turns would carry a black arrow angled to the right with a red line cutting through the arrow to show that turns in that direction are prohibited. A sign denying access to all motor vehicles would carry diagrams of a motor car and a motor cycle in black, in each case surrounded by a red circle. On occasions, additional information is provided by fixing a plate on the supporting post. In the case of the sign prohibiting the entry of motor vehicles, such a plate may read 'Except for access', indicating that residents in that street and their visitors may enter with motor vehicles. Signs which prohibit waiting include a red outer circle surrounding a blue background with a red band cutting across the face from the top left to the bottom right of the sign as seen by approaching drivers. Information is often provided on a surrounding yellow sign and, on occasions, on a plate attached to the post supporting the sign, giving particular information concerning the nature of the prohibition; for example, a yellow plate with the words 'At any time' painted in black, showing a continuous prohibition on waiting. Similar signs may carry the words '8.00 a.m.–6.00 p.m.' and carry an arrow pointing to the direction in which waiting is prohibited between these hours, or the words 'No loading at any time' in black on a white background. In instances in which waiting is limited, rather than prohibited altogether, the signs will consist of white lettering on a blue background.

There are other signs which may be placed on the roadway to reinforce prohibitions in relation to waiting. A single continuous yellow line running parallel with the kerb restricts waiting (other than for loading or unloading) for a period of at least eight hours between 7.00 a.m. and 7.00 p.m. on a minimum of four weekdays. A double continuous yellow line indicates these restrictions, but additionally there are restrictions on occasions which are outside the limits of 7.00 a.m. and 7.00 p.m. Broken yellow lines show waiting restrictions other than those shown by continuous lines, and usually appear for unilateral parking schemes, restricting waiting on certain sides of the road on particular days of the week. However, such road markings are only valid if used in conjunction with a plate of the type referred to above.

Restrictions upon waiting for the purpose of loading or unloading vehicles are shown by the provision of yellow lines running at right angle to the kerb line: two lines restricting the waiting of goods vehicles in the same ways as the single continuous yellow line for all traffic, three lines having the same meaning as a double continuous line, and a single line to restrict such waiting in any other way, quite often for unilateral schemes.

Equipment for detection of traffic offences

Section 40 of the Road Traffic Act 1991 inserts a new s. 95A into the Highways Act 1980 permitting a highway authority to install and maintain on or near a highway structures and equipment for the detection of traffic offences.

Provision is made by the Road Traffic Offenders Act 1988, s. 20, for records produced by prescribed devices to be evidence, and in Scotland sufficient evidence, of a fact related to an offence involving a driver's failure to comply with a traffic sign. The record must provide, in the same or another document, a certificate as to the circumstances in which the record was produced, signed by a constable or person authorised by or on behalf of a chief officer of police for the area in which the offence is alleged to have been committed. The device must be an approved device, and for these purposes the Secretary of State has approved a device designed or adapted for recording by photographic or other image recording means, the position of motor vehicles in relation to light signals.

A copy of such evidence must be served on the person charged not less than seven days before his trial. If the person charged, not less than three days before the hearing or trial, requires the attendance of the person who signed the document, the evidence of the circumstances in which the evidence was produced will not be admissible. The record produced by the device will.

Pedestrian crossings

In times during which an ever-increasing volume of vehicular traffic increases the dangers which pedestrians must face when attempting to cross roads, it becomes essential to provide crossings to safeguard pedestrians. There have been many experiments aimed at discovering the safest forms of pedestrian crossing and currently the two main types to be met on our roads are zebra and pelican crossings. The main purpose of a pedestrian crossing is to safeguard pedestrians.

Zebra crossings

The zebra crossing is quite easily identifiable by its alternate black and white stripes, its flashing beacons, and its zigzag approach lines.

The limits of the crossing itself (the walking area for pedestrians) are shown by outer lines of studs, the area between being marked with alternative black and white stripes. The presence of a crossing is indicated to approaching drivers by flashing yellow globes, mounted on posts marked by black and white stripes. There must be flashing globes at each side of the crossing and if there is a central reservation or street refuge on the crossing, globes may also be placed there. Failure of lamps, provided that one at least is lit, does not affect the legality of the crossing.

On each side of the crossing (or on one side only in the case of one-way traffic) an area is marked out which is known as the 'controlled area'. It is a defensive area before the crossing itself is reached and it is met by the approaching driver first coming to the 'terminal line' which is a broken white line reaching right across the carriageway. From this 'terminal line' three zigzag lines stretch, until they are halted 1 metre from the studs of the pedestrian crossing itself by a second broken white line which is known as the 'give way' line.

(1) Precedence

Foot passengers on an uncontrolled crossing have precedence over vehicles, and the driver of a vehicle must accord precedence if the foot passenger is within the limits of the crossing before any part of the vehicle has entered these limits. If the crossing is for the time being controlled by a police officer in uniform or by a traffic warden, it is no longer an uncontrolled crossing. In instances in which a crossing is separated by a street refuge or central reservation, each part becomes a separate crossing so far as precedence is concerned. The driver of a vehicle commits an offence only if the pedestrian is on the carriageway within the limits of the crossing before any part of the vehicle enters the limits. A pedestrian who is waiting on the kerb does not raise the issue of precedence until he steps into the carriageway. Once this has been done, drivers must stop at or before the 'give way' line.

It has been decided that, where a driver is satisfied that persons on the crossing are no longer in danger from his vehicle, he may proceed at a reasonable speed. There is, therefore, no need for him to wait until the crossing is absolutely clear. If pedestrians are pushing a pram or baby carriage, precedence must be afforded immediately the carriage enters the crossing.

The duty to accord precedence is absolute, unless control of the vehicle is temporarily taken from the driver, such as would occur if his vehicle was struck from behind while stationary outside the limits of the crossing. It is unnecessary to prove negligence, and convictions have been upheld in circumstances in which the view of a driver was obstructed on his approach in such a way that he could not see if there were persons on the crossing. When a driver was approaching a crossing at a reasonable speed and was only 10 yards from it, two children stepped on to the crossing without regard for traffic and he was unable to avoid one of them. He was found guilty of this offence. It is, therefore, clear that drivers must approach crossings in such a manner that they are able to stop in all circumstances if the issue of precedence is raised. The only circumstances which may excuse such lack of precedence are those involving a sudden defect in the vehicle; where a vehicle is pushed on to a crossing by another vehicle; or there is clear evidence that due to circumstances beyond his control the driver could not discharge his responsibilities. Such instances will be rare.

(2) *Stopping on a crossing*

Vehicles are not permitted to stop within the limits of a zebra crossing unless in circumstances beyond the driver's control or when it is necessary to prevent an accident. Pedestrians are also prohibited from remaining in such limits longer than is necessary to cross with reasonable dispatch.

(3) *Stopping in a controlled area*

The driver of a vehicle shall not cause any part of his vehicle to stop in a zebra controlled area, that is, the part marked by zigzag lines between the terminal and 'give way' line. The object of this regulation is to prevent obstruction of the view of approaching drivers and it is, therefore, not surprising to find that pedal cycles are not included. It is also clear that vehicles will have to stop within the controlled area to accord precedence to foot passengers and this is permitted, as is the presence of vehicles of essential services, such as fire, police, ambulance, building, demolition, road construction, gas, sewage, electricity or telephone. Vehicles waiting to make a

273

right turn and public service vehicles which have passed the crossing itself and require to set down or pick up passengers are also permitted to wait.

(4) *Overtaking in a controlled area*

It is an offence, when approaching a zebra crossing, to overtake another vehicle in the controlled area. Overtaking, for the purpose of this regulation, has been completed when any part of the vehicle moves ahead of the foremost part of another vehicle. The exceptions to the rule are, once again, common sense. If a number of vehicles are coming to a halt at a crossing to allow pedestrians precedence there will be a closing up towards the crossing itself. In these circumstances this offence is only committed if the moving vehicle nearest to the crossing is overtaken. If stationary vehicles are overtaken, it is only an offence if the vehicle overtaken has stopped to allow pedestrians to cross. If this was not so, a vehicle which was illegally parked in the controlled area would prevent other vehicles from proceeding.

Pelican crossing

The offences committed in relation to pelican crossings are largely the same as those outlined for zebra crossings. As pelican crossings are controlled by light signals it is an offence for a driver to cause the vehicle, or any part of it, to proceed beyond the stop line when a red light is showing. If the stop line is for any reason not visible, the vehicle must not proceed beyond the pole upon which the light signal is mounted. When a flashing amber signal is showing to drivers every pedestrian who is on the carriageway before the vehicle enters the limits of the crossing, has precedence and a driver who does not accord it commits an offence.

On each side of the crossing (or on one side only in the case of one-way traffic), an area is marked out which is known as the 'controlled area', which is similar to that encountered on approaching a zebra crossing; there being two or more zigzag lines stretching from the terminal lines to the 'stop' line, which is met before the limits of the crossing itself, are reached.

Light signals are synchronised to give clear signals to drivers and pedestrians. While a steady green light is shown to traffic, a steady red light is shown to pedestrians. Cautionary flashing lights which show to drivers are accompanied by similar cautionary signals for pedestrians, the light signals to pedestrians being reinforced by an illuminated sign which reads 'WAIT'. An audible signal may also be given when it is safe for pedestrians to cross.

School crossing patrols

Local authorities may appoint school crossing patrols for the purpose of assisting children, on their way to or from school, who are crossing or seeking to cross a road. School crossing patrols must wear a uniform approved by the Secretary of State (peaked cap or blue or black beret or yellow turban and a white dustcoat or raincoat which may carry fluorescent material) and must operate between the hours of 8.00 a.m. and 5.30 p.m.

They may require drivers to stop their vehicles by exhibiting a sign carrying the words 'Stop, children' in black letters, with a black bar on a yellow fluorescent background surrounded by a red fluorescent border. It is an offence to fail to stop before reaching the place of crossing or the point at which the children are waiting to cross, or to set the vehicle in motion again while the sign remains displayed.

The sign must be exhibited in such a way that the words 'Stop, children' can be read by approaching drivers, who will commit an offence if they move off while the sign remains displayed whether children are crossing or not.

Fixed penalty procedure

Introduction

The fixed penalty procedure is concerned with offences in respect of which an offender's liability may be discharged by the payment of a fixed sum by way of penalty without the necessity for the offender to appear before a court. The police officer dealing with the offence issues a 'ticket' which is in a prescribed form. Depending upon circumstances the ticket may be given to the offender or attached to the offender's vehicle.

The penalty with which we are concerned must be paid within a period of 21 days or such longer period as may be prescribed in the notice. At the time of writing, notices specify 28 days. If they are not paid and no request for a hearing before a court has been received, a penalty will be registered against that person equal to the fixed penalty, plus one half of that penalty.

The fixed penalty to be paid in respect of an offence is such amount as the Secretary of State may by order prescribe, or one-half of the maximum amount of the fine to which the person committing the offence would be liable on summary conviction, whichever is the less. The amounts currently prescribed by the Secretary of State are contained in the Fixed Penalty Order 1992. Under that order the penalty for offences involving obligatory endorsement is fixed at £40. Where the offence is a non-endorsable offence the penalty is normally £20. However, where the non-endorsable offence consists of a fixed penalty parking offence committed in London the penalty is £40 if committed on a red route or £30 if committed otherwise than on a red route.

The term fixed penalty parking offence means an offence under the Road Traffic Regulation Act 1984 which does not involve obligatory endorsement and is committed in respect of a stationary vehicle and road obstruction offences under a variety of statutory provisions. A 'red route' means a length of road on which there are traffic signs bearing the words 'red route' or red lines or marks.

The Road Traffic Act 1991 authorises the extension of the Function of Traffic Wardens Order to permit traffic wardens to deal with offences which involve obligatory endorsement provided that it is committed while the vehicle concerned was stationary.

The issue of a fixed penalty notice

Schedule 3 of the Road Traffic Offenders Act 1988 lists the offences which are fixed penalty offences. It indicates the sections of the relevant enactments and describes the offences. However, for enforcement purposes, police fixed penalty notices (tickets) are prepared separately to deal with those offences which are endorsable and those which are not.

Schedule 2 indicates the offences which carry obligatory endorsement. However, to assist in this respect, *aides-mémoire* have been prepared listing the various offences which are non-endorsable fixed penalty offences and those which are endorsable. That in relation to endorsable offences also indicates the number of penalty points which apply, and give a code number for each offence. That for non-endorsable fixed penalty offences includes advice concerning enforcement policies existing within a police force, particularly where a vehicle rectification scheme is in force.

Section 54 of the Road Traffic Offenders Act 1988 authorises a constable in uniform on any occasion upon which he has reason to believe that a person he finds is committing or has on that occasion committed a fixed penalty offence, to give him a fixed penalty notice in respect of that offence. These provisions, therefore, apply where the constable finds the driver and gives him a notice at the time of the offence. A fixed penalty notice for these offences must be issued at the time or immediately after the offence is committed and cannot be issued in circumstances involving the need for future enquiries to trace the driver. For example, a driver seen to enter a motor vehicle upon which there is no vehicle excise licence displayed, may be dealt with by a constable who so 'finds' him committing the offence. If he drives away before the constable has an opportunity to speak to him, and it, therefore, becomes necessary to carry out certain enquiries to trace the driver before speaking to him, a fixed penalty notice cannot be issued to him under s. 54 as the driver is not *found on that occasion* to be committing the offence. In such a case the conditional offer of a fixed penalty procedure (see below) will have to be used or a prosecution will have to be instituted.

Section 62 of the Road Traffic Offenders Act 1988 provides that where on any occasion a constable has reason to believe in the case of a stationary vehicle that a fixed penalty offence is being or has been committed in respect of it on that occasion, he may fix a fixed penalty notice in respect of that offence to the vehicle, unless the offence appears to him to involve obligatory endorsement.

One offence only – by fixed penalty

Only one fixed penalty notice may be issued on any one occasion. If more than one offence is committed on a particular occasion, a constable should either:

(a) report the offender for all offences; or
(b) give a verbal warning for all offences; or
(c) issue a fixed penalty notice for one offence and administer a verbal warning in respect of all other offences.

However, these restrictions would not apply to the instance where a constable has issued a fixed penalty notice for one offence which he knows to exist at the time that the notice is issued and, subsequently, further offences are disclosed. This could occur where vehicle or driver documents were produced later and found to be defective. Where this occurs, those offences subsequently disclosed will be reported by the officer with a view to proceedings by way of summons even though a fixed penalty notice has been issued for the original offence.

The issue of fixed penalty notices for non-endorsable offences, by traffic wardens, is restricted to offences included in the Function of Traffic Wardens Order 1970 as amended. The schedule to this order provides that traffic wardens may be employed to enforce law with respect to:

(a) offences of parking without obligatory lights or reflectors during the hours of darkness;

(b) offences of obstruction of a road by vehicles waiting, or being left or parked, being loaded or unloaded, on a road or public place;

(c) offences against the Vehicle Excise and Registration Act 1994 (e.g. no vehicle excise licence);

(d) offences related to parking places on highways where charges are made (e.g. by meters or machines); and

(e) offences committed by causing a vehicle, or any part of it, to stop in contravention of the pedestrian crossing regulations.

Types of fixed penalty notices

Fixed penalty notices are of two types; those issued for non-endorsable offences, e.g. breaches of parking regulations; and those issued for endorsable offences, that is those offences which attract penalty points, e.g. speeding.

Schedule 3 of the Road Traffic Offenders Act 1988 lists the offences to which the fixed penalty provisions apply.

Generally, non-endorsable fixed penalty offences are concerned with parking offences; failure to wear seat belts or crash helmets; offences connected with the display of vehicle excise licences and registration marks; driving elsewhere than on a road; failure to comply with certain traffic signs; obstruction and those offences against the Road Vehicles (Construction and Use) Regulations 1986 which are not concerned with the dangerous loading or condition of vehicles or any vehicle with defective braking, steering systems or tyres. Endorsable fixed penalty offences include the offences set out above in relation to the Road Vehicles (Construction and Use) Regulations 1986; failure to comply with 'Stop' signs; double white lines; traffic lights; directions of a constable; pedestrian crossing offences related to a motor vehicle in relation to stopping, parking and failure to accord precedence under both the 'Zebra' and 'Pelican' regulations; breaches of the conditions of provisional licences; offences committed by passengers on motor cycles; leaving a vehicle in a dangerous position, etc.

Fixed penalty notice – non-endorsable offence

The issue of a fixed penalty notice for a non-endorsable offence may be issued either to the offender, or attached to the unattended vehicle which is parked in breach of the regulations, or is defective, or is not displaying licences, etc. It is an offence for a person to interfere with or remove a fixed penalty notice which has been fixed to a vehicle in respect of a fixed penalty offence. Such a notice may only be removed by the driver; the person in charge of the vehicle; the person liable for the offence; or any person acting on the authority of any of these persons.

Fixed penalty notice – endorsable offence

For the purposes of the Road Traffic Offenders Act 1988 an endorsable offence is an offence involving obligatory endorsement (as set out in Schedule 2 to the Act), which is also specified in Schedule 3 (which lists fixed penalty offences). Occasionally, Schedule 2 limits the endorsable provisions of certain enactments by specifying particular offences within regulations which involve obligatory endorsement.

When an offender is dealt with, either by a court or by way of a fixed penalty for such an offence, he is liable to have his driving licence endorsed with the appropriate number of penalty points for the offence. The number of penalty points to be set against each offence is prescribed by Schedule 2 to the Road Traffic Offenders Act 1988. The procedure involving the award of penalty points has, as its ultimate aim, the disqualification of persistent offenders. The penalty points to be taken into account on the occasion of a person committing an endorsable fixed penalty offence are any which will be awarded for the existing offence, and any which are already endorsed on the licence for offences committed not more than three years before that offence. In determining whether a person convicted of an offence would be liable to disqualification, it shall be assumed, in the case of an offence in relation to which a range of numbers is shown, that the number of penalty points to be attributed to the offence would be the lowest in the range. However, if a court has disqualified a driver within that period this has the effect of rubbing out penalty points added to the licence prior to the date of conviction which led to that disqualification. However, this 'wiping clean' of a driving licence is restricted to a disqualification for repeated offences. Where a disqualification is imposed under the Road Traffic Offenders Act 1988, s. 34 (disqualification for a specific offence), the penalty points previously accumulated will remain effective at the end of the period of disqualification for the specific offence until the expiry of three years from the date of the offence for which they were imposed.

(1) *Full fixed penalty notice*

Section 54 of the Road Traffic Offenders Act 1988 deals with circumstances in which the fixed penalty offence involves obligatory endorsement. A constable may give the offender a 'full' fixed penalty notice if:

(a) he produces his licence and its counterpart for inspection by the constable;
(b) the constable is satisfied, on inspecting the licence and its counterpart, that he would not be liable to be disqualified if he were convicted of that offence (i.e. conviction for the fixed penalty offence) and the award of the appropriate number of penalty points would not cause the total number of relevant penalty points, to number or exceed 12; and
(c) he surrenders his licence and its counterpart to the constable to be retained and dealt with in accordance with the provisions of the Act.

So far as it is permitted by the existing policy applicable to a police force, the decision as to whether or not to issue a fixed penalty notice is a matter within the discretion of the constable. If the officer decides to deal with the matter by way of a fixed penalty notice, he has a duty to ensure that the offender is aware of the implications of the procedure. It is suggested that he uses a form of words which convey the following message:

'I propose to issue you with a fixed penalty notice for the offence of ... It will be necessary for me to examine your driving licence and any penalty points which may be endorsed on it. If, after examination I find that it is appropriate to issue you with a fixed penalty notice it will be necessary to surrender your licence to me.'

Police officers must not give the impression that the offender must permit the examination of penalty points endorsed on his licence or its counterpart or that he must surrender it. The 1988 Act requires constables to do things which they are not empowered to do. There is no power given by the Traffic Acts 1988 to examine penalty points on a licence or to require the surrender of a licence in these circumstances. However, the procedure is such that if a person refuses to permit examination of penalty points or to surrender his licence and its counterpart, he cannot be dealt with by this procedure. If he does and he is not liable to disqualification, he may be given a full fixed penalty notice. The officer should use words to the effect:

'Your licence indicates that you may have this offence dealt with by fixed penalty notice. Are you willing to surrender your licence to me? You will be given a receipt.'

If, after such a question, the driver refuses to surrender his licence and its counterpart he cannot be given a fixed penalty notice and he should be reported in the usual way for the offence. If he agrees, a receipt will be made out (it is incorporated in the fixed penalty notice). The notice also gives the offender details of the procedure to be followed if he wishes to arrange a court hearing. His attention should be drawn to this if he disputes any factor associated with the offence. It is helpful if police officers obtain the full postal code of offenders dealt with under this procedure as this assists the clerk to the justices in relation to the registration of the subsequent penalties with the offender's home court.

The receipt which is issued by an officer in respect of a surrendered driving licence and its counterpart is valid for two months from the date of issue (or such longer period as may be prescribed). In addition, a fixed penalty clerk may issue a new receipt on the application of the licence holder, which will expire on such date as is specified in the receipt. Any receipt ceases to be valid on the date the driving licence and its counterpart are returned to the offender. Such a receipt may be produced in place of a licence, subject to the usual conditions applicable to the production of a driving licence under s. 164 Road Traffic Act 1988. However, it is provided that, if required to do so, he must subsequently produce his driving licence and its counterpart at such police station immediately on their return.

Traffic wardens are empowered to require the production of a driving licence where the offence is one concerned with stopping on a pedestrian crossing, leaving a vehicle in a dangerous position and where employed as custodian of impounded vehicles.

(2) Provisional fixed penalty notice

Section 54 is also concerned with 'provisional fixed penalty notices'. Such notices may be issued in any case where:

(a) the offence appears to the constable to involve obligatory endorsement; and

(b) the person concerned does not produce his licence and its counterpart for inspection by the constable.

The constable may give such a person a notice that if, within seven days after the notice is given, he produces the notice together with his driving licence and its counterpart in person to a constable or authorised person at the police station specified in the notice (being a police station chosen by the person concerned), he must then be given a 'full' fixed penalty notice in respect of the offence, if:

(a) the constable or authorised person is satisfied, on inspecting the licence and its counterpart, he would not be liable to be disqualified if he were convicted of the offence; and

(b) he surrenders his licences and its counterpart to the constable or authorised person to be retained and dealt with in accordance with the Act.

In effect, the 'provisional' is made 'full' by completing the driving licence receipt section on the fixed penalty notice.

An 'authorised person', in relation to a fixed penalty notice given at a police station, means a person authorised for the purpose of the section by or on behalf of the chief officer of police for the area in which the police station is situated.

Fixed penalty notices are made out in such a way that they contain all of the details of the offence with which they are concerned and will form a basis of any report which may subsequently be required from the officer in the event of court proceedings.

However, no offence is committed by a person who fails to produce his driving licence as a result of a fixed penalty offer under s. 54. If a constable wishes to examine the licence for any other reason, he must make it clear that the requirement is made under the Road Traffic Act 1988, s. 164, and that the licence *must* be produced to permit examination of those matters set out in s. 164.

Practical points

The procedure does not apply to Scotland and it is therefore not permissible for a constable to issue a provisional fixed penalty notice with a request to produce a driving licence, together with the notice, at a police station in Scotland.

Fixed penalty notices should not be given to juveniles as there are other recommended procedures for dealing with juveniles in relation to offences generally. These procedures recognise the particular circumstances of each case.

Where the circumstances within which the issue of a fixed penalty notice is being considered involve an offence which is associated with a traffic accident, a fixed penalty notice must not be issued. This may occur where a driver has passed a 'Give Way' sign, or some other sign placing upon him a similar demand for action, and has become involved in a collision with another vehicle. In such circumstances it is quite possible that the prosecutor will wish to prefer additional charges when all of the available evidence is considered. The driver's failure to recognise the requirements of the sign may form the basis of such an additional charge.

Section 2 of the Road Traffic Offenders Act 1988 removes the necessity for an offender to be given notice of intended prosecution for an offence in respect of which a fixed penalty notice has been given or fixed under any provision of the Act.

Action by offender on receipt of notice

An offender who has received a fixed penalty notice shall not be subject to proceedings during a 'suspended enforcement period' which is the period of 21 days following the date of the notice, or such longer period as may be specified in the notice (28 days at present). During the suspended enforcement period he may: give notice requesting a court hearing (in which case the fixed penalty notice will be set aside and a court hearing will be arranged); pay the fixed penalty required by the notice (by completing part 2 of the notice and sending it with the fixed penalty required to the Clerk to the Justices at the Fixed Penalty Office); or he may do nothing. If he does not pay before the end of the suspended enforcement period or give notice of his requirement for a hearing, the sum required by way of fixed penalty, plus 50 per cent of that penalty, is registered with the court in the area in which he lives and becomes recoverable as a fine.

In cases in which a fixed penalty notice is fixed to a vehicle and the fixed penalty has not been paid and notice requesting a hearing has not been received, within the suspended enforcement period, a notice to owner may be served by or on behalf of the chief officer of police on any person who appears to him to be the owner of the vehicle (or a person authorised to act on such person's behalf). Such a notice shall give particulars of the offence and of the fixed penalty required and indicate the time allowed for response. If the fixed penalty is not paid before the end of that period, the person on whom the notice is served must furnish, before the end of that period, a statutory statement of ownership. The period allowed for response to such a notice is defined by s. 63(5) as 21 days from the service of the notice.

If such a person was not the owner of the vehicle at the time of the alleged offence he may furnish a statutory statement of ownership stating whether he was ever the owner, or when he ceased to be the owner, or became the owner after the date of the alleged offence. In the last two circumstances, if the information is in his possession he must give the name and address of the person to or from whom the vehicle was sold/bought together with the date of such transaction. If he does not furnish such a statement proceedings may be taken against him. These proceedings shall be by way of registering a penalty against that person equal to the fixed penalty concerned, plus 50 per cent. Provision is also made for statutory statements of hiring in the case of hire vehicles.

The Road Traffic Offenders Act 1988 recognises that there will be occasions upon which the person who receives the notice to owner will not have been the driver at the relevant time. The notice therefore indicates that within the period allowed, he may request a hearing. Alternatively, the person who was actually driving at the time may wish to request a hearing. If he does the owner should also provide a statutory statement of facts which has the effect of the actual driver requesting a hearing. (If such a driver is prepared to accept responsibility for the fixed penalty, the Act assumes that he will do so on behalf of the owner to whom the notice is addressed.)

Conditional offer of fixed penalty

In England and Wales where a constable has reason to believe that a fixed penalty offence has been committed and no fixed penalty notice was given at the time or fixed to the vehicle concerned, a notice of 'conditional offer' may be sent to the alleged offender by or on behalf of the chief officer of police. A conditional offer must give particulars of the circumstances and give reasonable information about the alleged offence; and state that proceedings cannot be commenced for the offence until the end of 28 days following the date of issue (or such longer period specified). Such a notice must indicate that if, within that period, the alleged offender pays the fixed penalty to the fixed penalty clerk and, where the offence concerned involved obligatory endorsement and the licence (and its counterpart) is delivered to the clerk at the same time and the clerk is satisfied that the alleged offender if convicted would not be liable to disqualification under the Road Traffic Offenders Act 1988, s. 35 (disqualification for repeated offences), liability to conviction shall be discharged. In assessing liability to such disqualification, it is assumed (where penalty points awarded for the offence are in a range) that the number to be attributed for the offence would be the lowest in the range.

A person issuing a conditional offer must notify the fixed penalty clerk. If payment is made in accordance with the offer and the licence is delivered, no proceedings will be taken for the offence to which the conditional offer relates. The fixed penalty clerk must endorse the licence or counterpart in appropriate cases and return the licence to the holder. Where the payment of a fixed penalty is made by means of a cheque which is subsequently dishonoured, the validity of the endorsement remains valid, even though the licence holder is then liable to prosecution for the offence. In such circumstances the fixed penalty clerk must, on the expiry of the period specified in the conditional offer, or (if that period has expired) forthwith, notify the person to whom the conditional offer was made that no payment has been made. Where proceedings are brought against a licence holder after he has been notified that a cheque tendered in payment has been dishonoured, the court must order the removal of the fixed penalty endorsement from the licence (or counterpart) and may make any competent order of endorsement or disqualification, in addition to sentence.

The fixed penalty clerk must notify the Secretary of State of any endorsement made on the licence in accordance with these procedures.

Dangerous and careless driving and exceeding speed limits

Speed limits

The maximum speed limit at which a motor vehicle can be lawfully driven on public roads depends on two factors, the first of which is the motor vehicle concerned. Motor vehicles are classified according to their weight, construction, and use, e.g. motor car, heavy motor car, goods vehicle or public service vehicle, and a maximum speed limit may be applied to the vehicle itself.

The second factor to consider is the road and particular restrictions which may be imposed in relation to a road which are of a temporary nature. Speed limits apply to public roads and these can be divided into classes, the most important of which is the restricted road.

All of the offences of speeding which we will consider are offences in respect of which there is discretionary disqualification; the endorsement of 3–6 or 3 (if fixed penalty) penalty points is obligatory.

Restricted road

The general rule is that a road is restricted if there is provided thereon a system of street lighting furnished by means of lamps placed not more than 200 yards apart. However, a direction may be given that a road which has such street lighting shall cease to be a restricted road, or that a road which is not provided with such lighting shall be a restricted road. If this is so, de-restriction signs (including repeater signs) shall be in place in the first instance, and restriction signs (including repeater signs) shall be in place in the second. If roads with such street lighting are subject to a 30 mph limit they will not necessarily show signs to that effect. The absence of any signs is an indication that such a limit is in force. If it is otherwise, the piece of road will show signs indicating any other speed limit which applies, or de-restriction signs, indicating that no speed limit applies. Other roads, which have no street lighting, may have speed limits applied by orders.

Roads other than restricted roads

The general rule is that where a road is not a restricted road then no speed limit applies to the road itself, although a motor vehicle may be limited because of its weight, construction, or use. However, the appropriate authority, i.e. the Minister or local authority, may, after giving public notice of the intention to do so, make an order prohibiting either generally or during certain periods specified in the order, the driving of motor vehicles at a speed exceeding that specified in the order. Thus, where there is a 40 mph or 50 mph speed limit in force, this is because the appropriate authority has made an order imposing such a speed limit. The restriction is indicated by signs showing the restriction, e.g. 50 mph, erected at the point where the restriction commences, together with repeater signs at set intervals along the road to indicate the length of road affected. Such orders are made under the Road Traffic Regulation Act 1984, s. 84, and may prohibit exceeding a specified speed limit at all times; during specified periods; or while a limit is for the time being indicated by traffic signs in accordance with the order.

Speed limits for particular classes of vehicle

The Road Traffic Regulation Act 1984, Schedule 6, sets out speed limits which apply to particular classes of motor vehicles. The limits apply quite apart from the limits which apply to roads. The restrictions imposed by the schedule relate generally to those vehicles which are larger or heavier than most vehicles (it does not deal with any vehicles, other than invalid carriages, which are less than 3.05 tonnes unladen weight, or goods vehicles which are less than 7.5 tonnes unless the particular vehicle is drawing a trailer). Buses exceeding 12 m in length; goods vehicles (other than those

283

up to 7.5 tonnes maximum laden weight, not drawing a trailer); and passenger vehicles or dual purpose vehicles drawing one trailer are generally restricted to a maximum speed of 60 mph on a motorway or dual carriageway (but articulated and other goods vehicles over 7.5 tonnes are restricted to 50 mph on a dual carriageway) and to 50 mph on other roads (but articulated and other goods vehicles over 7.5 tonnes are restricted to 40 mph on other roads).

Temporary speed limits

Under the Road Traffic Regulation Act 1984, s. 88, orders may be made to impose temporary maximum speed limits. Where the Secretary of State considers that, in the interests of safety or to facilitate the movement of traffic, such an order is desirable, he may impose a temporary maximum speed limit. In relation to such temporary limits, the order is deemed to have been made under s. 88. The 70 mph, 60 mph and 50 mph (Temporary Speed Limit) Order 1977 has been given indefinite validity. The effect of the order is that the maximum limit is 70 mph for any vehicle using an unrestricted dual carriageway and 60 mph for unrestricted carriageways unless a lower limit is particularly specified. (Schedules to the order impose limits of 60 mph on certain specified lengths of dual carriageway and of 50 mph on certain specified lengths of single carriageway. Signs must be provided on such roads.)

Motorways

Because of the special nature of motorways and the absence of junctions, traffic lights, etc., the speed limits placed on various classes of motor vehicles differ from those imposed on other roads, and these limits are laid down in the Motorways (Speed Limit) Regulations 1974. The maximum permitted speed on a motorway at present is 70 mph.

Offences

It is an offence for any person to drive a motor vehicle on a restricted road at a speed greater than 30 mph (ss. 81 and 89 of the Road Traffic Regulation Act 1984). Similarly, it is an offence to drive a motor vehicle at a speed which is in excess of that prescribed by a particular order (ss. 84 and 89); a motor vehicle of any class at a speed greater than the speed specified in Schedule 6 of the Road Traffic Regulation Act 1984 as the maximum speed for that class of vehicle (ss. 86 and 89 of the Road Traffic Regulation Act 1984) and in excess of a limit prescribed by a temporary order (ss. 88 and 89).

In addition, the Road Traffic Regulation Act 1984, ss. 14 and 15 (as replaced by the Road Traffic (Temporary Restrictions) Act 1991), is concerned with temporary prohibitions or restrictions made in consequence of the likelihood of danger to the public or serious damage to a road; or to enable cleansing or litter clearance. Such restrictions may be brought into force by notice in urgent cases. They may be concerned with regulating the use of roads, waiting, loading, direction of travel, restrictions on overtaking, *speed limits*, etc. Where such restrictions are in force, an offence is committed by any person who drives a motor vehicle at a speed in excess of that specified as the maximum.

Section 17 of the Act empowers the Minister to make regulations in relation to motorways and a person who drives a motor vehicle on a motorway in excess of 70 mph commits an offence against s. 17(4).

A person prosecuted for exceeding a speed limit is not liable to conviction on the evidence of one witness who states that, in his opinion, the accused was driving at a speed greater than the specified limit. This does not necessarily mean that there must be more than one witness. A person can be convicted on the evidence of one witness who is able to state as a fact, not an opinion, the exact speed at which the vehicle was being driven. In such cases, a police officer giving such factual evidence is supported by the reading of a speedometer or other mechanism which indicated the speed of the offending vehicle, supported in the case of speedometers by evidence of their accuracy. Similarly, evidence of speed given by a single police officer, which is based upon calculations made from skid marks existing at the scene of an accident, is factual evidence based upon objectively detectable phenomena, not opinion.

The law also recognises that pressure can be applied to persons who are employed as drivers and who, in order to comply with any timetable, schedule, or directions given by their employers, are forced to exceed the speed limit. In such cases the publication or issue of any such timetable or schedule, or the giving of such directions, may be produced to a court as prima facie evidence that the employer, as the case may be, procured or incited the persons employed by him to drive vehicles to exceed the speed limit.

Notice of intended prosecution

The provisions contained in s. 1 of the Road Traffic Offenders Act 1988, relating to notice of intended prosecutions, apply to an offence of exceeding a speed limit. It is, therefore, important to ensure that the provisions of that section are complied with when dealing with an offence of exceeding a speed limit, otherwise a subsequent prosecution may fail.

Exemptions from speed limit

Where a motor vehicle is being used for fire brigade, ambulance, or police purposes any provision imposing a speed limit will not apply if the observance of such a provision would be likely to hinder the use of the vehicle on that occasion. This does not mean that a police officer is free to ignore the speed limit as and when he chooses. He should, in fact, set an example to other road users by strict observance of all traffic laws; it is only in exceptional circumstances that a speed limit should be exceeded, and the utmost caution must be exercised. Exemption from the speed limit does not affect a police officer's liability to prosecution for dangerous or careless driving. The life of a police officer and that of any other road user is much more valuable than the arrest of a thief or intruder.

Evidence

The Road Traffic Offenders Act 1988, s. 20, provides that records produced by prescribed devices are evidence of a fact related to any offence of speeding. The record must provide (in the same or another document) a certificate as to the circumstances in which the record was produced, signed by a constable or a person authorised by the chief officer of police for the police area in which the offence is alleged to have been committed. The device must be of a type proved to have been approved by the Secretary of State and must be used in accordance with conditions subject to which the approval was given. The Road Traffic Offenders (Prescribed Devices) Order 1992 gave approval to devices designed or adapted for measuring by radar, the speed of motor vehicles. An identically named order in 1993 approved devices designed or adapted for measuring speeds by way of cables or sensors on or near the surface of a highway and those activated by means of a light beam or beams.

A copy of evidence obtained by means of an approved device must be served on the person charged with the offence not less that seven days before the hearing or trial. If the person charged, not less than three days before the hearing or trial, requires the attendance of the person who signed the document, the evidence of the circumstances in which the record was produced will not be admissible, although the record produced by the device will.

Radar meters are extremely accurate devices and the courts will accept evidence of speed which is based upon meter readings provided that there is evidence of use by a trained operator. Hand-held radar guns are similarly accurate (provided that the batteries are fully charged). They should not be operated within a quarter of a mile of powerful VHF or UHF transmissions or within 100 yards of high voltage cables. All such devices (and others which are in common use) are approved by the Secretary of State.

Introduction to dangerous and careless driving

It was recognised as long ago as the Motor Act 1903 that legislation was necessary to prevent misconduct in the management of motor vehicles towards the public on a highway. The relevant provisions are now contained in the Road Traffic Act 1988, covering both motor vehicles and pedal cycles. These provisions are concerned with standards, and it should be noted that there is only one standard of driving and this is an objective one, fixed and impersonal, governed by the essential needs of the public and fixed in relation to the safety of other road users. There is no distinction drawn between the person learning to drive and the professional driver who earns his living by driving all day. Invariably it is a question of facts whether, in particular circumstances, a person is guilty of driving or riding dangerously or carelessly, and it is the job of a police officer to present all the facts of a case to the court to enable the court to arrive at the correct decision. In connection with motor vehicles only, s. 1 of the Road Traffic Act 1988 creates the offence of causing death by dangerous driving. This offence is not intended to be an alternative to manslaughter, but is intended to be used as a substitute. Charges of manslaughter arising out of the driving of a motor vehicle are only preferred in the most serious cases where there is a high degree of negligence.

Driving

The word 'driving' in connection with these offences has not got an extended meaning as in other traffic offences. A person is driving if the vehicle, when moving, is subject to his control and direction and he has something to do with the propulsion of the vehicle. If a person was sitting in the driving seat of a stationary vehicle parked in such a manner to be dangerous to other road users and an accident occurred in which a person was fatally injured, the person sitting in the driving seat of the parked vehicle would not be liable for the offence of causing death by dangerous driving, although he may be guilty of other traffic offences. A man steering a car being towed by a tow rope is driving because he can both steer and operate the brakes. This would not necessarily be so on a fixed tow bar. A person who momentarily takes hold of a steering wheel while a motor vehicle is being driven by someone else, does not 'drive' that vehicle. 'Driving' involves more than such minimal action.

Dangerous driving

The offence of dangerous driving is provided in the Road Traffic Act 1988, s. 2, as substituted by the Road Traffic Act 1991, s. 1. The section provides that a person who drives a mechanically propelled vehicle dangerously on a road or other public place is guilty of an offence. Section 1 of the 1991 Act provides that, for the purposes of ss. 1 and 2 of the 1988 Act, a person is to be regarded as driving dangerously if, and only if:

(a) the way that he drives falls far below what would be expected of a competent and careful driver; and
(b) it would be obvious to a competent and careful driver that driving in that way would be dangerous.

This offence, being new, has not been interpreted by the High Court at the time of writing. However, the significant factors may be the words 'falls far below' and the words 'would be obvious' in their relationship to 'danger'. This standard applies to all drivers regardless of their experience. It will be no defence for an accused to claim that he was doing his incompetent best. The objective standard against which driving will be measured will vary according to the prevailing conditions and to exceptional circumstances which may have existed at the time. In fog, the competent and careful driver would drive differently than he would in clear conditions. High speed in a built-up area may amount to dangerous driving but is less likely to be so on a dual carriageway which is unobstructed. If the high speed driving in a built-up area occurred in the middle of the night when there were no other vehicles or pedestrians about, the element of 'danger' is not so apparent as it would be had that driving occurred in the middle of the day.

In a recent case which was concerned with the replaced offence of 'reckless driving', the judge made reference to acts which he described as 'a piece of deliberate *dangerous* driving' carried out with a manifest risk with a potentially lethal vehicle. The accused had closed up behind the car of an off-duty police officer, with the headlights of his car on full beam, and travelling at about 60 to 70 mph. He pulled out and overtook, at which the police officer 'flashed' the main beam of his headlights to alert him to the fact that his headlights were on full beam. The accused braked fiercely, then slowed until almost stationary. When the officer overtook, the accused moved to within one foot of the rear bumper of the officer's car with both head lamps and two long range driving lamps on full beam. The officer touched his footbrake pedal to warn him to drop back but to no avail. He decelerated at which the accused accelerated into the officer's car causing some damage.

The point was made that the actions of the accused caused a two-fold danger; the obvious inherent danger in driving in such a manner and the potentially more serious danger that an impetuous, perhaps inexperienced driver, harassed by the accused's aggression, might be tempted to retaliate with the consequences that the danger would be wider spread and more innocent road users might become involved.

To prove the old charge of reckless driving, the actions of the accused were considered collectively and this may be done in the future to establish dangerous driving which consisted of a course of conduct. In looking at the individual incidents, it could have been argued that the first, travelling at a fast speed on full beam regardless of traffic, might have been no more than momentary inattention (thus an incident of careless driving if that was established); that this conduct did not fall 'far below' that of a competent and careful driver. Contrast, however, the later incident where the accused deliberately closed to within one foot of the preceding car showing four main beam lights. This conduct does fall 'far below' that of a competent and careful driver and it must have been obvious to any such driver that driving in that way would be dangerous.

The section also provides that a person shall be regarded as driving dangerously for the purposes of ss. 1 and 2 if it would be obvious to a competent and careful driver that driving the vehicle in its current state would be dangerous. Thus, he who drives a vehicle, for example, with obviously defective brakes, drives dangerously if those defects would be obvious to a competent and careful driver. He who drives a goods vehicle and is aware that his vehicle's heavy load may fall off and kill or injure another road user, drives dangerously if the danger would be obvious to a competent and careful driver. A vehicle which was defective because of serious corrosion underneath the vehicle was held not to be such that a competent and careful driver would necessarily be aware of the defects.

When it has been established that the actual driving fell far below such standards, it becomes necessary to consider whether it would be obvious to a competent and careful driver that such driving would be dangerous. In this context 'dangerous' refers to danger either of injury to any person or of serious damage to property. In determining what would be expected of, or obvious to, a competent and careful driver, regard shall be had not only to the circumstances of which he could be expected to be aware, but also to any circumstances shown to have been within the knowledge of the accused. Where, for example, a rope securing a load was seriously weakened, this may be shown to have been within the knowledge of the accused, although it may not have been obvious to a competent and careful driver in a general sense. In determining the state of a vehicle, regard may be had to anything attached to it or carried on or in it and to the manner in which it is attached or carried.

Causing death by dangerous driving

This is the most serious offence that the driver of a motor vehicle can commit and is contained in s. 1 of the Road Traffic Act 1988 as substituted by s. 1 of the Road Traffic Act 1991 which reads:

'A person who causes the death of another person by driving a mechanically propelled vehicle dangerously on a road or other public place shall be guilty of an offence.'

This offence is punishable on indictment with ten years' imprisonment and, consequently, is an arrestable offence. It was created because of the reluctance of juries to convict a person of manslaughter in motor accident cases – a charge of manslaughter now being preferred only when there is clear evidence of criminal negligence. For explanation of term 'public place' see page 299.

Causes the death of another person

This does not mean that dangerous driving must be the sole cause of death; prosecution need only prove that the driving was a cause of the death, as opposed to the principal or substantial cause of death. The death must occur within a year and a day of the date on which the driving occurred. This limit is under review.

Where a fatal accident occurs, one of the important points to remember is the continuity of identification from the scene of the accident to the hospital and later the mortuary. If the person is not certified dead at the scene by a doctor, the usual practice is to convey him by ambulance to the nearest hospital where he is certified as being dead on arrival and then conveyed to the mortuary where a post-mortem will be carried out later. To avoid the necessity of having a number of witnesses to provide the chain of identification, a police officer will usually accompany the body from the scene to the mortuary via the hospital, and later will identify the body to the pathologist who performs the post-mortem examination.

The question of clothing worn by the deceased may be an important factor in any subsequent court proceedings, particularly where the person killed was a pedestrian. A note should be made of the top clothing worn by the deceased. If the accident occurred during the hours of darkness, one of the questions which will be asked is whether or not the pedestrian could have been easily seen by the driver of a motor vehicle. Similarly, if the motor vehicle concerned in the death failed to stop after the accident, an examination of the clothing may yield valuable evidence connecting the vehicle with the accident.

The death must be of another person; this includes a passenger in the motor vehicle involved in the accident. However, when a prosecution is being considered for causing death by reckless driving and the person killed (or all of the persons killed) was a relative of the driver but police nevertheless believe that in the light of all circumstances a prosecution should be brought, the case should be referred to the Director of Public Prosecutions before a decision is made to institute proceedings. Where the deceased is not a relative in a legal sense, but has a close connection with the driver, the case may still be referred to the Director for any advice he may wish to give.

Evidence of drink

Evidence that the driver was adversely affected by drink is relevant where the issue is whether he was driving dangerously. To be admissible, such evidence must tend to show that the amount of drink taken would adversely affect a driver or, alternatively, that the driver was in fact adversely affected. Thus, where it could be given that the alcohol content of the blood of a driver exceeded 80 milligrams per 100 millilitres of blood, that would be evidence tending to show that the amount of drink taken was such that it would adversely affect the driving of the person concerned. However, there must be evidence of the manner of driving. Consumption of alcohol is not, by itself, sufficient to justify conviction for dangerous driving. The section requires evidence of 'the way he drives' (as compared with the competent and careful driver) and evidence of the fact that it would be obvious to such a driver that driving in that way would be dangerous. The consumption of alcohol may be relevant to the first point; it cannot be relevant to the second as in that case we are concerned with the competent and careful driver, not with the accused in a direct sense. However, evidence of the consumption of alcohol will always be relevant to 'the way he drives' as it is a related fact.

Defences

Once it is proved that a person was in the driving seat of a moving vehicle there is an irresistible inference that he was driving, and if the driving was dangerous then that is likely to be regarded as conclusive evidence that the person in the driving seat was driving in a dangerous manner. However, a person cannot be said to be driving if he suffers a sudden mischance for which he is no longer to blame and which renders him unconscious or otherwise prevents him from controlling the movements of the vehicle. Examples of such situations are a sudden epileptic fit or coma, a blow on the head from a stone, or an attack by a swarm of bees.

This defence, now generally referred to as 'automatism', will only apply if the deprivation of all thought, which is caused by the affliction, was not connected with any deliberate act or conduct of the driver and arose from a cause which a reasonable man would have no reason to expect, and which the driver did not think might occur. In the absence of medical evidence the defence of automatism can only succeed in rare circumstances.

A good defence can be put forward when the driver of a vehicle is suddenly deprived of control due to some defect in the vehicle suddenly manifesting itself. Such a defect may be a defence if, because of it, the danger was created by a sudden total loss of control in no way due to fault on the part of the driver, but the defence has no application where the defect is known to the driver or should have been discovered by him had he exercised reasonable prudence.

Where a motor car is being hotly pursued by an armed gang or where it has been hijacked by an armed gang who order the driver to drive in a particular way, the driver may have a defence if he can prove that he drove dangerously in order to avoid a threat of death or serious injury.

Aiding and abetting

Although the offence of causing death by dangerous driving can only be committed by the person driving a vehicle, this does not preclude any other person who aided, abetted, counselled, or procured the offence from being punished. In relation to indictable offences the relevant legislation is contained in s. 8 of the Accessories and Abettors Act 1861, which states:

'Whosoever aids and abets, counsels or procures the commission of an indictable offence either at common law or by virtue of any Act passed or to be passed, is liable to be tried, indicted and punished as a principal.'

Thus, where a qualified accompanying driver is charged with aiding and abetting a provisional licence holder who was driving a motor vehicle when it was involved in a fatal accident, the accompanying driver could be convicted of aiding and abetting the provisional licence holder in causing death by dangerous driving if it could be shown that the provisional licence holder had been driving the car dangerously for a sufficient time to enable the accompanying driver to try to stop the driver from driving dangerously, and that he had not done so.

Alternative verdicts

The Road Traffic Offenders Act 1988, s. 24, provides that where a person is found not guilty of an offence of causing death by dangerous driving he may be found guilty of dangerous driving or careless or inconsiderate driving and that a person found not guilty of an offence of dangerous driving may be found guilty of careless or inconsiderate driving, provided that the allegations in the indictment or information amount to or include an allegation of an offence under the appropriate alternative provision.

Careless and inconsiderate driving

The relevant provisions are now contained in s. 3 of the Road Traffic Act 1988, as follows:

'If a person drives a mechanically propelled vehicle on a road or other public place without due care and attention, or without reasonable consideration for other persons using the road or place, he shall be guilty of an offence.'

A person commits an offence of careless driving if he was not exercising that degree of care and attention that a reasonable and prudent driver would exercise in those circumstances. No allowances are made for learner drivers; there is only one standard of care.

It is difficult to draw a distinction between dangerous driving and driving without due care and attention, or without reasonable consideration. The view most often taken is that where a driver has been merely careless, or momentarily inattentive, he is guilty of careless driving. Some examples will serve to illustrate the point. A driver who mounted the verge, hitting a pole almost 3 feet from the edge of the road, was held to be driving carelessly; similarly, it was careless driving where a driver gave

291

misleading signals. Examples of driving without reasonable consideration include driving with brilliant headlights which were not dipped for oncoming traffic and driving through puddles at speed, drenching pedestrians.

Sometimes the situation in which a vehicle is found raises a prima facie case of driving without due care and attention; for example, where a car left the road, mounted the footpath on its nearside, and collided with a structure on the other side of the footpath. Another example was where a car collided with a lamp standard and a shop, and although there were no eye witnesses there were tyre marks showing that the vehicle had been driven for 100 yards on the wrong side of the road and partly on the footpath. Paint of the same colour as the car was found on the lamp standard and the shop, and the position where the car, which was also badly damaged, came to rest was noted; these were all facts which were so eloquent in themselves that the court was entitled to find that the driver was guilty of driving without due care and attention.

On occasions a driver will have carried out an act which is contrary to the indications given by a traffic sign. This would be so if the requirement imposed by road markings which accompany such as 'Stop' and 'Give way' signs were ignored; that no vehicle shall pass the line markings on the road concerned in circumstances which will impede other traffic on the main road. While an offence of failing to comply with the indications given by the sign will always apply, a charge of careless driving may also lie where a collision, or near-collision occurs due to the driver's actions. It is submitted that the driver who impedes traffic by unreasonably remaining in the overtaking lane of a motorway or dual carriageway, and he who irresponsibly uses full beam headlamps, is driving without reasonable consideration for other road users.

The section creates two separate offences: careless driving and driving without reasonable consideration for other road users. Both cannot be charged in a single information.

Causing death by careless driving when under the influence of drink or drugs

The Road Traffic Act 1991, s. 3, added a new s. 3A to the 1988 Act. Section 3A provides:

'If a person causes the death of another person by driving a mechanically propelled vehicle on a road or other public place without due care and attention, or without reasonable consideration for other persons using the road or place, and:

  (a) he is, at the time when he is driving, unfit to drive through drink or drugs; or

  (b) he has consumed so much alcohol that the proportion of it in his breath, blood or urine at that time exceeds the prescribed limit; or

  (c) he is, within 18 hours after that time, required to provide a specimen in pursuance of s. 7 of this Act, but without reasonable excuse fails to provide it,

he is guilty of an offence.'

The term 'causing the death of another person' is discussed above. The terms 'unfit

292

to drive through drink or drugs', 'exceeds the prescribed limit' and 'without reasonable excuse fails to provide it' are explained in the section entitled 'Breath specimens and drinking and driving' on pages 294–315.

It is important to be able to establish clearly *careless driving* in the first instance, and

(a) that at the time the driver is either:
   (i) unfit to drive through drink or drugs;
   (ii) driving while over the prescribed limit; or
(b) that within 18 hours of that careless driving, he fails, without reasonable excuse, to provide a specimen for analysis; and that the careless driving was a cause of the death of another person.

Alternative verdicts

A person who is found not guilty of this offence may be convicted of an offence of careless or inconsiderate driving; driving when unfit to drive through drink or drugs; driving with excess alcohol in breath, blood or urine; or of failing to provide a specimen for analysis, if the allegations in the indictment or information amount to or include an allegation of such an offence.

Identification

As in all criminal cases, the identification of the driver and the linking of the driver to the alleged offence are most important. If the driver cannot be identified with the alleged offence, then a charge against him will generally fail.

Defences

As in dangerous driving, the defences of 'automatism' and 'mechanical defect' and perhaps 'necessity' apply to a person charged with an offence under s. 3 of the Act.

Aiding and abetting

Both the offences under s. 3 (careless and inconsiderate driving) are summary offences and, therefore, a person who is charged with aiding, abetting, counselling, or procuring the commission of an offence under s. 3 of the Act is dealt with under the Magistrates' Courts Act 1980, which states:

'A person who aids, abets, counsels, or procures the commission by another person of a summary offence shall be guilty of the like offence and may be tried (whether or not he is charged as a principal) either by a court having jurisdiction to try that other person or by a court having, by virtue of his own offence, jurisdiction to try him.'

The test to be applied in aiding and abetting cases is that if a person knows that the acts which constitute an offence are being done and he helps in any way, he is guilty of aiding and abetting that offence. It should be noted, however, that the passive conduct of the supervisor of a learner driver in circumstances which called for action on his part, could render the supervisor liable for aiding and abetting an offence committed by the learner driver.

Dangerous and careless cycling

The offences of dangerous and careless cycling are covered by ss. 28 and 29 of the Road Traffic Act 1988, and in each case the wording is similar to the corresponding sections of the Act relating to motor vehicles. What has been said about 'dangerous' for the purposes of dangerous driving also applies to the offence of dangerous cycling. Where a person is charged with dangerous cycling and is found not guilty of that offence and the allegations in the information amount to or include an allegation of careless cycling, he may be convicted of that offence.

Note of intended prosecution

The provisions contained in s. 1 of the Road Traffic Offenders Act 1988 relating to notice of intended prosecution apply to all the offences with which we have dealt, with the notable exception of the offence of causing death by dangerous driving. It is, therefore, important when dealing with an offence of dangerous or careless driving or cycling that the provisions of s. 1 of the Act are complied with. In practice, notice of intended prosecution is sometimes sent for the offence of dangerous driving, when a charge of causing death by dangerous driving is being considered.

However, s. 2 of the Road Traffic Offenders Act 1988 states that the requirements of s. 1 do not apply in relation to an offence if, at the time of the offence or immediately thereafter, an accident occurs owing to the presence on a road of the vehicle in respect of which the offence was committed. If, therefore, the dangerous or careless manner of the driving results immediately in an accident, there is no requirement to comply with the provisions of this section.

Police powers

The offence of causing death by dangerous driving is punishable with ten years' imprisonment and is, therefore, an arrestable offence. However, it should seldom be necessary to exercise such a power unless the driver is uncooperative.

Breath specimens and drinking and driving

Introduction

The driving of motor vehicles by persons adversely affected by drink or drugs has become a social problem not only in this country but throughout the western world. In 1967, Parliament introduced new legislation creating the offences of driving, attempting to drive and being in charge of a motor vehicle with a blood/alcohol concentration above a prescribed limit. This limit was set at 80 milligrams of alcohol in 100 millilitres of blood, or 107 milligrams of alcohol in 100 millilitres of urine.

294 Prior to the introduction of precise scientific methods of determining a blood/

alcohol, urine/alcohol level, successful prosecutions were dependent upon the evidence of the medical practitioner who examined the suspect and subjected him to certain tests most of which were concerned with coordination. It was hoped that these more precise methods would lead to a more effective enforcement of drink/driving legislation.

The early impact of the 1967 legislation, now incorporated in the Road Traffic Act 1988, led to a marked increase in prosecutions and an estimated saving of 1000 lives in the first year. However, complexities within the legislation led to difficulties in enforcement. A clear prescription was set out for the demand and the taking of preliminary breath tests by means of screening devices. To prove an offence, it became necessary to offer proof that procedures had been meticulously followed. Defects led to acquittals in many cases where analysis of blood or urine samples showed high levels of alcohol and the will to enforce legislation which included so many pitfalls was quite obviously affected.

The Road Traffic Act 1988 was drafted with a view to eliminating all of the difficulties encountered in enforcement and it has gone some way towards doing so. For example, the reason for many acquittals was seated in a procedural defect which was alleged to have invalidated the arrest. This, in turn, made evidence of alcohol content inadmissible. The 1988 Act does not require an arrest as an essential prerequisite to a successful prosecution. It also includes measures to eliminate the need for medical practitioners to become involved in most prosecutions, by introducing a requirement to provide two specimens of breath for *analysis* by means of a device approved by the Secretary of State. The approved devices accurately measure the alcohol in the breath and the prescribed limit is set at 35 micrograms in 100 millilitres of breath. Substantive breath testing machines in police stations will be operated by trained and approved operators.

However, care is essential in carrying out 'in station' procedures, within which irregularities may still lead to unmeritorious acquittals. There is currently an increasing tendency on the part of the High Court to allow appeals which are based upon the finer points of the procedure to be followed in a police station. The 'game' is once again becoming more important than the question of whether or not the driver was over the limit. Care must be taken in following the correct procedure in the police station.

Breath specimens at scene

(1) Roadside specimens

The enforcement of this legislation must begin with the driving, etc., of a motor vehicle on a road, or public place in circumstances in which a police officer suspects that the driver has alcohol in his body. The law allows the officer to demand a specimen of breath in certain circumstances. The suspect, by blowing into one of a number of approved screening devices, which indicate the presence of alcohol in the breath in such quantity that it is suspected that the prescribed limit might be exceeded, either confirms the officer's suspicion or provides evidence that he is not sufficiently affected. The operative word is 'screening device'. At this stage we are taking a breath specimen, measured roughly by a screening device, to confirm or set aside our suspicions. This procedure has nothing to do with the later requirement to provide breath for measurement by an evidential breath testing machine.

Section 6(1) of the Road Traffic Act 1988 provides that:

'Where a constable in uniform has reasonable cause to suspect:
  (a) that a person driving or attempting to drive or in charge of a motor vehicle on a road or other public place has alcohol in his body or has committed a traffic offence while the vehicle was in motion; or
  (b) that a person has been driving or attempting to drive or been in charge of a motor vehicle on a road or other public place with alcohol in his body and that that person still has alcohol in his body; or
  (c) that a person has been driving or attempting to drive or has been in charge of a motor vehicle on a road or other public place and has committed a traffic offence while the vehicle was in motion

he may, subject to Section 9 (protection for hospital patients), require him to provide a specimen of breath for a breath test.'

However, arresting officers must give direct evidence of their suspicion of the presence of alcohol in the accused person at the time at which they require a roadside specimen, where the issue of such suspicion is relevant to the arrest. The Divisional Court has ruled that the justices had the right to exclude the evidence of the subsequent analysis of a specimen, under the provisions of the Police and Criminal Evidence Act 1984, s. 78, on the grounds that the defendant had been denied the protection of the Road Traffic Act 1988, s. 6 (that a demand could only be made for a roadside specimen where that suspicion existed in the circumstances), and that the prosecutor had, in consequence of that denial obtained evidence which he would not have otherwise obtained and that this resulted in the defendant being significantly prejudiced in resisting the charge. This ruling would appear, to a considerable extent, to negative the purpose behind the phrasing of the Road Traffic Act 1988, s. 7 (see below), in its present form.

The constable's reasonable suspicion may arise as a result of an anonymous telephone call.

Section 6(2) provides that if an accident occurs owing to the presence of a motor vehicle on a road or other public place, a constable may require any person whom he has reasonable cause to believe was driving or attempting to drive or in charge of the vehicle at the time of the accident, to provide a specimen of breath for a breath test, subject to s. 9 (at a hospital – special provisions). The fact that an accident has occurred owing to the presence of the motor vehicle on a road or other public place does not entitle a constable to require a specimen under s. 6(2) from *anyone*. The requirement may only be made of a person whom he *has reasonable cause to believe was driving or attempting to drive or in charge of the vehicle* at the time of the accident. It is not enough for a constable to 'reasonably suspect', he must 'reasonably believe' that such a person was the driver.

Section 6(3) provides that such requirements, when made under any of these provisions, may be made either at or near the place where the requirement is made. If made under subs. (2), that is following an accident, and the constable making the requirement thinks fit, the specimen may be provided at a police station specified by the constable.

The power to require a screening breath test does not depend upon a person actually having alcohol in his body or actually having committed a moving traffic offence. It arises when a constable has reasonable cause to suspect such a thing. In addition, the power to require a screening breath test extends to circumstances in which a constable has *reasonable cause to suspect* that a person *has been driving, attempting to drive or is in charge of a vehicle* on any road or public place with *alcohol in his body* and that person still has alcohol in his body or has committed a moving traffic offence. Such a suspicion need not have arisen while the vehicle was in motion. Thus, in any case where a constable has stopped a motorist under his common law or statutory powers, and then has reasonable cause to suspect that the driver has alcohol in his body, he may require a screening breath test.

(2) *Screening devices*

The breath tests provided in accordance with this section are designed solely to assist police officers in deciding whether further action should be taken; the result of a breath test of this nature merely provides evidence on which to found reasonable suspicion that an offence is being committed. The specimen must be in sufficient quantity to enable the test to be carried out. The screening devices used must be those approved by the Home Secretary. At present the Home Secretary has approved certain devices comprising indicator tubes, mouthpieces and inflatable bags and four electronic screening devices. The 'blow in the bag' types are the 'ALCOTEST R80' and R80A and the Alcolyser. The correct assembly and use of the devices demands a special technique which must be mastered. The containers of these devices are marked with a date after which the device must not be used, and checks should be made to ensure that any device used has not become dated. The Home Secretary has approved four electronic screening devices, the LION SL2, SL2A, the DRAEGER ALERT and the DRAEGER ALCOTEST 7410. These devices give an electronic indication by means of lights, whether or not a motorist has provided a positive or negative specimen. Once again, it is important for police officers to master the correct usage of these devices. The instructions for use are set out clearly in a police officer's initial course lesson notes.

The instructions dealing with the operation of screening devices state that the breath test should not be given until at least 20 minutes have elapsed since the consumption of alcoholic drink. If an officer has reason to believe that such a drink may have been taken within the preceding 20 minutes, he should wait for such a period to elapse. This is because even small traces of mouth alcohol can give a positive indication. Breath should be supplied continuously for 10 to 20 seconds in the case of 'blow in the bag' devices, or until indicated in the case of electronic devices. If a driver is smoking, he should be asked to stop and allowed to take two or three breaths to void the lungs of smoke, before taking the test.

Section 9 is referred to above in relation to the taking of breath specimens. It provides that a person who is at a hospital as a patient shall not be required to provide such a breath test unless the medical practitioner in immediate charge of the case has been notified of the proposal to make the requirement. If the requirement is then made, it shall be for provision of a specimen *at the hospital*. If the medical practitioner objects, the requirement shall not be made. The grounds upon which a

297

medical practitioner can object are that the requirement itself, or the provision of the specimen, would be prejudicial to the proper care and treatment of the patient. The same provisions apply to the provision of laboratory specimens (see page 303). A person remains a patient until discharged by a doctor or when he discharges himself. A person is 'at a hospital' if he remains within a hospital complex, including its car park.

Driving, etc., while over the prescribed limit

Section 5 of the 1988 Act is concerned with driving, attempting to drive, or being in charge of a motor vehicle with an alcohol concentration above the prescribed limit.

'If a person drives, or attempts to drive a motor vehicle on a road or other public place, or is in charge of a motor vehicle on a road or other public place, after consuming so much alcohol that the proportion of it in his breath, blood or urine exceeds the prescribed limit, he shall be guilty of an offence.'

It will be seen that the word 'breath' precedes 'blood or urine'. In order to prove an offence the prosecution must bring evidence that the breath-alcohol concentration, as established by the correct use of an evidential breath testing machine, exceeds 35 micrograms of alcohol in 100 millilitres of breath. Only in particular circumstances, in which it has not been possible to obtain evidence of breath-alcohol concentrations, will it become necessary to show that one of the other prescribed limits was exceeded, that is either 80 milligrams of alcohol in 100 millilitres of blood or 107 milligrams of alcohol in 100 millilitres of urine. However, a police officer's involvement with such offences begins at an earlier stage, when he suspects that a driver, etc., has alcohol in his body, so it will be of assistance to follow the procedure through from this obvious beginning.

(1) Driving, attempting to drive or in charge of

Generally, we have little difficulty in deciding who is a driver and the term 'driver' is well discussed in other chapters. When a motorist stops before he has completed his journey, he may still be driving; an obvious example is when he is halted at traffic lights or a road junction. If a motorist is stopped by a constable in uniform, who immediately forms the suspicion that the motorist has alcohol in his body, the motorist should be regarded as still driving. If an appreciable time has elapsed before such a suspicion is formed, then it will be safer to allege 'in charge'.

In deciding whether or not someone is attempting to drive, a moment must arrive when the acts of the motorist amount to more than mere preparation. If an attempt to drive cannot be safely alleged, then an allegation of 'in charge' should be relied upon. It would be preparation to search for the ignition keys, while it would be an attempt to drive to use those keys to start the engine. A man who was trying to start the engine of his car with the wrong ignition key and who was not in possession of the correct key was held to be attempting to drive.

(2) *Motor vehicle*

The term 'motor vehicle' means a mechanically propelled vehicle intended or adapted for use on roads.

(3) *Road*

A road, as defined in the Act, is any highway and any other road to which the public have access, and includes bridges over which a road passes. It includes the footway as well as the carriageway. This definition can extend to privately maintained roads, if evidence can be brought to prove that the public have access; a quayside where the public are free to walk and drive, and where there is no notice of hindrance to stop them, is a road. Each case must be considered on its merits, the important factor being, in each case, the extent to which the general public, as opposed to any particular section of the public, have access.

(4) *Public place*

The term 'public place' is not defined in the Act and it is a question of fact and degree; if only a restricted class of persons is permitted or invited to have access, the place would be private, but if only a restricted section of the public are excluded, the place would be public. A private field to which members of the public were permitted access to watch racing was held to be a public place at the time. A car park at the side of a public house where members of the public were permitted to park their cars was held to be a public place when it was open for such use, but this decision should be compared with that in which a car park attached to a private club used by members was held not to be a public place; a public house offers its services to the public, but a private club only offers admittance to members and their guests. Justices are entitled to rely on their local knowledge in determining whether a car park is a public place.

Caravan sites which are open to members of the public are public places. It is irrelevant that payment is required for use of the roads and facilities within the site. A site which is owned by a club and where admittance is restricted to members is a private place. However, if members of the public are additionally admitted, the site becomes 'public'. A multi-storey car park is a public place at any time at which members of the public are admitted, so is the disembarkation lane at a ferry terminal as the persons using it are merely ticket-holding members of the public.

(5) *Is in charge*

This term should be given its ordinary meaning. A person is in charge of a motor vehicle, if he is in control of it. He does not need to be driving or attempting to drive it. However, distinctions must be drawn to be realistic and we must look at journeys and their purposes. A motorist remains in charge of his vehicle throughout a journey. If he sits in it at the end of that journey, he remains in positive control. Should he secure the vehicle and enter a public house, it is submitted that he is no longer sufficiently in control to justify a charge even though he retains the keys. Once he returns to the vehicle and begins to enter it, he has certainly regained his charge.

If, however, he has surrendered the keys to another person with instructions that that person assumes control of the vehicle, then it is clear that 'charge' has been relinquished.

Persons other than the owner or person in lawful possession or control of a vehicle may assume charge of it. In such cases consideration must be given as to whether and where he was in the vehicle or how far from it; what he was doing; whether he was in possession of a suitable ignition key; evidence of intention to take control by driving or otherwise; and the position and circumstances of other persons who were also in the vehicle.

(6) *Prescribed limit, etc.*

The prescribed limits are:

(a) 35 micrograms of alcohol in 100 millilitres of BREATH;
(b) 80 milligrams of alcohol in 100 millilitres of BLOOD;
(c) 107 milligrams of alcohol in 100 millilitres of URINE.

Note that the alcohol level in the breath is measured in *micrograms* – 35 micrograms in 100 millilitres of breath is roughly equivalent to the other two levels.

(7) *In uniform*

The test is whether or not the officer is identifiable as a constable and the fact that he is not wearing a cap does not affect the fact that he is in uniform, nor does the fact that he is wearing a raincoat loosely over his uniform. Note that this requirement to be in uniform when a breath test, using a screening device, is demanded does not apply to s. 6(2), in cases following an accident. A court is entitled to presume that a constable was in uniform unless the contrary is proved.

(8) *Suspicion of alcohol*

It is clear that the point is not whether the motorist has actually consumed alcohol but whether the constable has reasonable cause to suspect a motorist of having alcohol in his body. All factors will be taken into account in deciding whether actions merited reasonable cause to suspect alcohol. Lack of steering control would generally give cause to such suspicions, while selecting a wrong indicator would be unlikely to be enough standing alone. It is really a question of fact for the magistrates to decide upon the evidence put forward. It is possible that more than one officer may be involved in this process. A motorist whose driving gives rise to such a suspicion, may be seen driving erratically by one officer who passes a radio message to a colleague who actually stops the vehicle.

(9) *Traffic offence while vehicle in motion*

The term 'traffic offence' is defined by s. 6(8). It means an offence under:

(a) any provision of Part II of the Public Passenger Vehicles Act 1981 (fitness of vehicles, licences, etc.);

(b) any provision of the Road Traffic Regulation Act 1984;

(c) any provision of the Road Traffic Act 1988 except Part V (driving instruction);

(d) any provision of the Road Traffic Offenders Act 1988 except Part III (fixed penalties).

This includes offences contrary to the various regulations made under those Acts, for example, the Road Vehicles (Construction and Use) Regulations and the Road Vehicles Lighting Regulations. A common fault is to regard all offences committed in a moving vehicle as being included in the term 'moving traffic offence'. All offences under the Vehicle Excise and Registration Act 1994 and the regulations made under the authority of that Act – e.g. Road Vehicles (Registration and Licensing) Regulations – are not offences for which a motorist can be required to give a specimen of breath for a breath test.

(10) *Has been driving, etc.*

A sample of breath can be demanded if a constable reasonably suspects that a person has been driving, attempting to drive or has been in charge:

(a) with alcohol in his body and that that person still has alcohol in his body; or

(b) has committed a traffic offence while the vehicle was in motion.

These provisions are extremely helpful.

Difficulties existed in the past when drivers abandoned their vehicles and were later found after they had obviously ceased driving, etc. Now a reasonably held suspicion of the circumstances above empowers a constable to demand a sample of breath. It should be noted that when the requirement is made following an accident, this provision is only concerned with persons who the constable reasonably believes to have been driving, attempting to drive, or in charge of the vehicle at the time of the accident.

(11) *Accident*

There is no legal definition of the term 'accident' and an objective test should be applied, that is, would a reasonable man, applying everyday descriptions, describe what had occurred as an accident? It has been held that a deliberate motoring act which resulted in damage to a motor car was an accident because that is how a reasonable man would describe it.

Failure to provide a sample of breath

A person who, without reasonable excuse, fails to provide a specimen of breath when required to do in pursuance of s. 6(4) Road Traffic Act 1988 commits an offence. Section 6(4) is concerned with the screening test given to suspects by beat officers, using either tube and bag devices or electronic screening devices.

(1) *Reasonable excuse*

No excuse can be adjudged a reasonable one unless the person from whom the specimen is required is physically or mentally unable to provide the specimen of breath or its provision would entail a substantial risk to health. For example, a person suffering from chest or lung disorders such as bronchitis or asthma may be unable to provide sufficient breath for screening purposes. It is not a reasonable excuse that the person concerned has not consumed alcohol when a police officer, with reasonable cause, believes that he has alcohol in his body. Nor is it a reasonable excuse that consumption of alcoholic drink took place after an accident, or after immediate driving had ceased or that he mistakenly believed that the request was invalid. The term 'reasonable excuse' is strictly related to mental and physical factors which would prevent such a sample being given. It has been held that there was a reasonable excuse where a driver was concussed and where a foreigner was unable to understand the nature of the requirement.

(2) *Fail*

The term 'fail' includes a refusal to provide a specimen, and failure shall be construed accordingly. As long as clear words are used to show a person that he is being required to give a sample of breath, that is sufficient. The absence of a full reason for a request to provide a specimen does not render the request unlawful.

It has been held that once a person has been given an opportunity to do something and did not do it, there is a 'failure'. For example, where a motorist refused to wait until the testing device arrived at the scene, having been required by a police officer to provide a specimen, it was held that he had refused the test. On another occasion, a motorist refused a breath test and later the provision of samples, until his solicitor was present. It was decided that acceptance, subject to a condition, amounted to a refusal.

Where a person refuses to reply to a clear request, there has been a failure and it is no defence to allege that the refusal to reply was consequent upon a previous caution.

A person does not provide a specimen of breath for a breath test or for analysis (see below) unless the specimen is sufficient to enable the test (or analysis) to be carried out and it is provided in such a way as to enable the objective of the test (or analysis) to be satisfactorily achieved.

(3) *Arrest and entry*

Section 6(5) provides that a constable may arrest a person without warrant if:

(a) as a result of a breath test he has reasonable cause to suspect that the proportion of alcohol in that person's breath or blood exceeds the prescribed limit; or

(b) that person has failed to provide a specimen of breath for a breath test when required to do so in pursuance of this section and the constable has reasonable cause to suspect that he has alcohol in his body.

However, a person must not be arrested by virtue of either of these provisions when he is at a hospital as a patient. These powers are quite straightforward. Arrest may follow the provision of a positive breath sample or failure to provide a specimen, provided that in the second instance, the constable also believes that the person failing to provide the specimen has alcohol in his body. The person arrested must be under no illusion as to what is happening to him. An arrest is constituted when any clear form of words is used which conveys to the accused that he is under compulsion and thereafter he submits to that compulsion. The police officer must also make the reason for the arrest clear, and if the wrong reason is given the arrest could be unlawful. In circumstances where a man was in his home and he was required to submit to a breath test and refused, it was ruled that police officers had no power to enter private premises unless this is stated in the statute.

A person who, without reasonable excuse, fails to provide a specimen of breath when required to do so in pursuance of s. 6 of the 1988 Act commits an offence contrary to s. 6(4).

The offence is not committed where the required procedure has not been followed, such as the use of a defective device, or where the manufacturer's instructions are not followed in relation to assembly. Where a mistake is recognised, a constable may require another breath test to be taken on another device. Provided that a constable acts in good faith and is not negligent, non-compliance with the manufacturer's instructions as to the use of the device does not invalidate the test unless the non-compliance is prejudicial to the accused.

Section 6(6) provides a power of entry for the purpose of requiring a breath test if the constable has reasonable cause to suspect that the accident in which the driver's vehicle was involved, included injury to another person. Entry may be by force if necessary, to any place where that person is, or where the constable, with reasonable cause, suspects him to be. Where police officers followed an intoxicated driver into the driveway of his house without permission they were trespassers. The evidence of the analysis of the subsequent specimen was held to be inadmissible, being excluded under the Police and Criminal Evidence Act 1984, s. 78, because the police officers had acted quite deliberately outside their powers. The power given to police officers in these circumstances is a prime example of middle course legislation. The hit and run driver whose accident causes serious damage, but no injury to another person, can reach the privacy of his home and thus escape a breath test. The slightest injury to another person means that a police officer can effect entry to any private premises or property for this purpose. It will be seen later that s. 4 of the Act gives a right of forcible entry *to effect the arrest* of a driver, a person attempting to drive or person in charge of a motor vehicle while his ability to drive is impaired. If evidence of impairment is available, entry is permitted.

Provision of specimen for analysis

Section 7(1) Road Traffic Act 1988 now provides:

'In the course of an investigation into whether a person has committed an offence under Sections 3A or 4 or 5 of this Act, a constable may, subject to the following provisions of this Section and Section 9 below (hospitals) require him:

303

(a) to provide two specimens of breath for analysis by means of a device of a type approved by the Secretary of State; or

(b) to provide a specimen of blood or urine for a laboratory test.'

It will be seen that there is no pre-requisite for an arrest as the new provisions use the term 'in the course of an investigation, etc.'. It may be that there has been no arrest; a person may have come to a police station to report an accident or for some other cause or he may have been arrested for some other offence. The provision of the words 'in the course of an investigation, etc.' have been added to avoid unmeritorious acquittals when a mistake in procedure has invalidated an arrest and thus made the subsequently acquired evidence of alcohol concentration in blood or urine inadmissible. The new wording separates the arrest from the following station procedures which will now be independent of arrest. Thus, where a constable, in good faith, had administered a breath test on a public house car park which, at the time, was not a public place, the subsequent specimen for analysis was properly required 'in the course of an investigation'.

The procedure under s. 7 does not constitute an interview for the purpose of Code C of the Codes of Practice.

In addition, a person who alleges that he was a passenger, not the driver of a car at the time in question, may be lawfully required to provide a specimen as a 'person under investigation for an offence'. It is not necessary to show that he was driving.

Requirements under s. 7 to provide specimens of breath can only be made at a police station. The requirement to provide two specimens of breath must be made first. A requirement to provide a blood specimen or urine can only be made at a police station or at a hospital and it cannot be made at a police station unless:

(a) the constable making the requirement has reasonable cause to believe that for medical reasons a specimen of breath cannot be provided (because of inability) or should not be required (for some other reason such as suspicion of drug taking). Intoxication which prevents a breath specimen being provided is a medical reason, so is shock and distress; or

(b) at the time the requirement is made an approved device or a reliable approved device is not available at the police station, or it is then for any other reason not practicable to use such a device there; or

(c) the suspected offence is one under s. 4 of this Act and the constable making the requirement has been advised by a medical practitioner that the condition of the person required to provide the specimen might be due to some drug;

but may then be made notwithstanding that the person required to provide the specimen has already provided or been required to provide two specimens of breath.

A suspect must now be asked to provide two specimens of breath in the first instance. Blood or urine is only to be taken if medical reasons, lack of machine availability or suspected drug taking, makes this course essential. Where a defendant stated that he was taking a prescribed drug which would influence the outcome of a breath test, and this was believed by the constable, the constable had reasonable cause to believe that such a medical reason existed and was entitled to ask for an alternative specimen. Provided that a reasonable cause to believe that medical reasons exist, it is irrelevant that the constable himself does not believe that, for medical reasons, a breath specimen cannot be provided, or should not be required. Where a defendant has provided two specimens of breath on a machine which is then found to be defective, he may be lawfully required to provide two further specimens of breath for analysis by another device instead of being required to provide blood or urine. It must be remembered that where a person is charged with failure to provide a specimen of blood for laboratory analysis in circumstances in which a breath testing device was not available; if the validity of the request for a sample of blood is challenged the non-availability of the device must be proved in accordance with the laws of evidence. For the purpose of this section a 'reliable device' is one which the police officer concerned reasonably believes to be reliable. It is 'not practicable' to use a device if there is no officer available at the station who has been trained to use the device. A police officer must believe that a device is unreliable not that it might be unreliable before he is empowered to require an alternative specimen.

If, for some reason, it is not possible to take a breath specimen, the question of whether or not it is to be blood or urine shall be decided by the constable making the requirement. The only exception will be in circumstances in which a medical practitioner advises against blood for medical reasons, when it must be urine.

Where a constable requires a specimen of blood and the person refuses but offers urine as an alternative, there has been a 'failure' on the part of the motorist, unless such a medical reason exists. A belief does not amount to a reasonable excuse, thus a refusal to give blood because of a fear of AIDS is not in normal circumstances a reasonable excuse, but a medically recognised phobia in relation to contracting AIDS may be. It is advisable, therefore, that where a motorist alleges a genuine fear of AIDS, the opinion of a medical practitioner is sought so that the rare condition of 'phobia' may be eliminated.

In relation to urine specimens, they must be provided within one hour of the requirement being made and after a previous specimen has been provided and discarded. Blood samples must be taken by doctors and all police surgeons are aware of the techniques to be employed. The blood specimen kits are provided by the forensic science laboratories and are kept at police stations. When a police surgeon takes a specimen of blood for analysis, he completes a certificate and signs it, to show that he took the specimen of blood with the consent of the accused. This is evidence of the facts certified and, provided that a copy of such certificate is served on an accused not less than seven days before the court or trial, and the accused has not within three days of the court hearing or trial served notice on the prosecutor that he requires the attendance of the doctor, the certificate may be put in evidence and the police surgeon need not attend court.

When a specimen of blood or urine has been obtained from an accused, care should be taken that the labels are correctly made out and securely attached to the samples to be sent to the forensic science laboratory with the completed form FSLI. It should be remembered that continuity must be maintained from the time the sample is taken from an accused to the time it is handed over, or posted, to the forensic science laboratory. When at the time of the provision of a specimen of blood or urine, an accused asks to be supplied with a specimen, the specimen taken must be divided into two parts, the other part being supplied to the accused. If this is not done, the evidence of the proportion of alcohol will not be admissible. The most reliable analysis of a specimen of blood is that which takes place soon after the specimen was provided. There is a continuing loss of alcohol content even where a specimen is stored in controlled conditions. Where the doctor left the room for about two minutes and divided the specimen of blood outside the accused's view, such a division had taken place 'at the time'. 'At the time' means closely linked in time and a part of the same event. It is however, desirable that the division takes place in the presence of the accused.

Samples must be positively identified as those of particular defendants. To mark them with the surname of the defendant only is insufficient to ensure positive identification.

The use of the evidential breath testing machine

Approved devices may only be operated by trained operators authorised by chief officers of police. Instructors have been trained by the Home Office and authorised to teach the actual machine operators the correct procedures to be followed. The design of the machines is such that most of the likely problems in usage have been eliminated. At the outset the machine is correctly calibrated but its operating procedure is such that the machine checks its correct calibration both before and after each breath sample is provided and provides evidence on the printout slip that this has been done. The accused should be present throughout the running cycle of the machine. The police officer carrying out the test is not obliged to explain to the motorist that the second specimen must be provided within three minutes or the test will abort.

The operator must sign a certificate to the effect that the machine printout relates to the specimen provided by the accused at the date and time shown. The printout from the machine provides most of the details required and can be incorporated into the statement. The officer certifies all copies of the printout from the machine, declares the reading in respect of the lower proportion of alcohol in the accused's breath specimen to be at the specified level and certifies that copies of the statement were signed by him and signed (or signature refused) by the accused. He also declares that he has handed a copy of the statement to the accused who accepted, or declined to accept it.

However, the Act does not restrict evidence of the test to such documentary evidence. Oral evidence is admissible of the results of such a test but in such instances oral evidences must also be given of the calibration of the machine. It will be good practice, in such cases, to serve a copy of the evidence of the police operator on the defendant in accordance with s. 9 of the Criminal Justice Act 1967.

The machine, therefore, provides a timed, dated, identifiable printout which relates to a particular machine operator and a particular accused person. It shows that it has checked its own calibration both before and after samples and gives an immediate and accurate reading of alcohol concentration. Remember that two specimens are required and it is the lower of the two readings which may be given in evidence. This record is a statement within the meaning of s. 16 of the Road Traffic Offenders Act 1988 and is admissible in evidence as such.

Defence solicitors have no right to obtain intoximeter documents such as the log, repair reports and memory roll with a view to searching for material which might support a submission that the machine was defective. They must rely upon the prosecution to fulfil its duty to disclose material evidence which might be of assistance to the defence.

An approved device can only be shown to be defective by evidence which goes directly to the defective nature of the machine itself, or by the result of a blood analysis. However, the Divisional Court has ruled that where the in-built clock on an Intoximeter device is defective and recording incorrect times, the printout which it produces is not admissible in evidence as it cannot be said that the computer is operating satisfactorily.

The caution, which one would expect in relation to the introduction of such mechanical devices, is expressed by the requirement that if the lower of the two readings is no more than 50 micrograms of alcohol in 100 millilitres of breath, the accused may require that it may be replaced by a blood or urine sample for analysis. He must be informed of his right to exercise it, unless he makes this impossible (as where he refuses to listen and walks away). On the other hand, it is not necessary to invite him to express a preference as to whether the specimen should be of blood or urine (since it suffices that he is told that, if he exercises the right to have a replacement specimen taken, it will be for the police officer to decide whether that specimen is to be of blood or urine). If a police officer intends to require a specimen of blood, the person must be asked whether there is any reason why a specimen of blood should not be taken. The most recent, at the time of writing, decision of the Divisional Court is that there is no obligation for the constable to ask specifically whether there is any such reason based on medical grounds. However, this runs contrary to a previous decision of the same court that this must be specifically asked. Follow the procedure as prescribed by the existing forms used by your force. The constable will decide which of these alternatives is to be provided. In such instances, the evidence of the breath specimen is not used. Where an accused initially declined to exercise such option, but agreed to do so after legal advice one hour later, a court was entitled to decide that enough time had passed to bring the statutory procedure to an end, and admit evidence of the proportion of alcohol in his breath. If a motorist given the statutory option is asked to provide a blood specimen, but the police officer is unable to contact a doctor, the police officer has the power to ask the motorist to provide a urine specimen instead. If the motorist is unable to do so (e.g. because he has visited the lavatory in the meanwhile), the lower of the two breath specimens can be used in evidence since the statutory option procedure only prohibits either specimen of breath being used if a blood or urine specimen is provided under it.

There are two important factors to remember when dealing with evidential breath specimens. If a breath sample is analysed soon after the last drink has been taken the reading will be very high due to residual mouth alcohol. It is essential that a period of 20 minutes has elapsed since the last drink, to allow mouth alcohol to disperse. A wide variation in levels of alcohol as indicated in the two tests should raise the suspicion of mouth alcohol, which can sometimes be present even after a period of 20 minutes, if the accused has vomited or regurgitated. True measurements must be of deep lung air in sufficient quantity. If less quantity is provided, the machine will not accept it; it will abort and require a fresh specimen.

Failure to provide a specimen

A person who, without reasonable excuse, fails to provide a specimen when required to do so in pursuance of these requirements, commits an offence. The term 'reasonable excuse' has already been discussed. However, in a case related to the provision of two specimens of breath for analysis, it was held that where a defendant is young, fit and can provide no valid reason for his inability to provide two specimens of breath, justices are not entitled to 'assume', in the absence of direct evidence, that he was under some stress as a result of an accident and his arrest. In addition, in deciding whether or not an excuse is reasonable, justices are not entitled to go beyond the evidence which is before them. They should avoid using whatever knowledge they may have of physical or mental conditions which may have been affecting a motorist.

A Libyan national claimed that his command of the English language was such that he could not understand the requirement itself, or the consequences of failure. This was accepted as a reasonable excuse. In the same way as in screening tests, the imposition of conditions by an accused, for example, presence of a solicitor, or that he requires time to read the Detention Code, amounts to a failure. Unreasonable conditions concerning the method by which blood is to be taken, shall also amount to refusal. There has also been a refusal where a person fails to give a specimen on the advice of his solicitor.

Stress caused by self-precipitated agitation is not sufficient reasonable excuse. Almost invariably, medical evidence will be required for such a defence. Where a driver is so drunk that he is unable to understand the procedure which is being followed, such an excuse does not relate to his 'capacity' to provide a specimen. In such a case he is unable to respond due to self-induced drunkenness and this is not a reasonable excuse. However, where a driver failed to provide two specimens of breath and two police officers gave evidence that he appeared to be too drunk to do so, the Divisional Court refused to overturn a decision that the accused had a reasonable excuse due to stress resulting from adverse personal and family circumstances which had led to recent breathlessness, although no medical evidence was offered. It said that the justices had reached their decision on unimpeachable findings of fact and that they would not interfere. It is possible that the court was influenced by the fact that the accused had offered an alternative specimen, thus indicating that he was not attempting to avoid providing a specimen.

The Divisional Court has ruled that justices were entitled to accept that an accused was physically unable to provide the required two specimens of breath where, after providing the first, she broke down, sobbed continuously and experienced difficulty in breathing. She alleged that this was due to post-arrest shock. She was unable to provide a second specimen. The court acknowledged that, having successfully provided one specimen, the case was close to the borderline. It would not accept, in absolute terms, that there was a need for medical evidence to support such a claim. The circumstances of this case differed from that relating to 'stress' in that the woman concerned had been pursued by rowdy youths; involved in an accident while so pursued and was in an almost hysterical condition.

In addition, the Divisional Court overruled a decision by magistrates that an accused was unable to provide a second specimen of breath due to pain which he was suffering following an accident. He had already provided a roadside specimen and one specimen at a police station. The magistrates had ignored the fact that expert evidence had been given to the effect that it was more difficult to provide a specimen on the device used for a roadside breath test.

The section is now simplified in relation to warnings to be given to the accused. It is sufficient to warn him that failure may render him liable to prosecution. Failure to give such warning, however, will be a bar to conviction, as will failure to make the meaning of such a warning sufficiently clear to ensure that it was understood.

There is a failure if insufficient breath is provided for the purpose of analysis. A motorist has a duty, if he knows that a medical condition prevents him from providing sufficient breath, to inform the constable. If he does not do so, he may be found guilty of the offence of failure to provide a specimen.

A person only provides a specimen of blood if he consents to its being taken by a medical practitioner and it is so taken.

Section 7(6), which creates the offence of failing to provide a specimen, creates only one offence although the punishments provided by the Road Traffic Offenders Act 1988, Schedule 2, provide different penalties for those driving or attempting to drive a motor vehicle, as opposed to being in charge of it. An information framed in terms of s. 7(6) alone without reference to the circumstances in which the requirement was made is not bad for duplicity. However, the Divisional Court has pointed out that it will be good practice to inform an accused of the circumstances in which the investigation was taking place at the time when the specimen was demanded, that is, under s. 4(1), 4(2), 5(1)(a) or 5(1)(b) respectively, driving or attempting to drive while unfit; in charge while unfit; driving or attempting to drive while over the limit; and in charge while over the limit. The decision of the Divisional Court has now been endorsed by the House of Lords.

Hospital procedure

Section 9 requires that while a person is at a hospital as a patient he shall not be required to provide a specimen of breath for a breath test or to provide a specimen for a laboratory test unless the medical practitioner in immediate charge of his case has been notified of the proposal to make the requirement, and:

(a) if the requirement is then made, it shall be for the provision of a specimen at the hospital; *but*

(b) if the medical practitioner objects on the ground specified (that the requirement or the provision of a specimen, or in the case of a specimen of blood or urine, the warning required concerning failure being likely to render him liable to prosecution, would be prejudicial to the proper care and treatment of the patient), the requirement should not be made.

Let us consider this in stages and from the outset remember that we cannot, in any circumstances, demand a specimen of breath for analysis, from a patient at a hospital.

(1) Seek out the medical practitioner in charge of the case.

(2) Seek his consent to the provision of a screening breath test with a tube and

bag or electronic screening device, explaining what you intend to ask his patient to do.

(3) Secure that consent. He will give it if the procedure is not prejudicial to care or treatment.

(4) Obtain screening sample of breath observing usual procedures and warnings as to consequences of failure.

(5) If negative, explain, no further action (unless drugs suspected).

(6) If positive, obtain medical practitioner's consent to the taking of a specimen for laboratory analysis, explaining procedure. Remember that it must be blood or urine. Ask the driver if there is any reason why a specimen of blood should not be taken. There is no obligation for a constable to ask specifically whether there is any such reason based on medical grounds. This is the effect of the most recent decision of the Divisional Court at the time of writing but a contrary decision was made by the same court on an earlier date to the effect that this should be done. There is of course, no harm in doing so. Force procedure as set out on forms must be followed.

(7) If consent obtained, etc., obtain specimen of blood or urine by usual means.

Detention of persons affected by alcohol

A person may be detained until it appears to a constable that by driving, he would not commit a further offence. In practice, this means until he provides a negative screening specimen. However, there is no power to detain where there is no likelihood of his driving or attempting to drive while his ability to drive is impaired or the level of alcohol in his breath, blood or urine exceeds the limit. Many accused persons might be taken home by a responsible person in circumstances which would satisfy a constable that there is no likelihood of the accused driving, etc. If drugs are involved, medical advice should be obtained.

Offences of being unfit through drink or drugs

Section 4 of the Road Traffic Act 1988, states that a person who, when driving or attempting to drive or in charge of a mechanically propelled vehicle on a road or other public place is unfit to drive through drink or drugs is guilty of an offence. He is 'unfit' if his ability to drive properly is for the time being impaired.

'Drug' means any intoxicant other than alcohol, including medicine and glue. However, where a driver's condition is due to hypoglycaemic attack, this may or may not be due to insulin. There must be direct evidence that the attack was the direct result of an injection of insulin either because it was injected in too great a quantity, or because it was still clearly operative at the moment of the attack. Other factors such as neglect of diet, etc., may have been the direct cause of the attack.

Section 4 provides the only means by which we can deal with a person whose ability to drive is impaired by drugs. There is no purpose in requiring the specimens previously described as they will not identify drug content and it becomes necessary to depend upon observation. Witnesses may describe the manner of driving; speech and manner when interrogated by a police officer; the police surgeon's observations and the driver's responses to coordination tests carried out by the surgeon. It is

310

submitted that the use of this section in relation to alcoholic drink is likely to be extremely limited. The circumstances in which it is prudent to proceed with a charge of this nature when a subsequent analysis of a laboratory specimen has shown an alcohol concentration below any of the prescribed limits, are likely to be limited if not non-existent. Some forms circulated to police forces suggest that if an evidential machine indicates less than 35 micrograms, one should call a doctor if there is evidence of drugs, but if not and there is evidence of impairment, the person should be charged with the appropriate s. 4 offence. There can be little purpose in proceeding under s. 4 unless the evidence of impairment is really compelling and it is submitted that courts would always require evidence of a medical practitioner. It will be good practice to call a doctor in these cases too, should it ever be felt that proceedings are merited when there is little evidence of alcohol. There will be little prospect of a successful prosecution upon evidence unsupported by medical opinion.

Power of arrest and entry

A constable may arrest a person without warrant if he has reasonable cause to suspect that that person is, or has been, committing an offence of driving, attempting to drive or being in charge of a motor vehicle on a road or other public place while unfit through drink or drugs.

For the purpose of arresting a person under s. 4 a constable may enter (if need be by force) any place where that person is or where the constable, with reasonable cause, suspects him to be.

To summarise in relation to powers of entry, power to enter, by force if necessary, has been provided in respect of s. 5 offences (driving, attempting to drive or in charge while alcohol in the body is above prescribed limits), only following an injury accident for the purpose of obtaining a breath test but in all cases involving driving, attempting to drive or being in charge while ability is impaired, entry is authorised, by force if necessary.

Defence to 'being in charge of' in Sections 4 and 5 offences

For the purposes of charges relating to being in charge while there is alcohol in the body in excess of prescribed limits or while unfit to drive through drink or drugs, a person shall be deemed *not* to have been in charge of a motor vehicle if he proves that at the material time the circumstances were such that there was no likelihood of his driving it so long as he remained unfit to drive through drink or drugs, but in determining whether there was a likelihood, the court may disregard any injury to him and any damage to the vehicle.

A man who has taken steps to place his vehicle in someone else's charge while he remains affected by drink or drugs is entitled to use this defence. Prior to the final provisions allowing a court to disregard any injury to him or damage to his vehicle, it was possible for an accused to plead that there was no likelihood of his driving as his car had been too severely damaged to use, or that his injuries were such that driving was unlikely. The wording of ss. 4 and 5 is now such that a court may disregard these factors if other evidence shows guilt. It has been decided that a man who is in his car who is too drunk to drive it cannot rely upon this defence because he will be able to

311

drive on regaining consciousness, even though he may still be severely affected by alcohol.

Where the accused's car had been wheel-clamped and there was no evidence to show that the clamp could have been removed by any means other than paying for release and the accused had refused to do this, it was held that there was no likelihood of his driving at that time. The fixing of a wheel clamp does not damage a car; the vehicle itself is not altered in any way.

Evidence in proceedings for offences under Sections 3A, 4 and 5

The Road Traffic Offenders Act 1988, s. 15, provides that evidence of the proportion of alcohol or a drug in a specimen of breath, blood or urine taken from an accused shall, in all cases (including cases where the specimen was not provided in connection with the alleged offence), be taken into account and it shall be assumed that the proportion of alcohol was at least that found in the sample. However, in cases involving drink, that assumption shall not be made if the accused proves:

(a) that he had consumed alcohol before he provided the specimen; and
   (i) in relation to an offence under s. 3A, after the time of the alleged offence; and
   (ii) otherwise, after he had ceased to drive, attempt to drive or be in charge of a vehicle on a road or other public place; and
(b) that had he not done so the proportion of alcohol in his breath, blood or urine would not have exceeded the prescribed limit and, if it is alleged that he was unfit to drive through drink, would not have been such as to impair his ability to drive.

It is, therefore, for an accused who alleges that he has taken drink subsequent to the driving, etc., to prove this to the satisfaction of the court and additionally, that without such subsequent drink or drinks, he would not have been in excess of the limit or impaired. It will be necessary in such cases for a defendant to call expert medical or scientific evidence in order to discharge this burden of proof, unless the nature of non-expert evidence is such that it will enable a court reliably and confidently to reach a sensible conclusion without expert evidence. However, once justices have been given clear evidence from an expert as to the amount of alcohol necessary to cause a particular driver to exceed the legal limit and plausible evidence as to the quantity of alcohol consumed post-incident, then it is open to them, in spite of the fact that apparent discrepancies remain unexplained, to find that the defendant has discharged the burden necessary to establish a defence under s. 15(3).

The requirement that the results of a specimen analysis shall always be taken into account, eliminates the possibility that such evidence might be excluded by courts on the grounds that there had been an error in procedure prior to the obtaining of a sample. However, the High Court has recently approved the exclusion of such evidence under the provisions of the Police and Criminal Evidence Act 1984, s. 78, where the defendant had been wrongfully arrested, in that he was not told by the officer that he suspected him of having alcohol in his body at the time that a roadside specimen was required.

Remember that when, at the time of the provision of a specimen of blood or urine, an accused asks to be supplied with such a specimen, the specimen taken must be divided into two parts, the other part being supplied to the accused. If this is not done, the evidence of the proportion of drug or alcohol found in the specimen will not be admissible. It should be noted, however, that the legislation requires provision of a part of the specimen only if requested by the accused.

Documentary evidence

The Road Traffic Offenders Act 1988, s. 16, provides for documentary evidence to be given of the proportion of alcohol or drug in a specimen of breath, blood or urine. The statement automatically produced by a breath testing device together with a certificate signed by a constable that the statement relates to the specimen provided by the accused at the date and time shown in the statement, and a certificate signed by an authorised analyst as to the proportion of alcohol or drug found in a specimen of blood or urine identified in that certificate, are admissible in evidence. Similarly certificates of medical practitioners to the effect that a specimen of blood was taken from the accused with his consent is admissible.

Copies must be handed to the accused at the time, or served on him not less than seven days before trial. However, if an accused, not less than three days before the hearing (or lesser time if the court allows) serves notice requiring the attendance of the person producing any such document, the document itself is no longer admissible.

While this legislation permits the use of documentary evidence it does not require this procedure to be followed. A police officer may give oral evidence of the readings which he saw displayed on the Intoximeter, provided that he is also able to testify that the device was working properly and was accurately calibrated.

Police officers frequently give evidence while referring to pro forma completed at the time. Any reference to a person's previous convictions on such pro forma must be removed or concealed as there is always a possibility that, for one reason or another, the document may be examined by the court.

Alternative verdicts

A person charged with driving or attempting to drive while unfit or while over the prescribed limit and who is found not guilty of that offence, but the allegations in the information amount to or include an allegation of an offence of 'being in charge' in those circumstances, he may be convicted of that offence. A person charged with 'driving' may be convicted of 'attempting to drive'.

Courses for drink/drive offenders

The Road Traffic Offenders Act 1988 as amended by the Road Traffic Act 1991 gives the courts power to order that the period of disqualification imposed for an offence against s. 3A, 4, 5 or 7 of the Road Traffic Act 1988 may be reduced if the person concerned completes a course approved by the Secretary of State. This applies where the disqualification is for a period of not less than 12 months. The reduction may be of not less than three months and not more than one-quarter of the unreduced period. Consequently, a disqualification of 12 months may be reduced to one of nine months.

Regulations have provided for course managers to be appointed who may issue certificates of completion in a form approved by the Secretary of State. The areas within which courses are available are specified in Schedule 1 to the Courses for Drink-Drive Offenders (Designation of Areas) Order 1992.

Drinking – guided transport systems

The Transport and Works Act 1992 applies to transport systems which are used, or are intended to be used, wholly or partly for the carriage of members of the public. Its provisions are restricted to railways, tramways, or other *guided transport systems* specified by the Secretary of State. The guided transport systems at Birmingham International Airport; Merry Hill Centre, West Midlands; and Gatwick and Stansted Airports have been so specified.

The Act creates two offences involving drink or drugs on such transport systems which can be committed by the following workers:

(a) drivers, guards, conductors, signalmen or others who control or affect the movement of vehicles operating under one of these systems; or

(b) persons who couple or uncouple such vehicles or check that they are working properly; or

(c) persons maintaining the permanent way (or other support or guidance structures), signalling systems and power supply used by such vehicles; and

(d) supervisors of, and look-outs for, persons engaged in the functions set out in categories (b) or (c) above.

These two offences are committed where:

(i) a person in one of the above categories carries out his duties when unfit to carry out that work due to drink or drugs;

(ii) a person in one of the above categories carries out his duties after consuming so much alcohol that the proportion of it in his breath, blood or urine exceeds the prescribed limit (which is the same limit as prescribed by the Road Traffic Act 1988).

A constable in uniform is empowered to require a screening breath test where he has reasonable cause to suspect:

(a) that a person working on a transport system has alcohol in his body; or

(b) that a person has been working on a transport system with alcohol in his body and still has alcohol in his body.

This power is extended to circumstances in which there has been an *accident or dangerous incident* and a constable in uniform has reasonable cause to suspect that, at the time of the event, the person was working in one of the above capacities and that his act, or omission, while so working, may have been the cause of the accident or incident. A 'dangerous incident' means an accident which, in the constable's opinion, involved a danger of death or personal injury.

314   Similar powers to those under the Road Traffic Act 1988 are provided by the Act

in relation to arrest and entry; the provision of specimens for analysis; the option to have a breath specimen replaced if the alcohol content in it does not exceed 50 microgrammes in 100 millilitres of breath; failure to comply with a request; and hospital patients. The penalties for such offences are the same as those provided by the Road Traffic Act 1988, save, of course, that there is no power of disqualification from driving. However, the consent of the Secretary of State, or the Director of Public Prosecutions, is required before proceedings for such offences may be instituted in England and Wales.

The evidential provisions of the Road Traffic Act 1988 in relation to such offences are repeated in this Act.

Operators of such systems may be vicariously liable for some offences committed by employees.

These provisions are important to all police officers. Following a train crash, it is the first police officer on the scene who will be expected to require a screening breath test if it applies.

Pedal cycles – drinks or drugs

The offences set out above under the Road Traffic Act 1988 are concerned with motor vehicles. However, s. 30 of that Act deals specifically with cycles which are not motor vehicles. It creates the offence of riding a cycle, not being a motor vehicle, on a road or other public place while unfit to ride through drink or drugs. This means that such a person is sufficiently under the influence of drink or drugs as to be incapable of having proper control of the cycle.

Pedal cycles – drunk in charge

The Licensing Act 1872 states that it is an offence for a person to be drunk while in charge of a carriage, on a highway or any other public place. A bicycle is a carriage. A person in charge of a cycle, otherwise than riding it, is liable to be charged with this offence.

3 General police duties

Descriptions of persons and property

To be of any value a description should be a detailed word picture of a person or property. In the absence of photographs, a description may often be the only method by which a person or property can be recognised, therefore it is important to obtain accurate details when obtaining a description.

(1) *Description of persons*

Persons who are wanted or who are missing or found dead without any papers of identification can often be traced by means of a description. If a person is described in sufficient detail an identification may be quite a simple matter. Special attention should be paid to any personal characteristics which may attract attention and enable that person to be readily picked out from among other people; these include such things as peculiarities of appearance, manner, gait, speech, and any known habits.

Many witnesses will experience considerable difficulty in providing a description because they had never had reason to focus their mind upon the necessity to do so. Patience will be rewarded; while being unable to specify height they may be able to compare the suspect's height with that of someone else who is present.

A description can be compiled by covering the following points:

(a)	Name:	Whether known to be correct; include nicknames and aliases; if a married woman, her maiden name.
	Age:	Exact date of birth, if possible, otherwise approximate, also show place of birth if known.
	Occupation:	Present, past or possible, including where employed.
(b)	Appearance	
	Height:	Exact if known, otherwise approximate.
	Build:	Proportionate, stout, corpulent, heavy, thick set, thin, slim, well built, military bearing, erect, slouches, stoops, round shouldered.

Complexion: Fresh, ruddy, florid, pale, fair, sallow, blotchy, pimply, uses cosmetics.

Face: Round, oval, long, wrinkled, flabby, fat, thin, high cheekbones; expression – vacant, scowling, pleasant.

Hair: Colour, turning grey, going bald, wavy, straight, curly, frizzy, parted, unparted, brushed back, long, short, greased, unkempt, wears wig, bleached, dyed, sideburns.

Hair on face: Beard (shape and colour), moustache (size, shape, colour, waxed), dark chin.

Head: Large, small, narrow, square.

Forehead: High, low, broad, narrow, wrinkled, bulging, receding.

Eyebrows: Colour, thick, thin, bushy, plucked, pencilled, arched, meet in centre, sparse.

Eyes: Colour, cast, blind, missing, glass, red rimmed, long lashes, wears spectacles (for reading/habitually, type of spectacles).

Nose: Large, small, long, short, hooked, irregular, turned up, Roman, broken, bulbous, broad base, wide or narrow nostrils.

Mouth: Large, small, habitually open, close-shut.

Lips: Thick, thin, loose, hare-lip, well-shaped, upper or lower protrudes.

Teeth: Clean, discoloured, decayed, widely-spaced, irregular, over lap, dentures, fillings, gaps, gold-crowned, toothless.

Chin: Dimpled, cleft or double, round, protrudes, recedes, square jaw.

Ears: Large, small, protrude, cauliflower, lobeless, large lobes, pierced.

Hands: Long, short, broad, long fingers, short fingers, well kept, rough; nails – long, short, bitten, manicured, varnished (colour).

(c) Distinctive marks
(Especially those visible or on forearms – commence at top of head and work downwards): scars, birthmarks, moles, freckles, tattoos, deformities, amputations, limp.

(d) Peculiarities
Peculiar walking gait, accent – gruff, melodious, high pitched, deep, loud, soft, effeminate, affected voice, lisp, stammer or other impediment, difficulty in pronouncing certain words or letters.

(e) Characteristics and habits
Drinking habits, places used, type of drink – wine, beer or spirits, brand of cigarettes smoked, pipe smoker, brand of tobacco, type of associates, e.g. prostitutes; places frequented – billiard halls, night clubs or dance halls; particular bearing and mannerisms (such as strokes nose or ear when speaking), nervous cough, habitually uses certain words or phrases, peculiar walk, speaks of certain parts of the world or a particular country, or rich relatives (confidence trickster), experiences, skills or abilities.

(f) Dress

This can be extremely important in modern times. Although a good description of the style of dress usually adopted is unlikely to isolate an individual, it helps to identify the group to which a person belongs.

Always bear in mind that a description, however accurate or detailed, can never be as good as a photograph. Albums of known criminals are kept by police forces and a witness may be able to identify a suspect by examining them. This must be done in accordance with the Identification Code (see page 393).

Some police forces are equipped with a system known as E-FIT which creates a computer picture of a suspect's face from a witness's description. The picture can be modified as the witness supplies further details.

(2) *Description of property*

The object of obtaining a description of property is to enable the property to be identified. Remember that a photograph is often worth a thousand words and a detailed description may not be necessary if a photograph of the property is available.

Property falls into two classes: identifiable and non-identifiable. Identifiable in this context means that the property can be identified by any person who may see or examine the article in question usually by means of a serial number, engraving, laundry mark, or other distinguishing feature. When compiling a description be careful to identify the property and not the person; for example, it is correct to say a lady's green handbag but incorrect to say a green lady's handbag – we don't see many green ladies with handbags!

The appearance of the property should be noted; that is, the colour, shape, design and any blemishes, repairs, faults or other similar feature which may render the article in question to be more readily identified.

When dealing with motor vehicles obtain the registration mark, the make and model, the horsepower or cubic capacity, type of body, colour, year of manufacture, chassis or frame number, engine number, the colour of upholstery, number of doors, and any extra fittings such as radio, fog lamp and any distinguishing features such as dents, badges, mascots or homemade fittings which may have been added to the vehicle. If possible, always check the details given with the details given in the registration document relating to that vehicle.

In view of the number of cycles which are reported lost, found, or stolen an accurate description is essential. The best method of identifying a cycle is by the frame number, if a stolen pedal cycle is insured, this number may be obtained from the insurance company if it cannot be obtained from the owner of the cycle. Do not confuse the frame number with the patent or casting number; the frame number is always stamped into the frame while the patent or casting number is usually composed of raised numbers.

The next best method of identification is by make, colour, and any peculiarities. The make can usually be determined by a transfer or metal plate on a frame, but if these are absent an examination of the design on the chain wheel will often provide an indication of the maker. If there is cause to think that the bicycle has been repainted, indicate not only the present colour of the cycle but also the original

319

colour. Perhaps the most helpful information is that concerning modifications or extra or unusual items on the cycle which make it quite different from any other machine, e.g. saddle-bag, special lighting, mirrors, or a water bottle.

Special identifying marks such as dents, scratches, broken mudguards, transfers, or even the contents of the saddle-bag or tool-bag can help to identify a pedal cycle.

In each police station there is a chart classifying the various components of a bicycle, and by using the chart to assist in obtaining a detailed description you will always be sure of covering every component part of a bicycle and of using the correct description of each component part.

Lost and found property

Obligations and duties

There is no statutory duty imposed on a person to report to the police the finding of any property, or on the police to record and deal with lost or found property, but by custom the police have become the central agency for dealing with such property. It is the duty of the police to keep accurate records of all reports of property lost and found and to ensure that property coming into their possession is stored safely. For these purposes lost and found property registers are maintained by the police.

The owner of property always retains the best claim to it; the finder has the next best claim. A finder, although not required by law to hand over to the police property which he has found, is under a duty to take steps to trace or contact the owner where this is possible. If he does not do so, he leaves himself open to allegations of theft.

Report of lost property

Where a police officer in the street receives a report that property has been lost he should, at the time, enter in his pocket notebook the time, date, and place the report was received, the name and address of the person making the report, and a detailed description of the property, including any identifying means. If the lost property is likely to cause danger – for example, controlled drugs, firearms, or explosives – then the station should be informed immediately; in any other case a report will be made when the officer returns to the station. If the substance is dangerous, the officer in charge of the station will consider circulation of details and notification to PNC.

Where the report is received at the station, or where a police officer has received a report in the street and has returned to the station, the above details will be entered in the lost property register. An examination should be made of the entries in the found property register for any record of the property having been reported as found. The person reporting the loss, whether in the street or at the station, should be asked to inform the police if the missing property is subsequently found.

Where a report is received in one police area relating to property lost in another police area, the officer should record the required details as described above and, in addition, a telephone message containing the recorded details should be sent to the

320

police area concerned so that a record can be made of the loss in that area. The lost property register should be endorsed with the action taken.

Where lost property is found and restored to the owner, the entry in the lost property register should be endorsed accordingly. If the property comes into the possession of the police and it is returned to the loser by the police it should be treated as found property and the entries in the found property register and the lost property register should be cross-referenced.

Report of found property

When a report of found property is made to a police officer in the street he should, at the time, enter in his pocket notebook the time, date, and place the report was received, the name and address of the finder, and the time, date, and place found. A full description of the property should be entered in the pocket notebook in the presence of the finder. Particulars of any money or valuables should be carefully noted. When describing valuable articles precise descriptions should be avoided. It is better to describe an article as gold-coloured than as gold, and stones as stones of a particular colour, rather than as diamonds, etc. Once an article has been recorded as consisting of a precious metal or as containing precious stones, that is what an auditor would expect to find when found property is inspected.

Sealed pay packets or similar containers apparently containing money or other valuables should be opened in the presence of the finder so that the contents may be verified. If the finder does not wish to retain the property he should be asked to sign the entry in the pocket notebook. On his return to the police station the officer will immediately record the details of the finding, etc., in the found property register. If the property is retained by the finder a note is made of the address at which the property is being kept.

It is the general practice not to return to the finder keys, cheques, firearms, ammunition and other explosives, gambling instruments, hypodermic syringes, medicines, tablets, or weapons of any kind which have been handed to the police as found property and have not been claimed. Official documents which have been found and handed to the police should be forwarded to the appropriate authority and not returned to individual losers.

If letters, including registered, recorded or express letters, or bundles of letters or parcels are found which, although they appear to have passed through the post, do not seem to have reached the addresses, they should be deposited immediately at the police station. This course should also be adopted if a mail bag containing letters is handed in as found property. Unopened letters, whether stamped or otherwise, which have not been through the post, should, in the absence of any suspicious circumstances, be posted by the police officer who finds the letters or by the police officer to whom they are handed, and such action should be reported and recorded at the police station in the normal way.

Where the found property consists of perishable articles, the general police practice is to sell the property and retain the proceeds for the owner. If no claimant comes along, the proceeds of the sale may be paid to the finder after the lapse of the appropriate period, usually three months, although this may vary according to local procedures.

Property in public transport

Where a person finds property in a public service vehicle he is required by law to hand it over immediately to the conductor or, if there is no conductor, to the driver or operator's representative. The property is then deposited with the operator of the public service vehicle.

If a police officer is called to a case where a person has lost property on a public service vehicle and has claimed the property from the conductor or driver before either has deposited it with the operator, the driver or conductor should be told that by law he is required to restore the property to the loser, without fee, if the loser can give satisfactory proof of ownership of the property.

Particulars of found property must be recorded by the operator and made available for inspection by the police and traffic examiners at reasonable times. Unclaimed property vests in the operator after three months. Perishable goods found in public service vehicles may be destroyed by the operator or sold after 48 hours. Property found on railway property must be handed to the British Railways Board and in public hackney carriages, to the driver.

(1) Property found by police officers

Property found by police officers must be handed in at the police station. A police officer finding property is not allowed to receive either the unclaimed property or the proceeds from the sale of such property. If the property is not claimed after the lapse of the appropriate period, the property is sold and the proceeds credited to official funds.

(2) Restitution of property to loser

When a person claims property that has been found and handed to the police, the officer dealing with the matter should satisfy himself that the person claiming the property is the owner before handing the property over. A receipt should be obtained when the property is handed over, and the finder should be notified that the property has been returned to the owner. The name and address of the finder may be given to the owner.

Where the property has been retained by the finder, the name and address of the finder may be given to a person claiming the property who should be asked to notify the police if he identifies the property and it is restored to him. This will enable the lost property and found property registers to be endorsed accordingly.

(3) Restitution of property to finder

If found property is not claimed after the prescribed period has elapsed, which varies according to local procedure, it may be restored to the finder against his signature on a receipt and the found property register endorsed accordingly. If the finder does not want the property it may be disposed of by the police, by auction if the property is of any value, or destruction if worthless. Property found by a police officer is not returned to the police officer although he is not prevented from purchasing property where it is sold by auction.

The law relating to highways

Highway

The term 'highway' has many definitions, but is described most clearly in s. 328 of the Highways Act 1980 as being the whole or part of a highway other than a ferry or waterway. We are, therefore, considering roads along which vehicles or people pass, until they arrive at a river or estuary, the crossing of which involves going aboard ship. Section 328 of the Act goes on to include, within the term 'highway', bridges and tunnels over which or through which traffic passes. It is, therefore, clear that any road over which traffic actually passes is a highway, but such traffic need not be vehicular. The term 'bridleway' is defined as including a highway over which the public merely have a right of way on foot or on horseback. In addition, the Countryside Act 1968 has given pedal cyclists the right to use bridleways, in the absence of local by-lays prohibiting their use. A 'footpath' is a highway over which the public have a right of way on foot only and a 'footway' means a way comprised in a highway which also comprises a carriageway (for the passage of vehicles), being a way over which the public have a right of way on foot only.

A highway may, therefore, consist of many things: carriageways for the passage of vehicles, bridleways for horses, pedal cyclists and pedestrians, and footpaths or footways which are reserved for use by pedestrians. It is important to recognise that the term does not merely describe a 'road' but is wide enough to include any form of way over which any form of traffic passes. Section 137 of the Act says that it is an offence for any person, without lawful authority or excuse, to in any way wilfully obstruct the free passage of the highway.

The test of whether a particular use of a highway – for example, by a vehicle – amounts to an obstruction is whether the use is reasonable in all the circumstances. This means taking into account the duration, position and purpose, and any actual as opposed to potential obstruction. Such obstruction is 'wilful' if it is done with free will and causes an obstruction. An obstruction of a footway may be caused by a shopkeeper who causes a queue outside his premises by carrying on business in an unusual way. Selling or exposing goods for sale on a footway would similarly amount to an obstruction, as would the driving of a motor vehicle at a slow speed on the crown of the road so that faster vehicles are unable to overtake, although such an act may amount to an offence under the Road Traffic Acts. (See offence of driving without reasonable consideration for other road users.)

However, where a local authority was carrying out work on an area with a view to pedestrianisation and vehicles were permitted access for loading or unloading, it was held that there could not be an obstruction of an area which had been a footpath, by a shop blind, which, because of the presence of scaffolding opposite prevented the passage of vehicles. There must be evidence that exclusive use of the footway had been extinguished by resolution or otherwise and proof (beyond reasonable doubt) that a footway which had existed for many years had ceased to exist.

Where a supermarket left trolleys in a pedestrian precinct for the convenience of shoppers there was an unlawful obstruction even though no complaint had been made by a member of the public. In addition, the right to protest is not a reasonable excuse for obstruction of the highway.

323

'Lawful authority' exists, for example, where essential road works are carried out in a proper manner or where a road check is lawfully carried out by police officers.

Powers

Section 25 of the Police and Criminal Evidence Act 1984, which provides the general power of arrest to constables, makes specific provision in respect of highway obstructions. A constable who has reasonable grounds for believing that arrest is necessary to prevent a person causing an unlawful obstruction of the highway, may arrest such person without warrant. However, it should be recognised that this power was probably given to allow the police to deal with 'sit-down demonstrators' where such obstructions are caused on roads. Nevertheless, the power is not limited to such circumstances and it is for a constable to decide whether an arrest is necessary in accordance with the terms of s. 25.

Games

It is an offence contrary to the Highways Act 1980, s. 161, for any person to play at football or any other game on a highway to the annoyance of any user. Complaints are often received concerning children who are playing various ball games in the street. Frequently, the complaint is made by a householder who has viewed the nuisance through a window. Before there can be an offence, the game must cause annoyance to the *user of a highway*. In most instances, these matters are dealt with by way of advice.

Fires and fireworks

It is an offence contrary to the Highways Act 1980, s. 161, without lawful authority or excuse, to light any fire on or over a highway which consists of or comprises a carriageway, or to discharge any firearm or firework within 50 feet of the centre of such a highway, if as a consequence a user of the highway is injured, interrupted or endangered. It is important to recognise that this offence is only committed if the highway includes a carriageway. In the case of offences involving fireworks it is of advantage to consider the summary offence of supplying, offering to supply, or agreeing to supply fireworks to persons under the age of 16, against the person who supplied youngsters with such fireworks. This offence is included in Regulation 2 of the Fireworks (Safety) Regulations 1986. It is an offence contrary to the Explosives Act 1875 to throw or fire a firework in or on to a street or public place.

The Highways Act 1980, s. 161A, prohibits the lighting of fires on land not forming part of such a highway; or directing or permitting such a fire to be lit if as a consequence a user of the highway is injured, interrupted or endangered by, or by smoke from, that fire or any other fire caused by that fire. There is a statutory defence available to persons charged with this offence:

(a) that at the time the fire was lit, he was satisfied on reasonable grounds that such consequences were unlikely; and

(b) either

(i) that both before and after the fire was lit he did all that he reasonably could to prevent users of any such highway from being so injured, etc.; or

(ii) that he had reasonable excuse for not doing so.

Depositing litter

It is an offence to throw down, drop or otherwise deposit in, into or from any place specified in the Environmental Protection Act 1990, s. 87, and to leave anything whatsoever in such circumstances as to cause, contribute to, or tend to lead to, the defacement by litter of such a place, unless it was authorised by law or was done with the consent of the owner, occupier or person or authority having control over such place.

The Environmental Protection Act 1990, s. 87, is concerned with the *place* 'from which, in which or into which' litter is deposited so that it causes defacement by litter of such a *place*. The term *place* means any public open place (place in the open air to which the public are entitled or permitted to have access without payment and any covered place open to the air on at least one side and available for public use); special roads; Crown land; relevant land of statutory undertakers or educational authorities; or relevant land of a principal litter authority or within a litter controlled area. Thus, the act of depositing litter must be made from, in or into a specified place. It must be left and must cause, contribute to, or tend to lead to the defacement by litter of such a place.

A person who deposits litter in a lay-by commits this offence. It is deposited in a public open place and leads to its defacement. If that person threw the litter over the hedge into a field he would not, unless the field was a place particularly specified by the section, for example Crown land, commit an offence contrary to s. 87. Although the act of depositing was *from* a place specified by the section, it did not *lead to the defacement of such a place*. There would be an offence, however, against the provisions of the Refuse Disposal (Amenity) Act 1978, s. 2, see below.

Section 88 of the 1990 Act makes provisions for the payment of a fixed penalty in respect of an offence of depositing litter contrary to s. 78. Power is given to an authorised officer of the litter authority (authorised in writing) to give to a person whom he finds and whom he has reason to believe has on that occasion committed an offence contrary to s. 87 in the area of the authority, a fixed penalty notice. Where this is done, no proceedings shall be instituted for that offence before the expiration of a period of 14 days following the issue of the notice. A person may not be convicted of such an offence if he pays the fixed penalty before the expiration of that period.

The 1990 Act has, therefore, placed a significant responsibility for the enforcement of the provisions of the Act which deal with litter, upon local authorities. While the fixed penalty provisions are not extended to police officers, s. 87 creates an offence which may be dealt with by police officers.

A man and his family were living in a tent in a lane. Nearby was a lorry against which was a pile of scrap metal and the man was found sorting through it. It was held that he was guilty of depositing litter as he intended only to remove the scrap which had value. The High Court stated that 'leaves' does not mean 'abandons'. The

325

metal had been deposited and permitted to remain beside the road and had been left. An article deposited with no intention to remove it can be 'left' after being there only for a short time.

To prevent litter being deposited in structures such as bus shelters, the Act provides that any covered place which is open to the air on at least one side, and is available for public use, shall be treated as a place in the open air. It has been held that 'depositing and leaving' is a single act with two elements and it is, therefore, necessary to prove that the litter was left by the person throwing it down. If it is subsequently picked up, then no offence will have been committed.

The Refuse Disposal (Amenity) Act 1978 has previously been mentioned in relation to abandoned motor vehicles. Section 2 of this Act creates the offence of abandoning, without lawful authority, on any land in the open air or another land forming part of a highway, anything which has been brought to the land for the purpose of being abandoned there. There is no mention in this Act of depositing from particular places and prosecutions usually follow the discovery of identifiable waste which has been abandoned on any land in the open air.

When dealing with offences in relation to litter, the court will require a full description of the nature of the litter and the extent of the defacement caused.

Interfering with litter bins and notice boards

Local authorities are empowered by the Public Health Act 1961 to provide and maintain litter bins and notices concerning their use. Section 51 of that Act creates the offences of wilfully removing or otherwise interfering with such a receptacle or a notice.

Builders' skips

The Highways Act 1980, s. 139, allows builders' skips to be deposited on the highway with the permission of the highway authority. Such permissions must be in writing. Each skip must be authorised on each occasion; a general permission to place skips cannot be given. The owner of the skip must:

(a) ensure that it is properly lighted during the hours of darkness;
(b) ensure that the skip is clearly and indelibly marked with the owner's name and with his telephone number or address, and has attached to the sides which face in the direction of the carriageway two oblong plates of diagonal red and yellow fluorescent or reflective material, similar to those fitted to the rear of heavy goods vehicles;
(c) ensure that it is removed as soon as practicable after it has been filled;
(d) ensure that each of the conditions subject to which the permission was granted is complied with.

The requirement at (d) refers to the fact that the highway authority may grant permission with or without additional conditions. The additional conditions which may be attached to the use of a builder's skip may include conditions relating to:

(i) the siting of the skip;
(ii) its dimensions;

(iii) the manner in which it should be coated with paint or other material to make it immediately visible to traffic;

(iv) the care and disposal of its contents;

(v) the manner in which it is to be lighted or guarded;

(vi) its removal at the end of the period of permission.

An offence will be committed by the owner of a builder's skip if it is deposited on the highway without permission. Offences are also committed by the owner if he fails to comply with any of the duties set out at (a) to (d) above, or any conditions attached by the highway authority under the headings shown at (i) to (vi). The term 'owner' in relation to a skip which is hired for a month or more, or one which is the subject of hire purchase agreement, means the person in possession of the skip under the hiring agreement. In most instances in which a skip is left on the highway beyond its authorised date the offence of failure to comply with a condition, i.e. that it would be removed on a certain date, will have been committed. However, the term 'deposit' has been held to include 'leaving, remaining or leave lying' and it is, therefore, possible to charge depositing without permission if there are difficulties in relation to the particular conditions.

The highway authority or a police constable in uniform may require the owner of a skip to remove or reposition it, or cause it to be removed or repositioned and may either remove it or cause it to be removed. The expenses of removal may be recovered from the owner as a civil debt. It is an offence for the owner to fail to remove the skip as soon as reasonably practicable. A request by a constable must be made in person. A request by telephone, for example, is not sufficient.

Loudspeakers

Section 62 of the Control of Pollution Act 1974 states that loudspeakers shall not be operated in a street between 9 p.m. and 8 a.m. *for any purpose* or at any other time for the purpose of advertising any entertainment, trade or business.

There are certain exceptions, which include police, fire brigade, ambulance, the National Rivers Authority or a water undertaking in the exercise of its functions and travelling showmen using loudspeakers on land used as a pleasure fair and used in an emergency provided that the loudspeaker is so operated as not to give reasonable cause for annoyance to persons in the vicinity. For the purposes of this Act a street is defined as being a highway or any other road, footway, court or square open to the public for the time being. The most usual exception to be encountered is the use of loudspeakers to broadcast chimes from travelling shops or ice cream vehicles. Their use is permitted if the following conditions are served:

(a) the loudspeaker is fixed to a vehicle used for carrying perishable foods; and

(b) is operated solely to inform the public that such food is for sale;

(c) no words are used;

(d) it is operated so as not to cause annoyance;

(e) it is only used between 12 noon and 7.00 p.m.

Parking by disabled persons

The purpose of the specific legislation in favour of privileged parking by disabled persons is to permit them to park their vehicles in areas subject to parking restrictions, to prevent them having to walk long distances to reach amenities.

All no-waiting orders (other than those which prohibit the waiting of vehicles of all classes other than disabled persons' vehicles) made under the authority of the Road Traffic Regulation Act 1984, must contain exceptions in respect of vehicles displaying prescribed badges. Badges currently in use may be of different designs. Those issued before 2 March 1992 continue to be valid and will show a figure in a wheelchair, name, validity, name of issuing authority and the serial number. Those issued on or after that date will be in a form which includes a photograph of the holder. Badges issued to institutions must carry the stamp or seal of the organisation holding the badge. The background to all badges will be orange.

A disabled person's vehicle means a vehicle lawfully displaying a disabled person's badge and is a vehicle which, immediately before or after any period of waiting allowed by virtue of a provision in an order which makes special concessions for parking by disabled persons, has been or is to be driven by a disabled person or, as the case may be, has been or is to be used for carrying disabled persons as passengers. Therefore, before such a vehicle can take advantage of such concessions it must be being used, or about to be used, by or on behalf of a disabled person.

The badge must be fitted in the 'relevant position'. Those badges issued before 2 March 1992 may be displayed on the nearside behind the front windscreen, or where there is no front windscreen, in a conspicuous position on the vehicle. Those issued on or after that date must, where the vehicle is fitted with a dashboard or facia panel, be displayed thereon, in such a position that Part I (details of issuing authority) is legible from outside the vehicle. If there is no dashboard or facia panel, it must be displayed in a conspicuous position and be legible from outside the vehicle.

Badges issued by one local authority are generally valid in all other areas. It must be remembered that the driver of the vehicle may be an able bodied person, but the badge has been issued to his vehicle because he uses it to convey a specified disabled person. However, the exemptions will only apply while he is doing so.

Generally, a disabled person's vehicle which is correctly displaying a badge, is exempted from parking restrictions in the following instances:

(a) if the order restricts waiting to a specified period, that is not longer than a given time or to a period of time within a longer period, the vehicle is totally exempt;

(b) if the no waiting restriction is in respect of a period of time less than three hours, the vehicle may be left there for the whole of that period. If it is in respect of a period of more than three hours such a vehicle is exempt for three hours, but must then not return for at least one hour (parking disc must be used);

(c) if the order imposes parking charges, such a vehicle is exempt from that charge and may be parked without time limit.

When badges may be displayed, etc.

It is an offence contrary to the Chronically Sick and Disabled Persons Act 1970, s. 21, for a person to drive such a vehicle which is displaying such a badge otherwise than in a manner or in circumstances prescribed by regulations. It also creates an offence of displaying a badge which is not issued by a local authority. A badge, other than an institutional badge (a badge issued to an institution concerned with the care of disabled persons) may be displayed on a moving vehicle if it is being driven by the holder or where he is being carried in the vehicle. The only other circumstance is where the vehicle is being driven in a place subject to restricted access by vehicles but the order concerned provides for access where a disabled person's concession is available to a vehicle lawfully displaying a disabled person's badge, and it would not otherwise be practicable for the vehicle to be driven there to pick up such a person. Moving vehicles may also display such badges while leaving the vicinity of the place of disembarkation in such circumstances. When parked, a badge may be displayed if the vehicle has been driven to that place by the holder or has been used to carry him there, or is to be driven by the holder from, or he is to be carried from, the place where the vehicle is parked. The same rules apply to institutional badges where the vehicle is being used by the holder (the institution) for the benefit of a disabled person or persons.

What the orange badge scheme does not permit

The orange badge scheme does not permit parking:

(a) during the time a ban on loading or unloading is in force (indicated by one, two or three yellow marks on the kerb at the times shown on post mounted plates);

(b) where there are double white lines in the centre of the road even if one of the lines is broken;

(c) in a bus or cycle lane when it is in use as such;

(d) on a zebra or pelican crossing;

(e) on zigzag markings before or after zebra or pelican crossings;

(f) in parking places reserved for specific users, e.g. loading bays, residents, taxis or cycles; or

(g) in suspended meter bays or when the use of the meter is prohibited.

Wrongful use of disabled person's badge

It is an offence under the Road Traffic Regulation Act 1984, s. 117, for a person wrongfully to use a disabled person's badge. The offence is committed where a disabled person's badge is displayed on a vehicle when it is parked in circumstances in which a concession would be available to a disabled person and the vehicle was not at that time being used (by a disabled person) in such circumstances. In addition to this offence the person so parking would be guilty of the particular breach of the parking regulations.

329

Loss of memory and illness in the street

Introduction

The police service is one of the few civil agencies which provides a 24-hour service to the community on seven days of each week. Unlike other agencies, however, the police do not confine themselves to specialist matters such as those provided by hospitals, ambulance brigades, and fire brigades, but are available to provide help and guidance on any matter and often liaise with other agencies to ensure maximum efficiency. It is inevitable, therefore, that a police officer will usually make the first contact with persons requiring help, particularly when dealing with persons suffering from loss of memory, who fall ill in the street, or who are missing from home, destitute or homeless, and the responsibility for ensuring that such people receive the treatment or attention they require will fall on his shoulders.

Loss of memory

When a person suffering from loss of memory is found in a street or public place steps must be taken to obtain medical treatment as soon as possible. Because this condition is usually associated with injury or shock, a police officer must first ascertain if the person requires first aid treatment, particularly if he suspects concussion to be present, in which case the breathing will be shallow, the patient's face will be pale, the skin cold and clammy, and the pulse rapid and weak. The correct first aid treatment in such cases is the same as that for unconsciousness, i.e. to ensure an open airway and obtain urgent medical treatment.

The person should be removed to hospital by ambulance if necessary and any personal property should be safeguarded. If there has been an accident – for example, if the person has fallen or sustained an injury in any way – then the police officer should take the names and addresses of any witnesses present. On arrival at the hospital, the clothing and personal effects of the person should be examined to establish his identity. In the majority of cases personal documents will quickly establish identity, but when a person's identity cannot be established from an examination of his personal effects, a detailed description of the patient should be compiled, including details of any birthmarks, scars, or other distinguishing features. Arrangements should also be made to have the patient photographed. An examination of any clothing may reveal name tags or laundry marks which may subsequently lead to an identification.

The reporting officer should inform his immediate supervisor of any case where identity has not been established so that a decision can be made in relation to the circulation of the photograph, description, and circumstances of the finding of such a person to other police areas or to the public. The use of newspapers and television can be very helpful in such cases and lead quickly to an identification, thus obviating the necessity for a protracted police enquiry. Reports of persons listed as missing from home should be checked to see if the description tallies with that of the person in hospital. A check should be made of the names index with the PNC.

Where a police officer is called to a person who has been taken ill in a street or public place, the action he should take is similar to that taken in relation to persons found suffering from loss of memory, the most important consideration being the welfare of such a person. First aid should be administered where necessary, and an ambulance or other medical assistance summoned. Always check that an ambulance has been summoned; do not accept that it has been done. Very often such persons carry documentary evidence of their medical condition. An identification card, coloured blue, is issued to patients receiving steroid therapy; identification cards are also issued by the British Diabetic Association and by the Multiple Sclerosis Society to persons suffering from those diseases, and the Medic-Alert Foundation supplies, on payment, a metal wrist bracelet indicating a medical condition or allergy together with a serial number and telephone number by means of which information about the medical condition of the wearer can be obtained. The identity of such person should always be established and his relatives informed of what has happened.

Where a person declines assistance and refuses medical treatment he should be allowed to make his own arrangements, although the police officer should offer to contact a taxi or make other transport arrangements at that person's expense.

As in all cases of this kind, the personal property of any person taken to hospital, etc., should be safeguarded. If necessary, the constable should take possession of the property and, in accordance with local force orders, record each item and the eventual disposal of the property.

A word of caution: never assume that a person is drunk if found unconscious. The symptoms of some illnesses can be very similar. A person who is found alone and unconscious should be taken to hospital even if he smells of drink or there are other grounds for suspecting that he is in a drunken stupor.

Where a person is taken to hospital and detained, any relatives or friends should be notified as soon as possible to avoid any unnecessary concern on their part at the absence of that person.

Mentally disordered persons found in public places

Many people who are suffering from some form of mental disability or illness now receive treatment within the community. It is therefore probable that such persons when found in these circumstances are known to suffer from that disability or illness and are receiving treatment while continuing to live at home. Where possible, such persons should be taken home if found in distressed circumstances and their medical advisers contacted.

Where a constable finds, in a place to which the public have access, a person who appears to be suffering from mental disorder and to be in immediate need of care or control he may, if he thinks it necessary to do so in the interests of that person or for the protection of other persons, remove that person to a place of safety.

The Mental Health Act 1983 provides that such a person may be detained for a period not exceeding 72 hours for the purpose of enabling him to be examined by a doctor, to be interviewed by a mental welfare officer, and to make any necessary arrangements for his treatment or care. Such a person should normally be taken

331

direct to a hospital or, if this is not practicable, the assistance of the mental welfare officer should be sought to advise upon where he should be taken. When the person cannot be taken to a hospital immediately and is taken to a police station, every endeavour should be made to have that person removed as soon as possible to a more suitable place; preferably an appropriate hospital in the district.

In circumstances in which such a person is suspected of committing an offence, it must be remembered that specific procedures are set out in the Code of Practice for the Detention, Treatment and Questioning of Persons by Police Officers when dealing with the mentally ill and the mentally handicapped.

Missing persons, absconders, deserters, and escapees

Introduction

Thousands of people are reported missing from home each year. They frequently leave because of discontent with their existing lives, or because they wish to escape from a situation which they feel to be intolerable. On many occasions the reason for departure will be apparent; on other occasions there may appear to be no reason for a person dropping out of sight. Enquiries are important, particularly where young or other vulnerable people are concerned. It is important to recognise that many murder investigations begin with a report of 'missing from home'. On the other hand, it must also be recognised that the vast majority of such reports are concerned with people who had quite deliberately dropped out of sight. Even where that is so, such persons may, as a result, be exposed to danger.

Persons unlawfully at large

Escape is a common law offence. It is an offence for a person who is lawfully arrested to gain his liberty before he is given it within the due processes of law. The offence may be committed by the prisoner himself either by escaping, without the use of force, before he is put in hold, or with force, after he has been restrained. It may also be committed by other persons and may be committed by permitting such a person to escape, or by negligently allowing him to escape, or by rescuing such a person from custody.

A constable may arrest such a person without a warrant (but see below in relation to young persons).

Young persons absent from institutions

A child or young person who is absent, without the consent of the responsible person, from a place of safety or local authority accommodation in which he was required to live under the provisions of the Children and Young Persons Act 1969, s. 12AA (residence requirement imposed with supervision order), or to which that person had been remanded under s. 16(3A) (remand of person already under supervision), may be arrested by a constable anywhere in the United Kingdom or Channel Islands without a warrant. A person so arrested shall be conducted to the

332

place of safety; local authority accommodation; or such other place as may be directed, at the responsible person's expense. The 'responsible person' is the person who made the arrangements under s. 16(3A), or as the case may be, the authority designated under s. 12AA or 23 of the Children and Young Persons Act 1969.

Young persons in breach of conditions

Section 23A of the Children and Young Persons Act 1969 provides that a young person who has been remanded or committed to local authority accommodation who is subject to requirements that he will not commit further offences or will not interfere with witnesses or otherwise obstruct the course of justice, may be arrested without warrant by a constable if the constable has reasonable grounds for suspecting that the person has broken any of those conditions.

Missing persons

The police receive many reports of persons missing from their homes and police action will depend, to some extent, upon whether the report concerns a child or young person, a woman or girl under 21 years of age, or an adult other than such a woman or girl. On receiving a report of a person missing from home a police officer should first establish the relationship between the person making the report and the missing person, and the reasons or suspected reasons for disappearance. It is not usual to consider as missing persons, adults who have left home or employment intentionally, such as men who have deserted their wives or women who have run away from their husbands. In the absence of any special circumstances such as mental or physical illness or disability, suicidal tendencies, injury, loss of memory, or senility, no police action is normally taken beyond the recording of the report, unless police action is necessary in the interest of children or young persons who have been left by a parent or guardian.

Where the person reported missing is a child or young person, the steps taken are normally immediate and extensive, whatever the circumstances. Children have been known to travel considerable distances in a relatively short time and this should be borne in mind when considering the extent and circulation of information about the missing child and the fact that the child may have been a victim of serious assault or murder must not be overlooked. In the event of a woman or girl under 21 years being reported missing, it is usual for the enquiry to be immediate and for the assistance of a detective officer and a policewoman to be enlisted if it is likely that a criminal offence has been committed.

Where it is considered that police action is necessary, the officer receiving a report of a missing person should obtain the following information:

(a) Any previous similar behaviour? A check on the file kept of missing persons will quickly reveal this information. It may be that a person who has been missing previously may be quickly traced using the information from previous reports. Where a person has been missing on previous occasions this is usually a good indication that no harm has befallen him, although enquiries should not be curtailed because of previous conduct.

333

(b) Is there any suspicion of the missing person being involved in, or the subject of, crime? It may be that a person has left home to avoid arrest or prosecution, particularly in the case of children and young persons.

(c) The steps which have already been taken to trace the missing person? This will avoid duplication of enquiries. If enquiries have been made of all local relatives, these persons will have been made aware that the person is missing.

(d) Full name, age, and address of the missing person together with a full description and, if possible, a recent photograph. A photograph is worth more than the most detailed description and every effort should be made to obtain one.

(e) the usual haunts and acquaintances of the missing person. This includes clubs, public houses, dance halls, school friends, boy or girl friends and, if applicable, places of employment. Where the person is in employment, an enquiry at the place of work may reveal that the person has obtained his National Insurance cards and outstanding wages, which would be a good indication that he intended leaving and this may dispel any suspicion of foul play.

(f) Places where the person is likely to go. This is coupled with the information at (e) above, but may be more extensive. It may be that a person has discussed going to a particular area, in this country or abroad. This information may assist when deciding upon the extent of any circulation of the report of the missing person.

(g) the wishes of relatives regarding any publicity. Often persons do not wish the press or the news media to be made aware of the fact that a person is missing. The police should abide by the wishes of relatives except where the health and well-being of the person missing is likely to be endangered, in which case the overriding consideration must be the safety of that person and the assistance of the press may then be sought.

When dealing with children and young persons, one of the first places to be searched is the home of the child. Particular attention should be paid to discarded refrigerators, boxes, the luggage compartment of a car, all places where a child may have hidden and then been trapped by the door or lid closing with no means of escape from the inside. The use of police dogs at this stage should be considered. There has been at least one instance where, as a result of the prompt use of a police dog, a young child was found head down in a drum in the garage in which he would have died had he not been found at an early stage of the enquiry.

It is usual to check with the Criminal Record Office and with the descriptions of any bodies found, and to circulate particulars of missing persons in police informations. The BBC normally will only consider broadcasting particulars of missing persons exceptionally, the decision in this case being made by the chief officer of police of the area concerned.

Announcements concerning missing persons will be issued in the *Police Gazette* only on compassionate grounds such as loss of memory or illness, or if bodily harm is feared. The date of birth of the person concerned must be included and any request for details to be published in the *Police Gazette* should be signed by an officer not below the rank of inspector.

When a missing person is found, any further police action will depend on the circumstances in which that person is found. A child or young person is normally immediately restored to the parents or guardian or, where the child is in the care of the local authority, to an officer of that local authority. In the case of an older person, the circumstances may be that the individual does not wish his whereabouts to be disclosed. The police should, where advisable, try to persuade the person concerned to return home or, failing that, to inform parents or relatives that he is safe and well and that there is no cause for anxiety. Care should be taken about revealing the whereabouts of a person unless the express permission of that person has been obtained. The Department of Social Security will assist in tracing persons under 18 years of age reported missing from home. The procedure to be followed is set out in Home Office Circular 212/1978.

Destitute and homeless persons

When dealing with a destitute and homeless person, a police officer should try to establish the identity of the person; it may be that he or she has been reported missing from home – a check should be made with the PNC. If the person appears to be ill and in need of medical care, he should be treated in the same way as a person found in the street.

When a person is not of the vagrant type but appears in need of assistance, the social services department of the local authority should be contacted, particularly if a homeless family is found destitute and sleeping out. If such a family refuses assistance and, because of the way in which it is living, harm or unnecessary suffering is likely to be caused to a child or young person, then consideration should be given to removing the child to a place of safety. This may seem a rather harsh way to deal with a destitute and homeless family, but the interests of the child should be paramount; such a course of action safeguards the health and future of the child and is often the means of obtaining help and assistance for the whole family.

Local authority welfare officers can be of considerable assistance to the destitute and the homeless. It is the responsibility of the DSS to provide temporary board and lodging in such circumstances. The 'Shelter' organisation devotes much time and effort to these problems and is always willing to offer advice and assistance. Other organisations such a WVS and the Salvation Army allocate much of their time and resources to the comfort of such persons.

Persons who have become 'stranded' by losing travel tickets and money are usually helped by the police. Money may be advanced to such persons, provided that someone deposits a similar sum with the police in the area of that person's residence.

Absentees and deserters from armed forces

(1) *Arrest*

A constable may arrest any person whom he has reasonable cause to suspect of being an officer, warrant officer, non-commissioned officer or soldier of the regular forces who has deserted or is absent without leave. Persons so arrested must be brought before a summary court as soon as practicable. This power to arrest is provided by the Army Act 1955, Air Force Act 1955, and the Naval Discipline Act 1957 and such powers were preserved by the Police and Criminal Evidence Act 1984, s. 26 and Schedule 2. The Visiting Forces Act 1952 applies these provisions to members of visiting forces. Such a person is absent without leave if he is illegally absent from his unit at that time. He has deserted if he intends to remain permanently absent or goes absent temporarily to avoid a particular overseas posting or service before the enemy.

Where such persons are brought before a summary court and admit that they are illegally absent and the court is satisfied of the truth of that admission, then, unless he is in custody for some other offence, the court shall, and notwithstanding that he is in custody for some other cause, the court may, forthwith either cause him to be delivered into military custody or commit him to prison, a police station or other place for the confinement of persons in custody, to be kept there for delivery into military custody. Where the person concerned does not admit such absence the court must consider the evidence and the statement of the accused before coming to a decision.

(2) *Surrender*

Where a person surrenders to the police as being illegally absent from the armed forces the constable shall take him to a police station. The officer in charge of the police station, if satisfied that he is illegally absent, may cause him to be delivered into military custody without bringing him before a court.

(3) *Certificate of arrest and surrender*

Where, in either case, a person is handed over to a military escort, there shall be handed over with him a certificate signed by either a justice of the peace or clerk of the court, or where appropriate, by the officer of police who causes him to be delivered into military custody, setting out the particulars of his arrest or surrender.

(4) *No money for train fare*

In circumstances in which service personnel report to the police and claim that they do not have the necessary fare to enable them to rejoin their units they should be referred to a local service establishment or to a service careers information office. Where this cannot be done, railway travel warrants may be issued by the police to such a serviceman, provided that the unit is more than 10 miles distant.

Children and young persons

Purpose of law

The law of the land shows considerable tolerance towards offences committed by children and young persons and, additionally, gives them special protection by including offences which are only offences if committed by adults against them.

There are also provisions for ensuring that, in certain circumstances, special arrangements can be made for their care by removing them from an unstable family background. Juvenile courts were not established until 1908, and before this date there was little distinction between the methods by which adults and juveniles were tried, although an Act of 1879 did allow indictable offences committed by young people, in certain circumstances, to be tried summarily. When juvenile courts were set up in 1908, the legislation merely provided for separate courts but did not prescribe rules for their constitution. The matter was remedied in the metropolis in 1920, but was not resolved in relation to the remainder of the country until an Act of 1932 introduced a system of selecting, for juvenile court work, justices who were qualified to deal with young people. The Criminal Justice Act 1991 renames the juvenile courts, as 'youth courts'.

Ages

A 'child' for most purposes relevant to a police officer is a person under the age of 14 years, and a 'young person' is one who has attained the age of 14 years but is not yet 18 years of age.

It is frequently necessary to establish the age of young people appearing before the court and the best evidence available, when strict proof is required, is the production of a birth certificate with evidence from the mother to the effect that the child before the court is the child specified in the birth certificate. However, when such persons are appearing as defendants before a court, the issue seldom arises as the person concerned is quite prepared to give his age to the clerk of the court on request. The parents of such an offender are always aware of the proceedings as they are also served with a copy of any summons or sent notice by the police in other circumstances, and almost invariably are present in court if the issue of age should arise. The court is entitled to determine the age of an offender appearing before it by making enquiries and making its own ruling. If the age of the offender is later established and found to be different from that determined by the court, any order or judgment made will not be invalidated.

Liability of young offenders

The Children and Young Persons Acts 1933 and 1963 say that it shall be conclusively presumed that no child under the age of 10 years can be guilty of an offence. Conclusive presumptions permit no argument in law and it is a fact that no matter what a child under the age of 10 years may do, or why he may do it, the act is not punishable as he is beyond the law. However, a child under the age of 10 years, who is guilty of conduct which in an older person would constitute an offence, may be brought before a youth court under care proceedings.

It is also presumed that a child between the ages of 10 and 14 is incapable of committing crime, but that presumption can be rebutted by clear, positive evidence that he knew that his act was seriously wrong, such evidence not consisting merely in the evidence of the acts amounting to the offence itself. The prosecution must prove that a child defendant did the act alleged and that when he was doing it he knew that it was a wrong act as opposed to an act of mere naughtiness or childish mischief.

Secondly, there must be evidence of guilty knowledge and this must be more than the doing of the act, however horrifying or obviously wrong that act may be. Such evidence might be obtained by interviewing the suspect or having him psychiatrically examined, or on evidence from someone who knew him well.

However, in supporting the continued existence of this presumption, the House of Lords recently said that the time had come to examine this presumption further but that this should be done by Parliament, not the Appeal Courts.

Parents, guardians and their responsibilities

Where an application is made to a court by an individual, the court may by order appoint that individual to be the child's (for these purposes under 18), guardian if:

(a) the child has no parent with parental responsibility for him; or
(b) a residence order has been made with respect to the child in favour of a parent or guardian of his who has died while the order was in force.

Such an order may be made during family proceedings in a court even though no individual has applied for it to be made. Existing parents or guardians may appoint another to assume those responsibilities in the event of their death.

A court may, and in the case of a child under the age of 16 who is charged with an offence must, require the parent or guardian to attend court unless it would be unreasonable, in the circumstances, to do so. A local authority which has such responsibility for a child, may be so ordered. Parents or guardians *must* be required to pay any fine, costs or compensation awarded against a child who is under the age of 16. They *may* be so required where the child is 16 years or more. There are exceptions, where the parent or guardian cannot be found, or where it would be unreasonable to make such an order.

Courts are also empowered to require a parent or guardian to enter, with his consent, into a recognisance for an amount not exceeding £1000, requiring him to take proper care of such person and exercise proper control over him. If a parent or guardian refuses, and the court considers the refusal unreasonable, it may order the parent or guardian to pay a fine not exceeding £1000. In the case of a child or young person who has not attained the age of 16 years, it is the duty of the court to exercise these powers where it is satisfied, having regard to all the circumstances of the case, that it is desirable, to prevent him from committing further offences. If it does not so order, in these circumstances, it must give its reasons for not making such an order in open court.

Offences

(1) *Cruelty, etc.*

Section 1 of the Children and Young Persons Act 1933 provides that if any person who has attained the age of 16 years, who has responsibility for any person under the age of 16 years wilfully:

(a) assaults;
(b) ill-treats;

338

    (c) neglects;

    (d) abandons; or

    (e) exposes

him in a manner likely to cause unnecessary suffering or injury to health, he commits an offence. The offences outlined in this section are serious offences which can result in a sentence of up to 10 years' imprisonment when tried on indictment. The section requires that these acts are done 'wilfully', and the term means deliberately, intentionally, or by reckless act or failure as opposed to accidentally or by mistake. The offence, however, should not be judged against that which a reasonable parent would have done. It must be judged against the person responsible, allowing for his stupidity, ignorance or inadequacy. It has been held that the term 'ill-treats' covers most, if not all, forms of neglect which form a continuous course of conduct. 'Neglect' means the absence of such reasonable care as an ordinary parent would use for the care and protection of his child; while the terms 'abandon or expose' are concerned with leaving a child to its fate. Once a child has been so abandoned (e.g. being left on a doorstep) it is from that moment exposed.

A person is presumed to have responsibility for a child or young person if:

    (a) he has parental responsibility for him under the Children Act 1989 (which the mother and the father will both have if they were married to each other when the child or young person was born, or which only the mother will have if the mother and father were not so married, or which another person – including a father in the instance just given – or a local authority may acquire by operation of law); or

    (b) he is otherwise liable to maintain him; or

    (c) he has care of him.

In this way a burden of responsibility for the proper care of young people is placed firmly upon all persons of 16 years or more who have responsibility for them. Such persons include parents, foster parents, relatives who may be permanently or temporarily caring for children, or even baby sitters who have the care of the children for only a few hours, and all are responsible for the well-being of persons under 16 years of age in their care. If young people are not provided with adequate food, clothing, medical aid, or lodging, the parent or other person legally responsible for their maintenance shall be deemed to be guilty of neglecting them in a manner likely to cause unnecessary suffering, and where it is proved that a child under 3 years was suffocated by being overlain by a person of 16 years or over who went to bed under the influence of drink, the same shall apply.

These offences may be encountered in a number of ways, from the incident involving the father who brutally beats his child with a buckled leather belt to the mother who abandons her baby on a doorstep or in an underground station. Parents and teachers administering punishment to children are protected by the Act, provided that the punishment is reasonable.

(2) *Other offences under the 1933 Act*

Other offences include: allowing children between 4 and 16 years to reside in or frequent a brothel, causing children under 16 years to be used for begging, taking articles in pawn from persons under 14 years, giving intoxicating liquor to children under the age of 5 years unless in a medical emergency, exposing children under the age of 12 years to risk of burning, or employing a child under 13 years in circumstances other than those permitted by local by-laws, etc. In offences of exposing children under the age of 12 years to the risk of burning, the fact that such children were left in a room with an open fire or with an unguarded appliance and are burned so as to suffer death or serious injury, is sufficient to prove the offence.

(3) *Tobacco*

The selling of tobacco or cigarette papers to a person under the age of 16 is prohibited by s. 7 of the 1933 Act, whether the tobacco is for his own use or not. The term 'tobacco' includes cigarettes and any product containing tobacco intended for oral or nasal use and smoking mixtures intended as a substitute for tobacco. The offence is one of strict liability and the proprietor of a shop is guilty even when he has played no part in the transaction and knows nothing about it. However, s. 7 provides that it is a defence for an accused to prove that he took all reasonable precautions and exercised all due diligence to avoid the commission of the offence.

A constable in uniform may seize any tobacco or cigarette papers from a person apparently under 16 whom he finds smoking in any street or public place.

Where a cigarette machine is extensively used by persons under 16 a court may order the owner to take precautions to prevent such use, or if necessary, to remove the machine.

The Children and Young Persons (Protection of Tobacco) Act 1991 prohibits sale of unpackaged cigarettes by a person carrying on a retail business and requires notices to be displayed on premises and machines concerning sales to persons under 16.

The provisions of the Children Act 1989

Care proceedings

We have already discussed the conclusive presumption that a child under the age of 10 years is incapable of committing any offence and the rebuttable presumption that children between 10 and 14 years are equally unaware that what they are doing is wrong. Although such persons may escape punishment for offences that they commit, the Children Act 1989 makes various provisions for children and young persons to be brought into the care of a local authority. For the purpose of these provisions the use of the term 'child' is a reference to a person under 18. Local authorities are required to make provision for the reception and accommodation of children, including children who are in police protection and those whom they are requested, by a custody officer, to receive, where that custody officer has authorised an arrested juvenile to be kept in police detention.

Care and supervision orders

On the application of a local authority or authorised person (NSPCC or other body authorised by the Secretary of State), a family proceedings court (i.e. that part of a

340

magistrates' court hearing proceedings under the 1989 Act) may make an order:

(a) placing the child with respect to whom the application is made in the care of a designated local authority; or

(b) putting him under the supervision of a designated local authority or of a probation officer.

A court may only make a care or supervision order if it is satisfied:

(a) that the child concerned is suffering, or is likely to suffer, significant harm; and

(b) that the harm, or likelihood of harm, is attributable to:

   (i) the care given to the child, or likely to be given to him if the order were not made, not being what it would be reasonable to expect a parent to give to him; or

   (ii) the child being beyond control.

Such an order may not be made with respect to a child who has reached the age of 17 (or 16 in the case of a child who is married). On an application for a care order the court may make a supervision order and vice versa. 'Harm' means ill-treatment or the impairment of health or development.

It can be seen, therefore, that where a child has been the victim of an offence of cruelty or sexual abuse, an application may be made by a local authority or an authorised person for either of the above orders. In addition, the provision at (b)(ii) above, provides a means of obtaining a care order in circumstances in which a child who is below the age of criminal responsibility habitually commits crime, or where a child who is under 14, and therefore rebuttably presumed to be incapable of committing crime, does so.

Child assessment orders

The Children Act 1989, s. 43, permits a local authority or authorised person to apply to the High Court or a county court or magistrates' court sitting as a family proceedings court for such an order where difficulties are being experienced in making an assessment of the needs of such a child. This may be due to the lack of cooperation by those who have parental responsibility for the child. Such an order permits assessment to be made over a period not exceeding seven days and may require any person to produce the child to a person named in the order and to comply with specified instructions. However, a court should not make such an order if it is satisfied that there are grounds for making an emergency protection order and that it ought to do so rather than make an assessment order.

Emergency protection orders

There will be occasions upon which action must be taken immediately to protect a child. Section 44 of the 1989 Act empowers the High Court, a county or magistrates' court, on the application of any person, to make an emergency order for the protection of a child. It may do so if it is satisfied that:

(a) there is reasonable cause to believe that the child is likely to suffer significant harm if:
   (i) he is not removed to accommodation provided by or on behalf of the applicant; or
   (ii) he does not remain in the place in which he is then being accommodated;
(b) in the case of an application made by a local authority:
   (i) enquiries are being made with respect to the child under the authority's duty to investigate where a child is suffering, or is likely to suffer, significant harm; and
   (ii) those enquiries are being frustrated by access to the child being unreasonably refused to a person authorised to seek access and that the applicant has reasonable cause to believe that access to the child is required as a matter of urgency; or
(c) in the case of an application made by an authorised person:
   (i) the applicant has reasonable cause to believe that the child is suffering or is likely to suffer, significant harm;
   (ii) the applicant is making enquiries with respect to the child's welfare; and
   (iii) those enquiries are being frustrated by access to the child being unreasonably refused to a person authorised to seek access and the applicant has reasonable cause to believe that access to the child is required as a matter of urgency.

An emergency protection order directs a person to produce a child and authorises the child's removal to accommodation provided by or on behalf of the applicant or prevents the removal of the child from a hospital or other place. It also gives the applicant parental responsibility for the child. An emergency protection order has effect for such period, not exceeding eight days, as is specified by the court but the court has power (on one occasion only) to extend it for up to a further seven days.

Removal and accommodation of children by police in emergencies

Section 46 of the 1989 Act empowers police officers to take a child into 'police protection' in prescribed circumstances. It also places responsibilities upon 'designated police officers', that is officers designated by their chief officers of police to conduct enquiries into such cases. The details are as follows. Where a constable has reasonable cause to believe that a child would otherwise be likely to suffer significant harm, he may:

(a) remove the child to suitable accommodation and keep him there; or
(b) take such steps as are reasonable to ensure that the child's removal from any hospital, or other place, in which he is then being accommodated is prevented.

As soon as is reasonably practicable after taking the child into police protection, as above, the constable shall:

(a) inform the local authority within whose area the child was found of the steps that have been, or are proposed to be, taken with respect to the child and the reason for taking them;

(b) give details to the local authority within whose area the child is ordinarily resident (the appropriate authority) of the place at which the child is being accommodated;

(c) inform the child (if he appears to be capable of understanding):
  (i) of the steps that have been taken with respect to him and of the reasons for taking them; and
  (ii) of the further steps which may be taken with respect to him under this section;

(d) take such steps as are reasonably practicable to discover the wishes and feelings of the child;

(e) secure that the case is enquired into by a designated officer; and

(f) where the child was taken into police protection by being removed to accommodation which is not provided:
  (i) by or on behalf of a local authority; or
  (ii) as a 'refuge', i.e. a voluntary home or registered children's home certified as a refuge;
  secure that he is removed to accommodation which is so provided.

He must also, as soon as practicable, inform:

(a) the child's parents;

(b) every person who is not a parent of his but has parental responsibility for him; and

(c) any other person with whom the child was living immediately before being taken into police protection;

of the steps that he has taken under this section with respect to the child, the reasons for taking them and the further steps that may be taken with respect to him under the section.

When the case has been enquired into by the designated officer, he must release the child from police protection unless he considers that there is still reasonable cause for believing that the child would be likely to suffer significant harm if released.

No child may be kept in police protection for more than 72 hours. However, at any time while the child is in police protection, the designated officer may apply *on behalf of the appropriate authority* for an emergency protection order to be made with respect to the child. Such an application may be made whether or not the authority know of it or agree to its being made.

While a child is in police protection the designated officer must do what is reasonable in all the circumstances of the case for the purpose of safeguarding or promoting the child's welfare (having regard in particular to the length of the period during which the child will be so protected).

The designated officer must allow parents; any other person with parental responsibility; any person with whom the child was living immediately before he was taken into police protection; where there is a 'contact order' (an order permitting contact by named persons), any such person; and any person acting on behalf of any of these persons, to have such contact (if any) with the child as, in the opinion of the designated officer, is both reasonable and in the child's best interests. However, if a child taken into police protection is in accommodation provided by, or on behalf of, the appropriate authority, these contact responsibilities are those of the authority rather than the designated officer.

Police powers

An emergency protection order may include a requirement directed to a person to disclose the whereabouts of the child and it may authorise an applicant to enter premises specified by the order and search for the child. Such a warrant may authorise a constable to assist an applicant where entry is being, or is likely to be, denied. It may also direct that a constable be accompanied by a registered medical practitioner, registered nurse or registered health visitor.

If a child or young person is absent without the consent of the responsible person:

(a) from a place of safety to which he has been taken under the Children and Young Persons Act 1969, s 16 (3) (supervised person arrested on warrant and so placed for not more than 72 hours); or

(b) from local authority accommodation in which he was required to live as a condition of a supervision order; or

(c) to which he had been remanded by a court either awaiting trial or an offence, or having been convicted of such an offence;

the Children and Young Persons Act 1969, s. 32 as amended by Schedule 12 to the 1989 Act, continues to authorise a constable to arrest such a child or young person without a warrant. When so arrested he must be conducted to a place of safety; local authority accommodation; or such other place as the responsible person may direct. This power applies to a child or young person as defined by the Children and Young Persons Act 1933.

The 1989 Act requires local authorities to make provision for the reception and accommodation of children who are removed or kept away from home under these provisions. They must receive children in police protection whom they are requested to receive under s. 38(6) of the Police and Criminal Evidence Act 1984. That subsection requires that where a custody officer authorises an arrested juvenile to be taken into the care of a local authority, he must make arrangements for that juvenile to be taken into care of a local authority, unless he certifies that it is impracticable to do so.

This provision led to the constant transfer of juveniles who were persistent offenders into the care of local authorities, from which they had persistently absconded to commit further offences. However, following a High Court ruling that a custody officer need not do so if he is dissatisfied with the proposed detention arrangements, the subsection permits police detention for those of 12 years or over (when in force) 15 at present. The proven insecurity of the hostel, coupled with the likelihood of the commission of further offences are factors which he may consider if they are likely further to interfere with the administration of justice.

The 1989 Act permits local authorities to use 'secure accommodation' in respect of a child whom it is looking after, but such persons may not be placed in secure accommodation unless it appears that:

(a) (i) he has a history of absconding and is likely to abscond from any other description of accommodation; and

  (ii) if he absconds he is likely to suffer significant harm; or
 (b) if he is kept in any other description of accommodation he is likely to injure himself or other persons.

However, at first sight this provision does not appear to be very helpful in relation to the persistent offender who absconds from local authority care. The wording of the section is very precise and noticeably excludes any reference to the commission of further offences. Much may depend upon the interpretation of 'suffer significant harm'. In its narrowest sense it will mean exposure to undesirable consequences; in its broadest sense it could be held to embrace the commission of further offences, as those very acts could lead to significant harm in the long term, such as slipping into a life of crime, or short-term harm by association with criminals.

However, the Criminal Justice and Public Order Act 1994, s. 1, makes provision for 'secure training orders' to be made where:

 (a) a person of not less than 12 but under 15 years of age is convicted of an imprisonable offence; and
 (b) the court is satisfied:
   (i)   that the offender was not less than 12 years of age when the offence for which he is dealt with by the court was committed;
   (ii) that the offender has been convicted of three or more imprisonable offences; and
   (iii) that the offender, either on this or a previous occasion, has been found to be in breach of a supervision order under the Children and Young Persons Act 1969, or has been convicted of an imprisonable offence while he was subject to such a supervision order.

A 'secure training order' is an order that an offender in respect of whom it is made shall be subject to a period of detention in a secure training centre followed by a period of supervision. The period of detention and supervision shall be such as the court determines and specifies in the order, being not less than six months nor more than two years. The person concerned will be liable to serve one half of the total period of detention imposed by the order. An 'imprisonable offence' is one (not being one for which the sentence is fixed by law) which is punishable with imprisonment in the case of a person aged 21 or over. A person who is unlawfully at large from a secure training centre may be arrested without warrant and taken to the place from which he has absconded.

The Act provides for the age of 12, which it specifies, to be reached progressively by order, the age of 14 being substituted at first; then 13; with 12 being ultimately reached no doubt when sufficient secure accommodation is available.

Such an order may contain requirements with which the person concerned must comply. In the event of non-compliance he may be brought before a youth court by way of summons or warrant.

In addition, s. 23 of the Children and Young Persons Act 1969 was amended by the Criminal Justice and Public Order Act 1994 to allow the age at which a young person may be made subject to a security requirement when remanded or committed to the care of a local authority, to be progressively reduced, by order, from the present age of 15 to one of 12 years. The 1994 Act also increased the maximum

345

length of detention in a young offender institution to 24 months for offenders aged 15, 16, and 17.

Interrogation of children and young persons

The Code of Practice for the Detention, Treatment, and Questioning of Persons by Police Officers makes special provisions for persons who are particularly at risk in interview situations. Juveniles are persons considered to be at risk.

If anyone appears to be under the age of 18 then he shall be treated as a juvenile for the purposes of the Code and all other Codes of Practice issued under the Police and Criminal Evidence Act 1984, in the absence of clear evidence to show that he is older.

A juvenile, whether suspected of crime or not, must not be interviewed or asked to provide a written statement in the absence of 'the appropriate adult' unless an officer of the rank of superintendent or above considers that delay will involve an immediate risk of harm to persons or serious loss of or damage to property. However, in these exceptional circumstances questioning may not continue once sufficient information to avert the immediate risk has been obtained. A record must be made of the grounds for any decision to interview a juvenile in these circumstances. These instances must be exceptional to minimise the risk of interviews producing unreliable information.

Other than in these exceptional circumstances, all interviews with juveniles must take place in the presence of the 'appropriate adult'. The 'appropriate adult' in the case of a juvenile is his parent or guardian (or if he is in care, the care authority or voluntary organisation), or a social worker, or failing the attendance of these persons, another responsible adult aged 18 or over who is not a police officer or employed by the police. The parent or guardian of a juvenile should be the appropriate adult unless he is suspected of involvement in the offence, is a witness, is involved in the investigation or has received admissions. In such circumstances it will be desirable for the appropriate adult to be someone else. If the parent or guardian is estranged from the juvenile, he should not be asked to be the appropriate adult if the juvenile expressly or specifically objects to his presence. If a child in care admits an offence to a social worker, another social worker must be the appropriate adult.

If a juvenile has been cautioned before the arrival of the 'appropriate adult' the caution must be repeated in the adult's presence (unless the interview has by then already finished if conducted in the urgent situation described above). The 'appropriate adult' should also be informed of the juvenile's right to legal advice and if such adult feels that it is desirable, advice must be obtained.

Juveniles may only be interviewed at their place of education in exceptional circumstances and then only where the principal or his nominee agrees. Every effort should be made to contact both the parents, or other person responsible for the juvenile's welfare and the 'appropriate adult' (if a different person) and a reasonable time should be allowed to enable the 'appropriate adult' to attend. Where this would cause undue delay and unless the offence is against the educational establishment, the principal or his nominee can act as the 'appropriate adult' for the purposes of the interview.

Juveniles are particularly prone in certain circumstances to provide information which is unreliable, misleading or self-incriminating. It is necessary to exercise special care in questioning such a person. It is also good practice to obtain corroboration of any facts admitted in such an interview. The 'appropriate adult' is present to advise the person being questioned and to satisfy himself that the interview is being conducted fairly as well as to facilitate communication with the person being interviewed.

There will be few occasions upon which the arrest of a juvenile at his place of education could be justified. If, exceptionally, this must be done, the head teacher or his nominee must be informed.

Detention of juveniles

Where an arrested person is a juvenile he must be released on bail if his name and address are known; if it is not necessary to keep him in detention for his own protection or to prevent him from causing physical injury to another person or causing loss of or damage to property; there are no reasons for believing that he will fail to appear in answer to bail; it is not necessary to detain him to prevent him from interfering with the administration of justice or the investigation of offences; and the custody officer does not have reasonable grounds for believing that he ought to be detained in his own interests.

Section 38 of the Police and Criminal Evidence Act requires that where a custody officer authorises an arrested juvenile to be kept in police detention he must secure that the arrested juvenile is moved to local authority accommodation, unless he certifies:

(a) that, by reason of such circumstances as are specified in the certificate, it is impracticable to do so; or

(b) in the case of an arrested juvenile who has attained the age of 12 years, no secure accommodation is available and that keeping him in other local authority accommodation would not be adequate to protect the public from serious harm from him.

Evidence given by children

Section 33A of the Criminal Justice Act 1988 provides that a child's evidence in criminal proceedings shall be given unsworn. A deposition of a child's unsworn evidence may be taken for the purpose of criminal proceedings as if that evidence had been given on oath. While the matter of competence of a witness is a matter for a court, subs. (2A) of this section provides that a child's evidence shall be received unless it appears to the court that the child is incapable of giving intelligible testimony.

In addition, s. 34 provides that at a trial on indictment there is no need for the jury to be warned about convicting the accused on the uncorroborated evidence of a child.

Note At the time of writing some of the provisions of the CJPO Act 1994 have not been brought into force.

Railways

Introduction

The various laws concerned with our railway network in particular have been passed at different times and with different aims and objectives. Some regulate the running of the railway system while others are concerned with the comfort and protection of the travelling public. On occasions specific responsibility for the enforcement of laws protecting railway property and railway practices is given to bodies other than the police forces of England and Wales. A number of Acts authorise the appointment of railway constables. The British Transport Police are responsible for the protection of railway property and the enforcement of legislation which is particularly concerned with the railway system. However, it is only in instances in which particular enforcement problems are of such a nature that they are obviously the concern of the railways that the power to act tends to be restricted to constables of the British Transport Police, and, on occasions, to employers of the railway authorities in addition.

Railways pass through the areas of all police forces and on occasions there are miles of railway tracks within a force area. The officers of the British Transport Police tend to be rather thinly spread and they will not always be available, or available in sufficient numbers, to deal with incidents which arise. The football special passing through the area of a police force may present problems throughout its journey, and wherever it may halt, as it progresses through that journey. Damage to the track, the throwing of missiles and trespass upon dangerous sections of the track are all matters which are likely to be reported to any police officer. However, it is only in instances in which particular enforcement problems are of such a nature that they are obviously the concern of the railways that the power to act tends to be restricted to constables of the British Transport Police, and, on occasions, to employees of the railway authorities in addition.

Powers of entry

A constable may enter and remain on railway property to protect life and property and to prosecute offenders. Most offences which occur on railway property are offences in respect of which constables have the power of enforcement. The only exceptions to the general rule that constables may take action for all offences is where powers of enforcement are specially given to some other body. Some Acts dealing with railways restrict enforcement to railway personnel but, generally, these offences are of significance to the British Railways Board only. Some forms of trespass and some ticket offences related to production, etc., are restricted in this way.

Trespass on railway property

The British Transport Commission Act 1949 creates an offence of trespass upon any of the lines of a railway or siding, or in any tunnel or upon any railway embankment, cutting or similar work, or in dangerous proximity to any railway lines or to any electrical apparatus used for or in connection with the working of a railway. No person may be convicted of this offence unless it is proved that public warning has been given to persons not to trespass upon the railway by a notice fixed at the nearest railway station to the point at which the trespass occurred. That notice must be clear and not obliterated or destroyed.

Police powers

Police officers have a duty to prevent the dangers caused by foolish trespass upon railway property. It should be remembered, however, that the notice must be shown to have been properly displayed before this offence can be committed, although the effect of such a notice upon a trespasser who may be some miles from the station is likely to be limited.

Trespass and refusal to quit

The Railway Regulation Act 1840, s. 16, states that it is an offence for a person to wilfully trespass upon any railway, or any of the stations or other works, or premises connected with a railway and to refuse to quit when so requested by an officer or agent of the company. The word 'railway' in this section extends to all railways, constructed under any Act of Parliament, which are intended for the conveyance of passengers. There is no necessity to prove that notices are in place. Constables, other than those of the British Transport Police, are not officers or agents of the railways.

Police powers

An officer or agent of the railway, or any person whom these officers may call to assist, may arrest without warrant anyone committing this offence. This power to arrest is logical. If a trespasser refuses to quit, the only way in which he can be removed is by arrest. Constables must remember that s. 26 of the Police and Criminal Evidence Act 1984 removed all such statutory powers of arrest from constables. If a constable is the person called to assist, he does not have this power to arrest unconditionally. In any case, it is suggested that the exercise of such a power would in most instances be unnecessary as the refusal to quit is likely to be little more than a gesture. There is no doubt that in most cases the matter will be dealt with by means of a summons even if handled by a constable of the British Transport Police or an employee of the company.

A trespasser is a person who has entered upon, or who remains upon land or property without lawful authority.

Causing danger or obstruction – with intent

There are two almost parallel offences created by the Offences Against the Person Act 1861, s. 32, and the Malicious Damage Act 1861, s. 35. In common the two Acts deal with persons who unlawfully and maliciously commit certain acts; that is, the placing of any obstruction on any part of the railway; the moving of points or similar fittings or machinery; the showing of a false signal or the concealment of a real

349

signal; or carrying out any other act with certain intents. The Offences Against the Person Act is concerned with such acts being carried out with intent to endanger the safety of any person travelling, or being on the railway. This is reasonable; that Act is concerned with protecting people from injury. If the actions are carried out with the intention of obstructing, upsetting or overthrowing, injuring or destroying any engine, tender, carriage or truck which is using the railway, then the offence contrary to the Malicious Damage Act is committed.

The word 'malicious' can extend to acts done in sport and mischievously with a view to obstruct.

Both of these offences are arrestable offences. It will be a question of proof of actual intention in deciding which of the offences should be preferred. If such an act is carried out with the intention of derailing a train, it is quite obvious that there must be some intention to damage parts of the train. The additional question of intention to harm passengers will have to be considered before an offence contrary to the Offences Against the Person Act can be considered in the particular circumstances of each case.

Causing danger or obstruction – no intent

It will be appreciated that there will be occasions when it is impossible in the circumstances to prove a particular intention either to endanger passengers or to damage any part of a train. The reference to 'malice' is removed from the offences which we have already considered above, as is the reference to particular intentions. In all other respects the offences are the same. They are committed by persons who by any unlawful act, or by any wilful omission or neglect, in the case of the offence committed contrary to the Offences Against the Person Act 1861, s. 34, do so and as a result endanger, or cause to be endangered, the safety of any person conveyed or being in or upon a railway, or aid or assist any such act, etc., or in the case of the Malicious Damage Act 1861, s. 36, the offence leads to the obstruction of an engine or carriage using the railway. There is one essential difference between these two offences. In the case of the offence of endangering, etc., the placing of the obstruction wilfully in such way that potential danger is caused, even if that danger is removed by another person, is sufficient. The offence under the Malicious Damage Act requires that an obstruction is actually caused.

These are lesser offences because of the absence of malice and particular intentions and are only punishable by two years' imprisonment. They are not arrestable offences.

Throwing objects

In addition, the Offences Against the Person Act 1961, s. 33, deals quite specifically with particular offences of throwing objects at trains. It is an offence to unlawfully and maliciously throw, or cause to fall, or strike at, against, into, or upon any engine, tender, carriage, or truck used upon any railway, any wood, stone, or other matter or thing with intent to injure or endanger the safety of any person being in or upon such vehicles. This is an arrestable offence punishable by imprisonment for life.

For the purposes of this section an act can be malicious even if it is carried out in sport and mischievously with a view to obstruct.

While this offence deals with 'stone throwing' in a particular way, acts done which involve throwing missiles may also be punishable under the provisions which we have examined above. The fact that a specific intent need not be proved, increases the usefulness of the offences previously discussed.

Safety precautions

There are many occasions upon which it may be necessary for police officers to enter on to railway property. The dangers which exist on such occasions cannot be overstated. Many high speed trains travel at such fast speeds that there is little warning of their approach. There are a number of safety precautions which should be taken:

(a) wear clothing which is easily seen from long distances and in poor visibility conditions, when walking on or near to a railway track;

(b) walk beside the railway, keeping as far as possible from the nearest line;

(c) face towards oncoming trains wherever possible;

(d) trains approach at speed and not all have powerful headlights;

(e) never walk on the rails themselves, or on the sleepers or rodding and never stand on points which are likely to be switched at any time – step over all of these;

(f) do not enter a tunnel unless there is no other course of action open to you in the circumstances, always contact a signalman by lineside telephone to tell him of your entry and if in a tunnel when a train approaches, take refuge in the wall recesses which are provided for such circumstances; if a recess cannot be reached, lie down between the track and the tunnel wall until the train has passed;

(g) train drivers always sound a warning if they see anyone on or near to a track and such a warning should be acknowledged by raising the hand above the head and moving to a safer place if the circumstances necessitate such a move on the grounds of safety;

(h) bridges, viaducts and cuttings, etc., involve particular dangers because of their restricted clearance;

(i) when walking on or near a track which is electrified by a conductor rail (usually a third rail between the two tracks used by the train), do not touch the live rail or allow anything to come in contact with it;

(j) where overhead line equipment is in use on the track it is safer to treat all overhead wires as being 'live' and a potential threat to life; in no circumstances should broken, displaced or damaged wires be touched and it must be remembered that if there is sufficient moisture in the air it is not necessary that the wires be touched, before a fatal shock may be received as a charge can easily 'jump' a distance of 2 feet;

(k) the lineside telephones should always be used in any form of emergency such as a requirement that the electric power be switched off.

It is essential that officers restrict entry on to working areas of railway undertakings to situations which may be described as emergencies. Whenever possible, an officer should be accompanied by an officer of the railway undertaking or a British Transport Police officer. Where power has been switched off, overhead wires can remain live until residual electricity has been allowed to run to earth.

Although electrified track carries a high voltage of electricity, power from the 'third rail' does not normally arc. However, it must not be touched, even after the power has been switched off, until the residual electricity has been discharged. Where immediate action is essential because someone is lying in contact with the live track, he may be separated from it by pushing him aside with a dry object which is such that it will not conduct electricity.

Interviewing railway staff

In normal circumstances, police officers should not attempt to interview such persons as signalmen, guards, or look-outs while they are carrying out their duties unless the matter is extremely urgent, when arrangements should be made with a supervisor to have such person relieved. It is advisable not to enter a signal box unless extreme danger exists and it is essential to warn the signalman of it.

However, police officers must bear in mind their responsibilities under the Transport and Works Act 1992 in relation to such key railway personnel carrying out their duties when unfit through drink or drugs, or having consumed alcohol in excess of the prescribed limit (see page 314).

Bodies on railway lines

Bodies should be removed from railway lines as soon as possible, unless it is suspected that a crime has been committed. Where a crime is not suspected a police officer should not require that a body be left in position and if photographs are required, perhaps to assist a coroner, the photographs of the body should be taken after it has been removed from the track.

Crime prevention

Introduction

The prevention of crime, in the widest sense, requires the cooperation of many elements in society – parents, schools, churches, the probation service, youth clubs and leaders, voluntary organisations, the prison service, the police, and many others – who all have their part to play in ensuring that crime is not made easy and that people are discouraged from embarking on a life of crime.

The prevention of crime has always been one of the primary functions of the police; all officers have a general responsibility in this field. The following extract from *Instructions to Constables* by Charles Rowan, the first Commissioner of Police of the Metropolis, clearly illustrates this point:

'It should be understood, at the outset, that the principal object to be attained is the Prevention of Crime. To this great end every effort of the Police is to be directed. The security of person and property, the preservation of the public tranquillity, and all the other objects of a Police Establishment, will thus be better effected, than by the detection and punishment of the offender, after he has succeeded in committing the crime. This should constantly be kept in mind by every member of the Police Force, as the guide for his own conduct. Officers and Police Constables should endeavour to distinguish themselves by such vigilance and activity as may render it extremely difficult for any one to commit a crime within the portion of the town under their charge.'

Crime prevention officers

Crime prevention is the anticipation, recognition, and appraisal of a crime risk and the initiation of action to remove or reduce it. It has now been recognised as an integral and important part of all police work, and every force has a crime prevention department the members of which make a special study of this field. The Home Office Committee on the Prevention and Detection of Crime considered that the duties of a crime prevention officer should include:

(a) the cultivation of a two-way relationship between beat and patrol officers and the crime prevention officer, and encouragement of beat constables to report matters of crime prevention interest;

(b) the collection, coordination, and dissemination of crime prevention information on current trends of crime;

(c) the acquiring of a thorough knowledge of technical aids to security, by study of appropriate journals and visits to manufacturers of locks, safes, etc.;

(d) the inspection of property where there are special or difficult security features and the keeping of records of such visits to enable follow-up visits to be made at appropriate times;

(e) maintaining a firm relationship with local bank managers, local authorities, and all other bodies to whom advice can be given on crime prevention;

(f) the giving of talks, whenever the opportunity arises, to local bodies on crime prevention;

(g) ensuring that crime prevention literature is used to its best effect and displayed or distributed on all appropriate occasions; the crime prevention officer should always have available a collection of locks and, possibly, burglar alarms for selective display;

(h) the regular giving of lectures at probationer and refresher courses and the issue of a crime prevention booklet for the guidance of all members of all the force;

(i) the cooperation and liaison with children where the force operates a Juvenile Liaison Scheme; with the fire service to ensure that security standards do not conflict with fire safety precautions; with night watchmen in those parts of the country where Mutual Aid Schemes involving night watchmen have been introduced; and with burglar alarm companies on matters in respect of the installation of alarms;

(j) giving advice on security to builders and architects in the planning stages of buildings and, if necessary, to survey premises from plans.

353

This is a very comprehensive brief for a crime prevention officer and it is essential that all police officers assist in this area of police work. The bulk of the day-to-day crime prevention work inevitably and rightly falls to the operational uniformed police officer; his very presence on patrol is the best deterrent against crime, and any police officer should take every opportunity to give advice and assistance on prevention of crime matters to householders, vehicle owners, car park attendants, and other persons with whom a police officer comes into daily contact.

Most crimes are committed because an opportunity suddenly presents itself; few are carefully planned. The eradication of such opportunities is an essential part of a police officer's duties.

Motor vehicles, premises, and handbags

Thefts of motor vehicles and theft of property from parked and unattended motor vehicles are on the increase and police officers should advise drivers and owners of motor vehicles to take the following basic steps to minimise the risk of such offences:

(a) Never leave the ignition keys of a parked vehicle in the ignition switch, no matter how brief the time which the driver is likely to be absent from the vehicle.

(b) Never leave expensive articles lying on the seats or back window ledge of the vehicle. If it is not possible or convenient to remove such articles from the vehicle, the property should be placed in the boot of the vehicle which should be locked.

(c) Never leave a motor vehicle unlocked; a determined thief can start a vehicle in seconds if he can gain access to the vehicle quickly and quietly.

(d) The drivers of goods vehicles carrying valuable loads should be advised to park their vehicles off the road during an overnight stay, preferably in a lorry park if available.

(e) Advise drivers of motor vehicles to consider fitting an anti-thief device to their vehicles. Should they wish further details, the crime prevention officer will supply details of the various devices available.

Officers should also check the security of business premises to see if they have been left insecure and should offer advice to ladies who leave handbags or purses on top of shopping bags, or in perambulators, in crowded places.

Buildings

A patrolling beat officer will often see examples of people's carelessness towards their own property; e.g. notes left for the milkman or tradesman and newspapers or bottle of milk left on the doorstep, all indicate to a thief that the occupiers are absent and the house empty; ladders left available and garage doors open make entry into premises and the theft of property a simple matter. A word with the householder will correct such carelessness.

When a person is going away on holiday and seeks advice on the security of the house in his absence he should be advised to leave a key to the house with a trustworthy neighbour, to take any valuables to the bank, to cancel deliveries of bread, milk and newspapers, to leave curtains undrawn, and leave details at the local police station of the period of absence, and the name and address of the person with whom he has left the key.

If a beat officer is asked for advice on the security of shops or business premises, he should refer the person to the crime prevention officer whose specialised knowledge will assist. Often a police officer summoned to the scene of a crime will notice that the premises lack security, and in such cases he should advise the owners to contact the local crime prevention officer who would be only too willing to advise on appropriate security measures. Whether or not the owner follows up this advice, the officer should notify the crime prevention officer of his findings so that he can follow up by visiting the premises himself.

The locks fitted to many dwelling-houses and business premises are inadequate. Deadlocks and security catches fitted to windows make it much more difficult for a thief. If such devices are fitted to buildings and in addition, security lights are installed, it is more likely that a thief will seek an easier target. All householders can use approved marker pens to invisibly mark valuable property. This is best done by marking property with the post code followed by the number of the house. Householders should be advised that it is important to check after a period of time, that such marks are still distinguishable.

'Neighbourhood Watch' schemes can play a significant part in efforts to reduce crime, and should be encouraged. The more eyes which are tuned to recognition of the unusual, the more likely the prevention of crime becomes. In addition, those crimes which are committed are much more likely to be detected if public cooperation is encouraged. The success of the various 'crime watch' programmes provided by TV broadcasters, gives evidence of the value of full cooperation in every respect.

Local knowledge

A good knowledge of the locality and its residents will always assist a constable in efforts to prevent crime. He should make it his business to know the current crime trends in the area, and most vulnerable premises such as banks, jewellers, lock-up premises, and building sites. Such knowledge will enable him to concentrate his efforts and time to the best advantage. It is useful to have knowledge of wanted and suspected persons and any persons believed to be actively engaged in crime in his area. The local intelligence officer will have photographs of convicted criminals.

Dogs

Dog registration schemes

The requirement that the owner of a dog shall take out a licence authorising him to keep it was removed by the Local Government Act 1988. Section 37 of that Act authorises the Secretary of State to make provision by way of statutory instrument for the establishment and administration of a dog registration scheme by local authorities, or such other organisation as he may, after consulting with them, designate.

Dog collars

The Control of Dogs Order 1992 requires that every dog while on a highway or in a place of public resort must wear a collar with the owner's name and address inscribed upon it, or on a plate or badge attached to it. There are certain exceptions which refer to dogs which are working dogs used in the countryside in conditions which might make the wearing of a collar dangerous, or to other similar circumstances in other working environments. The exceptions apply to:

(a) any pack of hounds;
(b) any dog while being used for sporting purposes;
(c) any dog while being used for the capture or destruction of vermin;
(d) any dog while being used for the driving or tending of cattle or sheep;
(e) any dog while being used on official duties by a member of Her Majesty's Armed Forces or Her Majesty's Customs and Excise or by the police force for any area;
(f) any dog while being used in emergency rescue work; or
(g) any dog registered with the Guide Dogs for the Blind Association.

Where a dog is found in a highway or place of public resort without the requisite collar, the owner or the person in charge of the dog who, without lawful authority or excuse, the proof whereof shall lie on him, causes or permits the dog to be there without a collar, shall be guilty of an offence.

Dogs on leads

Section 27 of the Road Traffic Act 1988 gives power to local authorities to make orders designating certain roads within their areas as roads in which dogs must be held on a lead. The chief officer of police must be consulted before such an order is made; the local authority must publish the making of the order and provide the necessary signs to indicate that particular roads are designated roads. The local authority, for the purposes of this section, means the county council or other area authority.

Any person who causes or permits a dog to be on a designated road without the dog being held on a lead shall be guilty of an offence. The particular orders may contain certain exceptions to the general rule, and the Road Traffic Act permits the following dogs to be on designated roads:

(a) dogs proved to be kept for driving or tending sheep or cattle in the course of a trade or business;
(b) dogs proved to have been, at the time, in use and proper control for sporting purposes.

The Dangerous Dogs Act 1991 requires that designated dogs (see s. 1 below at page 358) be muzzled and kept on a lead in a public place.

Stray dogs

The Environmental Protection Act 1990, s. 149, requires every local authority to appoint an officer to deal with stray dogs found in its area. Where the officer has reason to believe that any dog found in a public place or on any other land or premises is a stray dog, he must, where possible, seize it and detain it. Where the place concerned is not a public place, he may only seize and detain the dog with the consent of the owner or occupier of the place. Notice must be served by the officer on the person whose address appears on the dog's collar, or on the owner (if known), stating that the dog will be liable to be disposed of if it is not claimed within seven clear days and the expenses of its detention met. After the dog has been detained for seven clear days (or where a notice has been served if it has not been claimed and the expenses paid within seven clear days) the dog may be disposed of by way of sale or destruction. Where a dog is sold under the provisions of this section to a person acting in good faith, the ownership of the dog is vested in the recipient.

The officer must keep a register giving particulars of all dogs so seized and disposed of. The register must be available, at all reasonable times, for inspection by the public without charge. The officer must ensure that all such dogs are properly fed and looked after.

Section 150 of the Act requires the finder of a stray dog to:

(a) return it to the owner; or
(b) take the dog
    (i) to the appointed officer of the local authority for the area; or
    (ii) to the police station which is nearest to the place where the dog was found;

and to inform the officer of the local authority or the police officer in charge of the station where the dog was found. Failure to comply with these requirements is an offence. Where the dog has been taken to the appointed officer, the finder may keep the dog if he wishes, on informing the officer of this and his name and address. In such a case the finder must keep the dog for at least a month; he commits an offence if he fails to do so.

The Dogs Act 1906, s. 3, makes similar provisions in relation to the seizure, detention and disposal of stray dogs by the police but it is anticipated that, in consequence of the 1990 Act, such dogs will be detained by the local authority officer. Section 4 of the 1906 Act makes similar provision to that in s. 150 of the 1990 Act concerning the situation where the finder takes a stray dog to a police station and wishes to keep it. It provides that, on informing the police officer of this and of his name and address, he must be given a certificate which includes a description of the dog and gives details of its finding. The finder is, in consequence, obliged to keep the dog for a period of one month. If he does not he commits an offence. This must be explained to him before he agrees to keep the dog. If the finder does not wish to keep the dog it must be dealt with by the police by sale or destruction in the same way as described above in relation to an appointed local authority officer.

Further offences of 'straying' are discussed below under the heading 'Specific offences in relation to dangerous dogs'.

Dangerous dogs

(1) *General provisions*

The Dogs Act 1871 empowers a magistrates' court to hear any complaint concerning a dog which is alleged to be dangerous and not kept under proper control. The court may make an order requiring the owner to keep the dog under proper control or may order that it be destroyed. It may specify the measures to be taken to keep the dog under control and may require neutering of a male dog. A police officer is authorised to prefer a complaint under this Act. The fact that the incident occurred on private property is not relevant if other persons are permitted access, and such proceedings may be taken in relation to attacks upon livestock, even though proceedings are taken for another offence. The owner may appeal to a Crown Court against the decision of the magistrate.

On receipt of such a complaint, a constable should interview the complainant, or person attacked, and should record all relevant details in a statement and in his pocket notebook. If the dog concerned is subsequently traced it should be identified by such person in the presence of the owner, if this can be arranged. The owner should be informed of the nature of the complaint, including the damage or injury caused to persons or animals. It can be helpful in determining the truth of such an allegation if a careful note is made of the attitude of the dog towards your presence, although this is not by itself significant as dogs are usually quiet in the presence of their owner.

The Dangerous Dogs Act 1989 provides that a magistrates' court may appoint a person to undertake the destruction of a dog, when it makes such an order under the 1871 Act, and may require the person who has custody of the dog to deliver it up. It may also disqualify the owner from having custody of a dog for a specified period. There is an appeal to the Crown Court.

The 1989 Act also creates offences of failing to keep a dog under proper control as ordered under the 1871 Act, s. 2, and failing to deliver up a dog for destruction as ordered. These offences are punishable by fine and disqualification from having custody of a dog for a specified period.

(2) Specific offences in relation to dangerous dogs

The Dangerous Dogs Act 1991, ss. 1 and 3, makes further provisions in relation to dangerous dogs. The most important provision is s. 1(3) which makes it an offence for a person to have in his possession or control a dog to which s. 1 applies. The section applies to pit bull terriers, Japanese tosas and any dog of a type designated by order of the Secretary of State, currently Dogo Argentino and Fila Braziliera. 'Type' is not synonymous with 'breed' and it is a matter of fact to be determined by a court, whether a particular dog is of a type specified. In reaching a decision, a court is entitled to refer to works describing breed standards but it is not essential that a dog should have all of the characteristics described. The behavioural characteristics of the dog may be taken into account. However, by the Dangerous Dogs Compensation and Exemption Schemes Order 1991, this offence does not apply to a dog born before 30 November 1991 if the following set of conditions is satisfied:

(a) the person wishing to keep the dog must have notified the police of its address, name, age and gender;
(b) the dog must have been neutered;
(c) there must be third party insurance in respect of bodily harm caused by it, a certificate of exemption must have been issued; and

(d) its terms must have been complied with.

Section 1 prohibits breeding, selling, exchanging; giving or offering to give, advertising or exposing of such matters, of the dogs specified above in relation to lead, etc., and makes it an offence for the owner to abandon such a dog, or for the owner or person in charge of it to allow it to stray. Voluntary intoxication is no defence to a charge of allowing a dog of such a type to be in a public place without being muzzled.

Section 3 creates two offences. First, where a dog is dangerously out of control in a public place, the owner or the person for the time being in charge of it is guilty of an offence. The offence is aggravated if the dog, while so out of control, injures any person. These are offences of strict liability and there is no need to prove negligence by the owner or handler. The owner has a defence if he can prove that at the time of the offence the dog was in the charge of a person whom he reasonably believed to be a fit and proper person to be in charge of it. Where a woman was looking after a dog on behalf of another person who was in prison and locked the dog in the house and went out, the Court of Appeal ruled that she remained in charge although another occupant of the house had returned when the dog escaped and bit a small boy.

Secondly, the owner or person in charge of a dog commits an offence if he allows it to enter a place which is not a public place but where it is not permitted to be and while it is there, it injures any person, or there are grounds for reasonable apprehension that it will do so. An aggravated offence is committed if the dog does injure any person in these circumstances. Section 3 offences apply to all dogs.

Where a person is convicted of an offence against s. 1 or 3 the court may order destruction of the dog concerned. It *shall* do so in the case of a s. 1 offence and those aggravated offences contrary to s. 3. A court may also order a person convicted of any of these offences to be disqualified from keeping a dog for such a period as it thinks fit. Dogs may not be destroyed during the period allowed for notice of, and determination of, any appeal.

Similar provisions are made in the 1991 Act to those set out above in the 1989 Act in relation to the appointment of a person to undertake the destruction of a dog and requiring it to be delivered up for that purpose.

Offences are committed against s. 4(8) where a person has custody of a dog while so disqualified, or where he fails to deliver up a dog for destruction as ordered.

(3) *Dogs owned by young persons*

Where a dog is owned by a person who is less that 16 years old, the term 'owner' in the above provisions includes a reference to the head of the household, if any, of which that person is a member.

(4) *Police powers*

By s. 4 of the 1991 Act a constable (or authorised local authority officer) may seize any dog which appears to him to be a dog to which s. 1 applies and which is in a public place when its possession or custody is unlawful by virtue of s. 1, or when it is not muzzled or kept on a lead. Such a person may also seize *any* dog in a public place which appears to him to be dangerously out of control.

(5) *Public place*

It will be noted that some of the provisions of the Act are limited to a public place. The Act defines a 'public place' as any street, road or other place (whether or not enclosed) to which the public have or are permitted to have access. A private garden is not a public place in this context and neither is any other type of place which people enter by express or implied invitation. On the other hand, a dog in a private car on a public highway is in a public place.

Protection of livestock

The Dogs (Protection of Livestock) Act 1953 provides that if a dog worries livestock on any agricultural land, the owner of the dog and, if it is in the charge of some person other than the owner, that person also shall be guilty of an offence.

The term 'worrying livestock' means either attacking livestock, or chasing them in such a way that injury or suffering may reasonably be expected to be caused. The effects of chasing cattle or sheep which are about to give birth can result in the loss of their calf or lamb, and the Act includes such action within the definition of 'worrying' as well as the diminution in produce which is likely to occur when milking cows are pursued by dogs.

The Wildlife and Countryside Act 1981 extended the meaning of the term 'worrying of livestock' to include a dog being at large, that is not on a lead or otherwise under close control, in a field or enclosure in which there are sheep. If livestock are disturbed with the effects described, this will be an offence now if it results from attacking, chasing, or being at large. (Dogs of the occupier of the field, police dogs, guide dogs, trained sheep dogs, working gun dogs and packs of hounds are exempted from the 'being at large' provisions.)

'Livestock' includes cattle, sheep, goats, swine, horses, or poultry. The term 'cattle' means bulls, cows, oxen, heifers, or calves; 'horses' includes asses and mules; and 'poultry', domestic fowls, turkeys, geese, or ducks. 'Agricultural land' means land used as arable, meadow, or grazing land or for the purposes of poultry farming, pig farming, market gardens, allotments, nursery grounds, or orchards.

It is a defence for the owner of a dog to prove that, at the time at which the offence was committed, the dog was in charge of some person whom he reasonably believed to be a fit and proper person to be in charge of the dog. In addition, animals which are straying on the dog owners's land are not protected by this Act, unless the owner urges his dog to attack.

Police officers serving in all forces are likely to receive complaints concerning dogs which have been worrying livestock. The definition of the term 'agricultural land' is so wide that it includes smallholdings and even allotments which appear even within our large cities. Poultry is kept in many places which are protected by this Act and complaints are quite frequent. A constable is empowered to seize any dog, found on agricultural land, which he has reasonable cause to believe has been worrying livestock there if there is no one present in charge of it. He may deal with it as if it has been taken possession of as a stray.

Proceedings under the Dogs (Protection of Livestock) Act 1953 may be taken by the occupier of the land, by the owner of the livestock, or by the police. If the police take action, the Act requires that the consent of the chief officer of police is obtained and it is the general practice to have the information authorised by the chief constable. It is good practice for the officer reporting to check that this has been done before the date of the hearing.

The owner of livestock that has been killed or injured frequently asks advice concerning his entitlement to compensation. The Animals Act 1971 places liability upon the keeper of the dog, and compensation can be obtained by way of civil claim. This Act also protects a person charged with killing or injuring a dog, if he acted in protection of his livestock and gave notice to the police of his actions within 48 hours.

Guard dogs

Guard dogs used on premises must either be under the direct control of a 'handler' or so secured that they are not at liberty to go freely about the premises. A man kept three Alsatian dogs in a yard and premises which he owned. The dogs were independently fastened on separate chains 12 feet in length which did not permit them to reach the entry gate to the yard, nor all parts of the premises. There was no handler present. It was held that a person may lawfully use a guard dog on premises without a handler if the dog is properly secured. Whether a chain of 12 feet is to be regarded as 'not at liberty to go freely about the premises' is a question of fact and will vary in differing circumstances. Offences are committed by those who use or permit the use of a guard dog on premises unless it is under control.

Warning notices must be clearly displayed at each entrance to premises upon which guard dogs are used. It is an offence to fail to do so. The term 'guard dog' means a dog which is used to protect premises, property kept on premises, or a person guarding such premises or property. 'Premises' means land other than agricultural land and the curtilage of a dwelling house, and buildings, other than dwelling-houses.

Animals

Cruelty to animals

(1) *Animals generally*

The Protection of Animals Act 1911 sets out various offences involving cruelty to animals and states that the offences may be committed by any person carrying out any act, causing or procuring an act to be committed, or in the case of the owner, permitting such an act.

The offences include cruelty, kicking, beating, ill-treating, overriding, overdriving, overloading, torturing, infuriating, or terrifying any animal, as well as acts of commission or omission which cause unnecessary suffering. Each of the terms used creates a separate offence, and if we consider all instances in which we have witnessed an animal being ill-treated in the past, it is quite probable that one of these words will describe the particular form of unpleasantness. The owner who savagely corrects his dog, the itinerant collector who overloads or overworks his horse, and

361

the owner or keeper of animals who neglects them are all guilty of offences contrary to this Act. Where it is alleged that there has been an unreasonable omission to act, the test to be applied is concerned with what a reasonably caring, reasonably competent owner would do in the circumstances. The tethering of horses, asses and mules under conditions or in such a manner as to cause unnecessary suffering is also punishable under this section.

Offences of cruelty can also be committed by transporting animals in a manner which causes suffering, by carrying out careless or inhumane operations, by administering poisonous or injurious drugs, or by fighting or baiting animals. In this way, amateur operations and such sports as bull fighting are made illegal. Cockfighting is still arranged in some parts of the British Isles and those concerned with its organisation are punishable under these provisions. In addition, the Cockfighting Act 1952 punishes the possession of instruments or appliances for use in this connection.

For the purposes of the Protection of Animals Act, the term 'animal' means any domestic or captive animal. 'Domestic animals' include fowl and all other animals which are tame or are being sufficiently tamed to serve some purpose useful to man. 'Captive animals' are those which are in captivity, confinement, or are subjected to any contrivance to prevent escape. This Act is not intended in normal circumstances to protect wild animals, and it has been held that wild rabbits caught and kept in confinement for a few days before being released for the purpose of being coursed are not captive animals, nor is a hunted stag which is temporarily unable to escape before being killed. Similarly, it has been held that the cruel maiming of a hedgehog by repeatedly beating it with a stick does not make that animal a 'captive animal' and that the trapping of a wild squirrel in a tree does not make it 'captive' for the purposes of the Act. Legislation to protect 'wild' animals is being considered.

The Abandonment of Animals Act 1960 punishes the owner, or person who has charge or control of any animal, if he, without reasonable excuse, abandons it whether permanently or not, in circumstances likely to cause unnecessary suffering. The offence is one of cruelty as set out in the Act of 1911 and carries the same penalty. Publicity is frequently given to the abandonment of puppies given as Christmas presents to children.

'Abandonment' in the present context does not require permanent abandonment, although it means something more than merely leaving unattended. For abandonment, there must be a leaving unattended of the animal in circumstances where suffering is likely and where there is sufficient evidence to prove that the accused had relinquished, wholly disregarded or given up his duty of care for the animal. Where a person has made or attempted to make arrangements for the animal's welfare during a period where he cannot look after it himself, there is no abandonment.

Persons who, without reasonable excuse, are present when animals are placed together for the purpose of fighting each other, commit an offence. Those who publish, or cause to be published, an advertisement for such a fight, knowing that it is such an advertisement, also commit an offence. The offences are particularly relevant to dog fights.

Further protection is given to animals by the Pet Animals Act 1951, which requires pet shops to be licensed and prescribes conditions under which animals must be kept.

(2) *Badgers*

The Protection of Badgers Act 1992 provides particular protection for wild badgers. It creates offences of wilfully killing, injuring or taking a badger or attempting to do any of these acts. If there is evidence from which it could be reasonably concluded that at the material time the accused was attempting to do any of these acts he shall be presumed to have been doing so unless the contrary is shown.

There are further offences of possession of a dead badger, a part of, or anything derived from a badger but it is a defence to show that the badger had not been killed in contravention of the Act, or the part, etc., of it was in the possession of a person who had no reason to believe that the badger had been killed in contravention of the Act. Offences of cruelty consist of cruel ill-treatment, the use of badger tongs, digging for badgers, or the use of other than prescribed heavy firearms. In addition, it is an offence to interfere with a badger sett by damaging, destroying, obstructing access to, causing a dog to enter, or disturbing a badger when it is occupying a sett. The sale of badgers is also prohibited.

Acts which consist of taking a badger which has been injured for the purpose of tending it, or killing a badger which appears to have been so seriously injured or in such condition that to kill it would be an act of mercy, are exempted from the provisions of the Act.

Police powers

A constable may arrest without warrant any person whom he reasonably believes to be guilty of an offence contrary to s. 1 of the Protection of Animals Act 1911 (the offences listed at (1) above), whether:

(a) in his own view; or
(b) on the complaint of a third person who gives his name and address.

The power of arrest does not extend to offences under s. 1(2), which is concerned with owners who permit cruelty by failing to exercise reasonable care and supervision in protecting an animal from cruelty. A constable is also empowered to take charge of the animal and vehicle where applicable, and to arrange for custody and care. If veterinary treatment is needed, the cost, in addition to the cost of custody, must be paid as costs of the case upon the owner's conviction. If some other person is convicted, such expenses may be recovered from the owner as a civil debt.

Arrests for these offences are now rare as it is usually possible to establish the offender's identity and to proceed by way of summons. The itinerant collector, who is often of no fixed abode, may have to be arrested to ensure that he appears before a court.

Where a constable has reasonable grounds for suspecting that a person is committing an offence under the Protection of Badgers Act 1992, or has committed such an offence and that evidence of the commission of the offence is to be found on that person or any vehicle or article he may have with him, the constable may without warrant stop and search that person, vehicle or article. He may seize and detain anything which may be evidence of the commission of such an offence.

Animals ill or injured

The section of the Protection of Animals Act 1911, which gives a constable power to deal with animals which are ill or injured, defines the term 'animal' as including a horse, mule, ass, bull, cow, sheep, goat, or pig. It is concerned with farm animals and, by exclusion of dogs and cats, eliminates the most likely instances which a constable will meet. However, to ensure that correct veterinary attention is given, most police forces follow a similar procedure when these animals are injured in road accidents.

When a constable finds an animal in such a condition through disease or injury that it cannot be removed without cruelty, he shall, if the owner is absent or refuses to have the animal destroyed:

(a) send for a veterinary surgeon; who may
(b) certify in writing giving the reasons why it would be cruel to keep the animal alive; and then
(c) arrange for the animal to be humanely destroyed; and
(d) if on a highway, removed.

If the veterinary surgeon certifies that the animal may be moved without causing unnecessary suffering, it is the owner's responsibility to arrange it, but if he cannot be found, or fails to do so, the constable may make the necessary arrangements. All expenses may be recovered from the owner as a civil debt.

Animals straying

The keeper, or person in whose possession animals may be, is guilty of an offence contrary to s. 155 of the Highways Act 1980 if horses, cattle, sheep, goats, or swine are found, at any time, straying on the highway or lying at the side of a highway. The provisions of this section do not apply to highways passing over any common, waste, or unenclosed land. Such highways usually carry signs which warn drivers that their way passes over unenclosed land and that animals are likely to be encountered.

Police officers who find animals straying on the highway may return them to the owner's or keeper's land, or to any other place provided for the safe custody of animals. Many years ago, common pounds were provided for the purpose of containing animals found straying, but are now extremely rare. Police officers, in instances in which the owner is not known, are compelled to make some arrangements for the security of the animals, but it is advisable to avoid securing them in any field in which other animals are already grazing. If non-tested cattle are placed in a field of tested cattle, a claim may lie against the police in respect of the expense involved in re-testing cattle.

When animals are impounded in this way, the person doing so is responsible for their well-being and must ensure that they are properly fed and watered until the owner is traced. When traced, the owner should be reported for the offence. He is responsible for any expenses involved in the care of the animals.

The Rabies (Importation of Dogs, Cats and Other Mammals) Order 1974 prohibits the landing of such animals in Great Britain if brought from a place outside Great Britain. However, the prohibition does not apply if the animal has been detained and isolated in quarantine for a period of at least six months before being landed in Great Britain. Otherwise, landing will only be permitted if it is in accordance with a licence granted by the Minister of Agriculture. One of the conditions of such a licence will be that it is similarly quarantined on arrival in Great Britain. In certain restricted circumstances, the importation of dogs and cats from another member State of the EU is permitted without a licence in accordance with the terms of Council Directive 92/65/EEC. The Directive is concerned with commercial transactions and requires vaccination and that the animals concerned were born on a registered holding and have remained there, in captivity, with no contact with wild animals susceptible to rabies. Certificates will be in existence authorising such importation.

Police powers

The Animal Health Act 1981, s. 61, provides that a constable may arrest without warrant any person whom he, with reasonable cause, suspects to be in the act of committing or to have committed an offence to which s. 61 applies. Section 61 applies to:

(a) the landing or attempted landing of any animal or importation or attempted importation through the tunnel system as defined in the Channel Tunnel Act 1987 of any animal in contravention of an order made under this Act and expressed to be made for the purpose of preventing the introduction of rabies into Great Britain; or

(b) the failure by the person having the charge or control of any vessel or boat to discharge any obligation imposed on him in that capacity by such an order; or

(c) the movement, in contravention of an order under s. 17 or s. 23 of the Act of any animal into, within or out of a place or area declared to be infected with rabies. (Section 17 is concerned with powers which relate to infected areas or places and s. 23 with orders made in relation to such areas or places.)

In addition, s. 62 of the Act provides that for the purpose of arresting a person under the power conferred by s. 61 a constable may enter (if need be by force) and search any vessel, boat, aircraft or vehicle of any other description in which that person is or in which the constable, with reasonable cause, suspects him to be.

For the purpose of exercising any power to seize an animal or to cause an animal to be seized, and:

(a) where that power is conferred on constables by an order made under this Act; and

(b) where that power is expressed to be made for the purpose of preventing the introduction of rabies into Great Britain, a constable may enter (if need be by force) and search any vessel, boat, aircraft or vehicle of any other description in which there is, or in which he, with reasonable cause, suspects that there is, an animal to which that power applies.

Fires and major incidents involving dangerous substances carried by road

Initial action – fire

There are a number of ways in which the presence of fire in buildings, or in other places at which there is a threat to public safety, may come to the attention of a police officer. In all circumstances, his initial action must recognise his duty to protect life and property. While patrolling a beat at night, police officers frequently discover fires and, because they are so easily visible in their early stages, it is often possible to take effective action immediately to extinguish or at least control the outbreak. It is, therefore, inadvisable to offer a list of rules which must be strictly observed; the constable must exercise his discretion and decide upon the most effective action to be taken at the time. Personal radio has removed the greater cause of delay: the necessity to reach a telephone in order to alert emergency services. Fires discovered by the police usually receive prompt attention as all constables are trained to act quickly and sensibly in times of emergency.

Difficulties can be encountered when reports are made to police officers by telephone, or orally, by members of the public who are usually highly excited and are not trained to give concise, essential information. It is important to establish whether or not the fire service has been informed, and it can be dangerous to assume that any telephone message passed to the fire service by a member of the public is sufficiently complete to ensure the arrival of tenders at the correct location. Many members of the public use the telephone badly in times of emergency and may have reported a fire, impressing upon the recipient of their message the need for speedy assistance, without giving its location before replacing the receiver. It is much safer to pass the correct information to your police office and to request that a check is made to ensure that the fire service telephone operator has all the information necessary to allow him to take effective action. When initial reports of this nature are received, it will be possible to decide whether other emergency services should be alerted. If it appears likely that people are trapped in the building, or will have difficulty in escaping, a request for the attendance of an ambulance is advisable to avoid unnecessary delay in their removal from the scene of the incident. Immediate medical attention is essential to persons suffering from severe burns or suffocation.

Usually, the radio message to Control requesting confirmation that the fire service operator has received a full report will ensure that supervisory officers and a keyholder are informed, but if the incident appears likely to be a serious one it is advisable that their attendance is specifically requested. As much information as possible should be obtained concerning persons who are likely to be in the building from the person making the report, from neighbours, or from the owners of the premises. It will be of considerable assistance to those responsible for the rescue of trapped people if information is also gathered concerning the likely places in which such persons may be located. If a fire is spreading rapidly, it is frequently impossible to search an entire building and it is preferable that limited search time is spent to the best advantage.

Duties and responsibilities

A police officer's first duty is always to preserve life, and if fire is discovered in a building the occupants should be warned and removed as speedily as possible, as should those occupying buildings in a dangerous proximity. After alerting the necessary emergency services, the constable should take any steps within his power to extinguish or at least contain the outbreak. If further police assistance arrives and is not required for immediate rescue operations, measures should be taken to ensure that easy access is maintained for rescue services. The Fire Services Act 1947 empowers the senior police officer present, or in the absence of the police, the senior fire officer, to close any street to traffic or to stop or regulate traffic in any street whenever, in the opinion of such officer, it is necessary or desirable to do so. If the fire is one which is likely to spread quickly, such measures will have to be considered and action taken quickly if chaos is to be avoided. Members of the public will arrive in considerable numbers – even in the early hours of the morning – if there is something unusual to look at, and their presence can seriously hinder effective fire fighting operations. Major outbreaks of fire involve the presence of a large number of pumping appliances, and hose reels are likely to be laid across sections of the roadway in considerable numbers. The fire service frequently provides ramps which can be laid in conjunction with their hose pipes to allow traffic to pass cautiously, but it is often more efficient to divert traffic and this becomes essential if there is any danger of building collapse.

Police problems are increased if it becomes necessary to pump water from rivers or canals over considerable distances as complex operations to control traffic movement become necessary. It is on occasions such as these that individual police officers carrying out traffic control duties some distance from the scene of the incident may question the necessity for their presence for lengthy periods of time performing functions for which the reasons are not apparent. Some incidents involve danger to members of the public over a considerable area, and where buildings used for the storage of highly flammable or explosive substances are involved, a complex scheme of evacuation must be planned and put into effect. Having ensured the removal of all persons from buildings, the preservation of animal life and property may be considered and during incidents which involve evacuation of certain areas, it must be remembered that the police are responsible for the safety of the property of those removed and that looting must be prevented. Causes of fire are always of relevance to the police, and the observations of the fire prevention officer when the outbreak has been finally controlled can be extremely important in subsequent enquiries to determine whether or not an offence of arson has been committed. The owners, occupiers, or keyholders of affected premises must be informed as soon as possible in all instances of fire and asked to attend as quickly as possible. Their knowledge of the inside of buildings can be of major assistance to the senior fire officer present.

The senior police officer present is in charge of police operations and is responsible for the control of the area surrounding the fire; in the same way, the senior fire officer is in charge of fire fighting operations. The Fire Services Act 1947 gives him this power and states that he shall be in sole charge and control of any operations for the extinction of fire, including the fixing of positions of fire engines and apparatus and the attaching of hose to any water pipes. Any person who wilfully obstructs or interferes with any member of a fire brigade who is engaged in operations for fire fighting purposes shall be guilty of an offence.

It is essential for the police to liaise closely with the senior officer present at every stage. If at any point there is the slightest doubt concerning the origin of the fire, or a hint that it may not have been an accident, a supervisory officer must be informed.

Remember that a burned building is a damaged building and it is therefore insecure. Thieves will take advantage of easy access, so be on your guard against the possibility of looting.

Rescue procedure

Most casualties are probably caused by smoke, fumes, and heat rather than by the flames themselves and it is important that all rescue personnel, including police officers, observe elementary safety procedures. On entering buildings one must shield against the impact of hot gases and smoke. These will instantly be released when a door is opened or entry is forced and a rescuer must keep out of line. Shelter behind the wall as the door is opened. Because of this surge effect, it is essential to keep as many doors and windows closed as is possible in the circumstances. It is also sensible to break in as far away from the seat of the fire as possible, unless there is a clear access closer to it which has proved to be safe. The opening of an access door, etc., will allow air to rush in which will accelerate the spread of the fire by feeding it with oxygen. Smouldering material will often burst into flames immediately a door is opened. In smoke filled rooms, cleaner air is always to be found closer to the floor and it can, therefore, be better to enter on all fours or to crawl on the stomach. If it is possible, keep close to walls as the floor joists are at their strongest at this point. They may have been weakened by fire closer to the centre of the room. A wet handkerchief placed over the mouth and nose will assist as it will exclude quite a proportion of the irritant fumes. If the hands are being used to attempt to locate casualties, use the back of the hand to feel around the room. If the open palm touches live electric wires, the fingers will automatically clasp the live wires.

Buildings should be searched methodically. The first task should be to examine the area in greatest danger quickly, so that casualties can be removed before the situation there becomes impossible. In all other circumstances search the top of the building where people will be in the greatest danger from rising smoke. Observe the rules and ensure your own safety at all times; you are of no use to the public if you make yourself a casualty. When the rescue of persons is obviously beyond you, ensure that the senior fire officer is quickly informed of places in the building where people are known to be, the number of persons who are likely to be there, and their probable location.

Persons with their clothing on fire should be laid flat to prevent flames creeping up towards their faces. Panic may have deprived them of their reason and it may be necessary to execute a flying rugby tackle to save their lives. When in the prone position the flames should be smothered with some heavy material such as woollen garments, coats or jackets. Fires caused by oil or electricity leaks present special hazards as the use of water is absolutely prohibited. When it can be done, the source of supply should be shut off.

Particular action when fire of doubtful origin

Collect as much information as possible from the senior fire officer and inform Control and a supervisory officer of your concern and give the reasons for that concern. A senior police officer will then attend the scene. Immediately the fire is under control, ensure that the scene is preserved for a careful and thorough examination by experts. No one must be allowed access to the scene unless authorised. Identify and take the names of persons present who were witnesses to the outbreak, or of any persons showing particular interest in the fire. Persons acting in any way suspiciously should be identified and if there are reasonable suspicions of implication, such persons should be detained.

Particulars to note

A comprehensive report will be required at the conclusion of any major incident involving fire, and on all occasions it will be necessary to make every effort to trace the cause of the fire. Fatalities will necessitate an inquest and accurate records of events as they occurred are essential. A simple rule to follow is to record the times of arrival of all persons and services and to record immediately the full particulars of the person who first reported the fire and any witnesses who may be present. In cases of extreme urgency, it may be difficult to record the personal details of the informant as the public become impatient if police officers do not effect immediate personal actions. In such circumstances, the person reporting should be asked to accompany the constable to the scene. Details should be recorded of all persons who have left the building. The last to leave is of particular importance as he will be able to give a more accurate account of the spread of fire, the parts of the building affected, and persons who are likely to be there.

When the fire has been extinguished, enquiries should be made of witnesses in an attempt to establish as clearly as possible the time of the outbreak, and an assessment of the extent of the damage should be made. The identity of the senior fire officer present and any fire prevention officer who may be called to the scene should be established. These officers will ultimately be able to provide a fairly accurate estimate of the extent of the damage and be able to give useful information as to the possible cause. If arson is suspected, detailed statements should be taken from such experts and any material they may discover which indicates the likelihood of the fire having been started deliberately should be preserved and packed for laboratory examination by crime officers at the scene. All forms of police fire reports require information concerning the insurance cover of the buildings damaged.

Force orders should be studied before reports are submitted as they are not always required following minor fires.

Police powers

The powers of the senior police officer at the scene of a fire have already been described. In addition, the Fire Services Act 1947 authorises constables to enter, if necessary by breaking in, any premises or place in which fire has, or is reasonably believed to have, broken out. Such an entry may also be made of adjoining premises in order to protect them from acts done for fire fighting purposes, or for rescuing persons. The consent of the owner or occupier of premises is not required on any of these occasions.

False alarms of fire

Any person who knowingly gives, or causes to be given, a false alarm of fire to any fire brigade shall be guilty of an offence.

Incidents involving dangerous substances

The Road Traffic (Carriage of Dangerous Substances in Road Tankers and Tank Containers) Regulations 1992 are concerned with the conveyance by road of various substances which, in the event of an accident, or a leak in a storage tank, would be dangerous.

Road tankers and containers which are used for carrying specified dangerous substances by road are required to display hazard warning panels on such vehicles and containers. The conveyance of dangerous substances by road cannot be undertaken without some element of danger existing for the public and particularly for rescue services, such as police and fire officers who will be called upon to deal with accidents or other mishaps which might occur in relation to such vehicles. Road tankers are vehicles with a tank which is an integral part of the vehicle or is structurally attached to it. The term includes 'tube trailers' which are vehicles with more than one gas cylinder structurally attached to it. A tank container is a container carried on a vehicle which is not in itself a road tanker and may be a tube container, i.e. a group of gas cylinders fitted into a framework suitable for lifting on or off a vehicle. Substances which are dangerous are specified in Schedule 1 to the Road Traffic (Carriage of Dangerous Substances in Road Tankers and Tank Containers) Regulations 1992 or which have been so specified by the Health and Safety Executive.

The driver of such vehicles will carry written information as to the load he is carrying. This document must be produced at the request of a constable or vehicle examiner. The operator and driver must ensure that hazard warning panels are fixed and displayed on the vehicle, one being at the rear on road tankers and one on each side of the vehicle, near to the front on road tankers and tank containers. The hazard warning panels must show certain information.

(1) The emergency action code

This will consist of a single number between 1 and 4 followed by a single letter, for example, 2R. Police officers carry a Hazchem Scale Card which sets out the meaning of these symbols. The Action Code will be on the top left of the plate. The number 1 indicates that the hazard may be tackled with water jets; 2 indicates 'fog' but in the absence of such equipment a spray may be used; 3 indicates 'foam'; and 4 a dry agent. The letters which follow indicate whether the substance may be diluted or needs to be contained (P, R, S, and T are used in relation to substances which may be diluted and W, X, Y, and Z are those which must be contained); and the need for protective clothing and breathing apparatus (P and R indicate that full protective measures are necessary, but S, if a black letter on a white background, means that breathing apparatus is required at all times and white on a black background means that breathing apparatus is required only if there is a fire involving the substance carried). The letter T is treated in the same way. W and X also require full protective measures at all times, while the significance of Y and Z varies in the same way as S and T. The letter E is most important as if that symbol is shown, evacuation needs to be considered. It is essential that the Hazchem Card is carried at all times as it is impossible to retain the meaning of each symbol and letter in the memory.

(2) *The substance identification number*

Each specified substance has a number. It appears in the section below the emergency action code. The name of the substance is also shown on many occasions, for example, hydrochloric acid. Where a multi-load is being carried (consisting of two or more dangerous substances carried separately), the plate will show, in place of the substance identification number the words 'MULTI-LOAD'.

(3) *The hazard warning sign*

This appears to the right of the previous two numbers. The sign is diagrammatic, for example acids, etc., will show liquid spilling from test tubes on to substances and on to the hand and will carry the word 'corrosive' below. When a multi-load is being carried, the diagram will be in the form of an exclamation mark.

(4) *Telephone number*

The telephone number at which specialist advice can be obtained at all times, together with the name of the manufacturer or owner will also be shown.

It is essential that police officers arriving at the scene of any incident involving dangerous substances initiate the correct action at once. Using their cards they should identify as much information as possible and give Control full details of the hazard warning panel.

Conveyance other than in tankers or tank containers

The 1992 Regulations require the drivers of vehicles which carry dangerous substances in receptacles to carry, and produce to police officers or traffic examiners on request, written information as to the nature of the load and its hazards. If 500 kilograms or more are carried on the vehicle it must display a rectangular orange plate to the front and to the rear. Vehicles carrying 3 tonnes or more must be parked in a safe place or be adequately safeguarded. The operator and driver shall ensure that no dangerous substance is carried in any vehicle in which food is being carried unless the food is carried in a part of the vehicle effectively separated from that containing the substance, or is otherwise adequately protected from the risk of contamination.

The regulations apply to certain dangerous substances, for example organic peroxides, when they are carried in quite small quantities. Most dangerous substances are only covered by the regulations when carried in receptacles with a capacity of 200 litres or more.

Explosives

The carriage of certain explosives is prohibited in a vehicle. The carriage of any form of explosives in a vehicle used to carry passengers for hire and reward is prohibited, otherwise than within strict conditions.

When explosives are carried, vehicles must carry at the front and rear reflectorised orange plates with a black border. They must also carry side-marker plates on each side of the vehicle, trailer, semi-trailer or freight container in which explosives are carried, of diamond shape, which are orange in colour with a black border, bearing certain letters in black according to the type of explosives carried. The letters may be 1.2E (with a symbol of an explosion above), or 1.4 with the letter 'E' below. If the explosives carried have not yet been classified, such plates may only carry the symbol of an explosion.

Offences

The operator must ensure that hazard warning panels are fixed and displayed correctly on road tankers and tank containers. The driver must ensure that such hazard warning panels are kept clean and are properly displayed.

It is also the duty of the operator to ensure that the driver is given written information concerning the nature of the load and the driver must ensure that this information is kept in the cab of the vehicle. Old written notices of loads must be removed, destroyed or kept in a locked container so that there can be no confusion in respect of the load which is carried.

Police powers

Chief constables may appoint certain officers, in writing, to be inspectors for the purposes of the Health and Safety at Work Act. An officer so appointed has the power to detain a road tanker or tank container for the purpose of examining its contents.

Training of drivers and police powers

The operators of vehicles used for the carriage of dangerous goods, including radioactive material, are required by the Road Traffic (Training of Drivers of Vehicles Carrying Dangerous Goods) Regulations 1992 to ensure that drivers of such vehicles are properly trained. Drivers must hold 'vocational training certificates' which must be carried in the vehicle and produced to a police constable or a goods vehicle examiner on request. Drivers who had been driving such vehicles for the period of five years preceding 1 July 1992 may alternatively hold 'provisional training certificates'. Other drivers may hold 'existing training certificates' some of which may continue in force until 1 July 1997, others until 1 January 2000.

Licensed premises, registered clubs, refreshment houses, and drunkenness

Licensed premises

(1) *Generally*

The term 'licensed premises' is defined by s. 200 of the Licensing Act 1964. This definition includes premises for which a justices' licence (or an occasional licence) is in force for the sale of intoxicating liquor to members of the public. Justices' licences are granted at the annual general licensing sessions or at transfer sessions which must be held at least four times a year. Licences are valid for a period of three years. There is a general renewal date every three years. A full on-licence generally authorises sale of all kinds of intoxicating liquor for consumption on or off the premises. An off-licence authorises sale for consumption off the premises only. The term 'intoxicating liquor' means spirits, wine, beer, cider, and any other fermented, distilled, or spirituous liquor of a strength of 0.5 per cent or more. Low alcohol drinks are, therefore, intoxicating liquor. Generally, any form of liquor which does not require an excise licence to permit sale by wholesale, is not intoxicating liquor – the exception being cider. A shandy, which is a mixture of beer and lemonade, is intoxicating liquor.

(2) *Restaurant and residential licences*

Restaurant licences may be granted for premises which are structurally adapted and bona fide used, or intended to be used, for the purpose of providing the customary main meal at midday, or in the evening, or both, for the accommodation of persons frequenting the premises. We are therefore considering establishments which provide either or both of the main meals of the day. Sale and supply of intoxicants is permitted to persons taking table meals on the premises, the drinks being consumed as an ancillary to the meal. Persons who are not eating there may not drink there.

Residential licences are granted to private hotels or boarding houses which provide breakfast and at least one of the customary main meals. Sale or supply of intoxicants is restricted to residents or their private friends who must be entertained at their expense. If meals are offered to the general public and drinks are to be supplied with those meals, a combined restaurant/residential licence would be required.

(3) *Occasional licence*

The definition includes premises in respect of which an occasional licence is in force. These licences are granted at magistrates' courts to allow intoxicating liquor to be sold at certain special events and are granted only to the holder of justices' on-licences (permitting sale of intoxicating liquor for consumption on the premises), allowing them to sell elsewhere than on their licensed premises the forms of liquor specified in their licence. An occasional licence may be valid for a period not exceeding three weeks. Such a licence may not be granted in respect of Good Friday, Christmas Day or any other appointed day of public fast or thanksgiving. At race meetings, sporting events, flower shows, dances, and other social events, beer tents or occasional bars may have been set up by an on-licence holder who is temporarily selling intoxicating liquor at premises other than his established licensed premises. In such circumstances, the hours during which he is allowed to sell liquor are specified in the occasional licence and normal permitted hours do not apply. During the validity of the licence, the premises are licensed premises and the various offences which may be committed by the holder of a justices' licence may also be committed by the holder of an occasional licence. Thus, he may not permit drunkenness, violence or unlawful gaming to take place on the premises, or unlawful sales to be made to persons who are under age.

However, drinking-up time provisions (explained below) cannot apply to occasional licences because the licence expires at a given time and when that occurs the premises are no longer licensed. If a sale takes place outside the hours specified in the licence, it is a sale other than as authorised by a justices' licence.

(4) Occasional permission

Licensing justices can grant to an officer of any organisation not carried on for the purpose of private gain, occasional permission to sell intoxicating liquor during any period not exceeding 24 hours, in respect of a function held by the organisation which is allied to its activities. Such permissions must specify the place, type of intoxicants to be sold and the hours. An organisation may not have more than four occasional permissions in any year. The justice may attach conditions to such permissions should they consider it proper to do so.

The Licensing (Occasional Permissions) Act 1983 was introduced to remove some of the inconsistencies within the system of occasional licensing. Before this procedure was set up, a non-licensed (registered or proprietary, see below) club was compelled to ask a licensee to obtain an occasional licence whenever it held a function upon the premises at which non-members would be allowed to purchase drinks, as such clubs are not permitted to sell to non-members.

Where the profits made from sales under the authority of occasional permissions go to the club or organisation, there is no *private gain*. Thus, a club may operate its own bar at a function to which non-members are admitted.

Section 3 of the Act gives authority to various offences contained in the schedule to the Act including permitting drunkenness and sales, etc., to persons under 18. The same powers of exclusion and expulsion are given as are given to licensees and the same powers are given to constables in this respect (see below). A power of entry exists for a constable at any time during the hours specified in the occasional permission.

(5) *Public entry*

A public house with open doors inviting the public to enter is a public place. The fact that certain people are excluded by law from entering and that others may be excluded at the will of the landlord does not prevent it from being public. A 'bar' in licensed premises is any place mainly or exclusively used for the sale *and* consumption of intoxicating liquor.

Licensing hours

A licensee, his servant, or agent shall not sell or supply any intoxicating liquor, whether to be consumed on or off the licensed premises, outside the general licensing hours described in the Licensing Act 1964. The hours prescribed are:

    (a) Weekdays (other than Christmas Day or Good Friday) 11.00 to 23.00;
    (b) Sundays (other than Christmas Days) and on Good Friday 12.00 to 22.30;
    (c) Christmas Day 12.00 to 22.30 with a break of 4 hours beginning at 15.00.

The hours prescribed in relation to off-licensed premises are from 08.00 to 23.00 on weekdays. On Sundays, they are the same as those which apply to on-licensed premises.

(1) *Special requirements of the district*

On weekdays, the licensing justices for any licensing district, if satisfied that the requirements of the district make it desirable, may by order modify the hours for the district so that the permitted hours begin at a time earlier than 11.00 but not earlier than 10.00 in the morning.

(2) *Meals*

In instances in which intoxicating liquor is supplied during the permitted hours, if supplied for consumption as an ancillary to a meal, it may be consumed during the half hour following permitted hours.

The legal meaning of the term 'meal' has never been strictly defined. In general circumstances it does not necessarily mean table meals. If meals are being served in premises which are fully on-licensed, advantage may be taken of this extended drinking-up time without full table meals being provided, but if the licence has been granted in respect of a restaurant it will be upon the condition that either the main midday meal, or evening meal, or both such meals will be provided. What constitutes a meal is a matter for the justices. It is unlikely that toasted sandwiches from a machine would be considered sufficient. The consumption of drink as an ancillary to a meal does not mean that it must be supplied at the same time as the meal or drunk with the meal. It can be taken as an aperitif prior to the meal or as a drink to follow up a meal, and in either case can be taken in the separate room usually set apart for such purpose. It is a question of fact to be determined by the magistrates, when drinking away from the table ceases to be ancillary to the meal.

Apart from this general provision in respect of premises supplying meals, in instances in which premises are structurally suitable and are bona fide used for providing substantial table meals with an ancillary supply of liquor, licensed premises or registered clubs may be granted a supper hour extension of one hour to the evening permitted hours on weekdays. This extension is granted at a magistrates' court and will only apply to the part of the premises set apart for table meals. The provisions permitting 'drinking-up' time of half an hour following a meal apply to premises with a supper hour extension, so that drinking with a meal can lawfully continue until 00.30 hours. A lunch hour extension permits such premises to serve intoxicants with a meal throughout the period between the first and second parts of licensing hours on Sundays, Christmas Day and Good Friday.

(3) *Entertainment*

The Licensing Act 1964, s. 70, states that justices may, by order, extend permitted hours until 01.00 on weekdays for premises in respect of which a supper hour certificate has been granted. Musical or other entertainment must be provided by persons who are actually present (which excludes recorded music) and the premises must be suitable for such entertainment and for the supply of meals. The sale and supply of intoxicants must be ancillary to the provision of meals and entertainment. The extension will only apply to the part of the premises set aside for these purposes.

While the section permits extended hours until 01.00 hours, the justices may limit the order to a time earlier than 01.00 hours if it appears to them reasonable to do so having regard to all the circumstances, particularly in relation to the comfort and convenience of those in nearby premises.

Such an order, in effect, permits sale and supply of intoxicating liquor up to the time at which the availability of meals, or the provision of such entertainment ceases and to allow the consumption of those intoxicants within the terms of the normal half-hour drinking-up time following the end of permitted hours where meals are being taken. Thus, if no meals or entertainment are offered after 23.30 hours, licensing hours end then and drinking must cease at midnight.

Sections 76–83 of the 1964 Act authorise a special hours certificate to be granted to licensed premises or a registered club which has a music and dancing licence, or in the case of a club, a certificate of suitability. The premises concerned must be structurally adapted and used or intended to be used in good faith for music and dancing and the supply of substantial refreshments, to which the sale of intoxicants is ancillary. In such cases the permitted hours on weekdays extend until 02.00 hours on the next morning (03.00 hours in specified parts of the metropolis). However, if on any day, music and dancing is not provided after midnight, permitted hours end at midnight. If the music and dancing end at any time between midnight and 02.00 hours permitted hours end with the music and dancing.

Sales out of hours

An offence is committed against s. 59 of the Act by any person who, himself or by his servant or agent, sells or supplies intoxicating liquor in licenced premises or in a registered club, whether to be drunk on or off the premises, outside permitted hours.

An offence is also committed by any person who drinks on the premises, or takes intoxicants away from such premises, outside permitted hours.

General and special orders of exemption

The holder of a justices' on-licence or the secretary of a registered club may be granted a 'general order of exemption' when the premises in question are situated in the immediate neighbourhood of a public market or place where people follow a particular trade or calling. Many market towns have a market day upon which farmers and residents gather from a large catchment area. The influx of such a large number of people makes it desirable that places of refreshment are open and available to them. The licensing hours are as specified in the order of exemption and registers are kept in police stations in which details of such orders are recorded. Orders are made in respect of named licensed premises.

The same persons may apply to a magistrates' court for a 'special order of exemption'. Here we are concerned with the extension of licensing hours in particular premises on a special occasion. That which is a special occasion has not been defined but the Divisional Court has indicated that the more frequently a particular 'occasion' arises, the less likely it is to be special. Weekly debates at the Oxford Union which were held over a period of eight weeks were held not to be special occasions. Special occasions are usually associated with weddings, twenty-first birthday parties and annual dinners. Each of these occasions is 'special' to the person or organisation concerned. Once it is granted, a special order automatically applies to the whole of the premises and is not restricted to the room in which the function is held. As a result, the justices frequently demand an undertaking that normal licensing hours will be observed in other parts of the premises. Nevertheless, if that undertaking is ignored, no offence is committed in relation to sales. Such an order may be valid for more than one day.

Exemptions to licensing hours

The permitted hours do not prohibit or restrict drinking in certain circumstances:

(a) A resident in licensed premises may drink outside permitted hours and may entertain guests at his own expense. Such guests must be private friends.

(b) These provisions extend to the licence holder and any of his servants who are resident on the premises. Whether such persons are true, as opposed to pretended, friends and were truly entertained at the resident's expense are matters to be determined by the magistrates.

(c) 'Drinking-up' time of 20 minutes is allowed at the end of normal permitted hours so that glasses may be emptied when sales have ended. Bottles purchased before the end of permitted hours may be taken from the premises during this time.

Police entry

For the purposes of preventing and detecting the commission of any of these offences against the Licensing Act 1964 a constable is empowered by s. 186 of the

377

Act to enter licensed premises, a licensed canteen (licensed by the Secretary of State), or premises for which (or any part of which) a special hours certificate is in force:

(a) in the case of licensed premises or licensed canteens, during permitted hours and during the first half-hour after the end of any period of permitted hours;

(b) where an occasional licence is in force, during the hours specified in the licence; and

(c) where a special hours certificate is in force, during the period between 11 p.m. and half an hour after the end of permitted hours for those premises.

These powers of entry might be described as the 'general' powers of entry as they are obviously concerned with inspections during, and immediately after permitted hours. However, in respect of licensed premises and licensed canteens an entry may be made *at any time* outside these hours where a constable suspects with reasonable cause that an offence against the Act is being, or is about to be committed. This power enables entry to deal with 'lock-in' after-hours drinkers.

It is an offence to fail to admit a constable who identifies himself as such. An employer commits an offence if an employee, or any other person acting with his consent, fails to admit a constable. The order issued by most chief constables requires that entry into licensed premises should normally only be effected in the presence of a supervisory rank. There are, however, many occasions upon which the urgency of the matter requires an immediate entry to be made, and it is good practice to make an accurate record of such entry, and the action which was taken, in the official pocket notebook.

Expulsion from licensed premises and exclusion

A constable is required to help to expel from licensed premises any person who is drunk, violent, quarrelsome, or disorderly or whose presence would subject the licence holder to a penalty, on being requested to assist by the licensee. A person who refuses to leave on being so required by the licensee, his servant or agent, or any constable, commits an offence. There is no power to arrest without warrant for this offence, but the Act authorises the use of such force as is necessary to expel such a person from the licensed premises. The Licensed Premises (Exclusion of Certain Persons) Act 1980 allows courts to make orders in respect of persons convicted of offences involving violence or threats of violence on licensed premises, prohibiting that person from entering specified licensed premises without the express consent of the licensee, his servant or agent. A person who enters in breach of an order commits an offence. A licensee, his servant or agent may expel a person who has entered, or whom he reasonably suspects of entering in breach of an order. A constable shall, on demand of such licensee, servant or agent, help to expel any person whom the constable reasonably suspects of being in breach of an exclusion order.

Restriction orders and licensed premises

Restriction orders apply to licensed premises or registered clubs, specifying any time between 14.30 and 17.30 (15.00 and 19.00 on Sundays and Good Fridays) hours as being non-permitted hours. They may apply to particular days of the week and to particular periods of the year and must not remain in force for more than 12 months.

An application for such an order may be made by a chief officer of police, persons living in the neighbourhood (or their representative), neighbouring businessmen or their managers or head teachers. Such an order may be made on the grounds of avoiding or reducing annoyance or disturbance to local residents or workers, to customers of businesses in the locality, or to people at schools. They may also be made on the grounds that it is desirable to avoid or reduce the incidence of disorderly conduct in the premises or in their vicinity.

Persons under 18

Section 169 of the 1964 Act requires that a licensee or his servant shall not sell intoxicating liquor to a person under 18. This offence *need not be committed knowingly*. However, it is a defence for a person charged with personally 'selling', to prove that he exercised all due diligence to avoid the commission of such an offence, or that he had no reason to suspect that the person concerned was under 18. Where a licensee is charged, as a result of an act of some other person, it is a defence for him to prove that he exercised all due diligence to avoid the commission of that offence.

In addition, the holder of the licence shall not knowingly allow any person to sell intoxicating liquor to a person under 18. Neither the licensee nor his servant shall *knowingly* allow a person under 18 to *consume* intoxicating liquor in a bar. The law so far is concerned with the sale of intoxicants to those under 18 and their being allowed to drink intoxicants in a bar. It goes on to make it an offence for the under 18 to buy or attempt to buy intoxicating liquor on licensed premises. In addition, it is an offence for him to consume intoxicants which he buys in a bar. Recognising that under age drinkers are often accompanied by older persons, it is declared to be an offence for any person to buy or attempt to buy intoxicating liquor for consumption by a person under 18 in a bar.

This seems to be complex at first until it is realised that persons under 18 years of age can lawfully consume intoxicants in parts of licensed premises which are not bars. Persons who have attained the age of 16 years may purchase beer, porter, cider or perry to drink with a meal in a part of the premises usually set apart for the service of table meals.

Let us consider licensed premises in which there is a licensee and his barman serving in the bar. A 16-year-old, who is known to them, enters the bar and purchases a pint of beer, sold to him by the licensee. At this stage, the licensee has committed an offence by selling and the 16-year-old an offence by purchasing. If the barman had sold the drink, he would have committed an offence by selling and the landlord one of knowingly allowing the drink to be sold.

If the 16-year-old then drinks from his glass, both the licensee and his barman have allowed him to consume in a bar and the 16-year-old is guilty of 'consuming' in a bar. If the 16-year-old had entered the premises with an 18-year-old friend who had bought two pints, one being for the 16-year-old to drink in the bar, the older commits an offence of buying intoxicants for consumption in the bar by the under 18-year-old. If he had intended to take the drinks outside the bar before consumption, he would not have committed an offence. He may have carried the

379

drinks to a seat outside the pub, or to a residents' lounge, or to a room of the hotel. In any of these events, he would not have committed an offence as the drink was not for consumption in a bar.

The term 'bar' is defined by the Licensing Act 1964 as including any place exclusively or mainly for sale or consumption of intoxicating liquor. It does not apply to rooms exclusively used for table meals in which the sale of intoxicants is restricted to persons taking meals as an ancillary to such meals. In all other instances the matter to be considered is the room's use. If it is mainly or exclusively used for the sale and consumption of intoxicants, it is a bar.

Where it is necessary to prove that most of these offences were committed 'knowingly', that is, in the knowledge that the person served, or drinking, was under the age of 18, it may be possible to show that the licensee or his servants positively knew the age of the person concerned, but such occasions will be rare. Most frequently the offences will come to light because the person concerned appears to be under the age of 18 and is in fact under the age of 18. This will be apparent to the justices.

Section 170 prohibits a licensee from employing a person under 18 in a bar of his licensed premises at any time when the bar is open for the sale or consumption of intoxicating liquor. This does not apply to persons who are employed to work elsewhere on the premises who may pass through a bar or deliver messages to persons in a bar. Equally, it would not apply to dining-room waiters who were asked by customers to deliver their coffee and brandy to an adjoining bar. The term 'employment' is given its general meaning of use and there is no necessity to prove payment of wages.

Persons under 14 years

By s. 168 of the 1964 Act, the holder of a justices' licence shall not allow a person under 14 years to be in the bar of the licensed premises during permitted hours. No other person shall cause or procure, or attempt to cause or procure any such person to be in a bar during permitted hours.

The previous offences which we considered were concerned with drinking intoxicants on premises but we are now examining the question of those persons who may be present. It is no offence for a 14-year-old to be in a bar on licensed premises drinking soft drinks. It is an offence for a 13-year-old to be there whether drinking anything or not. However, there are certain exceptions to the general rule that persons under 14 shall not be in a bar during permitted hours.

The licence holder's children are exempt as are those of residents on the premises provided that they are not children of resident employees. Children who are simply passing through a bar where there is no other means of access to another part of the premises are also exempt, and these provisions do not apply to railway refreshment rooms or premises in respect of which the holding of a justices' licence is merely ancillary to some other main purpose.

A licensee may prove that he used due diligence to prevent the person under 14 from being admitted, but if he is unable to do so he must be convicted of the offence if such a person is found there.

Licensed clubs

Clubs may be licensed or registered. The legal aspects of registered clubs are examined below. The term 'club' has not been defined but it can be described as a voluntary association of a number of people for a common object or purpose – for example, recreation, art, science, politics, or social welfare. When such an association has been formed and it is intended to serve drinks in the club, the members must decide whether to license or register the premises which are to be occupied and habitually used for the purposes of the club. If the decision is to apply for a justices' licence and it is subsequently granted, the licence will authorise the sale of intoxicants on the premises. A nominated officer of the club must apply for the justices' licence and, when it is issued in his name, he assumes the right and the obligations of a licence holder. The club must restrict sales to normal permitted hours and the legal restrictions which apply to the sale or supply of liquor to persons under 18 years of age will apply. In addition, conditions may be attached to the licence, prohibiting or restricting the sale of liquor to non-members. In this way, although a justices' licence is in force which would normally permit the licence holder to sell liquor to all members of the public, conditions attached to the licence probably restrict sales to members and, perhaps, their guests.

Registered clubs

We have already considered licensed clubs and other forms of licensed premises, and the common factor has been that a justices' licence is required before intoxicating liquor may be sold. A justices' licence is not required for the supply of liquor in a registered club which, to meet the conditions for registration, must consist of members who jointly own the property of the club, including the drinks. In this way the profits of the club are also shared by the membership and there is no direct profit to any individual. It is, therefore, considered that there is no sale of liquor in a registered club as the members actually own all of the intoxicating liquor in the first instance, it having been bought with money which they have paid as membership dues. When drinks are supplied in such a club, it is merely a release to a member of his own property.

The permitted hours in respect of the premises of a registered club shall be:

(a) on days other than Christmas Day, the general licensing hours; and
(b) on Christmas Day, the hours fixed by or under the rules of the club in accordance with the following conditions:
   (i) the hours fixed shall not be longer than six and a half hours and shall not begin earlier than 12.00 nor end later than 22.30 hours;
   (ii) there shall be a break in the afternoon of not less than two hours which shall include the hours from 15.00 to 17.00; and
   (iii) there shall not be more than three and a half hours after 17.00 hours.

So that the permitted hours which have been fixed by the rules of a registered club may be known, written notice of the hours fixed must be given to the clerk to the justices. In most police stations a record of licensed premises and registered clubs is maintained, in which the permitted hours are recorded. If offences of supplying intoxicating liquor during non-permitted hours are suspected in the premises of any registered club, the hours can be checked by reference to such records or by checking with the clerk to the justices.

There is no general power of entry into the premises of a registered club. If a special hours certificate is in force then the Licensing Act authorises entry to any part of the premises in respect of which the certificate applies during the period between 11 p.m. and half an hour after the end of permitted hours for those premises. Generally, entry into a registered club in which it is suspected that offences are being committed, is effected under the authority of two search warrants issued under ss. 54 and 187 of the Licensing Act 1964, authorising the seizure of documents and intoxicating liquor if sales to non-members and other unauthorised persons are suspected.

Late night refreshment houses

A late night refreshment house is a house, room, shop, or building which is kept open for public refreshment, resort, and entertainment at any time between the hours of 10 p.m. and 5 a.m., other than premises licensed for the sale of intoxicants. All such refreshment houses must be licensed by the county or district council and it is an offence for any person to keep a late night refreshment house without a licence.

It is a question of fact as to whether or not a particular building is kept as a refreshment house, and it is not essential that seating is provided for customers provided that refreshment is consumed on the premises. In most cases it is quite evident, as the premises involved will be late night cafés and restaurants.

Police powers

A constable may at any time enter a licensed late night refreshment house. It is an offence for the licensee, or any person acting on his behalf, to fail or refuse to admit a constable who demands admittance. On the demand of the occupier of such a house, a constable must assist in expelling drunken, riotous, quarrelsome, and disorderly persons.

Drunkenness

Drunkenness is not in itself an offence, but becomes punishable when it is accompanied by aggravating circumstances which interfere with other people. The most common offences of drunkenness are contained in the Licensing Act 1872 and in s. 91 of the Criminal Justice Act 1967.

(a) Any person who is found drunk in any highway or other public place, whether a building or not, or on any licensed premises, is guilty of an offence. The term 'public place' includes any place to which the public have access, whether on payment or otherwise.

(b) Any person who, while drunk in a public place, is guilty of disorderly behaviour, is guilty of an offence.

Where there is an intercom system and locks on the entrance to a block of flats, the landing area outside the flats is not a public place for the purposes of the offence of being drunk and disorderly.

Other offences, now quite rare, are also contained in this Act and include being drunk while in charge, on any highway or other public place, of any carriage (which includes bicycles), horse, cattle, or loaded firearm. The term 'loaded firearm' includes an air weapon.

The term 'drunkenness' is not defined, nor is the form of disorderly conduct which accompanies this condition. It has been held that an offence will be committed if the conduct is honestly believed to have been such disorderly conduct, if that belief is based upon reasonable grounds. The offence is most usually met in circumstances which involve disturbances by fighting or rowdy conduct involving persons who are obviously under the influence of drink.

The words 'found drunk' mean perceived to be drunk. When a person is expelled from a private place and is then perceived to be drunk on a highway, this offence is committed. In practice prosecutions for simple drunkenness are confined to circumstances in which the person concerned is incapable of taking care of himself. Often such persons are found lying in the street, having drunk themselves into a state of unconsciousness, or staggering through traffic with little control over their actions, causing danger both to themselves and to the drivers who are forced to take avoiding action.

A person who is drunk on a public service vehicle or railway passenger vehicle which is being used for the principal purpose of carrying passengers for the whole or part of a journey to or from a designated sporting event, commits an offence against s. 1(3) Sporting Events (Control of Alcohol, etc.) Act 1985. A person who is drunk in a designated sports ground at any time during the period of a designated sporting event at that ground, offends against s. 2(2) of that Act (see page 504).

Police powers

The general power of arrest which is provided by s. 25 of the Police and Criminal Evidence Act 1984 will usually be applicable to offences of drunkenness, where an arrest may be necessary for a number of reasons. A person who is 'found drunk' may often be in such a condition that he cannot establish his identity to the satisfaction of the constable, or arrest may be necessary to prevent him from causing injury to himself or suffering physical injury. The person who is guilty of disorderly behaviour while drunk may be arrested without warrant by any person, including a constable. His conduct in any case will invariably involve a breach of the peace.

Care must be taken in dealing with all persons who appear to be drunk. If there is any suggestion that they may be ill, or may have injured themselves because of their condition, medical assistance should be provided. It must be remembered that persons who are very drunk are quite likely to be sick, and if they are not carefully watched while in custody, are likely to choke if this should occur while they are lying on their backs. Frequent visits must be made by police officers responsible for the care and custody of prisoners.

Opinion

A necessary ingredient of these offences is that the person concerned was drunk, and this should be stated clearly by the constable in evidence. Although a statement to the effect that a man was drunk is largely a matter of opinion, the courts have always accepted the testimony of a police officer in this respect. The statement must be supported by evidence of the factors which caused the police officer to form the opinion that the man was drunk, and observable symptoms might include lack of coordination of movements, manner of speech, and the fact that the breath of the offender smelled of intoxicating liquor.

Particular offences involving police officers

The Licensing Act 1964, s. 178, provides that the holder of a justices' licence commits an offence if he:

(a) knowingly suffers any constable to remain on the licensed premises during any part of the time appointed for the constable's being on duty, except for the purpose of the execution of the constable's duty; or

(b) supplies any liquor or refreshment whether by way of gift or sale, to any constable on duty except by authority of a superior officer of the constable; or

(c) bribes or attempts to bribe any constable.

The holder of an occasional licence is the holder of a justices' licence for the purposes of this section. It must be proved that the licensee knew that person to be a constable *and* to be on duty. A constable is in the execution of his duty for the purposes of the section if he is assisting in the exclusion of drunkards or detecting offences under the Act.

Identification methods

Methods of identification

Section 66 of the Police and Criminal Evidence Act 1984 requires the Home Secretary to issue 'Codes of Practice for the Identification of Persons by Police Officers'. The Codes set out the methods by which such identifications may be made; that is identification by witnesses; by films and photographs; by fingerprints; by body samples; by swabs and impressions.

Witnesses may identify persons in a direct, personal way. It may be that they know the person who committed the offence; persons, particularly police officers, frequently identify wanted persons from descriptions which have been provided or from identikit or photofit impressions which have been created. The *modus operandi* system which has already been described, also provides a means by which criminals may be identified.

When a witness is being interviewed to establish the identity or description of a suspected person a police officer must exercise patience and considerable skill to obtain a worthwhile description. The average person is not equipped to provide such information and will be unable even to begin the process of description. In order to establish the height of the offender for example, it will probably be necessary to compare his height with some person who is present and the witness will have to be similarly guided through a description of each feature of the offender. Witnesses are frequently able to provide the information; they are unable to marshall it without assistance.

The Court of Appeal has provided general guidance to judges when summing up in disputed identity cases and this advice provides good guidelines for police officers to bear in mind.

(a) Warn the jury of the special need for caution in relying on correctness of identification.

(b) Make some reference to the possibility that a mistaken witness could be convincing and that a number of witnesses could all be mistaken.

(c) Direct the jury to examine closely the circumstances of the identification; how long seen, how far away, in what light, was observation impeded, had the witness seen the accused before and if so how often? If only seen occasionally had he any special reason for remembering the accused, how long was there between the original observation and the subsequent identification to the police, was there any material discrepancy between the witness's description of the accused given to the police and the accused's actual appearance? If the prosecution have reason to believe in any case that there is a material discrepancy between the witness's description and the accused's actual appearance they should supply the accused or his legal advisers with the original description, and in all cases such descriptions should be supplied to the defence on request, both in summary trials and trials on indictment.

(d) Remind the jury of any specific weaknesses in the identification evidence; recognition might be more reliable than the identification of a stranger but the jury should be reminded that mistakes in recognising close friends and relatives are sometimes made.

These matters are concerned with the quality of the evidence available. Observation over a long period will obviously be better than a momentary glimpse. The conditions existing at the time of the identification, for example, the light available at the time will also be important. Where evidence of identification is poor the judge may withdraw the evidence from the jury unless the evidence of identification is supported by other evidence. Such evidence must be sufficient to make a jury sure that there has been no mistaken identification. Most of these recommendations are now specifically incorporated in the Identification Code.

In a case involving disputed identification evidence, and where the identity of the suspect is known to the police and he is available, the methods of identification which may be used are:

(a) an identification parade;
(b) a group identification;
(c) a video film; and
(d) a confrontation by a witness.

A person is 'known' if there is sufficient information known to the police to justify the arrest of a particular person for suspected involvement in the offence. A suspect being 'available' means that he is immediately available, or will become so within a reasonably short time.

The arrangements for, and the conduct of, these four types of identification are the responsibility of an officer in uniform not below the rank of inspector who must not be involved in the investigation: he is called the 'identification officer'. No officer involved with the investigation may take part in these procedures. This includes the conveyance of witnesses to a police station at which an identification is to be attempted. Such contact permits the transfer of information concerning the identification.

Personal identification by witness

A written record shall be made of the description of the suspect as first given by a potential witness. This must be done before the witness takes part in the forms of identification listed in the Code. The record may be made or kept in any form provided that details of the description as first given by the witness can accurately be produced from it in a written form which can be provided to the suspect or his solicitor in accordance with the Code. A copy shall be provided to the suspect or his solicitor as soon as practicable, and, if available, before any interview takes place. Such a description must have been provided before a witness is shown photographs.

If identification is disputed in a case a parade must be held if the accused asks for one and it is practicable to hold one. This applies whether or not there is other evidence of identification which appears to be sufficient. Where a witness knows a suspect but does not know him well, an identification parade should be held.

Where a suspect who is agreeable to participate in a parade is released from custody because there is insufficient evidence to charge him, evidence of group identification outside the police station will not be admissible in evidence even though the person is no longer a suspect 'at a police station' when it takes place.

A parade may be held if the officer in charge of the investigation considers that it would be useful, and the suspect consents. If he refuses his consent, a record must be made of the refusal.

There are certain general rules for the conduct of an identification:

(a) A parade need not be held if the identification officer considers that, whether because a suspect is of such singular appearance or for some other reason, it would not be practicable to assemble sufficient people who resembled him to make a fair parade. If the identification officer considers that it is not practicable to hold a parade, he must tell the suspect why and record the reason. He must consider the practicality of holding one at a later date.

(b) Where a suspect refuses, or, having agreed, fails to attend a parade or if the holding of a parade is impracticable, arrangements must be made, if practicable, to allow witnesses to see the suspect in a group identification, video identification or confrontation. A video film or colour photograph must be taken of any identification parade. A group identification may also be arranged if the officer in charge of the investigation considers, whether because of fear on the part of the witness or for some other reason, that it is more satisfactory than a parade, in the circumstances. The suspect should be asked for his consent to a group identification. If he refuses consent, the identification officer has a discretion to proceed with a group identification, if practicable. A record must be made of the refusal.

(c) The identification officer may show a witness a video film of a suspect if he considers, whether because of the suspect's refusal to take part in an identification parade or group identification or because of other reasons, that this would in the circumstances be the most satisfactory course. The suspect should be asked for his consent to video identification. However, if he refuses consent, the identification officer has a discretion to proceed with a video identification if practicable. A record must be made of the refusal.

(d) If neither a parade nor a group identification nor a video identification procedure is arranged the suspect may be confronted by the witness. Such a confrontation does not require the suspect's consent but this procedure must not be used unless none of the above methods is practicable.

(e) A witness must not be shown photographs, photofit or identikit pictures for identification purposes if there is a suspect already available to be asked to stand on a parade or participate in group identification.

All decisions are those of the 'identification officer' who must arrange and conduct the procedures involved in such identifications. Such an officer must be in uniform and must not be involved with the actual investigation.

If it is decided by the identification officer that it is advisable to attempt to establish identity by means of a parade or group or video identification method, he must explain certain things to the suspect:

(a) the purpose of the parade or group identification or video identification;

(b) that he is entitled to free legal advice;

(c) the procedures to be followed (including the suspect's right to have a solicitor or friend present);

(d) where appropriate, the special arrangements for juveniles;

(e) where appropriate, the special arrangements for mentally disordered and mentally handicapped persons;

(f) that he does not have to take part in an identification parade, group identification or video identification procedure and, if it is proposed to hold a group identification or video identification, his entitlement to a parade if this can practicably be arranged;

(g) if he does not consent to take part in a parade or cooperate in a group identification or video identification his refusal may be given in evidence in any subsequent trial and police may proceed covertly without his consent or make other arrangements to test whether a witness identifies him;

(h) that if he should significantly alter his appearance between the taking of any photograph at the time of his arrest or after charge and any attempt to hold an identification procedure, this may be given in evidence if the case comes to trial, and the officer may then consider other forms of identification;

(i) that a video photograph may be taken of him when he attends for any identification procedure;

(j) whether the witness had been shown photographs, photofit, identikit or

387

similar pictures by the police during the investigation before the identity of the suspect became known;

(k) that if he changes his appearance before a parade it may not be practicable to arrange one on the day in question or subsequently and, because of his change of appearance, the identification officer may then consider alternative methods of identification;

(l) that he or his solicitor will be provided with details of the description of the suspect as first given by any witnesses who are to attend the parade, group identification, video identification or confrontation.

The identification officer must additionally give a written notice containing this information to the suspect and give him an opportunity to read it. The suspect will be asked to sign a second copy of the notice to indicate whether or not he is willing to participate in the parade or group identification or cooperate with the making of a video film. The signed copy shall be retained by the identification officer.

(1) *General*

Annex A to the Codes of Practice directs the form which an identification parade shall take.

A suspect must be given a reasonable opportunity to have a solicitor or friend present, and the identification officer shall ask him to indicate his wishes in this respect on the 'Notes to Suspect'. A parade may take place in a normal room or in one equipped with a screen permitting witnesses to see members of the parade without being seen. The procedures for the composition and conduct of the parade are the same in both cases (except that the identification does not take place in the accused's presence, etc.) and such a parade may only take place when the suspect's solicitor, friend or appropriate adult is present. This is an obvious safeguard, if the evidence of identification is to have any value.

The suspect or his solicitor should be allowed to view any material released to the media by the police for the purpose of recognising or tracing the suspect, provided it is practicable to do so and would not unreasonably delay the investigation.

(2) *Involving prison inmates*

If an inmate is required for identification, and there are no security problems about his leaving the establishment, he may be asked to participate in a parade or video identification. (Group identifications, however, may not be arranged outside the establishment.) A parade may be conducted in a prison department establishment and shall be conducted as far as practicable under normal parade rules. Members of the public shall make up the parade unless there are serious security or control objections to their admission to the establishment. In such cases, or if a video or group identification is arranged within the establishment, other inmates may participate.

If an inmate is the suspect, he should not be required to wear prison uniform for the parade unless the other persons taking part are other inmates in uniform or are members of the public who are prepared to wear prison uniform for the occasion.

The evidential value of a group identification in a prison exercise yard could be high. The similarity of dress of all participants will make identification difficult for witnesses who are not certain of the appearance of a suspect.

(3) *Conduct of a parade*

Immediately before the parade, the identification officer must remind the suspect of the procedure, and caution him. All unauthorised persons must be strictly excluded from the place where the parade is held.

Once the parade has been formed, everything following shall take place in the presence and hearing of the suspect, interpreter, solicitor, friend or appropriate adult who is present (unless the parade involves a screen, in which case everything said to or by any witness at the place where the parade is held must be said in the hearing and presence of the suspect's solicitor, friend or appropriate adult or be recorded on video). The investigating officer should not enter the room in which the parade is being held.

The parade shall consist of at least eight persons (other than the suspect) who so far as possible resemble the suspect in age, height, general appearance, and position in life. One suspect only shall be included in a parade unless there are two suspects of roughly similar appearance in which case they may be paraded together with at least 12 other persons. In no circumstances, shall more than two suspects be included in one parade and where there are separate parades they shall be made up of different persons.

Where police officers in uniform form an identification parade, numerals or other identifying badge shall be concealed. (It must be remembered that if a complaint concerns a police officer in uniform who was on duty at a particular time, all those on duty at the time who would have had an opportunity to be in the vicinity of any incident, whether in accordance with instructions or not, should be subjected to the identification procedure.)

When the suspect is brought to the place where the parade is to be held, he shall be asked by the identification officer whether he has any objection to the arrangements for the parade or to any of the other participants in it. The suspect may obtain advice from his solicitor, or friend, if present, before the parade proceeds. Where practicable, steps shall be taken to remove the grounds for objection. Where it is not practicable to do so, the officer shall explain to the suspect why his objections cannot be met.

The suspect may select his own position in the line. Where there is more than one witness, the identification officer must tell the suspect, after each witness has left the room, that he can, if he wishes, change position in the line. Each position in the line must be clearly numbered, whether by means of a numeral laid on the floor in front of each parade member or by other means.

The identification officer is responsible for ensuring that, before they attend the parade, witnesses:

(a) are not able to communicate with each other or overhear a witness who has already seen the parade;

(b) do not see any member of the parade;

    (c)   do not see or be reminded of any photograph or description of the suspect or be given any other indication of his identity;

    (d)   on that occasion, do not see the suspect either before or after the parade.

The officer conducting a witness to the parade must not discuss with him the composition of the parade, and in particular he must not disclose whether a previous witness has made any identification.

Witnesses shall be brought in one at a time. Immediately before a witness inspects the parade, the identification officer shall tell him that the person he saw may or may not be on the parade and that if he cannot make a positive identification he should say so but that he should not make a decision before looking at each member of the parade at least twice. The officer shall then ask him to look at each member of the parade at least twice, taking as much care and time as he wishes. When the officer is satisfied that the witness has properly looked at each member of the parade, he shall ask him whether the person he saw in person on an earlier relevant occasion is on the parade. The witness should make an identification by saying the number of the person concerned. Where this takes place behind a screen it is desirable for the witness to be asked to make a note of the number of the person identified so that he may give oral evidence of that number when the person identified appears in court. However, if a witness is unable to recall that number at the trial, evidence from the officer who conducted the parade as to the number which the witness called out is admissible as there is statutory authority for its admission. If the witness makes an identification after the parade has ended the suspect and, if present, his solicitor, interpreter or friend shall be informed. Where this occurs, consideration should be given to allowing the witness a second opportunity to identify the suspect.

If a witness wishes to hear any parade member speak, adopt any specified posture or see him move, the identification officer shall first ask whether he can identify any persons on the parade on the basis of appearance only. When the request is to hear members of the parade speak, the witness shall be reminded that the participants in the parade have been chosen on the basis of physical appearance only. Members of the parade may then be asked to comply with the witness's request to hear them speak, to see them move or to adopt any specified posture.

The usual rules (as set out above) apply if video films or photographs have been released to the media.

When the last witness has left, the suspect shall be asked by the identification officer whether he wishes to make any comments on the conduct of the parade.

(4) *Conduct of a group identification*

The arrangements must as far as practicable satisfy the requirements of an identification parade. A group identification takes place where the suspect is viewed by a witness among an informal group of people. The procedure may take place with the consent and cooperation of the suspect or covertly where a suspect has refused to cooperate with an identification parade or a group identification or has failed to attend. A group identification may also be arranged if the officer in charge of the investigation considers, whether because of fear on the part of the witnesses or for some other reason, that it is in the circumstances more satisfactory than a parade.

The procedure should follow that of a parade as closely as possible. Location is a matter for the identification officer, although he may take into account representations from the suspect, his solicitor, his appropriate adult or friend. It should take place where people are passing or walking around informally or in groups such that the suspect is able to join them and be capable of being seen by the witness at the same time as others in the group. Examples include an escalator, shopping centre, railway and bus stations, or standing groups in other public places. Where held covertly, locations will be limited by the places where the suspect can be found and the number of other people present. Regular routes travelled by the suspect may be useful.

An identification officer must consider the *general* appearance and number of people likely to be present. If he believes that because of the unusual appearance of the accused, none of these conditions can be satisfied, a group identification need not be held. When held, a colour photograph or video film should be made of the general scene. If practicable, the group identification should be video recorded. If all of this cannot be done at the time, the scene should be video recorded or photographed at a later date.

Before the group identification takes place, the suspect or his solicitor should be given the 'first description' by any witnesses. Material released by the police to the media should be similarly viewed. Where such photographs or video films have been released to the media, the officer shall ask each witness afterwards, if he has seen any broadcast or published film or photographs relating to the offence and shall record the reply.

Annex E to the Identification Code provides extensive details of procedures where the suspect consents to such identification; when identification takes place within a moving group; stationary group; and generally, in all such cases. The rules closely parallel those concerned with parades, where applicable. Where he does not consent, the difference is that he has no right to have a solicitor, etc., present as the identification will take place without his knowledge. Any number of suspects may be identified at the same time in these circumstances.

While group identification may take place in police stations, this may only take place where for reasons of safety, security, or because it is impracticable to hold them elsewhere. It may take place in a room equipped with a screen permitting witnesses to see the group without being seen, or in some other appropriate place.

A group identification involving prison inmates may take place at a prison or in a police station. Similar conditions apply to those governing a parade.

Copies of photographs or films shall be supplied on request to the suspect or his solicitor within a reasonable time. The usual conditions as to destruction apply. A record must be made on the forms provided and this shall include anything said by witnesses or the suspect about identifications or the conduct of the proceedings and any reason why it was not practicable to comply with any provisions of the Code.

(5) *Video film identification*

A video film must include the suspect and at least eight other people who so far as possible resemble the suspect in age, height, general appearance and position in life. Only one suspect shall appear, unless there are two of roughly similar appearance in which case there may be shown at least 12 other persons.

The same general rules apply as in the case of an identification parade in relation to the identification of persons by numbers and the special provisions relating to police officers and prison inmates.

The suspect and his solicitor, friend or appropriate adult must be given a reasonable opportunity to see the complete film before it is shown to the witness. Their objections should be met where practicable and if they cannot be met, an explanation of the reason should be given. All such matters must be recorded.

The suspect's solicitor, or where one is not instructed, the suspect himself, should be given reasonable notification of the intended identification. The suspect himself may not be present when the film is shown to the witness. Where the suspect's representative is not present, the viewing itself must be recorded on video. No unauthorised person may be present. The usual rules apply in relation to supplying details of the 'first description'.

The same general rules which apply to the showing of the persons on an identification parade to a witness, apply to a video identification. In addition, a witness may ask to see a particular part of the tape again or to have a picture frozen for him to study. It should be pointed out that there is no limit on the number of times he may view the whole or part of the tape. A witness should be asked to refrain from making a positive identification until he has seen the entire film at least twice. Only one witness may see the film at a time.

The identification officer will ask for an identification by number. When such a number is given, the film will be shown once more to confirm the identification given by the witness.

The identification officer is responsible for the security of the tapes. No officer involved in the investigation shall be permitted to view the film prior to it being shown to any witness.

(6) *Records*

If a parade is held without a solicitor or friend of the suspect being present, a colour photograph or a video film of the parade shall be taken unless any of the parade members objects. A copy of the photograph or video film shall be supplied on request to the suspect or his solicitor within a reasonable time. A photograph or video film must be destroyed or wiped clean at the end of the proceedings unless the suspect is convicted or admits the offence and is cautioned.

If the identification officer asks any person to leave a parade because he is interfering with its conduct the circumstances shall be recorded. A record must be made of all those present at a parade or group identification whose names are known to the police. If prison inmates make up a parade the circumstances shall be recorded.

(7) *Confrontation by a witness*

If neither a parade, nor a group identification nor a video identification procedure is arranged the suspect may be confronted by a witness. Such confrontation does not require the suspect's consent, but may not take place unless none of the other procedures is practicable.

The rules concerning confrontation are simple. The identification officer is responsible for the conduct of any confrontation of a suspect by a witness. Before the confrontation takes place, the identification officer must tell the witness that the person he saw may or may not be the person he is to confront and that if he cannot make a positive identification he should say so. Details of the 'first description' will be supplied to the suspect or his solicitor and the rules concerning media releases must be followed. The suspect shall be confronted independently by each witness who will be asked 'Is this the person?' Confrontation must take place in the presence of the suspect's solicitor, where he has one, unless this would cause unreasonable delay.

Confrontation should normally take place in the police station either in a normal room or one equipped with a screen permitting a witness to see the suspect without being seen. In both cases the procedures are the same except that a room equipped with a screen may be used only when the suspect's solicitor, friend or appropriate adult is present or the confrontation is recorded on video.

Where there has been a 'media release' each witness must be asked whether he has seen any broadcast or published films or photographs relating to the offence. His reply must be recorded.

Where the victim of an attempted rape which occurred at night pointed out a man who was some distance away and said 'I think that is him', it was held that it was sensible to take her closer to the man so that she could see him more clearly. The provisions of the Identification Code should be applied according to the circumstances of each case. The defendant had claimed that he should have been arrested when he was first pointed out and that he should have had the opportunity to stand in an identification parade. He alleged that what had occurred was a confrontation which should not have taken place unless none of the other identification procedures was practicable.

Identification by photographs

Annex D of the Identification Code sets out the procedures to be followed when an identification is to be made from photographs or photofit, identikit or similar pictures which are shown to a witness for identification purposes where the suspect's identity is unknown.

An officer of the rank of sergeant or above shall be responsible for supervising and directing the showing of photographs. The actual showing may be done by a constable or a civilian police employee. (This means that most of the responsibility remains with the sergeant, etc. The accountability of the constable or civilian employee will be limited to non-observance of the directions given.) The officer must confirm that the first description of the suspect given by the witness has been recorded before the witness is shown the photographs. If he is unable to confirm that the description has been recorded, he shall postpone the showing.

Only one witness shall be shown photographs at any one time. He shall be given as much privacy as practicable and shall not be allowed to communicate with any other witness in the case. The witness shall be shown not less than 12 photographs at a time which shall, as far as possible, all be of similar type.

When the witness is shown the photographs, he shall be told that the photograph of the person whom he has said that he has previously seen may or may not be among them. He shall not be prompted or guided in any way but shall be left to make any selection without help. If the witness makes a positive identification from photographs, then unless the person identified is otherwise eliminated from the enquiries, other witnesses shall not be shown photographs. However, they and the witness who has made the identification shall be asked to attend an identification parade or group identification or video identification if practicable unless there is no dispute about the identification of the suspect.

Where the use of photofit, identikit or similar picture has led to there being a suspect available who can be asked to appear on parade, or participate in a group or video identification, the picture shall not be shown to other potential witnesses.

Where a witness attending an identification parade has previously been shown photographs, or photofit, identikit or similar pictures (and it is the responsibility of the officer in charge of the investigation to make the identification officer aware that this is the case) then the suspect and his solicitor must be informed of this fact before the identity parade takes place.

None of the photographs used shall be destroyed, whether or not an identification is made, since they may be required for production in court. The photographs should be numbered and a separate photograph taken of the frame or part of the album from which the witness made an identification as an aid to reconstituting it.

(1) *Documentation*

Whether or not an identification is made, a record shall be kept of the showing of photographs and of any comment made by the witness.

Identification by fingerprints

The fingerprints, and other marks left by the hands of a person, provide a unique form of identification. Evidence of the comparison of prints found at the scene of a crime with those taken from a suspect, can only be given by an expert witness. The important factor is to ensure that prints left at the scene of a crime are not interfered with. The effectiveness of fingerprint and palmprint identification has diminished in proportion to thieves' awareness of such possibilities. Some simply wear gloves; others burn the cars which they have taken without consent in an attempt to destroy such traces. However, it is essential that the police service maintains a record of the prints of those persons who regularly commit crime.

The Police and Criminal Evidence Act 1984, s. 61, requires that generally, a person must consent in writing to the taking of his fingerprints at a police station. They may be taken without his consent on the authority of an officer of at least the rank of superintendent if he has reasonable grounds for suspecting the involvement of the person whose fingerprints are to be taken in a criminal offence and for believing that his fingerprints will tend to confirm or disprove his involvement. Such authority may be given orally or in writing, but if given orally, it must be confirmed in writing.

Fingerprints may also be taken without consent where the person has been charged with a recordable offence or informed that he will be reported for such an offence where he has not previously had his prints taken in the course of that investigation. Recordable offences are those which are punishable by imprisonment; offences under the Street Offences Act 1959, s. 1 (loitering or soliciting for the purposes of prostitution); Telecommunications Act 1984, s. 43 (improper use of public telecommunications system); Road Traffic Act 1988, s. 25 (tampering with motor vehicles); Malicious Communications Act 1988, s. 1 (sending letters, etc., with intent to cause distress or anxiety); and Criminal Justice Act 1988, s. 139 (having an article with a blade or point in a public place).

In either of these cases, the person concerned must be told of the reason why his fingerprints are being taken and that reason shall be recorded as soon as practicable after the prints are taken. A person whose fingerprints are taken with or without his consent shall be informed beforehand that his prints may be subject of a speculative search against other fingerprints and a record should be made of this. A 'speculative search' means that a check may be made against other fingerprints contained in records held by or on behalf of the police or held in connection with, or as a result of, an investigation of an offence. Reasonable force may be used to take fingerprints. He must also be told that the prints will be destroyed as soon as practicable if he is cleared of the offence or he is not prosecuted for it (unless he admits the offence and is cautioned for it). He must be allowed to witness the destruction of his fingerprints if he so requests within five days of such eventualities. There are certain exceptions to the requirement to destroy such prints and these are set out in subss. (3A) and (3B) of s. 64 of the 1984 Act. Where a right to destruction exists, any information derived from them shall not be used in evidence or for the purposes of the investigation of an offence. Similar provisions exist in relation to intimate and non-intimate samples taken from a suspect under the provisions of the 1984 Act.

If a person's fingerprints are taken at a police station, whether with or without the appropriate consent; before they are taken an officer must inform him that he may be subject to a speculative search and the fact that the person has been informed of this possibility shall be recorded as soon as practicable after the fingerprints have been taken.

Where a person has been convicted of a recordable offence his fingerprints may be taken without consent provided that he has not at any time been in police detention for the offence and has not had his fingerprints taken in the course of the investigation or since conviction.

In general, s. 63A of the 1984 Act provides that fingerprints and such samples taken under these powers from a person who has been arrested on suspicion of being involved in a recordable offence may be checked against other fingerprints or samples or the information derived from other samples contained in records held by or on behalf of the police or held in connection with or as a result of an investigation of an offence.

Showing of video recordings taken by security cameras

Nothing in the Identification Code inhibits an investigating officer from showing a video film or photographs of an incident to the public at large through the national or local media for the purposes of recognition and tracing suspects. However, when such material is shown to potential witnesses (including police officers) for the purpose of obtaining identification evidence, it should be shown on an individual

395

basis so as to avoid any possibility of collusion, and the showing should, as far as possible, follow the principles outlined in 'Video film identification' or 'Identification by photographs'. A police officer who is a witness is subject to the same principles and procedures as a civilian witness.

Identification generally

The Code is concerned with *formal* identification. Informal evidence of identification, where it is obtained in good faith, is valid. Where police officers who had been chasing a driver returned to the police station and while they were there, the suspect entered the police station and was instantly identified by the officers, the evidence of identification was admitted.

Where an accused and a witness know each other well, there is little need for a formal identification. However, if the accused asks for a parade he must be allowed one. Failure to provide a parade may result in the exclusion of the evidence of identification.

Where the result of a case depends substantially on the disputed correctness of one or more visual identifications of a person, the jury must be warned of the danger of convicting and the special need for caution. The judge must also explain the reasons for this; namely, that experience has shown that visual identification, even by way of recognition, is a category of evidence which is particularly vulnerable to error.

It must be appreciated that a witness who seeks to identify a suspect within the procedures set out in the Identification Code, may not always find him as he saw him. Defendants, following advice, can become masters of disguise. However, the new provisions introduced with the 1995 version of the Identification Code may make this practice a little more difficult.

4 Crime

Assaults

An assault is an attempt by force, or violence, to do bodily injury to another. The display of force should be such that the victim believes that force is about to be used against him. There are two important elements in the offence: a display of force by one party, and a genuine fear that force was about to be used in the mind of the person against whom the threat was made. The pointing of an unloaded gun at a person may amount to an assault. The act amounts to a display of force, and if the person at whom the gun is pointed fears that it may be used this is sufficient to constitute the offence. If a man threatens to throw a punch at another person who fears that his threat will be carried out, the assault is complete although the person assaulted has not been touched in any way. An assault has been committed when there is any act which intentionally, or because of the recklessness of the act itself, causes another person to fear immediate unlawful violence. It is important to consider whether or not such fear could have existed in the mind of the victim. If the threat is made at such a distance from the other party that it could not possibly have been carried out, then it is inconceivable that there was immediate apprehension that physical force was about to be applied. Provided that there is a present ability to carry out the threat, the nature of the act is only restricted in that it must contain an element of hostility. Urging a dog to attack, drawing a knife, throwing a stone or other missile, or raising a stick in a threatening manner each provides an example of the type of act which would cause a person to fear that violence was about to be used against him. If a gang of rowdy youths throw rubble from a building site at people who are passing in the street, a brick deliberately aimed at a particular person is clearly intended to cause that person to fear being hit; bricks showered at passers-by generally indicate a recklessness as to whether passers-by will be put in fear by these actions.

The law differentiates between an assault and a battery. The term 'battery' means the intentional or reckless application of unlawful force to another, however slight, and whether directly or indirectly. It would be applied directly where a person hits another with his fist or with some object and indirectly if he placed acid in a hand drier which is later blown on to the hands of some other person. Each battery includes the elements of an assault as it amounts to the eventual application of the threatened violence. A person who strikes another with his fist, or beats him with a stick, has both assaulted and beaten him, but the physical contact does not need to be so aggravated. Any hostile touching, pushing, striking with an implement or object which has been thrown, will amount to a battery. If a man throws a stone at his neighbour and misses him, he is guilty of an assault; if the stone finds its mark, he is also guilty of battery.

The High Court has ruled that where there has been an assault, if the assault is *by beating*, it should be so charged.

There are many instances in which such forms of physical contact are quite justified and are, therefore, not punishable, but in all such instances no more force must be used than is necessary upon that particular occasion.

Defences to assault

Questions concerning the nature of an assault usually establish whether or not valid defences may be put forward. Was consent given to the act which constitutes the allegation of assault? Was the assault justified in law?

Consent

Consent may, on certain occasions, be given to acts which would otherwise be an assault and these occasions would include blows exchanged in the course of friendly athletic contests or during innocent horseplay. If the act results in physical injury to another person, his consent is no defence to a charge of wounding. Thus, willing and enthusiastic participation in sado-masochistic acts of violence for the sexual pleasure engendered in the giving and receiving of pain can lead to a conviction for an assault or battery or for a more serious offence. If no physical harm amounting to a wounding or bodily harm results from an assault, it is necessary to prove the absence of consent, unless the actions themselves were injurious to the public or were accompanied by a breach of the peace. It has been held that injuries received in the course of a prize fight are injurious to the public and consent is, therefore, no defence. The distinction is made between the bare fisted public spectacle and the lawful sport of boxing, which is conducted in such a way that injuries are kept to the minimum possible in this form of contest. Persons who participate in sports such as soccer or rugby accept that there is a risk of injury from bodily contact permitted by the rules of the game. However, a head-butt or a deliberate kick aimed at a player on the ground would not be excused as no consent is given to such bodily contacts. If excessive violence is used during an assault the question of consent cannot arise as no legal consent can be given to such acts. In addition, the consent obtained must be a true consent and not one which was obtained by means of fear, fraud or ignorance.

Sometimes a consent which has been given will be invalid, for example where the person giving the consent is young or sufficiently mentally impaired to be unable to understand the nature of the act committed. The same would be true if consent had been obtained by duress.

Legally justified

(1) *Lawful correction*

It is a good defence that the assault was in the course of correction of a child by its parents, or other people in *loco parentis*, provided that it is moderate in manner and quantity, and that the instrument used is reasonable. Obviously, the force used is unreasonable if it is disproportionate to the wrongdoing, and is also unreasonable if the chastisement involved an uncontrolled response to wrongdoing. However, teachers in state schools do not have the right to chastise their pupils, but teachers at private schools do (except in relation to pupils whose fees are paid out of public funds).

(2) *Self-defence*

A person may be justified in assaulting another if the assault is carried out in self-defence. The justification is generally limited to circumstances in which the first act of hostility was carried out by the other party, although it is not essential that the other party struck the first blow. The Court of Appeal has ruled that it is both good law and good sense that a person who is attacked may defend himself, but that in doing so, he may only do what is reasonably necessary. In deciding upon his response, the facts as the person concerned believed them to be are the facts to be assessed. If a man raises a stick intending to strike another, the second party is not obliged to await the blow falling before taking action to defend himself. It is important, but not essential, that a person offering this defence is able to show that he did not wish to become involved in a fight. There is a limit to the action which must be taken to avoid conflict, and this need not include a willingness to run away in order to avoid a confrontation with a person who offers violence. It is not suggested that a man must avoid going to some place at which he knows persons are assembled who may offer him violence, but he must show that it was neither his wish nor his intention to become involved. A failure to retreat when this was possible is merely one factor which may be taken into account by a court when deciding whether the use of force was necessary and reasonable in the particular circumstances. A person may act in self-defence without temporising, disengaging or withdrawing in circumstances in which he will have a good defence.

(3) *Defence of wife, husband, parent, or child*

It has long been recognised that assaults committed in defence of persons who enjoyed these particular relationships may be justified and the common law recognised the special relationship which existed between masters and servants, so that similar defences are acceptable in respect of acts done in defence of one party, by the other. In 1967, the Court of Criminal Appeal refused to restrict this defence to these particular relationships.

There is, additionally, a right held by any person to intervene to prevent someone else from being assaulted, and it is permissible to do all that is necessary and reasonable to prevent such an assault. The Criminal Law Act 1967 provides a defence for anyone who commits an assault while acting in the prevention of crime.

(4) *Defence of property*

Assaults may be justified if they are committed in defence of property. This justification may relate to the unlawful removal of goods, or to the defence of an owner's right of possession of his property. If force is used to remove a trespasser from property, there must be a request made to the trespasser to leave before force may be used, and then it may only be such as is necessary to remove him from the premises. The essential question must always be 'was the force used reasonable in the circumstances?' A property owner does not have the right to use force against a trespasser who does not threaten violence.

(5) *During a lawful arrest*

An arrest can seldom be effected without some form of physical contact and the action of arrest must in some way indicate to the person arrested that he is subject to physical restraint and that he will be forcibly prevented from leaving, should he attempt to do so. The amount of force which must be used varies according to the degree of resistance of the prisoner, which can be considerable, particularly when persons are arrested for offences of drunkenness. The use of force by the constable is justified provided that it is reasonable in the circumstances and necessary to effect the arrest.

Certain other defences can reasonably be put forward in answer to a charge of assault. The physical contact may occur by misadventure, for example the accidental discharge of a missile; or in the course of a lawful sport, such as a wrestling bout or a soccer match.

Offences of assault and battery

The Criminal Justice Act 1988, s. 39, states that common assault and battery are summary offences. They are punishable by a fine or imprisonment for six months, or both. Offences dealt with by the police should be charged as offences of assault or battery depending upon the circumstances. Where a person has merely been 'put in fear' the person responsible should be charged with an assault contrary to this section. Where force has been applied to a person, the person responsible should be charged that he 'did assault by beating' and it is important that these words are used.

While there is a power of arrest for an assault committed in a police officer's presence, or where there is a danger that further violence will be offered, these are powers which will only be exercised where circumstances demand it. If an arrest is made for a breach, or threatened breach of the peace, proceedings must follow for those offences or be discontinued.

Police action

While police action may follow incidents involving an assault, it must be remembered that the circumstances in which such offences can be committed are so wide that prosecution for a criminal offence may not always be the best way forward. Where the nature of the assault is trivial, particularly in instances in which

400

family, friends or neighbours are the only persons involved, it may be more satisfactory, after a cautionary word, to ensure that the parties involved are aware of each other's names and addresses so that they may make a complaint to the clerk to the magistrates with a view to obtaining 'surety of the peace' from the other party. Any such action must be in accordance with force standing orders. An accurate record must be made of any such incident as constables are frequently called as witnesses in such cases.

Victims of criminal assaults may be entitled to receive compensation from the Criminal Injuries Compensation Board. They should be informed of this entitlement.

Assault – police

Section 51 of the Police Act 1964 states that any person who assaults a constable in the execution of his duty, or a person assisting a constable in the execution of his duty, shall be guilty of an offence.

The same section punishes persons who resist or wilfully obstruct a constable in the execution of his duty, or a person assisting him.

This section covers several important points and it is essential to prove that the person assaulted was a police officer and was acting as such, or, in the case of a person assisting him, both of these factors and that the second party was acting in his aid. It must also be shown that the officer was acting in the execution of his duty, and this is the essence of the offence. If an assault is directed at a police officer who is not acting in the execution of his duty, it is merely a common assault. The distinction is often a fine one, as illustrated by the following examples.

A police officer who witnessed an obstruction by a motor lorry, followed the vehicle into a garage in order to make enquiries. He did not have permission to enter the garage. The owner told him to leave and the officer refused, claiming that he had the right to remain, and was assaulted by the owner. It was held that even if the police officer had a right to enter the garage, he had no right to remain after being told to leave and so became a trespasser. As such he was no longer acting in the execution of his duty at the time at which he was assaulted. However, it would have been different if a breach of the peace had been taking place on the premises, as the common law permits a constable both to enter and *remain* on private premises to deal with an actual or apprehended breach of the peace. Such a constable is acting in the execution of his duty. A police officer, who believed that a breach of the peace would occur if a man addressed people assembled in a street, forbade him to do so but the man persisted and obstructed the officer when he attempted to prevent the meeting from being held. It was decided that as it is one of the duties of the constable to prevent breaches of the peace which he reasonably believes are about to occur, the man was guilty of obstructing him in the execution of his duty.

Where a constable witnessed an argument between a man and his girl friend which resulted in the girl running away, he was entitled, after giving the girl directions to her home, to speak to the man to ensure that he would not follow the girl, as he was acting in the course of his duties to preserve the peace. A sergeant and two constables passed through a garden gate and approached the door of a house at which they wished to make enquiries concerning a crime. The sergeant was invited into the house by the son of the occupier; the occupier immediately ordered him to leave and

401

as the sergeant was doing so he was attacked. The constables came to the assistance of the sergeant and a fight took place. In this case the defendants were convicted of assaulting the officers in the execution of their duty, it being held that they were not trespassers when they passed through the garden gate as they had implied leave to pass through the gate and approach the front door for the purpose of making enquiries. When the constables went to the assistance of the sergeant, they were acting in the execution of their duty by endeavouring to prevent a breach of the peace.

It has been held that in circumstances in which police officers arrested a man and it was not practicable to tell him of the reason for his arrest at the time, the arrest was lawful and the officers were acting in the execution of their duty, even though the arrest was subsequently made unlawful as the reason for arrest was not given when it was practicable to do so. Similarly, where a constable stopped a motor vehicle pursuant to the Road Traffic Act 1988, s. 163, and detained it, suspecting it to be stolen, he was acting in the execution of his duty provided that his 'suspicion' was justified.

Actual bodily harm

The Offences Against the Person Act 1861, s. 47, provides that it is an arrestable offence to assault any person causing him actually bodily harm. The term 'actual bodily harm' is self-explanatory, meaning some actual bodily injury which need not be extensive or of a permanent nature. Anything which interferes with the health or comfort of the victim in a more than trifling way, may be described as actual bodily harm and this would include black eyes, more serious bruising, and minor cuts. An injury includes an hysterical or nervous condition or psychiatric injury (but not emotions such as fear, distress or panic which are not themselves evidence of an identifiable clinical condition). Expert evidence should be offered of such a condition. It will be seen that this offence does not require a specific intent on the part of the accused; it is sufficient if there is an assault and, as a result of it, actual bodily harm is occasioned. There must be a direct causal connection between the assault and the bodily harm. If a man punches his victim this is apparent. If he chases him so that, in fear, he jumps out of a window and injures himself, there is still a direct causal connection between the assault and the bodily harm. Assaults resulting in serious nervous disorders have been held to be punishable under this section.

The *mens rea* required for this offence is that required for an assault or battery. It is not essential to establish that a defendant intended to cause some bodily harm, or was reckless as to the risk of doing so.

Woundings

Sections 18 and 20 of the Offences Against the Person Act 1861 deal with offences of wounding which are similar in some characteristics. It will be noticed that these offences require that the accused must have acted unlawfully and maliciously. The requirement that the act must have been done unlawfully excludes instances in which a constable or citizen may have used force to prevent a crime or to effect a lawful arrest. For an act to have been done maliciously the accused must have foreseen the possibility of the type of injury specified within each section. It is from this point, in the consideration of a charge, that the further facts of the case must be carefully considered as there is some difference in the seriousness of the offences. Offences contrary to s. 18, in respect of which specific intentions to effect particular types of harm must be specified, are punishable by life imprisonment, while those contrary to s. 20, in respect of which particular intentions need not be shown, are punishable by five years' imprisonment.

Wounding with intent

Section 18 of the Offences Against the Person Act 1861 states:

'Whosoever shall unlawfully and maliciously, by any means whatsoever, wound or cause any grievous bodily harm to any person, WITH INTENT to do grievous bodily harm to any person or with intent to resist or prevent the lawful apprehension or detainer of any person, commits an offence.'

The section creates two offences and the different intents mentioned in the section specify variations in the method by which the offences may be committed. There are various terms used within this section which require definition:

(a) *Wound.* To constitute a wound the continuity of the skin must be broken. The skin consists of two layers and both must be broken before an injury can be described as a wound. It is not necessary that this must be an outer skin covering, a break inside the cheek or the lip is a wound for the purposes of this Act.

Wounds may be inflicted in a variety of ways: by a kick, or with an instrument resulting in incised, punctured, lacerated, contused, or gunshot wounds. A broken bone cannot be a wound unless a part of it pierces the skin.

(b) *Grievous bodily harm.* This term means really serious bodily harm, but it is not necessary that it should be either dangerous or permanent. Where a man cut the private parts of an infant in order to commit rape, the injury not being serious although it caused considerable bleeding, he was convicted of causing grievous bodily harm with that intent.

(c) *With intent.* It is necessary to prove that the particular type of injury was inflicted with the intention of doing so, or with the intention to resist or prevent detention. It is reasonable to assume that a person intends the consequences of his deliberate acts unless he is able to prove that the result was accidental, but a court must consider all of the evidence available before deciding whether or not a particular intention existed. If a man attacks another in order to rob him and, in the course of doing so, inflicts grievous bodily harm, he may be convicted of this offence. By using violence to effect his purpose he shows an intention to cause grievous bodily harm, which is a natural consequence of his act.

The section specifies an intention to cause grievous bodily harm to any person and a man will be guilty of this offence if he strikes at or shoots at one person with such intent but injures another. In such circumstances the charge should specify that he caused grievous bodily harm to B with intent to cause harm to A. In all instances the particular intent must be shown in evidence. When a man heard an intruder in his house and fired a gun to frighten him away, but hit him and wounded him, it was held that he was not guilty of an offence contrary to this section as his intention had not been to cause harm, and this must be clearly shown before a conviction would be merited. It is not sufficient to establish mere recklessness, the specific intent alleged must be proved.

(d) *Resist or prevent lawful apprehension or detainer of any person.* If a charge alleges this particular intent it must be shown that the person concerned was told of the officer's intention to arrest him. By including the words 'any person' it is not only the person who is being arrested who may be convicted of this offence, but any person who attempts to prevent the arrest by use of force. Once again the intention of the person concerned is the preliminary factor for consideration. If a man trips a police officer who is chasing a criminal over grass and the officer falls on to broken glass, the presence of which was unknown to the accused, it cannot be said that it was the intention of his attacker to cause grievous bodily harm by means of broken glass or that such a result could be foreseen. If the police officer was tripped while running after a criminal in a street and was seriously injured when he fell, it can be assumed that such injury was intended as the results could be easily foreseen.

Unlawful wounding

Section 20 of the Offences Against the Person Act 1861 states;

> 'Whosoever shall unlawfully and maliciously wound or inflict grievous bodily harm upon any other person, either with or without any weapon or instrument, shall be guilty of an offence.'

The terms used within this section are similar to those used within s. 18, but the notable omission is the words 'with intent'. A particular intention to inflict the types of harm specified is, therefore, unnecessary, but it must be shown that the act was done 'maliciously'. It is sufficient to show that the act was such that the accused must have foreseen that he was likely to cause some harm, even if of a minor nature, to some other person. A person acts maliciously if he carries out an act deliberately and he was aware that some physical harm might result. He need not be aware that it *will* result. Nor is it essential that he foresaw harm of the gravity described in the section, foresight that some harm, albeit of a minor character, might result, is sufficient. In most cases with which police officers are involved, the malice is quite apparent from the circumstances of the case and need not be specified in any particular manner. If a blow is struck with the fist, which results in a wound requiring stitches, it is evident that it was done maliciously and the fact that a wound was inflicted is sufficient to justify a charge.

A wildfowler was using a punt on a river for the purpose of shooting and the accused fired a shot in the direction of the punt for the purpose of frightening the trespasser, but without the intention of hitting him, although the shot did in fact wound him. He was convicted of an offence contrary to this section as the act was malicious, being reckless in the circumstances, and it resulted in grievous bodily harm being caused. The case illustrates quite clearly the difference between the offences created by ss. 18 and 20. For a charge contrary to s. 18 to be proved, the prosecution would have had to prove that the shot was fired with the intention of causing that particular type of injury. A similar illustration of this difference is provided by the prosecution of the man who, with the intention of causing panic to the audience in a theatre, extinguished the lights and placed a bar across the exit door of a staircase leading from the theatre. In the resulting confusion, those coming first to the door were forced against the iron bar and seriously injured. The accused was convicted of an offence contrary to s. 20, as his act was malicious and resulted in grievous bodily harm to two persons. In such circumstances, an offence contrary to s. 18 had not been committed as it could not be said that the practical joker intended specifically to cause those injuries.

Where a man, believing an air rifle to be unloaded, although he had not checked it, aimed the rifle at another man and pulled the trigger thus wounding him it was held that, for the act to be malicious, it must be shown that the accused, on the facts known to him, actually foresaw that a particular kind of harm might be done. Malice must be concerned with foresight of the physical harm which is actually occasioned.

A person charged with unlawful wounding may be found guilty by a jury of assault occasioning actual bodily harm.

Police powers

All offences contrary to ss. 18 and 20 of the Offence Against the Person Act 1861 are arrestable offences.

Theft

The law relating to theft has generally followed the pattern of our society. At common law it was divided into petty larceny, the stealing of property not exceeding 12d. in value, and grand larceny if the value was in excess of that figure. The Larceny Acts of 1861 and 1916 varied the offence and the punishment in accordance with the degree of aggravation and having regard to whether or not the person who committed the offence was in a position of trust, or if particular forms of property were involved.

The Theft Act 1968 repealed previous legislation and deals with all forms of theft in a much simplified manner, being expressed in simple language which can be understood by the majority of people.

Section 1 of the Theft Act 1968 provides:

'A person is guilty of theft if he dishonestly appropriates property belonging to another with the intention of permanently depriving the other of it; and "the thief" and "steal" shall be construed accordingly.'

For there to be a theft it is not essential that the appropriation of property is made with a view to gain, or is made for the thief's own benefit. The person who appropriates a motor car and burns it, steals the car when he indicates his intention to permanently deprive the owner of his property by destroying it.

405

To be guilty of an offence of theft two main elements are necessary:

(a) the appropriation of property belonging to another (the *actus reus* of the offence); and
(b) the dishonest intention of permanently depriving the owner of his property (the *mens rea* of the offence).

Dishonesty

Whether or not an action was carried out dishonestly is a question of fact for a jury to decide.

Section 2 of the Act attempts to establish the dishonesty of the intention of the person who steals, by describing circumstances in which there is no dishonest intention:

(a) A person's appropriation of property belonging to another is not to be regarded as dishonest:
   (i) if he appropriates the property in the belief that he has in law the right to deprive the other of it, on behalf of himself or a third party; or
   (ii) if he appropriates the property in the belief that he would have the other's consent if the other knew of the appropriation and the circumstances of it; or
   (iii) (except where the property came to him as a trustee or personal representative) if he appropriates the property in the belief that the person to whom the property belongs cannot be discovered by taking reasonable steps.
(b) A person's appropriation of property belonging to another may be dishonest notwithstanding that he is willing to pay for the property.

It will be helpful to consider each of these circumstances in greater detail.

(1) *Belief in lawful right to deprive*

There is no dishonest intention if the act is done by someone in the belief that he has a legal right to do it. It is perhaps immaterial whether the belief is reasonable or not, or that there exists no basis in law for such a belief, if the person concerned honestly believed that he had a right. For practical purposes, the less reasonable a belief appears to be, the less likely it is that a court will accept it. Although the Act refers to a right in law, it does not necessarily imply that belief in a moral right will be sufficient to negate an allegation that an act is done dishonestly. Much will depend upon the nature of such belief, otherwise theft committed by anarchist organisations, the members of which believe that they have a moral right to finance their political activities with the money of other people, would become excusable.

Money is often taken by persons who have possession of it, but do not own it, with the intention of replacing it at some later date. Such persons may be employed as collectors and may use some of the money acquired on behalf of their employers in an emergency. It could be argued that this was not 'dishonest', if they knew with certainty that they could replace the money almost at once. This may occur if they used some of it on a Saturday while the banks were closed, knowing that they had more than sufficient in their account to replace it on Monday morning, but it certainly would be dishonest if the money was taken in circumstances in which it was not possible for them to replace it, or they merely enjoyed a vague hope that it would be possible, such as may occur if they had made a bet on the result of a horse race, which if successful would give them sufficient money to repay. A sound definition of dishonesty in such circumstances is: 'Does the person intend to act to the detriment of the owner against his wishes?'

(2) *Belief that the owner would have consented*

A similar defence was provided to charges of taking motor vehicles without the consent of the owner or other lawful authority under a repealed section of the Road Traffic Act 1960. This defence was provided to protect persons who had a special relationship with the owner of such a vehicle who, on finding the owner absent on calling to borrow his motor car, may nevertheless take it in the knowledge that consent would be given. The taking of motor vehicles and other conveyances is now dealt with under the Theft Act 1968, and the former defence to such charges available under the Road Traffic Act 1960 has been included in this Act. However, having been included as a general defence to a charge of theft on the grounds that such an act would not be dishonest, it would apply in all circumstances and would equally apply if such a person removed an alarm clock in the absence of the owner, knowing that the property would have been given had the owner been present. In most circumstances of this nature, the taker would leave a note explaining what he had done, but on occasion reports of such thefts are received from the owner of the property, to be followed by a further report that a relative had since telephoned to inform him that he had removed the property in his absence.

(3) *Belief that the owner cannot be discovered by taking reasonable steps*

The common law has always recognised the right of possession of property by the finder against all but the true owner or any other person having special rights in relation to such property. These rights have been preserved within the Theft Act 1968. Whether an owner is likely to be able to be traced is largely a question of fact. If a man finds a £10 note on the footpath in a busy shopping area he may be considered to be acting quite reasonably if he assumes that the owner cannot be traced. Although the property can be identified by its serial number, very few people are aware of the numbers of bank notes in their possession at any time. If, on the other hand, the £10 note was in a wallet which also contained a business card, a banker's card, or some other means by which the owner could be traced, the finder is clearly guilty of theft if he uses the money for his own purposes. The nature of the property, coupled with the circumstances of the finding, determines the form of steps which would have to be taken in order to attempt to trace an owner. In the case of the single £10 note little less than an extensive advertising campaign would have much hope of success, and this goes well beyond the term 'reasonable', whereas in the circumstances in which the bank note was contained in a wallet with some other personal, identifiable articles, quite a limited action would be sufficient to trace the owner and such action would certainly be within the term 'reasonable'. The question really turns upon the belief of the finder.

However, this defence is not limited to circumstances in which property is found. A person may be asked to take care of property for some other person who is subsequently not heard of for many years. In such circumstances, if he converts the property to his own use or even disposes of it for cash, the question of whether or not his act was 'dishonest' will have to be considered. If he believed that the owner could not be traced by taking reasonable steps, this defence will be open to him. In the circumstances in which he disposed of the property for cash, the owner of the property will have a claim upon it, but his belief that he could not be traced by taking reasonable steps is a defence to be considered in relation to a charge of theft.

(4) *Where taker willing to pay*

Section 2(2), by stating that a person's appropriation of another's property may be dishonest notwithstanding that he is willing to pay for it, resolves the situation concerning whether or not an act can be dishonest when full payment is made for goods which are taken. Such protection is necessary, otherwise rare, valuable property could be taken from collectors by persons willing to pay the market value. Payment for goods taken can be a mitigating factor to be considered by the court when considering the sentence to be passed. However, this subsection does say that such an action 'may' be dishonest and we must differentiate between the man who takes a newspaper from an unattended news stand and leaves payment, where he obviously believes that the owner would welcome such a sale, and the man who, being disappointed at not being able to purchase a rare painting, removes it from the owner's house and leaves payment. In the first instance there was no dishonest intention but in the second there clearly is an intention to act dishonestly against the interests of the owner.

(5) *Dishonesty in a general sense*

However, the Act merely describes particular acts which will not be dishonest. In a general sense, it is a matter for the justices or the jury to decide whether or not a particular act was carried out dishonestly. In deciding such an issue, they must consider whether or not a person's actions were dishonest according to the ordinary standards of reasonable and honest people.

If an employee in a grocery store takes provisions without paying for them, knowing that his employer would not consent, but claims that he intended to put the money in the till on the following day when he received his pay, he could not claim a belief in law that he had a right to take the provisions, nor that he believed that he would have the owner's consent if he knew of the appropriation. However, he could claim, that in the circumstances, he did not believe that what he was doing was dishonest and it will be for the prosecution to show that he did not intend to pay. The magistrates or jury must then decide whether his actions were 'dishonest' in the light of evidence offered by the prosecution.

In considering the term 'dishonestly' we have looked at the guilty state of the person's mind. or *mens rea*, but in considering the term 'appropriates' we are concerned with the guilty act, or *actus reus*.

Section 3(1) of the Theft Act 1968 defines appropriation as follows:

'Any assumption by a person of the rights of an owner amounts to an appropriation, and this includes where he has come by the property (innocently or not) without stealing it, any later assumption of a right to it by keeping or dealing with it as owner.'

Previous to the Theft Act 1968 an intention to deprive the owner permanently had to exist at the time of taking the property, but s. 3(1) now makes it clear that an appropriation can take place at any time, even if the property was acquired innocently in the first place. In most instances of theft reported to the police, the appropriation will have amounted to a straightforward removal of the property from the possession of the owner – for example, the stealing of a radio from a motor car, the removal of a wallet from a pocket, or the taking of a bottle of milk from a doorstep. Circumstances in which a later appropriation would amount to theft might involve a person handing over his radio to an acquaintance who, at that time, intended to repair it for him, but later decides to sell it and spend the money. The appropriation takes place at the time such person assumes the rights of the owner by disposing of the property. In determining when an appropriation has taken place, it is helpful to ask yourself the question, 'When did the accused first assume the rights of an owner?' This is not necessarily when property is sold or disposed of in circumstances in which original receipt of the goods was innocent. If, in the example given above, the accused had advertised the radio for sale, the offering of the goods for sale clearly indicates an assumption of the rights of an owner, and an offence of theft is complete. It is unlikely that a mental decision to keep or dispose of the property would be sufficient; the accused must in some way, by his actions, indicate an appropriation of the property.

Similarly, where a man hands over a sum of money to a second party who is to invest it on his behalf, the money continues to be the property of the owner as the second party is merely acting as his agent. If the second party later uses the money for his own purposes, he appropriates it at that time as he then assumes ownership rights.

A lorry driver is to deliver 100 toy train sets to a customer. On delivering his load he finds that there are five sets too many and decides to keep them. He then drives to his home and leaves the train sets there. In the first instance he came into possession of the surplus sets innocently, as he was unaware that his vehicle had been overloaded and on discovering the mistake, decided to keep them. When he begins to drive them to his home, he assumes the rights of an owner and appropriates the property. A workman on a building site knows that he is due approximately £100 as his weekly pay, but is given a pay packet containing £160. He realises that the money is not his, but later spends it. Once again the appropriation takes place not at the moment at which he decides to keep the money, but immediately that he assumes ownership rights by putting the money to use. Where an employee who is paid excess wages by means of a cheque, realises what has occurred and draws the money and spends it, he steals from his employer as he appropriates a 'thing in action' (see page 412), that is, part of the credit which the bank owes him. This is not uncommon.

When a man struck a woman causing her to drop her handbag it was ruled that he was trying to exclude the woman from her possession of the bag and had, therefore, appropriated it, this being an unlawful assumption of the right of the owner.

An appropriation may take place through an innocent agent. If a person in authority signs a false invoice, intending that innocent people take further steps which result in money being debited, and thus appropriated from a bank account, he is guilty of theft.

There may be an appropriation by deception where the goods are obtained in circumstances in which the consent which is obtained could not be described as a valid consent. Where a man obtained his shop manager's consent to release goods to another party by alleging that he had checked the validity of cheques which he knew to be stolen, it was held that he had appropriated the goods. Similarly, where a taxi driver took money from the wallet of a foreign visitor, in addition to the £1 which was offered in payment for a fare which was less than £1, he was held to have appropriated that money although no objection to its removal had been offered by the person concerned. The common factor within both of these cases is that neither of the injured parties would have consented to the taking had they known of the true circumstances of that taking. However, in such circumstances the persons concerned would also commit an offence of obtaining property by deception and that is the charge which would usually be preferred.

Where a person removes goods from a shelf in a supermarket and conceals them in his coat pocket to avoid having to pay for them, he clearly appropriates property as this amounts to an adverse interference with or usurpation of the rights of the owner (an unlawful act or *actus reus*). On the other hand, where an honest shopper takes goods from a shelf and puts them in a shopping trolley provided by the owner of the supermarket, there is no such interference or usurpation as this is an act which is authorised by the owner and is therefore not unlawful. If a person removes an article from a shelf and switches the price label for one indicating a lesser price and this is done with the intention of depriving the owner of a part of the true price of his goods, there is an appropriation with the required dishonest intent. A practical joker who switches labels for fun, would not steal because he did not appropriate those articles and in any case, had no dishonest intent.

Similarly, if a shop assistant sells goods to a friend at a price which is less than that fixed by the owner, she steals that property although she was in lawful possession of it at the outset, as what she does amounts to an assumption of the rights of an owner to fix the price at which goods should be sold.

The definition of the term 'appropriation' is such that a person who does not steal at the outset, may steal in consequence of some later action. If a person 'borrows' a raincoat from a coat stand in a public house because it is raining, intending to return it on the following evening, he does not steal at that time as he does not intend to permanently deprive the owner of his property. If he later sells the coat, he appropriates it dishonestly at that time, as he has assumed an ownership right; the right of disposal.

Section 3(2) of the Act is designed to protect the purchaser who innocently buys goods in good faith, paying full value, only to discover later that the seller had no title to the goods which still belonged to another person.

'Where property or a right of interest in property is or purports to be transferred for value to a person acting in good faith, no later assumption by him of rights which he believed himself to be acquiring shall, by reason of any defect in the transferor's title, amount to theft of the property.'

In the normal circumstances in which such a transaction may occur, the facts will be quite straightforward. A man may buy a watch from a market trader, paying full value for it, and it is later found that it is one of a consignment stolen at an entry port. This subsection protects him fully if he assumes the rights of an owner, thus 'appropriating' the property, as the act of appropriation in such circumstances is declared not to be contrary to the law. It is important to realise that this is so regardless of the mental state of the person concerned, which in normal circumstances will be innocent enough, as most people would feel that having paid a fair price they had a good claim to ownership; but even if the person who had come into innocent possession of the property, on discovering that it was the property of some other person, continued to use it as an owner, or even gave it away, he is not guilty of an offence of theft. If such a person sold the goods after discovering that they had been stolen, he may be found guilty of obtaining money by deception, the deception being that he pretends to be the true owner of the property.

The original receipt of property must be innocent in every sense of the word before the protection of s. 3(2) is valid. Property is frequently purchased in circumstances in which the buyer must have realised that it was stolen. Currently there is considerable illegal traffic in stolen home entertainment equipment and purchasers who receive such equipment at much reduced prices must be fully aware that there is some question as to title. However, where a man buys motor cycle parts for value and issues a receipt, but later suspects that such parts are stolen when he discovers that engine numbers have been removed, there can be no theft if he decides to keep them. Although such an act is clearly an appropriation, s. 3(2) prevents it from being theft.

Appropriation can be by act or omission, and acts of appropriation have already been discussed. An example of appropriation by omission is provided by the following circumstances. A child under the age of criminal responsibility brings home a pedal cycle which does not belong to him. The child commits no offence as it is conclusively presumed that he cannot commit crime. The child's father knows that the cycle must be stolen but does nothing about it, being quite content to allow his child to keep it, and, therefore, assumes ownership rights through the innocent agency of the child.

Property

Section 4(1) describes what is meant by the term 'property'.

' "Property" includes money and all other property, real or personal, including things in action and other intangible property.'

This definition deals with forms of property which we might describe as the tangible

411

and the intangible, or perhaps the things we can hold in our hands and the things which we cannot hold. Money requires no further description, and the terms 'real or personal' property may include articles, things, houses, or estates or may be used to indicate the owner's rights over that article, or estate. Things 'personal' are usually moveable, while those 'real' are not. 'Things in action' are intangibles. They include a debt, a copyright or a trademark in respect of which a person has ownership rights which may be dishonestly assumed by another person.

When a person has money in a bank account, the bank acknowledges that it owes that person a debt (the extent of the current balance). If a person dishonestly draws a cheque on that account, he steals from it as he has appropriated a part of the bank's debt to that person. It will be appreciated that in such circumstances, the drawer of the cheque could not steal money belonging to the holder of the bank account, as the money in the cashier's till which would be handed over does not belong to the holder of the account. The debt is a 'thing in action'. Similarly, a sum of money represented by a figure in a bank account is within the phrase 'other intangible property' and can be stolen by dishonest electronic transfer.

Subsection (2) provides:

'A person cannot steal land, or things forming part of land and severed from it by him or by his directions, except:
  (a) when he is a trustee or personal representative, or is authorised by power of attorney, or as a liquidator of a company, or otherwise to sell or dispose of land belonging to another, and he appropriates the land or anything forming part of it by dealing with it in breach of the confidence reposed in him; or
  (b) when he is not in possession of the land and appropriates anything forming part of the land by severing it or causing it to be severed, or after it has been severed; or
  (c) when, being in possession of the land under a tenancy, he appropriates the whole or part of any fixture or structure let to be used with the land.'

The subsection begins with a general statement to the effect that a person cannot steal land, or things which he detaches from it, or causes to be detached, and then gives various exceptions to the rule which cover many possibilities. Thus, a person who moves his boundary fence in order to enclose land belonging to a neighbour does not steal that land. Other remedies are open to him.

In the first instance this section deals with persons put in a position of trust in relation to land, who deal with it wrongfully by selling it or otherwise disposing of it in breach of the confidence placed in them. It may be, for example, that a firm of solicitors is authorised to act as agents on behalf of the owner in relation to the administration of an estate, and may be permitted to deal with tenancies and to appoint estate officers on behalf of the land owner. If a member of the firm sells sections of the land, or in any other way assumes rights of ownership, he is guilty of theft.

Secondly, it is concerned with people other than persons who are in possession of, or have a special responsibility for, the land. Such persons may steal fixtures, things growing, or even the land itself, provided that they sever them first. Examples would

be the unauthorised removal of gravel from a pit, the cutting of hay and its immediate removal from the land, the removal of stones fixed into land such as marker stones indicating the borders between England, Wales, and Scotland, which are occasionally dug up and removed by nationalist organisations. It will be noticed that both severance and the assumption of ownership rights are essential before an offence of theft is committed.

Finally, the subsection is concerned with persons who are in possession of land as tenants, and who are, therefore, in a position of trust. If the tenancy includes the right to use buildings and fixtures which are situated on the land, use and occupation of the building are permitted, but the removal of such buildings or fixtures would amount to the assumption of the rights of the owner and would make the tenant liable to prosecution for an offence of theft.

Subsection (3) provides protection for the person who picks mushrooms, blackberries, elderberries, or any other wild produce of the field or hedgerow. The protection of this subsection does not apply if the gathering of such wild produce is done for some commercial purpose, and one can appreciate the law makers excepting the casual hollypicker who requires one or two sprigs of holly to decorate his house at Christmas, but wishing to punish the trader who strips the hedgerows in order to make a big profit. The subsection provides:

> 'A person who picks mushrooms growing wild on any land, or who picks flowers, fruit or foliage from a plant growing wild on any land, does not (although not in possession of the land) steal what he picks, unless he does it for reward or for sale or other commercial purpose.'

This subsection is quite interesting: by permitting only the picking of flowers, fruit, or foliage, the removal of the plant by the roots is still prohibited. Such actions would, in any case, offend against the Wildlife and Countryside Act 1981, s. 13, in the case of 'protected plants'. The term 'picking' is quite clear; it permits the normal actions of the country rambler who wishes to pick flowers or berries, but would not be wide enough to permit someone to saw off the top of a Christmas tree. As Christmas approaches many police forces organise special patrols to prevent thefts of poultry, Christmas trees, and holly by thieves looking for a readily saleable commodity. Certain vehicles are checked as they leave the rural districts of counties and drivers are asked to provide documentary evidence to show that any poultry, trees, or large quantities of holly found in their vehicle have been purchased from recognised sources.

Finally, subs. (4) explains the law of theft in relation to wild animals. The common law always differentiated between tame and wild animals, and the position in relation to tame or domestic animals has always been clear; they are the property of some person and, therefore, may be stolen. On the other hand, wild animals have no owner and being free to roam from place to place are not generally the subject of theft at common law. The Poaching Prevention Act and Game Laws have the effect of making the killing and taking of such animals offences in many cases, and the Theft Act 1968 continues to recognise that such offences exist and it is, therefore, unnecessary to make the taking of wild animals punishable as theft:

> 'Wild creatures, tamed or untamed, shall be regarded as property; but a person cannot steal a wild creature not tamed nor ordinarily kept in captivity, or the

carcass of any such creature, unless either it has been reduced into possession by or on behalf of another person and possession of it has not since been lost or abandoned, or another person is in the course of reducing it into possession.'

The meaning of this subsection is quite clear: wild creatures cannot, in normal circumstances, be stolen, but let us consider instances in which birds or animals, which are wild by nature, may be stolen. Hawks and falcons are wild birds but are occasionally trained in captivity. Where this is so they are capable of being stolen because they are ordinarily kept in captivity. The carcasses of wild birds or animals may be taken into the possession of particular persons. This could occur if a land owner had been shooting over his land and stored dead pheasants and partridges in his shed. When they have been reduced into the possession of an individual or individuals in circumstances such as these, the birds may be stolen from the shed by some other party. The same would apply if the birds had been taken by a poacher; they are capable of being stolen from him as they have been reduced into his possession.

The reference to possession having since been lost or abandoned can refer to wild creatures which have been temporarily in captivity (but which are not ordinarily kept in captivity) and subsequently escape. A poacher may have driven game birds into a trap and in this way have reduced them into his possession, but if they are subsequently released or escape they return to their wild state and are incapable of being stolen.

The Deer Act 1991 creates specific offences of entering upon land without consent of the owner or occupier or other lawful authority, in search or pursuit of a deer with the intention of taking, killing or injuring it. There are further offences of taking, killing or injuring, searching for or pursuing with such intention or removing the carcass of any deer, once again without consent of the owner, etc. If a constable suspects with reasonable cause that any person is committing or has committed any of these offences, the constable may without warrant stop and search, search or examine vehicles, animals, weapons or other things and arrest that person, if he fails to give his name and address to the constable's satisfaction (as required by s. 25 Police and Criminal Evidence Act 1985) and seize or detain evidence of such offences. To exercise these powers a constable may enter any land other than a dwelling-house.

The Deer Act replaces previous offences included in Schedule 1, Theft Act 1968, but Schedule 1 still deals with fish, etc.

It distinguishes between fish which are in a wild state and those which can almost be proved to have been reduced into possession. It is an offence for anyone to unlawfully take or destroy, or attempt to take or destroy, any fish in water which is private property and in respect of which there is a private right of fishing. It is probable that in either of these circumstances the water concerned has been stocked by the owner or those persons who have been granted the rights of fishing.

The penalties for such offences vary, taking into account a previous conviction and whether the offence was committed during the day or by night. Night is defined as the period beginning one hour after sunset and ending one hour before sunrise. Although distinctions by way of penalties are unimportant to police officers, there is also a difference in police powers. A person committing such offences by night may be arrested by anyone who reasonably suspects him of committing the offence, but no such power applies during the day. Articles used in the taking or destruction of fish may be seized and a court may subsequently order their forfeiture. In the case of police officers, the power to arrest will be the conditional one provided by s. 25 Police and Criminal Evidence Act 1984.

However, fish which are securely contained within a pond or pool are the property of the owner of that pond or pool, or the person who, with the consent of the owner of that pond or pool, put them there. Where such fish are unlawfully taken, the offence is one of theft, which is an arrestable offence.

Belonging to another

Before property can be stolen it must belong to another. Section 5(1) states:

'Property shall be regarded as belonging to any person having possession or control of it, or having in it any proprietary right or interest.'

It appears at first sight that everything which we can imagine will be capable of being owned by someone, but the notable exception is a human corpse which is not the property of any person and, therefore, cannot be stolen. For this reason, special legislation was introduced many years ago to deal with 'body snatching' for medical experimentation. Even within this area, there are doubts as to whether courts would assume a lack of ownership *ad infinitum* as bones, skulls, and mummies are now prized possessions of many museums and if the matter is ever put to the test, will probably be deemed to have been taken into both the possession and the ownership of a particular organisation.

In considering all other property which is clearly capable of ownership, the problem is one of determining the 'owner' for the purposes of the Theft Act 1968, so that a correct charge may be preferred. If it is no one's property, then it cannot be stolen as the section requires that property 'belonging to another' is involved. Property which has been abandoned cannot be stolen. If a man is riding his pedal cycle home late at night and the tyre becomes punctured, he may leave it and walk home intending to return for it the following morning. The cycle can still be stolen as he intends to return for it and he has not abandoned it. It would be different if he threw the cycle into a field without the intention of returning for it, having made up his mind that it was of so little value that it was not worth reclaiming. To abandon property means that the owner had made up his mind that it is of no further use to him and he does not intend to exclude others from the use of his property. The owner of a coal mine does not necessarily abandon minerals which are thrown on to a tip; he may wish to exclude others from taking such minerals and has every right to do so.

Objects of gold or silver which were hidden by their owner at some time with a view to their later recovery, and his heirs are unknown, are treasure trove and the property of the Crown. Those which were lost or abandoned (as opposed to hidden) are not. Thus, ancient coins of gold or silver which have been scattered over a wide area of ground will not be Crown property; those concealed in batches will be Crown property.

Circumstances may be met in which property which appears to have been

415

abandoned is in fact still owned by some person and, in such cases, if the taker of the property believes that it has been abandoned his appropriation of it will not be 'dishonest' and no charge of theft will lie.

The term 'belonging to another' includes persons who have rights of ownership or possession or control. This is necessarily so to protect persons who have special interest in property. If a man buys a watch for £30, there is no difficulty in establishing that he has possession of it and that he is the owner, but if he subsequently takes the watch to a repairer, the repairer has a special interest in it. The owner can in these circumstances steal his own watch from the repairer if he recovers it by stealth to avoid paying the repair bill. It may appear strange that when the owner always has a better right of possession of his property than any other person, he may be charged with stealing it; but this must be so in certain circumstances. The example outlined above is quite clear because at least the possession of the article was transferred to another person who had a special interest in it, but it is possible for an owner to retain possession, merely giving control to another person, and to steal the property from that person. A jewellery store owner may provide his managers with goods to be sold in their departments and although retaining possession of all the goods in his store, in the same way as he retains possession of all the goods in his home, he gives 'control' to his manager. He may then steal the goods from his manager as the meaning of the term 'belonging to another' extends to persons having 'control'. It may be that the store owner, having made his managers responsible for the value of their stock, wishes to avoid payment of wages, or that he wishes subsequently to make a false claim upon an insurance company.

Husbands and wives may prosecute one another for any offence under the Theft Act, even if they are living together. On many occasions it may be that the parties are in the position of joint owners, and charges of theft will be appropriate if one party assumes the ownership rights of the other. If two men buy a car and one sells it without the consent of the other, the seller has assumed the ownership of the other party and has, therefore, 'appropriated' the property. A turnstile operator was held to be not guilty of theft when he took £2 from a man who did not have a ticket and allowed him entry to the ground. The High Court ruled that he had taken a bribe, and this being so, at no time did the £2 'belong' to his employer.

On occasions, property may be obtained by the mistake of some other person. Section 5(4) of the 1968 Act is concerned with such circumstances. However, the provisions of the subsection are limited to circumstances in which the property concerned is delivered to a person who is then under an immediate legal obligation to restore it, or its proceeds or value. This, in effect, limits the provisions to where a person receives ownership, possession or control of money under a mistake. That mistake must be on the part of the owner who wrongly believes that the person who receives the money is legally entitled to it. Thus, where an employer who, by mistake, overpays his employee and the employee is aware that this has occurred but nevertheless appropriates the money by spending it, that employee steals from his employer. This is so because s. 5(4) provides that at the time at which the money was spent (appropriated) it still belonged to the employer. In other words, ownership of the money did not pass to the employee when he received the wage packet.

With the intention of permanently depriving the other of it

The common law and all previous legislation concerning theft have preserved the rule that appropriation of property must be accompanied by an intention to deprive the owner permanently of his property. If it is merely intended to deprive him of the use of it for a limited period of time, it is not theft.

In most cases of theft, the presence of an intention to permanently deprive is easily proved. Where a person takes a bicycle belonging to another person, sells it and spends the money, the nature of his subsequent conduct clearly illustrates that he did not 'borrow' the bicycle. Where a thief steals money and uses it to purchase something, his actions clearly indicate an intention to deprive the owner of that money. A claim of an intention to repay is irrelevant, although it may be of significance in some cases in relation to 'dishonesty'.

Two exceptions to the general rule are included in the Act as it has become necessary, due in the first instance to legal difficulties and in the second to the prevalence of such action, to punish the removal of articles from places open to the public – for example, art galleries, and the taking of motor vehicles and other conveyances without authority. With these exceptions 'unlawful borrowing' is not punishable under the Theft Act. If a man takes his neighbour's lawn mower without his permission, but intends to return it in due course, he is not guilty of theft although he may have committed a civil trespass.

If the Act were to leave matters as simply as this, many anomalies would arise as property could be appropriated and sold back to the owner, thus showing that there was no intention to deprive permanently. For many years, boys have removed empty lemonade bottles from storage yards of business premises and have then taken them into the shop to claim the deposit charge of each bottle. Section 6(1) provides:

'A person appropriating property belonging to another without meaning the other permanently to lose the thing itself is nevertheless to be regarded as having the intention of permanently depriving the other of it if his intention is to treat the thing as his own to dispose of regardless of the other's rights; and a borrowing or lending of it may amount to so treating it if, but only if, the borrowing or lending is for a period and in circumstances making it equivalent to an outright taking or disposal.'

There are many examples of instances in which property can be returned to the owner in circumstances which would not deprive him permanently of his property but would certainly be dishonest, and this subsection is designed to protect owners from such actions. A man may take a £20 note from a bookmaker's satchel and immediately return it to him by placing a bet, but would have treated the £20 note as his own and have disposed of it regardless of the bookmaker's rights in the property, and thus be guilty of stealing it. Similarly, a thief may take a car and use it for a number of years until it is almost worthless and then return it to the owner, hoping to show that he did not intend to deprive him permanently of his car. This would amount to theft as his 'borrowing' was for such a period and in such circumstances that it is equivalent to an outright taking.

There can be certain complications when property which has been hired is unlawfully taken away as, if a man has hired a garden cultivator for a period of one week and his neighbour removes this without authority, returning it after the hire period is concluded, there is no doubt that he has permanently deprived the hirer of his interest in the machine. His interest is as one who has possession or control of the garden cultivator.

The meaning of the words 'regardless of the other's rights' was considered where the tenant of a council house removed doors from another council house to replace those for which he was responsible in his own home. While he had not, in a direct sense, deprived the council of the doors, he had treated them as his own to dispose of regardless of the other's rights. He had shown a clear intention to treat the doors as his own property.

Finally, s. 6(2) of the 1968 Act is concerned with circumstances in which a person who is in possession or control (lawfully or not) of property belonging to another, parts with the property under a condition as to its return which he may not be able to meet. This could occur where such a person pawns a valuable ring in circumstances in which it will be almost impossible for him to redeem it. Although in the absence of s. 6(2), he might have claimed that the act of 'pawning' was such that it did not indicate an intention to permanently deprive, s. 6(2) safeguards the owner's property by providing that the nature of the 'pawning' must be examined.

Abstracting electricity

The abstraction of electricity is dealt with separately because of difficulties which arise in alleging the theft of things which are not physical in form and cannot be held in the hand. Section 13 of the Theft Act 1968 provides:

> 'A person who dishonestly uses without due authority, or dishonestly causes to be wasted or diverted, any electricity shall, on conviction or indictment, be liable to imprisonment for a term not exceeding five years.'

The section has the effect of making electricity something which is as capable of being stolen as an apple or pear. Its dishonest use, waste, or diversion amounts to an offence. If an unauthorised person, perhaps someone who has left home and has no fixed address, enters a building and switches on electric heaters to dry out his clothes, he has dishonestly used electricity. Police officers sometimes encounter circumstances in which householders reconnect an electricity supply which has been disconnected by the electricity company, by-passing the company's meter to avoid payment. Where a building is in joint occupation and each of the persons living there had equal opportunity to carry out such an act as by-passing a meter, it must be proved that one, both or all of those persons committed the offence, as the case may be.

The source of electrical power is immaterial; an offence will be equally committed if electricity is used, wasted, or diverted dishonestly, which is provided by some form of battery. However, it must be remembered that Parliament has made such offences separate from common offences of theft. It is not theft for the purposes of burglary, i.e. a man who enters premises as a trespasser and switches on a light, will not be guilty of burglary in these circumstances only.

Offences of theft and the abstractions of electricity are arrestable offences.

Burglary

The Theft Act 1968 considerably simplified the law relating to burglary. The entry of premises with intent to steal was punishable according to the types of building which were attacked and the time of day or night at which the offence was committed. The offence of burglary, as defined by s. 9 of the Act, now covers all illegal entries into all types of buildings.

A person is guilty of burglary if:

(a) he enters any building or part of a building as a trespasser and with intent to commit any such offence as is mentioned in subs. (2) below; or

(b) having entered any building or part of a building as a trespasser he steals or attempts to steal anything in the building or that part of it or inflicts or attempts to inflict on any person therein any grievous bodily harm.

Subsection (2) provides that the offences referred to in subs. (a) above are offences of stealing anything in the building or part of a building in question, of inflicting on any person therein any grievous bodily harm or raping any person therein, and of doing unlawful damage to the building or anything therein.

Subsection (4) applies the above provision to inhabited vehicles or vessels and states that the provisions will apply equally whether the person is living there at the time, or he is not. The offences are considered so seriously that a maximum penalty of 14 years' imprisonment is provided by subs. (3) where the building is a dwelling and 10 years in any other case.

In considering fully the offences of burglary, it will be he helpful to examine the terms used separately.

(1) *Enters*

The common law rule concerning 'entry' is that the insertion of any part of the body, however small, will constitute an entry, as will the insertion of any instrument into a building if it is to be used for the purpose of committing the offence. However, in relation to the modern law of burglary, the Court of Appeal has adopted the test of 'effective entry' which excludes minimal intrusions such as might occur where a thief puts his hand across the top of a window frame to pull it downwards. Therefore, if a thief breaks a window and is seen to insert his hand, for the purpose of stealing goods, he has entered the building. If, having broken the window, he pushes in a walking stick for the purpose of hooking out a shopping bag, he has again entered the building. It should be remembered that the instrument must be used or intended to be used for the commission of a relevant further offence inside the building. It would be sufficient if a murderer broke a glass window, inserted a gun, and shot the occupier, but it would be insufficient if a thief, in using a drill upon a door, allowed the bit of the drill to enter the building as the bit would not be used, or be intended to be used for the commission of an offence inside. The old law recognised an entry by an innocent agent and there is little doubt that this will still apply. If a person uses a child, who is below the age of criminal responsibility, or a trained animal, to enter a building and to bring out articles, that will amount to an entry by that person.

For an entry to be an entry for the purposes of this section, it must be effected in

419

order to commit a relevant further offence, not merely to gain or facilitate entry to the building.

(2) *Building or part of a building*

The term 'building' is likely to be widely defined and will probably include any building made of any material which has some degree of permanence. If we think of the typical country mansion and its immediate surrounds, the house itself will be protected, as will those of employees; garages, greenhouses, barns, stables, or outhouses will also be buildings for the purpose of this section. In considering other buildings, shops, warehouses, factories, and similar structures will be equally protected. It is probable that the building must be fairly complete and quite solid, perhaps to the extent that it has a roof, before it may be classed as a building as it was obviously not the intention of the legislators to protect open structures such as walled gardens or bunkers. Tents, partially-built houses without a roof and open-sided barns are clearly outside the protection of s. 9. The inclusion of the term 'part of a building' is to protect premises which are subdivided into separate occupation, so that a man who rents a room in a lodging house may enter the room of another lodger or of the landlord as a trespasser, and a hotel guest may similarly enter the rooms of others as a trespasser.

A person who conceals himself on shop premises during opening hours and emerges when the shop has been closed enters as a trespasser when he enters any part of the shop as he knows that his permission to be there expired when the shop closed. While customers are clearly welcomed into shops, their permission to enter is restricted to those public parts of the building. There is no implied permission to go behind a counter and to do so would be a trespass into a part of a building.

Charges of burglary should indicate that the offence was committed against the person who is in possession or occupation of the building entered.

(3) *Inhabited vehicles or vessels*

The adjective 'inhabited' is of extreme importance. Many people in our modern society live in caravans or on boats, and it is reasonable that their homes should be protected in the same way as one built of bricks and mortar. The importance of the use of such a word as 'inhabited' is that it means more than mere presence; there must be someone living in the vehicle or vessel. If they are absent at the time, perhaps abroad for a long holiday, their residence remains protected by the section as it is an inhabited vehicle or vessel. On other occasions the vehicle or vessel attacked may not be inhabited in the general sense in that it is not a man's permanent residence. It appears that it will only be inhabited during periods of permanent residence, for example, during a family's summer holiday when such vehicle or vessel is taken into use as a home. In such circumstances it will remain an inhabited vehicle or vessel until such time as the holiday is over, regardless of whether or not the occupiers are present at the time. It may be that a family moves into a caravan for a period of one month but, at the time that it is unlawfully entered and property is stolen, the family is spending the day at the seaside some miles away. The caravan will be an inhabited vehicle for the purposes of this section throughout the period of the annual holiday.

The situation as it affects a motorised caravan is an interesting one, as it would seem that if it is used as a car for the majority of the year it cannot be classed as an 'inhabited vehicle', but immediately the family load it up and move into it as a place of residence it becomes inhabited for the purposes of the section.

It was necessary to add these words to give some protection to places of residence which were not buildings. It can be seen that a tent, whether or not it is permanently occupied, is not within this section as it is not a building. If protection was to be given to tented families, it would be necessary to add the word 'tent' to the places mentioned in subs. (3).

(4) Trespasser

If the building is in the possession of some other person who does not consent to entry, then entry is a trespass. To be charged with an offence of burglary it should be shown that the accused knew that he was a trespasser, or was at least unconcerned as to whether he was a trespasser or not. The section deals with criminal offences in respect of which *mens rea*, or guilty state of mind, should exist. For this reason it is submitted that the drunken man who enters his neighbour's house by mistake, may be a trespasser at civil law but would not be so for the purposes of this section. Instances occur where estranged husbands return to the matrimonial home to beat up unfaithful wives and, even though his wife may be the owner of the house, if he believes that he has a right to enter he may be a trespasser at civil law but does not have the guilty state of mind to make him so for the purposes of this section.

The law which was replaced by the 1968 Act recognised that where entry into premises was gained by means of deceit, it was unlawful. Although the Theft Act does not specify it, a 'constructive' illegal entry on such terms makes the person concerned a trespasser even though he has the householder's consent to enter. One television crime prevention film showed a lady answering the door in quick succession to bogus callers, each of whom falsely alleged that he represented an official organisation, so that when she finally opened the door to her husband, the living room of the house had been stripped bare of possessions. Although she had given permission to each of these men to enter, it was conditional upon their being official representatives of these organisations, and this not being so, the permission is null and void. As has been said by a judge of the High Court in considering trespass:

'When you invite a person into your house to use the staircase you do not invite him to slide down the banisters. So far as he sets foot on to so much of the premises as lie outside the invitation or uses them for purposes which are alien to the invitation he is not an invitee but a trespasser.'

This appears to summarise the position fairly.

Whether or not a person is a trespasser on any particular occasion is a matter of fact for determination by a court. Permission to enter may be given directly, or it may be implied, as is the case with a shop, restaurant, etc. There is an implied consent to entry by members of the public to all such places for the purpose of business. The owner of a dwelling-house either expressly or impliedly will have given permission to members of his family to enter. However, if persons enter a shop or restaurant for the purpose of damaging the property in order to induce the owner to

421

pay protection money, they enter as trespassers as their entry is outside the limits of the permission given to enter. The same would be true where someone who had been given permission to enter and use a dwelling-house, entered by stealth in order to steal property.

On occasions, permission is given directly to a person to enter a building under a mistake as to identity. If a person dresses as a meter reader and is given permission to enter to read a meter, permission is given to a meter reader, not to a person pretending to be such.

(5) *The forms of the offence of burglary*

It must be proved that a person entered a building or part of a building as a trespasser, knowing that he was a trespasser, or at least being reckless as to whether he was a trespasser or not (guilty state of mind), with intent to:

(a) steal;
(b) inflict grievous bodily harm;
(c) rape any person;
(d) commit unlawful damage to the building or anything therein;

or, having entered a building or part of a building as a trespasser, he

(a) steals or attempts to steal; or
(b) inflicts or attempts to inflict grievous bodily harm.

There are some important distinctions between the offences which may be committed by a trespasser who enters places protected by the section with one of the specified intents but subsequently commits offences. The offences of stealing and inflicting grievous bodily harm are included in both instances, but those of rape and committing offences of unlawful damage are only relevant in the case of one who enters with the intention of carrying out those acts. As the punishment for rape is one of life imprisonment, the reason for its exclusion in the second instance is quite clear, and the exclusion of unlawful damage to buildings or their contents prevents charges of burglary being preferred where damage is incidental to the trespass. For practical circumstances, the prosecution frequently relies upon the fact that an offence was committed to prove that the accused entered the buildings with that intention.

If a trespasser is apprehended in a building, part of a building, inhabited vehicle or vessel and admits that he entered with the intention of stealing, inflicting grievous bodily harm, raping, or committing damage to buildings or their contents, an offence of burglary is complete. Should he merely admit to entering as a trespasser, without other evidence to indicate a particular intent, it is necessary to prove that he stole property or attempted to steal it, or inflicted or attempted to inflict grievous bodily harm.

A tramp enters a building to find a place in which to sleep, but before leaving in the morning he makes himself a meal, eats it, and leaves the premises. He is guilty of burglary because he entered as a trespasser and stole property. On the following evening he again enters a building for the same reasons but is discovered there by a night watchman. In order to escape he assaults the watchman, breaking his jaw, and thus commits an offence of burglary; having entered as a trespasser he inflicts grievous bodily harm. Had he been disturbed in the first instance and forced to leave before eating the meal (having prepared it), or having aimed a vicious blow at the watchman with a crowbar and missed in the second, he would still have been guilty of burglary as he attempted to commit the specified offences in both cases.

If a young man has a dispute with his girl friend and enters her flat as a trespasser with intent to steal some of her property, to beat her up, rape her, or wreck the contents of her flat, he is guilty of burglary. (Since the Criminal Justice and Public Order Act 1994 extended the offence of rape to men, he would be equally guilty if he had entered with intent to rape his boy friend.) If he enters, still as a trespasser, but merely with the intention of talking matters over with her and, when she returns, does so without patching up his quarrel and, as a result of this lack of success, rapes her or wrecks the contents of her flat, he is not guilty of burglary. However, if he stole or attempted to steal her handbag, or caused her grievous bodily harm, or attempted to do so, he would be guilty of burglary.

In 1979 the Court of Appeal ruled upon previously conflicting decisions concerning burglary in two important areas. The defendant entered the 'till area' of a supermarket, opened the till further and shut it when he found it to be empty. It was held, in supporting a conviction for burglary, that it was a matter for the jury to decide whether an area was part of a building from which the public were excluded and that in the case examined, there was ample evidence to show that customers were prohibited and that the defendant knew it. When a person enters such a part of a building as a trespasser intending at the time of entry to steal, it is immaterial whether there is, in fact, anything worth stealing.

Aggravated burglary

Section 10 of the Theft Act 1968 deals with offences known as aggravated burglary. The aggravating circumstances are related to the possession of articles which are likely to be frightening to people in the building and the use of which might lead to serious consequences. The section provides:

'A person is guilty of aggravated burglary if he commits any burglary and at the time has with him any firearm or imitation firearm, any weapon of offence, or any explosive.'

The various terms are defined as follows:

(a) 'Firearm' includes an airgun or air pistol and 'imitation firearm' means anything which has the appearance of being a firearm, whether capable of being discharged or not.
(b) 'Weapon of offence' means any article made or adapted for use for causing injury to or incapacitating a person, or intended by the person having it with him for such use.
(c) 'Explosive' means any article manufactured for the purpose of producing a practical effect by explosion, or intended by the person having it with him for that purpose.

The use of weapons of all descriptions during the commission of offences of this nature is becoming quite common. The term 'firearm' includes air weapons, and all recognised forms of firearms are included. Bearing in mind that the aggravating circumstances are such that will cause fear or possible injury to persons, it is submitted that component parts of firearms, as defined in the Firearms Act 1968, would not be considered to be firearms for the purpose of this section.

'Weapon of offence' could include all offensive weapons made or adapted for causing injury, for example, coshes, knuckledusters, razors, caps with razor blades in the peaks, but in these circumstances would also include articles made or adapted for incapacitating a person such as handcuffs, or even knotted tights to be used for strangulation. Examples of those weapons intended to be used to cause injury could include almost all objects, for example, walking sticks or a golf club and those intended to incapacitate could include a chloroform pad, powder to be thrown in the face, or a length of rope to be used for binding a person.

The definition of the term 'explosive' is equally wide and includes anything manufactured for the purpose of producing a practical effect by explosion, or intended for that purpose. The use of explosives by certain organisations is certainly increasing, and although other serious offences are included in the various Explosives Acts, it is nevertheless an offence of aggravated burglary to enter a building or anything in the building by use of explosives. Fireworks are not within this definition.

In each case of aggravated burglary, it is essential to prove that an offence of burglary has been committed and, at the time, the accused had with him a firearm, imitation firearm, weapon of offence, or an explosive. It is not necessary that such a person was armed when he entered the building as a trespasser. The time at which a defendant must be proved to have with him a weapon of offence is the time at which he steals, attempts to steal, etc., where the burglary is contrary to s. 9(1)(b).

A person who commits a burglary and has with him at the time of the offence a knuckleduster is guilty of aggravated burglary because a knuckleduster is an article made for use for causing injury or incapacitating a person. However, if he was in possession of a small pocket knife the offence of aggravated burglary would only be committed if he showed an intention to use it for such purposes, as a small pocket knife is not an article made for use for causing injury or incapacitating. (See page 449 for further information re weapons of offence.)

For the purposes of aggravated burglary, an article not made or adapted to cause injury or incapacitate can be a weapon of offence even if the necessary intent is only formed an instant before it is used to injure or incapacitate (which is in contrast with the rule which applies to an offence of carrying an offensive weapon in a public place, see page 450).

A man used a screwdriver to break into a house. He was handling a video recorder when confronted by the occupier and another person. He took the screwdriver from his pocket and prodded the occupier in the stomach with the screwdriver. It was held that this was aggravated burglary as the screwdriver became an offensive weapon on proof that he intended to use it for injuring, or incapacitating, the occupier at the time of the theft, thereby aggravating the burglary.

All offences of burglary and aggravated burglary are arrestable offences.

Removal of articles from places open to the public

Where an art lover removes a valuable picture from an art gallery and alleges that he only did so to allow himself the luxury of enjoying it exclusively for a period of time before returning it to the gallery, there is a problem when attempting to prove theft or any associated offence. It would be necessary to show that this claim was false and that the taker intended to deprive the owner permanently of his property or that this was a 'borrowing' of such a nature that the period of time for which the article was 'borrowed' and the circumstances in which it had been kept were such that it amounted to an outright taking. To avoid these difficulties, the Theft Act 1968, s. 11, creates a specific offence to cover such cases while providing a safeguard, by careful drafting, to limit the offence to particular circumstances. It provides:

'Where the public have access to a building in order to view the building or part of it, or a collection or part of a collection housed in it, any person who without lawful authority removes from the building or its grounds the whole or part of any article displayed or kept for display to the public in the building, or that part of it, or in its grounds, shall be guilty of an offence.'

(1) The place from which the article is removed

There are two major points to prove. First, it must be shown that the article was removed:

(a) from the *building* to which the public have access in order to view the building or part of it, or a collection or a part of a collection housed in it; or

(b) from the grounds of the building.

Thus, in dealing with this first point we are considering removal of articles from national galleries, stately homes, etc., *which are open to the public in order to view the building, etc.*, or from the grounds of such buildings. The offence cannot be committed, therefore, from public buildings such as the offices of local authorities which, while they are open to the public, are not open for the purpose of 'viewing'. They are open to the public to carry out the functions of local government. We are also concerned with 'public access' so that, where access is limited to a certain section, or sections of the public, the offence, once again, does not apply. If the particular building was open to members of a local historical society, or a group of architects, it would not be open to the public for the purposes of this offence.

However, the offence does not apply to circumstances in which a collection of art treasures has been brought together for display with a view to sale or for any other commercial purpose. The removal of articles from a commercial art gallery, therefore, is not covered by s. 11. At the other extreme, articles which are merely brought together temporarily for display in a local village hall are protected by the section as they are displayed in a building to which the public has access in order to view.

In most instances, offences against s. 11 can be committed whether or not the gallery, etc., is open to the public at the time. The removal of paintings from the National Gallery, for example, will offend against this section at any time and this can easily be appreciated. Such a gallery exists for no other purpose than to give a home to such treasures so that they may be viewed by the public. On the other hand, this is not the case in relation to stately homes. While they are open to the public the treasures which they contain are vulnerable to such removal, but when they are not open to the public, the offence does not apply as they then revert to being dwelling-houses and the 'treasures' are merely a part of their decoration.

(2) *The nature of the article*

The second point is concerned with whether or not the article which was removed was *displayed or kept for display to the public*. If a member of the public is admitted to the building to examine articles and he takes one of them, for example an old sword, he commits an offence under the provisions of this section. If, however, it was a fur coat belonging to the owner of the house which was taken from a wardrobe in one of the bedrooms (an article which had not been on display), then the offence which was committed would be one of theft and it would not fall within the parameters of s. 11.

(3) *The nature of the removal*

The article concerned must be removed completely from the building or, as the case may be, its grounds. A visitor who places an article in his pocket with a view to removal does not commit an offence at that stage. He commits the offence when he walks out of the building and takes the article without lawful authority. If the article which he plans to remove is a statue which stands in the grounds, this offence is committed when it is removed from the grounds.

It is not essential that 'dishonesty' existed throughout the transaction as this is not a part of the offence. However, the section provides that a person does not commit the offence if he believes that he has lawful authority for the removal of the thing in question or that he would have it if the person entitled to give it knew of the removal and its circumstances. If, therefore, a man who had been asked by the owner or his agent to take certain items of furniture for restoration, took an item of furniture which was not meant to be taken for restoration, he would not commit an offence against s. 11 if he believed that he had lawful authority for its removal.

Police powers

This is an arrestable offence.

Criminal damage

Damage

Damage, or the causing of actual harm to property, is punishable if it is committed without lawful excuse. The Criminal Damage Act 1971 simplified the law by repealing a multiplicity of offences which were only distinguished one from another for the purpose of providing differing penalties. The Law Commission considered that the essence of the offences of criminal damage should be the destruction of, or damage to, the property of another and that such matters as the means used to commit the damage and the nature of the property should not affect the nature of the offence.

The Act creates one basic offence, which covers the whole field of damage to the property of another committed without lawful excuse, being punishable by 10 years' imprisonment, and a further aggravated offence which additionally involves an intention to endanger the life of another recklessly, which is punishable by life imprisonment. There are two further offences which deal with threats to commit damage and the possession of articles with intent to commit damage.

Lawful excuse

Acts which are committed 'without lawful excuse' become punishable. The term is not directly connected with any form of intention in all circumstances, as a police officer executing a search warrant may intentionally damage a door in order to gain access. This act is done with lawful excuse as it is backed by a warrant which authorises the use of force. It is also possible that a person may genuinely believe (although he is mistaken in that belief) that he has consent to carry out an act which causes damage. This could occur where a demolition contractor made a genuine error in relation to the building which was to be demolished. While he would undoubtedly be responsible for his act, he could not be said to be criminally liable as he believed that his act was lawful. However, a genuine belief, held by a vicar, that he was carrying out God's instructions by writing anti-war slogans on a concrete pillar, does not amount to a lawful excuse to offend against the laws of England and Wales. In the same way, a man who breaks down the door of his neighbour's house to extinguish a fire, is acting with lawful excuse although the damage is deliberate as he knows that he is acting in defence of his neighbour's property. The act would also be committed with lawful excuse if he broke down the door merely to preserve his own property, and this would probably be so, even if no fire was discovered in his neighbour's house, provided that he had honestly believed this to be so when the door was broken down. Similarly, where, for example, a car is parked in a field of valuable crops and a farmer damages it in order to gain access and remove it before irreparable damage occurs; provided that the damage to the car is not disproportionate, he may have a lawful excuse, as he is acting in defence of his property.

Property

The term 'property' is defined by s. 10 of the Act as meaning property of a tangible nature, whether real or personal, including money and:

(a) wild creatures which have been tamed or are ordinarily kept in captivity, any other wild creatures or their carcasses if, but only if, they have been reduced into possession which has not been lost or abandoned, or are in the course of being reduced into possession; but

(b) not including mushrooms growing wild on any land or flowers, fruit or foliage of a plant growing wild on any land.

The term 'mushroom' includes all forms of fungi and the term 'plant', any shrub or tree. The similarity between this definition and the definition of property given in the Theft Act 1968 will be noticed, and this is a useful comparison to make. However, in relation to offences of criminal damage there is no proviso that an offence will be committed in respect of mushrooms and plants if the damage is done for a commercial purpose . Damage to such articles, whether for a commercial purpose or not, is no offence. The term 'property' is, therefore, widely defined to cover all forms of tangible property except wild mushrooms and the flowers, fruit, and foliage of plants.

The references to animals is interesting as it would normally be anticipated that offences which are concerned with 'damage' to animals would be dealt with as offences of cruelty, but this need not be so. Injuring animals can be punishable under the Criminal Damage Act, and the classes of animals which may be stolen, as described in the text on the subject of theft, are the same as those in respect of which offences may be committed under this Act. All domestic animals are included within the terms 'real or personal property' and are protected because they are owned by some person, and zoo animals would be included in those which have been tamed or are ordinarily kept in confinement. Wild animals, because they have not become the property of any person while they remain in their wild state, are not protected unless they have been reduced into the possession of some person – for example, a pet hawk.

Belonging to another

Subsection (2) of s. 10 states that property shall be treated for the purpose of the Act as belonging to any person:

(a) having the custody or control of it;
(b) having a proprietary right or interest; or
(c) having a charge on it.

When a person hires a motor car, he gains both custody and control of it. If, while he has such custody or control another person damages the car, that person can be convicted of damaging *his* property. If a car is owned by two persons, each has a 'proprietary right or interest' in that car. Should the car be unlawfully damaged by one of them, he may be convicted of the offence of damaging property 'belonging to another'. The inclusion of the word 'proprietary' is for the purpose of restricting such ownership rights to those *directly* owning the property and has the effect of excluding bodies such as insurance companies which, although they have an 'interest' in the property, do not have a 'proprietary interest'.

For example, a building society has a 'charge' on property. Thus, where a house is being purchased by way of a mortgage the house belongs to both the purchaser and the building society. The owner/occupier who recklessly damages the property without lawful excuse, commits an offence in respect of property 'belonging to another'.

(1) *Damage (Section 1(1), Criminal Damage Act 1971)*

A person who, without lawful excuse, destroys or damages any property belonging to another intending to destroy or damage any such property or being reckless as to whether any such property would be destroyed or damaged shall be guilty of an offence.

It is an offence to destroy or damage any type of tangible property by any means. Property is obviously damaged if it suffers physical harm which involves permanent or temporary impairment of the property's use or value; a car which is scratched; a wall which is scribbled upon; or a radio aerial which has been broken from a vehicle – each one has suffered such physical harm and has been damaged. Where a person throws a stone at a passing car and dents it he commits damage. This is equally true if he aims at one car and hits another. Property which is rendered inoperative has also been damaged as it has been impaired. If a cog wheel is removed from a mill, the mill is inoperative and has been damaged. If the degree of impairment is minimal, for example, requiring no more than the replacement of the cog wheel which was left at the scene, there will be no 'damage' for the purposes of the Act. However, if the cog wheel has been concealed and could not be replaced, there would be a cost involved in rectification, the machine would have been 'impaired', and an offence of criminal damage would have been committed. In contrast it has been held that where a person's car is wheel-clamped without his consent, the car is not damaged as there is no intrusion upon the integrity of the vehicle. It has not been altered or affected in any way; the clamp was added to it. However, by the Computer Misuse Act 1990, s. 3(6), a modification of the contents of a computer shall not be regarded as damaging any computer or computer storage medium unless its effect on that computer or computer storage medium impairs its physical condition. However, where unauthorised alterations are made to a computer system which impair its proper use, an offence of criminal damage can be committed, although the damage to the magnetic particles in the disk are not perceptible without using the computer. Tangible property has been damaged, even though the damage itself is not tangible. Impairment of usefulness does not require physical damage to the thing itself.

The offence is restricted to damaging property belonging to some other person and it is no offence under this subsection to damage one's own property, even if it is done with the intention of making a fraudulent claim upon an insurance company. Such acts are punishable, in most circumstances, under the Theft Act. An honestly held belief, by the person committing the damage, that the property concerned belonged to him is sufficient to negate an offence, even though that belief is a mistaken one. A tenant of a flat installed a wiring system for stereo equipment with the landlord's permission. His adaptations included the addition of roofing material, asbestos wall panels, and floorboarding, which when fitted became the property of the landlord. On leaving the flat, the tenant removed the wiring causing £130 worth of damage in the course of doing so. It was held by the Court of Appeal that no offence was committed if the tenant honestly believed that the property damaged belonged to him. It is not essential to prove that the property belonged to a particular person, provided it is clearly shown that it is the 'property of another'.

A person is reckless as to whether or not any property would be destroyed or damaged if:

(a) he does an act which in fact creates an obvious risk that property will be destroyed or damaged; and

(b) when he does the act he either has not given any thought to the possibility of there being any such risk *or* has recognised that there was some risk involved and has none the less gone on to do it.

In relation to (a) the question is concerned with whether the risk would have been obvious to the ordinary, prudent person who gave thought to the matter. If it would have been obvious to such a person it is irrelevant that it was not obvious to the accused because he was too young or mentally retarded. This is important. If a wildfowler is shooting at ducks on a lake and, missing his aim, shoots through the side of a boat tethered behind the ducks, he cannot be said to have intended to damage the boat. However, his act, in the circumstances, created an obvious risk that property would be damaged and he was reckless as to that risk by not giving any thought to the possibility that such damage would occur. If he did recognise the risk, he was reckless in that he carried out the act in any case. On the other hand, if he had carefully considered the risk and concluded that there was none, he would not be guilty of criminal damage as there would be no recklessness as defined above.

(2) *Endangering life*

Subsection (2) does not make this distinction and if a person, without lawful excuse, destroys or damages property whether belonging to himself or another person:

(a) intentionally or recklessly; and

(b) intending by the destruction or damage to endanger the life of another or being reckless as to whether the life of another would be thereby endangered, he shall be guilty of an offence punishable by life imprisonment.

This subsection deliberately includes the property of the offender as it is possible that offences of this nature may be committed with the intention of killing or endangering the life of some person within the offender's family resident within his own property. Indiscriminate bomb attacks upon buildings, which involve the intention, or at least a reckless disregard for the life of others, are punishable under this section. The basic offence of criminal damage is aggravated by a disregard for the safety of other people. 'Recklessness' is to be judged in the same way in its relationship to 'endangering life' as in its relationship to offences of criminal damage contrary to s. 1(1). Thus, there may be a need to prove recklessness in relation to the destruction or damage and, in addition, similar recklessness in that the accused's act created an obvious risk that the life of another would be endangered, and when he carried out that act, he either had not given any thought to the possibility of there being any such risk or had recognised such a risk but had nevertheless gone on to take it.

It must be proved either that there was an *intention* to endanger life, or *recklessness* in that respect. If a man, after taking drink and tablets, either lights a fire or drops a cigarette upon papers which are scattered all around a bed, he is reckless both in relation to criminal damage and the endangering of lives of other residents in the house. Self-induced intoxication is no defence. His act and his state of mind both in relation to the act itself and its consequences must be viewed as if he had not been affected by drink or drugs at the time.

The word 'arson' is retained within the law relating to damage by subs. (3), which directs that acts of damage by fire shall be charged as arson. Self-induced intoxication can be relevant to a defence to a charge of arson where intent is alleged. It cannot be relevant to a charge of arson by recklessness.

(3) *Threats to destroy or damage property*

Section 2 of the Act deals with threats made, without lawful excuse, to destroy or damage another's property, or one's own property, in a way likely to endanger the life of another person. The essence of such an offence is that the threat is made to carry out an act which would be an offence against s. 1 of the Act, without lawful excuse with the intention that the person threatened would fear that it would be carried out. It does not matter how the threat is made, it may be verbal, by means of a letter or by telephone. Nor does it matter if the threat is made for the purposes of a joke; if it is made with the intention of creating fear in the recipient that it will be carried out.

The threat need not be made to the owner of the property; it may be a threat to damage someone else's property. For example, it would be an offence to make a threat to parents to destroy or damage property belonging to one of their children, if it was intended that the parents would fear that the threat would be carried out. If a person makes a threat to cause an explosion and his intention is to cause that person to fear that the threat will be carried out, he commits an offence against s. 2 of the 1971 Act. The offences which are separately created by s. 51, Criminal Law Act 1977, deal particularly with 'bomb hoaxes'. The section creates offences of placing articles anywhere, or dispatching them by any means whatsoever, with the intention of inducing a belief in some other person that they are likely to explode or ignite, thereby causing injury or damage to property. Similarly, communicating information known or believed to be false, to some other person with intent to induce a belief in any person that a bomb or other thing likely to explode or ignite, is present anywhere, is made a specific offence. Thus the placing or sending of innocent articles, or the communication of false information concerning such articles, becomes punishable if done to induce a belief in another party that such articles are likely to explode, etc.

(4) *Possessing anything with intent to destroy or damage property*

Section 3 states that a person who has anything in his custody or under his control intending, without lawful excuse, to use it or cause or permit another to use it:

(a) to destroy or damage any property belonging to some other person; or
(b) to destroy or damage his own or the user's property in a way which he knows is likely to endanger the life of some other person shall be guilty of an offence.

This section merely creates further offences of possessing articles which are intended to be used for either of the offences of criminal damage, or aggravated criminal damage, described in subss. (1) and (2) of s. 1 respectively. The term 'custody' means physical custody and 'control' means having the power to direct what shall be done with the property in question. These terms are more precise than the general term 'possession', which is difficult to define fully. The essential feature of this offence is the intention of the person having custody or the control of the article, rather than the nature of the thing itself. If a walking stick is in the custody of some person who intends to break shop windows with it, his possession of the stick is punishable. A person who is found with an explosive device in his pocket intending to use it to damage property has custody of it, as it is in physical possession. A man who owns a warehouse full of similar devices, if they are there with his knowledge, is in control of them, as he must have some power of direction over them. The possession of such articles would also be punishable under the Explosives Act. A petrol bomb is an explosive substance.

An offence is committed whether or not the person who has custody or control intends to use the article himself, or merely intends to cause or permit some other person to use it, to commit damage. Carrying a hammer which is to be used by another for the purpose of damaging cars is an offence contrary to this section.

Search warrants

A justice of the peace may issue a search warrant following information, on oath, that there is reasonable cause to believe that a person has anything in his custody or control or on his premises, reasonably suspected to have been used, or be intended to be used, to commit offences under the Criminal Damage Act 1971.

If a search warrant is granted, a constable may enter (if need be by force) any premises and search for the thing in question. He may seize anything which he believes to have been used or to be intended to be used for these purposes.

Police powers

All offences of criminal damage are arrestable offences.

Scenes of crime – police action

Introduction

Although police officers visit many scenes of crime they must never relax their attention to detail. An officer must always regard a scene of crime with great care. Much valuable evidence may be obliterated or lost by the first officer at the scene of a crime through his ignorance of its possibilities. In many cases valuable traces will have been obliterated by other persons who arrived on the scene before the police, and although this may be unavoidable in the present state of education of the public in these matters, after the arrival of the first police officer no more useful traces should be lost if he acts correctly. It should always be remembered that evidence may be found not only at the scene itself but on or near the line of approach and departure.

Such evidence will often be undetectable by the human eye; but wherever a criminal has been, there are likely to be traces of his presence.

Action at the scene and specialist assistance

The first police officer at the scene of a crime must take complete control of the situation tactfully and firmly. Any unnecessary movement should be avoided. The first fact to establish is whether or not a crime has been committed, although this is generally obvious. It is essential to note the time when the crime was committed (if this can be established); the time it came to your notice; and the time of your arrival.

If the first officer on the scene is not trained in searching the scene of a crime and it is possible to summon a specially trained officer, this should be done as soon as possible, and pending his arrival precautions should be taken to ensure that no unauthorised person approaches the scene. All persons including witnesses and the inmates of any building concerned should be warned not to touch or disturb anything and, in cases of serious crime, a guard should if possible be posted to prevent entry. If the scene is in the open all access to the area should be prevented and care taken to protect from the weather any traces (footprints, stains, etc.) which may be discovered.

It is usually the responsibility of the first officer at the scene of a crime to record the names and addresses of any witnesses present so that they can be seen later if they cannot be prevented from leaving the scene. It will also be his task to identify the complainant if he is present and to take particulars of the alleged crime and details of any property involved, together with the value if applicable. It will also be helpful if the officer records the identify of all persons visiting the scene, both police and public, together with the times of arrival. All this information will prove invaluable when compiling any subsequent report.

When examining the scene of a crime an officer should make very careful notes, in writing, of the scene and its condition; memory alone must not be relied upon. Specialist officers such as detective officers, fingerprint officers, photographers, and dog handlers are available to assist at the scene of a crime, but usually such specialists should be called to the scene as soon as possible to get maximum benefit from their specialist skills. Consideration should be given to taking photographs before anything is moved.

Any search for traces should be both thorough and systematic; and it must be kept in mind that very minute quantities of material or marks may afford invaluable evidence. Nothing capable of bearing a fingerprint or palmprint should be handled without proper precautions. It is said that whenever persons and objects come into contact with one another, traces of each are almost certain to be left on the other. Do not pick things up or move them; or attempt to match up implements with marks, or shoes with imprints. Such actions can result in the loss of valuable evidence. Human hairs, blood, saliva, etc., are all likely to provide some evidence of an offender's identity.

Avoid contact with areas with which the criminal may have made contact. Watch particularly where you are walking. In making any form of preliminary examination, attention should be paid to likely points of contact such as doors, windows, light switches, even telephones.

Where the offence concerned is one of burglary, the householder may have already begun to tidy up. Further tidying-up should be discouraged but do not attempt to replace objects in their original positions as this only leads to further handling. **433**

Objects which are commonly touched by thieves include bottles (particularly where the householder has been saving coins), coin boxes, boxes which have contained jewellery and the contents of wardrobes and drawers. Where a considerable time is likely to pass before a scenes of crime specialist can attend, it may be advisable to take some form of action to ensure that any marks are preserved after you leave the scene and that the house is in such a condition that the occupants can be reasonably comfortable. Where coin boxes have been removed from meters they can be put in a safe place. Most have a ring attached which can be used for lifting. It may be replaced within the meter by this method, where it should be safe from interference. Ensure however, that the fitter employed by the public utility concerned is not likely to remove it when he fits a new box, or securely replaces the old. Bottles, or other objects which have a 'neck' can be lifted by placing the fingers, or some object, inside the neck. Where bedrooms have been ransacked, the contents of drawers and wardrobes will probably be heaped upon the bed. In such cases, where there is likely to be an overnight delay before an examination can be carried out, all articles which will not carry prints such as clothing, may be returned to their storage places. Articles which are suitable for examination should be carefully set aside in a suitable place to await examination. However, where the crime which has been committed is a very serious one, such as murder or rape, nothing should be touched as examination will take place quickly. Footprints can be adequately protected by covering them with some object such as a box. If such a mark is in soft ground outside a building, they should be similarly protected. Documents which may have been handled by the criminal can be preserved in a polythene bag.

Where stolen vehicles are located, do not enter the vehicle or touch it in any way. Arrange for the vehicle to be examined before removal, or to be removed by specialists for later examination.

If a firearm has been left at the scene of a crime it must not be touched or moved in any way. If circumstances exist which necessitate its removal from its original position, it is best to take hold of the 'grip' itself which usually carries a rough surface. Use no more than two fingers and record the fact that the firearm has been moved. Care must be taken as some modern weapons are extremely sensitive and discharge easily. Television detectives frequently pick up firearms by placing a pencil inside the barrel. Avoid this, as forensic tests may later be carried out to match marks on spent ammunition with irregularities which exist on the surface of the barrel.

In searching vehicles, particular attention should be given to bumpers, lamps, wings, handles, tyres, etc., as well as the interior, under cushions, carpets, etc. Suspect vehicles should be immediately impounded and kept under cover until they can be examined. Where vehicles have to be moved a long distance, particularly over rough ground, the examination should be done on the spot to prevent the loss of material in transit.

In examining tools and weapons it should be remembered that the colour of blood varies with the action of the atmosphere and sometimes with the action of the chemicals in the article on which the blood lies. If blood is visible on a weapon, its distribution and general appearance should be noted and it should be observed whether or not the weapon has been wiped. Special care should be taken to see that all unevenness of surface joins, etc., is examined. The collection of traces from knives and weapons should be left to the expert, unless the traces are liable to become dislodged by the most careful method of transit. The material on a knife may indicate its previous history, and may also show whether it has been used for making more than one stab wound.

In examining splashes of blood on floors and walls the shape of the splashes should be particularly noted and photographed in order to establish the direction of fall.

If a suspect is being searched, then, after examination of the exposed parts of the body, particular attention should be paid to the fingernails and, where considered advisable, scrapings from under the nails should be taken if the suspect consents. It should also be remembered that the victim of an attack may bear traces left by the assailant during a struggle, e.g. small fragments of skin tissue under the fingernails.

At the scene of every crime the task of the first officer must be the preservation of any traces. However, where it is left to him to make a preliminary search, all the points above should be clearly borne in mind.

Serious crimes

Supervisory officers must be called to the scene of serious crimes and pending the arrival of such officers everything must be done to ensure that there is no disturbance of the scene and that the identity of all persons present at the scene when the officer arrived, is known. Talk to as many witnesses as you can while keeping the scene secure and gather as much information as possible.

Police action at scenes of homicides and abortions

It has already been stressed that the actions of the first police officer at the scene of a crime can have an important bearing on any later courses of action. Every care should be taken to preserve the scene and prevent unauthorised persons tampering or interfering in any way.

(1) Homicide

The first consideration must be the possible preservation of life, and in cases of suspected homicide medical assistance should be requested to confirm that life has ceased to exist, unless death is obvious, e.g. decapitation. The time at which the original information was received should be noted, together with the identity of the person from whom it was received. A supervisory officer should be notified at once.

The position of articles at the scene should be carefully noted and measures taken for their security, but they should not be moved without the authority of a senior officer, and then only under his direction. When possible, a rough sketch should be made pinpointing such articles in their relative positions. Witnesses at the scene should be carefully identified and a note made of their names and addresses. They should be asked to remain at the scene until the arrival of a senior officer so that their evidence can be obtained as soon as possible to avoid their recollections becoming distorted by discussing events with other people. It should also be remembered that such a witness may in some way be involved in the offence.

435

The scene of a homicide must be carefully protected and no unauthorised person should be allowed to approach it. An assurance that the scene has been protected will be required by senior detective officers immediately they arrive, together with precise information concerning the line of approach taken by the police officer, if this was necessary. An approved line of approach will subsequently be marked out by detective officers, and it is essential that this is followed by all specialist personnel who subsequently attend the scene of the crime. If anything has been touched by anyone, inform the supervisory officer as soon as he arrives. Any suspected offender should be detained but should not be questioned at this stage: this should be left to experienced detective officers. A note should be made of anything said by such a suspect.

In all cases of this kind the press will quickly learn of the occurrence and will ask questions of persons at the scene. It is the job of reporters to obtain a story and they cannot be blamed for trying to do their work well. They should be politely told that full information will soon be available from the forces press liaison officer or a senior detective officer. In no circumstances must the press be allowed to approach the scene or any witnesses who are awaiting the arrival of senior officers.

(2) *Abortion*

Although the general principles outlined above apply equally to cases of abortion, the nature of the incident requires that attention be given to other matters. Medical assistance will be urgently required as it is usually when things go wrong that illegal abortions come to the notice of the police. Many illegal abortions result in the death of the pregnant woman through lack of skill, hygiene, and care on the part of the abortionist. The varied nature of articles which can be used to effect an abortion should be recognised in protecting the scene from all except the doctor, who may arrive before specialist police assistance.

Conclusion

It is essential that police officers remain aware of the distress which has been caused to those who are the victims of crime and treat such persons accordingly. It is difficult for those of us who have not experienced that moment, when, upon returning home one finds that one's home has been burgled, to imagine the feelings of the lady of the house who sees what remains of her property strewn about the floor. It may be that considerable damage has been done to the property. The standing of the police service depends upon the impression which is created in the minds of such victims. The manner in which they are interviewed, the degree of sympathy shown, and the apparent concern of those charged with the task of investigation to do all that is possible to apprehend the offenders, are all factors of critical importance. The situation is a test of a police officer's qualities and professionalism, communication skills and ability to handle situations involving stress. Most of all it is a test of leadership.

Crime reporting and *modus operandi* system

The modus operandi *system*

Criminals frequently follow a general pattern of actions when committing crime. If it can be said that crimes have a 'personality' then it is because individual criminals, by the method which they follow, give their crimes noticeable characteristics. The criminal's method of working is known as his *modus operandi* or MO.

If care is taken when a crime is committed, all of the usual forms of identification of the criminal can be avoided. By wearing gloves he will avoid leaving fingerprints and by carefully selecting his form of dress, he will largely eliminate fabric traces left at the scene. A mask may make personal identification less likely and if he is careful when disposing of identifiable property, or avoids stealing identifiable property, the thief has considerably lessened his chances of being arrested. It is much more difficult to avoid acting in a way which is natural to the individual and, upon this human factor, the strength of the *modus operandi* system stands. The system tabulates information and the description of known criminals and the pattern of their actions and methods in committing crime. If MO is correctly reported when a crime is committed, these methods can be compared with similar methods recorded in the system. Suspects can thus be identified and this may limit the extent of the enquiry.

Collection of information

In order to build up a picture of the criminal's usual method of going about a crime it is necessary to record accurately details of each crime as it is reported. If a sneak thief is operating in your area and each offence is accurately reported upon by the investigating officer, it will soon become apparent to senior detective officers who examine reports submitted through your force area, that the same person is likely to be responsible for all crimes of this nature which are being committed. When the thief is eventually apprehended, it is then possible to clear up all offences for which he is responsible.

The information required can be obtained by examination of the scene of the crime; for example, the method of entry in burglary offences can be established in this way; witnesses will be able to tell you the particular lie which was told to them by the confidence trickster; or from the criminal himself who, when arrested, may wish to tell you exactly how he committed the crime.

The ten points of modus operandi

Details of crimes are entered in an index under each of ten headings.

(a) *Classword.* Under this heading is described the class of person or property attacked. The purpose of description is to make the person or property as individual as possible. A term such as 'dwelling-house' is abstract and describes all forms of dwelling. The words 'bungalow', 'detached villa', or 'farm cottage' are more helpful.

(b) *Entry*. The actual point of entry must be described. To use the word 'window' is helpful, but not as helpful as 'ground floor window at rear'.

(c) *Means*. The method used by the criminal in effecting an entry should be explained. The criminal may have used a jemmy, a drill, or bodily pressure in order to burst open the door. If entry has been effected through an upstairs window or via the roof, the approach to the point of entry should be described, for example, by scaling drainpipe.

(d) *Object*. Why did the criminal commit this crime? What was his motive? In instances of theft, it will be for personal gain; in sexual crimes, sexual satisfaction.

(e) *Time*. The actual time at which the crime as committed will be reported elsewhere. The importance of this factor for the purposes of MO is the occasion, indicating the opportunity which presented itself to the thief, for example, market day, lunchtime (office thefts), or early closing day (afternoon burglaries in shops).

(f) *Style*. This refers to the criminal's style of approach, his alleged trade or profession, and is, therefore, used in connection with offences involving deception. The bogus meter reader or alleged local authority rating officer provides an example of the types of person who adopt a 'style'.

(g) *Tale*. This means the account which a criminal gives of himself and is associated with the previous point, 'style', being applicable to offences of deception. The man who is posing as a vicar will also have some ready account of his reason for being in the area and for approaching members of the public. This is the most important factor to be described in all offences involving an element of criminal deception.

(h) *Pal*. If there has been more than one person involved in the commission of the crime, details of accomplices should be included. Some criminals prefer to work with accomplices, and this can be an important element in assisting to extract suspects from the index.

(i) *Transport*. Was a vehicle used in connection with the crime? Tyre marks may have been found at the scene or it may be evident, because of the quantity of property which was removed from the attacked premises, that some form of transport was used. Motor vehicles are becoming an essential part of the equipment of criminals, whose range of activities has thus become extensive.

(j) *Trademarks*. In the course of committing crime over a number of years, criminals establish their own methods of achieving their aims which can frequently become second nature. The aggressive type will commit unnecessary damage; the perverted will commit various forms of nuisances on the floor of a room or on a bed; some develop tidy, methodical methods of searching a room for property; and others cannot resist leaving a note for the householder. In instances in which such methods are observed, experienced detective officers can frequently limit their enquiries to a small number of criminals who are known to act in such a way.

It is not possible on all occasions to complete all ten points of *modus operandi*. If the offence does not involve deception, it is unlikely that 'style' or 'tale' will be applicable; there may be no 'trademark', 'pal', or 'transport' involved and in such instances these points should be left blank.

Details of these factors will be recorded in the police officer's pocket notebook at the scene of the crime and transferred to the crime report when submitted.

Crime complaint

A crime complaint is the first written record of a complaint of crime. A crime complaint form must be completed as soon as possible after a report of crime is received, and crime complaint forms are kept at all police stations. Usually the crime complaint form is combined with the crime report form. Copies are self-carbonating.

Information to the effect that a crime has been committed may reach police officers in a number of ways:

(a) by personal observation – the officer sees a crime being committed;
(b) by oral complaint at a police station;
(c) by oral complaint to a constable on the beat, or even at home;
(d) by telephone;
(e) by letter;
(f) while another crime is being investigated, information is received that further offences have been committed – for example, in fraud investigations, the examination of a firm's accounts;
(g) by admission, further offences admitted by a person in custody.

Whenever an allegation is made that a crime has been committed, an entry must be made in the crime complaint form even if the police officer concerned doubts the authenticity of the complainant's story. If it subsequently becomes clear that no crime has been committed, a report is submitted to this effect asking approval to have the entry endorsed 'No Crime'.

Contents of a crime complaint

A completed crime complaint should contain:

(a) the nature of complaint (offence as reported);
(b) the time and date the report was received;
(c) the name and number of the police officer receiving the report;
(d) the full name and address of the person making the report;
(e) the action taken and by whom (who was informed and attended to the complaint and at what time);
(f) how report was received, e.g. '999'.

Crime report

When an investigating police officer has visited a scene of a crime and has made his preliminary, on the spot enquiries, he will submit a crime report which provides the details which form a permanent record of the crime. These details are:

(a) name and address of aggrieved person, date and place of birth, occupation, and sex;

439

(b) place of offence and time and date committed;

(c) details of the offence (MO);

(d) injury to victim and type of weapon used (where appropriate);

(e) value of property stolen, recovered or damaged;

(f) property stolen which is identifiable, non-identifiable and any which is recovered;

(g) means of disposal of offence (Is crime detected? Was no crime in fact committed? Or other means or disposal);

(h) officers who attended scene;

(i) report of investigating officer;

(j) person wanted for offence, or suspected of it;

(k) information circulated by telephone, bulletin, etc.;

(l) date upon which a supplementary crime report is to be submitted setting out details of further enquiries;

(m) when and by whom complainant informed of result of investigation.

Police action

The strength of an investigation lies in the extent of the information gathered and the number of people who are contacted for information. The crime report includes full details of the offence, MO of the criminal, and details of suspected and wanted persons. The likelihood of the offender being identified increases with the extent of the information which is gathered from witnesses or the complainant. The accurate completion of a crime report is extremely important as it may have to be referred to months or years after it was completed, when some person is in custody for similar offences. It is important that investigating officers keep their supervisory officers and detective officers fully informed of the progress of their enquiries as their greater experience and knowledge of likely criminals will frequently assist in the identification of suspects.

Police officers must always ensure that a crime complaint is made out immediately upon a report of a crime being received. If enquiries quickly show that no crime has been committed, it is an easy matter to record that, in fact, no crime has been committed. The crime is, in effect, cancelled.

It is extremely important that the complainant is informed of progress in the investigation of the offence. If no progress is made, it is equally important that the complainant is aware of the efforts being made by the police to discover those responsible for the offence. The time spent doing this is small; the gain is large.

Taking conveyances

Introduction

The offences concerned with the unlawful taking of conveyances in the Theft Act 1968 differ from the other offences of theft in that they do not require that the taker had an intention to deprive the owner permanently of his property. The motive for moving a conveyance is immaterial, if it is taken and moved in a way which involves its use as a conveyance, the offence is committed. Similar offences were dealt with by the Road Traffic Acts prior to the passing of the Theft Act. If a conveyance is appropriated with the intention of depriving the owner permanently of his property, then the offence is one of theft of a conveyance.

Taking conveyances

Section 12(1) of the Theft Act 1968 provides:

> 'A person shall be guilty of an offence if, without having the consent of the owner or other lawful authority, he takes any conveyance for his own or another's use or, knowing that any conveyance has been taken without such authority, drives it or allows himself to be carried in or on it.'

(1) *Conveyance*

Subsection (7) defines the term 'conveyance':

> ' "conveyance" means any conveyance constructed or adapted for the carriage of a person or persons whether by land, water, or air, except that it does not include a conveyance constructed or adapted for use only under the control of a person not carried in it or on it, and "drive" shall be construed accordingly.'

The term is a wide one and will include most motor vehicles, railway locomotives, aircraft, hovercraft, ships, and dinghies. Some vehicles are excluded by the exception which describes forms of transport for the carriage of goods which are not controlled by a driver who is in or on the vehicle. Goods trailers, milk floats, and trolleys such as those used by railway porters are not conveyances for the purpose of this section. The offence is an arrestable offence. The Criminal Justice Act 1988 made the offence a summary one. As there can be no offence of 'attempt' in relation to a summary offence, the previous offence of attempting to take a conveyance was removed by the 1988 Act.

Where there is an attempt to take a conveyance, charges of 'vehicle interference' or 'criminal damage' will have to be considered as alternatives. Pedal cycles are dealt with separately.

(2) *Takes*

The word 'takes' means to acquire possession. However, the mere unauthorised assumption of possession or control is not enough to constitute a 'taking' of a conveyance, there must be some movement of it. A person who breaks into a car and is sitting in the driving seat has not taken it, but if he moves it only a few feet, he has taken it. A man who sits in a rowing boat and casts it adrift has taken it; he who stands on the shore and casts it adrift has not. Where two men pushed a motor car around a corner and hid it as a practical joke, this offence was not committed. The use did not involve use as a conveyance. The necessity to acquire possession without being authorised means that no offence is committed by a person who merely uses a vehicle for some purpose which has not been specifically authorised by the owner, as he is already in possession of the vehicle and, therefore, cannot 'take' it. It may be that a man is employed as a van driver and is authorised by his employer to use his motor vehicle for the purpose of delivering goods upon a prescribed route. If he decides to deviate without authority from this route, he is not guilty of taking the vehicle as it was already in his possession. The position is not quite so clear in circumstances in which the employee has completed his work for the day and parks his employer's vehicle outside his house and then returns to it later in the evening, outside his authorised working hours, and uses the vehicle for some private purpose. In such circumstances it has been held that when he parked the vehicle at the conclusion of his day's work, his authority to use it ceased and possession of the vehicle reverted to the employer, the employee merely having custody of it. Although the distinction appears to be a fine one, it can be appreciated that Parliament did not intend to punish professional drivers who merely deviated from a prescribed route, but probably did intend to punish drivers who used their employer's vehicle for private purposes outside their hours of employment, against the wishes of the owner. The High Court has also ruled that if a driver uses his employer's vehicle in a manner which is quite inconsistent with his terms of employment it may amount to a 'taking'. In this instance a driver had not only deviated from his route but had visited several public houses and had driven a number of friends to their homes, showing an intention to use the vehicle as he would his own. It has been held that merely to move a vehicle for convenience, because it was blocking a householder's doorway, does not in normal circumstances constitute an offence.

(3) *Without having the consent of the owner or other lawful authority*

Section 12(6) provides that a person does not commit an offence under the section by anything done in the belief that he has lawful authority to do it or that he would have the owner's consent if the owner knew of his doing it and the circumstances involved.

The consent which is obtained from the owner must be a true consent and not one which has been given as a result of threats of violence or any other form of intimidation. If a man with a pistol 'requests' permission to borrow a car, the consent which he obtains cannot be a valid one! On the other hand, a consent which has been obtained by fraud is nevertheless valid and prevents the offence from being committed. Where a hirer misrepresented his identity and falsely stated that he had a driving licence, he did not 'take' the car even though the consent was fraudulently obtained. If a man borrows his friend's car by alleging that he wishes to pick up his wife from the railway station, when in fact it was someone else whom he wished to meet, he does not take the car without consent. The consent gained is not invalidated by a deception as to the destination or purpose of the journey.

The term 'other lawful authority' recognises that the law authorises certain persons, including constables, to remove vehicles in certain circumstances without the consent of the owner and that an owner's representative, for example his wife, may on occasions give authority to some other person to use her husband's car. If X hired a car to Y subject to a contractual requirement for Y to return it on a certain day, X would have lawful authority to take it in the event of its non-return.

The term 'other' means, in relation to a conveyance which is the subject of a hire purchase agreement, the person in possession under that agreement.

(4) Drives it or allows himself to be carried in or on it, knowing it to have been taken without such authority

If special mention was not made of other persons who may knowingly use a conveyance which has been unlawfully taken by some other person, they would commit no offence provided that they were not a party to the original taking. If a man takes a car without the owner's consent, drives it to the home of his friends, tells them what he has done, and invites them to come for a drive with him, they cannot be charged with 'taking' the car as they were not present when it was taken nor were they a party to its taking. However, having accepted the offer, each of them allows himself to be carried in the car and is, therefore, guilty of an offence. If one of them should subsequently drive the vehicle he may be charged with that offence. When solo motor cycles are unlawfully taken it is not uncommon for others to drive the motor cycle at the taker's invitation, in the full knowledge that it has been so taken. On each occasion, the person concerned is guilty of driving the motor cycle knowing it to have been taken without authority; such a person cannot be charged with 'taking' as the act had previously been completed.

It may not always be possible to prove that the taker informed the persons concerned that the conveyance had been illegally acquired, but a court is entitled to take into account the surrounding circumstances which may make it clear that they must have known or, at least, have deliberately closed their eyes to the obvious.

Aggravated vehicle taking

The Aggravated Vehicle Taking Act 1992 creates offences of aggravated vehicle taking by adding a s. 12A to the Theft Act 1968. An offence is committed where a person has offended against s. 12(1) in any way in relation to a mechanically propelled vehicle and it is proved that at any time after the vehicle was unlawfully taken (whether by himself or another) and before it was recovered, the vehicle was driven, or injury or damage was caused in the following circumstances:

(a) that the vehicle was driven dangerously (as defined by the Road Traffic Acts, see page 287) on a road or other public place;
(b) that, owing to the driving of the vehicle, an accident occurred by which injury was caused to any person;
(c) that, owing to the driving of the vehicle, an accident occurred by which damage was caused to any property other than the vehicle;
(d) that damage was caused to the vehicle.

However, it is a defence for such a person to prove that such driving, accident or damage occurred before he committed the basic offence, or that he was neither in, nor on, nor in the immediate vicinity of the vehicle when such driving, accident or damage occurred.

The Act extends the concept of 'joint enterprise' to these offences. All who commit an offence against the Theft Act 1968, s. 12(1), where the motor vehicle is

443

subsequently involved in one of the sets of circumstances set out at (a) to (d) above, are guilty of aggravated vehicle taking. Section 12(1) embraces those who drive and those who allow themselves to be carried as well as those who 'take'. Thus, the difficult problem of proving who was actually driving at the time, or who actually took the vehicle in the first instance is avoided as all offend against s. 12(1). That those jointly involved in the enterprise should be similarly treated is reinforced by s. 3 of the 1992 Act which amends the Road Traffic Offenders Act 1988, s. 34, to provide that the fact that a person who is convicted of an offence under the Theft Act 1968, s. 12A, did not drive the vehicle in question at any particular time, or at all, shall not be regarded as a special reason for the purposes of s. 34(1). The offences under the 1992 Act are subject to obligatory disqualification and obligatory endorsement of 3–11 penalty points. The offence is triable only on indictment and punishable with two years' imprisonment, or where the accident causes the death of some person, with five years' imprisonment. Where a person is found not guilty of aggravated vehicle taking he may be convicted of the basic offence and the Crown Court shall have the same powers as a magistrates' court in such circumstances.

The offences must be tried summarily if the 'value' of damage to the vehicle or to property is less than the 'relevant sum' specified in the Magistrates' Courts Act 1980, s. 22, currently £5000. However, the restrictions placed upon imprisonment by s. 33 in such cases (maximum of three months), is removed in the case of aggravated vehicle taking.

Taking pedal cycles

As previously described, the taking of pedal cycles is dealt with separately because of the nature of the punishment provided for the unlawful taking of other conveyances. The maximum penalty for offences involving pedal cycles is a fine at level 3, and these offences are not arrestable offences.

Subsection (5) provides that a person who, without having the consent of the owner or other lawful authority, takes a pedal cycle for his own or another's use, or rides a pedal cycle knowing it to have been taken without such authority, is guilty of a summary offence. The defence of belief in lawful authority, or that consent would have been given, also applies to offences involving pedal cycles.

Differences between taking conveyances or pedal cycles and theft

As described in the introduction to this subject, theft requires an intention to deprive the owner of his property permanently, but such an intention is deliberately excluded from these offences to make joyriding, in all forms of conveyances described in this section, punishable. Because at times, particularly when a conveyance has been kept by the accused person for a considerable period of time, the dividing line between theft and these offences will be a fine one, the section provides that on trial on indictment an accused charged with theft of a conveyance may be found guilty of an offence under subs. (1).

Interference with vehicles

The Theft Act 1968 deals with offences of taking a conveyance, the term conveyance including motor vehicles. The offences under the Criminal Attempts Act deal with associated offences. If a person interferes with:

(a) a motor vehicle or trailer; or
(b) with anything carried in or on a motor vehicle or trailer, with the intention that an offence of
    (i) theft of the motor vehicle or trailer, or part of such vehicles; or
    (ii) theft of anything carried in or on the motor vehicle or trailer; or
    (iii) taking a conveyance, contrary to s. 12 of the Theft Act 1968,

be committed either by himself or another person, he shall be guilty of an offence of 'interference with vehicles', contrary to s. 9 of the Criminal Attempts Act 1981.

These offences cover a wide range of activities. A person interfering with the door locks of a vehicle is clearly interfering with the vehicle. As his actions develop and he enters the car his intention should soon become apparent, he either intends to steal the car, or to steal property within the car, or parts of the car. He may open the door to allow someone else to enter and steal property, or the vehicle itself, and in such circumstances would be guilty of this offence of interference. Additionally, interference with the load on a vehicle or trailer with the intention of stealing is an offence in itself. The removal of securing ropes and tarpaulins would amount to such interference. The terms 'motor vehicle' and 'trailer' have the meanings given to them by the Road Traffic Act 1988.

The distinction must be made between incidents of hooliganism and vandalism, as opposed to those involving theft or taking. Although those who 'rock' a vehicle to set off its alarm system, or scratch the paintwork with a coin 'interfere' with a vehicle they do not do so with the intention of theft or taking. He who breaks off a car aerial and throws it to the ground does not commit this offence; but he who pulls off a mirror with the intention of stealing it does.

Where an accused person can be shown to have intended to commit one of these offences, it is immaterial that it cannot be shown which offence it was.

Practical hints on investigation

Taking conveyances without authority is a common offence. It is unlikely that many conveyances will be taken before the eyes of a patrolling police officer. A much greater number *have been* taken when they are first observed by the police officer. He must remain conscious of the possibility that the vehicle with which he comes into contact may have been stolen or unlawfully taken.

Often the hour of the day and the circumstances of the use of the vehicle will attract suspicion but it must be remembered that vehicles are taken throughout the full 24 hours of the day in many of our cities and towns. Particular care should be taken when checking ownership of a vehicle by questioning the driver. Has he any documentary proof of ownership? Not many drivers carry their vehicle registration documents but they frequently have other documents which carry their names and the registration mark of the vehicle, such as service schedules. If the ignition circuit has been bypassed then the driver must have a very good explanation for the need to have done so. Does the driver know the registration number? Surprisingly, many true owners do not, but they can usually give some indication of the range of the symbols. Is the driver conversant with the keys? Does he know which key fits which lock? Most drivers have a sound knowledge of the contents of the car and its boot. Even the unobservant must notice something in the course of using the vehicle daily. The details of the excise licence should be known as should damage, marks or peculiarities affecting the vehicle. The driver and the occupants of the vehicle may be ill at ease if it has been unlawfully taken, although this need not necessarily be so. Many habitual car thieves do not expect to be caught and are used to dealing with such checks. Familiarity with the controls is somewhat reassuring but the regular thief tends to take particular models of motor car with which he is familiar.

A PNC check can be helpful as there may be a record of the driver, occupants or the vehicle itself. However, it is important to remember that a negative response from PNC does not mean that all is in order. It merely signifies that there is no record in the computer at that time.

Pedal cycles present additional difficulties because there is no registration system to assist enquiries. The observations to be made might include the size and suitability of the machine to the user. Does the user have cycle clips if wearing long trousers? The rider, if the owner, should have a knowledge of the make of the machine and the contents, if any, of the cycle bag. Are there any marks or peculiarities on the machine? Is the rider aware of this? Is he ill at ease?

The art of easy conversation, which demands the stimulation of an exchange of information, will assist in such situations. A staccato stilted form of questioning is artificial and unprofessional and leads conversation up a succession of blind alleys. Encourage suspects to be descriptive, give opportunities for them to enlarge upon their story; their explanation of where they have come from and where they are going to. The greater the opportunities given to allow them to talk, the greater the possibility of inconsistency.

Statutory preventive measures

The law has always recognised that many acts which are in some ways preparatory to the commission of crime, should be punishable if persons are found in possession of articles, or in circumstances which suggest that it was their intention to commit crime. Various Acts of Parliament deal with offences of this nature.

Criminal attempts

(1) *The offence*

Section 1(1) of the Criminal Attempts Act 1981 provides:

> 'If, with intent to commit an offence to which this section applies, a person does an act which is more than merely preparatory to the commission of the offence, he is guilty of attempting to commit the offence.'

446   Section 1(4) of the Act provides that the section applies to any offence which, if completed, would be triable in England and Wales as an indictable offence, except:

(a) conspiracy (at common law or under s. 1 of the Criminal Law Act 1977 or any other enactment);

(b) aiding, abetting, counselling, procuring or suborning the commission of an offence; and

(c) offences under s. 4(1) (assisting offenders) or s. 5(1) (accepting or agreeing to accept consideration for not disclosing information about an arrestable offence) of the Criminal Law Act 1967.

All attempts to commit indictable offences are therefore offences contrary to s. 1, with the exception of those specified. However, it will be seen that attempts to commit summary offences are not made offences under this Act. A number of statutes specifically create offences of 'attempt' and these are unaffected.

(2) The forbidden act

The section requires 'an act which is more than merely preparatory to the commission of the offence' and this relates to the full offence which he intends to commit. That which is 'merely preparatory' is not defined. One thing of which we can be sure is that a 'last act', because it is the last act which the accused could carry out with the necessary intent, even though the commission of the full offence would require an act on someone else's part is beyond preparation. If a man sends a parcel bomb to another with intent to kill or injure him, or places a poison in another's coffee with a similar intent, he has certainly attempted to commit the full offence even though the other party will have to open the parcel before it will explode, or will have to drink from the cup before he becomes poisoned. The act of the perpetrator is certainly more than preparatory. His preparatory acts would be the assembly of the device or the secreting of the phial of poison about his person.

However, the term 'more than merely preparatory' is not limited to such cases. All acts leading to an offence are 'preparatory' but they are not 'merely preparatory'. If a man buys petrol, boots and overalls with the intention of setting fire to a shop, he has carried out a number of preparatory acts which are all 'merely' preparatory to the commission of an offence of arson. If he then arrives outside the shop, and places the can of petrol on the ground, it is submitted that his act is still merely preparatory. However, his next step, pouring the petrol over the door of the shop, is likely to be held to be more than merely preparatory as it is a positive step on the road to completion of the offence. The striking of a match would certainly constitute an act which is more than merely preparatory. A man who intends to shoot another carries out acts which are merely preparatory when he takes his gun to a point of ambush and lies in wait. Things change as he takes aim; it is submitted that this is more than merely preparatory; and as he takes up pressure on the trigger he has arrived at a stage which allows only one further act before the full offence will be committed.

Where a man pointed a gun at another whom he intended to kill, and when foiled, placed a cord around his neck, it was held that these combined acts amounted to more than mere preparation and were sufficient evidence of attempted murder. In a case in which a man dragged a girl into a secluded spot and threatened her before putting his hand up her skirt in contact with her vaginal area, then moving his hand

447

to the top of her tights, it was held that there was sufficient evidence of attempted rape for consideration by a jury.

At the opposite end of the scale, a man was seen to approach a post office, ride around the area on a motor cycle and walk around that area before putting on sunglasses and placing his hand in a pocket which appeared to contain something heavy. These acts were all held to be merely preparatory to an attempt to rob the post office and this is understandable. They were far removed from an offence of robbery; the suspect had not even arrived at the scene of his intended crime. He was later found to be in possession of an imitation gun and a threatening note but these matters were related to his intentions when he arrived at the scene of his crime. The writing of the note was another 'merely preparatory' matter. Had the note subsequently been handed over the counter, that act would have been more than merely preparatory.

(3) *The guilty state of mind*

The intention of the person who attempts to carry out a particular act is important in 'attempt' cases. The accused must intend to commit an act or to continue with a series of acts which when completed will amount to or lead to an offence. He must *intend* the consequences of his act, as opposed to being reckless in relation to that consequence, even though recklessness may suffice in respect of the commission of the full offence. For example, for there to be a conviction for attempted murder the accused must be shown to have *intended* to kill. Where the person concerned had been killed as a result of such an act, it would be sufficient to justify a conviction for murder that he intended his act to cause grievous bodily harm.

However, where the act of the accused is merely forbidden if it occurs with lack of consent, the accused will have sufficient *mens rea* if he knew or believed that that state of affairs existed.

The standard of proof of intention in cases of 'attempt' is thus twofold; there must have been an *intention* to appropriate property belonging to another and a *dishonest intention* to permanently deprive the owner of his property, where an offence of attempted theft is preferred.

(4) *Impossibility*

A person may be guilty of attempting to commit an offence to which the section applies, even though the facts are such that the commission of the full offence is impossible. Thus, a man who puts his hand into another's pocket intending to steal, commits an offence of attempted theft even though the pocket is empty. He who shoots a man who is already dead can be convicted of an offence of attempted murder.

Section 1(3) reinforces this by stating that where apart from s. 1(3) a person's intention would not be regarded as having amounted to an intent to commit an offence, but if the facts had been as that person believed them to be, his intention would have been so regarded, he is to be regarded as having an intent to commit that offence. An accused was arrested carrying a package which he had brought from India which he believed contained heroin or cannabis. It in fact contained snuff. It was held that he had nevertheless attempted to import controlled drugs as he believed that the substance which he was bringing into the country was a controlled drug.

Other statutory offences of 'attempt'

The Criminal Attempts Act 1981, s. 3, applies the provisions of the Act to offences of 'attempt' created by other statutes, thus requiring proof of more than a merely preparatory act.

Offensive weapons – Prevention of Crimes Act 1953

The 1953 Act was passed at a time when the incidence of the possession of offensive weapons was on the increase. Flick knives and gravity knives were two of the types of weapons which were increasingly in evidence.

Section 1 provides:

'Any person who without lawful authority or reasonable excuse, the proof whereof shall lie on him, has with him in any public place any offensive weapon shall be guilty of an offence.'

The term 'offensive weapon' means any article made or adapted for use for causing injury to the person, or intended by the person having it with him for such use by him or by some other person. The definition specifies three different types of weapons: those made for causing injury; those adapted for that purpose; and others merely intended to be used.

Articles made to cause injury would include knuckledusters, swordsticks, a dagger (as opposed to a sheath knife) and flick knives or gravity knives because they are manufactured for no other purpose than to cause bodily injury. Those adapted to cause injury might include a bottle which is broken to form a weapon, a bicycle chain with sharpened links, or cap, the peak of which has been reinforced with metal. Weapons which are intended to be used for the purpose of causing injury can include any object which is ordinarily inoffensive: a walking stick, spanner, shoe, or sheath knife. It is at this point that the importance of the three categories of weapons specified in the definition can be observed. If persons are found in possession of weapons which are either made or adapted for the purpose of causing harm, and this fact is proved to the court, the burden of proof shifts to the defence to prove lawful authority or reasonable excuse for possession.

However, if the weapon concerned is merely an article, normally inoffensive, which is intended to be used for the purpose of causing injury, the burden of proof remains with the prosecution to show that the accused had it with him intending it to be so used. If a police officer finds a man in a public place in possession of a swordstick or a chain with sharpened links, he may immediately take action under this section, the responsibility being that of the defendant to establish lawful excuse. In the case of objects normally inoffensive, such as the walking stick, it is necessary to prove an intention to use them before the offence is committed. In normal circumstances the first step in proving that a weapon which an accused had with him was intended to be used for causing injury to the person is that it was used to assault

449

or attempt to assault another person. For many years, the High Court tended to accept that this was so. In 1975 a carpenter on his way home from work took a hammer from his case and assaulted another man with it. He was charged with an assault occasioning bodily harm and possessing an offensive weapon: the hammer. The second charge was dismissed in that the use of the weapon was part of the assault, and the dismissal was upheld by the High Court. It was said that in such circumstances the weapon must have been carried (i.e. the accused had it with him) with the intention to use it offensively *before* the occasion for its use had arisen. Therefore, in the case of a weapon 'intended to be used', it must be carried prior to its use 'without lawful authority or excuse' or, such a weapon not previously in lawful possession, must be taken up by the accused who must then show an intention to use it. A man who assaulted another in a public street and requested, and was given, a clasp knife by a companion, which he then held to his victim's head intending to cause injury, was held not to be guilty of this offence, having seized the weapon for instant use, rather than to have 'possessed' it for a sufficient length of time. In the case of articles already lawfully possessed which are used as offensive weapons, such use does not prove the intent by itself.

A person may have an offensive weapon 'with him' even though he is not carrying the weapon at the time, but he must be closely linked with it and it must be readily accessible to him. Thus, a man who has an offensive weapon with him in his car, still has it with him when he goes into a public convenience. A person does not have something with him when it has been slipped into his bag without his knowledge. If a person is at one time aware that there is a cosh in the glove compartment of his car it is no excuse that at the material time he had forgotten about it.

Circumstances which will be regarded as a reasonable excuse for possession of offensive weapons are quite restricted. A man was convicted when found in possession of a knuckleduster and truncheon which he alleged were kept for protection when collecting his firm's wages. The last occasion upon which wages had been collected was some days previously and the divisional court ruled that his possession was unreasonable. A taxi driver who carried a cosh for protection against violent passengers was also convicted.

Although the statute does not demand proof by the prosecution that those weapons which are made or adapted for use for causing injury to the person are possessed 'knowingly', it has been held that proof should be offered concerning knowledge. If a defendant alleges that he had put a weapon under the seat of his car and forgotten about it, he in effect admits knowledge of its presence. It is no excuse that he has since forgotten about it.

'Lawful authority' refers to those persons in the armed services, police, etc., who are authorised to carry such weapons.

The term 'public place' is given its normal meaning. Hospital grounds to which visitors and their friends were admitted have been held to be a public place. An interesting decision of assistance to police officers was that in which a man who produced a gun in a private dwelling-house was convicted on the grounds that the court was entitled to infer that it was brought to the house through the streets and that the defendant must have been in possession of the gun in a public place.

Restriction of Offensive Weapons Act 1959

A further Act was passed in 1959 which created the offences of manufacturing, selling, hiring, offering for sale or hire, exposing for sale, or having in possession for the purpose of sale or hire, or lending or giving to any person, flick knives or gravity knives. The importation of these knives is also prohibited by this Act, which made the transfer of such weapons from one person to another outside the law. Flick knives are those whose blade opens automatically on pressure on a button, and gravity knives those which open by the application of gravitational or centrifugal force.

Criminal Justice Act 1988

Section 139 of this Act punishes possession in a public place of articles which otherwise escape the definition of those which are made or adapted for use for causing injury. It declares it to be an offence for a person to have with him in a public place an article which is sharply pointed or with a blade, other than a folding pocket knife with a blade not exceeding 3 inches. A knife which is held in the open position by a locking device and can only be released from that position by pressing a button, is not a 'folding pocket knife' for the purposes of this section. A defence of 'lawful authority or good reason' for possession or that he had it with him for use at work, for a religious reason or as part of a national dress, is provided by the Act. Where a man was found in possession of a knife six days after he had used it at work, it was held that 'forgetfulness' was not a good reason for having it in his possession at the relevant time. The burden of proving 'good reason' is not discharged when an explanation is offered which is not contradicted by the prosecution. The justices were entitled to reject an excuse that a knife was to be used for food preparation later in the evening, as being improbable.

Section 141 of the 1988 Act also creates offences of manufacture, sale or hire, exposing for sale or hire, or lending or giving to another person, any weapon which the Secretary of State has specified in an order made to another person, any weapon which the Secretary of State has specified in an order made by statutory instrument. The Secretary of State has since made the Criminal Justice Act 1988 (Offensive Weapons) Order 1988 listing the knuckleduster, swordstick, handclaw, belt-buckle, knife, pushdagger, hollow kubotan (small truncheon with spikes in sides), footclaw, death star, butterfly knife, telescopic truncheon, blow-pipe, Kusari-game (sickle and chain), kyoketushoge (hook, knife and chain), and kusari (weights joined by chain), as weapons to which this offence applies.

A justice may issue a warrant authorising entry and search on the application of a constable if he is satisfied that there are reasonable grounds for believing that there are on those premises knives such as are mentioned in the Restriction of Offensive Weapons Act 1959, s. 1(1) or weapons to which the Criminal Justice Act 1988, s. 141, applies and that an offence under either of these provisions has been or is being committed in relation to them and that one of the essential conditions exists (see page 103).

Trespassing with a weapon of offence

The Criminal Law Act 1977 creates several offences the purpose of which is to prevent unlawful trespass upon buildings. Section 8 declares that it is an offence for any person, who is on premises as a trespasser, after having entered as such, if he has with him on the premises any weapon of offence without lawful authority or reasonable excuse. There are a number of points to consider. We are concerned with persons who enter premises as trespassers with weapons, who have no lawful excuse for possession of such weapons. The offender must enter as a trespasser. It is not sufficient to constitute an offence if a person enters lawfully and is subsequently asked to leave, thereby becoming a trespasser once his leave to remain is withdrawn. A thief who has a gun in his possession when he breaks into premises must always be guilty of this offence in addition to any other offence which he may commit. He enters as a trespasser and is unlikely to have any lawful excuse for his possession of a gun in such circumstances. However, persons may enter shops quite lawfully in circumstances in which they could not be described as trespassers while having knives in their possession. Provided that they remain in the public part of the shop they can never be trespassers unless required to leave. As they entered the shop lawfully, they do not commit this offence.

A 'weapon of offence' is any article made or adapted for use for causing injury to or incapacitating a person, or intended by the person having it with him for such use. The term 'premises' means any building, any part of a building under separate occupation, and land ancillary to a building, the site comprising any building or buildings together with any land ancillary thereto. The description of 'premises' makes it clear that offences can be committed by persons who although lawfully in one part of a building, trespass into another part which is in separate occupation; for example, hotel rooms or office blocks. Land ancillary to buildings is also included.

The extent of the s. 8 offence is such that offences may be committed in the course of theft in a very general sense. The other offences with which the Criminal Law Act of 1977 is quite specifically concerned are those caused by squatters and are strictly phrased to prevent the unlawful occupation of residential premises. The s. 8 offence would also deal with armed squatters.

Police powers

A constable in uniform may arrest without warrant anyone who is, or whom he reasonably suspects to be, in the act of committing this offence. For this purpose of effecting such an arrest, he may enter premises without a warrant in accordance with the provisions of s. 17 of the Police and Criminal Evidence Act 1984.

Going equipped to steal

Section 25 of the Theft Act 1968 provides that a person shall be guilty of an offence if, when not at his place of abode, he has with him any article for use in the course of or in connection with any burglary, theft, or cheat.

Unlike the provisions replaced by this section, this offence can be committed at any time of the day or night. Possession of articles in the home is excepted, but elsewhere is punishable if they are such that they are for use in the course of, or in connection with, any burglary, theft, or cheat. Under previous legislation it was held that the possession must be actual rather than constructive, and that actual possession by one of two persons acting in concert is possession by both. It is probable that these decisions will be followed in relation to the Theft Act offences. Once possession of articles has been proved, the burden of proof shifts to the accused, who must satisfy the court that his possession was for a lawful purpose.

The nature of the article carried is of importance from an evidential viewpoint. If it is made or adapted for use in committing burglary or theft, then proof of possession may be enough in itself to prove the charge. Possession of articles such as jemmies, skeleton keys, or picklocks can be for no other purpose than the commission of crime in most circumstances, although the exceptional case may arise in which the defendant can establish that they were carried for a lawful purpose. If the nature of the article is such that it can be used for these forms of crime as well as for some lawful purpose, then the court must decide from the evidence available – including the nature of the article and the circumstances in which the accused was in possession of it – the intention of the person concerned. This could apply to a bunch of car keys.

The reference to articles used for the purpose of 'cheat' is first met in this context in the Theft Act 1968, and means obtaining property by deception contrary to s. 15 of that Act. Such articles could therefore include false identification documents for the purpose of deceiving households into handing over rent money, in the belief that they were giving money to a representative of the local authority.

The person concerned must be equipped to carry out a burglary, theft or cheat which is to be committed in the future and it need not be proved that his possession related to a particular crime of this nature. Section 25(5) provides that for the purposes of this offence, an offence of taking a conveyance, contrary to the Theft Act 1968, shall be treated as an offence of theft.

Police powers

Going equipped to steal is an arrestable offence. It is declared to be arrestable by s. 24 of the Police and Criminal Evidence Act 1984.

Found on enclosed premises

Section 4 of the Vagrancy Act 1824 states that it is an offence for any person to be found in or upon any dwelling-house, warehouse, coach house, stable or outhouse, or in any enclosed yard, garden, or area for any unlawful purpose. The influence of the early nineteenth-century situation can be read within this offence. The buildings which are specified are associated with the residence of the middle and upper classes, which it was then necessary to protect from large numbers of vagrants (many of whom had been disabled during the Napoleonic wars) who were wandering throughout the country. However, this legislation is just as effective today in dealing with persons found in certain places in circumstances which suggest that they are about to commit crime.

There are a number of points which must be proved in these cases. Although it is unnecessary to specify the occupier of the building concerned, the address of the premises must be shown in the charge. The word 'enclosed' qualifies the terms 'yard', 'garden', or 'area' and it is, therefore, necessary to show that there was some form of enclosure. It is not necessary to establish that the yard is completely enclosed; there may be a form of access through an open gate, archway, or a gap between buildings. This is a common-sense approach adopted by the courts in looking at the usual forms of access to yards which accompany various buildings. A decision to the effect that railway sidings are not an 'area' for the purposes of this section perhaps provides a useful parallel. Most railway sidings do not have the strict form of enclosure envisaged by the legislators. The most significant factor for police officers is that the 'unlawful purpose' must be some criminal purpose, as opposed to acts of immorality. It is not an offence contrary to this section to be found in such a place for the purpose of prostitution. Following complaints, men are often found in the grounds of houses and hostels for the purpose of looking through lighted windows, and it is submitted that this is not an offence under this section as the commission of the actual offence would only lead to action by way of complaint, with a view to surety for good behaviour being given by the person concerned. The person committing an offence contrary to s. 4 must be found on the premises, but it is not necessary that he be arrested there.

Crossbows

The Crossbows Act 1987 is concerned with crossbows with a draw weight of at least 1.4 kg.

It is an offence for anyone to sell or let on hire a crossbow or part of a crossbow to a person under the age of 17 years. No offence is committed if the seller or hirer believes that the person so acquiring is of or over the age of 17, provided that he has reasonable ground for that belief. It is also an offence for such a person to purchase or hire such a crossbow or part of a crossbow, or for him to have with him a crossbow capable of discharging a missile, or parts which together (and without any other parts) can be assembled to form a complete crossbow, unless in either case he is under the supervision of a person who is 21 years of age or older.

Police powers

Where a constable suspects with reasonable cause that a person is committing or has committed an offence of having with him a crossbow or parts, he may:

(a) search that person for a crossbow or part of a crossbow; or
(b) search any vehicle, or anything in or on a vehicle, in or on which the constable reasonably suspects there is a crossbow or part of a crossbow connected with the offence.

A person or vehicle may be detained by a constable for the purpose of such searches and evidence may be seized. A constable may enter any land other than a dwelling-house to exercise these powers.

Intimidation of witnesses, jurors and others

The Criminal Justice and Public Order Act 1994, s. 51, creates offences which are concerned with the intimidation of witnesses before a trial, jurors during a trial and reprisals which are taken against such person after a trial has been concluded.

Acts of intended intimidation before or during a trial and acts which harm or are intended to harm such persons after a trial has been concluded must have been committed in the knowledge or belief that the person concerned was so involved. It does not matter that such a person was not so involved if the person carrying out the act believed that he was. Threats may be made to a third person (e.g. a wife) knowing that the threat will be 'passed on' to the person concerned. They may be directed at persons or property and 'harm' may be financial.

The intimidation must be intended to cause the investigation into an offence or the course of justice to be obstructed, perverted or interfered with. Where an act is done with the appropriate knowledge or belief it shall be presumed, unless the contrary is proved, that the accused did the act with the appropriate intent. In relation to offences committed in respect of harm or intended harm, offences which are committed after trial or appeal, if it is proved that the act was done or threatened within the 'relevant period', with such knowledge or belief, the accused shall be presumed, unless the contrary is proved, to have carried out the act with the required motive. The 'relevant period' covers the moment from the beginning of an investigation of an offence; the institution of proceedings; the act concerned of the witness or juror or person assisting; and one year from the anniversary of the particular relevant event.

In the case of proceedings, that period runs from trial or determination of appeal. However, 'relevant period' is only related to the time during which the presumption of intention or motive remains valid. Prosecutions may occur outside this period, but in such a case the intention or motive will have to be proved by the prosecution.

These are arrestable offences, being punishable by five years' imprisonment when tried on indictment.

Indecent language, exposure, and telephone calls

Indecent language

Although the use of language which borders upon the obscene has become almost socially acceptable in our modern society, mainly due to its use within the mass media, some control is still exercised by the Town Police Clauses Act 1847. Since the passing of the Local Government Act 1972, the provisions of this Act apply generally throughout England and Wales although there are certain administrative exceptions (e.g. licensing of Hackney carriages, and some other provisions do not apply in London). However, this is probably now of little significance to police officers, as the persons who are found to be using obscene language in places in which use is likely to offend other people, use it in conjunction with other forms of antisocial behaviour while under the influence of drink, and are arrested for being drunk and disorderly. In such circumstances, evidence of the obscene language used is usually given to the magistrates as supporting evidence of their disorderly conduct.

Section 28 of the Town Police Clauses Act 1847 lists various street nuisances which may be committed to the annoyance of residents or passengers in a street. For the purpose of this section, the term 'street' includes any road, square, court, alley, thoroughfare, or public passage, and a street will be taken to include the carriageway and the footway at its sides. The offence must be committed in the street, but as the annoyance may be to 'residents' it may include the occupiers of houses in that street, although they are not in the street itself at the time.

One of the offences listed is that committed by any person who uses any profane or obscene language or sings any profane or obscene song or ballad, in any street, including any place to which the public have a right of access, and any place of public resort, or unfenced ground adjoining a street, to the annoyance of residents or passengers. In the event of action being taken for this offence it is essential that evidence of such annoyance should be given to the court, and it is advisable to secure witnesses who will give evidence to the effect that they were annoyed by this conduct. The terms 'obscene' and 'profane' should be given their ordinary meaning; things 'obscene' being those which are disgusting, filthy, offensive, or repulsive and those 'profane' being disrespectful, irreverent, impious, or blasphemous. The current trend towards acceptance of many terms which the society of 1847 would not have tolerated, should be recognised as it is undesirable that police officers should be seen to interpret things which are offensive in an over-formal manner. The essence of the offence is the annoyance which is caused to residents or passengers and this should either be very apparent or be the subject of a complaint.

Indecent exposure – Vagrancy Act 1824

Section 4 of the Vagrancy Act 1824 as amended states that every person who wilfully, openly, lewdly, and obscenely exposes his person with intent to insult any female, commits an offence. This offence is one which can only be committed by a male, and the inclusion of the word 'openly' means that the act is done without concealment. It can be committed in any place, whether in public or in private, and the word 'person' means 'penis'. The inclusion of the word 'wilful' in the offence is provided to distinguish those exposures which are not committed deliberately.

Complaints are frequently received from women who have been subjected to this form of conduct on more than one occasion, particularly when the offence is alleged to have been committed by a man living nearby who may expose himself in front of a window or while in his garden. In such circumstances the complainant may give evidence of other occasions upon which exposures have taken place for the purpose of showing that she was not mistaken in her identification of the man, and that the act was wilful and carried out with intent to insult her. In addition, if the accused gives evidence on his own behalf, he may be cross-examined as to whether he has exposed himself to the complainant on other occasions. Generally, evidence of exposure to other women on other occasions is not admissible unless they are acts committed nearby on the same occasions, tending to show a systematic course of conduct. In such cases the evidence must not be offered until a defence of accident, mistake, or lack of intention to insult is raised.

Indecent exposure – Town Police Clauses Act 1847

It is an offence contrary to s. 28 of the Town Police Clauses Act 1847 for any person to wilfully and indecently expose the person in a public place to the annoyance of residents or passengers. No intention to insult a female needs to be proved; the offence is complete if the exposure is to the annoyance of residents or passengers, and it can be committed by a male or female.

Police officers on specific duties to apprehend persons committing indecent acts are not 'passengers' within the meaning of this section.

Indecent exposure – common law

An offence of indecent exposure also exists at common law but such an offence is rarely charged as, like all such common law nuisances, it is only triable on indictment. Occasions may arise in which no other offence can be charged. The exposure may not have been in a 'street' or done with intent to insult a female. In such circumstances no offence may be charged other than that at common law. Such a charge should allege that the accused unlawfully, wilfully, and publicly exposed his naked person. For an exposure to be public for the purposes of common law, it must be to more than one member of the public. It need not necessarily occur in a public place; it is sufficient if it is made where a number of persons may be offended by it and a number see it. The common law does not require that the act of indecency disgusted or annoyed anyone; the offence is indictable as a nuisance. It has been held to be an indictable offence for a man to undress himself on the beach and to bathe in the sea near inhabited houses from which he might be distinctly seen. Perhaps the greatest ever common law example of exposure which constituted an indictable nuisance occurred in 1663 when a man appeared naked on a balcony in Covent Garden before a huge assembly below.

'Peeping Toms'

This term is used to describe those individuals who gain pleasure from watching others undress or make love. It is not an offence contrary to any statute to do so, but such conduct may lead to a breach of the peace in the event of discovery. Although a power to arrest without warrant exists at common law where such a breach is imminent, it should seldom be necessary to exercise it. Proceedings should normally be by way of complaint with a view to binding over.

Indecent telephone calls and messages

The incidence of complaints concerning offensive telephone calls is increasing, and this can prove to be one of the most difficult offences to detect. Section 43 of the Telecommunications Act 1984 states that any person who sends, by means of a public telecommunication service, a message or other matter that is grossly offensive or of an indecent, obscene, or menacing character, shall be guilty of an offence. If indecent telephone calls are frequently received by a particular woman, it is usually only possible to trace the offender if she is willing to engage the speaker in conversation for sufficient length of time to allow the call to be traced.

By previous arrangement with the British Telecom telephone exchange supervisor, it is possible to arrange for all calls to be intercepted for a period of time, either with a view to tracing the call while the caller is engaged in conversation or, alternatively, to prevent nuisance calls from being connected to the complainant's number. It is frequently possible to keep such persons engaged in conversation for some time as they derive considerable pleasure from these conversations. In many cases, the complainant is more concerned about the prevention of further indecent calls, which invariably cease when the caller finds that the British Telecom exchange supervisor is intercepting the calls. However, new procedures being introduced by British Telecommunications lead to a quick identification of the source of the call.

The Malicious Communications Act 1988 makes it an offence to send to another person a letter or other article which conveys a message which is indecent or grossly offensive; a threat; or information which is false and known or believed to be false by the sender; or any other article which is, in whole or in part, of an indecent or grossly offensive nature, if the purpose, or one of the purposes, in sending it is that it should cause distress or anxiety to the recipient or to any other person to whom he intends that it or its contents or nature should be communicated.

A defence is available to a person who shows that a threat was used to reinforce a demand which he believed he had reasonable grounds for making; and that he believed that the use of the threat was a proper means of reinforcing the demand.

Indecent assault

Introduction

The Sexual Offences Act 1956, s. 14, states that it is an offence for a person to make an indecent assault on a woman. An indecent assault is an assault which in itself, or taken in conjunction with the surrounding circumstances, is capable of being considered an indecent assault by right-minded people. Section 15 of the 1956 Act makes it an offence for any person to make an indecent assault on a man.

The elements of an indecent assault

(1) The assault itself

An indecent assault involves the use of, or threats to use, any physical force to commit a sexual act. As can be seen from the provisions of the Sexual Offences Act 1956, it does not matter whether the person assaulted is a male or female, or whether the person committing the assault is male or female. It is as clearly an offence for a woman to commit an indecent assault upon a man as it is for the opposite to occur.

(2) The points to prove

It is necessary to prove two essential points: first, that there has been an assault (the use or threat of use of physical force upon another); and, second, the assault was accompanied by circumstances of indecency. In this way, kissing a girl against her will, accompanied by a suggestion either by words or actions that sexual activity should take place, is an indecent assault as the suggestion itself amounts to circumstances of indecency, and the forcible kissing is an assault. Similarly, a man was convicted of an indecent assault when he moved towards a woman with his person exposed, inviting her to have intercourse with him. Here there was a threat to use force, accompanied by indecent circumstances. However, in most cases of indecent assault, the circumstances will be quite straightforward, involving some form of indecent physical contact. The prosecution should seek to prove that the defendant intended to lay hands on his victim without her consent in circumstances of indecency. As it is necessary for a woman to have been touched, or put in fear of being immediately touched, an invitation to her to touch the accused person indecently can never be an indecent assault.

Thus, where a man is sitting still in a chair with his penis exposed and he invites a woman to touch it there is no indecent assault at that stage as he has done nothing to put the woman in fear of immediate bodily contact. There was, therefore, no assault. In the same way where a man exposed his penis to a nine-year-old girl and invited her to touch it there was no indecent assault as he had made no move towards her. It would be different if the man then took hold of the girl's hand and placed it upon his penis, as he would then have carried out an assault which, combined with the indecency, would become an indecent assault.

On most occasions the assault is indecent in itself and the basic intent sufficient to establish assault is enough. If a man walks up to a woman and places his hand on her breast, both the assault and the circumstances of indecency are direct and apparent. However, if this occurred on a crowded underground train the circumstances would be such that they would be capable of an innocent, as well as an indecent, interpretation. Similarly, a man may spank a girl which amounts to an assault if the spanking was not permitted by law in the particular circumstances, but if he did so because it gave him sexual satisfaction, it could be an indecent assault and evidence of his admission that sexual satisfaction was derived would be admissible. The test of indecency is that there has been a contravention of the standards of decent behaviour in the minds of right-thinking members of society.

Where an act is committed which amounts to an indecent assault, a defence based upon a submission that the person carrying out the act was too drunk to form the necessary intent, cannot succeed.

(3) Consent

If consent is given to the acts which take place then the actions cannot be an assault as an essential element of any assault is lack of consent, with the exception that the Sexual Offences Act 1956 states that if the person assaulted is under 16 years of age, consent is no defence. It is apparent that the legislators intended to offer full protection to persons under the age of 16 years, while still of such an age that they may give consent without fully appreciating the significance of doing so. There must, however, be an assault and the girl must, therefore, have been touched or put in fear. It is, however, no defence for a man to claim that he believed a girl to be 16 or over, no matter how reasonable that belief may be. A reasonable belief that a girl under 16 is his wife, having gone through a form of marriage, is a defence.

The consent given by a woman of any age must be a true consent, and if the

459

consent is obtained in circumstances involving force or fraud, the act will still amount to an indecent assault. Where an indecent assault occurred under the pretext of a medical operation (which it was not), the man concerned was convicted of an indecent assault. A man may be guilty of an indecent assault upon his wife by causing her to indulge in acts which she finds to be indecent, repellent or abhorrent.

Evidence

If the person assaulted is a child under 14, his evidence in criminal proceedings shall be given unsworn, and a deposition of such a child's unsworn evidence may be taken for the purpose of criminal proceedings as if that evidence had been given on oath. This is provided by the Criminal Justice Act 1988, s. 33A. The question of the competence of the child to give evidence is one to be considered by the court. The Criminal Justice and Public Order Act 1944 abolished the common law duty to give a direction to a jury to the effect that corroboration is required in relation to such sexual offences. Nor need magistrates direct themselves in a similar way. However, perhaps more particularly than in other cases, corroborative evidence will be of value otherwise the issue devolves to one person making a complaint, which is denied.

Anonymity of complainant

The Sexual Offences (Amendment) Act 1992, s. 1, makes provision for the anonymity of complainants in cases of indecent assault. Where an allegation has been made that such an offence has been committed, neither the name nor address, and no still or moving picture of the complainant shall be published in England and Wales during that person's lifetime, whether in writing or in a broadcast. Where a person has been accused of such an offence against a complainant, no matter may be so published during the complainant's lifetime, which is likely to lead members of the public to identify such a complainant.

A judge has the power to set aside these provisions on an application being made by an accused, if it is necessary to induce persons to come forward as witnesses and that the accused's defence is likely to be substantially prejudiced if such a direction is not given.

Police powers

Indecent assault is an arrestable offence.

Public order

Introduction

Throughout the years police involvement in the prevention of public disorder has developed from dealing with situations which involved little more than a Saturday night fight involving a number of people, to dealing with large-scale, organised protests which quickly degenerate into various forms of public disorder on a massive scale. Not too many years ago, the public would have been astonished if anyone had suggested that our police officers would appear on British streets in riot gear and would be compelled to become proficient in 'extinguishing' colleagues who had been set on fire by petrol bombs. However, no matter what may have caused large numbers of persons to assemble in the first instance, once there is danger, it is the duty of police officers to ensure that the Queen's Peace is maintained.

A crowd of people is a difficult thing to deal with. Where large numbers of people gather together for any particular single purpose, there is a possibility of disorder. Even where the gathering is of people who are intent upon making some peaceful form of protest, such a gathering may attract others who are opposed to their beliefs.

Shakespeare's *Julius Caesar* provides a fine example of the emotions which can be built up quickly in a crowd as the 'fever' spreads. Adolf Hitler had the ability to bring about a quick change in temperature within a crowd. Some pop groups have effected a style of performance which, quite apart from their music, tends to build up emotion. Once a 'common purpose' has been established within a group it quickly grows as individual members of the group become encouraged by the attitude of those surrounding them to believe that they have a 'cause'. Inhibitions which might normally have prevented individuals within the group from committing acts which are outside the law tend to disappear and people become prepared to act in a manner which is quite foreign to their normal pattern of behaviour.

Once a crowd has become unruly it is difficult to deal with the persons who constitute it; in the absence of someone who can influence the crowd to alter its behaviour, there is no way of making effective contact with such a large number of individuals. When it is seen that a situation is becoming potentially explosive, it may be possible to remove, or to influence those who are providing the 'crowd motivation'. Increasingly, in places such as football grounds, visible cameras are used to reinforce the message that individuals who cause disturbances within a crowd may not be able to preserve the anonymity which a crowd provides.

Public meetings

The Public Meeting Act 1908, s. 1, makes it an offence for any person, at a lawful public meeting, to act in a disorderly manner for the purpose of preventing the transaction of the business for which the meeting was called. This offence is punishable summarily. A similar offence is committed by any person who incites another to commit this offence. A public meeting is one held to discuss matters of public interest, or for the exchange of views on such matters. It includes any meeting in a public place and any meeting which the public or any section of the public are permitted to attend whether on payment or otherwise. The term 'public place' has its usual meaning.

Police powers

If a constable reasonably suspects any person of committing an offence under this Act he may, if requested to do so by the chairman of the meeting, require that person to give his name and address. If he refuses or fails to do so, or gives a false name and address, he commits an offence.

461

This Act has as its purpose the correct control of public meetings, the majority of which are likely to be of a political nature. It is not intended that such meetings should pass without comment or interruption by hecklers, and it is necessary for police officers to make their own judgment as to forms of conduct which are no more than protest and those which are purposely intended to prevent the transaction of business. If the person who is guilty of this conduct provides the constable with his name and address when requested to do so, the constable should provide the chairman of the meeting with those particulars. The issue at this stage clearly lies between the organisers and the person breaking up their meeting, and it is only when this information is refused that the constable becomes involved. It is unusual for police officers to be on duty at such meetings and their involvement is usually confined to instances in which they are summoned by the organisers, or events are such that their attention is directed to the meeting.

A constable's power to enter meetings which are held on private premises is restricted to circumstances in which they reasonably apprehend a breach of the peace. A meeting which is held on the highway is not necessarily unlawful, and consideration must be given to whether or not there is likely to be a nuisance or a breach of the peace. The High Court has ruled that it is the duty of the police to prevent any action likely to result in a breach of the peace by any person, and that the refusal of persons to desist from acts which may lead to such consequences amounts to obstructing the police in the execution of their duty.

Industrial disputes

The subject of trade disputes is so important that it merits examination in some depth. The law, from the time of the Industrial Revolution, has been increasingly concerned with finding the correct balance between the freedom of the unions to further their interests by industrial action and the freedom of individuals to exercise a personal choice. The Trade Union and Labour Relations (Consolidation) Act 1992 makes it an offence for any person to wilfully and maliciously break a contract of service knowing or having reasonable cause to believe that the probable consequence of doing so, either alone or in combination with others, will be

(a) to endanger life or cause serious bodily injury; or
(b) to expose valuable property, whether real or personal, to destruction or serious injury.

In other circumstances, the Act declares that an agreement by two or more persons to do, or to procure to be done, any act in contemplation of furtherance of a trade dispute within the meaning of that Act, shall not amount to a conspiracy if the act itself is a summary offence which is not punishable with imprisonment. Nothing in this section shall affect the law relating to riot, unlawful assembly, breach of the peace, sedition, or any offence against the state or the sovereign. As will be seen, there can be a fine distinction between the peaceful picket and an unlawful assembly when the number of the pickets becomes such that their purpose is effected by intimidation.

Section 241 of the 1992 Act deals with forms of intimidation designed to prevent workmen from exercising their right to work if they wish to do so, and provides a penalty of six months' imprisonment or a fine or both for any person who, wrongfully and without legal authority:

(a) uses violence to or intimidates such person or his wife or children, or injures his property;
(b) persistently follows him about;
(c) hides his tools, clothes, or other property to prevent or hinder his working;
(d) watches or besets his house or place of work, or the approach to it; or
(e) follows him with two or more persons through the street in a disorderly manner,

if such acts are done to compel that person to abstain from doing or to do any act which that person has a legal right to do or abstain from doing.

While the offence of 'watching and besetting' is normally associated with trade disputes it is not limited to such disputes. It is concerned with actions aimed at preventing people from doing what they wish to do. Anti-abortionists were found not to be watching and besetting an abortion clinic for the purposes of the section, as verbal abuse and reminders of the physical implications of abortion, did not amount to physical force or the threat of physical force.

It has been held that it is intimidation for an assembly to hurl abuse and missiles at a workman while on his way to work. In one case, all 13 men involved were convicted although only two could be proved to have thrown objects.

Police powers

A constable may arrest without warrant anyone he reasonably suspects is committing an offence under this section.

Peaceful picketing

Section 220(1) of the Trade Union and Labour Relations (Consolidation) Act 1992 provides that it shall be lawful for a person in contemplation of or furtherance of a trade dispute to attend:

(a) at or near his own place of work; or
(b) if he is an official of a trade union, at or near the place of work of a member of that union whom he is accompanying and whom he represents,

for the purpose only of peacefully obtaining or communicating information, or peacefully persuading any person to work or abstain from working.

A common-sense approach should be adopted in determining whether picketing is at or near the pickets' place of work. It has been held that pickets who stood at the entrance to a trading estate, 1200 yards distant from their employer's premises on that estate and who would have been trespassing if they had picketed on the estate, were attending near their place of work.

The only persons, other than those described above, who may lawfully be on a picket line are those employed by the company who do not work at any one particular depot, or it is otherwise impracticable for them to picket their place of work. Such persons may be included in pickets at any premises of the employer. This is interesting when considering the position of 'flying pickets'. Their presence is not authorised by the Act and they are not therefore protected from the 'watching and besetting' provisions of the Act.

Section 220(3) of the 1992 Act allows a person who is not in work, but whose last employment was terminated in connection with the trade dispute, or the termination of his employment was one of the circumstances giving rise to a trade dispute, to picket at his former place of work.

However, in the circumstances in which pickets are quite lawfully assembled at a particular place, the law must be observed in other respects and breaches of the peace must be prevented. It has been held that when persons who were acting as pickets in connection with an industrial dispute were requested to move by a police officer who was limiting the number of the pickets to a figure which was considered reasonable because of an apprehended breach of the peace, and refused to do so, they were rightly convicted of obstructing a police officer in the execution of his duty. In another instance, where an excessive number of pickets carried on a circling manoeuvre, obstructing the highway in such a way that vehicles were forced to stop, there was a similar conviction for obstruction of a police officer, although there was no threatened breach of the peace.

The effect of what is now s. 220 of the 1992 Act was discussed in both the House of Lords and the Court of Queen's Bench Division. In the House of Lords it was ruled that it is wrong to describe what is conferred by s. 220 as a 'right'. What was conferred was an immunity from prosecution in certain circumstances. It was held that s. 220 gave no right to a picket to stop a vehicle against the driver's will, although it had been widely believed in trade union circles that it did, if it was done for the purpose of persuading the driver to refrain from doing some act contrary to the interest of the pickets and their representative organisation. This ruling clarifies the position in relation to pickets who forcibly prevent vehicles from gaining access to premises during industrial disputes. The Court of Queen's Bench Division considered the actions of a man who assaulted and obstructed a police officer in the execution of his duty during an industrial dispute involving electricians at St Thomas' Hospital, London. Thirty to forty people had assembled at the entrance to the site, but only four were official pickets and wore armbands to identify themselves. Police officers under the command of a superintendent arrived at the scene and formed a cordon clearing the exit so that a bus containing electrical workers could leave. Although at first the four pickets were left inside the gate, they were finally cleared from the gateway and placed behind the cordon as the superintendent feared that, if the bus was stopped, a breach of the peace might occur. The man charged was an official of another trade union who had been asked to attend to speak to the bus driver, who was probably a member of his union. When the coach attempted to come out, he began to argue with police officers and eventually struck out at one of them. It was observed that it had already been established that pickets had no right to stop vehicles and that, therefore, the police superintendent and all of the officers were acting in the execution of their duty when the entrance was cleared in order to prevent an apprehended breach of the peace, and that the defendant was, therefore, guilty of both offences.

Other offences – Public Order Act 1936

The 1936 Act was passed at the time of vigorous activity by the British Fascist Party and its object was to resist political organisations which wished to fashion themselves on military lines. It prohibited the wearing, at public meetings or in public places, of uniforms signifying an association with a political organisation. The organisation, training, or equipping of members for the purpose of enabling them to usurp the functions of the police or the armed service, or to enable them to display or use force in promoting a political object, or to act in such a way that reasonable suspicion is aroused that such is their purpose, was also prohibited. The consent of the Attorney-General is required before proceedings may be taken for these offences.

Fear or provocation of violence

Section 4 of the Public Order Act 1986 states that a person is guilty of an offence if he:

(a) uses towards another person threatening, abusive or insulting words or behaviour; or
(b) distributes or displays to another person any writing, sign or other visible representation which is threatening, abusive or insulting,

with intent to cause that person to believe that immediate unlawful violence will be used against him or another by any person, or to provoke the immediate use of unlawful violence by that person or another, or whereby that person is likely to believe that such violence will be used or it is likely that such violence will be provoked.

An important point within this section is that the violence which is intended must be 'immediate'. However, this does not mean instantaneous. Violence will be 'immediate' if it is likely to result within a short period of time and without any other occurrence intervening.

The section covers a multitude of possibilities, particularly as the offence may be committed in public or in private, with the exception of a dwelling, where all persons concerned are in that dwelling. 'Dwelling' includes any form of dwelling, even including a tent. However, in this respect, communal landings outside individual flats do not form part of a person's home.

Things which are threatening indicate some immediate menace; those which are abusive are rudely addressed and those which are insulting, in this context, are likely to be scornful, offensive, contemptuous or an affront. Thus we are concerned with words, behaviour, writing, signs or other visible representations which may be said to be one of those things. The words, etc., may be used:

(a) with intent to cause the person towards whom these acts have been done to believe that immediate violence will be used against himself or another;
(b) to provoke such immediate use of unlawful violence;
(c) in such a way that the person addressed will believe it will happen; or
(d) in such a way that it is likely that it will happen.

If a man says, 'I am going to beat you up' and he intends that the person addressed **465** will believe that unlawful violence is about to be used, he commits the offence provided the threat is immediate. It would be different if he said that he would do so when a suitable opportunity presented itself as the threatened violence would not be immediate. If he is one of a group and says, 'We are going to beat you up now', and the person threatened is also one of a group, the offence is committed even though the person addressed does not know who is to do the beating, or indeed, who is to be beaten. The section also covers circumstances in which the person using the words does not intend to strike the first blow. He may say, 'Margaret Dixon says that you are only half a man', intending to provoke the young man so addressed to use unlawful violence. This offence is committed by the person using these words if he used them to provoke violence. The words need not be spoken; if they are written on a banner, or on a leaflet which is handed out, they are covered by the section. In relation to the offence of displaying, etc., writing, signs, or visible representations, the section specifically requires that the acts are done to another person. The acts must therefore be directed at a particular person and this offence will not be committed by a person who leaves leaflets in a shopping precinct or who pastes posters on a wall when there is no one about. A threat made against a person who is out of earshot and only learns of it through a third party who is not under the control or direction of the maker of the threat, is insufficient to constitute an offence against this section.

It has been held that a constable, having a common law duty to uphold the peace, is unlikely to respond to threatening, abusive or insulting language by the use of violence. However, an offence will be committed where such conduct is intended to cause a constable to fear that violence will be used against him.

Section 6(3) of the Acts provides that a person shall only be guilty of an offence under s. 4 if he intends his words or behaviour, or the writing, sign or other visible representation to be threatening, abusive or insulting or is aware that it may be threatening, abusive or insulting. This means that there are two propositions to consider: firstly, the intention behind the words, etc., themselves; and, secondly, the result which those words are intended to bring about.

Where a person ran on to a tennis court at Wimbledon and distributed leaflets, he was not guilty of this offence as his behaviour was not threatening, abusive or insulting, even if it was accepted that he caused anger, disgust or distress in spectators. In such circumstances, procedure by way of complaint with a view to obtaining 'surety of good behaviour', would, however, be appropriate. In the same way, if a person in addressing an audience uses words which in ordinary circumstances would be inoffensive but which are heard by persons to whom (unknown to the speaker) they are highly insulting, the speaker is not guilty of an offence against s. 4. It would be different where such a speaker ignored the mood of an audience once it was apparent. He must take an audience as he finds it. If he uses words which he knows will insult those persons and that they are likely to provoke violence on their part, it is irrelevant that a reasonable person would not so react.

Intoxication is no defence to such charges unless it as not self-induced or is a by-product of medical treatment.

This section is most likely to be used in circumstances which are quite direct where threatening behaviour is used and this may be by gestures or blows. Those engaged in fighting so engage with the clear intention of causing at least a belief in the immediate use of violence. It might be said that actions speak louder than words!

Charges under this section may be appropriate in many situations which arise in 'demonstrations'. If members of an unpopular organisation march through the streets people may gather to protest. If these protesters then threaten or offer immediate violence they commit offences, as they would do if they used insulting words with the clear intention of provoking the use of violence by members of the march. The section does not aim to prevent protest, it aims to prevent violent protest. It punishes threats and acts of violence wherever, and for whatever reason, they occur.

'Violence' for the purpose of this section means any violent conduct against a person or property and includes any violent conduct, e.g. throwing missiles capable of causing injury which miss or fall short of their target. The inclusion of 'unlawful' before 'violence' means that the common law defences to charges of assault (and the replaced common law offence of affray), of self-defence, reasonable defence of another person, and actions which do no more than restore the peace, will be valid.

Police powers

A constable may arrest without warrant anyone he reasonably suspects is committing an offence under this section.

Harassment, alarm or distress

Sections 4A and 5 of the Public Order Act 1986 deal with the offences of harassment. While s. 4 of the 1986 Act is primarily concerned with immediate threats to the peace, s. 5 is directed towards distressing forms of antisocial behaviour. The elderly and members of minority groups are particularly vulnerable. In order to provide protection against those who threaten, abuse, insult or who use written displays to cause harassment, alarm or distress, s. 5 is drafted in such a way that it erects a fine dividing line between criminal conduct and that which might be dealt with by other means.

A person is guilty of an offence if he:

(a) uses threatening, abusive or insulting words or behaviour, or disorderly behaviour; or
(b) displays any writing, sign or other visible representation which is threatening, abusive or insulting,

within the hearing or sight of a person likely to be caused harassment, alarm or distress thereby.

There are small differences at (a) and (b) when compared with s. 4. To (a) there has been added 'disorderly behaviour' and the words 'towards another person' have been omitted. The words used may, therefore, be generally addressed to an audience without being aimed at anyone, or any group, in particular. The addition of the words 'disorderly behaviour' may perhaps embrace some situations which would not be covered by behaviour which could be described as threatening, abusive or insulting. Persons who leave night clubs in the early hours of the morning in a disorderly manner might easily cause harassment or distress to persons in the

467

neighbourhood. At (b) the word 'distribution' is omitted in relation to writing, etc.

While s. 4 demands some element of unlawful violence or a belief that it will occur, this section is merely concerned with the act being 'within the hearing or sight of a person likely to be caused harassment, alarm or distress'. 'Harassment' may be defined as trouble, torment or confusion caused by persistent attacks; 'alarm' may be anxiety, fear, terror aroused by awareness of danger; and 'distress' may be to cause mental pain or to upset badly. It is sometimes less than difficult to use words which 'upset' some people and this section may cause problems for those charged with the enforcement of the law. Complaints may well be made by groups which are sensitive to critical comment.

It has been held that a police constable is a person capable of being subject to 'harassment, alarm or distress' for the purposes of the section. Where a man walked into the middle of the road and police officers and drivers were *seriously* alarmed concerning his safety, this offence was held to have been committed. It is submitted that the use of abusive and insulting words directed at police officers by lager louts and which have the effect of causing distress to police officers constitutes an offence under this section. However, it will be necessary to show clearly that the effect of such words was to cause harassment, alarm or distress. Anger is a different emotion, although it may be that it follows from the type of distress which the section describes.

This offence may be committed in public or in private with the exception of in a dwelling, where all persons concerned are in that dwelling. It is a defence for the accused to prove that he had no reason to believe that there was any person within hearing or sight who was likely to be caused harassment, alarm or distress, or that he was inside a dwelling and had no reason to believe that his words, etc., would be seen or heard by a person outside, or that his conduct was reasonable. Section 6(4) of the Act requires that the words, etc., must be intended to be threatening, etc., or the person using the words, etc., must be aware that they may be threatening, etc., or that the person intended his conduct to be disorderly or is aware that it may be disorderly.

Thus, statements made in a dwelling remain free from legal sanctions, as do those made in a private conversation which is accidentally overheard. A man at a bar who makes an insulting remark concerning 'punks' to a friend without knowing that one is in earshot does not commit this offence. Similarly, a man who makes such an offensive comment in his dwelling as a 'punk' passes his window does not commit an offence if he had no reason to believe that he would be heard by that person.

To commit the offence a person must intend or be aware that his words, etc., will be threatening, abusive or insulting and they must be used, etc., within the hearing or sight of a person likely to be caused harassment, alarm or distress. It is therefore restricted to 'face to face' situations. A newspaper editor may comment in his newspaper concerning homosexual acts and their relationship to the disease AIDS. If he does so in an address to a live audience he must avoid any words which might be considered to be 'insulting' and which might cause 'distress' to any member of his audience.

A person who gives no thought to the nature of his conduct or who honestly believes that there is no risk of it being threatening, etc., does not commit this offence. However, although the accused's conduct must be in the hearing or in the sight of a person likely to be caused harassment, alarm or distress thereby, the accused is not required to intend such a consequence or to be aware that it might occur.

When complaints are received in relation to alleged offences the following points should be considered before taking action:

(a) the intention of the person using the words, etc.;
(b) their likely effect;
(c) where they were delivered;
(d) was the use of the words, etc., reasonable in the circumstances?

Police powers

A constable may arrest a person without warrant if:

(a) he engages in offensive conduct which the constable warns him to stop; and
(b) he engages in further offensive conduct immediately or shortly after the warning.

For the purposes of this power 'offensive conduct' means conduct the constable reasonably suspects to constitute an offence under this section. The conduct mentioned in paragraph (a) above, need not be the same as the 'further conduct' at (b).

For a constable to be 'acting in the execution of his duty' under this section, the offender must be clearly told of the offensive conduct and that the constable required him to stop such conduct. However, where a man made racial remarks and behaved in a threatening manner, a police officer remonstrated with him and asked him to apologise. The man replied 'Or else you will nick me'. On being told that this was so he told her to 'get stuffed'; threatened her and the person to whom the racial remarks had been made, before being arrested by the police officer. It was held that, taken as a whole, the conversation was sufficient to convey to him that he should not engage in further offensive conduct and that it served as a warning for the purposes of the section. Nevertheless, the issue is best avoided by giving a direct warning to cease such conduct.

Harassment, etc., with intent

The Criminal Justice and Public Order Act 1994, s. 154, added a s. 4A to the Public Order Act 1986. It is an offence where a person *with intent* to cause a person harassment, alarm or distress:

(a) uses threatening, abusive or insulting words or behaviour, or disorderly behaviour; or
(b) displays any writing, sign or other visible representation which is threatening, abusive or insulting,

thereby *causing* that or another person harassment, alarm or distress.

This offence differs from that above in that the act is committed *with the intention* of causing harassment, alarm or distress, whereas that against s. 5 is concerned with

469

committing such an act within the hearing or sight of a person which is *likely to have* those effects. In addition, in the case of s. 4A, the prosecution must prove that one of the effects *was caused*. The penalty is the same, but in the case of s. 4A, the power to arrest without warrant exists on these facts. There is no need to give a warning.

The provisions set out above in relation to s. 5 which are concerned with dwelling-houses also apply to s. 4A. The defences (apart from that associated with having no reason to believe that there was a person within hearing or sight, which clearly could not apply to an offence of intent) also apply.

Acts intended to stir up racial hatred

For the purposes of the Public Order Act 1986 'racial hatred' means hatred against a group of persons in Great Britain defined by reference to colour, race or nationality (including citizenship) or ethnic or national origin.

Section 18 of that Act states that a person who uses threatening, abusive or insulting words or behaviour, or displays any written material which is threatening, abusive or insulting, is guilty of an offence if:

(a) he intends thereby to stir up racial hatred; or
(b) having regard to all the circumstances racial hatred is likely to be stirred up thereby.

The offence may be committed in public or in private with the exception of in a dwelling, where all the persons concerned are in that dwelling. The same defences apply as in cases of serious public disorder (see page 471). In addition, a person who is not shown to have intended to stir up racial hatred is not guilty of this offence if he did not intend his words, etc., to be, or was not aware that they might be threatening, etc. The section does not apply to words, behaviour, etc., used solely in a cable broadcast service.

Previous legislation required such acts to be in a public place or at a public meeting, or to be demonstrated to a section of the public. The offence may now be committed in a private meeting, attendance at which is restricted to members of a society. Thus, remarks made by a member of the Ku-Klux-Klan, to his fellow members at a closed meeting could be punishable under this section if those remarks were made with the necessary intent or in the required circumstances.

Section 18 does not apply to words or behaviour used, or written material displayed, *solely* for the purpose of being included in a television, sound broadcasting or cable service. In such a case, however, an offence may be committed under s. 22 when the programme is transmitted.

Police powers

A constable may arrest without warrant anyone he reasonably suspects is committing an offence under this section.

Publishing or distributing racially offensive material

Section 19 provides that a person who publishes or distributes written material which is threatening, abusive or insulting is guilty of an offence if:

(a) he intends thereby to stir up racial hatred; or

(b) having regard to all the circumstances, racial hatred is likely to be stirred up thereby.

However, the section requires that there must be a publication or distribution to the public or to a section of the public. For this to have occurred, the person must have made his written material available to sufficient people for it to be shown that it was made known to the public at large, or at least a section of it. Thus, if a man gives out racist leaflets at a National Front meeting to which admission is restricted to members of that organisation, he does not commit an offence against this section. The distribution is to members of a 'club' and not to the public. It would be different if persons other than members of the National Front had been admitted to the meeting and leaflets had been distributed to everyone. If a man hands a cartoon drawing to a friend, the contents of which are racially inflammatory, he does not commit this offence as his distribution is to only one person, and is therefore not 'public'. It would be different if he handed out such drawings to a number of people in a public bar.

The offence contrary to s. 19 is an arrestable offence, having been added to the Police and Criminal Evidence Act 1984, s. 24(2), by the Criminal Justice and Public Order Act 1994.

Offences also exist under this Act in relation to the publication or distribution of written material; the public performance of plays; the distribution or playing of a recording of visual images or sounds; or the broadcasting or inclusion in a cable programme service (other than those of BBC or ITC); in each case if there is an inclusion intended to stir up racial hatred, or having regard to all the circumstances racial hatred is likely to be stirred up. Defences exist where there is a lack of intent, or the act was unknown to the person charged and he had no reason to suspect it.

It is an offence contrary to s. 23 of this Act to possess written material or a recording which is threatening, abusive or insulting with a view to display, publication, distribution or inclusion in a cable service (other than BBC or ITC); or its playing, etc., if there is an intention to stir up racial hatred or having regard to all the circumstances, racial hatred is likely to be stirred up thereby.

Police powers

A warrant may be issued by a justice of the peace if he is satisfied by information on oath laid by a constable, that there are reasonable grounds for suspecting possession of such material on premises. Reasonable force may be used if necessary.

Offences of serious public disorder

The Public Order Act 1986 abolished the common law offences of riot, rout, unlawful assembly and affray. It introduced statutory offences of riot, violent disorder and affray.

471

(1) *Riot*

The Public Order Act 1986, s. 1, states that a riot takes place where 12 or more persons who are present together use or threaten unlawful violence for a common purpose and the conduct of them (taken together) is such as would cause a person of reasonable firmness present at the scene to fear for his personal safety. Each of the persons using unlawful violence for the common purpose is guilty of riot.

There are therefore a number of essential elements:

(a)   12 or more present together;
(b)   the use or threat of unlawful violence;
(c)   for a common purpose;
(d)   *collective* conduct which would cause a person of reasonable firmness present at the scene;
(e)   to fear for his personal safety.

If there are 12 or more present it is immaterial whether or not they threaten unlawful violence simultaneously. If there is a 'mob' therefore, and there is a constant threat or use of unlawful violence, this will suffice in relation to (a) and (b). 'Violence' means any violent conduct whether towards persons or property and includes the throwing of missiles capable of causing injury which miss their target or fall short. The mob must have a common purpose. If some are present to injure or inflict damage and others are merely awaiting an opportunity to steal from shops which have been damaged by others, at least 12 must be shown to have been present together and to be using or threatening use of unlawful violence. The common purpose may, of course, be inferred from the conduct of such persons. In addition, it must be the collective conduct of the 12 or more which causes, or would cause, a person of reasonable firmness to fear for his personal safety. The violence or threat must therefore be such that this stout-hearted bystander would fear for himself. However, the section states that no person of reasonable firmness need actually be, or be likely to be, present at the scene. A court will have to be satisfied that such a person, had he been present, would have feared for his personal safety.

If 12 or more supporters of a football team advance upon supporters of the opposing team, threatening to use unlawful violence against them, they have a common purpose and their collective conduct would undoubtedly cause supporters of the other team, who were of reasonable firmness, to fear for their personal safety. The 12 or more would therefore be guilty of riot. However, should such a group advance upon the empty coach which was to convey the supporters to their home town, threatening to overturn it, although they are offering violence to property, they would not be guilty of this offence unless they additionally posed a threat to the personal safety of some person, whether present or not.

Section 6(1) of the Act adds that a person is guilty of riot only if he intends to use violence or is aware that his conduct may be violent. Therefore a 'protester' who, in the course of expressing his protest is waving his arms about and pointing his finger at counter-protesters, or the police, cannot be guilty if he does not intend to use unlawful violence, or is unaware that his conduct may be violent in the eyes of some persons. Intoxication is no defence unless it is not self-induced, or it occurs in the course of medical treatment by taking some substance.

In addition, since the violence must be unlawful, riot will not be committed if the persons are acting in self-defence or in any other circumstances in which the violence which they were using, was legally justified.

Riot is an arrestable offence, triable only on indictment and is punishable by ten years' imprisonment. The consent of the DPP is required before a prosecution may be instituted. Unless there has been a true 'riot' situation, it is probable that the DPP will advise proceedings under one of the alternative sections even when all of the requirements of a riot have been fulfilled.

If 'riot' is being considered, it must be remembered that in addition to the use or threat of violence for a purpose common to at least 12 alleged offenders, that collective conduct, if taken together, must be such as would cause a person of reasonable firmness to fear for his *personal* safety.

(2) *Violent disorder*

This offence is committed against s. 2 of the 1986 Act where three or more persons who are present together use or threaten unlawful violence and the conduct of them (taken together) is such as would cause a person of reasonable firmness present at the scene to fear for his personal safety. Each person using or threatening unlawful violence is guilty of this offence. It is immaterial whether or not the three or more use or threaten unlawful violence simultaneously.

The ingredients of the offence differ from riot in that only three or more persons need to be present together and there is no requirement to prove a common purpose, although it is still necessary to prove collective conduct which would cause a person of reasonable firmness present at the scene to fear for his personal safety. Where evidence of the involvement of three or more persons is affected by the dismissal of the charges against all but one or two, the one or two may nevertheless be convicted of violent disorder if it is proved that others not charged with the offence were also involved. If it is not so proved, the one or two may be convicted of affray. However, if there is only evidence of violence towards property, a conviction for an offence of affray will not be possible.

The same considerations apply as in the case of riot in relation to intoxication; use or threat not necessarily being simultaneous; the places where the offence may be committed and the fact that the 'firm' person need not necessarily be present.

This is a useful section to police officers and its use need not be restricted to incidents which are on a large scale. Three or more who gather outside a dance hall using or threatening violence against persons may be guilty of this offence if it can be shown that they acted collectively and that their conduct was such that a 'firm' person would fear for his personal safety. Whereas a person charged with riot must be shown to intend to *use or threaten* violence or be aware that his conduct may be violent or threatening.

This is an arrestable offence being punishable by five years' imprisonment if convicted on indictment or by six months' imprisonment if convicted summarily.

473

(3) *Affray*

Section 3 of the 1986 Act states that a person is guilty of affray if he uses or threatens unlawful violence towards another and his conduct is such as would cause a person of reasonable firmness present at the scene to fear for his personal safety. By s. 6(2), a person is guilty of the offence only if he intends to use or threaten violence or is *aware* that his conduct may be violent or threaten violence.

While the common law offence of affray was seldom charged because it was triable only at Crown Court, the statutory offence is likely to be commonly used. We are concerned to a large extent with violent street fights. One person using or threatening unlawful violence towards another person in circumstances in which a person of reasonable firmness (which will almost invariably be the person assaulted), fears for his personal safety, commits this offence. Once again the offence may be committed in public or in private and the 'firm' person need not be present, although this is unlikely to be the case in most affrays. Usually there will be a direct threat to strike a blow, or a blow will be struck upon a person present. However, the section would extend to circumstances where a person was beating upon a closed door in an attempt to burst it open, while threatening a person who was inside, but only if that person, or someone else, whether present or not at the scene, would fear for his personal safety. It must always be recognised that in most circumstances courts will be unlikely to accept that persons who were not being threatened, or were not otherwise caught up in the violent situation, were actually in fear for their personal safety. In the situation outlined, it would be insufficient that a bystander feared for the safety of the man behind the door; he must fear for his own safety.

It is helpful when considering a charge of affray to remember that the offence is essentially concerned with three persons: a person using or threatening unlawful violence; a person towards whom the threat or violence is directed; *and* a person of reasonable firmness who need not be present at the scene. Thus, where a man attacks a police officer with a knife, it is not a question of whether another person of reasonable firmness, if he had been in the police officer's shoes at the time, would have feared for his personal safety, but whether such a person *if present in the room* at the time with the other two parties, would have so feared.

Affray is a serious public order offence and there are other ways of dealing with two people who fight.

The section demands a threat by *more than words.* Words must be accompanied by some action *which is sufficient to cause the 'firm' person to fear for his personal safety.* Therefore, a small threatening step and a lot of words will be insufficient, while a threat to break the nose which is accompanied by a swift rush forward, could amount to a 'threat' for the purposes of this section.

Where a man used words to urge an already excited dog to attack police officers there was an affray as more than words were involved. The combination of those words with the excited condition of the dog would be enough to cause the officers to fear for their personal safety. It would be different if a man merely said 'Seize him' to a docile dog which was unlikely to take notice. At that stage, there was no reason for any other person to fear for their safety. However, where persons who were sitting in their cars were asked for a lift by a man who used aggressive tones, there was no affray as there was nothing other than words at that stage.

A person whose awareness is impaired by intoxication must be taken to have been aware of that of which he would have been aware if he had not been intoxicated, unless that intoxication was not self-induced or followed medical treatment.

The offence is punishable by three years' imprisonment if convicted on indictment and by six months' imprisonment if convicted summarily.

A constable may arrest without warrant anyone he reasonably suspects is committing this offence.

Processions – Public Order Act 1986

The Public Order Act 1986, s. 11, requires that written notice must be given to a police station in the police area within which it is proposed to hold a public procession to demonstrate support for or opposition to the views or actions of any person or body of persons; to publicise a cause or campaign; or to mark or commemorate an event. The notice, naming the organisers and specifying the times, route, etc., must be delivered six days in advance unless it is not practicable to give any advance notice of the procession, i.e. when it is spontaneous. The chief officer of police (or the senior officer present at a spontaneous procession) may impose conditions relating to time, route or circumstances if he reasonably believes that such procession may result in serious public disorder, serious damage to property, or serious disruption to the life of the community; or the purpose of the person organising it is the intimidation of others with a view to compelling them not to do an act they have a right to do, or to do an act they have a right not to do.

Summary offences are committed by organisers who do not give notice, or if the details given in the notice differ from the reality, and by organisers and participants who knowingly fail to comply with conditions. Those who incite others to fail to comply with a condition also commit offences.

Chief officers may apply to the council of a district for an order prohibiting, for a period not exceeding three months, the holding of all public processions (or processions of a class), within that district. The Commissioners of the Metropolitan and City of London Police Forces may make such orders. All orders are subject to the consent of the Secretary of State.

The provisions of the section do not apply to processions commonly or customarily held (for example, a procession held as part of an annual gala), or to funeral processions.

Police powers

A constable in uniform may arrest without warrant anyone he reasonably suspects is committing an offence or organising a public procession and knowingly failing to comply with a condition, or holding a prohibited procession; or a participant who knowingly takes part in a prohibited procession, or who knowingly fails to comply with a condition or a person who incites a participant to commit such an offence.

Assemblies – Public Order Act 1986

The Public Order Act 1986, s. 14, permits a chief officer to impose conditions in relation to the place at which any public assembly may be, or continue to be held; its maximum duration or the maximum number of persons who may constitute it, as appear to him necessary to prevent serious public disorder, serious damage to property or serious disruption to the life of the community; or the purpose of the persons organising it is the intimidation of others with a view to compelling them not to do an act they have a right to do, or to do an act they have a right not to do.

Police powers

A constable in uniform may arrest without warrant anyone he reasonably suspects is committing an offence of organising such an assembly and knowingly failing to comply with a condition, or of participating in such an assembly and so failing to comply, or of inciting another to commit such an offence.

Trespassory assemblies

Section 14A of the 1986 Act was added by the Criminal Justice and Public Order Act 1994. It permits a chief officer of police where he reasonably believes that an assembly of 20 or more persons is intended to be held in a district at a place on land in the open air to which the public has no right of access or only a limited right of access and that assembly is likely to be held without permission of the occupier of the land, or to conduct itself in such a way as to exceed the limits of any permission given, or the limits of the public's right of access and may result in serious disruption of the life of the community, or where the land, or a building or monument on it, is of historical, architectural, archaeological or scientific importance, in significant damage to the land, building or monument, to apply to the council of the district for an order prohibiting the holding of trespassory assemblies in the district or part of it. The Commissioners of the City of London and Metropolitan Police may make similar orders with the consent of the Secretary of State.

Where an order is made it shall not be for a period exceeding four days. It may not apply to an area represented by a circle with a radius of five miles.

These provisions are intended to prevent disorder at such places as Stonehenge which attract large numbers of persons at particular times.

Offences and powers

It is an offence to organise, take part in, or incite another to take part in such a prohibited assembly.

A constable in uniform may arrest without warrant anyone he reasonably suspects to be committing any of these offences.

Where a constable in uniform who is within the prohibited area, reasonably believes that a person is on his way to such a prohibited assembly he may stop that person and direct him not to proceed in the direction of the assembly. A person who fails to comply commits an offence and may be arrested without warrant by the constable.

Exclusion orders

Part IV of the 1986 Act empowers a court by or before which a person is convicted of certain offences to make an exclusion order prohibiting him from entering any premises for the purposes of attending any prescribed football match. The court must be satisfied that the making of such an order in relation to the accused will help prevent violence or disorder at or in connection with prescribed football matches. It is therefore unlikely that the court will make an order if a bishop is found in possession of a whisky miniature! Such an order must be in addition to any other sentence, probation order or order of absolute or conditional discharge.

A 'prescribed football match' is one involving a football league or a Football Association Premier League team or one which is an international match or a match in the European Champion Clubs' Cup, the European Cup Winners' Cup or the UEFA Cup.

An offence is committed by any person who enters premises in breach of such an order. See page 508 for those offences to which this legislation applies.

Police powers

A constable who reasonably suspects that a person has entered premises in breach of an exclusion order may arrest him without warrant.

Contamination of goods

The Public Order Act 1986, s. 38(1), provides that it is an offence for a person to contaminate or interfere with goods, or make it appear that goods have been contaminated or interfered with, or to place goods which have been contaminated or interfered with, or which have that appearance, in a place where goods of that description are consumed, used, sold or otherwise supplied, with the intention:

(a) of causing public alarm or anxiety; or
(b) of causing injury to members of the public consuming or using the goods; or
(c) of causing economic loss to any person by reason of the goods being shunned by members of the public; or
(d) of causing economic loss to any person by reason of steps taken to avoid any such alarm or anxiety, injury or loss.

It is an offence contrary to s. 38(2) for a person to threaten that he or another will do, or claim that he or another has done, any of these acts with such an intention as is shown in (a), (c) or (d) above. The possession of contaminated goods, apparently contaminated goods, materials with which to contaminate goods or make it appear that goods have been contaminated is also punishable.

Individuals are attracted to such acts, or threats, as a means of extracting large sums of money from large companies. In addition, groups of activists who know better than we do, what is good for us, employ such methods in an attempt to ensure that whether we agree, or do not agree, we will not dare to use the products of targeted companies. By making the offence punishable either way, it is possible to separate the prankster from the seriously ill-intentioned. On indictment, the offence is punishable by ten years' imprisonment or a fine or both; on summary conviction, by imprisonment for six months, or a fine.

It is important to recognise that while this charge may be appropriate, the actions of such persons may be such that a charge of attempted murder may be appropriate. The placing of a poison in an article with the intention of killing is more than a merely preparatory act. If someone actually eats or drinks the product then such a person is guilty of the full offence of murder (should that person die) or causing grievous bodily harm with intent, should that be the case.

While a defence is provided by the section it does not relate to such a person as we have described above. It exists in favour of a person who, in good faith, reports or warns that such a danger exists. In this way, the broadcast of a warning is protected, as without that protection, the broadcaster would have, technically, made it appear that goods had been contaminated in circumstances in which he must have known that economic loss would follow by reason of those goods being shunned.

Trespass or nuisance on land

The Criminal Justice and Public Order Act 1994, s. 61, is the result of the tendency of certain groups to trespass upon private property in large numbers. As a result of such trespass, considerable damage is caused to property. The 'Peace Convoys' which currently seek places to stay, have attracted the attention of the media.

If the senior police officer present at the scene reasonably believes that two or more persons are trespassing on land and are present there with the common purpose of residing there for any period, that reasonable steps have been taken by or on behalf of the occupier to ask them to leave the land and

(a) that any of those persons has caused damage to the land or to property on the land or used threatening, abusive or insulting words or behaviour towards the occupier, a member of his family or an employee or agent of his, or

(b) that those persons have between them six or more vehicles on the land,

he may direct those persons, or any of them, to leave the land and to remove any vehicles or other property they have with them on the land. Such a direction may be communicated to such persons by any constable, where it is not delivered by the officer giving the direction.

Where the original entry on to land was not trespassory (where campers outstay their welcome, for example) he must be satisfied that these things occurred after such persons became trespassers (after their permission to stay had been withdrawn).

Persons who, knowing that such a direction has been given, fail to leave the land as soon as reasonably practicable, or who, having left, again enter the land as trespassers within three months from the date of the direction, commit an offence. This offence is punishable by three months' imprisonment, a fine, or both. A person reasonably suspected of committing this offence may be arrested by a constable without warrant.

It is a defence for such a person to prove that he was not trespassing on such land or that he had a reasonable excuse for failing to leave it as soon as reasonably practicable, or as the case may be, for again entering the land as a trespasser.

Such trespass may occur on common land against the commoners' rights. While

478

the offences do not apply to buildings in a general sense they apply to agricultural buildings and scheduled monuments. They cannot be committed on land forming part of a highway unless it is a footpath, bridleway or byway open to all traffic or road used as a public path or is a cycle track.

The term 'vehicle' includes a vehicle which is not in a fit state for use on a road and includes any chassis or body with or without wheels, appearing to have formed part of such a vehicle, and any load carried by, and anything attached to, such a vehicle and a caravan is any structure designed for human habitation which is capable of being moved from one place to another whether by being towed, or by being transported on a motor vehicle or trailer, and any motor vehicle so designed and adapted.

Section 62 provides a power of seizure where there is a failure to remove such a vehicle or where the vehicle is returned within three months.

Raves – police powers of removal from land

A 'rave' is a gathering on land in the open air of 100 or more persons (whether or not as trespassers) at which amplified music is played during the night (with or without intermissions) and as such is, by reason of its loudness and duration and the time at which it is played, likely to cause serious distress to the inhabitants of the locality.

Such a gathering continues throughout intermissions in the music. Where the rave extends over several days, the section applies to those periods during the night when amplified music is played. 'Music' can include the emission of a succession of repetitive beats.

Where a police officer of at least the rank of superintendent reasonably believes that:

(a) two or more persons are making preparations for the holding there of a such a gathering;
(b) ten or more persons are waiting for such a gathering to begin there; or
(c) ten or more persons are attending such a gathering which is in progress,

he may give a direction that those persons and any other persons who come, to prepare or wait for, or to attend the gathering are to leave the land and remove any vehicles or other property which they have with them on the land.

Persons will be treated as having received such a direction if reasonable steps have been taken to bring it to their attention and the direction may be communicated to them by any constable at the scene. It will be appreciated that there may be difficulties in making announcements at such gatherings and these provisions foresee those difficulties.

Offences and powers

An offence is committed against s. 63 of the 1994 Act by any person who, knowing that such a direction has been given, fails to leave the land as soon as practicable or, having left, enters the land within seven days of the direction being given. These offences are punishable by three months' imprisonment, a fine, or both.

A constable in uniform who reasonably suspects that a person is committing an offence under the section may arrest him without warrant.

479

It is a defence for a person to show that he had reasonable excuse for failing to leave the land as soon as reasonably practicable or, as the case may be, for again entering the land. In addition, the section does not apply where an entertainment licence has been granted by a local authority. A direction to leave cannot apply to an exempt person, that is an occupier, member of his family, or his employee or agent, or to any person whose home is situated on the land.

The authorising superintendent, under powers given by s. 64, may authorise constables to enter land to establish that such circumstances exist and to exercise powers. Where such a constable reasonably suspects that any person to whom the direction applies has, without reasonable excuse, failed to remove any vehicle or sound equipment on the land which appears to belong to that person or to be in his possession or control, or has entered the land as a trespasser with a vehicle or sound equipment within seven days of that direction being given, he may seize and remove that vehicle or sound equipment of any person other than an exempt person.

Under powers given by s. 65, where a constable in uniform reasonably believes that a person is on his way to such a gathering he may stop that person and direct him not to proceed in the direction of the gathering. However, this power may only be exercised within five miles of the boundary of the site of the gathering. A person who, knowing that such a direction has been given, fails to comply commits an offence punishable by a fine. A constable in uniform who reasonably believes that a person is committing this offence may arrest him without warrant.

The court is empowered in such cases to order the forfeiture of sound equipment.

Aggravated trespass

Section 68 of the 1994 Act introduces an offence of aggravated trespass which is aimed at hunt protesters. Where a person trespasses on land in the open air and, in relation to any lawful activity which persons are engaged in on that or adjoining land in the open air, does there anything which is intended by him to have the effect:

(a) of intimidating those persons or any of them so as to deter them or any of them from engaging in that activity;

(b) of obstructing that activity; or

(c) of disrupting that activity,

he commits an offence.

For the purposes of the section an activity is lawful if it is carried out without trespass. The term 'land' does not include highways and roads.

The offence is punishable by three months' imprisonment, a fine, or both.

Police powers

A constable in uniform who reasonably suspects that a person is committing this offence may arrest him without warrant.

Powers given by s. 69 permit the senior police officer present at the scene, where he reasonably believes that a person is committing this offence, or intends to commit it, or that two or more persons are so trespassing and are present there with the common purpose of intimidating persons so as to deter them from engaging in a lawful activity or of obstructing or disrupting a lawful activity, to direct that person, or persons, or any of them, to leave the land. Any person who, knowing that such a direction has been given which applies to him and who fails to leave the land as soon as practicable or, who having left again enters the land as a trespasser within a period of three months of that direction commits an offence punishable by three months' imprisonment, a fine, or both.

A constable in uniform who reasonably suspects that a person is committing this offence may arrest him without warrant.

Module 4

Domestic disputes

Introduction

The Working Party on Police Probationer Training of 1971 first reported upon the need for some form of training which assisted uniform police officers to determine the best course of action which might be taken when domestic disturbances occurred in the home. Young officers had commented upon the complexity of some of the situations which they met, and felt that their youth and inexperience made them ill-equipped to deal with many of them. Offering advice upon such occasions is often difficult as the causes of these disputes are so varied. Basically, police officers become involved because of their duty to ensure that there is no disturbance of the peace and, upon occasions, the forms of violence which are used are sufficient to cause serious injury if there is no intervention.

If the officer's decision invoked no more than a choice to arrest or not to arrest, then that officer's initial training need include no more than a knowledge of police powers. Life is no longer so simple and the police service is becoming increasingly involved in the social affairs of a community. The police officer must apply the law with an appreciation of the needs of the parties involved, and make some attempt to change the course of conduct which led to the situation arising. It is often possible to talk away doubts and suspicions which have existed in the minds of individuals for some time. The dispute is often a climax to much that has remained unsaid for a longer period of time, and once the washing is put out for airing, it may as well be completely dried. This would not be possible without the presence of someone who was recognised by both parties as being in a position of authority, to give some form of order to the proceedings.

As the advice which is to be given to police officers concerning the 'interaction' involving the disputants and police officers is constantly changing as the problems which are encountered during day-to-day policing lead to the identification of new priorities, the information provided in this chapter will be restricted to those matters which involve the enforcement of the law in such situations. The *detailed* social factors involved in such disputes will be dealt with by instructors during probationary training.

Social factors

There are many factors which affect family life in such a way that violent arguments are bound to occur. The human requires reasonable living space and, like many animals, becomes aggressive if crowded by others. This is perhaps the basis upon which domestic disputes, or breakdowns in the day-to-day family relationships, occur and most of the other factors are merely consequences of this form of pressure. Disputes are most frequently met within certain social groups and this is not because of the personalities of the persons included in these groups. The need to provide for large families often means residence in a poor neighbourhood, in indifferent housing, or in crowded conditions. Occasionally the mother of the family becomes a little discontented with her day-to-day life and father spends a lot of time at his local as a means of escape from the home. Such conditions are endured by many without serious conflict arising, but occasionally disputes are bound to occur. It would be incorrect, however, to convey the impression that domestic disputes are restricted to the lower classes as disputes occur between partners at all social levels. It is frequently more difficult to deal with those arising in the middle and upper classes, as the parties concerned may not so readily accept the advice which is offered by the police officer, even though he or she has been called for advice and assistance.

Initial contact

The method of approach adopted by a constable is of the utmost importance, as the first impression that the constable creates will establish his or her certainty of purpose in the minds of both parties. If the officer appears calm, assured, and helpful, a working relationship will be quickly established with the parties involved in the dispute, particularly if he or she can give the impression of being there to assist rather than to make demands, unless continuing violence necessitates a more immediate form of police action. Most frequently, the physical action has passed and the establishment of degrees of blame within the parties forms the basis of the dispute at the time of police intervention. On occasions, injuries to the parties must be attended to and consideration given to the desirability of charges being preferred because of the nature of those injuries. Frequently a wife will give wholehearted support to action being taken against her husband for an assault occasioning actual bodily harm in the heat of the moment, but will be found to be unwilling to continue with the matter on the following day when she has had an opportunity to consider the implications. However, in most circumstances no criminal offence has been committed and the police officer's role is strictly that of an adviser.

Police powers of entry

The difficulties of police officers are increased because of the delicate situation in which they find themselves when attending disputes in the home. In English law there is no such thing as a general power of entry, and a constable must have been invited into the premises or no objection must have been raised to the constable's entry. In normal circumstances, the constable must remain no longer than the invitation remains. If entry is to be considered without invitation, it must be made to

486

quell a breach of the peace or to prevent its occurrence. This power of entry to prevent a breach of the peace is invaluable when attending violent domestic disputes as constables will frequently meet circumstances which will not permit their departure at the request of either party because of the danger of a renewal of a breach of the peace at that time. The Court of Appeal has ruled that where a police officer is invited into a house by a wife to resolve a domestic dispute involving her husband, the officer is entitled to remain long enough to ensure the safety of the complainant and her children and to ensure that there is no further danger of a breach of the peace, even though the officer is ordered to leave by the husband.

Landlord/tenant disputes

On occasions police officers are called to disputes involving the owner of furnished accommodation who has let a part of his premises to tenants and wishes to be rid of them for some reason before the expiration of the term of lease. These can be difficult situations as the conduct of the tenants is frequently the cause of the dispute and it is, therefore, possible to feel considerable sympathy for the owner of the property. However, the Protection from Eviction Act 1977 gives a considerable degree of protection to tenants and the effect of the Act should be explained to such landlords.

Section 1(1) of the Act defines the term 'residential occupier' in relation to any premises as a person occupying the premises as a residence whether under a contract or by virtue of any enactment or rule of law which gives a right to remain in occupation, or restricting the right of any other person to recover possession of the premises. It is an offence contrary to s. 1(2) to unlawfully deprive or attempt to deprive a residential occupier of his premises or part of them unless it is proved that the person believed, and had reasonable cause to believe, that the residential occupier had ceased to reside in the premises. By s. 1(3) it is an offence to do any act calculated to interfere with the peace or comfort of a residential occupier or his family, or to withhold services reasonably required for the occupation of the premises as a residence with intent to cause such residential occupier to quit, or to refrain from exercising his rights of pursuing a remedy. Such an offence would be committed if a landlord shuts of gas, electricity, water supplies, etc. These offences may only be committed in relation to a 'residential occupier' and this does not include, for example, persons hiring holiday accommodation on a short-term basis other than under a contract. Section 3A creates a similar offence where the act is not done with 'intent' but where the landlord or his agent *has reasonable cause to believe* that the conduct is likely to cause the residential occupier to give up occupation or to refrain from pursuing remedy.

Although the Protection from Eviction Act 1977 creates these offences, it must be noted that the Act specifically authorises councils to institute proceedings. The action to be taken by a police officer should be restricted to preventing a breach of the peace at the time and to giving advice. A landlord should be warned, if it appears that a breach of the provisions of the Act has occurred and, on all occasions, the officer should submit a full report to be sent to the local housing authority. In appropriate cases, a complainant should be informed in writing by the police, that the complaint has been passed to that authority.

Once a person becomes a residential occupier, his lease cannot be forfeited while he is still residing in his premises, otherwise than by proceedings in a county court, or in exceptional circumstances, the High Court. This even applies when the tenancy agreement has come to an end, if the occupier is still on the premises. The owner may only enforce his right to recover the property through the court.

Similar provisions are made to protect the 'residential occupiers' of caravans by the Caravan Sites Act 1968.

Husband/wife

The subject of 'battered wives' is an important one. However, we are not considering here the various offences of assault which may be appropriate as these have been dealt with under that heading. Disputes involving a husband and wife present difficult situations. While a wife who has been assaulted by her husband is both competent and compellable to give evidence, her reluctance to do so, on occasions, can be appreciated. Some women are reluctant to break up such a marriage as, despite its difficulties, it is all that they have. Help is available from social workers.

When dealing with domestic disputes involving husband and wife, one of the parties will frequently request a police officer to remove the other party from the house. A rent book bearing the name of one party may be produced to prove who is the 'occupier'. It must be remembered that the law gives protection to both parties of the marriage, regardless of proprietary interest in the home. A court order is necessary before either party can be deprived of occupation.

Domestic violence

The Domestic Violence and Matrimonial Proceedings Act 1976 allows a spouse or cohabittee to obtain an injunction from a county court judge restraining the other partner from using violence against him or her or any children living with the applicant. The injunction may also exclude the other partner from the matrimonial home. A judge may attach a power of arrest for breach of specified parts of the order or injunction if he is satisfied that violence is likely to be repeated.

The provisions apply regardless of the ownership of the home or the marital status of the partners. However, the Act is not intended to apply to unmarried people in casual relationships and it only applies where a common household is maintained. The parties must be living as husband and wife to the exclusion of other relationships, such as housekeeper and employer, brother and sister, co-tenants.

If a power of arrest has been attached to the injunction by the judge, police will be informed when the injunction or order is made, varied or revoked. When such a power is given, if a police constable has reasonable cause to suspect that the person named has disobeyed the injunction, he may arrest him and take him before a judge to be dealt with within 24 hours of the arrest. The injunction or order does not have to be in the possession of the constable at the time of the arrest. The power to arrest is permissive, rather than mandatory, allowing a constable to exercise his discretion in particular circumstances. In reckoning a period of 24 hours, no account shall be taken of Christmas Day, Good Friday, or any Sunday. Police officers must use their discretion concerning the necessity for arrest on each occasion.

The Domestic Proceedings and Magistrates' Courts Act 1978 empowers a magistrates' court to make orders for the protection of a party to a marriage or a child of a family, in urgent cases. Such orders will require the person named not to use or threaten violence against the party concerned. If there is a history of violence a party may be required to leave the matrimonial home and/or not to enter it. The court may attach a power to arrest without a warrant on reasonable suspicion that a person is in breach of the order. The same provisions concerning appearance within 24 hours, etc., apply to such arrests.

As the 1978 Act permits immediate action to be taken, battered wives may be advised to consult the clerk to the justices, or a solicitor, in the first instance, but not to the exclusion of any appropriate police action in the particular circumstances.

Sudden death

Introduction

This section is concerned with deaths which are reported to and dealt with by HM Coroner. They are referred to as 'sudden deaths' and this term covers not only a sudden death of which the cause is unknown but also violent or unnatural deaths. The police usually receive the first report of such deaths and investigate the circumstances and notify HM Coroner of their findings. Once a coroner has been informed of a death it is for him to consider whether it will be necessary to hold an inquest or order a post-mortem examination to be made, or whether, after due enquiry, he should notify the Registrar of Births and Deaths that an inquest or post-mortem examination is unnecessary. A police officer investigating a sudden death has to keep two things in mind: the possibility of the death being a criminal homicide and the necessary information required by the coroner. We have dealt with homicide and the need to approach all deaths with caution, and now it is necessary to examine the procedure to be followed when reporting 'sudden deaths' to the coroner.

Initial action

On receiving a report of a possible sudden death the first thing is to determine whether or not a death has occurred; if there is any doubt, first aid should be given and medical assistance called for including an ambulance. It would not be the first time that a police officer has been called to a reported sudden death only to find that there are signs of life, and prompt action by the police officer has resulted in the 'corpse' surviving. This has happened on a number of occasions with persons suffering from a condition of deep coma resembling death. Even where death is apparent a doctor must be summoned to certify that a person is dead. In no circumstances should the police officer be content with his own opinion; there could be a tragic error if the first time a person is seen after death is when the pathologist commences the post-mortem!

In the majority of deaths coming to the knowledge of the police an enquiry with the deceased's doctor will establish the fact that the deceased was suffering from an illness, and was receiving treatment from the doctor, who is quite prepared to certify

489

the cause of death. Usually the doctor will not issue such a certificate if he has not seen the deceased within the 28 days prior to his death. If there are any suspicious circumstances the coroner should be informed notwithstanding that the deceased's doctor is prepared to certify the cause of death.

If the circumstances are such that the deceased's doctor is not prepared to issue a death certificate, for whatever reason, the reporting officer should notify his supervising officer via Control, and request that the coroner's office be informed. Some forces have a police officer whose sole duty is to act as the coroner's officer for a particular area, and he reports all sudden deaths in that area. If there are any suspicious circumstances, Control should be informed as soon as possible and the action taken should follow that for a suspected criminal homicide. Do not move the body or interfere with the scene.

If there are no suspicious circumstances, police action depends on the place where death has occurred. If, as in the majority of cases, a person dies in his own home, the first act after death has been certified is to examine the body for any marks or signs of violence. This will usually be done or directed by the coroner's officer. It is not a very pleasant task but one which should not be overlooked. The procedures to be followed when dealing with bodies are set out in force orders. These may differ from force to force. The essential thing is to take care to avoid any form of contamination which may occur due to the presence of saliva, blood, excreta, etc.

Where death occurs out of doors or on business or industrial premises, there are not the same facilities to examine the body. Make sure that the body is screened from public view and that the property of the deceased person is protected. In such circumstances, if a doctor has not certified death, the body is removed by ambulance to the nearest hospital where the deceased will be certified as dead on arrival and placed in the mortuary. If possible, a cursory examination should be made of a body before it is moved in case there is the slightest possibility of life being present, in which case medical assistance should not be delayed. Where a person has died out of doors, etc., it is important for the purposes of identification to have continuity from the scene of the death to the mortuary. If the body has not been moved before the arrival of the police one police officer should accompany the body to the hospital and to the mortuary. In the event of an inquest, this procedure will obviate the necessity of having statements from the ambulance personnel and the mortuary attendant as well as the police officer reporting the death to provide continuity of identification. On arrival at the mortuary the body should be thoroughly examined for any marks or signs of violence.

The next step in the reporting of a sudden death is to identify the deceased. Where death occurs at the home of the deceased it may be possible to have a relative identify the body before it is removed. In situations where death has occurred outside or at a hospital and the body has been removed to the mortuary the identification should be made at the mortuary. This can be a very distressing experience for the relatives, particularly in cases of fatal accidents or where the death was not expected, and relatives should be treated tactfully and with sympathy. Where the death has resulted from an accident and a police officer is given the task of breaking the news of the death to relatives, he should be both tactful and sympathetic. If the relative lives alone, the assistance of a neighbour should be sought so that the relative is not left alone after hearing such distressing news.

Usually the statement of identification is coupled with a history of the deceased's employment and health. This should include details of any disability pension which a deceased may have been in receipt of, such as a pension for an industrial disease. Where the death has occurred at home, usually one statement will suffice and, as well as identifying the deceased and giving details of his employment and medical history, it will also incorporate details of when, where, and by whom the deceased was last seen alive and any other details connected with the death.

Suicide

When the death appears to be a suspected suicide the reporting officer should immediately notify his supervising officer and if there is the slightest suspicion of another person being involved in the death, the CID should be informed and the police procedure as for criminal homicide should be followed. An officer must ensure his own safety. Care must be taken with live electric wires, caustic agents, etc.

In uncomplicated cases of suicide the means employed in the killing should be seized where applicable (e.g. tablets), or noted where seizure is inapplicable (e.g. gas oven). Any letters or suicide notes found should be handed to a supervising officer for onward transmission to the coroner. In no circumstances should a letter addressed to a coroner be opened by the reporting officer. In cases involving hanging the rope should be cut rather than the knot untied. The type of knot tied might be important.

There should be no delay in notifying the coroner of the death, giving as much information as possible. The coroner will then authorise the removal of the body to a mortuary in cases where the body is not already at a mortuary, and arrange for a post-mortem to be carried out by a pathologist to determine the cause of death.

Essentials details for sudden death report

The sudden death report is designed to include all information which is essential to HM Coroner. It contains the name, address, age, occupation, sex, date and place of birth, etc., of the deceased person; details of the person who identified the deceased; the time and place at which death occurred together with details of the suspected cause; particulars of the person who found the deceased including how, when, and where the body was found; the identity of the person who identified the deceased; the identity of the person who last saw the deceased alive and when and where that occurred; any history of illness and the name of the doctor who certified death; evidence of neglect, particularly in the case of children; marks on the body; the names and addresses of any other witnesses who may be able to assist; information as to the location of the body and details of the removal of the body to the place at which it rests to allow continuity of evidence as to the identity of the deceased person at all stages.

Post-mortem

This is arranged by the coroner, although, having ordered a post-mortem, the coroner often leaves the task of liaising with the pathologist to the police officer reporting the death. The body of the deceased must be identified to the pathologist before a post-mortem can be performed, and to ensure continuity the police officer to whom the deceased was identified provides this information. It is not part of a police officer's duty to assist or remain in the mortuary while a post-mortem examination is being carried out. The only purpose for which a police officer remains at a mortuary during a post-mortem is to prevent a breach of the peace, e.g. if relatives of the deceased object to the post-mortem and attempt to stop the pathologist from carrying out his examination.

The pathologist is responsible for informing the coroner of the results of the post-mortem and, in cases where death has resulted from natural causes, the coroner will normally dispense with an inquest and will issue a certificate authorising the Registrar of Births and Deaths to register the death. In connection with the registration of death, the coroner must know if it is intended to have the deceased buried or cremated in order to issue the correct documents with the correct information for the registration of death.

Property of deceased

The property of a deceased person should be safeguarded by the police until it can be handed over to a relative or personal representative of the deceased against his signature. Where the next of kin cannot be traced and the deceased lived alone, the local authority should be contacted to see if assistance can be given to store the effects of the deceased until arrangements are made for eventual disposal.

Whenever possible, a police officer should have a witness, either another police officer or a responsible person, when checking any money found on a deceased person. This will protect him from any subsequent complaint from relatives that the deceased was thought to be in possession of more money than was actually found, the implication being that some money had been stolen after death.

In fatal road accidents any property found in the deceased's vehicle should be safeguarded if it cannot be secured in the vehicle itself.

Details of all property coming into the possession of the police should be recorded in detail and the record should be endorsed as to the subsequent disposal of the property.

Coroner's court

The coroner makes the decision whether or not an inquest should be held into the circumstances of a death. He is required to hold an inquest when he is informed that the body of a person is lying within his jurisdiction and that there is reasonable cause to suspect that such person has died a violent or unnatural death, or a sudden death of which the cause is unknown, or has died in prison or in such circumstances as to require an inquest in pursuance of an Act of Parliament. Such inquests may be with or without a jury. The Coroner's Act 1980 authorises him to request the coroner of another district to hold the inquest in his area if it is more expedient to do so.

A coroner may decide to hold an inquest with a jury of not less than seven and not more than eleven persons who are summoned by a warrant addressed to the coroner's officer and to members of the police force for the area, setting out the number of jurors to be summoned. On receipt of the warrant the coroner's officer, or the police officer dealing with the death, makes out the summonses to be served on the persons selected as jurors. These summonses should preferably be served personally, although service by leaving with a person at the juror's house would appear to be sufficient compliance.

A coroner's inquest is not bound by the laws of evidence. In practice, however, the laws of evidence are usually observed by coroners. A witness is not bound to answer any questions which might incriminate him, but this does not entitle a witness to refuse to enter the witness box on the grounds that he may be asked such questions.

Section 56 of the Criminal Law Act 1977 removed the power previously held by coroners to find a person guilty of murder, manslaughter or infanticide, and prohibits any person being charged with any such offence by coroner's inquisition. The section also removed the mandatory requirement for a coroner to sit with a jury in any case involving murder, manslaughter, infanticide or death caused by an accident arising out of the use of a motor vehicle in a street or public highway. Schedule 10 to that Act substitutes a new s. 20 to the Coroner's (Amendment) Act 1926 relating to the adjournment of inquests when relevant criminal proceedings are pending. If, at any time before an inquest is concluded, the coroner is informed by a clerk to magistrates that a person has been charged with murder, manslaughter, infanticide, causing death by dangerous driving, or an offence contrary to s. 2(1) Suicide Act 1961 (aiding and abetting suicide) or is required by the Director of Public Prosecutions to do so, he shall adjourn the inquest.

After the conclusion of the relevant proceedings, a coroner may proceed; if with a jury, with the jury previously convened, or he may begin again with a new jury. He may alternatively supply the Registrar of Deaths with the result of the criminal proceedings (by certificate).

Police action generally

Dealing with a sudden death is a distressing experience. People have never been able to come fully to terms with death. The person who was loved and respected by all has now gone; the body which is left behind represents something quite different and this is difficult to come to terms with. The closer a person is to the deceased, the greater the difficulty becomes. Police officers do come to terms with this situation but the process can be damaging if it is not handled correctly. If a researcher was to question a large number of long-serving police officers to establish those incidents which occurred during their service which had a lasting effect upon them, it is suggested most would be concerned with incidents which involved a death. The more tragic the circumstances, the more likely it becomes that the effect would be considerable.

When dealing with relatives and close friends, the distress of the situation generally, being equally felt by the police officer, tends to ensure that the enquiry is dealt with in a sensitive manner. However, it helps to remember that such persons may appreciate additional help, and offers to contact other persons or associations who will be willing to help may be much appreciated. There are so many things which need to be done following a death and, on many occasions, close relatives need advice and assistance in this respect.

It is also important to keep an eye on yourself. Such situations can have a

493

considerable effect upon you. If you feel that dealing with the situation has left you with questions which need to be answered, ask them. Other police officers will have moved through the same experiences. You will be surprised at the quality of the advice which can be given by an experienced officer; and perhaps to find that they will readily admit that they have travelled the same journey, will provide assurance. If the problem which you have encountered goes beyond this, then seek help from other qualified agencies.

Drugs

Purpose – need for control

The Misuses of Drugs Act 1971 both reformed and strengthened the law related to the misuse of drugs. Previous Acts of Parliament had been passed with a view to controlling different types of drugs as they came to be more commonly used. The 1971 Act, by setting up an Advisory Council on the Misuse of Drugs, has established a system whereby trends in drug taking can be quickly identified and measures taken to set up effective forms of control. The Advisory Council has three functions: to keep under review misuse of various forms of drugs which are likely to have a harmful effect and to advise the Secretary of State upon measures which should be taken; to advise the Secretary of State concerning regulations which he may wish to make under the Act; and, finally, to act as an advisory body upon all matters relating to drug dependence or the misuse of drugs, which may be referred to the Secretary of State or any other Minister.

There is so much debate concerning the need for the use of drugs to be controlled, as opposed to the rights of the individual to choose his own path, that it will be helpful to study the nature of that path.

In the first instance, drugs are essential, as their medical applications are both useful and varied. From the diabetic who needs insulin to the worried businessman who needs something to relax him sufficiently to enable him to sleep, a medical need for the prescription of drugs has become a part of our modern society. Many general titles are applied to different forms of drugs: the sleeping capsules or sedatives, the pain killers or analgesics, and the antidepressants or tranquillisers. The stimulation of various forms of drug taking is known to most of us, from the small uplift given by the caffeine in a cup of tea or coffee, to the effect of the nicotine in a cigarette, or the alcohol in a pint of beer.

Addiction

Drug dependence can be socially, physically or mentally related. It frequently develops within those who are too inhibited to enjoy themselves within a modern society, or those who seek new 'experiences'. An inability to face up to social or personal problems can be the initial cause, but the boredom and restlessness which follow the passing of the drug's effect, lead to further compulsion for the drug taker. As the body's tolerance towards the drug increases, it becomes necessary to increase the dose to compensate for this resistance. A drug addict is a sick person and should

494

receive medical treatment as a matter of urgency. It is the duty of a police officer to ensure that he receives it, whether such person is identified as a drug user by an officer on patrol, or by a custody officer at a police station.

Offences generally

(1) *Unlawful possession*

The Misuse of Drugs Act 1971, s. 5(2) states that it is an offence for a person unlawfully to have a controlled drug in his possession. Drugs which are controlled are classified as A, B or C controlled drugs but the important factor is that they are all controlled drugs.

Controlled drugs may lawfully be in the possession of certain persons. Regulations made under the Act describe such lawful possession. In addition to forms of possession which are particularly dealt with by regulations, it is a defence for a person to prove that he took possession of a controlled drug for the purpose of preventing someone else from committing an offence and that, as soon as possible, he took steps either to destroy it or deliver it to some person lawfully entitled to take possession of it. Section 7 of the Act directs that the Secretary of State shall exercise his power to make regulations to ensure that it is not unlawful for doctors, dentists, veterinarians, pharmacists, scientists, and other similar persons to possess drugs in the course of their profession. These other persons include police, customs, carriers, forensic scientists and post office employees. In addition, persons who have been prescribed drugs or are conveying them to a person may lawfully possess controlled drugs in those circumstances.

The term 'possession' is defined in s. 37(3). For the purposes of the Act, things which a person has in his possession shall be taken to include anything subject to his control which is in the custody of another. 'Possession', therefore, extends to circumstances in which a controlled drug is being held for someone else; for example, by a servant on behalf of his master. In such an instance, both would be in possession of controlled drugs, and it has been held that a person is not in possession of drugs if he is unaware that they are in some place over which he has control – for example, his house or room. Guilty knowledge is necessary, and if a drug has been placed in a man's house or in his jacket pocket without his knowledge, he is not in possession of it for the purposes of the Act. The knowledge required is knowledge that the substance is within one's control and knowledge of the nature of the substance if its nature is the same, such as a drug in a tablet form, as opposed to something else in that form. Knowledge of the quality of the substance is not necessary. If a man is in control of tablets which he believes to be aspirin but which in fact consist of cocaine, he is in possession of cocaine. Possession of cigarettes believed to contain tobacco is possession of cannabis cigarettes if that is what they contain.

It is not necessary to prove that a minimum quantity of a controlled drug was unlawfully in the possession of the person charged, but it should be measurable. Persons who are found under the influence of a controlled drug cannot be said to be in possession of it, even though traces are found in a urine sample. If a thing is consumed it changes its character and can no longer be considered to be a controlled drug in its true form. However, evidence of the presence of such a drug in a urine sample can be given to support an allegation of possession at some earlier time. Police officers executing a search warrant found a letter on a hall table addressed to the defendant. He was invited to open it and amphetamine hydrochloride was found. It was held that the defendant, having given directions to the supplier to send the drug by post, became the possessor when the letter passed through the letter box.

A person may be guilty of an attempt to possess if he takes possession of a substance which he believes to be a controlled drug, but which is in fact a harmless substance.

(2) *Supplying and possession with intent to supply*

These offences are those which form a part of 'drug trafficking'. Section 4(3) of the 1971 Act states:

> 'It is an offence for a person unlawfully to supply a controlled drug to another or to be concerned in the supplying of such a drug to another, or to offer to supply a controlled drug to another, or to be concerned in the making to another of an offer to supply such a drug.'

Those persons who may lawfully supply drugs are considered above.

Drug pushers supply drugs directly to addicts. A person who passes drugs around at a party supplies them contrary to the section. There is no requirement that the act must be for personal gain. Each person who passes a cannabis cigarette to his neighbour supplies a controlled drug. Many people may be concerned in 'supply'. Those who arrange delivery; allow premises to be used; or who arrange for young persons to attend a party with a view to making drugs available to them, are all 'concerned' in supply.

It is not necessary that controlled drugs are actually supplied. If an offer is made and the person concerned refuses to accept the controlled drug, an offence of 'offering to supply' has been committed. In fact, it does not matter that the substance proves to be other than a controlled drug if the offer is made in the belief that it is a controlled drug. Where a person supplied vitamin C tablets alleging that they were ecstasy tablets, it was held that he could be properly convicted of offering to supply a controlled drug. In such cases it is not necessary to prove that, pursuant to the offer, a controlled drug would be supplied.

An offer may be made by words or conduct. Where an offer to supply is made in words the nature of the substance is irrelevant, even where the person offering to supply is aware that the substance is not a controlled drug. Where an offer is made by way of conduct, the issue of whether or not the substance is controlled may be relevant as the conduct must have been sufficient to have indicated that it was a controlled drug which was being offered.

Section 5(3) prohibits possession of controlled drugs with intent to supply. A 'pusher' who is found in possession of large quantities of drugs and can be proved to have been supplying to some persons, is obviously in possession of the remainder with intent to supply.

(3) *Controlled drugs on premises*

Section 8 of the 1971 Act is concerned with persons who, being the occupier or concerned in the management of any premises, knowingly permits or suffers any of the following acts to take place on the premises:

  (a) unlawful production or attempted production of a controlled drug;
  (b) unlawful supply or attempted supply of a controlled drug to another, or offering to supply a controlled drug unlawfully to another;
  (c) preparation of opium for smoking; or
  (d) smoking cannabis, cannabis resin or prepared opium.

A person is the occupier of premises if he is entitled to exclusive possession of them having sufficient control to exclude persons who would carry out forbidden activities. Thus, we will normally be concerned with owners, tenants, etc., at this level. To be an 'occupier' two factors must be present: legal possession of the premises, and control over them. In circumstances in which two sisters aged 20 and 15 years were charged with permitting cannabis smoking as the occupiers of premises while their parents were absent on holiday, it was held that there could be no conviction as they were not occupiers, not being, in law, in possession of the premises during the temporary absence of their parents.

In contrast, a person may be 'concerned in management' without having any ownership or tenancy rights. In this category we will find managers, persons in control of rooms or a part of the premises, provided that all of them have the power to exercise control over activities which take place there.

Persons who occupy premises as trespassers can commit this offence. If drug parties are organised in 'squats', all concerned in the organisation of those parties commit this offence.

(4) *Other offences*

The Misuse of Drugs Act 1971 is a very comprehensive piece of legislation. It prohibits the unlawful import or export (s. 3) and the unlawful production (s. 4(2)), of controlled drugs. In relation to importation, where a person believes that a package which he is carrying contains a controlled drug, it is immaterial that it in fact obtained snuff rather than heroin or cannabis.

The term 'production' covers the conversion of cocaine hydrochloride into a freebase cocaine, in which form it would vaporise and be capable of being inhaled. The same would be true where cocaine hydrochloride is converted into 'crack' by mixing it with other chemicals.

Statutory defences generally

The Misuse of Drugs Act 1971, s. 28, provides a defence which is applicable to charges contrary to s. 4(2) (unlawful production), s. 4(3) (unlawful supply), s. 5(2) (unlawful possession), s. 5(3) (possession with intent to supply), s. 6(2) (unlawful cultivation of cannabis) and s. 9 (opium smoking, frequenting places used for opium smoking or possessing utensils used for opium smoking).

Where a person has been proved to have been in possession of a controlled drug he may be convicted of that offence even if it has not been proved that he *knew* that he was in possession of a controlled drug. However, an accused may prove, on the

497

balance of probabilities that he *neither knew of, nor suspected, nor had reason to suspect* the existence of some fact alleged by the prosecution which it is necessary for the prosecution to prove to gain a conviction. However, this is subject to the proviso that where the issue is the nature of a controlled drug alleged to have been possessed and the accused proves that he did not know, suspect or have reason to suspect that the thing in question was the particular controlled drug alleged, this is not a sufficient defence in itself. In such circumstances an accused must also prove:

(a) that he neither believed nor suspected, nor had reason to suspect, that the thing in question was a controlled drug at all; or

(b) that he believed that the thing in question was a controlled drug which he was, in fact, legally entitled to possess (or supply or produce as the case may be).

If, therefore, a person is given a packet of powder which she is told is baking powder but is, in fact, cocaine, that person is in possession of cocaine and she is knowingly in possession of the powder. However, she will have a defence to a charge of unlawful possession if she can prove that she did not believe or suspect that the powder was a controlled drug. It would, of course, be no defence to prove that she believed the powder to be heroin as heroin is merely an alternative controlled drug.

The defence provided by (b) is aimed at less common circumstances. A registered addict may be entitled to receive heroin on prescription. If he is provided with an alternative drug by mistake, he is in unlawful possession as the drug is not that prescribed. If he believed that he was in possession of heroin, this part of the defence would apply.

Controlled drugs

The misuse of certain drugs is controlled by the Act. These are called 'controlled drugs', and are divided into three categories, depending upon their harmfulness. The 1971 Act allows new drugs to be added to lists of controlled drugs by the passing of an Order in Council. The reason for dividing controlled drugs into three subgroups is that penalties for offences vary according to the type of controlled drug to which the offence relates. Class A drugs can be divided into two groups: narcotic drugs such as cocaine, morphine, opium, pethidine, and heroin; and hallucinogenic, such as mescaline, LSD, and MDMA (ecstasy). Class B drugs include amphetamines (which are stimulant drugs) such as mandrax, cannabis, and cannabis resin. Class C drugs include benzyphetamine, pipradol, chlorophentomine, mephentermine, methaqualone, phendimetrazine, and other drugs. The only significance of differing classifications to constables enforcing the provisions of this Act is that the more serious offences are arrestable offences.

The term 'controlled drug' includes preparations or other products containing a substance or product specified as a controlled drug. Possession of a naturally occurring material which contains a controlled drug, for example a mushroom, is not unlawful, but if it is subjected to some process which prepares it for future use as a drug, such as packaging and freezing for later separation of the drug, such possession is unlawful.

Recognition

The most difficult problem which faces the operational police officer is the impossibility of recognising substances found in the possession of persons suspected of drug offences as being particular drugs of certain classes. It would be a simple matter to reproduce coloured representations of the most common forms of controlled drugs in an effort to assist identification, but it would serve little purpose. These drugs appear in many forms and there is no limit to the variations which can be made in an effort to avoid their identification. Recognising that a detailed analysis will have to be carried out by forensic scientists before the type of drug can be established, identification of the substance cannot be taken as the starting point of a police officer's investigation. A police officer will become suspicious of persons observed to be passing tablets or capsules to one another in discothèques or cafés. Their appearance – their air of detached serenity, a look of intoxication without its accompanying tendency to become over-verbose – are all factors which give rise to a reasonable suspicion that such persons are in possession of controlled drugs. It is safe to say that if the tablets are the type used by young people looking for kicks, they will be listed in Schedule 2 of the 1971 Act as controlled drugs. In the absence of some medical reason for possession of such tablets, there is every reason to suspect that they are controlled drugs. Powers to arrest for such offences require suspicion on the part of the arresting officer, and this must be so because of the impossibility of positive recognition of controlled drugs. Provided that there are grounds for such suspicion, the person concerned can be arrested, searched, suspected substances may be taken into possession by the arresting officer, and that person can be taken to a police station, and thoroughly searched before being released on bail on a delayed charge procedure, requiring his presence at the police station at a particular time to finalise the proceedings. If subsequent analysis proves possession of a controlled drug, such person will be charged with an offence when he answers his bail, and if it does not he will be told by written notice that his presence at the police station is not required.

The main offences which police officers on the beat are likely to encounter are those of possession of controlled drugs, the unlawful cultivation of cannabis plants, or persons occupying or managing premises knowingly permitting cannabis smoking, or preparing or smoking opium. The possession of controlled drugs has already been discussed.

The cultivation of cannabis plants is not uncommon. It will grow quite well in most parts of the British Isles and could be found anywhere. The word 'cultivate' indicates some form of labour in order to raise crops and, therefore, some positive act is required by an accused person either by planting or caring for the plant. It is probable that a mere omission on the part of the occupier of land to destroy plants planted by a previous occupier will be insufficient to merit a conviction. In such circumstances, the new occupier has carried out no positive act in the process of cultivation. If, however, he had done as little as to water the plant, this would be evidence of caring for the plant and this amounts to cultivation. Cannabis (except in the expression cannabis resin) means any plant of the genus *Cannabis*, or part of any such plant. The definition does not include the mature stalk, the stalk fibre or seeds once they have been separated from the plant.

499

Police powers

Search, seize, and detain

By s. 23 of the 1971 Act, if a constable has reasonable grounds to suspect that any person is in possession of a controlled drug in contravention of the provisions of the Act, he may:

(a) search that person and detain him for the purpose of searching him;

(b) search any vehicle or vessel in which the constable suspects that the drug may be found and for that purpose require the person in control to stop it;

(c) seize and detain, for the purpose of proceedings under the Misuse of Drugs Act 1971, anything found in the course of the search which appears to the constable to be evidence of an offence under the Act.

Other powers are given by the Act in relation to entry to inspect documents which are of little concern to most police officers and are well known to those who are concerned. A justice of the peace may issue a search warrant authorising entry to premises within one month, if satisfied by information on oath that controlled drugs are on the premises in the possession of any person, or there are documents connected with drug dealing.

The powers of the constable are dependent upon the words 'reasonable grounds to suspect' and in no way include the right to stop and search all persons encountered late at night in an effort to discover drug offences. Matters which afford reasonable grounds to suspect possession cannot be defined. There is no general right to search persons who are found by night in areas which drug users frequent. However, if their presence there is noted together with the fact that substances which have the appearance of being drugs, are being passed from one to another, this may give rise to a reasonable suspicion in the mind of the police officer concerned. It should be remembered that precise advice is given within the Code of Practice for the Exercise by Police Officers of Statutory Powers to Stop and Search. In essence, the suspicion must arise from the nature of the property observed, coupled with the significance of the time, place and suspicious behaviour of the person concerned. Suspicion must *not* be based upon the fact that person's membership of a group creates a higher than average chance that he may be in possession of controlled drugs. However, reasonable suspicion may exist as a result of information received from another party but this would depend upon the reliability of the person providing the information and the likelihood of that information being true in all the circumstances. The most important factor to bear in mind is that the Code requires the degree or level of suspicion which would justify arrest in any case.

Infection

Persons who are drug takers may be in the high risk category in relation to AIDS or hepatitis. Be careful when carrying out searches of such persons. The hand which is placed into a pocket risks being pierced by a dirty needle; the hand which is run over the outside of clothing is similarly at risk. The saliva or blood of an infected person must enter your body in order to contaminate you and this may occur through the eyes, mouth or any cut in the skin. Do not take unnecessary chances and if there is any form of contact about which you are concerned, ask to consult the police surgeon. It is advisable to wash carefully after contact with persons who may be infected.

Arrestable offences

The offences with which police officers are most likely to be concerned – i.e. possession of controlled drugs, possession with intent to supply another (drug pusher), the occupier or manager of premises permitting certain drug-taking activities on premises, supplying controlled drugs, or offering to supply them to another – are all arrestable offences regardless of the class of the controlled drug concerned, with the exception of possession of a Class C drug. As already discussed, the precise nature of the drug found in the possession of a particular person can only be established by analysis, but reasonable suspicion that an arrestable offence is being committed is sufficient to make an arrest lawful.

Drug trafficking offences

The Drug Trafficking Offences Act 1986 provides that where a person is sentenced at a Crown Court for one or more drug trafficking offences, if the prosecutor asks it to proceed under this section, or if the court considers that, even though the prosecutor has not asked it to do so, it is appropriate for it to so proceed, the court shall determine whether or not that person has benefited (payments received) from such drug trafficking and shall determine any amount to be recovered. The standard of proof required to determine such questions is that applicable to civil proceedings, that is the balance of probability. Where a court considers that it requires further information it may postpone the making of a determination.

The Act permits the court to assume that property held by that person since his conviction or within six years preceding the institution of proceedings was payment or reward in connection with drug trafficking. Such assumptions must be based on prima facie evidence which entitles that court to make that assumption. This will extend police enquiries considerably when persons are arrested for offences of drug trafficking, which include persons concerned in producing, supplying, transporting, storing, importing or exporting a controlled drug, whether in England and Wales or elsewhere. In the beginning the prosecutor is required to offer a statement of such dealings to the court. A copy of this statement must have been served on the accused and he may have accepted the facts set out in the statement totally or in part.

It is also an offence to assist a drug trafficker but the procedures related to confiscation of benefits do not apply to such a person. However, the High Court has ruled that there must be direct or inferential evidence that drugs have been sold for profit, a strong suspicion is not enough.

Solvent abuse

It is a summary offence contrary to the Intoxicating Substances (Supply) Act 1985 for a person to supply, or offer to supply, a substance other than a controlled drug to a person under 18 years whom he knows or has reasonable cause to believe to be under that age, or to a person who is acting on behalf of someone under 18, and whom he knows or has reasonable cause to believe to be so acting, if he knows or has reasonable cause to believe that the substance is, or its fumes are, likely to be inhaled by the person under 18 for the purpose of causing intoxication.

A person charged with supplying or offering may offer in defence that at the material time he was under 18 and was not acting in the course of furtherance of a business.

Control of alcohol at sporting events

Introduction

Dealing with crowds of people who could be described, at best, as being somewhat indifferent towards the laws of the land and towards the well-being of other members of the public, is perhaps the most difficult task which faces the police officer today. A person who shows little individual courage within his day-to-day life, becomes all that he would really like to be when submerged in the anonymity of a crowd of pretended football supporters. All of the advice and training offered to police officers which is concerned with dealing with the individual and the group, is of little purpose when the group has reached its fever pitch of excitement and has engaged itself within a course of conduct which at best could be described as a 'massive breach of the peace' and at worst a 'riot'. When such a stage has been reached, only the effective use of force will prevent a bad situation from becoming an impossible one.

Parliament has therefore directed its attention towards preventive measures calculated to decrease the likelihood of such a large-scale breach of the peace occurring at soccer matches. The provisions of the Sporting Events (Control of Alcohol, etc.) Act 1985 are aimed at the soccer hooligan. The provisions of that Act were extended by the Public Order Act 1986.

Designation of grounds and events

The Act is concerned with 'designated sporting events' which occur at 'designated sports grounds'.

A 'designated sports ground' is any place:

(a) used (wholly or partly) for sporting events where accommodation is provided for spectators; and
(b) for the time being designated, or of a class designated, by order made by the Home Secretary.

The Home Secretary has designated the home grounds of all football clubs which are members of the Football Association or the Football Association of Wales; and any other ground in England and Wales used occasionally or temporarily by such a club, grounds used for international matches; Wembley Stadium (which is not solely a football ground); and the ground of Berwick Rangers (specially mentioned because the Club plays in the Scottish League).

A 'designated sporting event' is any one of the following classes:

(a) (i) Association football matches in which one or both teams represent a Football League or a Football Association Premier League club;

(ii) International Association football matches, matches in the European Champion Clubs' Cup, European Cup Winners' or UEFA Cup;

provided that in each case the match takes place at the ground of an Association Football club which is a member of the Football Association or the Football Association of Wales, or at Wembley Stadium;

(b) Association football matches within the jurisdiction of the Scottish Football Association;

(c) Association football matches outside Great Britain:

(i) in which one or both teams represent the Football Association or Football Association of Wales or a Football League club (whether a full or associate member); or

(ii) in competition for the European Champion Clubs' Cup, European Cup Winners' Cup or UEFA Cup and one or both teams represent a club which is a member of the Football Association or the Football Association of Wales.

Similar provisions exist in Scotland by an Order of 1980. Rugby internationals at Murrayfield are also designated sporting events.

Permitted hours within designated sports grounds

The purpose of designating particular grounds and particular events is to apply special provisions of those grounds and events, which would not ordinarily apply. Section 3(1) of the 1985 Act states that permitted hours within licensed premises or registered clubs which are situated in designated sports grounds shall not include any part of the period of a designated sporting event at the ground, nor must there be any off-supply during that period. The period of a designated sporting event is the period beginning two hours before the start of the event or, if earlier, two hours before the time at which it is advertised to start, and ending one hour after that event. If a match is postponed or cancelled, the period includes the period in the day on which it is advertised to take place, beginning two hours before and ending one hour after that time. Thus, the Act prevents bars within these sports grounds from being open pre-match and after match. However, a magistrates' court is authorised by s. 3(2) to allow by order, supply in the premises (or part of those premises) subject to any conditions which the court may impose. Such an order must not apply to any part of the premises from which the designated sporting event may be directly viewed. There must be a condition requiring that a person must be in attendance throughout, who is responsible for compliance with the order. Such an order may be cancelled or varied and it expires on the coming into force of a further order, or after 12 months. In an emergency situation, where there is no time to refer the matter to a magistrates' court, the order may be temporarily cancelled or varied by written notice from a police inspector (or above) if he is of the opinion that such sale or supply is likely to be detrimental to the orderly conduct or safety of spectators at a particular designated sports event.

503

These provisions ensure that there is no public, or near-public bar open while spectators are present in designated grounds and attending designated events, other than bars from which there is no view of the match. Therefore a 'directors' bar', for example, could be open in a part of the ground from which the match could not be directly viewed. It could be watched on closed circuit television.

However, s. 5A permits variations in the case of private facilities for viewing these events. Sale, supply or possession of intoxicants is permitted in a room from which the event may be viewed, which is not open to the general public, at times other than within a 'restricted period' which is defined by that Act as a period which begins 15 minutes before the start of the event (or advertised start of the event if earlier) and ends 15 minutes after the end of the event. The same considerations apply in relation to postponed fixtures. The Secretary of State may by order shorten this restricted period or may abolish it. Drinking in the directors' box is, by these means, partially restored and may be fully restored by order.

Offences of selling, etc

A person who sells or supplies, or authorises the sale or supply of intoxicating liquor at a time which is excluded from the permitted hours by s. 3 of this Act, or in contravention of conditions imposed under s. 3(2) does not commit an offence under the Licensing Act 1964, s. 59(1)(a). He offends against the Sporting Events (Control of Alcohol, etc.) Act 1985, s. 3(10), if he is the holder of a justices' licence or an officer of the club. Any other person who sells or supplies in these circumstances is guilty of a similar offence if he knows or has reasonable cause to believe the sale or supply to be such a contravention.

Police powers

Section 6(1) of the Act provides that if at any time during the period of a designated sporting event at a designated sports ground, it appears to a constable in uniform that the sale or supply of intoxicating liquor at any bar within the ground is detrimental to the orderly conduct or safety of spectators, he may require the person having control of the bar, to close it and keep it closed until the end of that period. It is an offence to fail to comply with such a requirement.

A constable may enter *any part* of a designated sports ground during the period of a designated sporting event for the purpose of enforcing the provisions of the Act.

Travel to and from the ground

(1) *The vehicles concerned*

The provisions set out above are provided to prevent spectators from becoming intoxicated while at these sporting events. The Act also seeks to control the behaviour of supporters who are travelling to and from these grounds.

A person who knowingly causes or permits intoxicating liquor to be carried on a public service vehicle or railway passenger vehicle which is being used for the principal purpose of carrying passengers for the whole, or part of a journey, to or from a designated sporting event, is guilty of an offence against s. 1 of the 1985 Act. These provisions apply to the operators of public service vehicles, their servants or agents, and to the hirer of such vehicles, his servant or agent. Each person who is on such a vehicle, who has intoxicating liquor in his possession in such circumstances, commits an offence. It is also an offence to be drunk on such a public service or railway passenger vehicle. The prohibition created by the Act is concerned with travel to and from a designated sporting event, wherever it may be held. Thus, travel to soccer matches which are being played abroad is subject to these provisions if the match is one of those specified, i.e. one of the teams involved represents the Football Association (including that of Wales) or a Football League club, or the match is in competition for one of the European cups and one of the teams represents those Football Associations. As association football matches within the jurisdiction of the Scottish Football Association are also designated sporting events, the 'travel' provisions also apply to such matches.

Section 1A applies these provisions to motor vehicles which are not public service vehicles, but are adapted to carry more than eight passengers, and are being used for the principal purpose of carrying *two or more* passengers for the whole or part of a journey to or from a designated sporting event. The same offences apply; but it is the driver or keeper or the servant or agent of the keeper, or the person to whom the vehicle is made available (by hire, loan or otherwise), or his servant or agent who commits the offence of causing or permitting intoxicating liquor to be carried. This extension is to embrace the use of owned or hired 'Transit' type vehicles which are used for the conveyance of soccer supporters.

Possession of intoxicants by an individual within the vehicle is an offence by that individual. A person who is drunk on such a vehicle is guilty of an offence.

(2) The person who 'causes or permits'

Section 1(2) provides that a person who knowingly causes or permits intoxicating liquor to be carried on a vehicle to which s. 1 applies is guilty of an offence:

(a) if the vehicle is a public service vehicle and he is the operator of the vehicle or the employee or agent of the operator; or

(b) if the vehicle is hired (e.g. a chartered train or football special) and he is the person to whom it is hired or the employee or agent of that person.

It can be seen, therefore, that the secretary of a supporters' club or some other person who hires a vehicle on the club's behalf is guilty of an offence if he permits intoxicating liquor to be carried on the vehicle or passenger train.

Section 1(2A) provides that a person who *knowingly* causes or permits intoxicating liquor to be carried on a motor vehicle to which s. 1A applies is guilty of an offence:

(a) if he is the driver; or

(b) if he is not the driver but its keeper, the servant or agent of its keeper, a person to whom it is made available (by hire, or loan or otherwise) by its keeper or the keeper's servant or agent, or the servant or agent of the person to whom it is made available.

The act must be carried out *knowingly* and it must therefore be proved that the accused actually knew of the presence of intoxicating liquor or was wilfully blind to the fact. In the case of responsible persons present in the vehicle, the open carriage or drinking of intoxicants will provide such proof.

Police powers

Section 7 permits a constable to stop a vehicle to which s. 1 or s. 1A applies and to search that vehicle or a railway passenger vehicle if he has reasonable grounds to suspect that an offence of possession of intoxicants, or one of drunkenness, is being or has been committed in respect of the vehicle. Thus, a 'football special' upon which there is seen to be drinking, or upon which such drinking is suspected, may be stopped and searched. The power to search vehicles is restricted to a search *for intoxicants*. This is important. The Act also provides a power to arrest without warrant for offences under the Act. It would not be an offence under this Act to possess 'articles' (see below) on such a vehicle. A constable may, therefore, arrest those who are drunk, or those who are in possession of intoxicants upon such a vehicle. 'Reasonable grounds to suspect' such offences will be those as described in the Code of Practice.

At the ground

(1) *Possession of articles*

Section 2 of the 1985 Act is concerned with the designated sports ground itself and its provisions are mainly related to intoxicating liquor or 'articles' as defined by the Act. (See page 502 for meaning of designated sports ground.)

An article is, for the purposes of the Act, any article capable of causing injury to a person struck by it, being:

(a) a bottle, can or other portable container (including such an article when crushed or broken) which:
   (i) is holding any drink; and
   (ii) is of a kind which, when empty, is normally discarded or returned to, or left to be recovered by, the supplier; or
(b) part of any article described above.

However, the definition expressly does not apply to anything which is for holding any medicinal product.

Section 2A(1) extends the definition of 'article' to include articles or substances whose main purpose is the emission of a flare for purposes of illuminating or signalling (as opposed to igniting or heating) or the emission of smoke or visible gas; and in particular to distress flares, fog signals and pellets or capsules intended to be used as fumigators or for testing pipes but *not* matches, cigarette lighters or heaters. It is a defence to prove 'lawful authority'.

(2) *Offences of possession*

It is an offence for a person while entering, or trying to enter a designated sports ground at any time during the period of a designated sporting event, to have intoxicating liquor or an article to which the Act refers, in his possession. Similarly, it is an offence to have intoxicating liquor or an article in one's possession at any time during the period of a designated sporting event when in any area of a designated sports ground from which the event may be directly viewed. The only places in which intoxicants could be lawfully possessed, therefore, are those bars such as 'directors' bars', from which there is no direct view of the game, or where there are private viewing facilities.

These are useful provisions. Any form of intoxicating liquor is banned from spectator areas, as are 'articles capable of causing injury' if they are 'empties' of a disposable kind and most pyrotechnic devices. An empty beer bottle is certainly capable of causing injury, but it is doubtful if an empty beer can (which is made of aluminium), would do so in its original form. If such a can is crushed, it becomes a more effective and harmful missile and may well be capable of causing injury. The article must be of a disposable kind, so that the spectator who is in possession of an expensive 'hip flask' is not in possession of an article within the meaning of this Act. However, if the flask contains intoxicants, he is guilty of possessing intoxicants. Pyrotechnic devices include all those which cause danger or nuisance to persons.

Police powers

A constable may search a person he has reasonable grounds to suspect is committing or has committed *an offence under the Act* and may arrest such a person. The Act therefore provides wide powers of search and arrest. It must be remembered that the term 'reasonable grounds to suspect' is now quite precisely defined in Annex B to the Code of Practice for the Exercise by Police Officers of Statutory Powers to Stop and Search. Although reasonable suspicion does not amount to certainty, it must be founded on fact. There must be a concrete basis for the officer's suspicion which is related to the individual concerned. A constable is not entitled to search soccer supporters who are entering a sports ground because he suspects that football fans, generally, take intoxicants into football matches. However, if the constable noticed the distinctive bulge of a 'four-pack' in a spectator's pocket, it is submitted that this would be reasonable. The suspicion is related to an individual and there is a concrete basis for the officer's suspicion. Note 1D to the Code of Practice says:

> 'nothing in this code affects the routine searching of persons entering sports grounds or other premises with their consent, or as a condition of entry.'

There is no doubt that this note of guidance was added because of public concern over soccer hooliganism but it is submitted that it is unhelpful. A search, with a person's genuine consent, a consent which is freely given, is quite lawful but this would not realistically occur outside a sports ground. If fans submit to a search, they do so because they believe that police officers have a right to search them in such circumstances. A search as a condition of entry into the ground must be a matter between the proprietor of the ground and his intended customer. As such, any search must be carried out by some person other than a police officer. The position is no different if the proprietor is paying for the services of the police officer. It is no part of an officer's duty to enforce the rights of proprietors.

The police powers under this Act are very wide, extending to the stopping of 'football specials' where there is reasonable suspicion of there being intoxicants, or drunken persons, aboard. Search powers extend to those occasions; to entry or attempted entry to the ground; and within the ground itself (for both intoxicating liquor *and* articles in relation to the ground itself). The power to arrest extends to reasonable grounds to suspect that *any* offence under the Act is being committed or has been committed.

Exclusion orders

Section 30 of the Public Order Act 1986 empowers a court by or before which a person is convicted of certain offences to make an exclusion order prohibiting him from entering any premises for the purpose of attending any prescribed football match there. The court must be satisfied that the making of such an order in relation to the accused will help to prevent violence or disorder at or in connection with prescribed football matches. Thus, an order is unlikely to be made where an elderly gentleman is convicted of possessing whisky in a hip flask at a soccer match. The order must be *additional* to a sentence, probation order or order of conditional or absolute discharge. A 'prescribed football match' is one involving a football league or Football Association Premier League team, an international, or European Champion Clubs' Cup, Cup Winners' Cup or UEFA Cup.

The section applies to any offence which fulfils one or more of the following conditions:

(a) an offence committed during the period of a designated sporting event, while at, entering or leaving or trying to enter or leave, a football ground; or

(b) the offence involved the use or threat of violence by the accused towards another person while one or each was on a journey to or from an association football match; a threat towards property while on such a journey; or an offence which was committed under s. 5 (harassment, alarm or distress) or Part III of the Act (racial hatred); or

(c) offence was one of possessing intoxicants on prohibited vehicles on a journey to such association football matches.

For the purpose of such orders the term 'journey' in its relationship to these offences includes breaks in the journey, including overnight breaks. An order must be for a period of at least three months. If an order has been in force for at least a year, there may be an application for cancellation.

A person who enters any premises in breach of such an order commits a summary offence punishable by imprisonment for a term not exceeding one month, or a fine or both.

Restriction orders: football spectators

The Football Spectators Act 1989 provides that persons convicted of relevant offences may be made subject to a 'restriction order'. Restriction orders are concerned with attendance at designated football matches outside England and Wales. Exclusion orders are inapplicable to matches abroad as our courts have no power to exclude persons from football grounds outside the United Kingdom. No restriction order may be made unless a court is satisfied that making it in relation to the accused would help to prevent violence or disorder at or in connection with designated football matches outside England and Wales. Persons made subject to restriction orders are required to report to a specified police station within five days of the making of the order. Such orders may only be made in addition to a sentence or probation order.

Subsequently, such persons may be made to report to a police station on the occasion of a designated football match at such times as are specified in a notice sent by the 'enforcing authority', which is the Football Spectators Restriction Orders Authority, a body set up as a police common service. Persons so required to report may apply for exemption and it is likely that they will make such an application by attending the police station at which they are required to report. Such matters must be referred to the officer responsible for the police station who will liaise with the enforcing authority.

Persons who commit offences associated with matches outside England and Wales which 'correspond' with relevant offences may be dealt with by a magistrates' court in England and Wales for the purpose of making a restriction order.

'Relevant offences' are those contrary to the Sporting Events (Control of Alcohol, etc.) Act 1985; those involving violence or threats of violence, harassment, alarm or distress, or racial hatred; those involving violence or threats of violence against property; drunkenness; offences contrary to the Road Traffic Act 1988, s. 4 or 5 (drinking and driving offences), committed while the accused was on a journey to or from such a match; offences involving the use or threat of violence by an accused towards another person while one or each of them was on a journey to or from a designated football match, or towards property, these offences being 'relevant' to the match; and offences against the Football (Offences) Act 1991.

Where it is relevant in the above that the offence was committed while on a journey to or from a designated football match, a 'designated football match' includes one in this country or one outside England and Wales and a restriction order can only be made if the court declares that the offence related to football matches. Designation of football matches has been made under the 1989 Act by two orders. By the Football Spectators (Designation of Football Matches in England and Wales) Order 1993 a football match is designated if it is played either at Wembley Stadium, the National Stadium at Cardiff, or at any sports ground in England and Wales which is registered with the Football League or the Football Association Premier League at the time the match is played. The Football Spectators (Designation of Football Matches Outside England and Wales) Order 1990 designates away international matches involving Football Association National sides; matches outside England and Wales involving full or associate member clubs of the Football League or the Football Association Premier League; or matches involving club sides participating in UEFA competitions outside England and Wales.

A person who, without reasonable excuse, fails to comply with the duty to report imposed by a restriction order, commits an offence. A constable who reasonably suspects that a person has entered premises in breach of an exclusion or restriction order may arrest him without warrant.

Misbehaviour at a designated football match

The Football (Offences) Act 1991 creates a number of offences. They can only be committed at a 'designated football match'. Such matches are designated by the Football (Offences) (Designation of Football Matches) Order 1991. The order designates any association football match played in England and Wales which is a UEFA match, which involves a football league or FA Premier League team or a team representing any country or territory, and which is played at a designated sports ground or one occupied by a team in one of the two leagues.

Reference in the Act to things done at a designated football match includes anything done there in the period beginning two hours before the start of the match or (if earlier) two hours before the advertised start time and ending one hour after the end of the match. If the match does not take place, the period is two hours before the advertised start time until one hour after that time.

(1) *Throwing objects*

The Football Offences Act 1991, s. 2, creates offences of throwing anything at or towards:

(a) the playing area or any area adjacent to the playing area to which spectators are not generally admitted; or

(b) any area in which spectators or other persons are or may be present;

without lawful authority or excuse (which it is for the accused to prove).

Thus, those who throw objects on to the pitch, into the players' tunnel, etc., or into spectator areas, will commit offences. Those who may prove 'lawful authority or excuse' would include vendors who throw packets of crisps, etc., into the crowd, or spectators who throw money to such persons.

(2) *Chanting*

Section 3 of the 1991 Act makes it an offence to take part in 'chanting' of an indecent or racist nature. 'Chanting' means the repeated uttering of words or sounds in concert with one or more others and 'racist nature' means consisting of or including matter which is threatening, abusive or insulting to a person by reason of his colour, race, nationality (including citizenship) or ethnic or national origin.

(3) *Pitch invasion*

By s. 4, it is an offence for a person to go on to the playing area, or any area adjacent to the playing area to which spectators are not generally admitted, without lawful authority or lawful excuse (which it is for the accused to prove).

This offence could be interesting in circumstances in which spectators surge forward on to the pitch. Most will contend that they were carried forward unwillingly by the momentum of the crowd. However, if this is so, it is submitted that they should be able to establish that they retreated from the playing area at the first opportunity. However, such an incident is not likely where all spectators are

510

seated. Those who would have lawful excuse for going on to the pitch would include trainers and official first aiders.

The Criminal Justice and Public Order Act 1994, s. 166 provides that it is an offence for an unauthorised person to sell, or offer or expose for sale, a ticket for a designated football match in any public place, place to which the public has access, or in any other place in the course of a trade or business. An authorised person must be authorised in writing by the home club or the organisers of the match. The section also provides that the powers of search of persons and premises (including vehicles) upon arrest under the Police and Criminal Evidence Act 1984 shall apply as if the power to enter and search any vehicle extended to any vehicle which the constable has reasonable grounds was being used for a purpose connected with the offence.

This is an arrestable offence under the amended provisions of s. 24(2) of the 1984 Act.

Firearms

The Firearms Act 1968 deals with, among other things, the sale, transfer and possession of firearms. Such sales and transfers are prohibited, other than those carried out in accordance with the provisions of the Act. The failure to comply with instructions in a firearm certificate when transferring a firearm to a person other than a registered dealer, or the failure to report that transaction to the police, is an arrestable offence. Within the United Kingdom, only a minority of firearms (mainly air weapons) may be possessed without authority. It is one of the functions of chief officers of police to control possession of firearms by issuing various forms of certificates and permits to those who have sufficient reason to possess firearms.

Explanation of terms

(1) *Firearm*

A firearm is a lethal barrelled weapon of any description from which any shot, bullet or other missile can be discharged. The term also includes:

(a) any prohibited weapon, whether it is a lethal weapon or not;
(b) any component part of such a lethal or prohibited weapon; and
(c) any accessory designed or adapted to diminish the noise or flash caused by firing the weapon.

The first important word within this definition is 'lethal', and the High Court has ruled that it will include a weapon which is not designed to kill or inflict injury, but is capable of doing so if it is misused. This decision was made after considering the status of a Very light pistol, which is designed to give a distress signal but is capable of killing. Most air weapons are likely to cause only minor injuries, but if they are capable of causing serious injury they may be classified as 'lethal' and if they are so capable, they may be declared to be specially dangerous.

511

A prohibited weapon is:

(a) any firearm which is so designed or adapted that two or more missiles can be successively discharged without repeated pressure on the trigger;

    (ab) any self-loading or pump-action rifle other than one which is chambered for .22 rim-fire cartridges;

    (ac) any self-loading or pump-action smooth-bore gun which is not chambered for .22 rim-fire cartridges and either has a barrel less than 24 inches in length or (excluding any detachable, folding, retractable or other moveable butt-stock) is less than 40 inches in length overall;

    (ad) any smooth-bore revolver gun other than one which is chambered for 9 mm rim-fire cartridges or loaded at the muzzle end of each chamber;

    (ae) any rocket launcher, or any mortar, for projecting a stabilised missile, other than a launcher or mortar designed for line-throwing or pyrotechnic purposes or as signalling apparatus.

(b) any weapon of whatever description designed or adapted for the discharge of any noxious liquid, gas or other thing; and

(c) any cartridge with a bullet designed to explode on or immediately before impact, any ammunition containing or designed or adapted to contain any such noxious thing as is mentioned in paragraph (b) above and, if capable of being used with a firearm of any description, any grenade, bomb (or other like missile), or rocket or shell designed to explode as aforesaid.

It is important to remember when considering prohibited weapons of a type used for the discharge of a noxious liquid, gas or other thing, that such weapons, to be prohibited, must have been 'designed or adapted' for that purpose. A water pistol is designed to eject water and its design purpose does not change simply because someone puts acid in it. The same applies to a 'Fairy Liquid' bottle.

The fact that a 'stun-gun' designed for the discharge of an electrical charge is not working due to some unknown fault, does not change its character as a prohibited weapon.

Section 5(1A) was added to the 1968 Act and specifically prohibits the sale, transfer, purchase, acquisition or possession of a weapon 'prohibited' by the section, except with the authority of the Secretary of State for Defence. It prohibits any firearm which is *disguised as another object* and any launcher or other projecting apparatus designed to be used with any rocket or ammunition which is designed to explode on or immediately before impact. In relation to these weapons and ammunition, there are a number of exemptions which are concerned primarily with collectors and use in connection with slaughtering animals, sporting purposes, shooting vermin, estate management purposes, and competition and target shooting purposes.

A component part of a weapon is some part which is essential to its functioning as a firearm. A telescopic sight is not a component part as the weapon would function without it, whereas the trigger mechanism is such a part as the firearm could not function without it. It is for the courts to decide whether or not a particular weapon is a firearm for the purposes of the Act, but a decision of the High Court ruled that a dummy revolver, which could be readily converted into a lethal firearm by boring through a solid barrel, consisted of component parts of a firearm and fell within the definition. Some starting pistols are outside this definition as they are incapable of conversion, while others, with small modifications, can be made to kill. Where there may be doubts concerning whether a weapon may be 'lethal barrelled' it is useful to recognise that it is as essential to be authorised to possess a component part, as it is to possess the whole weapon.

Noise and flash eliminators would not be component parts as defined because a weapon would function as a firearm without them, and Parliament has, therefore, found it necessary specifically to include them because of their nature. They have no other purpose than to allow firearms to be used without the user being detected.

(2) *Ammunition*

Ammunition means ammunition for any firearm and includes grenades, bombs, and other like missiles whether capable of use with a firearm or not; it also includes prohibited ammunition.

This definition is extremely wide and includes all forms of ammunition, including blank cartridges, for use with guns and, because the purpose of the Firearms Act 1968 is to prevent sections of the public from arming themselves in any way (unless they can show cause for doing so), includes other offensive explosive devices such as grenades and bombs. Prohibited ammunition is ammunition which contains noxious substances. A 'bomb' is any explosive substance in a case, or a case containing poisonous gas, smoke, or flammable material which might be dropped from an aircraft, fired from a gun or thrown or placed by hand.

Certain ammunition is 'prohibited' including bullets which are designed to explode on, or immediately before impact (e.g. dum-dum bullet), ammunition containing, or designed or adapted to contain any noxious liquid, gas or other thing and, if capable of being used with any firearm, any grenade, bomb or other like missile, or a rocket or shell designed to explode on or immediately before impact.

Section 5(1A) makes specific prohibitions in respect of similar military rockets and ammunition; military ammunition which ignites on or immediately before impact; military armour piercing ammunition; expanding bullets for use with pistols and similar prohibited ammunition designed to be projected as a missile.

(3) *Public place*

A public place for the purposes of this Act includes any highway and any other premises or place to which, at the material time, the public have or are permitted to have access, whether on payment or otherwise.

Classification

The Firearms Act 1968 controls the purchase of and the possession of firearms by members of the public. It can be appreciated that having defined, in the broadest sense, those weapons which are firearms and those things which are ammunition, the law begins to make provisions in respect of different types of firearms. There can be no reason for a member of the public to possess a sub-machine gun, so it is declared to be a prohibited weapon and cannot be possessed by the public. There are many

513

different types of rifles and although members of the public may not be encouraged to own some of them, there are many sporting uses to which rifles and revolvers can be put, and considerable enjoyment can be experienced by enthusiasts. Ownership of such weapons is not, therefore, prohibited, but it is carefully controlled and persons wishing to possess them must show sufficient reason for doing so. Shotguns are perhaps less offensive, being primarily designed for sporting purposes, but when it was lawful to buy and possess such weapons without any form of control, they were found to be increasingly used by criminals and control became essential. Air weapons are not usually a danger to life but can become so in the hands of young people. There is no control over the purchase or possession of such weapons generally, but there are restrictions in relation to young people.

In effecting different forms of control, the Act divides firearms into three groups for practical purposes. We shall examine each in turn.

Firearms and ammunition controlled by Section 1 of the Act

Section 1 applies to all firearms except:

(a) a shotgun within the meaning of this Act, that is to say a smooth-bore gun (not being an air gun) which:
   (i) has a barrel not less than 24 inches in length and does not have any barrel with a bore exceeding 2 inches in diameter;
   (ii) either has no magazine or has a non-detachable magazine incapable of holding more than two cartridges; and
   (iii) is not a revolver gun; and
(b) air weapons (air gun, air pistol, or air rifle, not declared specially dangerous under rules made by the Secretary of State);

and to all ammunition except:

(a) cartridge containing five or more shot, none of which exceeds 0.36 inch diameter;
(b) ammunition for air weapons; and
(c) blank cartridges not more than 1 inch in diameter.

This section applies to all firearms which are particularly dangerous, merely omitting some shotguns, air weapons, and their ammunition. It declares that it is an offence for a person:

(a) to have in his possession, or to purchase or acquire, such a firearm or ammunition without having a firearm certificate in force, or otherwise than as authorised by the certificate; or
(b) to fail to comply with a condition subject to which a certificate is granted.

(1) Possession

It is not essential that a person has physical custody of a firearm to have it in his possession. A person who keeps a firearm in his home, or in a desk at his office, remains in possession of that weapon no matter where he may be. The offence is one of strict liability, so much so, that a person can be in possession of a firearm even though he is unaware that he has control of it. If a man briefly has custody of a grip containing a firearm and does not consider the nature of its contents, he is nevertheless in possession of them. Brevity of possession, or lack of knowledge of the contents is no defence. The nature of the legislation is deliberately strict.

(2) *Control of possession*

(a) *A firearm certificate.* A certificate for a firearm controlled by s. 1 of the Act is granted by the chief officer of police for the area and is valid for five years. An application form must be completed and it is an offence to make any statement known to be false for the purpose of obtaining a certificate. Similar provisions and offences apply to applications for shotgun certificates (see below). Chief officers of police will only grant certificates if they are satisfied that the applicant has a good reason for requiring a firearm and can be permitted to have it in his possession without danger to the public safety or peace. Persons who are prohibited from possessing firearms, or who are of intemperate habits or of unsound mind or are considered for any reason unfitted to be entrusted with a firearm, should be refused.

A person who is under 18 who applies for such a certificate is capable of having a good reason for possessing it *only* if he has no intention of using it for a purpose other than a purpose authorised by the European Firearms Directive. An authorised purpose is a sporting purpose, the shooting of vermin, a purpose related to estate management activities, competition or target shooting.

If the grant of a certificate is not precluded by any of these factors, chief officers will consider whether or not the applicant has a good reason for requiring the firearm or ammunition in respect of which the application is made, and if the use of the firearm in the manner described in the application can be permitted without danger to the public. Police officers make enquiries at the direction of their chief officer of police to determine the general reputation of the applicant to ensure that he is not given to bouts of irrational behaviour, to examine the secure place in which it is intended that the firearm will be kept, and to ensure that the reason given for wishing to possess the firearm is genuine. If it is intended to shoot over land, the officer will ensure that this can be done without danger to the public.

The certificate issued by the chief of police will identify the serial number of the particular weapon which the holder may possess, and if this information is not available at the time of application it will be added to the certificate at a later date. Conditions may be imposed restricting the use of the firearm; for example, if it is the applicant's wish to shoot over open land, conditions may be made limiting use to a certain area of land. In such instances, if the area over which the applicant wishes to shoot is to be changed, he must apply to the chief officer of police for variation of this certificate, and this provides a further opportunity to have land assessed with a view to ensuring public safety. It is unusual for conditions to be attached to certificates held by persons who regularly use firearms in the course of their employment, such as

515

gamekeepers, RSPCA inspectors, and recognised sportsmen who are used to handling firearms and appreciate the general rules to be observed.

Ammunition is carefully controlled. Applicants for certificates are required to state the total amount of ammunition which they are likely to use in the course of a year, the maximum amount which they would wish to purchase on any occasion and the maximum to be in their possession at any one time. Conditions are attached to the grant of the certificate controlling the sale and use of ammunition. If the amounts applied for appear to a chief officer of police to be excessive, the conditions imposed will limit the purchase, possession, and use of ammunition to a reasonable level.

(b) *Shotgun certificate*. Shotguns are controlled in a similar way: s. 2 of the Act states that it is an offence for a person to have in his possession, or purchase or acquire, a shotgun without holding a certificate authorising him to do so. A shotgun certificate shall specify the description of the shotguns to which it relates including, if known, the identification numbers of the guns. Although ammunition sales are not strictly controlled in terms of quantity, it is an offence to sell ammunition to a person who is not a registered firearms dealer, or a person who sells such ammunition by way of trade or business, unless that person produces a shotgun certificate, or shows that he is exempt from the necessity to hold one, or produces someone else's certificates with that person's written authority to purchase ammunition on his behalf.

It is an offence to shorten the length of the barrel of any shotgun. When the barrel has been so shortened to less than 24 inches, it is no longer a shotgun for the purposes of the Firearms Act and becomes a firearm to which s. 1 applies. A firearm certificate, rather than a shotgun certificate, would then be required to authorise its possession. It is difficult to imagine any lawful use which could be made of such a weapon, and the grant of a firearm certificate is most improbable.

The Firearms (Amendment) Act 1988 creates an offence of shortening the barrel of any smooth bore gun to which s. 1 of the Act of 1968 applies, to a length less than 24 inches, other than a gun which has a barrel with a bore exceeding 2 inches in diameter. Therefore pump-action and revolver-type shotguns are similarly protected.

A person who is under 18 who applies for such a certificate is capable of having a good reason for possessing it *only* if he has no intention of using it for a purpose other than an authorised purpose (see page 515). It has been held that when deciding whether to revoke a shotgun certificate, a chief constable is entitled to take into account irresponsible conduct by the holder which does not involve the use of the shotgun. It is a matter for the chief constable's discretion to what extent he should investigate a particular offence.

(c) *A permit to possess*. On occasions, some form of authority is required for a person to hold a firearm or shotgun for a relatively short period of time, usually to permit disposal. If the holder of a firearm certificate dies, his widow may wish to sell the weapon, but from the moment she becomes the owner she must have some authority to possess it. Chief officers of police are authorised to issue permits in such circumstances, giving details of the weapon and ammunition. The expiry date must be shown and it is unusual to issue permits valid for longer than one month.

Exemptions

There are certain exemptions from the necessity to hold either a firearm certificate or a shotgun certificate:

(a) Persons carrying a weapon belonging to another person who is the holder of a certificate which is to be used for sporting purposes by some other person. Such a person might be described as 'gun bearer'. He is not authorised to use the weapon.

(b) Possession at a miniature rifle range, usually at a side show, provided that only rifles and ammunition not more 0.23 inch calibre are used. (These provisions may also apply to rifle clubs.) The owner is entitled to purchase and possess weapons for such use. (Weapons in his possession are recorded.)

(c) Starters at athletic meetings may possess firearms without a certificate for the purpose of starting races only but cannot possess ammunition other than blanks not exceeding 1 inch in diameter.

(d) Persons taking part in theatrical performances, rehearsals, or films may possess a firearm without a certificate during such events (not ammunition).

(e) Firearms dealers do not require certificates for guns in their possession in the course of business, but if a dealer wished to possess one for his own use for sporting purposes, a certificate would be required. He is required to register as a dealer with the chief officer of police and must keep records of firearms and ammunition in his possession. However, this exemption only applies to firearms and ammunition kept on registered premises.

(f) Persons in the service of the Crown and police may possess firearms in their capacity as such.

(g) Auctioneers, carriers, warehousemen and their servants may frequently be required to handle firearms in the course of their business, and this is permitted without a certificate. They must take reasonable precautions for safe custody and report forthwith to the police any theft or loss.

(h) Slaughtering instruments, and ammunition for them, may be possessed by a licensed slaughterman without the necessity for a firearm certificate.

(i) Firearms may be possessed as part of a ship's equipment without a certificate being in force, and may be removed from the ship on the authority of a police permit.

(j) Signalling apparatus on aircraft or at an aerodrome, for example, Very light pistols, may be held without a certificate.

(k) A member of an approved cadet corps may possess a firearm and ammunition when engaged as such a member in, or in connection with, drill or target practice.

(l) A member of an approved rifle club, miniature rifle club or pistol club may possess a firearm and ammunition when engaged as such a member in, or in connection with, target practice. An approval of a club may be subject to limitation to specified weapons.

517

Although at first sight this list of exemptions appears to be very difficult to memorise, the items are more easily remembered by recalling instances in which firearms have been seen in the possession of various persons in the course of their trade or business. There are further exceptions in relation to shotguns which may be possessed without a shotgun certificate:

(a) guests and other persons who are loaned shotguns by the occupier of private land, for use on that land in the occupier's presence;
(b) clay pigeon shoots approved by the chief officer of police;
(c) visitors to Great Britain who have not been here for more than 30 days in the preceding 12 months.

The Firearms (Amendment) Act 1988 permits a person of or over the age of 17 to borrow a rifle from the occupier of private premises, without such person holding a firearm certificate, for use on those premises in the presence of the occupier or his servant provided that the person accompanying the borrower holds a firearm certificate in respect of that rifle and the borrower's possession and use of it complies with any conditions as to those matters specified in the certificate.

The 1988 Act also makes provision for 'visitors' permits' for both s. 1 firearms and shotguns.

In addition, the Firearms Acts (Amendment) Regulations 1992 introduced provisions which permit the issue of a European Firearms Pass to citizens of a member State. The holders of such passes are entitled to be in possession of the firearm or firearms specified within that pass. The pass will record the authorisation given by the State such person is visiting. Such a pass must be produced on demand by a constable.

Police powers

Since the Criminal Justice and Public Order Act 1994, all offences of possession of s. 1 firearms or shotguns without having a certificate are arrestable offences, as are offences of possessing or distributing prohibited weapons, and offences selling firearms to another person who does not have a certificate.

Air weapons

Air weapons operate by the release of compressed air. They contain no explosive charge. No form of certificate is required to authorise possession unless the particular weapon has been declared by the Secretary of State to be specially dangerous. If so, the weapon become a s. 1 firearm.

Offences

(1) *Carrying a firearm in a public place*

A person commits an offence against s. 19 of the 1968 Act if, without lawful authority or reasonable excuse (the proof whereof lies upon him), he has with him in a public place a loaded shotgun or loaded air weapon, or any other firearm whether loaded or not, together with ammunition suitable for use in that firearm. A certificate for a firearm and ammunition is not in itself lawful authority for a holder to have the firearm and ammunition in a public place. This is an arrestable offence.

There are certain points which require amplification. Although lawful authority or reasonable excuse for possession must be established by the person charged, this burden is less than that placed upon the prosecution, who are required to prove all matters beyond reasonable doubt. If it appears that a reason put forward by an accused is probably correct, this will be sufficient. There will be occasions upon which there can be a reasonable excuse for carrying a loaded shotgun in a public place and it must be recognised that possession of a shotgun certificate is irrelevant in relation to this offence.

A gamekeeper who is merely crossing a public road in the course of his duties might be considered to have such an excuse, but the courts are unlikely to place any wider interpretation upon the term 'reasonable excuse'. Even in that event, the justices may feel that a professional gamekeeper should have known better and, therefore, did not have a reasonable excuse. While a person who is going to a rifle club for the purpose of target practice might be considered to have such an excuse for possession of his rifle and ammunition, much will depend upon the club rules. If the rules of the club insist that ammunition is left in a secure place within the club premises, a court may consider that such a person did not have a reasonable excuse for such possession. An air weapon is loaded for the purposes of this section if there is a missile which is available for discharge in the weapon, although the necessary compression is *not* yet present, and in the case of either a shotgun or an air weapon having a loaded magazine, it shall be treated as loaded even though there is no round in the breech. The aim of this section is to prevent criminals from having weapons in their possession in public places in a state of readiness. The offence is a serious one if the loaded weapon is a shotgun and is punishable by five years' imprisonment if tried on indictment.

This section uses the term 'has with him' not the word 'possession'. However, this does not mean that he has the firearm and/or ammunition on his person, but he must have a close personal link with it and it must be readily accessible to him. This could be so where they are in a bag which he is carrying, or in the glove compartment of a car which he is driving, or where the car has been parked sufficiently close to make the weapon readily accessible. It has been held that a person has a firearm with him if it is readily available to him when he is committing a robbery. The emphasis should not be so much upon the exact distance between the criminals and the guns but rather on the accessibility of those guns judged in a common-sense way in the context of criminals embarking on a joint enterprise.

(2) *Trespassing with a firearm*

A person commits an offence against s. 20 if, while he has a firearm or imitation firearm with him, he enters or is in any building or part of a building or on any land as a trespasser, without reasonable excuse; the proof of which lies on him.

In this offence the words 'lawful authority' are omitted, as such authority would prevent the entry from becoming a trespass. It is immaterial whether or not the firearm is loaded, or if ammunition is carried, as the essence of these offences is that

519

the presence of such a person as a trespasser is made more ominous by his possession of firearms. The expression 'land' includes water. If the trespass is upon buildings, the offence is more serious and can be tried on indictment.

Where the weapon possessed is an air weapon it is necessary to show that it is one from which a shot could be fired, or was one which could be adapted to do so and that it was 'lethal barrelled'. The offence is an arrestable offence.

General police powers

(1) Production – handing over of firearms

Section 47(1) of the Firearms Act 1968 authorises a constable to require any person whom he has reasonable cause to suspect:

(a) of having a firearm, with or without ammunition, with him in a public place; or

(b) to be committing or about to commit, elsewhere than in a public place, an offence of 'having with him' a firearm or imitation firearm with intent to commit an indictable offence or to resist arrest or an offence of trespassing with a firearm,

to hand over the firearm or ammunition for examination. It is an offence to fail to hand over the firearm when required to do so.

The purpose of subs. (1) of s. 47 is to enable a constable to require a firearm to be handed over for his examination so that he may establish its type and, therefore, what type of authority should be held to authorise its possession. In the case of a shotgun or air weapon carried in a public place, he will also wish to establish whether or not it is loaded.

(2) Stop and search

Subsection (3) of s. 47 authorises a constable to search persons reasonably suspected of having firearms in public places, buildings, parts of buildings, or on land and to detain them for that purpose. This power is an extension of that above. After the person concerned has failed to hand over a firearm which he is suspected of possessing, the power to search can be exercised. The power of search is extended by subs. (4) to vehicles, and constables, by subs. (5), may enter any place to exercise these powers.

(3) Production of certificates

Following the probable process of enquiry, a person may fail to hand over a firearm at (1) above which he is suspected of possessing, and his actual possession can only be established by exercising the search powers outlined at (2) above. Having established that the person is in possession of a firearm, the Act must give a constable power to determine whether or not the person is authorised to possess a weapon of the type produced. Section 48 provides:

(a) A constable may demand, from any person whom he believes to be in possession of a firearm or ammunition to which s. 1 applies, or of any shotgun, the production of his firearm certificate or shotgun certificate.

(b) If such a person fails to produce his certificate, or to permit the constable to read it, or to show that he is exempt from the necessity to hold a certificate, the constable may seize the firearm or ammunition and require such person to give his name and address.

(c) It is an offence for a person to refuse or fail to give his true name and address.

An added s. 48(1A) provides that where a constable has made a demand under s. 48 and there is a failure to produce the relevant certificate and that person fails to show that he is not a person entitled to receive a European Firearms Pass, or to show that he is a recognised collector of a another member State, he may demand the production of a European Firearms Pass. It is an offence for the holder of such a document to fail to comply with such a demand. The powers of seizure, etc., then apply.

(4) *Search with warrant*

A justice of the peace may issue a search warrant under s. 46 if satisfied by information on oath that there are reasonable grounds for suspecting that an offence has been committed against the Act except offences relating to air weapons or possession of an uncovered shotgun by an unsupervised person under 15 years of age – and to seize and detain firearms, imitation firearms and ammunition in respect of which an offence is reasonably suspected to have been committed or to be about to be committed.

Children and young persons

It is an offence for a person under the age of 17 to purchase or hire *any* firearm or ammunition. Persons under 14 years of age may not be granted a firearm certificate in any circumstances. Possession of s. 1 firearms is restricted as described below. Persons between 14 and 17 years may be granted firearms certificates but are not permitted to purchase or hire firearms or ammunition, but may acquire them in other ways, for example, as a birthday gift. Such a person could also borrow or receive an air weapon as a gift. In the case of shotguns, persons over 15 years of age but less than 17 years may also accept weapons as a gift, provided that they are in possession of a shotgun certificate. There are a number of restrictions placed upon the possession of firearms by young persons.

The Firearms Acts (Amendment) Regulations 1992 extend the Firearms Act 1968 to create a requirement that the holder of a firearm or shotgun certificate who is under 18 may only use that firearm for a purpose authorised by the European Weapons Directive. It is an offence to use the weapon for a purpose other than those specified. It is probable that such purposes will be specified in the certificate.

(1) *Section 1 firearms and ammunition*

A person less than 17 years of age may not purchase or hire any such firearm or ammunition, but may acquire it by way of a gift or loan, if he is 14 years of age or over. In such circumstances he must have been granted a firearm certificate, and if it is the wish of an adult to make such a present, the adult must obtain a firearm certificate to allow him to purchase the weapon, which can then be transferred. The transfer must be notified to the chief officer of police within 48 hours by registered post or recorded delivery service. On occasions in which persons less than 17 years are granted firearms certificates, they are endorsed to the effect that firearms and ammunition must not be sold or let on hire until a given date, which will be the date of the person's 17th birthday.

It is an offence to give or lend s. 1 firearms or ammunition to persons under 14 years of age, or for such persons to possess them, except:

(a) when carrying for another, who is the holder of a firearm certificate, for sporting purposes;
(b) as a member of an approved cadet corps, while engaged in target practice or drill;
(c) at a miniature range or shooting gallery using air weapons or rifles not exceeding 0.23 calibre; or
(d) when, as a member of an approved rifle club, he is engaged in, or in connection with, target practice.

(2) Shotguns

It is an offence for a person less than 17 years of age to purchase or hire any shotgun and an offence for a person to sell or hire a shotgun to such a person. It is also an offence to make a gift of a shotgun to a person under 15. No one less than 15 years shall possess an assembled shotgun, except:

(a) while under the supervision of a person of 21 years or more; or
(b) while it is securely fastened with a gun cover so that it cannot be fired.

The sale or hire of a shotgun to such a person is an offence. It should be noted that the Act does not prohibit the grant of a shotgun certificate to a person of any age. It is for chief officers of police to decide whether or not a shotgun certificate can be granted to a person under 15 without the public safety being endangered. Young persons must have a certificate authorising their possession of shotguns when shooting under supervision or when carrying a covered gun.

A holder of a shotgun certificate who is under 18 may not use the weapon for a purpose which is not authorised by the European Weapons Directive.

(3) Air weapons

It is an offence for a person less than 17 years to purchase or hire air weapons or ammunition. The seller or person who lets on hire in such a case also commits an offence. He may accept them as a gift or loan, and there being no requirement to possess any form of certificate they may be handed over immediately after purchase by an adult. However, such a gift or loan may not be made to a person under 14. The restrictions in respect of these weapons relate to possession.

A person less than 17 years of age commits an offence if he has with him an air weapon in any public place, except:

(a) as a member of an approved rifle club, for the purpose of target practice;

(b) at a shooting gallery or miniature range using air weapons or rifles not exceeding 0.23 calibre; or

(c) an air rifle which is so covered with a securely fastened gun cover that it cannot be fired.

The exception at (c) does not apply to air pistols. It is an offence for persons under 17 years of age to possess air pistols in a public place whether or not they are in a gun cover.

It is an offence for persons under the age of 14 years to possess air weapons or ammunition in any circumstances (including on private premises), except:

(a) while shooting under the supervision of a person of 21 years or over on private premises (including land) and provided that the missile is not fired beyond those premises;

(b) at shooting galleries, as above;

(c) as a member of an approved rifle club for the purpose of target practice.

Offences are committed by persons supervising shooting on private premises if they allow shots to be fired beyond those private premises, and also by those who part with possession of air weapons or ammunition to persons less than 14 years of age.

Criminal use of firearms

(1) Possession of firearm with intent to injure

Section 16 of the 1968 Act states that it is a serious offence, punishable by life imprisonment, for any person to possess any firearm or ammunition with intent to endanger life, or enable any other person to do so, whether any injury has been caused or not. If criminals are found in a post office in possession of firearms that is some evidence to suggest an intention to endanger life. If they produce the firearms in the course of a robbery the inference becomes compelling. A person who carries a firearm for another, intending to hand it to him should it be needed, commits this offence.

It has been held not to be an offence contrary to this section, to possess a firearm with intent to endanger one's own life.

Section 16A creates offences which are committed by a person who has in his possession any firearm or imitation firearm with intent by means thereof, or to enable any other person by means thereof, to cause any person to believe that unlawful violence will be used against him or another. These offences are punishable by ten years' imprisonment.

(2) Use of firearm to resist arrest

It is an offence contrary to s. 17(1) to use or attempt to use a firearm or imitation firearm with intent to resist or prevent the lawful arrest or detention of oneself or any other person. To possess a firearm or imitation firearm at the time of arrest for, or when, committing any offence mentioned in Schedule 1 of the Firearms Act 1968 is an offence against s. 17(2) unless it can be shown that it was possessed for a lawful

523

purpose. These offences include theft, robbery, burglary, blackmail, taking a conveyance, assaulting a constable in the execution of his duty, assaulting a prison custody officer or secure training centre custody officer, rape, abduction of women or children, offences of criminal damage, malicious woundings, assaults occasioning actual bodily harm, and assaults with intent to resist arrest. These offences are punishable by life imprisonment.

An imitation firearm is anything which has the appearance of being a firearm (other than for the discharge of noxious liquid, gas or other thing) whether or not it is capable of discharging any bullet, shot or other missile. An automatic pistol with the firing pin removed has been held to be an imitation firearm. On many occasions the circumstances of the use of an object will be important in establishing whether or not it was being used as an imitation firearm. A child's plastic gun may be clearly identifiable as such in daylight, but when used in a darkened room it may have the appearance of being a firearm.

Possession at the time of assaulting a prison custody officer at a contracted out prison is now also included under the provisions of the Criminal Justice Act 1991, s. 90(2).

(3) *Carrying firearms with criminal intent*

A person who has with him a firearm or imitation firearm with intent to commit an indictable offence, or to resist arrest, or to prevent the arrest of some other person, commits an offence against s. 18. It is necessary to prove:

(a) possession of the firearm or imitation firearm;
(b) an intention to commit an indictable offence, or resist arrest, or prevent the arrest of some other person; and
(c) that he intended to have the firearm with him.

If the first two factors can be proved, it is evidence that he intended to have the weapon with him at the time of committing the indictable offence or of resisting or preventing the arrest. The accused must show that there is a reasonable doubt of his intention to have the firearm at the material time.

A person 'has a firearm with him' if it is readily available to him when he is committing a robbery. The emphasis should not be so much upon the exact distance between the criminals and the guns but rather on the accessibility of those guns judged in a common-sense way in the context of criminals embarking on a joint enterprise to commit an indictable offence. This offence is punishable by life imprisonment.

Possession of firearm after conviction

Restrictions are placed, by s. 21 of the 1968 Act, upon the possession of any firearm or ammunition by a person who has been convicted of a crime and been sentenced to:

(a) custody for life, imprisonment or youth custody or detention in a young offenders' institution for three years or more – such a person is banned for life; or

(b) imprisonment or youth custody or detention in a young offenders' institution from three months to three years; or who has been subject to a secure training order – such a person is banned for five years.

For these purposes suspended sentences are discounted unless they are actually served at a later date. This is an arrestable offence.

Converting a firearm or shortening the barrel of a shotgun

It is an offence for anyone other than a registered firearms dealer to convert into a firearm anything which, though having the appearance of a firearm, cannot discharge a missile through its barrel.

It is an offence to shorten the barrel of a shotgun or any smooth-bore gun to which s. 1 of the 1968 Act applies (other than one which has a bore exceeding 2 inches in diameter) to a length of less than 24 inches. It is not an offence in either case for a firearms dealer to shorten a barrel for the sole purpose of replacing a defective part so as to produce a barrel not less than 24 inches in length. These are arrestable offences.

Handling stolen goods

Offence

Section 22 of the Theft Act 1968 provides:

> 'A person handles stolen goods if (otherwise than in the course of stealing) knowing or believing them to be stolen goods he dishonestly receives the goods, or dishonestly undertakes or assists in their retention, removal, disposal or realisation by or for the benefit of another person, or if he arranges to do so.'

It can be seen that there are a number of ways in which offences can be committed in respect of the handling of goods which have been stolen. It will be of assistance if the terms 'goods' and 'stolen goods' are examined before looking at the various forms of these offences.

Goods

Section 34 states that for the purposes of the Theft Act 'goods', except in so far as the context otherwise requires, includes money and every other description of property except land and includes things severed from the land by stealing. It therefore seems that property which can be dishonestly handled is almost identical to property which may be stolen. There are, perhaps, minor differences which are restricted to things in action, e.g. assets handled by an executor, etc.

Stolen goods

The meaning of 'stolen' is set out in s. 24 of the Act and can be summarised as follows:

(a) goods which have been stolen in circumstances contrary to s. 1;

(b) goods which have been obtained as a result of blackmail (s. 21);

(c) goods which have been obtained by means of deception (s. 15);

(d) goods which have been stolen abroad contrary to the law of that land, the stealing of which would, in England or Wales, have been contrary to ss. 1, 15, or 21 of the Theft Act 1968.

The circumstances set out above are likely to cover the dishonest handling of stolen goods in all circumstances in which police officers are likely to be involved.

The goods must be stolen goods at the time of the handling. When the taker of the property is under the age of criminal responsibility, the law conclusively presumes that such a person is incapable of theft and there being no original stealing, there cannot be a handling of stolen goods. It is not essential that the thief has been found guilty of stealing it; it is for the court to decide whether or not the property is stolen property. These issues can be some distance apart; it may frequently be quite clear to a court that property which is produced in the course of proceedings is stolen property, but it may be much more difficult to establish that a particular person is responsible for its theft. Frequently, offenders are dealt with for dishonestly handling stolen property when the person responsible for the original theft has not been apprehended or is perhaps unknown. In any case, evidence of the conviction of a thief is not admissible at the trial of a person charged with dishonestly handling, for the purpose of proving that the property is stolen. The status of the property is most frequently established by the evidence given by the owner of the property.

Goods ceasing to be stolen

It is extremely important that police officers realise that there comes a moment when goods cease to be stolen. Section 24(3) provides:

'But no goods shall be regarded as having continued to be stolen goods after they have been restored to the person from whom they were stolen or to other lawful possession or custody, or after that person and any other person claiming through him have otherwise ceased as regards those goods to have any right to restitution in respect of the theft.'

It is quite obvious that if the owner discovers the whereabouts of his property and recovers it, it ceases to be stolen property, otherwise property once stolen would continue to be classified as stolen indefinitely. The addition of the words 'or to other lawful possession or custody' is most important to police officers. When, in the course of an investigation, a police officer recovers property on behalf of an owner, it ceases to be stolen property. The property has been taken into 'other lawful possession or custody'. This point is important, as no charge of dishonest handling will lie in circumstances in which police officers arrest a thief and take possession of stolen property on behalf of the owner, then subsequently allow the property to pass to a receiver.

If a police officer arrests a thief in his home and takes possession of the radio he has stolen and then discovers that a prospective purchaser, who knows that the radio is stolen, is about to call, and as a result returns the property to the thief before concealing himself, the purchaser does not handle stolen property when he 'buys' the radio. The property is in 'lawful possession and custody' of the police officer and is no longer stolen.The words 'lawful possession or custody' are important. A thief stole cartons of cigarettes and loaded them on to a lorry. A security officer discovered them, initialled them for later identification and then informed the police who allowed the lorry to be driven away. The goods were delivered to two men who admitted that they knew they were stolen. It was held that the security officer never took 'physical' possession of them; he merely wrote his name on them. He was, therefore, not exercising control over them and the goods at the material time remained stolen goods. At all material times the goods remained in the thief's possession and in his custody and he had full power to dispose of them as he saw fit. The goods remained stolen at the time of handling.

The moment at which an owner or other person with a title to goods ceases to have a right to restitution is not so apparent and is a question of fact. The owner himself can waive title at any time at which he chooses, and this occasionally occurs when property has been obtained as a result of deception. On discovering the deception, the owner may nevertheless be quite satisfied with the contract which has been made and give his approval. In such circumstances, although the property was originally classed as stolen property (having been obtained by deception contrary to s. 15 of the Act), the owner has waived his title to it and no longer has a right to have the property restored to him (restitution). The passage of time has no bearing upon the matter; goods stolen today will remain the property of the owner as long as he does nothing to set aside his title. The subsequent sale of stolen property to a person acting in good faith, allows such a person to assume the rights of an owner without being guilty of theft, and he acquires a good title to the goods if bought in open market. In certain circumstances, it is possible for the original owner's right to restitution to become affected by later dealings in respect of the property.

Goods representing those originally stolen

It is possible for there to be a dishonest handling of goods other than those which were originally stolen, as s. 24 also provides that references to stolen goods shall include, in addition to the goods originally stolen:

(a) any other goods which directly or indirectly represent or have at any time represented the stolen goods in the hands of the thief as being the proceeds of any disposal or realisation of the whole or part of the goods stolen or of goods so representing the stolen goods; and

(b) any other goods which directly or indirectly represent or have at any time represented the stolen goods in the hands of a handler of the stolen goods or any part of them as being the proceeds of any disposal or realisation of the whole or part of the stolen goods handled by him or of goods so representing them.

The effect of these provisions is that goods which an accused is charged with handling must, at the time of the handling or at some previous time,

(a) have been in the hands of the thief or of a handler; and

527

(b) have represented the original stolen goods in the sense of being the proceeds, direct or indirect, of a sale or other realisation of the original goods.

The 'thief' is the person by whose conduct the goods were originally stolen. A 'handler' is any person who has committed the act of handling with the necessary dishonest intention.

If a thief steals a transistor radio he is then in possession of a stolen radio set which may subsequently be dishonestly handled by some other person. Should be exchange the radio for a cigarette lighter, the lighter represents the stolen goods, being the proceeds of the disposal of the stolen property. Had the thief sold the radio set, then the money obtained as a result of the sale represents the stolen property, and if subsequently used to purchase a bicycle, the bicycle then represents the stolen property, being the proceeds of its disposal. The process is one which could continue indefinitely and police officers investigating handling offences frequently find the tasks of tracing the origin of any article in the possession of a thief or a receiver to be quite impossible. The principle to bear in mind when dealing with such offences is that when a person's property is wrongfully converted into another form, he continues to own the property in its changed form. The only difficulty which can arise for police officers is in circumstances in which the actual stolen property is recovered from some other person who bought it quite innocently, and money is also recovered from the offender which represents the original property. The legal position is that immediately the stolen property is returned to the owner, it ceases to be stolen property and at the same time, money, or other goods received in exchange for it, cease to represent 'stolen' property. In such cases a court may give directions as to the disposal of money, or other goods representing this property, found in the possession of a thief or receiver.

Where an accused handles goods believing them to be stolen, although they were not stolen or those goods had lost their status as stolen goods, he may nevertheless be guilty of an attempt. The Criminal Attempts Act 1981 states that a person may be guilty of an attempt to commit an offence even though that offence could not, for some reason, be committed.

Forms of handling

The term 'handling' is a collective term, describing different ways in which an offence can be committed contrary to s. 22 of the Act. There is only one offence created by the section and it may be committed:

(a) by receiving stolen goods; or
(b) by dishonestly undertaking or assisting in their
    (i)   retention;
    (ii) removal;
    (iii) disposal;
    (iv) realisation;
(c) by or for the benefit of another person, or arranging to do so.

Before the passing of the Theft Act 1968, the only offence known was that of receiving, one of the requirements of which was that the receiver must have had the goods in his possession or control. It is essential to remember that the section specifically excludes those who handle goods in the course of the original stealing. Such persons are guilty of theft.

(1) *Receiving*

Receiving still remains somewhat distinct from the other forms of handling, as in all other instances the handling must have been by or for the benefit of another person. This provides a useful starting point in considering the correct form of charge in particular cases. If there is no evidence of handling for the benefit of another person, the only charge which will be appropriate is one of receiving or arranging to receive. Evidence must be available to show that the person concerned received the goods, and this might be done directly or by authorising employees to receive them on his behalf. It is not essential that the receiver acquires any profit or advantage from his actions, and it would be sufficient if he merely agreed to receive them into his warehouse for a short period of time to conceal them. However, it must be shown that he, knowing or believing the goods to be stolen, took them into his possession or under his control. If the stolen property has not yet been taken into possession or under control, the only charge to be considered would be one of arranging to receive stolen property. In considering charges of arranging to receive stolen property, it must be remembered that the arrangement must have been made after the theft had taken place, as it is essential that the receiver knows or believes the goods to be stolen.

Where goods are found on the premises of a particular person, but the premises are not in his sole occupation and there is no evidence that he received them, possession by that person can only be proved if it can be shown that the goods had come into the premises by arrangement and that an employee or agent had instructions from him to receive them. Such an employee or agent would also be guilty if he knew or believed that the goods were stolen.

A person may 'arrange to receive' stolen goods where there is an arrangement between him and another person (most frequently the thief) to receive stolen goods. If a person, having stolen property, approaches another and that person agrees to accept the property which he knows or believes to be stolen, he is guilty of arranging to receive those goods, whether or not they are subsequently delivered.

(2) *Undertaking and assisting*

In cases other than receiving or arranging to receive the forbidden act must be done 'by or for the benefit of' a person other than the handler. 'Undertaking' and 'assisting' are the two key words which can be qualified by the words 'retention', 'removal', 'disposal' or 'realisation'. 'Retention' means keeping possession of, not losing, continuing to have. 'Removal' refers to the movement of stolen goods from one place to another, for example, taking stolen goods by means of a vehicle to another place. 'Disposal' is concerned with giving away, destroying, melting down or reducing to scrap. 'Realisation' means the exchange of the stolen goods for money or some other property.

If thieves take a motor lorry loaded with goods and, on arrival at a warehouse, are

529

assisted with the unloading of the vehicle by others who know that the property is stolen, such persons have assisted in the removal of stolen goods, although they have no intention of receiving them. The person who lends the motor lorry for that purpose assists in the removal of those goods. Arranging to commit any of the offences of handling is also punishable, therefore, if the men had merely agreed to assist with the unloading of the vehicle but had not begun to do so, they would still be guilty of an offence. If a wife brings home household goods stolen from a shop and the husband allows such articles to remain in the house knowing that they have been so obtained he is assisting in their retention, and if he later helps her to remove some of the goods, he is assisting in the disposal of the goods.

Verbal representation made for the purpose of concealing the identity of stolen goods, if made dishonestly and for the benefit of another, can amount to handling stolen goods by assisting in their retention. This might be so, if a wife dishonestly denied that goods in the house were stolen and told lies about them to assist her husband to retain them.

(3) *For the benefit of another person*

In all cases of undertaking and assisting in the retention, removal, disposal, or realisation of stolen goods (i.e. all charges other than those of receiving), it must be shown that such undertaking was for the benefit of another person, who should be named in the charge if his identity is known. If his identity is not known, the charge should indicate that the acts were done for the benefit of some person unknown.

Guilty knowledge

The guilty state of mind, or *mens rea*, necessary in handling offences is described by the words 'knowing or believing them to be stolen goods'. Before the Theft Act 1968 it was essential to prove actual knowledge that the property was stolen, and this was occasionally difficult to prove beyond doubt. If a man was offered property at a figure below the market price, he may have suspected that it had been stolen but may not have been sure. Now the question is simply: Did he know or 'believe' that the property was stolen? A man might be said to 'know' that goods were stolen if he is told by someone with first-hand knowledge that this is so. 'Belief' is less than knowledge. It exists where a person says to himself, 'I do not know that these goods are stolen but there can be no other reasonable conclusion in the light of all the circumstances'. Mere suspicion is insufficient. If a man says to himself, 'I suspect that these goods are stolen but on the other hand they may not be stolen', this is insufficient as a 'belief' does not exist. The knowledge or belief must exist at the time that the goods are received, supervening belief or subsequent dishonesty is insufficient. A second-hand dealer bought a watch worth £29 for £5. He admitted that he had taken a chance that the watch might be stolen. The Court of Appeal ruled that the prosecution must prove knowledge or belief. It is not necessary to prove that the handler was aware of the precise nature of the goods. If he believes that crates contain stolen television receivers it is no defence that they in fact contained stolen radios.

The word 'dishonestly' qualifies 'knowing or believing' by requiring that the very act itself is criminal. It is possible that a man might handle property knowing that it was stolen, but may intend to return it to the owner. In such circumstances his act would not be dishonest.

In practice, when stolen property is found in the possession of some person other than the thief, full enquiries are made to establish the transactions which took place between the thief, handler, and any other person. Factors which assist in establishing knowledge or belief that property had been stolen are: property which has been carefully concealed on premises, the owner having denied its presence prior to its being found; identification marks destroyed; immediate, furtive (perhaps at night), or secret disposal; purchase of property at a price well below market value; or the lack of records by persons who normally keep records of all goods upon the premises.

Recognising the difficulty which may be encountered by the police in proving knowledge or belief that property had been stolen, s. 27 of the Theft Act allows special evidence to be given in certain circumstances, but only in respect of handling charges. Provided that evidence has been given of possession, arranging, undertaking or assisting in the retention, removal, disposal or realisation, the following evidence may be given to help to prove knowledge, or belief, that the property was stolen:

(a) evidence that he has had in his possession or has undertaken or assisted in the retention, removal, disposal, or realisation of stolen goods from any theft taking place not earlier than 12 months before the offence charged; and

(b) (provided that seven days' notice in writing has been given to him of the intention to prove the conviction) evidence that he has, within the five years preceding the date of the offence charged, been convicted of theft or of handling stolen goods.

Although advantage is not always taken of the provisions of this section by the police, its value is readily apparent. If premises are raided upon which it is suspected that there is stolen property, it is likely that goods stolen upon many separate occasions will be recovered by the police. The court may be reluctant to accept that the owner of the premises knew or believed that property was stolen if property connected with only one offence of theft is found, but is unlikely to accept that the owner could innocently come into possession of property connected with a number of offences of theft. In the same way, the provisions outlined at (b) allow a court to take notice of the fact that the owner of the premises is either a thief or a receiver of stolen property. The Court of Appeal has ruled that (a) above does not permit the introduction of details of a previous conviction for an offence of handling and this seems to be a reasonable approach. It appears obvious that the Act is concerned with other property found at the time.

Evidence of recent possession of stolen goods in the hands of receivers or handlers may be offered. A court may infer guilty knowledge if the defendant offers no explanation, or the court does not believe the explanation offered. However, where stolen goods are found in the premises of a particular person, to establish that those goods were in his actual or constructive possession it must be shown that the goods came to the premises by his arrangement and that he accepted the goods, or a servant or agent had instructions to accept them on his behalf.

531

Police powers

The handling of stolen property is an arrestable offence. Because of the nature of these offences, it is frequently necessary for premises to be searched for stolen property. Section 26, therefore, authorises a justice, on receipt of information on oath that there is reasonable cause to believe that a person has stolen goods in his custody or possession, to grant a search warrant authorising a constable to search for and seize the property at any time.

Robbery

The Theft Act has simplified the law relating to robbery as previous legislation distinguished between various offences of robbery, some with aggravation, in order to increase penalties. Section 8 (1) of the Theft Act 1968 provides:

> 'A person is guilty of robbery if he steals, and immediately before or at the time of doing so, and in order to do so, he uses force on any person or puts or seeks to put any person in fear of being then and there subjected to force.'

The subsection requires that in every offence of robbery there is a theft. It is probably more accurate to say that robbery is merely an aggravated form of theft, the person responsible being liable to a maximum sentence of life imprisonment. In considering charges of robbery it is helpful to examine the theft of the property first in order to ensure that all the essential points to prove are evident within the circumstances. A man who genuinely believes that he has the right to recover property to which he has a claim of right, is not guilty of robbery if he does so by force provided that he genuinely believes that he has a claim of right as, in those circumstances, his actions are not dishonest. However, it is not sufficient merely for him to claim that he had a right to the property.

A previous tenant returned to the property to forcibly take goods from the landlord's possession, to the value of his cash deposit which had not been returned to him. He accepted that he was aware that he had no legal right to the property which he took but needed a bargaining counter to ensure that his property was returned. While admitting that this was not the best way to achieve his aims, he claimed that what he did was fair and was not dishonest. His appeal against conviction for robbery was dismissed. The jury had been properly directed and came to the conclusion that his actions were dishonest. The facts of this case clearly illustrate the difference between a genuine claim of right and that which might be described as 'a convenient excuse'. Whatever else he might have believed he could not realistically have believed that he had a claim of right to the goods which he took.

A man who forcefully dispossesses another of his motor car and drives away does not commit robbery if he takes it for the purpose of escaping from a pursuer and with the intention of abandoning it when he has escaped from the scene. If he takes the car with the intention of permanently depriving the owner of it, he commits robbery.

Having established that a theft has occurred, the circumstances should be examined for evidence of the use of force (which is the exercise of physical strength against another), or the threat to use force. There must be the use of force, or the threat of such use, in order to steal. The offence commonly known as 'mugging' provides a good example of robbery. The victim is assaulted and on occasions may be knocked unconscious before being relieved of his wallet and other valuables. On such occasions force is used for the purpose of making the completion of the theft much easier. If, however, two men fight outside a public house and one knocks the other unconscious, then later decides to relieve the other of his wallet, there is no robbery as the force was not used for the purpose of theft, the decision to steal having been made when the assault had been completed.

A threat of force must be directed at the person. To threaten the use of force against a man's home or his motor car is insufficient to justify a charge of robbery. Similarly, if the force used is merely sufficient to gain possession of the property – for example, to snap a watch chain – the offence will be one of theft rather than robbery as no force was directed against the person. The dividing line is frequently a fine one and it is a question of fact whether or not a charge of robbery should be preferred. If a man snatches a lady's handbag and runs away he has committed theft as the force was merely sufficient to gain possession of the property, but if the lady holds on to her handbag and it become necessary to use force to overcome her resistance, then force is used before or at the time of the theft and is directed against the person, and the offence is robbery. A threat of the future use of force is insufficient, it must be to use violence then and there.

The force or threat of force must be used immediately before or at the time of the theft. If a threat is involved, it must refer to force which is to be used then and there, so that the property is given up while fear is acting upon the victim. Examples of force being used immediately before a theft have already been given. Instances of theft at the time at which force is applied are not quite so clear, as a theft occurs at the time at which property is appropriated. It may be argued that an appropriation has taken place immediately a thief grips property with a dishonest intention, but it is unlikely that the interpretation will be so narrow. If this view is taken, then as soon as a thief places his hand into a man's pocket and takes hold of his cigarette case an appropriation has taken place and if, on being discovered, he uses force against his victim to enable the removal of the cigarette case, a charge of robbery would not be possible. For this reason it is more realistic to look at an act of appropriation as continuing until the property is completely removed. The distinction is important, as force offered after a theft has been completed will not constitute an offence of robbery in any circumstances. If a pickpocket steals a wallet and is pursued by his victim whom he subsequently assaults when he is caught, there is no robbery as the offence of theft was complete before the assault took place. In such circumstances it would be proper to charge theft and to include a separate charge of assault according to the degree of violence used, the intention of the assailant, and the injury caused to the victim.

The force or threatened use of force may be directed at any person. It is not essential that it is directed at the person from whom property is stolen. If a thief is about to steal property from a market stall and is seen by a shopper who has no connection with the stallholder, but who nevertheless attempts to prevent the completion of the theft, the use of force against him in order to steal would amount to robbery, provided that the theft is completed.

In circumstances in which a theft has not been completed, it may be possible to charge assault with intent to rob. It must be clearly shown that there was assault and that it was carried out with the intention of stealing property.

Police powers

The offences of robbery and assault with intent to rob are both arrestable offences.

Criminal deception

Obtaining property by deception

Section 15 of the Theft Act 1968 deals with the obtaining of property by deception:

(a) A person who by any deception obtains property belonging to another, with the intention of depriving the other of it, shall on conviction on indictment be liable to imprisonment for a term not exceeding ten years.

(b) For the purposes of this section a person is to be treated as obtaining property if he obtains ownership, possession or control over it, and 'obtains' includes obtaining for another or enabling another to obtain or to retain.

(1) Dishonestly

The deception must be made with a dishonest intention, and the meaning of the term has already been discussed when dealing with theft.

(2) Obtains

Subsection (2) describes the extent of the meaning of this word, which includes obtaining ownership, possession, or control for oneself, for another, or enabling another to obtain or retain it.

(a) *Ownership.* When a person buys an article in a shop, upon payment of the full agreed price he obtains the property in the article and has first claim to it. As opposed to everyone else he has the right of ownership and may do as he pleases with that particular article. If a person buys a car and pays full price for it, from the moment that the agreement is signed the retailer surrenders his rights of ownership to the purchaser. The purchaser may then do as he pleases with the car, provided that his actions do not conflict with the law, and may change the colour of it, apply stickers to it, or even destroy it if that is his wish. The law recognises that property may be jointly owned by two or more persons and provides that offences may be committed by one owner who deals with the property in some way which is against the interests of the others, for example, by assuming full rights over the property.

(b) *Possession and control.* It is an advantage to examine these terms together as it is difficult, on occasions, to separate their meaning. Possession is often described in two forms, actual and constructive, and it is when considering forms of constructive possession that a certain identification with the term

534

'control' can become apparent. The man who buys a car from a retailer is in actual possession of it as he drives it home. If, on arriving home, he sends his gardener on an errand and instructs him to drive his car, the gardener is now in actual possession of the car, but the owner also retains possession through his servant, and such possession is frequently described as constructive possession. 'Control' is a word of more general meaning which could be fittingly applied to both the gardener and the owner in the circumstances described above, but can also be more extensive in meaning. If the gardener was allowed to take his master's car to his home for the evening and parked it outside his house, he would no longer be in actual possession of it, but it would still be under his control. The inclusion of all three words in the section illustrates quite clearly the extent of the term 'obtains', which covers obtaining property from an owner or a person who, in any way, has a special interest in the property. Possession by an owner is identified by the fact that, no matter where the article may be, he retains control over it and can exercise his rights of ownership whenever he may wish to do so. For the purposes of the law relating to criminal deception, it is equally important to be aware of the term 'ownership' as, on occasions, the deception practised is such that an owner is induced to surrender his rights of ownership, in addition to his possession of the article, believing some false story to be true.

(c) *When does ownership pass?* Property has been obtained for the purposes of this section immediately that ownership, possession, or control has passed to another person. An owner of property may be induced by means of deception to sell 100 soccer balls to the party practising the deceit. The ownership in this property passes immediately that the deal has been completed, although no payment has been made and delivery has not been effected. This is normal business procedure; the ownership in articles being passed to retail traders on the promise of later payment. In examining circumstances which may include an offence of criminal deception it is important not only to identify the passing of physical possession or control of property but also to look for a possible transfer of ownership, by the original owner surrendering his ownership at some particular moment, intending delivery at a later date. In most circumstances a written contract will have been made out, but it is not necessary that it should be in writing. If an offer has been made by a person making false statements, or by a person whose conduct is misleading, and this has been accepted by the owner of the property, who surrenders his rights of ownership, then a contract has been completed, although this will later be voidable if the deceit is discovered.

(d) *Who may obtain?* In most circumstances the offender will have acted in order to benefit himself, but subs. (2) makes it clear that an offence will equally have been committed if the act is done for another, or to enable another to obtain or retain possession, ownership or control.

A man may tell a false story to an official of a charitable body concerning the circumstances of his friend, thus inducing the charity to make a payment to the friend. In such circumstances the man concerned obtained money for another by means of deception. Similarly, it may be that a man is offering rings for sale to a group in a public house, when another party deceives the potential buyers as to the quality of the rings in order to allow the seller to obtain a better price. He is, therefore, guilty of enabling the seller to obtain money by means of deception. In such circumstances, it is possible that the man telling the false story and the seller were acting in concert and the seller is, therefore, also guilty of an offence under this section. It is less likely that circumstances will be met in which some form of deceit has been practised to enable someone to retain property. This could occur, for example, if the owner had allowed someone the use of valuable paintings, and upon requiring their return was falsely told by another party that the borrower had arranged for various interested parties to visit his home over the following months to view the paintings and that it would cause him considerable embarrassment to be unable to meet his obligations. In this way, as a result of deceit, another person would have been enabled to retain property belonging to someone else.

(e) *What may be obtained from whom?* The terms 'property' and 'belonging to another' have already been examined under the heading of theft. Although there may be marginal differences in interpretation of the term 'property' for the purposes of the offence of criminal deception, all forms of property described by s. 4 in relation to theft are included and persons to whom property may belong are as described by s. 5 of the 1968 Act. Money represented by a credit figure in a bank account falls within the term 'other tangible property' and is capable of being obtained by deception by means of the electronic transfer of cash from that account.

However, property cannot be obtained from a machine by deception. A machine has no mind and therefore cannot be deceived.

(3) *The deception*

Subsection (4) of the Act states:

'For the purposes of this section, "deception" means any deception (whether deliberate or reckless) by words or conduct as to fact or as to law, including a deception as to the present intentions of the persons using the deception or any other person.'

(a) *Deliberate or reckless.* By including both of these words the prosecution is not required to prove beyond reasonable doubt that the offender knew that his story was false; it is sufficient to show that he was at least reckless as to whether or not it was true. 'Reckless' means more than being careless or negligent and involves an indifference as to whether the statement is true or false. A man may say that the watch he is selling has an 18 jewel movement, knowing that this is untrue, but he also may make this claim without having any knowledge of its truth or falsity, therefore showing recklessness. If his statement proves to be untrue and, because of it, another person pays money for the watch, the seller is guilty of an offence under this section. It is, however, important to recognise the difference between recklessness as to the falsity of a statement and mere negligence, as the basis of offences of criminal deception is that the act is done dishonestly. If the statement is such that any reasonable person should have known that it was false, this is good evidence that the accused knew of its falsity or was at least reckless in this respect. In the same way, a court is expected to listen to the explanation given by the accused and, if he feels that he genuinely believed that his claim in respect of the property was true, he is entitled to be acquitted. There must be a dividing line between criminal claims in relation to property and accepted forms of advertising. The Trade Descriptions Act 1968 makes punishable any misleading trade descriptions in forms of advertising.

(b) *By words or conduct*. Police officers experience little difficulty in identifying a deception by words. If a man tells another that the ring he is selling is gold, knowing that it is of some lesser metal, it is clearly a deception by words. Fortunately, most cases involve a deceit of this nature. However, the conduct of the man can be sufficient. If he wears a badge representing that he is an accredited bookmaker and receives bets from punters, his conduct inducing them to part with their money to him, his actions become dishonest if he has no intention of honouring the bets which are placed with him. A common form of criminal deception is the purchase of goods, by means of a cheque, by a person who knows that he has not sufficient funds in his account. The signing of a cheque implies three things; that the drawer has authority to draw that sum; that he has a bank account with that particular bank; and that the cheque is good and valid for that amount of money. If the drawer of the cheque has been notified by his banker that he has a certain sum of money in his account (by bank statement, verbally, or in answer to an enquiry) and he signs a cheque for an amount in excess of that sum knowing that no further funds are likely to be paid into his account, he has practised a deception, his actions are dishonest, and he has obtained property as a result of his deception. It would be different if he had authority to overdraw. However, banks guarantee that cheques up to a certain amount will be honoured and consequently a person using such a card, as authorised by his bank, cannot be guilty of deception in representing that such a cheque will be met. It would be different if the bank had withdrawn his authority to use the card. However, it has been held that a *genuine* belief that a cheque would be honoured provides a defence to a charge of deception, even if the belief is not based on reasonable grounds. Where a cheque book and cheque card are stolen and the thief forges a signature on one of the cheques and supports it with the card, he obtains money by the deception that he has authority to use the card.

There can also be a deception by omission. If a woman is in receipt of benefits which are calculated on the basis that she is separated from her husband and is receiving no help from him; and she continues to draw those benefits after her husband has returned to her, she commits this offence. Her original representation is a continuing one existing on each occasion upon which she draws benefit.

Instances in which customers in restaurants have left without paying for their meal are frequently reported to the police and it can be a difficult matter to decide when such conduct is criminal and when it is not. A person who

537

orders and consumes a meal in a restaurant has incurred a debt for which he is then obliged to pay. This can be described as a normal debt. If he then finds that he is unable to pay he may, by arrangement with the owner, defer payment until a later date. His conduct becomes criminal when his intentions are dishonest and he deceives the owner of the restaurant or his servant either by words or conduct. If it can be proved that he had no intention of paying when he sat down for the meal, he is clearly guilty of obtaining the meal, which is property, by deception, and he is therefore guilty of an offence against s. 15. However, unless this is admitted, it is seldom possible to show that this was his intention at the time he ordered the meal.

(c) *Deception as to present intentions.* Promises concerning future conduct were not generally punishable under the legislation which was replaced by the 1968 Act and this created considerable difficulties for the police. Bogus jobbing builders and interior decorators, who had received deposits for work which had not been carried out, were frequently reported to the police, who were powerless to proceed against them provided that they maintained that they did intend to carry out the work in due course. Section 15 is now wide enough to permit proceedings in such cases provided that it is possible to prove beyond reasonable doubt that the accused had no intention of fulfilling his promise at the time that he made it. It is important to differentiate between the man who intended to carry out the work at the time and later finds it impossible to do so, and he who did not intend to do the work at the time at which he received money in consideration of doing so.

(d) *Injured person must be deceived.* The person who is deprived of his property must believe that the false story is true, or be deceived by the conduct of the accused, before the full offence can be committed. The section requires that the accused 'obtains property by deception' and before this can be true the owner must believe the falsehood and because of this, part with ownership, possession or control of his property. If he is not deceived, the person practising the deceit is guilty of attempting to obtain property by means of deception. Statements taken from injured parties should, therefore, include evidence of their belief in the particular deceit involved in the offence. Where an unlicensed taxi driver picked up a foreign passenger at an airport, he falsely represented by his conduct that he was a licensed taxi driver and that his fares would be reasonable. When he charged grossly excessive amounts, although his passenger suspected by then that he was not a genuine taxi driver, he felt obliged to pay the extortionate rate. It was held that he had obtained the money by deception. If the deception is the effective cause of the property being obtained it is irrelevant that, at the final moment, the victim suspected or even believed that he was being swindled. However, in such cases it would be better to charge theft as theft can occur where an atmosphere of menace is the cause of a person parting with his property.

The meaning of the term 'intention of permanently depriving' has already been discussed on page 417.

Obtaining pecuniary advantage by deception

Section 16 of the Theft Act 1968 provides:

'A person who by any deception dishonestly obtains for himself or another any pecuniary advantage shall on conviction on indictment be liable to imprisonment for a term not exceeding five years.'

The offence is similar to that created by s. 15, the difference being that for an offence to be committed contrary to s. 15, property must be obtained as a result of the deception, whereas s. 16 requires that a 'pecuniary advantage' be obtained.

Pecuniary advantage

Subsection (2) of s. 16 defines 'pecuniary advantage':

'The cases in which a pecuniary advantage is to be regarded as obtained for a person are cases where:

(a) this subsection was repealed by the Theft Act 1978;
(b) he is allowed to borrow by way of overdraft, or to take out any policy of insurance or annuity contract, or obtain an improvement of the terms on which he is allowed to do so; or
(c) he is given an opportunity to earn remuneration or greater remuneration in an office of employment, or to win money by betting.'

Although s. 16 creates only one offence, it is essential that the charge specifies the pecuniary advantage which the accused is alleged to have obtained. It is, therefore, important to examine the meaning of each of these conditions.

(1) *Overdraft, insurance policy, or improved terms*

An authority to overdraw may be given by a bank manager upon being deceived by a customer into believing that he had assets which he did not in fact have. In addition, when a bank's customer with an overdrawn account uses a cheque card to obtain goods after a warning that no more cheques would be met and after having been requested to return the bank card, the customer commits the offence of obtaining a pecuniary advantage from his bank by his deception of the owner of the goods. This was an interesting decision of the Court of Appeal as it had been submitted that the customer, who obtained a railway ticket and a dog by use of her banker's card, had deceived the railway booking clerk and the pet shop owner, not the bank. It was held that her deception had indeed been practised upon these two individuals, but as the bank was bound to honour cheques which were supported by its card when presented, she had obtained a pecuniary advantage from the bank. It is not necessary that the person deceived is the person from whom the pecuniary advantage is obtained, although there should be some connection. Where a person uses a cheque card to obtain money in excess of the limit imposed by the bank, he is borrowing by way of an overdraft and if this is done dishonestly, he is guilty of this offence.

Policies of insurance or annuity contracts with insurance companies may be

539

obtained by deception as to the past medical history of the applicant, or it may be that the terms offered are improved because of a similar deception.

(2) *Opportunity to earn remuneration, greater remuneration, or win money by betting*

Before the passing of the Theft Act 1968 there was no criminal offence of obtaining an office or employment by deceit. Section 16 now deals with such conduct. If a man obtains a post as a school teacher by dishonestly representing that he had successfully completed a training course at a college of education, he is guilty of an offence. On the other hand, it may be that he is a qualified teacher, but on appointment he falsely alleges that he is the holder of an honours degree in order to obtain a higher salary; such conduct would amount to securing a greater remuneration by deception. There is a difference between applying for an office *carrying* remuneration and having an opportunity to *earn* remuneration. Thus, a man who makes a false statement to obtain a brewery tenancy does not commit this offence because, as a tenant, he would not be in the *employ* of the brewery company, nor could the post be described as an *office*. However, where a man falsely represented that he was a member of the Chartered Institute of Management Accountants and agreed to complete accounts and VAT returns for customers and claimed that the nature of the contract existing between himself and his customers was such that he was self-employed, it was held that he would be an employee in the eyes of ordinary literate men and women. To say differently would offer the opportunity for dishonest persons to arrange matters so that they became self-employed and thus escape the consequences of their deceitful conduct.

A person may gain the opportunity to win money by betting, by deceiving a bookmaker into allowing credit betting. A pecuniary advantage is obtained – that is, the opportunity to win money – and that advantage is gained by deception.

Powers of arrest

All of the above offences of pecuniary advantage by deception are arrestable offences.

The Theft Act 1978

The Theft Act 1978 repealed s. 16(2)(a) of the Theft Act 1968 in respect of which there had been many problems of interpretation. Although problems in relation to the dividing lines which might exist between offences may have been simplified for the courts, this quite short Act is not one which fits easily into the understanding of those who are required to enforce the law. The 1978 Act deals with three offences: obtaining services by deception; the evasion of liability by deception; and making off without payment.

Obtaining services by deception

Section 1 makes it an offence for any person, by any deception, to dishonestly obtain services from another. We have already considered the obtaining of goods or

540

pecuniary advantage by deception. The first is concerned with 'tangible' goods, the second with 'intangible' benefits in the sense that one cannot take hold of them. We now consider 'services' which are also intangible in the sense that they cannot be taken hold of. A ride in a taxi, a manicure, or the services of a mechanic to start a troublesome car, are all services provided by someone else. So is permitted entry to a theatre or a sports ground.

The section goes on to say that it is an obtaining of services where the other is induced to confer a benefit by doing some act, or causing or permitting some act to be done, on the understanding that the benefit has been, or will be paid for. The essence of this offence is seated in 'deception', 'dishonesty', and the 'obtaining of services'. It is calculated to identify the criminal offences, as opposed to instances of debt. A man may, by means of a dishonest deception, induce a builder to carry out work on his behalf. If he issues a worthless cheque, he has then induced the builder to believe that his services *have been* paid for. If he induces him to believe that he will pay on completion of the work, knowing that he is not and will not be, in a position to pay at that time, he has by deception, dishonestly caused the builder to believe that his services *will be* paid for. The prosecution must prove the dishonesty and the deception which, in effect, convert a civil debt into a criminal offence.

There are certain factors to remember. The debt does not need to be one which is legally enforceable; the services must be for reward and there may be an offence even though the person practising the deception intends to pay, if the deception is concerned with some other related matter. In examining these factors in turn, it is realised that the obtaining of the services of a prostitute by deception (a debt which is not legally enforceable) is nevertheless an offence under this section. A man who pays a prostitute with a worthless cheque knowing that it is worthless, in advance of receiving her services, is clearly liable under this section. There is a deception, his intentions are dishonest and it does not matter that the debt is not legally enforceable. However, if he pays the prostitute after the event with a worthless cheque it would be necessary to prove that he did not intend to pay from the outset, that is at the time at which he obtained the services. If he discovered afterwards that he had no money and paid with a worthless cheque merely to avoid embarrassment, there would be no offence under this section. To illustrate the second point, if a man hires a car and deliberately pays for that hire with a worthless cheque, he is clearly guilty of this offence. However, if he paid for the hire, but produced a friend's driving licence with the intention of concealing the fact that he was disqualified from driving, he would still be guilty under this section, although he had paid for the services. The deception is not limited to matters concerning payment, it is broadly attached to the 'obtaining of services by deception'. The aim of the section is to limit consideration of things done commercially; a man who 'hires' a lawn mower by deception without an intention to pay is guilty, he who borrows one from his neighbour is not.

The term used in subs. (2) 'confer a benefit' as related to the services which may be obtained gives width to the section; we are not only considering a job done, but a benefit provided, for example the services of an estate agent or surveyor who does no physical work; or admission to theatres, soccer grounds, etc., by deception.

It must be shown that an accused made his deception deliberately or recklessly and that he obtained his services dishonestly.

If a man books into an hotel intending not to pay, he obtains accommodation (a service) by deception. If he then takes breakfast, although the food represents goods, he continues to obtain services by deception as the waiter is not deceived by any words or conduct on the guest's part; he supplies the food because he believes that person to be a guest in the hotel and that is true.

Evasion of liability by deception

Section 2 deals with three offences which are seated in securing remission of a liability by deception: dishonestly securing remission of liability; inducing a creditor to wait for, or forgo payment; and obtaining exemption from, or abatement of, an existing liability. In all such instances the liability must be a legally enforceable one and this represents the first difference from offences which we have considered contrary to s. 1. Thus, the man who receives services from a prostitute by deception, or waiver of gambling debts, etc., by means of deception, cannot commit any of the offences outlined below. A non-accepted claim for compensation is in the same way not legally enforceable at that stage.

(1) Remission of liability

Section 2(1)(a) makes it an offence for any person who, by means of any deception, dishonestly secures the remission of the whole, or part of an existing liability to make payment whether his own liability or another's. To 'remit' means to 'refrain from exacting' so that any cancellation, whether in whole or in part, as a result of deception is sufficient for this offence. To separate this offence in our minds from that described in s. 1 we must remember that s. 1 was concerned with 'services', while s. 2 is concerned with 'liabilities'. To commit offences contrary to s. 1, the deception must be practised in order to obtain services, so that the man who deceives a radio dealer into repairing his radio by means of deception is guilty of a s. 1 offence as he 'obtained services' by deception. A second man, who merely places a radio with the dealer for repair, practising no deception and even intending at that time to pay has committed no offence. When the radio is returned to him he has a 'liability' to pay the repairer his charge. If he dishonestly, and by means of deception at this stage, secures remission either in full or in part, of that liability, he is guilty of an offence against s. 2(1)(a). Similarly, a man may borrow money from a friend and thereby have a liability to repay. If he later tells a false story to the effect that his mother has died and that he is required to meet the funeral expenses, as a result of which his friend either cancels or reduces the debt, the man is guilty of this offence. The term 'existing liability' means that there must have been some previous transaction which has been completed. It may amount to a credit sale, a borrowing, or a debt in respect of repair, etc.

(2) Wait for or forgo payment

Section 2(1)(b) deals with a person who, by means of a deception *with intent to make permanent default* in whole, or in part on any existing liability to make payment, or with intent to let another do so, dishonestly induces the creditor or any person claiming payment on behalf of the creditor, to wait for payment (whether or not the due date for payment is deferred), or to forgo payment. A person is induced by deception to forgo payment if the deception causes him to give up waiting for payment and (although he does not necessarily agree to extinguish it) to write off the debt, or he is convinced by deception that there is no liability to pay.

As these offences are all concerned with deception, understanding of the differences between particular offences becomes difficult. Previously we have been concerned with *services which are obtained* by deception and *debts which are cancelled or reduced* by means of deception. Now we are concerned with *criminal intentions*, deceptions practised 'with intent to make permanent default', which result in an inducement to persons to wait for payment or to forgo it. The subsection is concerned with 'stalling debtors' who embark upon a course of conduct which tends to indicate an intention to make permanent default. There must come a time in the course of such processes when the reasonable man would decide that a debtor intended to make permanent default. This is the reason why subs. (3) specifically declares that when a creditor takes a cheque in conditional satisfaction of a pre-existing liability, he is to be treated not as being paid, but as being induced to wait for payment. Therefore, a defendant who gives a creditor a worthless cheque commits an offence contrary to s. 2(1)(b) if he is dishonest and intends never to pay. However, where a man pays off a debt with a cheque which he knows to be worthless merely to get the creditor 'off his back' and intends to pay when funds are available, he does not intend to make permanent default and does not, therefore, commit this offence.

If customers in a restaurant dishonestly deceive the proprietor by alleging that they have already paid the bill, they deceive with intent to make permanent default.

We have considered the first part of this offence, 'waiting for payment', in the light of the deception with intent to make permanent default, by a stalling debtor.

The second provision of this subsection uses the word 'forgo' and we are concerned with the man who by means of deception, with intent to make permanent default, dishonestly induces his creditor to 'decide' that he will never seek repayment. If we consider two students who rent a room from a landlord, and one of them informs the landlord that the other has left owing rent without leaving a forwarding address and that story is false, the landlord may decide that it will not be worth his trouble to try to trace the student and may cancel the debt. If the student who left intended to make permanent default, he is guilty of this offence. So is the student who practised the deception if his intention was to allow his colleague to make permanent default. The words 'with intent to let another do so' make him a principal offender. In the same way, a man who is about to leave the country or the district, who pays a small garage bill by means of a worthless cheque and thereby similarly induces the garage owner to decide to cancel the debt, would be guilty if he intended to make permanent default. If the garage owner did not decide to cancel the debt, he would have been induced to wait for payment in these circumstances.

(3) *Exemption or abatement*

Section 2(1)(c) makes it an offence for a person dishonestly, by any deception, to obtain an exemption from or abatement of liability to make a payment. Although this appears at first sight to bear many parallels with the offences already described, it adds a new dimension. So far we have been concerned with obtaining services, evasion of existing liabilities and inducing creditors to wait for or forgo payment. Now we are considering a dishonest deception which from the outset was concerned with securing some form of 'exemption' or 'abatement', the term 'abatement' signifying a reduction of liability. The offender may obtain services at a reduced rate, for example a railway ticket by use of a student's union card, to which he was not entitled, thus obtaining 'abatement of liability to make payment' or free passage on a public service vehicle by use of a pensioner's pass to which he was not entitled, which would amount to an 'exemption'. A consultant who had a duty to give information to a NHS hospital concerning patient services received by private patients, but who deliberately and dishonestly refrained from giving that information, was held to be guilty of this offence because, by his deception (by omission) he had obtained exemption from patient charges which otherwise would have arisen.

Section 1 could not apply to any of these offences as the benefit was not conferred on an understanding that it would be, or had been paid for; it was given on a false belief that the offender was entitled to concessions. This subsection will also apply to the dishonest, deceptive claim made to a tax inspector or local authority council tax officer to secure allowances or rebates to which the person submitting the claim is not entitled. Perhaps this illustrates the purpose of ss. 1 and 2 of the 1978 Act to cover deceptions related to concessions.

(4) *Making off without payment*

The Theft Act 1978, s. 3, makes it an offence for a person who, knowing that payment on the spot for any goods supplied or service done is required or expected from him, dishonestly makes off without having paid as required or expected and with intent to avoid payment of the amount due.

This offence was included to cover offences known as 'bilking', for example, leaving a restaurant or a self-service petrol station without paying. The previous theft law left gaps in relation to such activities as it was necessary to prove dishonest intentions at the beginning of the transaction and did not cover 'opportunist' offences. The section states that the term 'payment on the spot' includes payment at the time of collecting goods on which work has been done, or in respect of which service has been provided. The payment must be one which is legally enforceable. This offence does not require 'deception' and the dishonesty need only be present at the time of 'making off'.

The offender must have known that payment on the spot is required or expected *of him*. This means immediate 'on the spot' payment. Therefore, if Jones takes two friends into a restaurant and orders meals on the clear understanding that it is his party and he will pay the bill, and the whole party leave without paying, only Jones commits this offence as payment was expected from him. The wording of the section is such that it distinguishes between instances in which an account may be settled at a later date and instances in which payment on the spot is required. If a garage mechanic goes to his firm's wholesalers and collects goods on behalf of his employer and leaves without signing for them there can be no offence. A debt exists between his employer and the wholesaler. No one expected the mechanic to pay on the spot, his employer will settle the account and it is his employer who is expected to pay, but not on the spot. It would be different if the next customer is a private customer who has no account with the wholesaler and who wishes to make a credit card transaction. If the goods which he requires are supplied and he, seeing an opportunity, leaves without presenting his credit card so that the purchase can be recorded, he commits an offence. In this case, payment was clearly expected of him on the spot and such payment has not been made until the credit voucher has been made out.

This offence will frequently be associated with self-service garages; restaurants; and taxis (where there is a clear requirement to pay on the spot), as opposed to the hiring of a car for a wedding, where payment is not required on the spot.

The section does not require the payment to be made at any particular spot. The words 'on the spot' relate to the knowledge which a customer must have of *when* payment must be made. The words 'dishonestly make off without payment' involve a departure without paying, from the place where payment would normally be made.

Police powers

The offences against ss. 1 and 2 are arrestable offences.

Post-foundation training

The Cinemas Act 1985, s. 1, requires that premises which are to be used for a film exhibition must be licensed for the purpose. A film exhibition is any exhibition of moving pictures which is produced otherwise than by the simultaneous reception and exhibition of programmes included in a programme service (within the meaning of the Broadcasting Act 1990). This definition has been held not to embrace coin operated video games in an amusement arcade. The nature of the definition is such that, for example, the exhibition of a live football match by way of 'cable' would not be included.

Section 2 of the Act requires that, in addition, no premises must be used, except with the consent of the licensing authority, for a film exhibition organised wholly or mainly as an exhibition for children.

There are certain exemptions in favour of exhibitions within a private dwelling-house to which the public are not admitted and there is no element of private gain, and the sole purpose is for demonstration, advertising or the provision of information, education or instruction; where the exhibition is non-commercial; in relation to licensing generally, where exhibitions in the premises concerned are occasional (not more than six days in a year), provided that notice is given to the licensing authority, fire authority and the chief officer of police; and in respect of exhibitions in moveable buildings in similar circumstances.

The licensing authority may:

(a) impose conditions or restrictions prohibiting the admission of children to film exhibitions involving the showing of works designated, by the authority or by such other body as may be specified in the licence, as works unsuitable for children; and

(b) to consider what (if any) conditions or restrictions should be imposed as to the admission of children to other film exhibitions involving the showing of works designated by the authority or by such other body as may be specified in the licence, as works of such other description as may be so specified.

The Children and Young Persons Act 1933, s. 12, contains various provisions intended to ensure the safety of children at such entertainments.

Where such an exhibition is for children, or where the majority of the persons attending are children, if the number of children attending exceeds 100, the person providing the entertainment must station, and keep stationed, a sufficient number of adult attendants who have been properly instructed in their duties, to prevent more children or other persons being admitted to the building, or to any part of it, than the building or part can properly accommodate, and to control the movements of the children and other persons admitted while entering and leaving the premises, and to take all other reasonable precautions for the safety of children.

Police powers

Under the Children and Young Persons Act 1933 a constable may enter any building in which he has reason to believe that such an entertainment is being, or is about to be, provided, with a view to seeing whether these provisions are being carried into effect.

In addition, under s. 13 of the 1985 Act, where a constable has reasonable cause to believe that:

(a) any premises in respect of which a licence of either kind (s. 1 or s. 2) is in force, are being, or are about to be used for an exhibition which requires a licence of that kind;

(b) and premises in respect of which a licence under s. 1 is in force are being or are about to be used for an exhibition at a non-commercial exhibition; or

(c) any premises in respect of which notice has been given under s. 7 or s. 8 (premises used occasionally and exhibitions in movable buildings) are being or are about to be used for an exhibition which, but for that section, would require a licence under s. 1.

Offences

Offences are committed by persons concerned in the organisation or management of premises upon which such an unlicensed exhibition is given, as well as the licence holder and persons who, knowing or having reasonable cause to suspect that the premises would be so used, allowed the premises to be used, or let them or otherwise made them available where:

(a) there is no licence;

(b) there is no consent, s. 2;

(c) there is a use outside the terms of a condition imposed;

(d) there is a contravention of regulations made by the Home Secretary under s. 4 (currently the Cinematograph (Safety) Regulations 1955).

Foreign citizens in the United Kingdom

Introduction

The Immigration Act 1971 sets out the general principles with which the Act is concerned.

It is concerned with those who have a right of abode within the United Kingdom and with ensuring that such persons shall be allowed to live in the United Kingdom freely, and to come and go into and from, the United Kingdom without let or hindrance except such as may be required under and in accordance with the Act.

Secondly, it is concerned that persons not having such a right of abode, may live, work and settle in the United Kingdom by permission and subject to such regulation and control of their entry into, stay in and departure from the United Kingdom as may be imposed. The Act provides that rules laid down by the Secretary of State dealing with such persons shall include provision for admitting persons coming for the purpose of taking employment, or for the purpose of study, or as visitors, or as dependants of persons lawfully in or entering the United Kingdom. Indefinite leave to enter and remain in the United Kingdom shall be treated as having been given to those who were in the United Kingdom under these conditions at the time of the 1971 Act coming into force.

Right of abode in United Kingdom

A person has a right of abode if:

(a) he is a British citizen; or
(b) he is a Commonwealth citizen who:
    (i) immediately before the commencement of the British Nationality Act 1981 was a Commonwealth citizen having the right of abode in the United Kingdom at the time at which the 1971 Act was passed; and
    (ii) has not ceased to be a Commonwealth citizen in the meanwhile.

The British Nationality Act 1981 is now the principal Act dealing with citizenship. It deals with three categories of citizen:

(a) those who have British citizenship because of a right which is associated with descent, birth, adoption, naturalisation, etc.;
(b) persons who are citizens of British Dependent Territories which are set out in Schedule 6 to the Act, for example, Gibraltar, Hong Kong, Falkland Islands and Bermuda; and
(c) persons who are British Overseas Citizens and became such, having been a citizen of the United Kingdom and Colonies, while not becoming a British citizen or a citizen of the British Dependent Territories, at the commencement of the British Nationality Act 1981.

There are no restrictions upon the movements of persons who are classed as *British citizens*.

Immigration controls

Control over immigration is exercised in the first instance by immigration officers who have the power to give or refuse leave to enter the United Kingdom. Thereafter, the power to give leave to remain in the United Kingdom, or to vary the original leave granted by the immigration officer, is exercised by the Secretary of State.

551

Generally, the Secretary of State exercises his powers by notice in writing to the person concerned.

The Act also empowers the Secretary of State to make regulations requiring some persons who have been permitted entry to the United Kingdom to register with the police. The regulations which have been made include a requirement that such persons shall be issued with a police registration certificate. In connection with the purpose of this Act, the Secretary of State is also permitted to make regulations requiring records to be made and kept of persons staying in hotels and at other premises where lodging or sleeping accommodation is provided.

Common travel area

Arrival and departure from the United Kingdom from or to any of the Islands (Channel Islands and Isle of Man) or the Republic of Ireland are within this area and are not subject to the controls effected by this Act if they are connected with a 'local journey'.

A 'local journey' is one which begins and ends in the common travel area and is not made by a ship or aircraft which began its journey outside the common travel area, or is due to end its journey at a place outside that area.

Conditional leave to enter the United Kingdom

Persons not having a right of abode in the United Kingdom may be admitted subject to such restrictions as may be provided by rules of the Secretary of State which may provide that such entry shall be subject to conditions as to length of stay or otherwise. A person's leave to enter may be varied by altering its limits, or by adding, varying or revoking conditions.

Breach of conditions and deportation

A person who is in the United Kingdom in breach of such conditions is liable to deportation and the Secretary of State may make a deportation order against him.

In addition, a person who is not a British citizen is liable to deportation if, after he has attained the age of 17 he is convicted of an offence punishable with imprisonment and such deportation is recommended at the time of his conviction.

The Secretary of State may also order deportation if he deems it conducive to the public good, or if another person to whose family he belongs is, or has been ordered to be, deported.

Illegal entry and similar offences

The Immigration Act 1971, s. 24(1), states that a person who is not a British citizen is guilty of an offence if:

    (a) contrary to the Act he knowingly enters the United Kingdom in breach of a deportation order or without leave;

    (b) having only a limited leave to enter or remain in the United Kingdom he knowingly either:

(i) remains beyond the time limited by the leave; or

(ii) fails to observe a condition of the leave;

(c) having lawfully entered the United Kingdom without leave by virtue of s. 8(1) of the Act (crew member of ship or aircraft), he remains without leave beyond the time allowed by that section;

(d) without reasonable excuse, he fails to comply with any requirement imposed upon him under Schedule 2 of the Act to report to a medical officer of health, or to attend or submit to a test or examination, as required by such an officer;

(e) without reasonable excuse, he fails to observe any restriction imposed on him under Schedule 2 or 3 of the Act as to residence, as to his employment or occupation or as to reporting to the police or to an immigration officer;

(f) he disembarks in the United Kingdom from a ship or aircraft after being placed on board under Schedule 2 or 3 with a view to his removal from the United Kingdom;

(g) he embarks in contravention of a restriction imposed by or under an Order in Council under s. 3(7) of the Act (provisions aimed at preventing persons from going to specified places on the grounds of safety).

Section 24(1A) provides that a person who commits an offence under (b) above by remaining beyond the time limited by the leave commits that offence on the day when he first knows that the time limited by his leave has expired and continues to commit it throughout any period during which he is in the United Kingdom thereafter. However, a person may not be prosecuted under (b) more than once in respect of the same limited leave.

A constable or immigration officer may arrest without warrant anyone who has, or whom he, with reasonable cause, suspects to have, committed or attempted to commit an offence under s. 24 other than an offence under (d).

Assisting illegal entry, and harbouring

Section 25(1) of the 1971 Act provides that a person who is knowingly concerned in making or carrying out arrangements for securing or facilitating the entry into the United Kingdom of anyone whom he knows or has reasonable cause for believing to be an illegal entrant commits an offence. This is an arrestable offence. Immigration officers are given statutory power to arrest in these circumstances. Subsection (2) makes it an offence for a person knowingly to harbour any person whom he knows or has reasonable cause for believing to be either an illegal entrant or a person who has committed an 'overstaying' offence under (b) or (c) of s. 24.

European Union Nationals

European Union nationals are admitted on proof of European citizenship.

Registration with police

The Immigration (Registration with Police) Regulations 1972 deal with the registration of aliens. An 'alien' is a person who is neither a Commonwealth citizen, nor a British protected person, nor a citizen of the Irish Republic. Such persons may be required to register with the chief officer of police for the area in which they reside. They will have been granted limited leave to enter which will be subject to a condition of registration and their passports will have been endorsed accordingly. If, in any circumstances, EU nationals are required to register, the Home Office will notify the appropriate police force. Where this occurs, the residence permit will be endorsed in the space provided and this endorsement fulfils the purpose of a police registration certificate.

In respect of other persons who must register with the police, a police registration certificate will be issued which carries the photograph of the person concerned. Police forces maintain records of aliens living within their areas who are subject to registration requirements. Changes of residence must be reported within seven days and changes in other registered particulars, within eight days. This may be done by post but personal attendance may be required.

An immigration officer or constable may require an alien to whom the Regulations apply either to produce a certificate of registration, or to give to the officer or constable a satisfactory reason for failure to produce it, forthwith. Where alterations are being made in registered particulars, a registration officer may require the alien concerned to produce his certificate of registration so that necessary amendments can be made. Where there is a failure to produce at the time, the officer or constable may require that person to produce a certificate of registration at a police station specified by the officer or constable within the following 48 hours.

A person who fails to register as required or to comply with any registration requirement offends against s. 26(1) of the 1971 Act.

Goods vehicles – plating and testing: driving licences and operators' licences

Introduction

A 'goods vehicle' is a motor vehicle or trailer constructed or adapted for the carriage of goods. The carriage of goods includes haulage. If a vehicle is adapted it is 'altered physically so as to make fit for the purpose'. If the seats are taken out of a minibus which is then fitted out as a mobile shop, the vehicle has been adapted as a goods vehicle. The test is to ask oneself whether, if the motor vehicle had been originally constructed in the form in which it then exists, it would have been classified as a goods vehicle?

The driver of a goods vehicle

(1) *Minimum age for driving goods vehicles*

Different minimum ages are prescribed for different vehicles. A goods vehicle may be a small, medium or large goods vehicle for this purpose.

(a) A *small goods vehicle* is a motor vehicle (other than a motor cycle or invalid carriage) which is constructed or adapted to carry or haul goods, *and* is not adapted to carry more than nine persons inclusive of the driver, *and* the permissible maximum laden weight of which does not exceed 3.5 tonnes.

Persons of 17 or over (16 if in receipt of a mobility allowance) may drive small goods vehicles.

(b) A *medium-sized goods* vehicle is a motor vehicle which is constructed or adapted to carry or haul goods, *and* which is not adapted to carry more than nine persons inclusive of the driver, *and* the permissible maximum weight of which exceeds 3.5 tonnes but does not exceed 7.5 tonnes. Persons of 18 or over may drive medium-sized goods vehicles.

(c) A *large goods vehicle* is a goods vehicle which exceeds 7.5 tonnes permissible maximum weight or which has more than nine seats inclusive of the driver's. Persons of 21 or over may drive large goods vehicles.

The carriage of passengers is referred to in these definitions of goods vehicles because of the existence of Transit-type vehicles which although constructed for the carriage of goods, retain a quantity of seats. Such vehicles are frequently used for the carriage of goods as well as the transport of workers to a site.

The 'permissible maximum weight' of a vehicle is usually the relevant maximum weight of the vehicle and this will be shown on the plate of the vehicle (see below). In the case of an articulated goods vehicle the permissible maximum weight will be its relevant maximum train weight which is the gross weight of the unladen motor vehicle and its unladen trailer plus the maximum weight which the combination is permitted to carry. Again, this will be shown on the 'plate' in the column marked 'gross train weight'.

It is important to recognise that while persons of less than 21 may be permitted to drive certain types of goods vehicle, the addition of a trailer to the vehicle can make a difference. A person of 17 may drive a goods vehicle of a permissible maximum weight of 3 tonnes but if a trailer is attached which has a relevant maximum weight of 1 tonne, the sum of the weights exceeds 3.5 tonnes and the combination becomes a medium-sized goods vehicle.

There are some exceptions to these rules in relation to age. Medium and large goods vehicles owned and used by naval, military or air force authorities may be driven by persons aged 17. In addition there is a heavy goods vehicle training scheme; if a person is registered and employed by an employer who is also registered in the heavy goods vehicle training scheme, he may, at 18, drive a large goods vehicle, provided that it is of a class approved by his training agreement or that it is used by a registered heavy goods vehicle training establishment.

(2) Large goods vehicle drivers' licences

For licensing purposes a 'large goods vehicle' is:

(a) an articulated goods vehicle; or

(b) a motor vehicle (not being an articulated goods vehicle) which is constructed or adapted to carry or haul goods and the permissible maximum weight of which exceeds 7.5 tonnes.

It is an offence contrary to the Road Traffic Act 1988, s. 87, for a person to drive a large goods vehicle on a road otherwise than in accordance with a DVLA vocational driving licence. Previous legislation required that the drivers of such vehicles held a

DVLA licence and, in addition, a heavy goods vehicle driver's licence. Transitional arrangements allow such holders to drive large goods vehicles on the authority of those two licences.

The Motor Vehicles (Driving Licences) (Large Goods and Passenger-Carrying Vehicles) Regulations 1990 include two categories of vehicles for the purpose of driving tests:

(a) *Category C*. This category includes vehicles used for the carriage of goods and whose maximum authorised mass exceeds 3.5 tonnes including such a vehicle drawing a trailer with a maximum authorised mass not exceeding, in the case of a trailer with a single axle, 5 tonnes or, in the case of any other trailer, 750 kg, but not including a vehicle in category C1.

(b) *Category C plus E*. This includes combinations of motor vehicles in category C and a trailer with an authorised maximum mass exceeding, in the case of a trailer with a single axle, 5 tonnes or, in the case of any other trailer, 750 kg.

'Maximum authorised mass' has the same meaning as 'maximum gross weight'.

However, although category C vehicles as defined by the regulations are such that the definition includes all goods vehicles exceeding 3.5 tonnes, those who apply for a test in respect of large goods vehicles must provide a category C vehicle which the regulations specify as suitable for such a test. Such a vehicle will not be suitable, if the test is taken before 1 July 1996:

(a) and the test is for category C unless it has a maximum authorised mass which exceeds 7.5 tonnes;

(b) and it is a test for category C plus E unless it is either an articulated goods vehicle combination, or a combination of vehicles comprising a vehicle in category C and a trailer with at least two axles with a permissible maximum weight in relation to the combination of at least 15 tonnes.

If the test is taken on or after 1 July 1996, the vehicle must be capable of a speed of at least 80 kph. If the test is for category C entitlement, the vehicle must have a maximum authorised mass of at least 10 tonnes and an overall length of at least 7 metres. If it is for category C plus E entitlement, it must be either an articulated goods vehicle combination with a permissible maximum weight of at least 18 tonnes and an overall length of at least 12 metres, or a combination of vehicles with a maximum authorised mass of at least 18 tonnes and an overall length of at least 12 metres, comprising a vehicle in category C with a maximum authorised mass of at least 10 tonnes and an overall length of at least 7 metres and a trailer with an overall length of at least 4 metres.

It can be appreciated therefore, that to gain a DVLA vocational licence to drive large goods vehicles, a considerable degree of driving ability must be shown to exist.

(3) *Trainee drivers*

The 1990 Regulations permit persons (including those of 18 or over 18 years who have training agreements) to be issued with provisional driving licences.

They are of two types; one concerned with such persons; the other with those issued with a standard provisional driving licence for large goods vehicles.

Conditions applicable to both types of provisional licence

Holders of provisional licences may not drive an authorised vehicle unless:

(a) under the supervision of a person who is present with him in the vehicle and who holds a full standard licence or a full existing licence to drive a vehicle of that category;

(b) there is displayed in a conspicuous manner on the front and on the back of the vehicle a distinguishing mark which may be, before 1 April 1996 of the type which consists of an 'L' plate with the letters HGV above or of the ordinary type which consists of the red letter 'L' on a white background, and on or after that date may only be those which display a red letter 'L' on a white background.

However, once a holder has passed a test, he need not observe these conditions although he may still be the holder of a provisional licence.

Those who hold a large goods vehicle trainee driver's provisional licence which is being used as such are additionally subject to the condition that they must not drive such a vehicle if it is being used to draw a trailer, unless the licence is for category C plus E and the combination of vehicle and trailer would fall into that category.

Where a person under 21 passes a test for a category of large goods vehicle for which the licence is, or acts as a provisional licence, these conditions no longer apply, except that, where the vehicle is in category C and it is being used to draw a trailer, or is in category C plus E, he must be under the supervision of a full licence holder.

A full standard licence to drive a particular category of large goods vehicle may be used as a provisional standard licence to drive such vehicles of a different category. A trainee driver's licence in respect of category C may be used as a provisional licence in respect of category C plus E after a period of two years from the date on which the test was passed in relation to category C vehicles.

(4) Drivers from abroad

European Union citizens who become normally resident in the United Kingdom may be granted exchange licences to drive large goods vehicles.

Holders of convention or domestic driving permits who are resident in a member State of the European Union, may drive any goods vehicle which they are authorised to drive by that permit during a period of 12 months from the date of their last entry into the United Kingdom.

Plating and testing of goods vehicles

(1) Manufacturer's plate

The Road Vehicles (Construction and Use) Regulations require the following vehicles to be fitted with a manufacturer's plate:

(a) every heavy motor car and motor car first used on or after 1 January 1968, which is not a passenger vehicle or dual-purpose vehicle; and

(b) every bus (whether or not it is an articulated bus) and first used or after 1 April 1982; and

557

(c) every locomotive and motor tractor first used on or after 1 April 1973; and

(d) every trailer manufactured on or after 1 January 1968 which exceeds 1020 kg unladen weight (although living vans not exceeding 2040 kg are exempted if fitted with pneumatic tyres); and

(e) every trailer which is a converter dolly manufactured on or after 1 January 1979.

There are the usual exceptions in favour of land, works, pedestrian-controlled and plant, etc., vehicles.

Motor tractors and locomotives are 'pulling' vehicles which do not themselves carry a load. All such vehicles must be plated. Motor cars and heavy motor cars are vehicles which will themselves carry a load and if they are goods vehicles, unless they are exempted, they must carry a plate. Converter dollies are trailers used to support the front of a trailer which is normally attached to an articulated vehicle, when it is not so attached.

A manufacturer's plate must be fitted in a conspicuous and readily accessible position. The particulars which the plate must contain are prescribed in Schedule 2 to the regulations. In some instances, the only plate to be carried by a goods vehicle during the first year of its life will be the manufacturer's plate. However, vehicles to which the Motor Vehicles (Type Approval for Goods Vehicles) (Great Britain) Regulations 1982 apply will be examined and fitted with a 'Ministry Plate' within 14 days. For practical purposes, all such vehicles will be fitted with a plate which contains details of authorised weights, etc. These weights are shown as 'gross weights'. The maximum gross weight of a vehicle is the unladen weight of the vehicle plus its maximum permitted load, thus it represents the weight transmitted to the road surface. The weights which are shown on the plate are the weights which we look at for enforcement purposes when goods vehicles are being examined.

(2) Ministry plate

The Goods Vehicles (Plating and Testing) Regulations 1988 require that most goods vehicles and trailers are subject to annual testing, the first test being not later than 12 months after first registration, or, in the case of trailers, not later than 12 months after retail sale. At the first annual inspection, if this has not already been done, such a plate will be fitted to the vehicle. Authorised weights are then recorded on this plate.

The following goods vehicles must be *Ministry* plated and thereafter subject to annual tests:

(a) heavy motor cars and motor cars constructed or adapted to form part of an articulated vehicle;

(b) other heavy motor cars;

(c) other motor cars, the weight of which unladen exceed 3500 kg;

(d) semi-trailers;

(e) converter dollies of any unladen weight manufactured on or after 1 January 1979; and

(f) other trailers, the weight of which unladen exceeds 1020 kg.

A semi-trailer is the type of trailer which is normally attached to an articulated tractive unit and it therefore has no wheels at the front as this part of the trailer is usually supported by the drawing vehicle.

Some vehicles are exempt from these requirements, e.g. dual purpose vehicles not constructed or adapted to form part of an articulated vehicle (although they are subject to MOT testing). In addition, breakdown, firefighting or snow clearance vehicles are exempt as are living vans whose unladen weight does not exceed 3500 kg; police vehicles and those temporarily in Great Britain.

At this stage we must recognise that the requirements at manufacture are prescribed by the Road Vehicles (Construction and Use) Regulations and that the requirements at the time of plating are concerned with annual tests and are prescribed by the 1988 Regulations.

The first examination is a joint exercise leading to the affixing of a Ministry plate and the issue of the first goods vehicle test certificate. Those vehicles which were subject to the Motor Vehicles (Type Approval for Goods Vehicles) (Great Britain) Regulations 1982 would be issued with a certificate of conformity or approval which acts in the same way as the Ministry plate.

(3) *The nature of the plate*

The manufacturer's plate is a metal plate fixed to the vehicle at the time of manufacture. Once a Ministry plate has been attached, the manufacturer's plate is of no significance. The weights, etc., shown on the Ministry plate are those with which we are concerned. The Ministry plate is a paper plate which is fixed in a conspicuous place in the cab of the vehicle or elsewhere in a trailer. Where the vehicle is an articulated vehicle, plates will be attached to both parts of it.

In addition to the plates which are attached to vehicles, a 'plating certificate' is issued in respect of the vehicle.

(4) *Offences in connection with plating*

It is an offence for a person to use, or to cause or permit a goods vehicle to be used on a road which is of a class required to have been submitted for an examination with a view to plating, where no *plating certificate* is in force in respect of that vehicle. This certificate will normally be held at the company office. A constable may demand its production in the same circumstances as apply to the production of other vehicle documents.

A Ministry plate will specify the maximum laden weight of any trailer which may be drawn by the vehicle. It is an offence to draw a trailer other than one which complies with the plated requirements of the vehicle.

If alterations are made to a vehicle after it has been plated, the nature of those alterations must be notified to the Ministry and it is an offence to fail to do so.

(5) *Goods vehicle testing*

The examination of a goods vehicle with a view to plating is solely concerned with establishing its safe operating weights, etc. It must also be submitted for testing at the same time and it is, thereafter, subject to the requirement that it shall be tested

559

annually. It is an offence to use a goods vehicle on a road, at any time after the relevant date upon which it was required to be tested, where no test certificate is in force. He who causes or permits such a vehicle to be so used, also commits an offence.

Trailers will carry a disc which shows the date upon which a test is due.

Exemption is afforded to vehicles and trailers which are going, by previous appointment, to (and from) a testing station, while it is undergoing a test, or where the vehicle is refused a certificate, it is going to or from a place of repair or to the breakers.

A goods vehicle test certificate must be produced to a constable in the same instances as a certificate of insurance and within the same time limitations. It is an offence to fail to produce it.

Operators' licences

The nature of goods vehicles and the tasks which they undertake make it essential that there is a strict form of regulation in respect of their use on a road. The traffic commissioner for the area is responsible for goods vehicle licensing.

The Goods Vehicles (Licensing of Operators) Act 1995, s. 2, states that no person shall use a goods vehicle on a road for the carriage of goods for hire or reward, or for or in connection with any trade or business carried on by him, except under the authority of an operator's licence. Section 2(5) provides that it is an offence to do so.

For licensing purposes, where a person who owns a vehicle, or has it in his possession under an agreement for hire, hire purchase or loan is driving it on a road, he is deemed to be the owner. In other cases, the owner will be the person whom the driver is serving or whose agent he is at the time. The offence of using a goods vehicle without an operator's licence is therefore one which is committed by he who owns, has hired, or in some other way is 'operating' the vehicle. Thus, if a man drives his own vehicle on a road for the carriage of goods for hire or reward without an operator's licence he commits this offence. If another person is driving the vehicle for him in these circumstances it makes no difference; the owner commits the offence of using the vehicle without an operator's licence; the driver does not as he is not the operator of the goods vehicle.

(1) Hire or reward

The best example of a use of a goods vehicle for hire or reward is where the vehicle and its driver are hired to another person. This occurs where a person hires a firm of furniture removers as, in effect, the proprietor hires both his vehicle and his driver to the person who is to move house. Firms which 'rent-a-van' do so for hire or reward. Where earth is removed from a site by contractors for a fixed fee, there is such a use and this is also so where septic tanks are emptied and the effluent dumped on land elsewhere if this is done on a contract basis.

(2) For or in connection with his trade or business

If, in the last two examples above, these tasks had been carried out by, in the first instance, the firm which was engaged in the earth removal, for example an open-cast mining company, the removal would have been in connection with the remover's trade or business and, in the second, if the septic tank had been that of the company itself, the removal would also have been connected with his trade or business. There would be no element of 'hire or reward'. Supermarket chains operate their own fleets of vehicles for delivering goods to their retail outlets. Such deliveries are made for or in connection with a trade or business carried on by them.

A local authority is carrying on a business for the purposes of this legislation and requires operators' licences in respect of its vehicles.

Types of operators' licences

(1) *Standard operators' licences*

These licences authorise a holder to carry goods for hire or reward or in connection with a trade or business carried on by him. Where a licence is held by a company, a restricted licence may be used to carry goods for hire or reward instead of a standard licence, but only if the goods are the property of a subsidiary or holding company.

A standard licence may authorise operations both nationally and internationally, but may be limited to national operations. Transport operators who have dealings throughout the European Union require an international licence. If they do not hold one, they will be restricted to delivery of goods to a port for dispatch.

(2) *Restricted licences*

These licences are restricted in that they merely authorise the use of the vehicle for, or in connection with, a trade or business carried on by the holder of the licence.

(3) *General points in relation to licences*

An operator's licence is issued to the operator of the vehicles and will be kept at the office of the operator. The licence may authorise the operator to use any specified vehicles and the registration numbers will be set out in the licence. Trailers will be identified by type and the number which may be used will be specified.

So that it is possible to establish, on the spot, that a vehicle is being operated under a licence, an identity disc is issued for each vehicle and must be fixed to the vehicle in a waterproof container next to the vehicle excise licence. On rare occasions, where a vehicle is found without an identity disc, it will be authorised on a temporary basis (not exceeding one month) within the terms of the operator's licence. An identity disc will specify the type of licence which is in force, that is, whether it is 'standard' or 'restricted' and whether it is 'national' or 'international'.

It is an offence if a licence holder does not cause a disc to be displayed at all times whether the vehicle is being used under the licence or not.

The holder of a licence must produce it at any time if required to do so by a constable, vehicle examiner or a person authorised by the licensing authority. He may elect whether to produce it at his operating centre, head office or principal place of business within the traffic area of the licensing authority by whom the licence was granted.

Exceptions to the rule that licences must be in force

The Goods Vehicles (Licensing of Operators) Act 1995, s. 2(2), exempts small goods vehicles as defined by sch. 2 and vehicles of a class specified in regulations.

A 'small goods vehicle' is a goods vehicle which:

(a) does not form part of a vehicle combination and has a relevant plated weight not exceeding 3.5 tonnes or (not having a relevant plated weight) has an unladen weight not exceeding 1525 kg; or

(b) forms part of a vehicle combination (not being an articulated combination) which is such that the total plated weight of the combination (except any small trailer) does not exceed 3.5 tonnes (or, if one or more of the vehicles in the combination, other than a small trailer, is not plated, if the total unladen weight of those vehicles, excluding such a trailer does not exceed 1525 kg); or

(c) forms part of an articulated combination which is such that the total of the unladen weight of the tractive unit and the plated weight of the trailer does not exceed 3.5 tonnes (or if the trailer does not have a plated weight, the total of their unladen weights does not exceed 1525 kg).

This appears to be terribly complex until it is realised that we are only concerned with 3.5 tonnes and 1525 kg, which is 30 cwt 3.5 tonnes applies to vehicles and combinations where plated weights are available and 1525 kg applies where there is no plated weight and we therefore have to deal with unladen weight.

Certain vehicles are exempted from these provisions by the Goods Vehicles (Operators' Licences, Qualification and Fees) Regulations 1984. Schedule 5 to those regulations lists a large number of vehicles which are exempt but generally they fall within what might be described as 'public services'. Defence force, firefighting, rescue and ambulance vehicles are exempt, so are vehicles used for snow clearance, gritting and refuse disposal. Outside the description 'public services' we have agricultural tractors or machines, dual purpose vehicles, showmen's goods vehicles, recovery vehicles, cement mixer lorries, hackney carriages, and vehicles used for funerals.

Vehicles temporarily in Great Britain

From 1 January 1993, the Goods Vehicles (Community Authorisations) Regulations 1992 established a Community-wide authorisation allowing goods vehicles access to the market in the carriage of goods by road between member States. The Goods Vehicles (Licensing of Operators) Act 1995, s. 2 consolidates these provisions requiring that each member State must issue a Community authorisation to any haulier established in that State who is entitled to carry out international carriage of goods by road for hire or reward. Holders of such authorisations do not require operators' licences in other Community countries. The Community Regulation provides for the appointment of 'authorised inspecting officers' who are empowered to demand the production of a certified copy of the authorisation which must be carried on each vehicle operating under its authority. The 1992 Regulations appoint police constables and examiners appointed under the Road Traffic Acts as authorised inspecting officers.

In consequence of the 1992 Regulations, the definition of 'foreign goods vehicle' which is provided by the Goods Vehicles (Operators' Licences) (Temporary Use in Great Britain) Regulations 1980 is altered to exclude all such authorised vehicles. The effect of the 1980 Regulations is now therefore restricted to non-EC countries with which Great Britain has an agreement. A 'foreign goods vehicle' is, by Regulation 3 of the 1980 Regulations, as amended, one which:

(a) has been brought temporarily into Great Britain and does not remain in Great Britain for longer than three months;

(aa) is not being used for international carriage by a haulier established in a member State other than the United Kingdom and is not established in the United Kingdom;

(b) is engaged in carrying goods by road on a journey some part of which lies outside the United Kingdom;

(c) is not used at any time to transport goods from a place in the United Kingdom to another place in the United Kingdom (unless it carries a 'cabotage authorisation' issued under Community Regulation (EC) No. 4059 of 21 December 1989).

A 'cabotage authorisation' lays down conditions under which non-resident carriers may operate national road haulage services within a member State.

The 1992 Regulations, in effect, remove the necessity for international road haulage permits under the International Road Haulage Permits Act 1975 and the Goods Vehicles (International Road Haulage Permits) Regulations 1975 in respect of journeys to other member States. With the acceptance of Austria within the EU, the 1975 Regulations were revoked as they had no further application.

Offences of entering and remaining on property

The offences themselves

The Criminal Law Act 1977 creates several offences the purpose of which is to prevent unlawful occupation of residential premises. These offences are as follows:

(a) For a person without lawful authority to use or threaten violence for the purpose of securing entry into premises for himself or another person provided that there is someone present on the premises at the time who is opposed to entry and the person seeking entry knows that to be the case, s. 6.

(b) For a person to fail to leave premises on which he is trespassing and which he entered as a trespasser, when required to do so by a displaced residential occupier or by a protected intending occupier of the premises, s. 7.

(c) For a person to resist or intentionally obstruct an officer of a court in the execution of a High Court or county court judgment or order for the recovery of any premises or for the delivery of possession of any premises, s. 10.

We are concerned with premises and 'premises' for the purposes of the Act includes any building, any part of a building under separate occupation, any land ancillary to the building, and the site comprising any building or buildings together with any land ancillary thereto. The definition would therefore cover a block of flats, a single flat or even the grounds within which the block has been erected. The term 'building' includes any immovable structure, and any movable structure, vehicle or vessel designed or adapted for residential use. Thus, caravans, houseboats, etc., are covered by the Act.

Violence for securing entry

(1) The offence

By s. 6 of the Act, it is an offence for any person, without lawful authority, to use or threaten violence for the purpose of securing entry into any premises either for himself or any other person, provided that:

(a) there is someone present on those premises at the time who is opposed to the entry which the violence which the entry is intended to secure; and

(b) the person using or threatening the violence knows that to be the case.

However, this does not apply to a person who is a 'residential occupier' or a 'protected intending occupier' of the premises in question or who is acting on behalf of such an occupier. Where a person who is accused of such an offence adduces sufficient evidence that he was, or was acting on behalf of, such an occupier, he shall be presumed to be, or to be acting on behalf of, such an occupier unless the contrary is proved. These terms are explained below.

(2) Use or threat of violence

The essence of the offence is the use or threat of violence for the purpose of securing entry into premises upon which is present, a person who is opposed to entry. An intention to secure possession is not an issue.

(3) Entry

Actual entry is not required, it is the use or threat of violence for the purpose of securing entry into premises upon which a person opposed to entry is present, which is the essence of the offence. The section does not require that the violence is for the purpose of securing possession of the property. Persons who used or threatened violence to gain entry to the annual hunt ball would commit this offence if they were aware that there were people inside who opposed their entry. Similarly, protesters who tried to secure entry to premises upon which animals were kept in captivity would commit offences in the same circumstances.

The violence used or threatened may be directed against persons or property. The section requires the use of 'violence' which differs from 'force'. The press of a crowd may force entry into premises without any of the persons thus forced into the premises intending or threatening violence.

To kick down a door to secure entry amounts to violence directed against property, but it is submitted that the use of a key to gain unlawful entry would not involve a violent entry, although it would amount to a forceful one.

(4) *Person on premises who is opposed to entry*

There must be someone on the premises who is opposed to entry. If squatters attempt, by violence, to take possession of premises which are guarded by a watchman who is opposed to their entry they commit this offence.

However, once they have gained occupation of the premises the owner of the premises may commit this offence if, by violence, he seeks to regain occupation of the premises. This does not apply where the person concerned is a displaced residential occupier or a protected intending occupier or a person acting on their behalf. In the case of business premises there can be no displaced residential occupier or protected intending occupier.

(5) *Without lawful authority*

The offence contrary to s. 6 must be committed *without lawful authority*. Obviously those executing orders of the courts would have lawful authority for such entry and in the case of s. 6, this is as far as this may go. It would be reasonable to assume that an owner of property would always have lawful authority to re-occupy his property but this is not so. Section 6(2) states quite clearly that the fact that a person has any interest or right to possession or occupation of any premises does not give him lawful authority to use or threaten the use of violence for the purpose of securing his entry into those premises. The section recognises the need to ensure the keeping of the peace as opposed to an owner's right of occupation of his own property. Thus, where business premises are taken over by squatters, the owner of those premises has no right to re-possession other than that which might be established by other means. It may be, however, that such an owner or occupier might gain entry to his property by means other than the use, or threat of violence and if he does so he will not offend against the section by evicting those who are trespassing upon the premises.

(6) *Displaced residential occupier and protected intending occupier*

The provisions of the section do not apply to displaced residential occupiers or protected intending occupiers.

A 'displaced residential occupier' is:

> 'any person who was occupying any premises as a residence immediately before being excluded from occupation by anyone who entered those premises, or any access to those premises, as a trespasser is a displaced residential occupier of the premises as long as he continues to be excluded from occupation of the premises by the original trespassers or by any subsequent trespasser.'

The section makes clear however, that a person who was occupying the premises as a trespasser before being excluded is *not* a displaced residential occupier.

A 'protected intending occupier' is a person who:

(a) has in those premises a freehold interest or a leasehold interest with not less than two years still to run;
(b) requires the residence for his own occupation as a residence;

565

    (c) is excluded from occupation of the premises by a person who entered them, or any access to them, as a trespasser; and

    (d) has, or a person acting on his behalf holds a written statement which specifies his interest in the premises; states that he requires the premises for occupation as a residence for himself; and it is signed in the presence of a magistrate or commissioner for oaths, who has subscribed his name as a witness to that signature.

Tenants and those holding a licence to occupy premises granted by an authority (local authority, housing corporation, etc.) are similarly protected in the circumstances set out above.

Adverse occupation of residential premises

(1) The offence

Section 7 (as substituted by the Criminal Justice and Public Order Act 1994) gives a residential occupier or an individual who is a protected intending occupier of premises a quicker remedy in relation to re-occupation than would be afforded by civil process. He, or a person acting on his behalf, may require the trespassers to leave. They commit an offence if they fail to do so.

(2) Defences to charges under s. 7

There are three defences provided by s. 7. The burden of proof in each case is upon the accused:

    (a) where the accused believed that the person requiring him to leave was not a displaced residential occupier or a protected intending occupier of the premises, or someone acting on his behalf, he has a defence. However, it is of limited effect when one recognises that there is a requirement that protected intending occupiers will be in possession of a written statement or certificate to this effect. Most displaced residential occupiers will be in possession of documentary proof of ownership and residence;

    (b) where the accused proves that, although asked to do so by the accused at the time the accused was requested to leave, the person requesting him to leave failed at the time to produce a written statement or certificate as required by the Act;

    (c) it is a defence that the premises in question are or form part of premises used mainly for non-residential purposes and that the accused was not on any part of the premises used wholly or mainly for residential purposes. This ensures that strikers, or protesters who are upon private property do not commit the offence if they fail to leave when required to do so, provided that they are not in occupation of any part of the premises which might be used, for example, by a resident watchman.

Police powers generally

A constable in uniform may arrest without warrant anyone who is, or whom he with reasonable cause suspects to be, in the act of committing these offences. For this purpose the police officer may enter (by force if need be) and search any premises where he has reasonable grounds for believing the person to be.

A similar offence of entering diplomatic missions and similarly inviolable premises is included and the power to arrest persons committing that offence is extended to constables in uniform. However, proceedings for this offence require the consent of the Attorney-General and the question of action by a constable on his own initiative does not arise.

Offences related to interim possession orders

The Criminal Justice and Public Order Act 1994, ss. 75 and 76, deals with 'interim possession orders' which are to be made under rules of court for the bringing of summary proceedings for possession of premises which are occupied by trespassers. Where such an order has been made and served in accordance with rules of the court a person who is present on the premises as a trespasser at any time during the currency of the order commits an offence. However, no offence will be committed if he leaves the premises within 24 hours of service of the order, or where a copy of the order was not fixed to the premises in accordance with the rules of court. These rules are to be made at the time of writing.

A person who was in occupation of the premises at the time of the service of the order, commits an offence if he re-enters, or attempts to re-enter as a trespasser within one year of service of the order. The powers of entry and search granted by the Police and Criminal Evidence Act 1984, s. 17, have been applied to these offences.

Police powers

A constable in uniform may arrest without warrant anyone who is, or whom he reasonably suspects to be, guilty of this offence.

Powers to remove unauthorised campers

The Criminal Justice and Public Order Act 1994, s. 77, empowers local authorities to give a direction to persons residing in a vehicle or vehicles within their area on land forming part of a highway, unoccupied land, or occupied land without consent, and to other persons with them, to leave the land and remove the vehicle or vehicles and any other property from the land and not to return within three months of the date of the direction. Persons who fail to do so as soon as reasonably practicable, commit an offence. Within proceedings for such an offence, it is a defence for an accused to show that his failure to leave or to remove the vehicle or other property as soon as practicable or his re-entry with a vehicle was due to illness, mechanical breakdown or other immediate emergency. 'Vehicle' and 'caravan' have the same meaning as set out above.

567

Section 78 permits a magistrates' court to make an order, where it is satisfied that persons are in contravention of such a direction, requiring the removal of any vehicle or other property and any person residing in that vehicle. It is an offence to wilfully obstruct any person in the exercise of any power conferred on him by the order. Such action will be taken by officers and servants of the local authority who are required to give land owners 24 hours' notice of their intention to enter the land.

Road checks

Statutory powers for road checks

The conduct of road checks is governed by the Police and Criminal Evidence Act 1984, s. 4. They may be conducted for the purpose of finding out whether a vehicle is carrying:

(a) a person who has committed an offence other than a road traffic offence or a vehicle excise offence;

(b) a person who is a witness to such an offence;

(c) a person intending to commit such an offence; or

(d) a person unlawfully at large.

A 'road check' consists of the exercise in a locality of the power conferred by the Road Traffic Act 1988, s. 163 (power of a constable to stop a mechanically propelled vehicle or pedal cycle on a road) in such a way as to stop all vehicles or vehicles selected by any criterion. They are therefore concerned with the apprehension of actual or intending criminals or escaped prisoners. The purpose of a road check is to stop all vehicles or all vehicles of a particular type if it is selective. If the person being sought is known to be in a particular model and colour of motor vehicle, it may be that only vehicles of that description will be stopped. However, the circumstances may be such that that person will have had ample opportunity to change vehicles and in such a case, all vehicles will be stopped.

The powers given to a police officer to deal with traffic matters in the ordinary course of his duties are unaffected by this legislation. A constable may stop as many vehicles as he wishes if he has reason to do so under powers granted by the Road Traffic Acts. The 1984 Act is concerned with what might be described as 'road blocks'.

Authorisation of road checks

A road check must be authorised in writing by an officer of the rank of superintendent or above. Such authorisation may only be given:

(a) if the commission of an offence, or the intention to commit an offence is involved, the officer must have reasonable grounds for believing that the offence is a serious arrestable offence and for suspecting that the person is, or is about to be, in the locality of the proposed check;

(b) if it is to trace a witness to an offence, the officer must have reasonable grounds for believing that the offence is a serious arrestable offence; and

(c) if it is to arrest a person who is unlawfully at large, the officer must have reasonable grounds for suspecting that the person is, or is about to be, in that locality.

The term 'serious arrestable offence' is defined. The offences are treason; murder; manslaughter; rape; kidnapping; incest with girl under 13; buggery with a person under 16; an indecent assault which constitutes an act of gross indecency; causing an explosion likely to endanger life or property (Explosive Substances Act 1883, s. 2); intercourse with a girl under 13 (Sexual Offences Act 1956, s. 5); possession of a firearm with intent to endanger life or use to resist arrest or carrying a firearm with criminal intent (Firearms Act 1968, ss. 16, 17, and 18); hostage-taking (Taking of Hostages Act 1982, s. 1); and hijacking (Aviation Security Act 1982, s. 1); torture (Criminal Justice Act 1988); causing death by dangerous driving and by careless driving when under the influence of drink or drugs (Road Traffic Act 1988, ss. 1 and 3A); endangering safety at aerodromes, hijacking of ships and seizing or exercising control of fixed platforms (Aviation and Maritime Security Act 1990); (indecent photographs and pseudo-photographs of children (Protection of Children Act 1978); and publication of obscene matter (Obscene Publications Act 1959). In addition s. 116 of the 1984 Act includes certain drug trafficking offences (in Drug Trafficking Offences Act 1986, s. 38(1)).

By s. 116 of the 1984 Act, any other arrestable offence is serious *only if its commission has led to, or is intended to lead to*:

(a) serious harm to the security of the State or to public order;
(b) serious interference with the administration of justice or with the investigation of offences or of a particular offence;
(c) the death of any person;
(d) serious injury to any person;
(e) substantial financial gain to any person; and
(f) serious financial loss to any person.

'Loss' is serious for the purposes of the section if, having regard to all the circumstances, it is serious for the person who suffers it. Thus, the life savings of a pensioner, although this may not be a large sum of money in a general sense, may represent the difference between 'subsistence' and 'meaningful existence' to such a person. A much larger sum would be less important to a wealthy person and may not represent a serious financial loss.

Emergency authorisation

In an emergency situation in which there is insufficient time to obtain the authorisation of a superintendent, authorisation may be given by an officer below the rank of superintendent. Where this has been done, the officer who gives such emergency authorisation must, as soon as practicable:

(a) make a written record of the time of the authorisation; and
(b) cause a superintendent (or above) to be informed.

In such a case, the superintendent (or above) may then authorise, in writing, the road check to continue. Should he decide that it should not continue, he must record the fact that it took place, and its purpose (including the relevant serious arrestable offence).

Time limits for road checks

The maximum period for which a road check may be authorised is seven days. However, written authorisation may be given for a further period not exceeding seven days if a superintendent (or above) believes that a road check ought to continue.

There may be limitations in respect of the periods of a day in which such a check may be carried out, or no limitations may apply in the circumstances.

Records

A written authorisation will show:

(a) the period during which the road check is authorised to continue;
(b) the name of the officer who authorised it;
(c) the purpose of the road check (including any relevant serious arrestable offence); and
(d) the locality in which vehicles are to be stopped.

Persons in charge of vehicles which are stopped at a road check are entitled to obtain a written statement of the purpose of the road check if they apply for such a statement within 12 months of the road check. The notice need only contain information concerning the purpose of the road check.

Searches

While the 1984 Act does not give a constable power to search vehicles which are stopped at a road check, the power exists to do so:

(a) if he has reasonable grounds for suspecting that it contains stolen or prohibited articles (s 1); or
(b) for the purpose of arresting someone for an arrestable offence if he has reasonable grounds to suspect that the person is there (s. 17); or
(c) under powers granted by any other statute, e.g. the Firearms Act 1968.

Common law powers

It is submitted that s. 4 of the 1984 Act does not affect the previously existing common law powers to set up road blocks which are related to apprehended breaches of the peace. If there is an *immediate threat of a breach of the peace* the divisional court has ruled that if the police, on reasonable grounds, believe that a breach of the peace may be committed, the police officer is not only entitled but under a duty to take reasonable steps to prevent the breach occurring. Provided they honestly and reasonably form the opinion that there is *a real risk of a breach of the peace in the sense that it is in close proximity both in time and place,* then the conditions exist for reasonable preventive action. The possibility of a breach must be real to justify preventive action. The imminence or immediacy of the threat to the peace determines what action is reasonable.

If a vehicle is stopped under this power an officer is also entitled to search it. A person in such a vehicle who insists on continuing his journey may be arrested under common law powers to prevent the apprehended breach of the peace.

This is not to say that where there is sufficient time in such circumstances a check should not be authorised under the provisions of s. 4, but the circumstances existing at the time may not necessarily fall within the parameters of such a check.

Road Traffic – associated offences

Introduction

While most of the offences which we have so far considered have been concerned with roads and places to which the public have access, there are other offences involving the use of vehicles which may be committed elsewhere. It is also important to consider how the identity of a driver may be discovered, in circumstances in which that vehicle was not stopped at the time and the identity of the driver established.

Driving elsewhere than on a road

(1) *Common land, etc.*

The Road Traffic Act 1988, s. 34(1), creates an offence of, without lawful authority, driving a motor vehicle:

(a) on to or upon any common land, moorland or land of any other description, not being land forming part of a road, or
(b) on any road being a footpath or bridleway.

Subsection (2) provides that it is not an offence under the section to drive a motor vehicle on any land within 15 yards of a road, being a road on which a motor vehicle may lawfully be driven, for the purpose of parking the vehicle on the land.

The provisions of the section do not, therefore, prevent the parking of vehicles on the land immediately abutting upon a road, but are useful in preventing 'off-road' events which are unauthorised. While motor rallies may be specifically authorised to use areas of such land, or parts of footpaths or bridleways which cross private land, the unauthorised use of trials motor cycles would amount to an offence. A 'footpath' means a way over which the public have a right of way on foot only, and a 'bridleway' means a way over which the public have a right of way on foot and a right of way on horseback or leading a horse, with or without a right to drive animals of any description along the way. Subject to any orders made by a local authority and to any by-laws, the public have a right to ride a pedal cycle on a bridleway, but cyclists must give way to pedestrians and persons on horseback.

Subsection (3) provides that a person shall not be convicted of an offence against s. 34 if he proves to the satisfaction of the court that the vehicle was driven in

571

contravention of the section for the purpose of saving life or extinguishing fire or meeting any other like emergency.

(2) *On a footpath*

A person who wilfully drives a carriage on a footpath offends against the Highways Act 1835, s. 72. The Road Traffic Act 1988, s. 191, states that a motor vehicle or a trailer is a 'carriage' for the purposes of any Act of Parliament or any rule, regulation or by-law made under any such Act. Bicycles and tricycles and other similar machines are declared to be 'carriages' by the Local Government Act 1988, s. 85.

Tampering with motor vehicles

The Road Traffic Act 1988, s. 25, is concerned with persons who, while a motor vehicle is on a road or on a parking place provided by a local authority:

(a) get on to the vehicle; or

(b) tamper with the brake or other part of its mechanism,

without lawful authority or reasonable cause.

The vehicle must be on a road and/or on a 'parking place provided by a local authority'. For whom or for what purpose the parking place is provided is irrelevant. The word 'tamper' is not defined by the 1988 Act and should be given its ordinary meaning of improper interference. The words 'other part of its mechanism' are wide enough to refer to any mechanical part of the vehicle.

Information as to identity of driver

(1) *The requirement to give information*

The Road Traffic Act 1988, s. 172(2), provides that where the driver of a vehicle is alleged to be guilty of an offence to which the section applies:

(a) the person keeping the vehicle shall give such information as to the identity of the driver as he may be required to give by or on behalf of a chief officer of police; and

(b) any other person shall if required as stated above give any information which is in his power to give and may lead to the identification of the driver.

The section applies to:

(a) all offences against the provisions of the Road Traffic Act 1988 except an offence under Part V (driving instruction), or s. 13 (promoting motoring events on highway), s. 16 (wearing of protective headgear), s. 51(2) (certain test conditions – goods vehicles), s. 61(4) (certain types of approval requirements), s. 67(9) (obstructing a vehicle examiner), s. 68(4) (failing to proceed to place of vehicle inspection), s. 96 (driving with uncorrected defective eyesight), or s. 120 (offence against regulations dealing with licensing of drivers of large goods vehicles and passenger-carrying vehicles);

(b) an offence under s. 25 (information as to date of birth and sex after conviction), s. 26 (interim disqualification), or s. 27 (production of a licence on conviction) of the Road Traffic Offenders Act 1988;

(c) any offence relating to any other enactment relating to the use of vehicles on roads, except an offence under para. 8 of Schedule 1 to the Road Traffic (Driver Licensing and Information Systems) Act 1989 (relating to drivers' licences of large goods and passenger-carrying vehicles); and

(d) manslaughter by the driver of a motor vehicle.

A requirement may be made by way of written notice and served by post. Where it is so made:

(a) it shall have effect as a requirement to give the information within the period of 28 days beginning on the day on which the notice is served; and

(b) the person on whom the notice is served shall not be guilty of an offence under the section if he shows either that he gave the information as soon as reasonably practicable after the end of that period or that it had not been reasonably practicable for him to give it.

(2) *The offence*

A person who fails to comply with such a requirement commits an offence. However, he shall not be guilty of the offence if he shows that he did not know and could not with reasonable diligence have ascertained who the driver of the vehicle was.

(3) *Procedural points*

There is no requirement that the police specify the nature of the offence which it is alleged has been committed. A notice signed by an inspector with the authority of his superintendent, that superintendent having implied delegated authority from the Commissioner of Police to further delegate to his inspector, has been held to be a good and valid notice. In addition, it has been held that where a notice has been produced from an official source and has every appearance of authenticity, justices may draw an inference as to the validity of the notice. However, at the other end of the scale, it cannot be said that a police officer acting in the course of his duties is necessarily acting on behalf of his chief officer of police.

The expression 'any other person' as used in the section includes the driver himself.

In all cases involving extended enquiries in order to trace a driver it is important to ensure that any complainant is informed of what is being done.

Street offences

Introduction

The offences which are concerned with various activities associated with 'prostitution' are made punishable more because of the fact that those engaged in such activities constitute a nuisance, than that they commit offences which are blameworthy in the normal sense. The actual sexual activities in which the people concerned engage are not, where those acts take place with consent, etc., criminal offences. They become criminal offences where the 'contact' which precedes such activities takes place in public places. The nature of the offences is such that cautions are given in respect of many of them; it is when the persons concerned persist in their conduct that the criminal law is invoked.

Common prostitute

A prostitute is a woman who offers her body commonly for sexual intercourse or acts of lewdness, in return for payment. The term 'acts of lewdness' covers all of the other activities which are associated with prostitution, such as masturbation and whipping. Thus, 'massage parlours' can offer the types of sexual activity which are associated with prostitution if the service extends to masturbation. A virgin may therefore be a prostitute.

For a woman to be a *common* prostitute she must offer her services commonly, that is, to more than one man. A girl who adopts a 'sugar daddy' who sets her up in a luxury flat and pays all of the expenses involved, does not thereby become a prostitute as she limits the services which she 'sells' to one man. She who offers herself commonly for no other reasons than she enjoys intercourse, is not a prostitute as she does not do so for payment.

However, it is not an offence to be a prostitute *per se*, but it becomes an offence in certain circumstances.

(1) *Loitering or soliciting*

The Street Offences Act 1959, s. 1, creates the offence committed by a common prostitute who loiters or solicits in a street or public place. To prove that such an offence is committed, there must be evidence of the accused's recent behaviour in a street or public place. She should have been seen on at least two previous occasions accosting men in a street or public place and that she was seen to leave with them. The fact that she leaves with them will frequently eliminate the possibility of an innocent explanation. While a woman may approach different men in an effort to find out the location of a particular place, she is unlikely to leave with them and this increases the likelihood that she is soliciting. However, it is not necessary that a woman should approach men. Many prostitutes dress in a manner which leaves little doubt concerning the reason for their presence on the street. They may be approached by men who see them as 'loitering' for the purposes of prostitution. There may be soliciting from a slowly moving vehicle and soliciting need not involve the use of words. A deaf and dumb prostitute solicited by making grunting noises accompanied by a gesture involving the folded right arm being bent and then straightened. No one ever doubted what she had for sale!

Solicitation may take place even though the prostitute is not in the street or public place. Standing, scantily dressed in front of a lighted window while indicating with the fingers the price charged; tapping on the window and indicating the door of the house; or placing a card in the window offering services are all forms of solicitation. The test is whether it is clear to those men that they are being offered sex for money.

(2) *Cautions*

In practice, at least two cautions are given before proceedings are taken against a woman in these circumstances. Particulars of cautions given are entered in an official cautions register maintained at the police station. A woman so cautioned, who wishes to deny that her actions were such that she merited a caution, can apply to a court within 14 days for an order directing that the caution be expunged. The procedure is as follows:

(a) On the first occasion that a woman is suspected of this offence, obtain the assistance of a colleague as a witness (joint observation);

(b) Tell her what you have seen and caution her. Obtain name, date of birth, address and description to aid later observation. Check name and address, if possible from documents. There is no power to use or threaten force to detain a woman for these purposes; consequently, the use or threat of force in such circumstances is unlawful.

(c) Ask her if she is willing to be put in touch with a welfare, social or probation service or help, or attend at a police station to see a policewoman, at her convenience.

(d) If seen on a second occasion, the same procedure should be followed.

(e) All cautions must be officially recorded.

(f) If seen loitering or soliciting after having been cautioned twice, she may be arrested and charged. A custody officer must satisfy himself that two cautions have been so recorded and that they are sufficiently recent (some forces require that they must have been given within the preceding 12 months) before accepting the charge.

(g) A complaint from a woman to the effect that she has been cautioned without cause requires investigation in the same way as any other complaint. If the complaint is justified it may be expunged without the need to refer the matter to a court.

(h) When a hearing is in progress it is not necessary to mention cautions. However, the conduct which occasioned those cautions will probably have to be given to prove that she is a common prostitute.

(3) *What is a street or public place?*

For the purposes of the Act, a street includes any bridge, lane, footway, subway, square, court, alley or passage, whether a thoroughfare or not, which is for the time being open to the public; and doorways and entrances to premises abutting upon a street and the ground adjoining and open to a street are treated as forming part of the street. The terms of this definition therefore prohibit loitering and soliciting in places which are on private property if they open on to streets. Prostitutes who solicit from balconies or from behind closed windows are therefore caught by the Act. The mischief which the Act seeks to prevent is the molestation of persons who merely wish to walk along a street and a form of solicitation which is 'projected' into a street is forbidden.

The Act does not define 'public place' but it is a place where the public go, no matter whether they have a right to go or not. Places which are 'private' for most of

575

the time may be 'public' at other times, for example, where the grounds of a private house are opened to members of the public.

Police powers

A constable may arrest without warrant anyone he finds in a street or public place and suspects, with reasonable cause, to be committing an offence against the Act.

Brothels

Premises become a brothel if they are used by persons of opposite sexes for illicit intercourse or other indecent behaviour. The Sexual Offences Act 1956, s. 33, makes it an offence for a person to keep or manage a brothel, or to act or assist in its management.

The offence is not associated with those relating to prostitutes and it is not necessary to show that the women in a brothel were prostitutes. It is not therefore necessary to prove that the women concerned received payment for their services. The premises must be used by at least two women before the premises can be a brothel, but it does not matter that only one of them uses the premises at any one time. Where many flats in one building are so used, if each is used by only one woman, none are brothels. However, where a number of single rooms in one building are so used it is probable that the whole building will be looked upon as a brothel housing a number of women.

A residential landlord is likely to be a 'keeper', a day-to-day manager, or a madame, is likely to be a manager and all other persons associated with the 'trade' will be assisting in the management of the premises. To assist in the management of a brothel does not necessarily involve any element of 'control' but it must involve some element of 'management'. Thus, a person who arranges for advertisements to be placed in respect of the premises assists in management, but she who cleans out the rooms does not.

Kerb crawling

The Sexual Offences Act 1985, s. 1, makes it an offence for a man persistently to solicit a woman, or different women, for the purpose of prostitution, from a motor vehicle while that motor vehicle is in a street or public place, or for a man persistently to solicit a woman, or different women, for the purpose of prostitution, in a street or public place while in the immediate vicinity of a motor vehicle which he has just got out of or off. The offences are designed to remove the nuisance caused to respectable women who are mistaken for prostitutes in areas which become 'red light' districts.

The man must indicate to the woman or women by words or actions that he requires her or their services as a prostitute. Men who drive through such districts persistently addressing such requests to women, where the vehicle is in a street or public place, commit the offence. If a man travels to the general district in a vehicle; parks and leaves it; persistently solicits a woman or women in the immediate vicinity of the place where he has parked the vehicle, he similarly commits an offence. It does not matter that the vehicle was parked in an official car park; if it was parked and left there while the driver or an occupant solicited a woman or women in the immediate vicinity, an offence is committed. The test to be applied is whether the vehicle was used directly for, or was connected with, the solicitation.

There are alternative charges under s. 1 which are useful where 'persistent' soliciting cannot be proved. It is an offence if there is soliciting in such a manner or in such circumstances as to be likely to cause annoyance to the woman (or any of the women) solicited, or nuisance to other persons in the neighbourhood. Justices are entitled to use their local knowledge of the area in which the offence is alleged to have occurred when considering whether particular behaviour was likely to cause nuisance to other members of the public.

Section 2 of the Act deals with the offence of a man persistently soliciting a woman, or different woman, in a street or public place for the purpose of prostitution. There is no mention of the use of a motor vehicle within this section. Where there is a doubt concerning whether the solicitation occurred 'in the immediate vicinity' of a motor vehicle, it will be preferable to charge under s. 2.

Police powers

The offences under the Sexual Offences Act 1985 are not arrestable offences. The general power to arrest provided by the Police and Criminal Evidence Act 1984, s. 25, will therefore apply unless there are exceptional circumstances which would justify the use of common law powers.

Male importuning

It is an offence contrary to the Sexual Offences Act 1956, s. 32, for a man persistently to solicit or importune in a public place for immoral purposes.

In this sense 'immoral' does not indicate that the conduct must be contrary to law. However it must be associated with sexual activity whether of a homosexual or heterosexual nature. The standards of ordinary, right-thinking people should be applied when considering the circumstances and the nature of the overtures being made. Persistently suggesting homosexual acts between consenting adults in private is an 'immoral' purpose and it is irrelevant that no offence would be committed by those who took up those suggestions. This is true also in relation to women prostitutes. What they eventually do is not an unlawful act, the essence of the crime lies in the way in which they arrange that activity.

The offences under the Sexual Offences Act 1985 do not include male prostitutes soliciting women for the purposes of prostitution, but such conduct would be punishable under the 1956 Act, s. 32.

Other sexual and indecent offences

Indecent conduct towards young children

The Indecency with Children Act 1960 was passed to remedy a defect in the law, where the High Court ruled that there could be no indecent assault where a child had merely accepted the accused's invitation to touch him in an indecent manner. It is an offence for any person to commit an act of gross indecency with or towards a child under the age of 14 years, or to incite any child to commit such an act with that person or another. The term 'gross indecency' is limited to activities involving indecent contact with the genitalia including contact through clothing. A person incites another to commit an act if he, by any form of arrangement, promise, inducement, or invitation, encourages him to commit that act. The words of the section extended the offence to circumstances in which the accused incited the child to commit the act of gross indecency. An act of gross indecency with or towards a child is committed if a person does something grossly indecent against or directed towards a child, or if he cooperates in or invites some act of that nature which is done by the child. If a man masturbates in the presence of a child and gains his 'thrill' by the fact that the child is watching, he is guilty, whether or not he has attracted the child's attention towards his act. Alternatively, if he was doing this secretly while looking at the child, the offence would not have been committed as the act was not directed towards the child, nor was there any form of cooperation. Where a man encourages a child to touch his genitalia and the circumstances are such that he can be said to permit the child to touch him in this way, he commits the offence.

An act of incitement must be judged on its own. Where a man left notes in a public lavatory inviting boys to be his 'pretend son' those notes in themselves did not amount to incitement to commit acts of gross indecency. Entries in a diary kept by such a man disclosing his desire for sexual activity with such boys were held merely to relate to 'intention' and to be inadmissible in evidence. It is submitted that there is an alternative view; that the diary entries were sufficiently 'related' to the alleged offence to be admissible in evidence.

Police powers

Offences of indecent conduct towards children are not arrestable offences. However, the circumstances of the offence, if current, may be such that a breach of the peace is immediately apprehended. If not, the general power to arrest under the Police and Criminal Evidence Act 1984, s. 25, will apply.

Unnatural sexual offences

The Sexual Offences Act 1956, s. 12, makes it an offence, other than in certain circumstances, for a person to commit buggery with another person or an animal. Because of the reference to persons and animals the offence is frequently described as either sodomy or bestiality.

(a) Sodomy is committed where sexual intercourse takes place per anum between males or between a male and a female per anum.
(b) Bestiality is committed where either a man or a woman has sexual intercourse with an animal in any manner; which could involve a man with an animal per vagina or per anum, or an animal with a man per anum, or a woman with an animal per vagina or per anum.

The circumstances referred to above are that the act of buggery takes place in private and both parties have attained the age of 18. Such an act of buggery by one man with another shall not be treated as taking place in private if it takes place:

(a) when more than two persons take part or are present; or
(b) in a lavatory to which the public have or are permitted to have access whether on payment or otherwise.

Offences of buggery are arrestable offences if committed by a person of or over the age of 21, where the other person is under the age of 18. If the other person is under 16, the punishment is life imprisonment. An assault with intent to commit buggery is also an arrestable offence. It is for the prosecutor to prove that the act took place otherwise than in private or that one of the parties to it had not attained the age of 18.

Where buggery remains an offence, both the active and passive parties are guilty if both consent to the act.

Prior to the Criminal Justice and Public Order Act 1994, intercourse per anum with a female was always punishable as an offence of buggery, but that Act decriminalised such acts committed with consent in private.

Gross indecency – male with male

It is an offence for a man to commit an act of gross indecency with another man, whether in public or in private, or to be a party to the commission, or to procure the commission of such an act. This offence is set out in the Sexual Offences Act 1956, s. 13. The Wolfenden Committee, which studied the problems of homosexuality in the 1960s, described the usual acts of gross indecency as including mutual masturbation, indecent contact or oral/genital contact. Consent to such acts is not generally an offence as the nature of the acts is not such that an assault is involved. Both parties are guilty when such an offence is committed. If a third man procures the commission of such an offence (and this will usually apply to a man who arranges meetings of others for such a purpose), he is equally guilty. A person who is a party to the commission of such acts will usually be he who is present as an observer but is a non-participant. He is equally guilty of the offence.

Lawful homosexual acts

The Sexual Offences Act 1967, which resulted from the recommendations of the Committee, described circumstances in which homosexual acts could be carried out lawfully. It legalised all homosexual acts (which term is so defined as to include acts of buggery between males *and* acts of gross indecency), provided that both parties consent, the acts are carried out in private, and both have attained the age of 18 years. Those acts which take place when two or more are present, or which take place in a public lavatory are not carried out in private.

The Criminal Justice and Public Order Act 1994, s. 146, provides that nothing in the section shall prevent a homosexual act (with or without other acts or circumstances) from constituting a ground for discharging a member of HM Forces from the service or a member of the crew of a UK merchant ship from his ship.

579

The legality of such acts is dependent upon a number of factors. Firstly, was there consent? (Men suffering from severe subnormality within the meaning of the Mental Health Act cannot give such consent.) However, it is a defence for a man to prove that he did not know and had no reason to suspect that subnormality. Secondly, was the act in private? In order to decide this the surrounding circumstances must be carefully examined, including the place, time of day or night, and the likelihood of another person arriving on the scene.

Police powers

If the act of gross indecency is committed, or there is an attempt to procure its commission, by a man who is of, or over, the age of 21 with a man who is under the age of 18, the maximum penalty for the man of 21 years is five years' imprisonment. This is an arrestable offence in such circumstances. In all other instances the penalty is one of two years' imprisonment and the offence is not an arrestable one.

Rape

The Sexual Offences Act 1956, s. 1(1), as amended by the Criminal Justice and Public Order Act 1994, states that it is an offence for a man to rape a woman or another man. A man commits rape if:

(a) he has sexual intercourse with a person (whether vaginal or anal), who at the time of the intercourse does not consent to it; and

(b) and at the time he knows that the person does not consent to the intercourse or is reckless as to whether that person consents to it.

For this offence to be committed, per vagina, with a woman, it is necessary to prove penetration of the female organ but it is not necessary to prove rupture of the hymen, should the girl attacked be a virgin, nor that there was any emission of seed. Evidence of penetration can be given by the complainant herself, supported by the evidence of a doctor who conducted a medical examination as soon as possible following the commission of the offence. Absence of consent is an essential factor, and the consent obtained must have been a true consent and not one obtained by intimidation or fraud. There is no requirement that the sexual intercourse be 'unlawful' in the sense that it is extra-marital intercourse. A husband can be convicted of raping his wife if the elements of the offence can be proved. Section 1(2) of the Act provides that a man who induces a woman to have sexual intercourse with him by impersonating her husband, is guilty of rape. Thus, if a man climbs into bed with a sleeping woman and induces her to respond to his sexual advances by pretending to be her husband, he commits rape, as any form of consent given is negatived by s. 1(2). This only applies to impersonation of a *husband*.

Where consent is gained in consequence of violence or threats of violence, there can be no true consent. However, threats of the exposure of an extra-marital affair will not suffice for the offence of rape, but such a person would commit an alternative offence under s. 2 of the 1956 Act.

580   Consent gained by fraud is not a true consent, thus a doctor can commit rape by gaining consent to intercourse by falsely claiming that the act is a recognised part of medical procedure.

In addition, a consent gained from a woman who is mentally deficient or drunk is not a true consent.

The definition of the offence of rape was amended by the Criminal Justice and Public Order Act 1994 to extend the offence to the rape, by a man, of another man.

A man commits rape if he has sexual intercourse with a person who at the time of the intercourse does not consent to it and at the time he knows that there is no consent or he is reckless as to whether there is such consent. To show such recklessness it is necessary to prove that the man was indifferent and gave no thought to the possibility that the person might not be consenting, or being aware that the person was probably not consenting in the circumstances, he persisted regardless. It must be remembered that there is a difference between consent and submission induced by fear of physical harm.

The question of consent can be a difficult one for the jury. If a girl permits a casual acquaintance to take her to a remote spot and then to kiss and fondle her, the man concerned may be encouraged to attempt to have intercourse with her. If she refuses, no matter how far the preliminaries have gone, it will be rape to proceed with the act. Bearing in mind recent decisions of the High Court, if the intercourse is proceeding, it will be rape to continue after a request to desist.

'Recklessness' in its relationship to consent in a case of rape, is concerned with the state of mind of the accused on the occasion in question; not some hypothetical reasonable person.

Offences of procurement

The Sexual Offences Act 1956, ss. 2 and 3, deals with further offences which are similar to rape in many respects. It is an offence to procure a woman, by false pretences or false representations, to have sexual intercourse, or to procure her by means of threats or intimidation. At first sight, because it has already been said that it will be rape if consent is obtained by fraud or intimidation, these offences appear to be unnecessary. However, in these cases intercourse must have taken place. Although these offences can be committed by a man who procures a woman to have intercourse with himself, they may also be committed by those who procure a woman for the purpose of intercourse with some other person. If committed with the procurer, the offence could be rape, but it must also be recognised that only a threat of immediate personal violence (or possibly of violence to another person such as a woman's child) will negative consent for the purposes of rape while lesser threats will suffice for the purpose of procurement by threats. A threat to inform a husband of his wife's past indiscretions, or an employer of her past dishonesty, will be sufficient.

An offence, contrary to s. 4, is committed by any person who applies, administers or causes a woman to take any drug, matter or thing with intent to stupefy or overpower her so as to enable any man to have sexual intercourse with her. This offence is complete when the substance has been taken with this intention in the mind of the person responsible, and it is immaterial whether he intends to seek intercourse himself or to facilitate matters for some other person. The words 'drug,

581

matter or other thing' are wide enough to include intoxicating liquor where the intention can be established.

When dealing with offences of rape, etc., it is important to include evidence of early complaint, as the fact that a complaint is made immediately is good evidence that there was no consent to the act which took place.

Police powers

Rape is an arrestable offence. The offences of procurement by threats, false pretences, or the administration of drugs to facilitate intercourse are not arrestable offences.

Unlawful sexual intercourse with young girls

It is an offence contrary to s. 5 of the 1956 Act for a man to have unlawful sexual intercourse with a girl under 16. A further offence under s. 6 is concerned with such intercourse with a girl under 13. If a man marries a girl who has not reached the age of 16 and genuinely believes that his marriage is valid, he commits no offence if he has intercourse with her.

For the purposes of 'intercourse' proof of penetration is sufficient. A certified copy of a birth certificate, supported by proof of the identity of the girl, is sufficient for the purposes of the sections. 'Unlawful' in such cases means 'illicit'; outside the bonds of matrimony.

In the case of a s. 6 offence, it is provided that a man shall not be guilty of an offence under this section if, at the time of commission, he is under the age of 24 and has not been previously *charged* with such an offence, and he believes the girl to be 16 or more and has reasonable cause for such belief. An accused must satisfy a court of his belief and that it was reasonable. The law recognises the possibility that girls not yet 16 may frequently appear to be much older. It at the same time recognises that males of 24 or more should be able to identify, or at least suspect, their true age.

Police powers

It is an arrestable offence to have unlawful sexual intercourse with a girl not yet 13 years. Although the imprisonment to be awarded for an offence in respect of a girl who is 13 but not yet 16 is only two years and it is therefore not an arrestable offence it should be remembered that an indecent assault upon a woman is an arrestable offence. Such offences will almost invariably involve an indecent assault.

In relation to both offences the question of consent does not arise, but if the act is done without consent, the man would be, additionally, guilty of rape.

General

It is essential to obtain assistance from CID when these offences are reported and the place at which a rape is alleged to have occurred is protected. An accurate record must be made of the actual complaint made by the person concerned, as evidence of early complaint, and the nature of that complaint, is important in relation to the question of consent. It is admissible (although hearsay) if it was made to someone at the first opportunity and was not made in response to leading questions.

On occasions it may be found that the victim has returned to her home and she may have changed her clothing and be preparing to wash her undergarments. These will be required for forensic examination.

Evidence

Unsworn evidence will be given where the person concerned is under 14. A deposition of such a child's unsworn evidence may be taken for the purposes of criminal proceedings as if that evidence had been given on oath. These provisions appear in the Criminal Justice Act 1988, s. 33A. The competence of a witness is a matter for the court, but s. 33A(2A) of the 1988 Act provides that a child's evidence shall be received unless it appears to the court that the child is incapable of giving intelligible testimony.

Incest

The history of the offence of incest begins with society's (and the church's) desire to ensure that children were not affected by the close blood ties of the parents. The ingredients of the offence therefore become predictable. If we are to prevent a male from siring children of closely-related females of child-bearing age, sexual intercourse with the mother, daughter, granddaughter and sister must be prohibited. A 'grandmother' is not included as it is extremely unlikely that a liaison between the two would produce a child.

They say that it takes two to tango so we must look at the other side of the bed. Women who have intercourse which is likely to result in the birth of child must be of child-bearing age and the law currently requires that they must be 16 or more before they can be guilty of the offence. When we consider the males within her close family who are likely to make her pregnant, her grandfather must be included as males remain sexually potent into late life. The banned relationships are therefore with her grandfather, father, brother or son. There is no purpose in including 'grandson' as, by the time he reaches sexual maturity, grandmother will be past child-bearing.

The terms 'brother' and 'sister' include 'half-brother' and 'half-sister'. The offence being concerned with blood relationship, it is immaterial that the relationship is illegitimate, provided that at the time that the intercourse took place the accused was aware of the relationship.

The Criminal Law Act 1977, s. 54, makes it an offence for a man to incite a girl under 16 whom he knows to be his granddaughter, daughter or sister to have sexual intercourse with him.

Anonymity of complainants

The Sexual Offences (Amendment) Act 1976, s. 4, provides for the anonymity of complainants in rape cases. The Sexual Offences (Amendment) Act 1992, s. 1, makes identical provisions (with a few exceptions) for the anonymity of complainants in respect of offences of indecent assault (whether committed against a man or a

583

woman); indecency with children; procurement of women by threats, false pretences or the administration of drugs; and attempts to commit these offences. The common provisions of the two Acts are as follows.

Where an allegation of one of the offences to which the two Acts applies is made, neither the name nor address, nor a still or moving picture of that person shall, during that person's lifetime, be published in England and Wales in a written publication available to the public, or be included in a programme for reception in England and Wales, if it is likely to lead to the identification of the complainant. Where a person has been accused of an offence to which one of the Acts applies, no matter, whatsoever, which is likely to lead to the identification of the complainant, may be so published. Provision is made for the requirements of the Acts to be set aside on application being made to the trial judge where it is considered necessary to induce persons to come forward as witnesses and that the applicant's defence will be substantially prejudiced if the direction is not given. A judge is also given a 'public interest' discretion to set aside these provisions.

Certain offences can be committed in the case of proprietors, editors or publishers of newspapers or periodicals, or by a body corporate or programme editor in the case of a programme.

The provisions of these Acts apply equally to offences of incitement or conspiracy to commit an offence of rape in which case the protection is afforded to the intended victim of the offence.

Indecent literature through the post

The Post Office Act 1953 prohibits sending, attempting to send, or procuring the sending of a postal packet which encloses an indecent or obscene print, painting, photograph, lithograph, engraving, cinematograph film, book, card or written communication, or any indecent or obscene article, whether similar to the specified article or not. The section also prohibits marks, works or designs on the packet or cover of any postal package which are grossly offensive or of an indecent or obscene character.

The forms of material which may be used to reproduce indecent or obscene matter are widely defined, and the addition of the words, 'or any indecent or obscene article whether similar to the specified article or not' will permit charges to be preferred provided that the matter is indecent or obscene, regardless of the material with which it is produced. The issue of whether or not such article is indecent or obscene is one for the court to determine, and particular evidence on the point should not be given. It is sufficient to prove the sending, attempting to send, or procuring to send the matter which appears to be indecent or obscene.

A person commits an offence against the Malicious Communications Act 1988 if he sends to a person a letter or article which conveys a message which is indecent or grossly offensive; a threat; or information which is false and known or believed to be false, by the sender; or any other article which is wholly or partly of an indecent or grossly offensive nature; if his purpose, or one of his purposes, is to cause distress or anxiety to the recipient or to another person to whom he intends that it, or its contents or nature, should be communicated.

A defence exists if a threat is to enforce a demand the person has reasonable grounds for making and he believed that it was a proper means of reinforcing the demand.

The Obscene Publications Act 1959 creates the offence of publishing an obscene article, whether for gain or not, or having an obscene article for publication for gain, whether for himself or another. Therefore, a person who publishes such an article commits an offence whether or not the question of gain arises. He who merely possesses, must so possess with a view to publication for gain. An article for the purposes of the Act is anything to be read, looked at or both, any sound record or film or other picture record (such as a video cassette). 'Article' for the purposes of the Act, also includes any matter included in a television or sound broadcast or in a cable programme service. Such an article is published if it is distributed, circulated, sold, hired, given or lent, or so offered. In relation to films, sounds, etc., they are published if they are shown, played, projected or, where the matter is data stored electronically, when they are transmitted. An article is obscene if its effect is to deprave or corrupt those likely to read, see or hear it. Whether or not it is obscene is a matter to be determined by the jury.

A photographer who develops obscene pictures publishes them when he distributes or sells them. The photographs are 'records of a picture' and are articles for the purposes of the Act.

It is a defence for a person to prove that he had not examined the article and had no reasonable cause to suspect that it was of such a nature that his publication of it, or possession of it, would make him liable under the Act. There is also a defence of 'public good' on the grounds that it is in the interests of science, literature, art or learning, or of other objectives of general concern. Expert evidence is frequently given in relation to such matters.

Proceedings must be approved by the Director of Public Prosecutions as such prosecutions lead to complexities because of conflicting expert evidence which tends to be offered in relation to that which is obscene and that which is not.

This offence is declared to be an arrestable offence by s. 24(2) of the Police and Criminal Evidence Act 1984, as amended by the Criminal Justice and Public Order Act 1994. It is also now included in the list of 'serious arrestable offences' in Schedule 5 to PACE.

The Indecent Displays (Control) Act 1981 makes it an offence to display publicly any indecent matter. An offence is committed by the person who makes the display and any other person who causes or permits the display to be made. If matter is visible from any public place, it is deemed to be publicly displayed. The term 'public place' has its usual meaning, that is a place to which the public have or are permitted to have access (whether on payment or otherwise), at the time at which the matter is displayed. To protect certain art exhibitions, premises are exempt when the payment taken includes payment for the display and shops, or parts of shops, to which the public can only gain access by passing beyond an adequate warning notice, provided in both instances persons under 18 are not admitted while the display is in progress. The warning notice must read, 'WARNING. Persons passing beyond this notice will find material on display which they may consider indecent. No admittance to persons under 18 years of age.'

The provisions do not apply to BBC or ITV broadcasts, art galleries, museums, Crown or local authority buildings, theatres and cinematograph exhibitions under the appropriate regulating legislation.

A constable may seize any article which he has reasonable grounds for believing to be, or to contain indecent matter and to have been used in the commission of an offence under the Act.

Indecent photographs of children

The Protection of Children Act 1978, s. 1, states that it is an offence for a person to take, or permit to be taken or made, any indecent photograph or pseudo-photograph of a child. Thus, the person who takes such a photograph and he who permits it to be taken (perhaps a parent or guardian) commit offences. The term 'photograph' includes a negative and data stored on a computer disk or by other electronic means which is capable of conversion into a photograph. A 'pseudo-photograph' is an image, whether made by computer graphics or otherwise in any way, which appears to be a photograph. The definition of 'photograph' was extended by, and the term 'pseudo-photograph was introduced by, the Criminal Justice and Public Order Act 1994. These provisions are aimed at the trade in indecent material which is read by a computer, such material being concerned with paedophile activities. Copies of indecent photographs are covered by the Act, as is data stored in a computer disk or by other electronic means which is capable of conversion into a pseudo-photograph.

The 1978 Act also prohibits the distribution; possession with a view to distribution; and publication, or causing publication of an advertisement for photographs or pseudo-photographs.

These offences under the 1978 Act are arrestable offences, having been added to s. 24(2) of the Police and Criminal Evidence Act 1984 by the Criminal Justice and Public Order Act 1994. They have also been added to the list of 'serious arrestable offences' set out in Schedule 5 to PACE.

The Criminal Justice Act 1988, s. 160, creates the offence of possession of an indecent photograph or pseudo-photograph of a child.

Both Acts provide defences if there is proof of a legitimate reason for distribution, showing or possession, as the case may be, or proof that the person concerned had not seen the photograph and did not know, or have reason to suspect, the photograph to be indecent.

A person shall be taken to be a child at the material time if it appears from the evidence as a whole that he was under 16. If the impression conveyed by a pseudo-photograph is that the person shown is a child, it shall be treated as showing a child and so shall a pseudo-photograph where the predominant impression conveyed is that the person shown is a child, notwithstanding that some of the physical characteristics shown are those of an adult. This represents a commendable attempt to deal with the problem of 'computer images' in their relationship to 'photographs'. No matter how these images are presented, it is the overall impression which will be important.

Wildlife and countryside

Introduction

Until the passing of the Wildlife and Countryside Act 1981 very little protection was given to wild creatures and wild plants. While game birds, etc., were protected, little existed to prevent interference with other wild birds. Game birds were primarily given protection because so many of them were reared or 'encouraged' by land owners who demanded that that which they saw as their property, was protected from the attentions of poachers. In the same way, plants which were grown by farmers were protected by law, but those which grew wild were largely ignored as they were not seen as being sufficiently identified as anyone's property.

Wild birds

It is an offence contrary to the Act to intentionally kill, injure or take any wild bird, or to intentionally take, damage or destroy the nest of such a bird, or to intentionally take or destroy an egg of such a bird. The possession of a wild bird, whether alive or dead (including one which has been stuffed and mounted), or any part of it, or an egg (or part of an egg) of such a bird, is also an offence. Offences of possession are offences of strict liability.

The term 'wild bird' includes all wild birds which are resident in, or are visitors to, Great Britain, with the exception of poultry (which could not in any case be truly described as wild) and game birds (protection for which is provided by other Acts, see below). The foremost problem in relation to the enforcement of this legislation has been the fact that the term 'wild bird' does not include a wild bird bred in captivity. For a bird to be bred in captivity the parent birds must have been in captivity when the egg was laid. Licensed keepers of birds of prey frequently take eggs or chicks from the nests of protected birds of prey and have the eggs hatched under captive birds, and in either case, offer the chicks for registration in due course. In this way the number of captive birds for the sport of falconry is increased.

It is also an offence to disturb any wild bird mentioned in Schedule 1 to the Act while it is building a nest, or is in or near such a nest containing eggs or young birds. Schedule 1 contains all but the commonest of birds. It includes all resident birds of prey with the exception of the commoner kestrel and sparrow hawk. Nest robbers target the nests of peregrine falcons, goshawks, kites and eagles. If chicks are found in the possession of persons suspected of offences against this Act, assistance should be obtained from the RSPB who will try to establish, by means of DNA fingerprinting, that they could not belong to the captive adult birds lawfully kept.

If persons are found killing wild birds, or in possession of their eggs, it is almost certain that they will have committed offences against the Act. However, some birds

587

may be killed or taken outside their close season (generally their nesting season) and predictably they are the commoner species of duck, goose, plover, snipe, and woodcock. These birds are listed in Part I of Schedule 2 to the Act.

'Authorised persons' may be permitted to kill or take certain common birds, or to damage or destroy their nests. Crows, magpies, wood pigeons, starlings, and the commoner of the gull families may be 'culled' in this way. Land owners, occupiers of land and persons authorised by them, or by a local authority, the National Rivers Authority, a water undertaker, a sewage undertaker, a fishery board or the Nature Conservancy Council are 'authorised persons'. However, even in the case of these 'pest' birds, killings, etc., must be so authorised. There are other exceptions relating to wild birds in general, where acts are carried out in respect of disabled birds, etc.

Wild animals

The wild animals which are protected by the 1981 Act are listed in Schedule 5 to the Act. It is an offence to intentionally kill, injure or take any animal so listed, or to possess such an animal alive or dead (in whole or in part), without lawful authority. These provisions of the Act are more difficult to enforce. It is fairly safe to assume that any wild bird will be protected with the narrow exceptions offered to 'authorised persons'. The animals listed in Schedule 5 include most of the less common butterflies, moths, frogs, lizards and newts, porpoises and dolphins, red (but not grey) squirrels, and the common otter.

Wild plants

It is an offence for anyone to *uproot any wild plant*. 'Authorised persons' are excepted and the same classes of persons are within this classification as in the case of wild birds. A person who is digging up wild daffodils and primroses is committing an offence unless he is the land owner or properly authorised.

However, it is more likely that persons will be found picking the flowers from such plants. The picking of such flowers is only an offence if the plant concerned is one which is listed in Schedule 8 to the Act. Many wild plants are protected even from the 'pickers' and the list contains all but the commonest of our wild flowers and plants.

Police powers

If a constable suspects, with reasonable cause, that any person has committed or is committing these offences, he may, without warrant, stop and search that person and search and examine anything which that person may then be using or have in his possession. In each case, if he with reasonable cause suspects that evidence of the offence is to be found, he may seize and detain for the purpose of proceedings under the Act anything which may be evidence of the commission of the offence or may be liable to be forfeited.

For the purpose of exercising these powers, or for the purpose of arresting a person under the Police and Criminal Evidence Act 1984, s. 25, for any of the offences under the 1981 Act, a constable may enter on to any land other than a dwelling-house. A justice may issue a search warrant subject to the usual conditions in respect of the offence disclosed.

The Protection of Badgers Act

The Protection of Badgers Act 1992, s. 1, creates offences of wilfully killing, injuring or taking any badger, or attempting to do any of these things. The Act provides that if there is evidence from which it could be reasonably concluded that at the material time the accused was doing so, he shall be presumed to have been doing so, unless the contrary is shown. It is an offence to be found in possession of a dead badger, or any part of it, unless the person concerned can show that the badger had not been killed in contravention of the Act, or that it, or the part, had been sold (whether to him or another) and, at the time of the purchase, he had no reason to believe that the badger had been killed.

Licences may be granted by the Ministry of Agriculture to permit badgers to be killed or taken where they are causing serious damage to crops, or where it is necessary to prevent the spread of disease, or it is for scientific purposes.

Where dogs are used in the taking or destruction of badgers, a court may order their destruction.

Section 2(1) of the Act makes it an offence to cruelly ill-treat, use badger tongs, or dig for badgers. By s. 2(2) a person found digging for badgers is presumed to have been doing so in contravention of the Act, unless the contrary is shown. The use of firearms, other than smooth-bore weapons of not less than 20 bore or a rifle using ammunition having a muzzle energy not less than 160 footpounds and a bullet weighing less than 38 grains, is prohibited.

Section 3 makes it an offence to interfere with a badger sett by intentionally or recklessly damaging, destroying it, obstructing access to it, causing a dog to enter it or disturbing a badger when it is occupying that sett. Fox hunters are permitted to obstruct entrances to keep their hounds out of the setts. The section also makes it an offence to sell, offer for sale, or have a badger in one's possession or control.

Mercy killings and taking for the purpose of caring for an injured badger are exempted by the Act. Farmers, etc., are exempted if they kill or take badgers to prevent serious damage to land, crops, poultry or other property but this is subject to conditions. If it was apparent before the act was carried out that it would be necessary to prevent such damage (i.e. there is no urgency) such a person is not exempted if he had not applied for a licence as soon as reasonably practicable after it became apparent, or if an application for such a licence was under consideration at the time.

Police powers

Where a constable has reasonable grounds for suspecting that a person is committing an offence under this Act, or has committed such an offence, and that evidence is to be found on that person, or in any vehicle or article he has with him, the constable may without warrant stop and search that person, vehicle or article. He may seize and detain anything which may be evidence of the commission of such an offence.

Poaching

(1) Day poaching

The offence of poaching by day is contrary to the Game Act 1931, s. 30. Anyone who trespasses by entering or being upon land in the daytime in search or pursuit of game, woodcock, snipe or rabbits commits an offence. 'Game' includes hares and pheasants, partridges, grouse, heath or moor game, and black game, for the purposes of this Act. 'Daytime' begins one hour before sunrise and ends one hour after sunset.

A person trespasses on land if he is there without authority. The occupier of that land is empowered to order that person to leave at once and is authorised to use reasonable force to eject him if he refuses to go. For an offence to be committed under this section, there must also be evidence of a search for, or the pursuit of game. The Act exempts persons who trespass on land when coursing or hunting with hounds or greyhounds.

Where five or more persons so trespass together the offence attracts a higher penalty under s. 31. There is a threat offered to land owners or occupiers by the presence of such a large party. Section 32 creates a further offence. If any of these persons is armed with a gun and he uses violence, intimidation or menaces to prevent any person from exercising his powers under the Act, he and those with him commit a further offence. In addition, s. 4A of the Game Laws (Amendment) Act 1960 provides that where a person is convicted as one of five or more persons so liable and the court is satisfied that any vehicle belonging to him or in his possession or under his control at the relevant time has been used for the purpose of committing or facilitating the commission of the offence, the court may make an order for forfeiture in respect of that vehicle. This may be done regardless of any other way in which the court deals with the offender and without regard to any restriction on forfeiture in any enactment.

Police powers. A constable has power to require trespassers in search or pursuit of game to quit and give their names and addresses. If a constable has reasonable cause for suspecting that the person is committing the offence of trespassing in pursuit of game in the daytime he may enter on to land for the purpose of exercising this power.

(2) Night poaching

Poaching by night is covered by the Night Poaching Act 1828. 'Night' commences one hour after sunset and continues until one hour after sunrise. There are two specific offences under s. 1:

(a) unlawfully taking or destroying by night any game or rabbits on land, open or enclosed (including a public road, highway or path); and

(b) by night unlawfully entering or being on any land, open or enclosed, with any gun, net, engine or other instrument for the purpose of taking or destroying game.

'Game' as defined under this Act includes hares, pheasants, partridges, grouse, heath or moor game, black game or bustards; it does not include rabbits, but it will be noted that rabbits are added to the offence under (a).

He who commits an offence under (a), i.e. killing or taking, commits it in respect of game *or rabbits* killed or taken anywhere; in a field, street or public place. He who commits an offence under (b), i.e. trespass with instruments, etc., for the purpose of taking or killing, must commit it on land, open or enclosed. The offence cannot be committed in a street or public place. Anyone who commits an offence under s. 1, who assaults or offers violence with a gun or other offensive weapon towards any person authorised to apprehend him, is liable to an increased penalty. By s. 9, if three or more people together enter or are on land at night to take or destroy game or rabbits, and one of them is armed with a gun or other offensive weapon, all are guilty of an aggravated offence.

Police powers. A constable who has reasonable grounds for suspecting that one of these offences is being committed may enter land to deal with the offences.

(3) *Game licences*

Whether authorised to take game or not, all persons who kill or take game must have a game licence. Game licences are required in respect of game, woodcock, snipe, rabbits or deer. Exemption is limited to coursing and hunting, the authorised killing of deer and the killing of rabbits by land owners. The occupiers of land, and persons authorised, do not need licences for the taking of hares. The Game Act 1831 requires that a licence be held if a person searches for game, but 'game' for the purposes of that Act does not include rabbits.

(4) *Close season for game*

The taking or killing of game is prohibited on Sundays or Christmas Day by the 1831 Act, which also prohibits the killing or taking of game during their close seasons, which are as follows:

(a) partridges – 1 February to 1 September;
(b) pheasants – 1 February to 1 October;
(c) black game – 10 December to 20 August;
(d) grouse – 10 December to 12 August.

The following subjects are retained in the book at the request of the reviewers as probationer constables have no other access to the material.

Betting

Betting has been defined as the staking of money or other valuable things on the event of a doubtful issue. It follows that within our own experience, some forms of betting have been witnessed or undertaken and we are equally aware that in many circumstances it is lawful. We have all seen betting offices in which bets may be received; we have visited race tracks and perhaps staked a few pence on a horse or greyhound, and realise that these are legally accepted practices. Betting is not in itself unlawful, but can be so in certain circumstances.

Betting in a public place

It is an offence for any person to frequent or loiter in a street or public place, either on his own behalf or on behalf of someone else, for the purpose of bookmaking, betting, agreeing to bet, or paying, receiving or settling bets. Although this offence is now included in the Betting, Gaming and Lotteries Act 1963, it has been in existence in various Acts of Parliament for some considerable time and is intended to prevent bookmakers, or persons acting on their behalf, from becoming a nuisance by carrying out their day-to-day business in the eyes of the general public.

Section 8 of this Act prohibits frequenting or loitering in a street or public place for such purposes, and the use of the words 'frequenting or loitering' signifies that the person concerned must have placed himself in a street or public place for that purpose. A police officer observing such an offence being committed, should therefore note the offender's continued presence in a particular area over a period of time together with details of the number of persons by whom he is approached. It is equally important to note the form of the transaction which takes place on each occasion, including details of things which change hands, for example, money and pieces of paper.

The term 'street' is defined for the purpose of the section as including:

(a) any bridge, road, lane, footway, subway, square, court, alley or passage, whether a thoroughfare or not, which is for the time being open to the public; and

(b) the doorways and entrances of premises abutting upon, and any ground adjoining and open to a street, shall be treated as being a part of the street.

This definition is extremely wide and the inclusion of doorways and entrances at (b) removes any doubt that persons frequenting or loitering in such places are in a street for the purpose of such offences. The term 'public place' is not defined within the section and should be given its usual meaning: a place to which the public have or are permitted to have access, whether on payment or not. The words which describe the purpose of any person frequenting or loitering are wide enough to cover any part of a normal betting transaction, including the arranging, acceptance, or settling of bets.

A constable may seize and detain any article liable to be forfeited. Articles which may be forfeited are books, cards, papers, and other articles relating to betting which may be found in the possession of a person arrested.

Betting on premises

It is an offence to use, cause or knowingly permit premises to be used for the purpose of betting transactions, unless the use of the premises for such purposes is specifically permitted by the Betting, Gaming and Lotteries Act 1963. Permitted forms of use are:

(a) *Premises which have a betting office licence.* No offence is committed by a person who is the holder of a valid betting office licence, using the premises to which the licence refers for the purpose of betting. His servants and agents employed upon the premises are also entitled to complete betting transactions on behalf of the holder of the licence. These licences are controlled and can only be granted to holders of a bookmaker's permit or a betting agency permit.

(b) *At approved racecourse or tracks on special days.* Betting is permitted on approved horse racecourses, that is, courses approved by the Totalisator Board, on any day upon which horse races are lawfully taking place. The term 'track' includes any premises on which races of any description, athletic sports, or other sporting events are taking place and betting can be authorised at such places by the grant to the user of the premises of a track betting licence. The users of all approved dog tracks have obtained such a permit which specifies the number of days upon which betting can take place.

(c) *On private premises in particular circumstances.* It is a common practice for persons to organise forms of betting in works or residential establishments. These forms of betting are usually referred to as sweepstakes. All persons willing to pay a certain fee are permitted to draw the name of a horse from the hat, prizes being awarded to the holders of tickets naming the first, second and third horses in the race concerned. This and other similar forms of betting are permitted by s. 1 of the 1963 Act, provided that the organiser and all persons with whom the betting transactions are effected either work or reside on the premises. Such sweepstakes organised by members of a family in their home, residents in private hotels, or persons working together on particular premises are lawful.

Bookmakers

Section 2 of the 1963 Act prohibits persons from acting as bookmakers unless they are the holders of a bookmaker's permit, or are registered pools promoters. Applications for a bookmaker's permit are considered only by a committee of justices acting for the area, and in this way the suitability of applicants can be impartially judged. Copies of all such applications are sent to chief officers of police. Bookmakers may authorise other persons to act as their agents and to receive and negotiate bets on their behalf, and such persons, upon being granted a 'betting agency permit' may take out betting office licences in their own name. Applications for such permits are dealt with in the same way as applications for a bookmaker's permit.

Licensed betting offices

The rules applicable to licensed betting offices include:

(a) a requirement that they must close daily between midnight and 7 a.m., and between 10 p.m. and midnight between April and August inclusive, and between 6.30 p.m. and midnight at any other time of the year;

(b) a requirement that they must be closed on Sundays, Christmas Day and Good Friday;

(c) they must not be used for any purpose other than betting;

(d) no person apparently under the age of 18 years may be admitted;

(e) the betting office licence must be displayed;

(f) no person should be encouraged to bet while on the premises;

(g) no visual or sound apparatus shall be used on the premises unless the information is related to a sporting event (including betting on that event); or other related, incidental matters (including advertisements) and betting transactions made on the premises;

(h) no music, dancing or other entertainment shall be provided or allowed on the premises, other than that set out at (g) above;

(i) drinks, other than alcoholic drinks, may be sold on the premises and there may be sold by any means whatsoever pre-packaged sandwiches and other pre-packaged snacks including, without prejudice to the generality of the foregoing, confectionery, biscuits, and cakes.

Police powers

A constable may enter any licensed betting office for the purpose of ascertaining that the law is being complied with, and it is an offence for any person to obstruct a constable exercising his powers of entry. Many police forces refer to the exercise of these powers in general orders, requiring that certain conditions be observed.

At the request of the licensee, his servant or agent, a constable may help to expel any person who is drunk, quarrelsome, or disorderly, or whose presence would subject such person to a penalty – for example, a person under 18 years of age – and may use such force as may be required. Any person liable to be expelled who, when requested to leave by the licensee, his servant or agent, or a constable, fails to do so, commits an offence.

Vagrants and dealers

Introduction

The Vagrancy Act 1824 attempts to exercise some control over beggars. The Scrap Metal Dealers Act 1964 regularises dealings in scrap metals.

594

Vagrancy

Section 3 of the Vagrancy Act 1824 deals with persons who wander abroad, or place themselves in public places, streets, etc., for the purpose of begging, or causing or encouraging children to do so. Offences of begging still occur and, in a society which claims to have adequate welfare facilities, these offences can be annoying to members of the public. Instances of begging with children are rare, but do occur. The Vagrancy Act offence does not specify the age limits of a 'child', and it was held in 1867 that justices may form their own judgment from the appearance of the child, or receive evidence of actual age. It is a matter of fact which they must decide. It is probable that, in a modern setting, the age would be one under 14 years of age to coincide with other matters affecting children. In any case, where a child is involved, it is more likely that proceedings would be taken under the Children and Young Persons Act 1933, s. 4, which creates an offence of causing or allowing a person under 16 to be used for begging. However, for an offence to be proved under that section it would have to be shown that the person charged had responsibility for the child or young person at the time of the offence.

Scrap metal dealers

The Scrap Metal Dealers Act 1964 was passed to regulate the trading of persons engaged in dealings in old metals. The definition of a scrap metal dealer is quite a complex one, but includes all persons who, by way of business, buy or sell scrap metals. The provisions only apply if the business is conducted for that purpose and do not apply to persons who take in metal only for the purpose of manufacture of other goods; for example, manufacture of finished goods such as cars. Most scrap metal dealers have settled premises upon which their business is conducted, but some are itinerant collectors who gather metals by visiting houses, farms, or works depots.

'Scrap metal' is defined as old metal, broken, worn out, defaced, or partly manufactured articles made wholly or partly of metal.

The Act requires local authorities to maintain a register of persons carrying on business in their areas as scrap metal dealers, and no one may carry out business as a dealer in the area of any local authority unless so registered. Such a person, to qualify for registration, must occupy premises; if an itinerant collector, must reside; or if no place is occupied as a scrap metal store, a place must be used wholly or partly for such business in the area of that authority. The register must contain the full name and address of the dealer and the addresses of each of his places of business. If the dealer alters his premises or ceases to carry on business, he must inform the local authority so that the register may be amended.

Registered scrap metal dealers must keep records at each of their places of business. They must contain details of:

(a) all scrap metals received at that place; and
(b) all scrap metal processed at, or dispatched from, that place.

Separate books may be used to record items at (a) and (b), but other than this, all records must be kept in one book to avoid a confusing multiplicity of records.

595

The records of dealings which must be kept are in respect of metals received at that place and include:

    (i)   its description and weight;
    (ii) date and time of receipt;
    (iii) full name and address of person from whom received;
    (iv) price paid, if settled at time of receipt;
    (v) if not settled, an estimated price; and
    (vi) registration mark of vehicle delivering metal.

In the case of metal processed at or dispatched from that place:

    (i)   its description and weight;
    (ii) date of processing or dispatch and process applied;
    (iii) if disputed on sale or exchange, the full name and address of the person to whom the scrap is sold, or with whom it is exchanged and the consideration for which it is sold or exchanged; and
    (iv) if processed or dispatched otherwise than on sale or exchange, the value of the scrap before its processing or dispatch as estimated by the dealer.

These forms of records would be difficult for the itinerant collector to maintain, and local authorities are empowered to exempt them from these provisions. Collectors so exempted must, on sale of any metal, obtain a receipt from the purchaser showing its weight and aggregate price and must keep all such receipts for a period of two years.

(1) *Offences*

    (a) Carrying on business as a scrap metal dealer without registration by local authority, or failing to notify local authority of change of particulars.
    (b) Failing to comply with any of the requirements in relation to records or receipts of sale.
    (c) Acquiring scrap metal from a person apparently under the age of 16 years, whether offered on his own behalf or on behalf of some other person.
    (d) Selling scrap metal to a dealer and giving a false name or false address.

(2) *Police powers*

A constable is empowered to enter registered premises at any reasonable time and may inspect the premises, metals, books, or receipts. He may also take copies of, or extracts from, any book or receipt.

Index